CORRECTIONAL ADMINISTRATION

Integrating Theory and Practice

Richard P. Seiter, Ph.D.

Director, Criminal Justice Program
Saint Louis University

Prentice
Hall

Upper Saddle River, New Jersey 07458

Library of Congress Cataloging-in-Publication Data

Seiter, Richard P.
   Correctional administration : integrating theory and practice / Richard P. Seiter.
     p. cm.
   Includes bibliographical refrences and index.
   ISBN 0-13-087147-8
    1. Corrections—Administration. 2. Correctional institutions—Administration. 3. Prison
administration. I. Title.

HV8665 .S29 2002
365'.068—dc21

                                         2001034009

Publisher: Jeff Johnston
Executive Editor: Kim Davies
Production Editor: Lori Dalberg, Carlisle Publishers Services
Production Liaison: Barbara Marttine Cappuccio
Director of Production & Manufacturing: Bruce Johnson
Managing Editor: Mary Carnis
Manufacturing Buyer: Cathleen Petersen
Senior Design Coordinator: Miguel Ortiz
Marketing Manager: Ramona Sherman
Editorial Assistant: Sarah Holle
Interior Design and Composition: Carlisle Communications, Ltd.
Printing and Binding: R. R. Donnelley & Sons

Pearson Education LTD.
Pearson Education Australia PTY, Limited
Pearson Education Singapore, Pte. Ltd.
Pearson Education North Asia Ltd.
Pearson Education Canada, Ltd.
Pearson Educación de Mexico, S.A. de C.V.
Pearson Education—Japan
Pearson Education Malaysia, Pte. Ltd.

                                       10 9 8 7 6 5 4 3 2 1
                                  ISBN 0-13-087147-8

To my son, Matt, who every day, brings me pride and joy.
Love, Dad

Contents

CHAPTER 8   CREATING A SAFE AND SECURE ENVIRONMENT   205

CHAPTER 9   MANAGING VIOLENT AND DISRUPTIVE INMATES   234

CHAPTER 10   THE BASICS: FOOD, HOUSING, AND MEDICAL CARE   271

Foreword

It was a great pleasure to be asked to review this exciting new text and discover that Professor Richard P. Seiter has finally been able to fill the need for a corrections management text that benefits from the long career that this scholar/practitioner provides to the corrections profession. He has carefully and meticulously developed a linear and comprehensive examination of the history and growth of this huge industry we refer to as "corrections." This text provides a clear road map of where correctional management has been and where it might be heading in the twenty-first century. Especially commendable is the fact that, rather than simply cranking out another "how-to" handbook for correctional managers at all levels, this text includes the "why to" based on theory, research, practice, and history that informs and provides discussions of guidelines that have worked in the "real world."

Professor Seiter clearly describes and explains the basic differences between leadership and management in an environment of often-totalitarian control over those who have been incarcerated. His discussions of planning, organizing, staffing, directing, and controlling not only revisit those basic tenets of management but also provide an explanation of why these are essential and effective in the correctional environment. He emphasizes the differences among management and leadership of the offenders, the environment, and the correctional employees toward coordinated and mutually compatible actions for positive results that are both observable and measurable.

This text presents a substantial contribution to the field of corrections and a superb example of the blending of theory and practice. Parts of the text dealing with managing offenders and managing the environment are the best we have ever read. In addition, sections on managing correctional staff provide excellent explanations of the roles, approaches to, and empowerment of correctional staff. As such, the text is a welcome addition to the teaching of students interested in understanding correctional management and for students considering entering the field.

Professor Seiter has drawn on a long and illustrious career in almost every aspect of correctional management: from major research; to the Secretary of Corrections for a major state; to top leadership positions in the Federal Bureau of Prisons; to planning and directing the construction, opening, and operating of a major "new style" prison. As the editor of *Corrections Management Quarterly,* he has been able to review and present hundreds of articles that cover the full spectrum of management thinking in corrections and share them with the profession in order to develop new approaches to handling the problems that beset so many correctional institutions and programs.

This book is a "must have" reference for the desks of current correctional leadership and a perfect vehicle for the training of newly appointed managers as well as educating students of corrections. The correctional profession is fortunate to have forward-looking scholars and experienced practitioners such as Professor Seiter to help move corrections away from the often Draconian correctional management systems of the past and into an enlightened management style for the future.

Clifford E. Simonsen, Ph.D.
Harry E. Allen, Ph.D.
Co-authors: *Corrections in America* (9th ed.)
January, 2001

Preface

This textbook has been written to help you understand the past, present, and future of corrections; the functions of correctional administrators; and the issues that drive administrators as they create new operational approaches to respond to new challenges. It is organized into five sections, each providing readers with essential history and background, an understanding of critical issues, the important functions of correctional operations, and projections for future needs and adjustments to correctional administration. The goal of the textbook is to provide a framework for understanding and action. As correctional practitioners confront some of the issues and critical functions presented in this text, they should be able to put them in both historical and managerial perspective, and avoid mistakes that might occur without such an orientation.

Part I of the text (Correctional Management and Administration) provides a discussion of the correctional surroundings from past to present. The information presented includes a description of management development in the private sector and how that management expertise was transferred and reorganized to meet public sector bureaucracies. There is a presentation of the specific development of correctional administration and how the evolving theories and criminal justice philosophies resulted in certain management practices.

Part I also includes a description of management as it differs from leadership and how the complex issues of the future will require leaders to modify traditional styles of leadership. Finally, the section includes a discussion of how administrators can guide their organizations through planning exercises to identify future challenges and appropriate responses. By the end of Part I, you have a solid background of management and leadership, the issues that drive correctional administration, and the approaches to "reach ahead" and proactively confront their agencies' futures.

In Part II (Managing Offenders), you learn the history of various correctional goals and philosophies that influenced the development of correctional administration. Correctional goals often seem almost contradictory to one another, because administrators must try to balance the need to punish, deter, and rehabilitate criminal offenders. Key elements enabling administrators to reduce criminals into smaller, and somewhat homogeneous groups include risk assessment and offender classification. During the past several decades, corrections has progressed beyond subjective and even judgmental approaches to handling offenders. More recently, offender classification is "actuarial" and attempts to quantify risk or dangerousness and chances for success for criminal offenders.

With the help of objective classification instruments, correctional administrators create and offer offenders a variety of programs and services to meet their individual needs, and it is hoped, prepare them for a crime-free future. The variety of programs provided by correctional agencies is described and examined. These programs may address individual offender needs, such as substance abuse and lack of education; they may be critical in reducing idleness and peacefully managing prisons, or they may have some positive affect on both of these areas. At this point, you realize the difficulty correctional administrators face in meeting conflicting correctional goals, but you understand the methods used to maintain balance in the operations.

In Part III (Managing the Environment—The Prison Setting), you learn the organization and activities critical for creating a safe and secure prison environment. Prisons are complex organizations, with difficult missions and a variety of client groups, many of whom have different goals and objectives for their involvement with the organization. There are a multitude of components (such as physical security, inmate disciplinary programs, contraband control, and inmate accountability) that must be effectively administered to achieve a safe and secure prison. Today, more than ever, there are many violent and dangerous individuals in prisons. The correctional administrator must, therefore, understand the tools available to manage this population in order to protect staff and other inmates.

No correctional administrator can be successful in managing offenders or the environment without paying particular attention to the development and performance of their most important resource—correctional staff. In Part IV (Managing Correctional Staff), you learn the functions of human resource management within correctional agencies, including how agencies recruit, hire, train, and develop staff. One of the keys to effectively using human resources in a correctional environment is supervision, which involves how supervisors assign work, monitor and evaluate performance, and prepare staff for upward mobility. Finally, in this section, there is a thorough description of the various jobs available to those who choose correctional careers. These descriptions include the type of work required, pay and working conditions, and opportunity for advancement. Also, there is a presentation of the critical role of leadership and how it affects staff throughout a correctional organization.

Finally, the study of correctional administration is concluded with a look toward the future. Many issues that will confront correctional administrators over the next decade are presented and discussed. You will realize that correctional administration is not a static event; it evolves in response to issues that must be confronted. One critical issue involves managing tightened budgets under increasing fiscal pressure. Many approaches to fiscal administration are considered, and there is an in-depth review of the current role of the private sector contracting for the delivery of correctional services. Our study of correctional administration ends with a look to new issues of the future and to new approaches that are likely to evolve as corrections continues to change.

This text was written with several goals in mind, but the most important goal was to give those who are considering corrections a realistic appraisal of it as a career opportunity. It is important to convey the difficulty of the work in this arena, as well as the potential enjoyment and fulfillment that can accompany doing a challenging job well, while contributing to the public good. With the combination of background, philosophy, policy, and current practice, you get an authentic and pragmatic understanding of the world of correctional administration.

This text includes a variety of learning tools and aids. Practical Perspectives present real case studies of correctional administrators, the challenges they faced, and the decisions they made to handle a situation in a certain manner. In the Problems and Solutions you have the opportunity to discuss how to deal with certain issues and challenges that are likely to confront correctional administrators. In the feature You're the Correctional Administrator, you must use knowledge and resources to respond to a problem and develop a solution. The Web Link Exercises provide you with Web site addresses that relate to the topics being studied. Not only are you instructed to visit the Web sites but you are also assigned learning activities to complete. The Key Terms reinforce your understanding of the terminology of corrections and correctional administration. Like any discipline, correctional administration has a language unto itself, and familiarity with the terms and their uses helps you learn and become comfortable in your study.

Overall, this text is geared toward building a knowledge of correctional administration that can be used throughout your careers. The examples and case studies not only convey the types of substantive issues that must be addressed but also the thought processes that are often used in considering optional solutions to problems. Corrections is not a career for those who do not want to be challenged, who do not want to be in a "people business," and who do not want to contribute to the protection and safety of society. It is for those who are willing to expose themselves to public scrutiny, second-guessing, and even life-and-death decision making. This text is designed to help you consider whether correctional administration is the right career for you.

Richard P. Seiter, Ph.D.

Acknowledgments

I wish to acknowledge the many people who helped, in a variety of ways, to make this book possible. First, thanks to my colleagues, both at Saint Louis University and across the country, who advised and encouraged me as I developed this book. Special thanks go to Harry Allen and Cliff Simonsen, two outstanding scholars and authors. They originally encouraged me to write a textbook, and we discussed many ideas before settling on the topic of correctional administration. They both gave me considerable advice over months of research and writing.

Second, I would like to thank the many students at Saint Louis University who went to the library, found books and articles, and researched topics and materials. These include Josh Pope, Cathryn Jacko, Pam Marstall, Steve Holt, Julia Staten, Karin Tusinske, Carrie Menendez, Megen Siebelts, and Krista Hall. Krista was especially helpful requesting the many permissions. And thanks to Cindy Lennox, department secretary, who helped in numerous ways with the development of this book.

Thanks to the many correctional agencies that provided information and photographs. Particular thanks goes to the Federal Bureau of Prisons and the Ohio Department of Rehabilitation and Correction. Anne Diestel, archivist at the Federal Bureau of Prisons, in particular, helped me sort through and select photos, and Tessa Unwin and Virginia (Ginny) Lamneck both helped me find and photograph pictures in the Ohio Department of Rehabilitation and Correction.

I thank the staff at Prentice Hall, who assisted in many ways, and Kim Davies, executive editor of criminal justice for her guidance and support. I especially appreciate the work of Kelly Curtis, developmental editor. Kelly not only gave me considerable advice and information but she also helped find Web links to aid students and faculty using this book. I also wish to thank Eric Metchik (Salem State University), Angela West Cockfield (University of Louisville), and Barbara Peat (Indiana University-South Bend). They reviewed the first draft of this textbook. I found their suggestions extremely valuable to improving the text, and making it more readable and useful for students of correctional administration.

Finally, I thank my many friends and family members who encouraged and supported me during the writing of this book. My son Matt, to whom this book is dedicated, and who seems well beyond his 18 years, regularly provided common-sense advice on research and writing the book. When I was tired of the work, his humor and encouragement always pushed me back to it. And thanks to my friend, Riffi O'Brien, who heard all of the complaints of how hard I was working, offered to assist in many ways, and was my constant source of motivation.

I owe you all a debt of gratitude. Thank you.

Richard P. Seiter, Ph.D.

PART

I

Correctional Management and Administration

CHAPTER

1

Correctional Administration: Past to Present

WHAT IS CORRECTIONAL ADMINISTRATION?

Is management the same as administration? Is leadership the same as management? Does the administration of a correctional agency differ from the administration of some other public agency? These are the kinds of questions this textbook is designed to answer, while providing the student or practitioner of correctional administration a framework for understanding the essential functions of a correctional agency, and the role of managers and leaders in that agency.

First, it is important to have a common understanding of terms. For purposes of this textbook, *administration* is a broad term, which encompasses both leadership and management, and includes all the activities and functions that leaders and managers must do to guide and direct an agency toward today's mission and tomorrow's challenges. **Correctional administration** is guiding and directing an agency responsible for the safekeeping of criminal offenders. As such, correctional administration includes all of the traditional management functions of planning, organizing, staffing, directing, and controlling. It includes the importance of having a thorough substantive knowledge of corrections and correctional issues. And, it includes showing leadership by empowering staff and guiding them toward the future. Although there are currently many private, for profit companies that contract with governments to conduct this function, this textbook primarily addresses the role of public correctional administration.

As we begin our study of correctional administration, you should keep in mind the definition of correctional administration—*guiding and directing an agency responsible for the safekeeping of criminal offenders. Safekeeping* of criminal offenders is herein used as a broad term to include protecting the public from further crimes committed by offenders, both through supervising offenders and preparing them to be successful and law-abiding citizens after release from the supervision of a correctional agency. In that sense, safeguarding of criminal offenders can take place in the community as well as in a prison or other secure institutional setting. Safeguarding also represents a balance or supervision of and programming for offenders, and cannot be achieved to it fullest with an emphasis on one function over another.

Guiding and directing an agency convey a unique aspect of administration. When most people think of administration, they think of "running something" and a boss telling people what to do. Administration is far more complex than that. Organizations must have a mission and goals; they must have a focus, and all staff must work together to move the organization forward toward accomplishing the goals. Administrators have a very challenging function of bringing together the resources of an agency (staff, budgets, facilities) in a coordinated fashion to put the organization in the best position to accomplish its mission. In that sense, an administrator is like a football coach who puts certain players on the field, gives them scouting reports of what to expect from their opponent, and modifies the game plan as the game progresses and the situation changes. The coach's job is to put the team in the best possible position to win the game and allow the players to accomplish as much as they can with their own abilities.

Guiding and directing has a future as well as a present context. Not only must an administrator maximize the use of resources and coordinate functions so the agency can accomplish the mission it currently faces but the administrator must also envision the future and guide the agency in a direction to increase their chance of success in coming years. This requires an understanding of the forces and pressures of an agency, anticipating change and developing issues, and preparing the agency to meet expected and unexpected challenges.

For the purpose of definition, the textbook uses four levels of delineation of correctional staff. **Line staff** are the employees or personnel responsible for carrying out the procedures and activities of the agency. Line staff include correctional officers in a prison who conduct security functions and supervise inmates, parole or probation officers who monitor whether offenders meet the conditions of their parole or probation, and drug treatment counselors who conduct group and individual counseling for addicts who are required to participate in programs as a part of their criminal sanctions. **Supervisors** are the next level of staff; they direct the functions of line staff. Their specific duty is to oversee the work of staff in any segment of an organization, while promoting efficiency and compliance with agency policies.

The third level of staff are **managers,** responsible for setting department or division goals and objectives, and ensuring their successful completion. Managers are responsible for controlling resources, such as budget dollars and staff allocations, and disbursing those resources in a manner that best accomplishes their goals and objectives. At the final level are **leaders.** Leaders provide direction, empower staff, and deal with external agencies and political leadership. Their external interactions are essential in order to create resources and establish authorities under which the agency functions.

This delineation of four staff levels (as illustrated in Figure 1–1) is an oversimplification of a general table of organization for a public agency. There can be, and

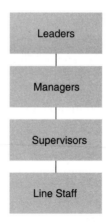

FIGURE 1–1 A "simple" organization chart indicating the hierarchy of staff roles.

usually is, overlap in these roles and functions. Many supervisors are also managers under these definitions. Many managers are also leaders. Although perhaps an over-simplification, these broad definitions will assist the reader in understanding material presented later in this text.

WHY IS IT IMPORTANT TO STUDY CORRECTIONAL ADMINISTRATION?

Correctional administration is one of the most challenging, unpredictable and diverse professions of any public or private management operation. You as students of correctional administration should understand the diverse challenges that face a modern-day correctional administrator. Corrections is the most rapidly growing public sector function and, perhaps, other than information technology, the most rapidly growing "business" in the American economy. Corrections is growing in the number of offenders it handles, it is growing in the number of staff required to carry out its functions, it is growing in the volume of tax dollars directed to its operations, and it is growing in public interest. Consequently, the administration of correctional agencies is also becoming more complex, and there is a need to rethink how corrections operates, and even its historically accepted goals and objectives. Correctional administrators of the future will face many challenges and must be prepared to step into leadership positions in an aggressive and bold manner.

Unfortunately, this growth of corrections is expected to continue. Despite the fact that crime (both violent and property) has been on a continual decline since the early 1990s, the public fear of crime continues. One poll indicated that 38 percent of those surveyed often worry about being the victims of sexual assault, 35 percent worry about being victimized, and 90 percent felt safe when alone at night only by staying home.[1] With fear of crime continuing, even with the actual reduction in the likelihood of victimization, elected officials respond by increased spending on law enforcement, expanded definitions of criminal activities, and enhanced penalties for criminal offenses. With the demographic prediction that a growing number of teenagers are moving into the high crime ages of 18 to 30, it is possible that crime rates could again increase. If so, the public's fear of crime will ensure that corrections remains a growth industry.

This growth creates a need for talented, educated, and well-trained individuals to enter the field of corrections, and work their way up the ladder to administrative positions. The issues correctional administrators must confront are some of the most complex in the public sector. And there is a great public misunderstanding of corrections, its operations, costs, and effectiveness. Correctional administrators must, therefore, educate the public, elected officials, and even their staffs. It is important for you to study correctional administration because proficient and professional correctional administrators are needed today and tomorrow to guide corrections through this rapid growth and uncertain future.

THE ORGANIZATION OF THIS TEXT

This book is organized to build your broad knowledge of the theories and development of correctional administration and the factors and issues that have been driving forces throughout its history. When you understand the dynamics between correctional administration and the environment in which it operates, you develop the ability to deal with problems you will encounter when you are in decision-making positions. Therefore, the text moves from general administrative challenges to more specific issues, such as creating a safe and secure prison environment, maximizing staff resources, and stretching tight budget dollars.

Part I of this text concentrates on the broad issues of management, administration, and leadership. In Part 2, a review of the background of correctional administration, and the link between philosophy and practice, results in your understanding the critical policy roles that administrators play in a correctional environment. You are then provided information regarding functions of correctional managers and correctional leaders. You discover how leaders have a responsibility to reach into the future, identify issues that challenge their agencies, and use strategic planning to position their agencies to meet those challenges.

We then move into a section of study to understand the philosophical underpinnings of corrections and how the need to balance punishment, rehabilitation, and other correctional goals impacts correctional administration. Administration does not occur in a vacuum without an overriding philosophy to guide policy and anchor decisions. It is important for you to learn how the need to meet a variety of societal goals must be factored into the practice of administration. Correctional administrators, whether they work in community or institutional settings, should understand the relevance of the overall correctional goals and theories to their individual programs and agencies.

In order to optimize the balancing of correctional goals within each criminal sanction, it is necessary to differentiate offenders by their program needs and security risks. One way in which correctional administrators attempt to do this is by using "risk assessments," or actuarial formulas, to identify levels of risks and needs. You learn how these tools are used to classify and manage offenders. By separating criminal offenders by risk and need, they can be placed in programs that will contribute to their rehabilitation, yet not undermine the importance of punishment and deterrence.

Approaches to managing criminal offenders can take place either in the community or in a prison. Although most offenders are supervised in the community, most of the correctional resources in the United States are directed to institutional corrections. Therefore, in Part 3 of this text, you learn how prisons are organized, what they try to accomplish, and how administrators must successfully juggle many balls (prison operations and programs) without dropping any in order to meet the overall mission of a prison. You learn how the basics of housing, food service, and medical care are provided in a prison setting, and how administrators gain compliance from and maintain order with a group of individuals who are detained against their will. Many of these individuals are violent and dangerous to staff and other inmates, and you learn the extraordinary measures that are taken to ensure safety within a prison.

With an understanding of what must be done, we move to a study of "how" it is accomplished. Corrections is a business, even though prisons are formidable structures and corrections often makes use of high-technology devices, that is, based on "people." Correctional staff are the most important resource for correctional administrators, and there are many key activities that must occur to optimize the staff's contribution to an agency mission. In Part 4 of this text, you learn about the management of human resources, and how important supervision is to effective staff utilization. You also learn about the functions and roles of certain staff positions in corrections, and information to help them make choices about their own careers in corrections.

Finally, in Part 5 you look toward the future. Although a variety of challenges for present correctional administrators are presented throughout the text, Part 5 begins with a review of some of the issues that will present even more difficult challenges for correctional administrators of the future. One of these is the cost of corrections, and considerable time is spent illustrating a variety of budgetary approaches to manage scarce financial resources. One of these is the somewhat controversial contracting with the private sector for delivery of correctional programs and services. The study of correctional administration ends with a visualization of the world of correctional administrators over the next few decades, as technology, politics, and changing administrative techniques evolve and influence the practice of correctional administration.

This textbook provides an extensive theory and background, and presents a wide variety of practical issues regarding correctional administration. Before moving further into the study, you must clearly understand the history and background of the correctional administration. Developments of management practices in the private sector, the public sector, and corrections have all had an impact on the current status of correctional administration.

THE BACKGROUND OF CORRECTIONAL ADMINISTRATION

As you begin your study of correctional administration, you must understand its historical perspective from two approaches. The first is how the discipline of both private and public sector management have developed throughout the history of the United States. The second is how the more specific discipline of correctional administration has developed, mirroring the prevalent theories of corrections, and how those theories have influenced the practice of correctional administration.

In this regard, correctional administration should be studied as an interactive entity, influenced by general management theory and by public expectations regarding the role of correctional agencies. When referring to the private sector, the term *management* is used rather than administration. *Administration* is almost exclusively a public sector term, without parallel in the private sector. Yet administration as defined for the public sector is similar to a more general term of management in the private sector.

It is easily argued that corrections is both influenced by the broader approaches to private and public management, and by public opinion and political reaction regarding the issue of crime. What makes correctional administration and management so complex is that corrections is a highly visible activity, a large percentage of public funds go toward its operations, and criminal justice is one of the top issues confronting every elected official and legislative body.

The next section of this chapter presents a brief history of public versus private management approaches, and continues with the development of correctional theory, and the impact theory had on management practices. As noted previously, it is important to understand general management practices, and how such practices develop incrementally to where they are today. Theory and practice in any discipline are not simply created; they evolve in an incremental fashion from past theory and practice. By understanding where a discipline has come from, it is possible to understand where it will go.

Private Sector Management

Throughout the years, public sector governments have copied the private sector in terms of management and organization styles. For that reason, it is helpful to review the history of private sector management to see how we got where we are today in government.

No matter how they started or how technologically sophisticated their product or processes have become, most private companies today can trace their work styles and organizational roots back to the prototypical pin factory that Adam Smith described in *The Wealth of Nations*, published in 1796.[2] Smith recognized that the technology of the industrial revolution had created unprecedented opportunities for manufacturers to increase worker productivity and thus reduce the cost of goods, not by small percentages, which one might achieve by persuading an artisan to work a little faster, but by orders of magnitude. From his studies of industry, Smith developed what he called the principle of division of labor.

Smith's principle embodied his observations that some number of specialized workers, each performing a single step in the manufacture of a pin, could make far more pins in a day than the same number of generalists, each engaged in making whole pins. Today's airlines, steel mills, accounting firms, and government agencies all have been built around Smith's central idea—the division, or specialization, of labor. Usually, the larger the organization, the more specialized the worker and the more separate steps into which the work is divided.

Another development in the way in which organizations operate resulted because of innovative changes in the ways in which goods could be shipped. In the 1820s, Americans began to build railroads. To prevent collisions on single-track lines that carried trains in both directions, railroad companies invented formalized operating procedures, and organizational structures and mechanisms to perform them. Management created a rule for every contingency they could imagine, and lines of authority and reporting were clearly drawn. The railroad companies literally programmed their workers to act only in accordance with the rules, which was the only way management knew to make their one-track systems predictable, workable, and safe. Educating or training people to conform to established procedures remains the essence of bureaucracy even now. The command-and-control systems in place in most companies (and governments) today embody the same principles introduced in the railroad industry almost two centuries ago.

Another important management development resulted from Henry Ford improving on Smith's concept of dividing work into small, repeatable tasks, inventing the assembly line, and thereby bringing the work to the worker. Alfred Sloan, head of General Motors, soon thereafter created the prototype of the management system that Ford's efficient factory system demanded. Sloan created smaller, decentralized divisions that managers could oversee from a small corporate headquarters simply by monitoring production and financial numbers. He was applying Smith's principle of division of labor to management just as Ford had applied it to production, because corporate executives did not need general expertise in all areas, for example, manufacturing or marketing. They could oversee these operations simply by creating quantitative goals and monitoring "the numbers." Companies created divisions dealing with production, quality, shipping, and finances. Likewise, government organizations created departments such as finance, human resources, delivery of program services, and operations.

The final evolutionary step in the development of private sector management came about in the United States between the end of World War II and the 1960s, a period of enormous economic expansion. Through elaborate planning exercises, senior managers determined the various types of businesses in which they wanted their corporations to be involved, how much capital they should allocate to each, and what returns they would expect the operating managers of these businesses to deliver. Large staffs of corporate controllers, planners, and auditors acted as the executives' eyes and ears, ferreting out data about performance, and intervening to adjust the plans and activities of operating managers. During this period, consumers had money to spend, and after being deprived of material goods (first by the depression, then by the war), customers were more than happy to buy whatever companies had to offer them, regardless of quality or service. The chief operational concern of managers, and how they responded to the needs placed on them, was to expand capacity, or increase the ability of the company to produce and deliver their products to their customers. Most corporations were organized as a pyramid, well suited to expansion by simply adding workers as needed to the bottom layer, and then filling in the management layers above them. This type of organization is also well suited to control and planning, and, therefore, proliferated throughout the 1960s and beyond.

The Public Sector

Following the private sector models, government similarly developed its organization and structure. Government has always been based on a bureaucratic model. However, 100 years ago, the word *bureaucracy* had a positive connotation—as opposed to how it is perceived today. It then suggested a rational, efficient method of organization. Mirroring the division of labor as created by Adam Smith and the need for procedures and control developed by the early railroads, bureaucracy was to take the place of the arbitrary exercise of power by authoritarian regimes. Following periods when strong political bosses operated government agencies as they desired, policies and procedures, command and control, and civil service systems were put in place as reform measures for government agencies. Bureaucracy was seen as facilitating precision, speed, and reduction of ambiguity.

Things have changed. The bureaucratic model of government developed when conditions were different from today—society was slower paced and change was incremental. Bureaucracy began with the use of a top-down hierarchy, when only those at the top of the organization had enough information to make informed decisions. It developed in a society of people who worked with their hands, not their minds. It developed in a time of mass markets, when most Americans had similar wants and needs.

We now live in an era of rapid change. There is a global marketplace; and information is available to ordinary people almost as fast as it is to their leaders. The economy is knowledge based; educated workers bridle at commands and demand autonomy. In the public sector, employees are important customers, and managers and administrators must recognize the culture and expectations of their employees/customers.

In this fast-paced and continually changing environment, bureaucratic institutions developed during the industrial era often fail. Today's environment demands organizations that are extremely flexible and adaptable, that deliver high-quality goods and services, that are responsive to customers, and that empower workers and citizens. Management and leadership must create organizations that can function effectively in these situations. Correctional administration was modeled after these traditional, bureaucratic organizations. They have historically been inflexible, highly structured, and with strong central authority. To be successful in the changing world in which we live, these traditional correctional organizations must modify their operations and management approaches.

Staff at the McNeil Island (Washington) Federal Penitentiary (c. 1895). Correctional administration was much simpler in the 1800s, when there were few staff or inmate issues. (Courtesy of the Federal Bureau of Prisons)

THE EVOLUTION OF CORRECTIONAL PHILOSOPHY AND ITS EFFECT ON ADMINISTRATION

As is generally true with public agencies, management practices reflect the mission and philosophical approach taken to accomplish that mission. Throughout the history of corrections in the United States, there has been a general evolution of the elements of the mission of corrections. During certain periods in U.S. history, correctional agencies focused almost exclusively on the punishment of offenders. At other times, the focus was on the need for rehabilitation. Recently, the primary emphasis has been on public safety. The following sections provide a brief overview of how the evolution of correctional philosophies has influenced the varying approaches to correctional administration.

The Mission and Goals of Corrections

For as long as corrections has been a discipline in the United States, its mission and goals have changed very little. Although not formally stated by most correctional agencies until the twentieth century, the **mission of correctional agencies** has been *to protect the citizens from crime by safely and securely handling criminal offenders, while providing offenders some opportunities for self-improvement, and increasing the chances that they will become productive and law-abiding citizens.*

Corrections has traditionally emphasized the goals of punishment, incapacitation, deterrence, and rehabilitation. There have been general swings in focus around which of these goals should warrant the highest priority. Goal priorities influence policies and procedures, budget decisions and staffing allocations, research and efforts to advance the state of the art of corrections, and public positioning for support by elected officials and the public.

Stages of Correctional Development

Throughout the history of corrections, the overriding philosophies and expectations of correctional sanctions influenced what correctional administrators did and the practices they put in place. Authors of corrections describe the history in a variety of ways. Allen and Simonsen list several trends during the "Age of Prisons" from 1800 to the present time.[3] When the United States was in its infancy, methods and approaches for dealing with criminals were related to prior experiences in England, yet they often reflected a desire to do things differently from what was done in the "mother country." The first use of prisons as criminal sanctions was in the United States. During this period, prisons were supposed to have a reformative effect on offenders, and therefore, prison managers emphasized strict control, hard work, and reflection on the crimes offenders had committed.

From 1870 until 1910, corrections was in the "**reformatory era,**" driven by a need to respond to the overcrowding of prisons and the building and operating of prisons to alleviate the overcrowding. U.S. prison administrators followed the early work of Captain Alexander Maconochie, who in 1840 took over the British penal colony on Norfolk Island, and Sir Walter Crofton, who built on the ideas of Maconochie as head of the Irish penal system. These two men used the concept of indeterminate sentencing, which emphasized preparing offenders for release, providing an opportunity for inmates to gradually reduce restrictions and work their way to a less controlling environment, and facilitating release on a conditional basis when administrators determined the offender was prepared to return to the community. The early use of conditional release led to the development of modern-day parole. Correctional managers in the reformatory era within the United States had to move beyond the earlier stage of prison operations, with its sole emphasis on punishment and reflection on the past. In the reformatory era, they provided an environment that expanded educational and other programs, and focused offenders' attention more on their future than on their past.

The twentieth century brought the "**industrial prison era**" from 1910 to 1935, and led to the first major interest in how correctional managers operated prisons by external parties. During this period, the number of inmates in U.S. prisons grew more than 170 percent,[4] resulting in the construction of several new prisons designed to hold large numbers of inmates in harsh, work-oriented environments. The emphasis was on inmates working to produce products that could help make the prisons self-sustaining. Using their free labor, prisons became very successful at this; prison management emphasized production as much as security and rehabilitation, and the volume of prison-made products sold on the open market increased considerably.

The success of prison industries brought challenges from organized labor to the continuation of large-scale prison industries. The U.S. Congress passed two laws, the Hawes-Cooper Act in 1929 and the Ashurst-Sumners Act in 1935 and amended in 1940, which severely limited the sale of prison-made products on the open market.

Inmates Clearing Timber at McNeil Island (Washington) Federal Penitentiary (c. 1910). The wood might be used in the prison industries. An emphasis on work during the industrial prison era resulted in large numbers of inmates assigned to work and produce products, later sold on the open market. (Courtesy of the Federal Bureau of Prisons)

As a result, these statutes tolled the death knell for the industrial prison, resulting in almost total idleness of thousands of inmates who had previously been working, and forced prison administrators to find another approach to operating prisons. From 1935 until 1960, described by Allen and Simonsen as the "**period of transition,**"[5] enforced idleness, lack of professional programs, and the excessive size and overcrowding of prisons resulted in an increase in prisoner discontent and prison riots. Prison managers were constrained in what they could do with the large facilities they had inherited and struggled to find alternative approaches to maintain control of prisons that were very difficult to operate.

Both external and internal pressures to reform prompted the "**modern era.**" This era was moved forward when the U.S. Supreme Court ended its **hands-off doctrine,** which had restricted judicial intervention in the operations of prisons and the judgment of correctional administrators. By accepting cases filed by inmates under the Fourteenth Amendment to the U.S. Constitution, the Court opened a "Pandora's box," and the floodgates opened for decisions by federal courts demanding certain procedures or operations be instituted in prisons.

Correctional officials also looked for reform themselves. They realized that they could not provide a safe and secure environment for inmates or staff with the current situation. One avenue for reform was to accept some level of inmate involvement in shaping prison policies through inmate councils or the use of ombudsmen as links between inmates and the administration. Other reforms included the professionalizing of staff through recruitment and training, and implementation of many self-improvement programs to take the place of the industrial work programs.

Inmates Working in the Prison Factory at the Lewisburg (Pennsylvania) Federal Penitentiary (c. 1935). The prisons built and operated during the 1920s and 1930s had large factories, and a major administrative emphasis was to maximize prison industry production. When these factories and the inmate workers were idled, new ways to administer prisons were needed. (Courtesy of the Federal Bureau of Prisons)

The Past Twenty-Five Years

Developments during the past 25 years of correctional history represent the most dramatic changes in philosophy, policy, and practice by correctional administrators. In the early 1970s, the **medical model** of corrections was clearly the most dominant theory influencing practice. With the medical model, offenders were believed to be sick, or "inflicted" with problems that caused their criminality. A medical approach was, therefore, appropriate, and offenders were diagnosed and treated in a hospital-like setting. It was believed that offenders' problems could be resolved through programming, and they could be returned to the community "well," successfully crime-free.

Many correctional officials realized that the medical model needed a little tweaking, and the community and institutional links had to be strengthened to be successful. "Reintegration" as a key principle was adopted but without forfeiting rehabilitation. After the offender completed treatment in the institutional setting, "step-down" care, or a transition from the institution to the community, was needed. **Reintegration** represented the inclusion of the community into the medical model, because it was understood that the transition from prison to free citizen in society was a difficult step for most offenders to make. Community correctional programs were in their heyday, and dollars and ideas on how to bridge the gap from the prison to the community were readily available.

The Death of the Medical Model

In the early 1970s, Robert Martinson reviewed all the correctional research to determine "what worked."[6] In the review, Martinson and his cohorts analyzed more than 200 separate studies of the effectiveness of correctional treatment programs in reducing recidivism. Although there were a few isolated correlations between a treatment program and a reduction in recidivism, there were no consistent findings of the effect of any single treatment program significantly reducing recidivism. Therefore, the Martinson review concluded that **"nothing works."** This revelation was the death knell for the medical model, and public officials looking for a way to reduce costs and make corrections more punitive had their statistical support. Soon, rehabilitative programs were not funded in many jurisdictions, and parole was eliminated in several states. The theory was that if these programs did not enhance public safety or change offender behavior, why spend money on them.

Correctional administration sought safe cover, and their retreat led to a philosophy and practice of improving management and focusing on the criminal justice process. The emphasis was on managing the criminal justice process in an efficient manner. Corrections could not change offenders; they had to make a decision to change themselves. The role of corrections was to efficiently provide program options, and it was the offenders' responsibility to take advantage of opportunities and change if they wanted. This period emphasizing efficient management unfortunately resulted in almost a generation of correctional administrators who forgot why most people seek careers in corrections, which is to make a difference in offenders.

The practical advantage of this time period was that the profession of corrections advanced in terms of improved management. It is interesting that during this period, the most career-enhancing, postgraduate degree for correctional workers moved from masters in social work to masters in public administration. Other positive changes included a better system for classifying and predicting risk in decision making, the rapid advancement in the use of computers and other technologies, a better understanding of organizations and managing people, and improved budget development and administrator's ability to deal with legislatures and elected officials. In addition, this era resulted in corrections strengthening their links with other criminal justice components, because there was not much difference between the perceived mission of corrections, law enforcement, or the court system.

The "Get Tough on Crime" Mentality

With the increase in crime, especially crimes of violence, during much of the 1980s, crime and corrections became very important to the public and elected officials. Throughout this time, constant media coverage of tragic and senseless violence created a fear of and anger about crime. Political rhetoric emphasized the need to be tough on criminals, to keep them away from law-abiding citizens, and to make them serve "hard" time. Correctional administrators, therefore, were forced to rethink and reposition their priorities. Over the past few years, corrections has had to react to the need to be tough, offer few amenities, and emphasize public safety over all

Inmates Wearing Stripes. The current "tough on crime" mentality has even resulted in going back to inmates wearing striped clothing, chain gangs, and other activities to make prison and jail punitive. (Courtesy of the Maricopa, Arizona, Sheriff's Department)

else. This "get tough" approach has resulted in a great reduction in managers and administrators taking even minimal risks to avoid problems that are hard to explain through the media. In a retrenchment and nonrisk-taking approach, there is little advancement in knowledge and professional development.

PUBLIC OPINION AND REPOSITIONING REHABILITATION

Corrections is now moving into another era of correctional management: one of implementing programs that 20 years ago would have been labeled as "treatment" or "rehabilitative." Today, they are called "programming," and the emphasis is not on helping the offender but on providing public safety by forcing offenders to deal with their problems, which may reduce their likelihood of recidivism. In this era, offenders are considered responsible for their pasts and their futures. They are not, as under the medical model, considered sick but rather irresponsible and lacking in respect for others and society.

This new era has been influenced by several developments, most of which occurred naturally, without correctional leadership strategically pushing the field in a particular direction. First, there is a new generation of correctional workers who did not experience the rehabilitative and medical model era. They entered corrections philosophically with a more criminal justice and individual-offender responsibility mind-set. But they bring with them an interest in implementing programs that can improve offenders' chances for success and hopefully reduce recidivism. They have not been burdened by the failure of the medical model, criticized by the media or the public for using community sanctions instead of focusing on incapacitation, or faced budget cuts for programs that could not be proven effective.

Second, although the principle interest of the public is to be protected, once they believe their safety concerns are met through incarceration of offenders, they support rehabilitative programs, such as educational and vocational training, drug abuse support groups, work programs, and counseling for inmates. Public support can lead to funding, and funding and encouragement from political officials leads to innovation and enthusiasm by staff implementing such programs.

Third, a positive economic climate has created a renewed interest in offenders as human capital. Across the United States, business and industry are experiencing a challenge in finding workers for entry-level jobs, particularly in the service industry. Twenty years ago, it was very hard to get past the fact that an offender had a criminal record when looking for a job. Today, this has changed significantly, and employers are even recruiting employees from correctional programs and institutions.

Finally, correctional programs have been repositioned to better fit into the current philosophical approach to criminal justice and corrections. The repositioning represents a shift toward holding offenders responsible for their criminal activity and changing their own behavior to prepare for successful reentry into the community. There is no consideration of how society may have let these people down, how their lack of educational and employment skills resulted in their inability to compete in society, or how their poor upbringing caused psychological problems that did not allow them to cope with challenges and problems. The focus is on acknowledging that people have free will and that they make lifestyle decisions that move them toward work and law-abiding activities or toward crime and violence. Schmalleger discusses the public perspective of this philosophy as such:

> This point of view holds that individuals are fundamentally responsible for their own behavior and maintains that they choose crime over other, more law-abiding courses of action. . . . This viewpoint, which we shall call the social responsibility perspective, tends to become increasingly popular in times when the fear of crime rises.[7]

The Responsibility Model

In this repositioned era, correctional administrators can offer correctional programs, but within a philosophy and in a manner that holds offenders responsible, both for their crimes and for their correction. For purposes of discussion, this approach to correctional programs is the responsibility model.[8] Current correctional programs in the **responsibility model** are often mandatory, and offenders are expected to participate and comply with the program requirements. They often must go to school, participate in substance-abuse counseling, work in a prison job, or do community service. The bottom line is that more is expected from offenders, and excuses for past behaviors are unacceptable. The eras of rehabilitation and reintegration have almost naturally evolved into the era of responsibility. This responsibility model is easy to support by correctional staff, the public, and elected officials.

ADDITIONAL HISTORICAL DEVELOPMENTS OF CORRECTIONAL ADMINISTRATION

Another method for studying the historical development of correctional administration is through Freeman's division of correctional organization and management into two periods: Pre-DOC Corrections covers the years from 1812 to the early 1940s, and DOC Corrections extends from the 1940s until the present.[9] Freeman notes that the Pre-DOC (prior to the organizational formulation of centralized departments of corrections [DOC]) period had a simple mission of controlling prisoners, which was accomplished by an autocratic prison management independent of any central correctional authority. The DOC Corrections period (after the formulation of central departments of corrections) developed around a more complicated correctional mission, in which rehabilitation was a comparable goal to custody and control. Freeman notes how states created centralized departments of corrections to provide centralized organization to both prisons and community-based correctional programs, which developed extensively during this period. Phillips and McConnell cite a similar transition regarding the nature and mission of correctional organizations. They note, "Many prisons of the past century provided only custodial care. For all practical purposes, there was only one occupation: the custodial (or security) service,"[10] and that there were "very few, if any, self-improvement programs."[11] They go on to describe, however, that by the end of the twentieth century, the role of the prison had evolved into an organization that not only provided security and safety but also "programs and services that inmates can use, if they so choose, to reach the point where they can live lawfully after release."[12]

In general, correctional administration has evolved from a simple, single mission organization, controlled by a single, autocratic leader. These earlier organizations had few written policies and no central department to coordinate operations, give guidance, and set goals. As the mission of corrections became more complicated, and as the operations became more visible and of interest to the general public, this trend changed significantly.

CORRECTIONAL ORGANIZATIONS TODAY

With this background, you can see how corrections has developed. However, correctional administrators currently face a much different environment than they did 100 or even 25 years ago. Before continuing to a discussion of the issues that confront correctional administration, it is important to present how the current situation facing correctional administrators differs from the past and to put this current environment into the context of our study of correctional administration. There are several ways in which today's situation is different from that of the past.

First, public opinion and political involvement in correctional policy and practice are active, whereas in past years it was passive. Crime is one of the most visible issues in the United States, and it affects almost every citizen. Although most citizens have an interest in public policy regarding defense, the environment, or economic development, they usually leave the details of the policy and practice to professional experts. However, with crime policy, there is not only high public interest but also most people have a strong opinion and take positions regarding how policies should be developed and implemented.

Second, correctional agencies now use a large percentage of the public budget of the federal, state, and local governments. When a high volume of dollars is directed toward any one area, a high amount of scrutiny is likely to follow. Big budgets get the attention of everyone, general citizens, interest groups for other social service programs, and elected officials. Supporters of increased budgets for education, child-development programs, economic development, and other public programs see the increasing correctional budget as a threat to their interests. As such, these special interest groups generate support for their budget concerns, which are frequently in conflict with the growth of correctional budgets. Elected officials would like to avoid pouring money into correctional operations. However, they usually do not want to modify legislation that would reduce the supply of offenders that require correctional supervision. These types of budgetary tensions, with the push to increase service but at less cost, bring increased attention to correctional agencies, their mission, and their operational approaches.

Finally, because of the extensive media coverage of high-profile crimes and sentencing practices, citizens develop a strong interest and opinion of criminals' treatment. Most people are fed up with crime, support criminals receiving sentences they perceive as punitive, and hold offenders accountable for their behavior. As elected officials try to react to this concern and continue to enhance sentences, they end up confronting the same policy issues: how tough to be and how much it costs. Debates regarding these issues create even more visibility and interest in how correctional agencies operate and spend their public dollars.

Correctional administrators face difficult challenges in this highly charged environment. There is great interest in what they do; they require more resources to carry out their mission, yet there is little philosophical support for allocating the resources it takes to operate continually growing agencies. Even the most supportive and responsible elected officials would rather spend less on corrections and more on "politically popular" public programs. As a result, although corrections received little interest 25 years ago, correctional administrators in today's environment face a variety of issues.

ISSUES FACING CORRECTIONAL ADMINISTRATION

These are not times for weak-spirited correctional managers and leaders. There are few public departments and organizations that face a more difficult challenge and a more rapidly changing environment. To be successful correctional administrators must be some of the best leaders and managers in government service. Throughout the remainder of this text, there will be an identification and detailed description of many practical issues that confront correctional administrators. To put these specific issues into perspective, the following discussion presents these issues in four general categories: (1) substantive correctional issues, (2) administrative correctional issues, (3) policy and philosophy correctional issues (what agencies should do and how they should do it), and (4) issues in managing the external environment.

Substantive Correctional Issues

Correctional administrators face a variety of challenging issues that require futuristic planning, innovation, and the effective management of change. **Substantive issues** within corrections involve that knowledge specific to the practice and profession of corrections and include such factors as dealing with increasingly overcrowded prisons and managing prisoners who are serving extremely long (possibly life without parole) terms. Managers of community-based correctional operations must consider what is often referred to as a new narrative for community supervision, one that deals more with supervision and public safety than with assistance and counseling for offenders.[13] Both prison and community correctional staff must deal with offenders who are younger, more violent, and more likely to be associated with gangs, and respond to the needs of a diverse offender population in terms of gender, age, and program needs.

From 1980 to 1996, the number of prisoners in state and federal prisons rose from 330,000 to 1,054,000, an increase more than threefold.[14] During this period, the prison population grew more rapidly than at any other period of time since prisons were first established.[15] In 1985, there were 256,615 inmates held in local jails, a number that more than doubled to 567,079 by 1997.[16] These increases present several issues for administrators: the prediction of the number and offender categories of growth, the development of policy on managing (for example, added bed space or diversion of offenders) the expected increase, public and political support for the approach, and the implementation of plans for managing the increase in offenders.

Each year, the average length of prison confinement increases. State legislatures and the U.S. Congress have consistently lengthened criminal sentences for all crimes, adopted three strikes laws for repeat offenders, and extended the number of crimes for which offenders must serve a "natural life" sentence, without the chance of ever being released from prison. Flanagan notes, "Prisoners incarcerated for long periods present correctional policy makers and administrators with several formidable problems. These problems stem from two principal characteristics of this prisoner population: (1) its diversity and (2) the serious offenses that eventuated in the inmates' long prison sentences."[17] These changes create unique and complex problems. Not only must correctional administrators determine the appropriate design and construction of prisons to house these inmates, but they must also look at how these longer sentences affect traditional approaches for inmate discipline and rewards to promote safe environments for staff and other inmates.

Proponents of longer sentences argue that longer sentences maximize the correctional goals of incapacitation and deterrence and result in maturation of offenders (offenders usually reach their peak criminal activity during their late teens to early twenties[18]). They suggest that these longer sentences effectively reduce crime and, therefore, justify the significant increase in the number of inmates.[19] Opponents, however, argue that this increase in prisoner term creates collateral issues that must be factored into the consideration of the benefit of this policy. Clear notes 10 unintended consequences of the growth of duration of imprisonment, including social consequences such as the recruitment of younger offenders to replace those criminals arrested and incarcerated, and the depreciation of the family that results from removing the parent-age male from the home. He also points out the fiscal consequences such as the reduction of funding for schools and other public services and the growth of future generation debt to fund prison construction and operation, even at a time when crime is decreasing.[20]

For most of the 1990s, community supervision (probation and parole) has undergone a transition from helping and counseling offenders to risk management and surveillance.[21] The focus on risk management is accompanied by new allocations of resources for incarceration, rather than probation and parole, and management of internal system processes. Greely and Simon describe this perspective as the "new penology."[22] Rhine describes this perspective as one in which:

> crime is viewed as a systemic phenomenon. Offenders are addressed not as individuals but as aggregate populations. The traditional corrections objectives of rehabilitation and the reduction of offender recidivism give way to the rational and efficient deployment of control strategies for managing (and confining) high-risk criminal populations. Though the new penology refers to any agency within the criminal justice system that has the power to punish, the framework it provides has significant analytic value to probation and parole administrators.[23]

Although community corrections and prison administrators struggle with how to deal with longer sentences and new strategies of supervision, they also must confront a basic and critical issue: managing an offender population that has changed dramatically during the past 25 years. Seiter describes these changes as follows:

> A variety of characteristics separate the contemporary offender from his or her historical counterpart. As a group, today's offenders are more prone to gang involvement and violence, are younger and more impulsive, are serving longer sentences, and have little hope or belief that they will successfully return to the community as law-abiding citizens. The number and percentage of females involved in crime have increased too. Many more offenders are dealing with medical and mental health issues. Last, juvenile offenders increasingly act like adults in their sophistication and types of crimes.[24]

A changing offender population requires correctional administrators to deal with several new problems, including handling violent, impulsive inmates while ensuring staff safely, providing medical and mental health programs to respond to increased offender needs and demands, and planning facility construction or renovation to house an increased number of female and juvenile offenders. These examples illustrate that correctional administrators cannot be singly focused, because they must confront a wide variety of problems in substantive areas such as prison security, offender programming, and facility and bed space management.

Administrative Correctional Issues

The substantive issues described previously require new responses for leadership and management in terms of **administrative issues,** or those traditional topics dealt with by managers and administrators, and include areas such as budgeting, human resource management, construction and planning, and projecting for the future. Budgeting for correctional agencies used to be a relatively simple process, with few controversial issues, resulting in little attention or concern by elected policy makers. However, as budgets have grown, demanding a larger share of governmental resources, there has been increased political scrutiny. In 1981, it was reported that correctional expenditures totaled more than $7.9 billion.[25] This amount has increased almost 400 percent in less than 20 years; the budgets for state correctional agencies were reported to be more than $29 billion in 1999.[26]

The challenge for correctional administrators is twofold. First, as a result of public concern the large amount of dollars being spent on corrections, administrators must convince elected officials that maintenance of their budgets is essential and probably will need to increase, because they usually have an increased supply of offenders to handle each year. Second, as the private sector becomes involved in operating correctional programs, competition develops, and public correctional administrators must ensure their budgets are not out of line with operating expenses of the private sector.

Another very complex administrative issue is the multitude of human resource management problems and challenges that result from rapid expansion, particularly when the work environment is difficult and sometimes dangerous. These challenges include recruitment, training and staff development, professionalizing staff, and labor relations. Most correctional agencies recognize the importance of staff above all else to accomplish their mission. Freeman even names an era in correctional management history after this recognition. He calls the period from the 1970s to the 1980s the human capital school, and notes how this approach "emphasized that employees are much more than just factors of production or individuals who only respond on the basis of feelings or needs. Employees are valuable investments that provide long-term returns to the organization if they are effectively developed and utilized."[27]

In periods of rapid growth, correctional agencies must obviously add staff, train them, and prepare them to take over challenging duties. However, new staff are only the bottom level of the organizational pyramid—with supervisors, managers, and administrators at each step above this level. With each new prison or community-based unit, there must be new supervisors, managers and administrators, as well as new line employees. Rapid growth requires rapid development of staff, because they must be prepared to advance in the organization and take over added responsibilities. Historically, much of the "maturation" and development of staff to assume upper-level positions came from years of experience. Unfortunately, during this period of rapid expansion, there is usually not time for the normal maturing of staff to occur. Correctional agencies, therefore, must ensure they have specialized training capabilities to accelerate the development of staff.

The human resource issues also include dealing with labor organizations. Phillips and McConnell note, "Labor management relations are an integral part of prison management; the question is whether you are dealing with the issue within a contractual bargaining structure or not. In the public sector, unions are a fact of life."[28] There are several reasons for the large number of unions representing correctional employees. First, with the decline in the number of industrial jobs in the United States, unions have concentrated on organizing and representing employees in the public sector. Second, in environments in which employees face risks to their personal safety (such as policing and corrections), there is likely to be strong employee involvement in unions. It is natural for employees to seek all of the support they can for the safest and most comfortable working conditions they can have. Finally, with the private sector entering corrections, public employees for the first time believe their job security could be threatened. Therefore, they turn toward unions for job protection.

A third administrative issue involves planning for the future. Correctional agencies have had almost two centuries of very slow change, and most strive for routine and consistency rather than organizational preparation for change. Times have changed. Freeman notes, "Correctional managers must constantly respond to changing circumstances in the internal and external environment."[29] Change should be anticipated, and the dilemma administrators face is how to position their organizations to adapt to this change. Implementing change requires an organizational ability to recognize factors that could bring about a need to change, establishing efficient decision-making processes, and the capability to modify policy and procedures as required. Many inexperienced managers think that making changes is easy. However, effectively managing change is one of the most difficult things a manager must do.

Policy and Philosophy Correctional Issues

It is generally understood that policy and philosophy issues drive the substantive and administrative issues. This certainly has been the case in the 1990s, and it is expected to continue into the millennium. Never in the history of corrections has there been so much attention and action by elected officials to dictate correctional policy. In *Corrections Management Quarterly* in 1997, Seiter wrote, "However, in an attempt to seem tough on crime, many correctional professionals believe that they [elected officials] may go too far in trying to influence what professional administrators should be doing."[30] Courtless continues this theme in a 1998 publication:

> As we have seen, corrections must deal with legislative actions and judicial decisions. Legislatures have been moving toward statutes based on philosophies such as "truth in sentencing," "just deserts," with determinate sentences, and variations on life without parole terms of imprisonment such as "three strikes and you're out," and harsher forms of probation and parole. The correctional administrator has little choice but to follow these laws when offenders enter the correctional domain.[31]

Some **issues of policy and philosophy** that confront correctional administrators include responding to the current emphasis on punishing offenders, managing risk and reducing the opportunity for offenders to commit further crimes, the types of amenities that should be available in prisons, the number of support programs to divert offenders from prison, and the types of rehabilitative programs to provide to offenders. A recent issue that is getting increased consideration by elected officials involves the proper role for the private sector in the operation of correctional activities and facilities.

Perhaps the greatest challenge for correctional administrators is to maintain balance in a system that is constantly bombarded with admonitions to be tough on crime and punish criminals. **Mandatory sentences** of imprisonment for first-time drug offenders, **three strikes** laws requiring life without parole, and removing amenities from prisons are all the result of the public and elected officials' belief in a need to ensure criminals are punished. Although punishment is a valuable and legitimate goal of corrections, all four goals (punishment, incapacitation, deterrence, and rehabilitation) must be balanced to maintain a professional organization that continues to meet its mission to protect society over the long term. Correctional administrators must understand public desires that criminal offenders be punished for their crimes. However, they should not simply accept punishment as marching orders and must take the responsibility to advise and counsel elected officials on the importance of rehabilitation, deterrence, and incapacitation as well as punishment to ensure a safe environment for staff and improved opportunity for the future success of offenders.

Correctional agencies are also urged to develop policies that move offenders deeper into more restrictive correctional sanctions thereby reducing the use of diversion and community-based programs. The public has little tolerance for offenders who commit additional crimes while under community supervision. As correctional administrators try to retain the effective use of community sanctions, they do so with great peril. As a result, there is a greater use of classification and risk management (attempting to predict the chance of success) to help guide these decisions and make community supervision explainable when it results in failure.

Along with a harsher public attitude focusing on punishment, corrections often faces an increased supply of offenders without a comparable increase in dollars and staff resources. Yet correctional administrators must find ways to carry out programs that can improve the likelihood that offenders will become productive and law-abiding citizens. They must be guided by research findings that determine those programs most likely to be successful, and they must implement them in an efficient and committed manner. During the 1960s and 1970s, there was ample supply of federal money available to jurisdictions through the Law Enforcement Assistance Administration grants for initiation of new programs. Today, in an environment of scrutiny and scarce resources, implementation of new programs designed to do anything other than be more restrictive to offenders is difficult.

Issues in Managing the External Environment

Linked closely to the challenges of dealing with policy and philosophy is the issue of managing the external environment. The **external environment,** as related to corrections and correctional administration, includes interest groups outside the correctional organization, such as the media, political supervisors, the legislature, other criminal justice and social service agencies, and a variety of interest groups from victims to offender families. The external environment is the arena in which the philosophy of correctional issues evolves into public policy.

For correctional administrators to effectively influence public policy, they must be adept at managing within the external environment. Historically, correctional administrators did not do this well. With little public interest in correctional policy or practice, correctional administrators could do almost whatever they wished with little oversight or concern. Today, correctional administrators must be much more sophisticated and have a broad base of leadership skills. In acknowledging the breadth of talents required of high-level executive positions in correctional agencies, Riveland writes:

> I would suggest that the ideal candidate for corrections director positions in the future would have the following qualities: well-grounded experientially and academically in correctional operations and theory; in management skills and techniques; and in major public policy development and political skills. Many have the first two, few have all three.[32]

Many correctional administrators note, and often bemoan the fact, that they spend more time on issues external to the organization than on dealing with their agency's central mission. They regularly deal with interest groups, who may either support or disagree with the agencies' policies. They often give media interviews to explain a policy or describe a situation or incident. They respond almost daily to their executive branch leaders or to members of the legislature. If they want their policies to be supported by these elected officials, they must educate and convince them that they are in the public and the officials' best interests.

There are two types of external issues: those to which the administrator must react and those that require a proactive approach of education and coalition building. For correctional administrators, the reactive type of issues often result from a serious incident, such as a prison escape, a serious crime committed by a parolee, a disturbance or riot, or a union picket or walkout. The proactive issues usually result from a challenge to an established policy or the administrator's interest in changing a policy. Both types of issues require considerable time, and both require considerable patience, excellent communication skills, and a foundation of trust and confidence in the administrator by others. The case study on page 26 is an outstanding example of how many of the issues discussed are involved as a result of one serious incident in a prison.

SUMMARY

This chapter outlines the history of correctional administration, the evolution of correctional theory and how it impacts correctional administration, and the issues confronting corrections now and in the future. The remaining chapters of this text will expand on these topics. You should now have an understanding of how correctional administration is one of the most difficult roles in the public sector. As well, you should have an idea of how important it is to study correctional administration as a distinct profession requiring a combination of education, experience, and personal preparation to perform effectively.

PRACTICAL PERSPECTIVES

An Administrator's Worst Nightmare

The call came about 3:00 A.M. A correctional supervisor in the state's maximum security prison was on the telephone as the state prison director sleepily answered. "I am sorry to have to wake you up," started the supervisor, "but we just had an inmate die here at the prison after an altercation with staff. The warden is out of town, and the associate warden is on his way but said I should call and inform you." Now fully awake, the state director got more information, and asked the supervisor to tell the associate warden that he would be at the prison in about two hours. He called the deputy director, and they soon left for the 100-mile drive to the prison.

When they arrived at the prison, the director and deputy director received more details. An inmate with a history of mental health problems, who was violent and was isolated in a cell identified for mental health troubled inmates, had started to destroy his cell and act up at about 11:00 P.M. He jumped head first from the top bunk to the floor, and appeared to be injured. The supervisor in charge at the time ordered a group of correctional officers to assemble, remove the inmate from his cell, and move him to another cell where he could be restrained, medicated, and checked for injuries.

When the group of eight officers was assembled, they discussed how to move the inmate. The inmate was very big, very strong, and they suspected he would not come out peacefully. They decided to use a Plexiglas riot shield, move into the cell as a group, and pin the inmate against the back wall. They would then handcuff him, and move him to the other cell. However, when they opened the cell door, the inmate came charging out at them, knocking down many of the officers. They were in a large area, and did not have close walls to use to help control the inmate. Most of the officers were untrained in self-defense, were out of shape, and were not prepared to handle the inmate in this situation.

The single inmate was successful at holding off the officers, and they were having a difficult time grabbing his arms and legs to control him. Finally, they got him down on the floor, and started to restrain him with handcuffs. The inmate was struggling and flailing his head around, making it difficult for the staff to hold him still. One of the officers yelled at another to hold the inmate's head to the floor. Tired from the fight, instead of reaching down with his hands, the officer took his foot and placed it on the side of the inmate's neck to hold his head. The inmate was successfully restrained and taken to the other cell. However, when a medical person went into the cell to check on his injuries about 30 minutes later, the inmate was dead. It was believed that the officer's foot was pressed on the carotid artery, cutting off blood to the brain, and resulting in death by asphyxiation. The state police were called in to do an investigation.

The death of the inmate under these conditions was bad enough, but the circumstances made it worse. Exactly one week before, a staff member at that prison had been murdered by an inmate. The prison had a history of racism, with only one African American of 500 staff members. The state director had been on the job for less than one year and was targeting this area for change. The staff member who was murdered was a well-liked, over age 60, white staff member who worked in the prison industry area. The inmate who killed him was African American, had a history of mental health problems, and was mad because the staff member had threatened to fire him from his job unless he improved his work performance.

The death rocked the spirit and morale of the prison staff. They questioned the leadership of the prison and the department, they complained that there were not enough staff for security and safety, and they threatened a union action of some type if things didn't improve. The prison was in the district of the most powerful member of the state legislature (the speaker of the house of representatives), and he had to do something to respond to his constituents. So, there was already an emotional and inflamed environment at the prison at the time of the inmate's death.

When the circumstances of the inmate's death became public, there were cries from the African American community and many media reports hinting at racism and retaliation by prison staff. Another very powerful state legislator, a leader of the African American elected officials in the state, called on the governor for action, including criminal prosecution and the firing of all officers responsible for the death. The racial issue was even more inflamed by the fact that about one month before an African American woman, who was director of the department of mental retardation was fired by the governor for poor management, in part because of the death of a patient who had suffered neglect by staff at one of state hospitals.

The state director of corrections refused to take any immediate disciplinary action against the staff involved. He believed there had not been intent to injure the inmate and knew that the investigation by the county grand jury would result in criminal prosecution if intent was believed to exist. He also believed the staff had not been properly trained in handling mentally ill inmates or in safely and humanely removing a violent inmate from a cell. He did not believe that the inmate's death was racially motivated, yet it was difficult to deter that appearance. However, there were calls for his firing for not taking more aggressive and immediate action.

Although the director reacted to media and legislative requests to explain findings to date and his decision not to immediately discipline the staff, he used the opportunity to get additional resources and implement some changes at the prison. With the support of the speaker, he received approximately 30 new correctional and mental health staff positions. He candidly discussed the racial issues with African American members of the state legislature and secured their support for recruiting African American staff to apply for the new positions and to implement racial sensitivity training at the prison. He worked

Continued

with the state department of mental health to expand their services to the prison, and used some of the positions to open a special unit at the prison to manage mentally ill and violent inmates. As these changes were being implemented, the county grand jury decided to not seek an indictment against the correctional officers involved in the death with a crime.

The director continued to push for the changes at the prison in a deliberate, persistent manner. He demanded the prison leadership to increase the number of African American staff, and within 12 months, added approximately 25 minority employees to the prison. He required physical renovations to be quickly completed to house the new mental health unit and added cells in the hospital for inmates suffering from serious, yet temporary, mental health problems. He oversaw new training on the removal of violent inmates from cells in a manner that reduced the chance of injury to staff and inmates. Although these changes did improve the situation at the prison, without working hard to respond to the external pressures surrounding this incident, the director states he probably would have been fired and not able to implement the needed changes.

Correctional administration did not develop as an independent discipline without the influence of administration in both the public and private sectors. It has been influenced by the correctional philosophy prevalent during various periods and eras throughout its history. Especially during the past 25 years, the public and political interest in correctional policy has caused administrators to look not only internally but also to interests external to the agency. Successful correctional administrators have found that they must become adept at managing the external environment as well as successfully performing traditional management roles.

This chapter includes a description of the four types of issues that must be addressed by correctional administrators: substantive correctional issues, traditional administrative issues, policy and philosophy issues, and issues that evolve from external sources. The rapid growth of corrections, the changing political environment, the challenge of getting additional resources, the multiple missions and conflicting goals, and the need to create stability in the midst of chaos makes the job of a correctional administrator one of the most unique and challenging in either the public or private sector. It requires strong leadership, the ability to plan and predict the future, and the knowledge of how to empower and motivate employees to be successful in the new millennium.

The case study presented is an illustration of a real-life situation that includes almost all the categories of issues. You can see how the state director referenced in the case study had to be knowledgeable in improving the functions of a prison by addressing areas that undermined its safe and secure operation, and managing administrative issues such as budget needs and staff training. He also had to address the policies that he wanted to change at the prison, and both react and be proactive with interests groups in the external environment, in order to make desired changes. At this early point in your study, you have the framework and understand the general background of issues linked to administration in a correctional agency. The remainder of this text builds on this framework and continues to challenge you to integrate the theoretical and practical applications of correctional administration.

ENDNOTES

1. "Poll: More Fear Being Murdered," *USA Today,* 26–28 November 1993, A1, A8.
2. Adam Smith, *An Inquiry into the Nature and Causes of the Wealth of Nations* (Philadelphia, PA: Thomas Dobson, 1796).
3. Harry E. Allen and Clifford E. Simonsen, *Corrections in America: An Introduction,* 8th ed. (Upper Saddle River, NJ: Prentice Hall, 1998).
4. Margaret Calahan, *Historical Corrections Statistics in the United States: 1850–1984* (Washington, DC: U.S. Department of Justice, 1986), p. 36.
5. Allen and Simonsen, pp. 46–47.
6. Douglas Lipton, Robert Martinson, and Judith Wilks, *The Effectiveness of Correctional Treatment and What Works: A Survey of Treatment Evaluation Studies,* (New York: Praeger, 1975).
7. Frank Schmalleger, *Criminology Today: An Integrative Introduction,* 2nd ed. (Upper Saddle River, NJ: Prentice Hall, 1999).
8. Richard P. Seiter, "A Rebirth of Rehabilitation: The Responsibility Model," *Corrections Management Quarterly,* 2 no.1 (1998): 89–92.
9. Robert M. Freeman, *Correctional Organization and Management: Public Policy Challenges, Behavior, and Structure* (Boston, MA: Butterworth Neinemann, 1999), p. 5.
10. Richard L. Phillips and Charles R. McConnell, *The Effective Corrections Manager: Maximizing Staff Performance in Demanding Times* (Gaithersburg, MD: Aspen Publishers, 1996), p. 4.
11. Ibid. p. 5.
12. Ibid. p. 5.
13. Edward E. Rhine, "Probation and Parole Supervision: In Need of a New Narrative," *Corrections Management Quarterly* 1 no.2 (1997): 71–75.
14. Jill Furniss, "The Population Boom," *Corrections Today* 58 no.1 (1996): 38–43.
15. Albert Blumstein "Prison Populations: A System out of Control?" in *Crime and Justice: A Review of Research,* edited by Michael Tonry and Norval Morris (Chicago, IL: University of Chicago Press, 1988).
16. Bureau of Justice Statistics, *Prison and Jail Inmates* (Washington, DC: U.S. Department of Justice, 1997).
17. Timothy J. Flanagan, "Correctional Policy and the Long-Term Prisoner," in *Long-Term Imprisonment: Policy, Science, and Correctional Practice,* edited by Timothy J. Flanagan (Newbury Park, CA: Sage Publications, 1995), p. 249.
18. Albert Blumstein et al., *Criminal Careers and "Career Criminals,"* Vol. I, Chap. 3 (Washington, DC: National Academy Press, 1986).
19. Edwin W. Zedlewski, "Why Prison Matter: A Utilitarian Review," *Corrections Management Quarterly* 1 no.2 (1997): 15–24.

20. Todd R. Clear, "Ten Unintended Consequences of the Growth of Imprisonment," *Corrections Management Quarterly* 1 no.2 (1997): 25–31.

21. J. Simon and M. M. Freely, "True Crime: The New Penology and Public Discourse on Crime" in *Punishment and Social Control*, edited by T. G. Bloomberg and S. Cohen (New York: Aldine De Gruyter, 1995).

22. M.M. Greeley, and J. Simon, "The New Penology: Notes on the Emerging Strategy of Corrections and Its Implications," *Criminology* 30 no. 4 (1992).

23. Edward E. Rhine, "Probation and Parole Supervision: In Need of a New Narrative, *Corrections Management Quarterly* 1 no.2 (1997): 71–75.

24. Richard P. Seiter, "Offenders and Issues Force Managerial Change," *Corrections Management Quarterly* 1 no.4 (1997): iv.

25. Edmund F. McGarrell, Timothy Flanagan. *Sourcebook of Criminal Justice Statistics—1984* (Washington, DC: U.S. Department of Justice, 1985), p. 2.

26. Camille Graham Camp and George M. Camp, *The Corrections Yearbook, 1999: Adult Corrections,* (Middletown, CT: Criminal Justice Institute, 1999), p. 85.

27. Freeman, p. 24.

28. Phillips and McConnell, p. 406.

29. Freeman, p. 363.

30. Richard P. Seiter, "Setting Correctional Policies," *Corrections Management Quarterly* 1 no.2 (1997): 81.

31. Thomas F. Courtless, *Corrections and the Criminal Justice System: Laws, Policies, and Practices* (Belmont, CA: Wadsworth Publishing, Co., 1998), pp. 387–388.

32. Chase Riveland, "The Correctional Leader and Public Policy Skills," *Corrections Management Quarterly* 1 no.3 (1997): 24.

KEY TERMS

correctional administration	medical model
line staff	reintegration
supervisors	nothing works
managers	responsibility model
leaders	substantive issues
mission of correctional agencies	administrative issues
reformatory era	issues of policy and philosophy
industrial prison era	mandatory sentences
period of transition	three strikes laws
modern era	external environment
hands-off doctrine	

YOU'RE THE CORRECTIONAL ADMINISTRATOR

1. You are a probation administrator in a large metropolitan county. You have been increasingly concerned over the past decade about the trend toward surveillance and monitoring of probationers, and the lack of support for rehabilitative programs such as substance abuse prevention and vocational training. There are more and more rules being passed down about the need

for urine tests for drug use and a "zero tolerance" once someone tests positive. Probation revocation rates are going up dramatically. Although you agree that probationers that fail to meet their responsibilities should be revoked and sent to prison, you think the current reactive approach doesn't put enough emphasis on helping offenders, and many who are trying but have relatively small failures end up being sent to prison. Can you consider the responsibility model that is discussed in this chapter as a way to reposition rehabilitation and try to move for a more balanced approach to supervising probationers? How would you do this? What type of public message would you create about rehabilitative programs? How would you try to sell the need for these programs to your politically sensitive leadership?

2. You are in charge of planning for a correctional agency. You believe that challenges for correctional administration are usually influenced by the development of new correctional philosophies. You have been asked to speculate on the next era of correctional philosophy that will develop from the current get tough approach. This is important so the agency can begin to consider how the philosophy might impact the operations. How do you go about thinking about the future? What type of information is important to consider? How do you go about the task of predicting the future? Once you decide how you will make the prediction, what do you think is the "next era" of correctional philosophy?

◼ WEB LINK EXERCISES

Federal Bureau of Prisons www.bop.gov

Go to the Web site for the Federal Bureau of Prisons (BOP). Find the section on public information, and search for documents regarding the history of the BOP. Pick any of the historical documents or articles, and read it. From this history, identify what era of prisons it primarily references and the types of issues that administrators would have had to deal with in regard to this topic in history.

CHAPTER 2

Leadership and Management of Corrections

LEADERSHIP AND MANAGEMENT IN CORRECTIONS

In this chapter, you examine correctional leadership and management, and clarify how the two terms are similar and distinct. *Webster's* defines *management* as the judicious use of means to accomplish an end, and *leadership* as directing the operations, activity, or performance of an organization. These definitions imply a subtle difference between "doing" and "guiding," or "making something happen" and "showing the way." Although some authors argue that management and leadership are different, others suggest that they are similar. Carlson almost combines the two, noting how "strong, involved management does not preclude the chief executive officer from exuding many intrinsic leadership qualities."[1] In practice, these terms are often used interchangeably.

In this book three terms are used to discuss the roles of those responsible for correctional agencies or operations and distinguish among the three. The first term is **leadership.** Correctional leaders are responsible for the broad-based setting of direction and guiding the agency through both internally and externally created challenges. Leadership is associated with the higher-level functions of mission and vision. Managers conduct traditional supervision of activities to ensure that the day-to-day functions of an organization are accomplished. In this regard, **management** is more likely linked to policy and procedure than mission and vision. **Administration** is the third term. Simply put, correctional administration encompasses both the functions of leadership and management. The term *correctional administrators* includes both leaders and managers of correctional agencies and the roles they play in the organization.

▮ TRADITIONAL CORRECTIONAL ADMINISTRATION

Historically, correctional administrators focused their activities on managing the internal organization. Throughout the history of corrections, the terms *leadership* and *management* had a very different meaning than they do today. Through most of the history of corrections, prior to the establishment of state- or countywide departments of corrections, prison wardens and agency heads wielded almost autonomous authority, establishing policy and procedures, and hiring and firing staff as they desired. This was understood to be leadership, more in the General George S. Patton mode than in the staff involved mode of today.

Currently, leadership brings to mind guiding an organization through difficult times, setting agendas and priorities, and empowering staff. Historically, when leadership was discussed, it was not envisioned as empowering employees with a vision and urging continuous improvement through total quality management.[2] Whereas leaders do the right things, managers do things the right way. Throughout the history of corrections, there was a different understanding of management than there is today.

Management came about with the advent of bureaucracy, and managers were those people who made sure operations were efficiently completed according to the dictates of those in charge. Management was soon thought of as the typical functions of planning, organizing, directing, and controlling. Midlevel management positions were created to supervise organizational entities (departments, divisions, or sections). Managers were charged with these four functions of management within their area of responsibility, were held accountable to ensure the entity completed the tasks for which they were responsible, and were responsible for contributing to the overall mission of the organization.

These roles and functions of leadership and management continued with little change until the 1980s, when elected officials and politicians became more interested in corrections. Until that time, corrections was generally a small part of state or federal budgets and, therefore, did not attract the attention of elected officials. Elected officials paid little attention to correctional operations, assuming that correctional administrators were good managers if there were no problems that surfaced and had to be dealt with at a level above the correctional department. Policy and practice were the responsibility of the correctional administrator with little political intervention. Today, public correctional administration has changed radically. Politicians are interested in what is done, how it is accomplished, how much it costs, and how successful the results are. Therefore, the role of both leaders and managers of correctional agencies has changed dramatically.

PRACTICAL PERSPECTIVES

"How Things Have Changed"

Recently, a state correctional director from a decade ago was musing about the political oversight of current state directors. She told the story of using new technology to change policy and practice to improve the prison environment and benefit taxpayers. The state had many prisons built in the 1930s through 1950s. These prisons used traditional methods for perimeter security to keep prisoners from escaping. The prisons usually had a set of two fences around them, and armed guard towers every one hundred yards or so to watch the fence and shoot inmates who tried to escape.

The problem with guard towers is that they are only as effective as the staff member's ability to see the fence, and accurately shoot an escaping inmate. The staff member also has few options to using deadly force. They cannot leave the tower and respond to the area of attempted escape. However, new developments in physical fence security offer new approaches. Many medium security prisons have moved to upgrading the fence security using layers of razor ribbon, which makes it extremely difficult for inmates to move through and get to the fences without being seriously cut and injured. As well, electronic detection devices can be set up on the fences, and alert staff to an attempted breach of the fence, even if the staff are not present or cannot see because of fog or other bad weather conditions. Finally, instead of having eight to ten guard towers around the prison fence line, two or three armed "roving" patrols are often used. Roving patrols are correctional officers in vehicles specially equipped with electronic pictures of the fence line which visually show the point of attempted breach. The vehicles continuously drive around the perimeter, and two or three patrols provide more improved coverage than eight or ten towers.

The director told of how she had staff research the possible replacement of the towers at the medium security prisons in the state. The findings were that for approximately $150,000 per prison, the physical security of the fences could be improved with razor ribbon, electronic detection devices could be installed, and roving vehicles could be purchased and equipped. Two roving patrols operated 24 hours per day, seven days per week could replace ten towers which also had to be operated continuously, saving eight staff posts. These eight posts required forty staff to cover. A post that must be covered 24 hours per day, seven days per week, is calculated at approximately five to one. In other words, calculating the need for around the clock coverage, sick and annual leave by staff, it takes five people to fill one post. At an average of $35,000 dollars in salary and benefits, these forty staff not needed could save $1,400,000 per year.

The director decided to invest the money in upgrading the fences, and eliminate all the towers in the medium security prisons. The staff saved from the tower posts would be used to implement unit management (discussed in Chapter 7). When the plan for the first prison was announced, the local union objected. They suggested that the change would not be as effective as the current guard towers. However, in reality, some of the correctional officers liked working alone in the towers, with no contact with inmates and little contact with their supervisors. The union even put an advertisement in the local newspaper saying how eliminating the towers would increase the chance of inmate escape and endanger the local community.

The prison warden and director developed a plan to reduce the union opposition and inform staff of the benefits of the change and of implementing unit management. First, they sent several staff to another state prison about seventy miles away, to observe the non-tower fence system, and talk to staff at that prison about its effectiveness, and the benefits of unit management. Second, the warden let union leadership try to get through the razor ribbon and climb the fence without setting off the alarm and having the roving patrol quickly respond. They could not do it. Finally, the warden and director briefed local politicians about the effectiveness, benefits, and potential cost savings of the new system. These efforts were successful, and six medium security prisons eliminated towers, and several new prisons were built without towers.

The director enjoyed telling how the change was beneficial to her state. She then bemoaned how she had just read a January, 2000 Associated Press article about New Jersey Governor Donald T. DiFrancesco ordering state prisons to continue manning guard towers, reversing a cost-cutting measure imposed by his predecessor, Governor Christie Whitman. The Whitman administration had previously ordered prisons to begin vacating the towers as new electronic perimeter fencing was installed. The article noted how complaints from correctional officers and community residents persuaded DiFrancesco to change course.

WHAT CORRECTIONAL ADMINISTRATORS MANAGE

To understand the functions of management and leadership in corrections, this section describes the traditional areas that administrators manage. After a general discussion of these areas, a new model of correctional leadership and management is presented. As with any public administration function, correctional administrators have a dual role. First, they must manage the administrative areas standard in public administration, such as budgeting, human resources, and facility maintenance. Second, they must manage the substantive areas of corrections, such as security, offender programs, and operational procedures. In addition to this dual role, correctional managers conduct those functions required to accomplish the day-to-day activities of their organization. Phillips and McConnell suggest that management is the effective use of resources to accomplish the goals of the organization.[3] Koontz and O'Donnell point out that managers are responsible for planning, organizing, staffing, directing, and controlling.[4] These traditional management functions are the mainstay of correctional managers, as they are with other public sector or private sector managers.

Planning

For the first three-quarters of the twentieth century, correctional administrators were not required to conduct any extensive level of planning. Simply put, **planning** is looking into the future and deciding what an agency and its workers must do to respond to the issues and challenges they face. Historically, planning has been deficient for correctional administrators, because most correctional planning that was accomplished was neither complex nor long term. Chapter 3 discusses strategic planning, or charting the long-range activities for an agency. However, most planning in corrections has focused on short-term (perhaps six months) issues such as dealing with staff shortages, expanding to meet an increasing institutional or community program population, or developing a budget for the next fiscal year.

As noted previously, the history of correctional management is not replete with discussions of planning activities or how administrators planned to respond to changes in policy or philosophy. Correctional planning for the most part has been incremental, meaning that staff begin with the status quo and decide if they need to change what they are doing in moderate ways. Planning is seldom a perfect process; a major planning activity does not often result in a listing of goals and objectives for the future. Forces thrust on corrections more often spur planning, as administrators decide how to respond to these forces, which frequently results in knee-jerk reactions and "Band-Aid" solutions.

For instance, in the 1930s, when the Ashurst-Sumners and the Taft-Hartley acts forced idleness in prisons by almost eliminating prison industry work opportunities for inmates, prison wardens had to modify operations to ensure the secure and safe operation of their facilities. They did this by increasing security and limiting programs. These changes were not the result of a regular planning activity to anticipate the future but reactions to a change forced on wardens at that time.

Today's correctional managers have to be more sophisticated about their planning processes. For one, most government operations require detailed budget information regarding the changes expected by an agency, what these changes will mean for management, and how the agency's budget submission responds to these changes. Second, the environment in which correctional managers operate today is fluid, and because of rapid changes in conditions, corrections managers must be flexible and plan and replan throughout the year. Most correctional agencies have created an organizational unit responsible for planning. Staff assigned to the planning unit complete several planning tasks, collect information that will be important to consider in the planning process, monitor compliance and progress on the current plan, and coordinate the actual planning processes.

Organizing

The development of bureaucracy and the division of work forms the basis of the process of organizing. By **organizing** work, an agency links staff functions to the accomplishment of the organization's mission. The first step in organization work in a public agency involves understanding the product or outcome expected by the agency or organizational entity. Administrators then organize the specific tasks that must be accomplished to produce the product or outcome into a table of organization. A typical table of organization for a prison is presented in Figure 2–1. Tables of organization are narrower at the top than at the bottom. They often include department or unit titles, and they communicate expected lines of authority and reporting. Each person noted in the table of organization has a specific responsibility that is to be accomplished, and each contributes to the overall agency mission. The method for completing tasks at each level is detailed through written policy and procedure.

Organizations generally have a similar hierarchy of policy and procedures that somewhat mirrors the table or organization. As an example of how this might look organizationally, see Figure 2–2. Upper-level administration is responsible for setting policy for activities to be accomplished. Midlevel managers create

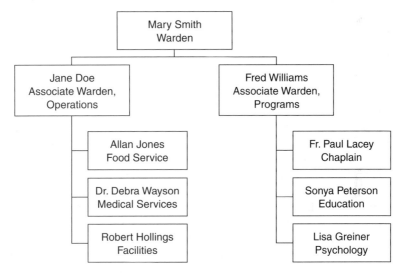

FIGURE 2–1 Typical organizational chart for a prison.

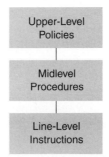

FIGURE 2–2 Organizational hierarchy of policy, procedure, and instructions.

procedure—how policies are to be carried out. And the lowest levels (individual employees within an organization) have specific instructions about how to perform their functions.

In a prison or jail setting, the instructions are often called **post orders,** and they detail how a correctional officer or other line employee completes their assigned daily tasks. Examples include conducting a security check of a building or area, searching inmates, or applying handcuffs and escorting offenders. In a community setting, such as probation and parole, officers may have procedure manuals regarding writing presentence investigations, conducting home visits of supervised offenders, or conducting interviews.

Staffing

Staffing has to do with matching people capable of carrying out specific tasks with the assignment of those tasks within the organization. In contemporary management texts, staffing is not always listed as one of the key management functions, because it is considered a more specific function of the human resource department, rather than a general management activity. However, managers must take responsibility to ensure they have the right people in place to carry out the duties. The human resource departments complete the more technical activities, such as recruiting staff, following rigorous hiring practices endemic to public agencies, and ensuring that performance appraisals are done in a timely and fair manner.

Managers, however, are the key staff positions that monitor performance, suggest additional training, take disciplinary actions for nonperformance, and mentor and develop staff to effectively perform their duties, as well as prepare to take over assignments with additional responsibility. In this regard, staffing is the responsibility of managers. No one in an organization can better take action to ensure that employees' skills and the jobs assigned are a satisfactory match.

Directing

An area in which correctional managers excel is directing operations. **Directing** involves the supervision of functions to be accomplished, through clear policies, procedures, and a chain of command. Perhaps because corrections is a "paramilitary" organization, supervisors are very good at giving direction to line staff regarding how to understand policy, follow procedures, and accomplish work. The success of a correctional agency is often the result of clear direction to staff, with little or no variance in carrying out established policy. The role of supervisors is, therefore, to ensure that written policies are followed, both by staff and by inmates.

In correctional agencies, directing staff comes from two elements: written policy and procedures, and a clearly understood chain of command. Prisons and community correctional agencies usually have a lengthy policy and procedure manual, guiding staff on how to carry out all types of tasks in detailed fashion. As noted previously, prisons use post orders to direct correctional officers on particular shifts regarding the activities they are to perform at certain times during their shifts. There are regular checks by supervisors to ensure that these activities are accomplished.

The second element of directing staff involves a clear chain of command. As illustrated in Figure 2–1, correctional agencies have tables of organization that indicate who works for whom. As in the military, lower-ranking staff take orders and direction from their higher-ranking officials, and according to the culture of these agencies, orders are communicated and passed through the ranks. These traditional lines of authority have historically been very rigid, and it was considered a "cardinal sin" to not follow the chain of command. With more modern methods of leadership and empowerment, these traditions are changing, and communications are more flexible and free flowing.

Controlling

Controlling is a management function most often viewed as taking action to ensure that activities and procedures are completed as directed, and result in accomplishing the organizational objectives. Correctional managers have probably been somewhat ineffective in conducting evaluations of the effectiveness of programs and operations. Little time and few resources have been focused on determining the effectiveness of programs or procedures. It is relatively easy to create a policy and give a directive to carry it out. However, it is much more difficult to follow it up, measure results, and ensure the policy results in the intended outcome.

Supervisors monitor activities of line staff in a variety of ways. In some situations, they may actually watch activities being performed and make adjustments on the spot. Once they know staff have performed a specific procedure, supervisors may follow up procedures by discussing with the staff any problems the staff encountered or any questions they had about the task. Or, supervisors may be able to determine the successful completion of the procedure by reviewing the end results. Prison managers can move throughout the prison and quickly get feedback from staff and inmates as to the effectiveness of a procedure or program. In this sense, correctional managers effectively control their operations with continuous and regular feedback, even though they are less formal than a more rigid evaluation of policy effectiveness. There are formal process evaluations of policies and procedures to determine whether managers have achieved the results anticipated.

◾ A CHANGING VIEW OF CORRECTIONAL LEADERSHIP

Correctional agencies are paramilitary organizations, taking many of their key operational functions from the military model of command. Line correctional officers wear uniforms, ranks such as sergeants, lieutenants, and captains are often used; and the need to follow the chain of command is understood by both staff and offenders. Wardens were historically perceived as generals in that successful wardens had to be assertive, strong, and let it be known that they were the bosses. Wardens were thought of as autocratic leaders, wielding power over all things in their domains, totally controlling the prison, staff, and inmates. They were not only thought of as the authoritative boss but also as the highest ranking person in the organization; they were believed to be the smartest and most powerful, the person who always knew what to do and how to do it.

Today's complex environment for corrections, as well as the development of theories of quality management emphasizing new roles for leaders, requires a change in what is expected of correctional leadership. Much of the impetus for change has been the public arena in which corrections operates. Traditional correctional leaders, in the stereotypes noted previously, had much greater control than contemporary leaders. Historically, leaders managed the *internal* operations of the correctional agency with very little *external* interference. With few policy directives from their political supervisors, these historical leaders were allowed to focus on the internal operations of the agency and were not accountable to anyone about why they made a particular decision or took a particular action. As noted, traditional correctional leaders were very autocratic, not only because they wanted to be but also because every process and procedure was not identified in a step-by-step manner. In fact, in the early years of correctional administration, there were few written policies. Therefore, correctional leaders were left to their own devices and whims about what should be accomplished and how it should be done. Today, there are rules and regulations for every activity, from hiring staff to spending a budget to supervising an offender.

Traditional correctional leaders had few demands on them to be *external managers,* because corrections was of little interest to elected officials, the courts, or the media.[5] Today, the operations of corrections are of interest to everyone. With crime as a high domestic priority, what correctional agencies do, how they do it, and how much it costs is of great interest to the public and elected officials. Only a few decades ago, the courts would not get involved in correctional management issues. Today, they are regularly and intensively involved in corrections and even direct how some correctional agencies must be managed. Media sources seldom reported on activities or occurrences in prisons. However, print and television media now regularly present stories about criminal justice and correctional programs and operations. They have found these stories are of high interest, sell newspapers, and attract viewers.

Leadership in the New Millennium

Needless to say, correctional leadership in the twenty-first century will have to be very different than leadership in the past. Leadership was historically associated with a position rather than a person. Leaders were those in the top position who exercised power by giving orders and making decisions. Leaders offered rewards and resources to followers in exchange for assistance in reaching the organization's goals. This type of leadership of the past was defined as "transactional," involving exchange relationships between leaders and followers.[6] **Transactional leadership** involves essentially immediate, short-run exchanges. It is often very bounded in that it affects the immediate organization only and has little consideration for the public or society as a whole.

Transactional leaders were the traditional authorities, those with the position, power, and knowledge of a substantive area. These leaders were able to provide an-

Leadership Training for Ohio Correctional Employees. The increasing demands on correctional leadership for dealing with the media has prompted some correctional agencies to include training on conducting a media interview.
(Courtesy of the Ohio Department of Rehabilitation and Correction)

swers and direction for any issue the agency confronted. Staff respected them and looked to them for guidance and direction. Transactional leadership worked fairly well in the relatively stable correctional environment of the past, with routine situations within the experience of the leader.

It is easy to think of the traditional role of the warden as transactional leadership. The warden was the substantive expert with the experience and background to know how to deal with any situation. The warden was the person who knew where to find answers for responding to any circumstance. In this model of leadership, the person in the highest position of authority is frequently expected to know more than they actually do. This puts pressure on the leaders and often forces them to "play the expert" even when they know they are not, because it is what staff expects of them.

Leadership of the future will relieve some of this pressure, but in exchange, there will be demands for more sophistication and intellect in dealing with issues and followers. The challenges of the future are based on the fact that there will be rapid change and, therefore, fewer guiding policies for dealing with many issues. There will also be fewer substantive experts who have experience dealing with problems, because with rapid change, many problems will be new or have a new twist to them.

The type of leadership required for the future is referred to as "transformational." **Transformational leadership** is much broader than transactional leadership. It is based on principles rather than practice and on motivating people to jointly address challenges and find solutions to new problems. Transformation leaders begin with a vision that has a set of values and principles as guidelines to use in responding to issues. They inspire staff to focus on the broader vision and higher-level goals, and help staff and the organization to learn and work through problems in an adaptive manner. Transformational leaders know they cannot jump to conclusions or rush to find quick and easy answers to many questions. They must involve staff in creative and innovative solutions. This conflicts with the traditional leader who searches for an expedient way to respond to problems to find a quick fix. The future requires developing the ability for leaders, managers, and line staff to work together, involving and empowering staff to adapt to change and deal with difficult and frustrating issues.[7]

CHALLENGES FOR THE FUTURE

Only a few decades ago, corrections involved a simplistic system, ignored and undisturbed by outside intervention. Since approximately 1980, however, corrections has changed dramatically and is now a multibillion-dollar industry that is as complex and visible as any public service agency in the United States. Moving into the new millennium, change and demands on correctional administrators will be even more dramatic. There will be many new challenges, or continuing challenges that will grow in intensity or will require a different approach. Following are a few of the more significant challenges.

   1. Scrutiny will intensify from the media, elected officials, and the public.   It is expected that this increased scrutiny will lead to a greater "politicalization" of correctional departments and institutions. Since the mid-1980s, elected officials have become very involved in the philosophies and operations of corrections. In many cases, the conservative emphasis of being tough on crime has resulted in correctional administrators being forced to establish chain gangs, boot camps, and "supermax" prisons. Many recreational, educational, and treatment programs, and "inmate privileges" have been stripped from prisons. Some correctional administrators believe these are the right approaches during conservative times, because the public demands that offenders be punished for their crimes. However, there are also many correctional administrators who disagree with these policies but see no alternative other than their implementation. Therefore, correctional administration has taken a "reactive" approach to these activities, and in most cases, correctional administrators have not been involved in the discussion and decisions of whether these practices were adopted.

   Another result of the increased scrutiny has been an increased "politicalization" of correctional agencies. Historically, elected officials were uncomfortable appointing anyone without extensive correctional experience to the highest positions of leadership, believing that the most critical challenges for correctional leadership occurred during a prison crisis, and wanting the confidence in their correctional leaders' abilities to handle these types of situations. However, it is now common for elected officials to appoint individuals without backgrounds in correctional management to leadership positions. The individuals appointed are usually politically sensitive and involved, and can be counted on to factor public and political perceptions into their correctional decisions. This indicates that elected officials now see more risk in poorly handled "political" situations than in poorly handled "crisis" situations. Even when "correctional professionals" are appointed or stay in charge of correctional agencies, they find increased pressure to make "political" rather than "correctional" decisions.

2. Rising incarceration rates will mean more inmates but not a proportionate increase in dollars or staff resources.   Even though there has been a reduction in all types of crime rates since the early 1990s, there has been a continued increase in numbers of offenders and money funneled into the correctional system. Most members of the general public, if asked, would respond that crime continues to increase rather than decrease. The political response to the perceived public fear of crime and criminals has been to push for long terms of incarceration as the primary sanction for criminal activity. Unfortunately, although the public continues to pour more money into building and operating prisons, there has not been a rethinking about preventative approaches to deal with the social causes of crime or a serious examination of community versus institutional sentencing choices. Therefore, the increase in incarceration rates will continue.

Meanwhile, there is an increasing concern about the total amount of money directed toward correctional systems. During the 1990s, the number of offenders under correctional supervision and the amount of money allocated to correctional agencies grew exponentially. Although state legislatures and the U.S. Congress will probably not change these policies resulting in expanding prison populations, they have shown a hesitance to obligate operating funds in proportion to the inmate growth. This may seem irresponsible. However, as legislators try to respond to many other demands (such as educational programs, health care, and economic development) for tight budget dollars, it is only natural that they will try to reduce the growing correctional budgets so they can fund more popular public ventures.

3. The number of young, violent, gang-oriented inmates will continue to rise. Prisons and community correctional agencies are difficult to manage, even when there is a high degree of homogeneity among offender groups, resulting in a relatively low level of conflict and high level of stability. However, with more competing factions (street and prison gangs) under correctional supervision, it is expected there will be more strife and problems to confront. More violent acts among offenders, as well as by offenders against staff, will create concerns for staff and offender safety. How to control these gang-oriented offenders will be a major challenge for administrators. With an increase in violent incidents, the media, elected officials, and employee unions will question the ability of correctional leadership to safely manage the environment.

4. "Generation X" has different motivators, skills, and needs for involvement. The correctional workforce of the 1990s (even more so in the future) is very different from the workforce of 20 years earlier and is often called the **generation X workforce.** These employees are perceived as less dedicated and committed to their employers, seeking immediate gratification for their work performance, and expecting to be involved in organizational decisions. In some ways this is a very positive trend. There are indications that a higher percentage of employees entering corrections have some college education or a degree in criminal justice. In addition, most of these new employees are computer skilled and easily adapt to rapid changes in technology. However, the new workforce is very different in the way they expect to be supervised and managed, and the amount of involvement they expect in the workplace.

This workforce is less dedicated to the agency and more focused on themselves and their career advancement. They want to be involved in not only the practice but also in the decision-making process for operations, because they want to know the background and reasons for decisions before they support them.

5. For public sector correctional administrators, the private sector will be a "competitor."   It is hard to imagine that there could be competition for the government carrying out functions that have traditionally been the purview of the public sector. This is especially true when considering that probation, prison, and parole functions oversee and deter freedom from citizens. However, public correctional agencies are no longer the only possible providers available to operate prisons and other correctional sanctions. Private, for-profit companies now operate several prisons and supervise offenders in communities.

Private companies argue that they can do just as good a job as the public sector and that they can do it for less money. With the noted concern for reducing the money allocated to correctional agencies, without having fewer people in prison and under supervision, the private sector message of cost reduction is attractive to elected officials. This is expected to result in pressures for increased use of the private sector in the future. Public correctional agencies often become very defensive about private corrections companies, and in many cases, fight their involvement. The challenges for future correctional leadership are to find ways to work cooperatively with the private sector, while accomplishing the correctional mission for the overall good of the taxpayers and considering the interests of current public employees.

6. There will be continued, rapid change in technology and information availability.   There is no reason to believe that the rapid changes in technology and information availability will decline. Society is inundated with new technology and what it can do for correctional management. The current approach to managing prisons and community correctional agencies is several years old, and even with technological advances, there have been few changes in correctional procedures or approaches. Technological advances provide an opportunity to reconsider the mission of corrections and to determine whether technology can better be used to help accomplish the correctional mission.

These challenges make the task of correctional administrators even more difficult. Leaders must guide their staffs through times of change and through public questioning about what they do and how they do their jobs. Correctional leaders will be required to learn to manage externally, to create a vision for staff, and to empower staff to carry out this vision. The future presents an opportunity to "reinvent" correctional practice and find more efficient ways to accomplish missions. The old paradigms of correctional administration are decades old. The future provides opportunities to create new ones.

THE NEED TO MANAGE (AND LEAD) EXTERNALLY

Throughout the history of the United States, the American public and their elected officials have paid little attention to corrections. Few people cared about what went on in jails, prisons, or even about how offenders were supervised in the community.

But with the media attention on crime, fear of potential victimization is high, and the public demands government action to make communities safer. Elected officials respond by creating policies and passing legislation that directs (and possibly micromanages) correctional agencies and programs. Working in corrections under these conditions generates a sense of "operating in a fishbowl."

As a result, correctional leaders strive to find ways to effectively manage in this very public arena. Too often, correctional administrators are not consulted and their professional judgments are not sought when a change in correctional policy is considered by elected officials. By learning to better manage the external environment, correctional administrators are more likely to be invited into the discussions of such issues of correctional policy.

I have advocated several proactive activities that can facilitate correctional administrators' becoming involved in the external decision making surrounding correctional policy.[8] First, correctional administrators must understand the point of view of elected officials. Second, correctional administrators must indicate an ability and willingness to effectively put in place programs important to the general public and political leaders. Third, correctional administrators must communicate their own messages about the importance of what they do. Fourth, correctional administrators must know the results of correctional programs, and where there are none, create them. Finally, correctional administrators must understand and practice compromise. When they are confronted with a proposal for a correctional policy that they oppose yet believe is inevitable, they should find ways to accept some of the elements that have strong public support and incorporate them into more acceptable practice.

The first rule of politics is that elected officials want to get reelected. Even dedicated elected officials who support correctional programs will make decisions counter to the professional judgment of correctional administrators if that judgment endangers their reelection. There are certain issues that the public supports as elements of the criminal justice and the correctional systems. For example, the public wants offenders to be punished; they want offenders to be held accountable and to pay back society for their crimes. In this regard, the public supports public works programs as well as prison industries if inmates produce goods or somehow repay society with a portion of their earnings. An Ohio public issue survey regarding correctional issues found an overwhelming majority of respondents favoring prisoners working, being paid for their work, but requiring the earnings be used to repay victims for their loss or paid to the state for the cost of the inmates incarceration.[9]

The public wants to be protected yet understands that every offender cannot be sentenced to prison. The public, therefore, supports intermediate sanctions for nondangerous offenders. Another Ohio survey illustrated how respondents supported community corrections programs but were more in favor of using them to deal with scarce prison space instead of paying for new prison construction.[10] A more recent random survey of respondents from all 50 states also found that "while over half of the American public agrees that community corrections programs are too lenient, a much stronger majority appears to support certain programs that keep offenders in the community."[11] However, it was noted that this support for community corrections "appears to be dependent on how effective those programs are at protecting citizens against crime.[12] These surveys also indicate that the public does not want prisoners and other criminal offenders treated too well, and they do not want to spend money on prison "amenities" or treatment programs they believe lessen the impact of the punitive aspects of the sentence.

The public also expects there to be a focus on the victim, believing that victims deserve to be informed and to be involved in decisions regarding perpetrators of their crimes. Since the beginning of the formal criminal justice processes in the United States, society (the government) took responsibility for processing and punishing criminals. As a result, victims were soon removed from any direct involvement in judicial and administrative decision making. Victims were to "assist" the criminal justice system by providing evidence and testifying against the individual alleged to have committed the crime. The overall emphasis was the notion of justice for the state, rather than justice for the victim.

The role of victims in the criminal justice process began to change during the 1960s, as advocates of the **victim rights movement** endorsed the victim as the primary person needing to be heard and as influential in the decision making process. As a result, victim assistance programs began to offer support to victims, counseling them as to the justice process and providing services that could educate and assist them with their continued involvement. There has also been a renewed emphasis on requiring offenders to pay victim restitution, taking responsibility for the harm they have done to their victims.

A key to effective management of the external environment is for correctional administrators to be sensitive to these issues and proactive in implementing such programs. By putting programs in place that are supported by the public, before being asked or having the programs legislated into law, correctional officials can create confidence that they are acting in the public's best interest. In turn, it is expected that elected officials will trust and more often support positions important to correctional administrators. When elected officials believe they will not have to worry about correctional administrators implementing politically unpopular policies that could ultimately damage their chances for reelection, the professional judgments of correctional administrators will more likely be sought and valued.

There are two sides to the issue of the proper role of correctional administrators in the policy-making process. Some authors argue that correctional administrators serve the public and should not try to influence policy. Garrett suggests the following:

> Institution administrators should not become involved in the political process. As experts in corrections, professional administrators are sometimes called upon to share such expertise and facilitate the consideration of proposed changes in the law. While senior institution staff should always welcome the opportunity to educate lawmakers, they must be cautious not to give the appearance that they are trying to influence the legislative process.[13]

Others suggest that correctional administrators are "experts" and have a responsibility to be involved in the process and to influence policy development. As experts, correctional administrators influence policy by giving opinions based on information and experience, and they argue for policy that best meets the overall purpose or mission of the agency. Important to this debate is the approach a correctional administrator takes to influence public policy. In a thoughtful and practical article, Chase Riveland identifies the many ways that correctional leaders can be involved in public policy creation and suggests ways to be involved in the political process in the proper role of expert.[14] Some of his suggested steps for involvement in public policy include the following:

- Facts should drive the policy. However, it is often done backwards, as ideas for policy are put forward, and facts are then developed to justify them.
- Leaders have to sell every reason a policy makes sense and benefits the stakeholders, and when it doesn't, that should be explained.
- Take time (have patience) and let parties become comfortable with the ideas, issues, and solutions.
- Involve a diversity of opinions in big issues. Involving critics presents other sides of an issue and legitimizes the decision.
- Build constituencies for topics that do not have much political support. Issues such as overcrowding and inmate health care have few supporters until a crisis hits.
- Be honest and candid with the media. Explaining background information to the media, especially editorial boards, can go a long way toward influencing policy in a beneficial manner.

Another way correctional administrators manage externally is by informing the public about important correctional issues, and the philosophy and practical needs for certain practices. One responsibility of a leader is to shape public opinion and confidence in corrections. By reaching out to the public, the media, and elected officials, increased trust, support, and understanding of what corrections does can be built, even if there is not total agreement about how it is accomplished. U.S. Senator Mike DeWine from Ohio notes that correctional administrators should not sit back and let public opinion be shaped by sensational media coverage of extreme cases, offender failures, and stories that the news media find interesting.[15]

For years, corrections officials have been hampered in attempting to argue for programs without good research data to confirm that what they do is effective. Since the 1970s when Robert Martinson wrote about what worked and argued that "nothing works," correctional officials have been on the defensive.[16] Corrections is a big business, with billions of dollars directed to the operation of correctional agencies. Yet there has been very little information to prove which programs are effective or which archaic programs, such as chain gangs, are ineffective. Allen Ault, former commissioner of corrections in three states and former chief of the NIC National Academy of Corrections noted,

> I do not believe that we in corrections will ever be a "profession," or that we in it will ever be considered professionals or listened to by the public or the politicians, until we have our own body of knowledge—the distinction of a profession—that is backed by solid research. We have adapted other knowledge from many other professions and attempted to apply it in the correctional setting, but too often we did not have any research component to consider if it worked or not. It is hard to sell programs when you do not have facts to back up their effectiveness.[17]

Until recently, there have been very few sound research studies that conclusively determined that certain correctional programs work. However, there are now several studies that show a relationship between drug programming, job readiness classes, and education that link program completion with reduced criminality.[18] It is important for correctional administrators to know the results of program effectiveness and to be able to use data to argue for correctional programs they believe improve their ability to manage or reduce recidivism.

LEADERSHIP AND EMPOWERMENT

As noted previously, leadership in the twenty-first century will require a very different way of managing the external environment. In addition, the future will also require changes in the way leaders manage "internally" and interact with employees. The transactional leader, who sends commands down the chain of command, through layers of bureaucracy, will not be successful in the new millennium. The future-oriented, transformational leader, who creates a vision and empowers employees to fulfill that vision, will be the preferred leadership style for at least the next decade. Changes in how leaders operate will also require changes in how managers and line employees function within the correctional organization.

One way to structure this new leadership approach in a manner that integrates leaders, managers, and line staff is illustrated in the leadership and empowerment triangle in Figure 2–3. The triangle is not the same as an organizational chart with an increasing number of employees from top to bottom, and it does not indicate lines of reporting or authority among staff. It relates to the types of tasks that each layer of the triangle should perform.

At the top of the triangle are the tasks that should be key functions for leadership in the new millennium in any organization. These tasks focus on providing staff with tools and opportunities to better manage and operate the agency. The leader's role has changed considerably over time, from directing specific actions to empowering employees to take the actions they recognize are necessary. Therefore, the following four key functions are those recommended for contemporary public leadership.

1. Create a vision and set the direction for the organization.   Agencies and organizations must have a vision, a road map or understanding, of where they want to go and what they want to be. Leaders must create this vision for their agencies. This does not mean that the leaders do this for the organization. In fact, leaders should not individually create or define the vision but should involve employees in setting the vision. Leaders do not have a monopoly on understanding where the agency should go or what the agency should be. Leadership of an organization, instead, acts as the primary resource for information and even opinion for employees as they develop a vision and should be personally involved with employees in any group process to discuss the vision. In reality, even though it is often understated, employees are many times more vested in the future of the organization than leadership. The leaders are usually older, and will retire or move to another position before the

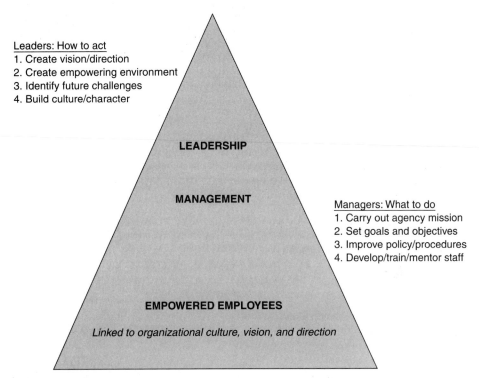

Leaders: How to act
1. Create vision/direction
2. Create empowering environment
3. Identify future challenges
4. Build culture/character

LEADERSHIP

MANAGEMENT

Managers: What to do
1. Carry out agency mission
2. Set goals and objectives
3. Improve policy/procedures
4. Develop/train/mentor staff

EMPOWERED EMPLOYEES

Linked to organizational culture, vision, and direction

FIGURE 2–3   Leadership and empowerment triangle.

typical line correctional employee. Therefore, it is critical to involve employees in creating a vision, and setting the direction for the future of a public agency.

2. Create an empowering environment.   Leaders have a unique opportunity to create an environment where employees can maximize their own skills, complete assigned tasks, and make decisions that enhance the agency mission. It is critically important for leaders to recognize that employee morale, commitment, and enthusiasm for their jobs increase in direct proportion to their feelings of importance and recognition for what they have to offer. Leaders must recognize this, create an environment that pushes decisions down to the lowest level, share information on a continuous basis, and encourage the pursuit of excellence by all staff within the organization.

3. Identify areas of challenge for the future.   Leaders have the opportunity to learn from other organizational leaders, from their political supervisors, and from key constituents and stakeholders that employees often do not see and hear. As leaders process this information, they have the unique opportunity to identify trends and anticipate future challenges. A myth in most organizations is that leaders must be smarter than line employees, because they seem to have a broader picture of how the organization fits into the political and public environment in which they operate. This is not the result of more brainpower. It is the result of access to information and individuals that line employees do not enjoy. Therefore, it is the responsibility of leaders to pass on this information, and identify and prepare the organization for future challenges.

4. Build (or reinforce) the organization culture and character.   There is considerable discussion about the importance of agency culture. Most agencies have developed a culture, hopefully one that encourages professionalism and dedication to the mission. However, negative cultures can also develop, and it is a true test of leadership to change a negative into a positive agency culture. Character of leadership receives more discussion now than it has in the past. This is partially because of the public perception that many other public officials take advantage of their positions for self-benefit. Leaders are responsible for setting the tone and character of an organization. The organization takes on their moral personality and character in ways that even the leaders may not recognize.

The second level of the leadership and empowerment triangle is the management level. Managers are the doers, those who make sure things are done the right way. Just as the role of leaders has moved beyond traditional tasks, the role of managers has also increased in the level of sophistication required to take over some of these functions. Managers should be those people who ensure that the agency mission is accomplished. They do this by working within their divisions or departments to set goals and objectives, to refine and improve policies and procedures, to develop staff though training and mentoring, and to continually reinforce the agency mission in employees' minds.

The biggest change in functions in the leadership and management triangle comes in the role of line employees. It has always been important to clearly describe tasks for employees, oversee their work, and hold them accountable for completing those tasks. However, it is seldom recognized that every line correctional employee makes dozens of decisions during an eight-hour shift. How do they deal with a somewhat noncompliant offender? How do they handle a minor security breach? How do they counsel an offender who has an issue that needs immediate attention? How do they respond when they see a co-worker being less than professional?

The end result of leadership in an organization is to empower employees to make decisions and respond to situations in a manner consistent with the culture, principles, ethics, and values desirable within an agency. Through the four roles of leaders described, employees will come to understand the culture, organizational direction, and professional approach that is desired, and hopefully, their actions will be consistent with those. Leaders and managers cannot be everywhere to observe operations. By creating the proper empowering environment and ensuring employees understand the vision and direction of the agency, employees are better prepared to make appropriate decisions and function in a professional manner.

SUMMARY

The issues facing corrections have changed dramatically over the past few decades, requiring correctional leadership and management to change accordingly. Historically, leaders were autocratic and ruled correctional organizations with an iron fist. Few states had central departments of corrections, none had standardized policies and procedures, and prison authorities decided on their own how the prisons would operate. Managers performed the traditional functions of planning, organizing, staffing, directing, and controlling. Even those functions, however, were unsophisticated and performed without guidelines or bureaucratic standards.

Today's environment for corrections is sophisticated, complex, and requires standard, bureaucratic processes for almost everything. Change is rapid, and new problems must be confronted. Corrections has become a very visible discipline, with high public interest and intense involvement by political officials. No longer are correctional administrators left alone to manage their organizations without interference. The public demands to be protected and that offenders be held accountable. Elected officials look for ways to toughen penalties, yet they do so without taking too many resources from their more favored government functions. Correctional leaders, therefore, must understand and be actively involved in managing the external environment.

This situation requires a modification of how correctional leaders and managers perform. Leaders must now be as concerned with understanding and managing the external environment as they are with the internal organization. Therefore, they must spend their time looking forward, identifying new trends and challenges, being proactive, creating a vision, and empowering staff with that vision. They must become transformational leaders by focusing on the principles, values, and vision of their organization rather than on efficiency and procedures. Because procedures must still be performed efficiently and consistently, leaders must encourage mid-level managers to oversee day-to-day operations, meet agency goals, improve policy and procedures, and mentor and develop staff.

The challenges faced in today's correctional organizations also require a new focus on empowering line staff. The process of empowerment requires leaders and managers to open lines of communication and continuously pass information down the organization to line staff. It requires the organization mission and vision to be clearly understood by staff, and for decisions to be consistent with and contribute to the agency vision and mission. When each level of staff in an organization modifies their behavior to incorporate these functions, corrections can move to the next level, that of flexible organizations, ready and capable of meeting the unknown in a rapidly changing world.

ENDNOTES

1. Peter M. Carlson, "Management Accountability," in *Prison and Jail Administration: Practice and Theory,* edited by Peter M. Carlson and Judith Simon Garrett (Gaithersburg, MD: Aspen Publishers, 1999), p. 42.
2. For a discussion of the impact of total quality management of correctional agencies, see Clifford E. Simonsen and Douglas G. Arnold, "Is Corrections Ready for TQM?" *Corrections Today* (July 1999): 164–169.
3. Richard L. Phillips and Charles R. McConnell, *The Effective Corrections Manager: Maximizing Staff Performance in Demanding Times* (Gaithersburg, MD: Aspen Publishers, 1996), p. 21.

4. H. Koontz and C. O'Donnell, *Principles of Management,* (New York: McGraw-Hill, 1968).

5. For an excellent discussion of the "new" role of correctional leaders in this era, see Chase Riveland, "The Correctional Leader and Public Policy Skills, *Corrections Management Quarterly* 1 no.3 (1997): 22–25.

6. See James MacGregor Burns, *Leadership* (New York: Harper & Row, 1978).

7. See M. Kay Harris, "A Call for Transformational Leadership for Corrections," *Corrections Management Quarterly* 3 no.1 (1999): 24–29.

8. Richard P. Seiter, "Contemporary Issues in Corrections," unpublished monograph prepared for the National Institute of Corrections (Washington, DC: U.S. Department of Justice, 2000).

9. F. T. Cullen et.al., "Public Support for Correctional Treatment: The Tenacity of Rehabilitative Ideology," *Criminal Justice and Behavior* 7 no. 1 (1990): 6–18.

10. S. E. Skovan, J. E. Scott, and F. T. Cullen, "Prison Crowding: Public Attitudes Toward Strategies of Population Control," *Journal of Research in Crime and Delinquency* 25, no. 2 (1988): 150–169

11. Barbara A. Sims, "Questions of Corrections: Public Attitudes toward Prison and Community-Based Programs," *Corrections Management Quarterly* 1 no. 1 (1997): 55.

12. Ibid. p. 56.

13. Judith Simon Garrett, "Political Involvement in Penal Operations," in *Prison and Jail Administration: Practice and Theory,* edited by Peter M. Carlson and Judith Simon Garrett (Gaithersburg, MD: Aspen Publishers, 1999), p. 440.

14. Chase Riveland, "The Correctional Leader and Public Policy Skills" *Corrections Management Quarterly* 1 no. 3 (1997): 22–25.

15. Mike DeWine, "Public Opinion and Corrections: A Need to Be Proactive," *Correctional Management Quarterly* 1 no. 3 (1997): 6.

16. Douglas S. Lipton, Robert Martinson, and Judith Wilds, *The Effectiveness of Correctional Treatment: A Survey of Treatment Evaluation Studies,* (New York: Praeger, 1975).

17. Richard P. Seiter. "Managing Within Political Comfort Zones: An Interview with Allen Ault," *Corrections Management Quarterly* 1 no. 1 (1997): 74–75.

18. For a good overview of the results of correctional treatment in reducing recidivism, see Gerald G. Gaes, Timothy F. Flanagan, Laurence L. Motiuk, and Lynn Stewart, "Adult Correctional Treatment," in *Prisons,* edited by Michael Tonry and Joan Petersilia (Chicago, IL: The University of Chicago Press, 1999), pp. 361–426.

KEY TERMS

leadership
management
administration
planning
organizing
post orders
staffing

directing
controlling
transactional leadership
transformational leadership
generation X workforce
victim rights movement

■ YOU'RE THE CORRECTIONAL ADMINISTRATOR

1. You have been appointed as an associate warden of a prison that has operated in a very traditional fashion for the past 40 years of its existence. The warden has been there for a long time, operates in a very autocratic fashion, but is becoming increasingly ineffective. Line staff have been joining the union at increasing numbers, their morale is very low, and they complain that they are never told what is going on or when a threat of conflict is developing between inmate groups. The midlevel managers or departments believe they do not have the authority to make any decisions without getting them approved by the warden. Do you simply blend in and accept the situation as it is, or do you try to make change? If you want to change things, what risks do you run, and how do you gain the approval of the warden? What types of changes should be made, and what are some actions you would take to make the changes? What end results do you hope for from the changes?

2. You are the director of corrections for a midwestern state. The agency has operated well, and there have not been any serious incidents for a while. However, the state legislature has become increasingly interested in the department and has passed some bills to lengthen sentences, reduced the ability of corrections staff to award good time to inmates, and reduced what they consider "amenities" in the prisons. There seems to be a continuous increase in the political rhetoric around how the prisons should be managed, in order to make offenders feel punished for their crimes. You believe that the legislature's involvement in the operation of the department will continue but do not know what to do to change it. They do not consult you when considering new legislation. Where do you begin, what can you do, and how do you go about it? Develop a plan that will ensure thoughtful discussion of correctional legislation and, hopefully, result in the department not being required to implement policy that you believe will have a negative impact on your ability to run safe and controlled prisons.

■ WEB LINK EXERCISES

California Department of Corrections (CA DOC) www.cdc.state.ca.us

Go to the section regarding news releases for the California Department of Corrections. Pick one news release and read it. In this chapter, there was a discussion of the importance of managing the external environment to include constituencies, the media, and the political arena. From the news release, what do you think was the intent of the CA DOC? What message were they trying to send? What group(s) were they trying to influence and how?

CHAPTER

3

Creating a Vision, Mission Statement, and Strategic Plan

INTRODUCTION

The concepts of strategic planning, vision, and mission statements are "old hat" to the private sector and have recently become a regular concept used in most public sector agencies. However, these concepts have not been used for a long period of time by correctional administrators. Corrections has historically been very reactionary in its management, and thoughtful, strategic planning, including an examination of external factors and forces, agency strengths and weaknesses, and expected future challenges, has historically not been used extensively. Gibbons and Pisciotta note,

> As the corrections industry begins to look more and more like a multibillion dollar business, so must the leadership of each individual agency and facility, given the dynamic and complex operating environment of corrections and the limited funding, stringent federal regulations and exploding offender populations. Correctional agencies need a vision and a plan for how to manage burgeoning inmate populations while retaining a motivated workforce.[1]

Recently, correctional agencies faced intense public scrutiny, rapid technological and environmental changes, continually increasing demands for services (more offenders), and a proportionately reduced supply of resources (budgets and staff). To address these challenges, correctional agencies need to constantly look to the future and plan for how to respond to known and potential challenges. The traditional approach to planning for public agencies has been to identify needs for resources around the budget cycle. This was all that was required during times of stagnant growth, minimal internal changes in operations and conditions, and few outside pressures on an agency. However, this type of planning is no longer acceptable to meet the current fluid environment that confronts corrections.

This chapter outlines approaches used by private corporations, public organizations, and correctional agencies in order to understand the future, educate staff, create a vision, and develop a plan that meets their needs for the twenty-first century. The process of planning for the future is a complex one, requiring commitment and effort from leadership, management, and line staff. All play a critical role in the process, and all must be involved and contribute at every step along the planning route. Only with a concerted effort by all staff within an organization, as well as with input from political leaders and other constituent groups and stakeholders, can a planning process be useful in meeting future challenges that confront the field of corrections.

This chapter provides an understanding of the overall process of strategic planning. This description of process is to be much more than a step-by-step account of how to conduct a planning initiative. It also describes the more subjective issues of the role of leaders in the planning activities, the creation of a vision and its impact on organizational culture, and the critical importance of leaders and managers tending to the communications and change process that line staff will go through when implementing the strategic plan. This chapter also includes a discussion of vision, mission, objectives, and goals; a description of the planning process; and the need for emphasis on the implementation of the plan.

DISTINGUISHING VISION AND MISSION

Organization mission statements have been around almost as long as organizations. It would be nearly impossible to read organizational literature without there being some discussion of the purpose, or mission, of the organization. However, the concept of **vision** for an organization is relatively new in organizational literature, and it is seldom found in practice with public correctional agencies. What is meant by vision in an organization or agency?

Vision is often confused with mission, goals, statement of purpose, and many other terms used by organizations. In the context used in this textbook, and in the context used by most agencies that really understand vision, it is not the same as the other terms. Kouzes and Posner define *vision* as "an ideal and unique image of the future."[2] In *The Empowered Manager*, Peter Block notes, "A vision is the preferred future, a desirable state, and ideal state. It is an expression of optimism despite the bureaucratic surrounding or the evidence to the contrary."[3] Bennis and Nanus state, "a vision articulates a view of a realistic, credible, attractive future for the organization, a condition that is better in some important ways than what now exists."[4] As is apparent, vision is a general statement encompassing the direction an agency wants to take and the desired end result once it gets there. As employees of an organization think of their vision, it is simply that, a vision of what they want the organization to be.

A **mission**, however, is more focused on the specifics of what an organization is to accomplish. It differs from a vision in that it focuses on function, is accomplishable and measurable, and is often statutorily or bureaucratically established. Eadie states that the mission of an organization "is a statement of its basic purposes, often in terms of broad outcomes that it is committed to achieving or the major function it carries out."[5]

A mission can also be the reason an agency exists. When staff meet to write a mission statement, they often begin by asking themselves the questions, "Why do we exist? What is it we are supposed to accomplish?" That is why the mission is often legislatively established. When a legislature creates an agency, it almost always states its purpose, function, or mission. For a state correctional agency, a common mission often is "to supervise criminal offenders during the period of their sentence, protect the public, and offer programs that assist in the rehabilitation of criminals."

As well as stating the purpose or function of an organization, a mission can also be value laden, going beyond what is to be accomplished, and communicating some of the principles and values that accompany the function. Freeman states, "A well-developed mission statement also states the strategies, values and commitments that provide guidance and direction to both managers and employees as they pursue accomplishment of the objectives."[6] The incorporation of values into the mission statement is not the usual approach, because most correctional mission statements are very focused on function. Mission statements that emphasize values and principles, blur the usual distinctions between mission and vision.

An Example of Mission and Vision

The Federal Bureau of Prisons (BOP) has been a leader as a correctional agency in strategic planning, communicating, and reemphasizing the mission of the organization to employees. The mission statement of the Federal Bureau of Prisons, as stated in the 1997 annual report, is

> The Federal Bureau of Prisons protects society by confining offenders in the controlled environments of prisons and community-based facilities that are safe, humane, and appropriately secure, and which provide work and other self-improvement opportunities to assist offenders in becoming law-abiding citizens.[7]

Many federal prisons restate that mission statement as their own purpose or function within the overall Bureau of Prisons operation. For instance, the Federal Correctional Institution (FCI) at Greenville, Illinois, which was constructed and opened in 1994, states the mission as

> FCI Greenville protects society by confining offenders in a controlled environment that is safe, humane, and appropriately secure for both staff and inmates. FCI Greenville provides work and other self-improvement opportunities to assist offenders in becoming law-abiding citizens. As stewards of the public trust, cost efficiency will be a guiding principle at this facility.[8]

However, to be more future oriented, FCI Greenville also created a vision statement in 1998. The vision statement was value laden, future oriented, and an ideal of what the staff wanted the organization to be. The vision of FCI Greenville is, "We [the staff] envision FCI Greenville as a safe, pleasant and empowered workplace."[9]

One of the positive characteristics of the FCI Greenville vision statement is its simplicity. Although the vision clearly presents certain key values in describing and defining the institution, it is not so complex that it is difficult to communicate. One of the problems often associated with vision statements is that they are extensive, hoping to cover all aspects of the company's or agency's values and principles. They, therefore, end up being difficult to communicate to employees, clients, customers, and external stakeholders. And, as discussed later in this chapter, the communication of the vision is the most important reason to have one. If all associated with the agency do not know the vision, it is a waste of time to develop one. As an example, the vision for the Federal Bureau of Prisons is as follows:

> The Federal Bureau of Prisons, judged by any standard, is widely and consistently regarded as a model of outstanding public administration, and as the best value provider of efficient, safe and humane correctional services and programs in America. This vision will be realized when . . .
>
> The Bureau provides for public safety by assuring that no escapes and no disturbances occur in its facilities. The Bureau ensures the physical safety of all inmates through a controlled environment, which meets each inmate's need for security through the elimination of violence, predatory behavior, gang activity, drug use, and inmate weapons. Through the provision of health care, mental, spiritual, educational, vocational and work programs, inmates are well prepared for a productive and crime free return to society. The Bureau is a model of cost efficient correctional operations and programs.
>
> Our talented, professional, well trained, and diverse staff reflects the Bureau's culture and treat each other fairly. Staff works in an environment free from discrimination. A positive working relationship exists where employees maintain respect for one another. The workplace is safe and staff performs their duties without fear of injury or assault. Staff maintains high ethical standards in their day-to-day activities. Staff is satisfied with their jobs, career opportunities, recognition, and quality of leadership.[10]

Although this vision statement is excellent at communicating values and principles when it is read, it is too complex to communicate to staff. The FCI vision of a "safe, pleasant and empowered workplace" is probably remembered and easily repeated by most staff that works there. However, it is unlikely that many staff could recite more than one or two elements of the Bureau of Prisons' vision. Vision statements should be brief and clear. Brevity allows communication of the message through mottos, posters, symbols, or any other approach used to communicate and remind employees and stakeholders of the vision. A vision statement must also be clear and precise so it is easily understood. Acceptance of a vision statement by stakeholders cannot occur unless they fully understand it.

LEADERSHIP AND THE VISION

When establishing a vision for an agency, leaders must first determine their role in the process. Most current literature on organizational leadership notes that providing a vision for an organization is the responsibility of a leader, and even goes so far as to conclude that all good leaders have a vision for their organization. As quoted in Kouzes and Posner's *The Leadership Challenge,* Robert L. Swiggett, chairperson of Kollmorgen Corporation, stated, "The leader's job is to create a vision.[11] Bennis and

Nanus note that an essential element of leadership is the articulation of direction or vision.[12]

There are others that dispute the almost sole responsibility of the leader to create a vision for the organization. Ensuring and guiding the development of a vision for an organization is one of the key activities of leadership:

> Agencies and organizations must have a vision and understanding of where they want to go and what they want to be. Leaders must provide this for their agencies. This does not mean that the leaders do this for the organization, as leaders involve employees in setting the vision. . . . it is critical to involve employees in creating a vision and setting the direction for the future of a public agency.[13]

Leaders have the opportunity to hear firsthand the opinion of elected, political officials regarding their expectations of correctional agencies. They spend more time talking to external stakeholders than other agency managers and line employees. They also deal with other agencies in developing budgets and acquiring resources. As a result of these opportunities, leaders should be aware of trends, expected changes, and future challenges to the agency. Leaders should have a strong cognitive ability to process this information, understanding what is important, and what issues are most likely to impact the future of the agency. The end result of this gathering and processing of information is that the leader becomes the repository of information that is essential when creating a vision for an agency.

Practically, organization leaders should use this knowledge in the creation of a vision. From the preceding statements regarding the leader's responsibility to create the organization's vision, one gets the impression that after processing the information, the leader may already have a vision of what the future of the agency should be. However, this individual formulation of a vision neglects to take advantage of the congregate experience and information that lies within other employees of an organization. It is better for leaders to share and communicate their acquired information with staff. The leader then participates in, and may even direct, the process of staff discussing historical situations, current operations, and future trends and challenges, as they jointly create a vision for the agency.

Developing and Promoting the Vision

Although it can be argued that it is not the sole responsibility of the leader to create a vision, it can also be argued that it is the sole responsibility of the leader to guide staff through the vision development process and to promote the vision in every way possible. After a vision is created, the leader should do everything possible to make it a part of the agency culture. The case study on page 59 provides a good examination of a vision being established.

The case study is a good demonstration of a process that can be used to create a vision for an organization. Based on the activities presented, several key steps can be enumerated:

1. Educate staff about what a vision is and why it is important.   In this case, the warden began talking about a vision for the future, not what it should be, but what it could mean for the agency. It would not have been wise to simply jump into

PRACTICAL PERSPECTIVES

Creating a Vision Statement for an Organization

In a midwestern prison, the warden had read the recent leadership and management literature and wanted to establish a vision for the institution. However, she was convinced the vision would mean more to all staff if they participated in developing it rather than it being her idea only. Although the staff respected the warden's intellect and believed she was forward thinking, they had been through a rough few years. The institution had a serious riot, with several staff injured. After the riot, the employee labor union went on the offensive, demanding certain changes to ensure staff safety. This created a divisive situation, whereby staff were not sure if they were to support the union or the administration. Because the prison had been in operation less than three years, there was no entrenched culture to reemphasize as a guiding principle to staff.

As a result of these problems, the warden and her executive staff had been emphasizing the need to involve staff in decision making, push decisions down to the lowest possible level, empower midlevel managers to take charge of their areas, and be very visible in communicating with line staff about issues, problems, operations of the prison, and why certain decisions were made. These activities seemed to be working, but the warden wanted a single focus for building a positive culture for the institution. Creating a vision, an impression in every employee's mind, of what the prison should be and could be, was important, and it would make an excellent activity to give these individuals an overarching goal or approach.

The warden began talking about a vision statement, what it was, and what it could mean to the future of the institution. She emphasized it was the staff's responsibility to take the best of what the institution was, and build that into a model for the future. The institution had several small groups of staff, in addition to the various departments that made up the formal organizational structure. These included the department heads, the labor union, the lieutenants (the ranking security officers who supervised correctional officers), the employees club (a voluntary group of employees that sponsored social functions for staff), a line staff advisory committee (created by the warden to hear directly from line staff about issues important to them), and the executive staff. The warden used these groups as discussion groups about the vision. She asked each group to discuss what the vision should be for the institution, seeking their input on the most important elements of what they do. Flyers were put up notifying all staff that their input was important and giving them ways to communicate their ideas and suggestions even if they were not a part of any of the groups.

The warden then organized a retreat to discuss the vision. Representatives of all the groups were invited to attend. It was to be a roundtable discussion,

Continued

with no hierarchy. All employees were equal in their roles, regardless of their job or rank in the institution. The warden played the role of facilitator, organizing the discussion, providing information, and getting everyone involved. She sought out opinions from each group and the kinds of things that were important to them in the operation of the prison. As ideas were presented, the warden began to blend them into similar areas and shape them into a vision statement. At the end of the discussion, the group agreed on a brief, clear statement that espoused the values that were important to them. This became the accepted vision for the future.

a planning session to create a vision before the staff understood and had the chance to discuss and accept why a vision was as important. It also would not have been wise to simply announce and present the warden is vision for the prison. Staff hear all types of pronouncements from upper-level management, and announcing a vision would have been little different than announcing a minor change in procedures.

2. Develop a process to involve all staff in creating the vision.   The positive steps taken by the warden to begin to seek input from staff, giving every staff person the opportunity to be involved, not only ensures a better product but it also ensures increased acceptance. And acceptance by the staff increases, the likelihood that the vision will be integrated into the organizational culture also increases.

3. Ask for specific input from the various groups within the organization.   In this case, the warden asked each group to provide input so it could be considered at the planning retreat. Not only is there the opportunity to provide input but it also practically forces each group to discuss and consider the topics important to them. This can be particularly important when there are groups of staff who do not contribute but will criticize decisions or processes after the fact. Although no one likes to admit it, all organizations have such groups. Through this process, if a group is hesitant to discuss and provide recommendations, peer pressure by the other groups encourages them to do so. If they do not contribute to the discussion, it is less likely that staff will give their after-the-fact criticism much credibility.

4. Hold a planning session or retreat to gather input and shape the vision statement.   In the case study, the warden held a retreat, inviting all groups to send a representative, and treating each person as an equal in terms of the value of their input. The retreat allows excellent discussion, each group hears what is important to the others, and they most likely find out that they all share common ground and are interested in the same things.

5. The leader should share information, lead the process, and shape the vision statement.   It is important for the leader to "be the leader" in this group process. Some argue it is better to use a trained facilitator and let the leader only be a participant in the process. But the leader cannot totally abdicate leadership, even if she or he is trying to get everyone involved. A facilitator would naturally seek the leader's opinion throughout the discussion, and the other participants would simply wait to see what the leader says and wants. This stymies discussion. If the leader facilitates the discussion, he or she can encourage input yet still provide personal opinions and desires during the process.

6. Draft the vision statement.   At the end of the retreat, the vision statement should be drafted, at least for distribution and further comment. The retreat should not end without a product. After the staff has experienced the process, there is no better time to bring it to a conclusion. Some leaders are hesitant to end a process and do not want to create a vision without more opportunity for comment. This delay can have negative consequences. If a process with the opportunity for staff involvement, as in the case study, has been completed, it is time to draft the vision. There is nothing wrong, however, with calling it a draft and encouraging comments. However, it is unlikely there will be any significant suggestions after such a thorough process and opportunity for discussion.

7. Communicate and reinforce the vision to staff.   Once the vision is established, it is critical to communicate it to all levels of staff throughout the organization. The vision does little in guiding staff and giving direction if middle management and line staff are not aware of it and use it as guidance. It is, therefore, critical for leaders, and other staff who have been involved in the vision development process to constantly reinforce the vision. Typically, an organization develops signs and posters to communicate the vision to staff, discusses the vision at staff meetings, and takes advantage of opportunities addressing large groups of staff to reinforce the vision. These are important steps, but the most effective way to reinforce the vision is to use it to begin the planning process, to build it into supervisor–employee discussions of performance, and to create awards and recognition programs based on activities and accomplishments that are consistent with the agency vision.

This process describes the specific steps that can be taken to develop a vision statement for an agency, as well as the key role of leaders in making the process a success. The vision is a desired state, sets a direction for the future, and guides employees in the day-to-day functions within their job responsibilities. After establishing and communicating the vision statement throughout the organization, it is important to link it to the agency mission, and established goals and objectives. The next section explains the meaning of these terms, and later sections explain a strategic planning process used to develop activities to accomplish the mission.

MISSION, OBJECTIVES, AND GOALS

A vision statement provides a direction of where an agency wants to go. The mission, objectives, and goals are developed through a planning process by an agency to create and promote shorter-term activities that should occur. These activities are designed to overcome obstacles and move the agency toward reaching the vision. King and Cleland note that, "The objective of the planning process is the establishment of a mission, goals, strategies, programs, and allocations of resources that will enable the organization to best cope with and influence an uncertain future."[14]

FIGURE 3-1   Relationship of strategic choice elements.

Figure 3–1 illustrates a simple hierarchy of organizational plans, and the elements that can link the organizational purpose with the activities to accomplish that purpose.[15] It should be noted that the use of these specific terms to describe these linkages is not universal, and many agencies use "goals" as the broader activities between mission at the top, and specific steps to be taken at the bottom of the hierarchy. The terms and definitions in the hierarchy can vary. The key concept is that there is a broad mission statement that is to be accomplished, and more detailed and specific activities at the bottom of the hierarchy that, when successfully completed, support the accomplishment of the mission.

At the top of the hierarchy is the organization's mission. As previously stated, the mission is the key function that the organization is to accomplish. As an example, a shortened version of the mission of FCI Greenville is "confining offenders in a controlled environment that is safe, humane, and appropriately secure for both staff and inmates." At the next level are **objectives,** which specify the accomplishments that need to be completed to fulfill the mission statement. As an example, three objectives that could be listed for the prison include the following:

1. Have no inmate escapes.
2. Have no serious staff or inmate injuries from assaults by inmates.
3. Have a positive pattern of staff and inmate interaction and communications.

King and Cleland suggest that, based on these objectives, the organization chooses its next level of the hierarchy, "its strategy (general direction), goals (specific targets), and programs (objective- or goal-focused collection of activities). . . . A strategy may be oriented toward the accomplishment of a single objective, or an array of objectives. Goals are more detailed and specific states to be achieved within the framework of objectives and strategy. Programs may relate to goals or objectives

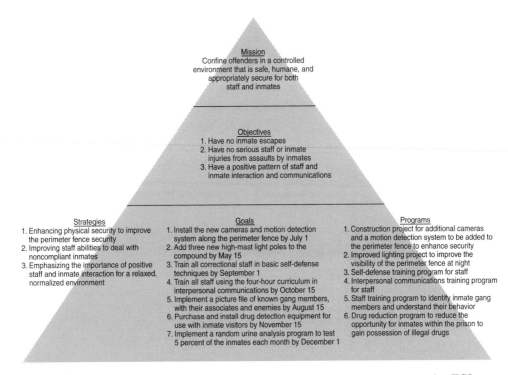

Mission
Confine offenders in a controlled environment that is safe, humane, and appropriately secure for both staff and inmates

Objectives
1. Have no inmate escapes
2. Have no serious staff or inmate injuries from assaults by inmates
3. Have a positive pattern of staff and inmate interaction and communications

Strategies
1. Enhancing physical security to improve the perimeter fence security
2. Improving staff abilities to deal with noncompliant inmates
3. Emphasizing the importance of positive staff and inmate interaction for a relaxed, normalized environment

Goals
1. Install the new cameras and motion detection system along the perimeter fence by July 1
2. Add three new high-mast light poles to the compound by May 15
3. Train all correctional staff in basic self-defense techniques by September 1
4. Train all staff using the four-hour curriculum in interpersonal communications by October 15
5. Implement a picture file of known gang members, with their associates and enemies by August 15
6. Purchase and install drug detection equipment for use with inmate visitors by November 15
7. Implement a random urine analysis program to test 5 percent of the inmates each month by December 1

Programs
1. Construction project for additional cameras and a motion detection system to be added to the perimeter fence to enhance security
2. Improved lighting project to improve the visibility of the perimeter fence at night
3. Self-defense training program for staff
4. Interpersonal communications training program for staff
5. Staff training program to identify inmate gang members and understand their behavior
6. Drug reduction program to reduce the opportunity for inmates within the prison to gain possession of illegal drugs

FIGURE 3–2   Mission, objectives, strategies, goals, and programs for FCI Greenville.

or both."[16] Figure 3–2 illustrates an example of an entire hierarchy that could be created for FCI Greenville to accomplish its mission.

The **strategies** give the general directions that must be taken to reach the objectives. Strategies listed in Figure 3–2 include enhancing physical security to improve the perimeter fence security; improving staff abilities to deal with noncompliant inmates; and emphasizing the importance of positive staff and inmate interaction for a relaxed, normalized environment. These strategies are approaches that should be targeted to reach the objectives. Strategies, as well as programs and goals at the bottom of the pyramid, are the basis for accomplishing objectives and the institution mission.

Programs are made up of projects and activities that link with a strategy to accomplish a specific goal. In this sense, all three of the elements at the bottom of the pyramid link together to accomplish the goals. Examples of possible programs to accomplish the goals for the prison are as follows:

1. Construction project for additional cameras and a motion detection system to be added to the perimeter fence to enhance security.
2. Improved lighting project to improve the visibility of the perimeter fence at night.
3. Self-defense training program for staff.
4. Interpersonal communications training program for staff.

5. Staff training program to identify inmate gang members and understand their behavior.
6. Drug reduction program to reduce the opportunity for inmates within the prison to gain possession of illegal drugs.

The **goals** are specific targets to be reached through the strategies and programs. In kind, by accomplishing the goals, the objectives are therein met. Goals are measurable and usually have a timetable for completion. Examples of goals for the prison are as follows:

1. Install the new cameras and motion detection system along the perimeter fence by July 1.
2. Add three new high-mast light poles to the compound by May 15.
3. Train all correctional staff in basic self-defense techniques by September 1.
4. Train all staff using the four-hour curriculum in interpersonal communications by October 15.
5. Implement a picture file of known gang members, with their associates and enemies by August 15.
6. Purchase and install drug detection equipment for use with inmate visitors by November 15.
7. Implement a random urine analysis program to test 5 percent of the inmates each month by December 1.

As can be seen, goals are outputs from strategies and can be achieved through the identified programs. Programs are the approaches to implement the strategies. Goals accomplish the agency objectives. And finally, meeting objectives are the activities that fulfill the mission. The hierarchy in Figure 3–2 illustrates how to visualize the linkages of all these activities to successfully reach the mission of a safe, humane, and secure prison.

STRATEGIC PLANNING: IDENTIFYING MISSION, OBJECTIVES, AND GOALS

How does an organization create a mission statement, and identify objectives and goals (as well as strategies and programs)? The answer is through a process called strategic planning. Strategic planning originated in the private sector during the 1960s. One early definition is as follows:

> Strategic planning is the process of deciding on the objectives of the organization, on changes in those objectives, on the resources used to attain these objectives, and on the policies that are to govern the acquisition, use and disposition of these resources.[17]

Strategic planning is a process involving many staff, resulting in a linkage of the mission statement to objectives and goals, and identifying actions to be taken by the agency to accomplish these objectives and goals. In essence, it results in a "road map" for how an agency gets to where it wants to go. Strategic planning is future oriented and is not concerned about where the agency has been. In a strategic plan, agencies clarify future directions, obstacles to getting there, and steps that must be taken to overcome the obstacles.

Why (or When) to Plan?

Most purists would suggest that strategic planning be continuous and that there is no particular time or issue generation that spurs planning. Most would also agree that an agency should always be reaching into the future, searching the environment, and modifying plans. In reality, the planning process is not continuous, and is usually bounded and defined. There are many reasons to conduct a planning activity, and many issues that spur planning. An agency can experience a variety of activities, which prompts leadership to initiate the development of a new plan. Following are some of the opportunities for beginning or conducting a planning activity.

A change in leadership. A change in leadership often is an opportunity for developing a new plan. New leaders want their own "thumbprint" on the organization, and a planning process allows them to add it. Not only will it result in a plan that they endorse but also the process of planning allows leaders opportunities to communicate with employees, hear their concerns as well as their optimism about the future, and identify employees who have specific skills they may be looking for in their administration.

Changes in the external environment that necessitate a response by the organization. Outside issues that may confront correctional agencies include new sentencing laws, a major change in budget allocations, an identified change in the types of offenders supervised, or expected growth or even reductions in the number of offenders. These influences warrant an agency implementing a planning process to be sure they understand the change, to identify the potential impact of the change, and to develop activities to respond to the change.

Changes in the internal environment of the organization. At times, agencies reorganize and modify the responsibilities of various units. When this occurs, it can be useful to conduct a planning process, because various staff interactions and roles can shift. The planning process is a good opportunity to discuss these in relationship to the desired outcome and to clarify who will be responsible for certain activities.

When staff morale is low or when staff need direction. It is naive to think that staff are always dedicated and excited about their jobs and their position in the agency. At times, even the best of staff can become disenchanted with the agency, certain policies or procedures, or their leadership. A planning process can be a useful forum to address these concerns with a positive motive, not as a "gripe session," but with an emphasis on addressing the future successfully. Staff get the opportunity to be involved in setting the direction for the future in a planning session, and with this, they also can be reinvigorated and recommitted to the agency and its goals.

When there is a major change in policy or procedure. Many things can prompt a need to change an agency's policies and procedures. If the changes are significant enough to affect a large number of staff, it is valuable to have a planning session to be sure staff understand how the new policy will be implemented and to determine whether there are any unexpected outcomes that may be identified by staff that also need to be addressed.

In addition, there are many situations that undermine an agency's ability to meet its potential. King and Cleland identify several symptoms that require a planning process to change the focus of the organization from reactionary to future oriented. These include

1. A tendency for managers to view a current domain from the standpoint of the discipline in which credentials were first acquired, regardless of its broader scope and the requirements for more diverse considerations.
2. A "tunnel vision" phenomenon, in which managers fail to recognize the multiple objectives of the organization even though they have moved to a general management position and can no longer afford the luxury of the simplistic efficiency-oriented objectives that are the forte of managers at lower levels.
3. A bureaucratic organizational structure designed more for maintaining efficiency and control in current operations than in fostering long-range innovation.
4. The lack of an "organization" or process designed specifically for fostering the managerial participation and innovativeness for developing new products and services.
5. An assumption that the chief executive or, alternatively, a professional planning staff should *do* the planning.
6. An incentive system wherein performance oriented toward the production of short-range results is rewarded more highly than that oriented toward long-range opportunities.
7. The introduction of radically new planning systems into organizations without proper concern for their effect on the motivations and behavior of those managers who must use them.[18]

When these symptoms occur, an agency should reconsider their leadership and management approaches and ensure they have a culture that involves staff in planning and focusing on the future.

Organizational Culture and Strategic Planning

Every organization has a **culture,** in terms of the way employees interact; the manner in which the organization interacts with other entities; the emphasis that is placed on certain traits, processes, and goals; and the style of leadership and management that is utilized. Wilson defines organizational culture as "a persistent, patterned way of thinking about the central tasks of and human relationships within an organization."[19] The culture of an organization can also be viewed as "the integrated system of acquired behavioral patterns in the organization that are characteristic of the members of the organization and that influence the attitudes and the modus operandi of the organization."[20]

There are two ways in which organizational culture links to strategic planning. First, when an organization has a culture endorsed and appreciated by employees, they have a sense of mission about the agency's work. In contrast, when the agency mission is vague, employees are less committed to the organization's role, and there is little sense of dedication to the organization and what it is trying to accomplish. Strategic planning can clarify mission, goals, and everyone's role in accomplishing the mission, resulting in a culture focused on this accomplishment. Second, if an agency has a culture that accepts strategic planning as a basic part of their operations, they are likely to be more focused on the future. Those organizations that do not share such a culture are unlikely to be successful at planning. Therefore, effective planning can assist in the development of a culture being mission driven, and a future-oriented culture can lead to effective planning. Both culture and planning contribute to one another.

To effectively plan, and to effectively communicate and implement a plan, an organization must have developed a culture that looks toward the future, accepts change, is mission driven, and constantly strives to improve its operations. All organizations do not have this culture, and culture cannot be developed overnight. For correctional agencies, it may be particularly difficult to establish a culture of focusing on the future. Correctional agencies are, by nature, reactionary. As explained in earlier chapters, routine and consistent repetition of practices is a desirable trait in a correctional agency. For a correctional leader to suddenly declare that the agency must look for different ways of doing things and not be wedded to the past is almost counterintuitive to the way a generation of correctional workers have learned to do their jobs.

Take, for example, the case of J. Michael Quinlan, who became director of the BOP in the mid-1980s. Quinlan was a visionary, constantly thinking of future challenges and how to better understand the external environment and the functions of the private sector. He took over the BOP at a time of unprecedented growth in the number of inmates and, therefore, in facilities and staff. He envisioned a changing BOP, from one that efficiently functioned through personal relationships and informal communications, to one that would double in size over a 10-year period. This entailed a variety of changes, including management using key indicators of success, computer literacy by staff, and more formal lines of communications. His vision was an accurate one, undisputed by any expert in organizational development, yet his attempts to move the organization in that direction were very difficult for established staff to accept.

Quinlan created a strategic planning unit, not to do the planning, but to travel throughout the United States to educate staff on strategic planning, train them in the process, and encourage them to conduct training sessions at the local level. He also established organizational and individual awards for strategic planning, lead planning efforts for his top administrators, and built organizational strengths in research and information systems to capture and more efficiently communicate new information.

Even so, it took five to seven years before planning became "second nature" to the Bureau of Prisons. It is now considered one of the cultural anchors of the BOP. A 1997 statement of the Bureau of Prisons Fundamentals states, "The active participation of staff at all levels is essential to the development and accomplishment of organizational objectives."[21] Although Quinlan's focus on planning was not fully appreciated while he was director of the BOP, after he retired in 1993, he was hired as the director of planning for a private corrections company, Corrections Corporation of America. So important is planning to the private sector, that in 1999, he became president of this company, the largest private corrections company in the United States, with assets of more than one billion dollars.

Leaders and managers must be committed to a culture of planning, and constantly lead and manage to reinforce this emphasis. Perhaps the most effective activities by leaders and managers is to constantly discuss the future and how the organization must respond to it, and to value planning and employees' involvement in the process. Even if leaders and managers do function in this manner, a culture that emphasizes planning will not quickly develop. But with persistence, the end result will be an organizational culture emulating these traits.

THE PLANNING PROCESS

For purposes of simulating a planning activity, two assumptions will be made. First, an agency has an event that creates an opportunity for planning, or the agency has recognized symptoms that reflect the need for developing a plan. Second, the agency has a culture that values planning, and seeks to identify future challenges and create responses to them. The organization is now ready to conduct a strategic planning exercise.

There are a variety of steps that can be listed as key elements in strategic planning. The following steps are identified by Sorkin, Ferris, and Hudak as basic to the process:

1. Scan the environment.
2. Select key issues.
3. Set mission statements or broad goals.
4. Undertake external and internal analysis.
5. Develop goals, objectives, and strategies with respect to each issue.
6. Develop an implementation plan to carry out strategic actions.
7. Monitor, update, and scan.[22]

These steps should result in the end product of the planning process. It is important to remember, "Plans are not the objectives to be achieved through planning. The objective of the planning process is the establishment of a mission, goals, strategies, programs, and allocations of resources that will enable the organization to best cope with and influence an uncertain future."[23]

Before describing each of these seven steps, it is important to understand two issues of logistics: how long strategic planning should take and who should participate. Planning cannot be accomplished in only a few hours, and it also should not take several days. The first part of strategic planning (steps 1 though 5) can be accomplished, if a strategic planning process is well organized, in two to three days. The required follow-up of developing an implementation plan and monitoring progress and making necessary modifications is a long-term and continuous process.

The first two- to three-day session should be organized to take each of steps 1 through 5 sequentially, because each builds on the information developed and the discussion points made in the earlier steps.

The second logistical determination is who should attend the planning exercise. As noted earlier, a benefit in strategic planning is that it is an opportunity for many people to be involved in a problem-solving exercise, so they bring their knowledge to the discussion, and take a commitment to implementation away from it. In the early days of strategic planning, planning usually only included small groups of upper-level management. However, diverse participation from all levels of staff results in more thoughtful and realistic planning.

A good example of diverse participation is the development of a strategic plan for Federal Prison Industries (FPI) in 1989. FPI is a government corporation that manages the prison industry program within the Federal Bureau of Prisons. FPI executives included approximately 30 FPI staff and other interested parties in the planning process. Included staff were all of the corporate officers (approximately five), all of the division managers (approximately eight), three or four factory managers, one or two quality control supervisors, representatives from the sales staff, representatives from the financial department, and a three-person planning group. Interested parties included six to eight wardens who oversee the factories within the prisons they supervise, and three or four other executives from the Bureau of Prisons.

To ensure that the group had input from outside parties, yet to prevent the group from getting too large, a facilitator conducted interviews with additional individuals prior to the planning session. Those interviewed were all seven members of the corporate board of directors, a few representative customers (federal government officials who purchase FPI products), a few private sector company officials who sell products in competition with FPI, and some selected members of the U.S. Congress. At the outset, the results of these interviews was presented to aid in setting the stage and understanding the environment in which FPI was operating. At relevant times throughout the planning discussions, additional input from the interviews was also considered. Those involved in the FPI planning process recognized that not only did they benefit from the diversity of the planning group but they were also able to broaden the input considered without expanding the number of planning participants.

Although the size of the group should not be too large so as to allow and encourage all participants to present their points of view and allow for active discussions, strategic planning processes usually can accommodate fairly large numbers, perhaps as many as 75 or even 100. The large group may stay together to hear presentations of important data and information; however, they should break into smaller groups for discussion. These small groups are then tasked with presenting a summary of their discussion back to the larger group.

Scan the Environment

Environmental scanning is usually considered the first step in a planning process. In this process, the organization looks both internally and externally, and determines what current or future forces will have an impact on the organization's ability to accomplish its mission. Denhardt, in describing environmental scanning, states that, "the organization is not assumed to exist in a vacuum, but rather both the organization's objectives and the steps to achieve those objectives are seen in the context of the resources and constraints presented by the organization's environment."[24]

The strategic planning group engages in a variety of activities to seek input on significant issues that will impact their organization. In correctional planning, this is especially important. Over the past 25 years, the environment has changed on almost all fronts—legal, political, supply and demand, financial, types of clients, and even levels of competition. The following represents some of the sources to review to identify potential changes in the correctional organization's environment:

▮ Trends in the number of offenders the agency supervises.
▮ Budgets approved by the legislature, and the proportional increases (or decreases) related to the number of clients.
▮ New legislation or political proposals regarding the agency policy or operations.
▮ The make-up of clients (age, offense, history of violence).
▮ Changes in staff retentions rates.
▮ Changes in incidents of violence by clients/inmates.
▮ Changes in rates of program completions.

Select Key Issues

The next step in strategic planning is to select key issues that will have the most impact on the organization and need to be addressed. For correctional agencies, these usually include the growth in the number of offenders to be supervised, fewer per capita financial and staff resources, offenders who are becoming violent and dangerous, the effectiveness of treatment modalities, advancements in technologies of equipment available to supervise offenders, the threat of the private sector expanding their role in corrections, and increased scrutiny from the public and political leaders.

Develop an Implementation Plan

Surprisingly and regretfully, even the best developed plans are often poorly implemented. It would be expected that an agency which completed every step of planning would also do a good job of implementation. Because this is not the case, correctional administrators must tend to the implementation of the plan even more than to the development of the plan. The plan is not the objective. The **end objective in a planning process** is the effective implementation of goals, objectives, strategies, and programs in a way that improves the agency's ability to meet its mission in the face of any challenges.

A rather common phenomenon occurs some months after a plan is developed when top managers realize that they have not been effective in meeting the challenges they identified during the planning process. They are often quick to doubt the plan and whether they accurately identified goals, strategies, and programs that would effectively meet their objectives. They may even begin another planning process to identify where they went wrong. However, if they look closely enough, they find that the plan was not faulty; their implementation of the plan was ineffective. A focused implementation plan is critical to the success of the planning process.

There are four steps that are essential to effective implementation: (1) communicating the plan; (2) empowering middle management with responsibility for the implementation; (3) developing action steps, measures of outcome, and target dates for completion of the steps; and (4) monitoring progress and rewarding staff for positive progress. All four steps are essential, but the most critical is effectively communicating the plan.

Communication of the plan begins when organizing the planning process. The reasons for the planning process, how the process will occur, and interest in staff input should be made known to staff. All these activities are important to effectively communicating the plan once it is complete. Selection of a diverse group of staff to attend the planning function allows them to become informal communicators of the plan and its importance to the organization. The completed plan should be documented in writing and communicated to as many staff as possible. The key is to then widely distribute the plan in whatever form is available to the agency (intranet, employee bulletin boards, or at staff meetings).

Organization leaders should then discuss the plan with as many staff groups as possible. This could be through staff meetings, union meetings, or even videotape or written communications if staff is dispersed over a large geographic region. Effective communication of the plan lets staff know the plan is important, that it should be taken seriously, and it allows leaders to explain some of the reasons for the plan and its strategies and programs. Staff are able to ask questions and provide input on implementation strategies. Through these communications efforts, staff feel involved in and committed to the planning process.

After the organization leadership has communicated the plan, and demonstrated their commitment to it, the plan should become the responsibility of middle management for implementation. There are several reasons for this, but the most important is that a plan's success or failure rests in the hands of middle management. Middle managers should meet with the line staff they supervise; develop action steps and target completion dates for implementing goals, strategies, and programs; and identify measures of outcome. Because they are charged with its implementation, middle management and their staff should develop the activities necessary to accomplish the plan.

The final step in the plan is to monitor its implementation, hold middle management accountable for the target dates they set, and recognize and reward staff for making positive progress toward the plan's accomplishment. An old, but still true, strategy for implementing change is to identify success stories and reward staff responsible for the success. This creates momentum toward completion of the overall plan. Completion of activities by the identified target dates should be publicized, and staff should be visibly recognized and rewarded. This recognition is an incentive for those who have not yet reached their target dates and shows all staff that progress is being made in the plan.

Monitor, Update, and Scan

Even when a plan is effectively implemented, it should never be considered "set in stone." Situations and conditions change, especially in today's fluid and rapidly changing correctional environment, and leaders and top managers must constantly monitor the plan, continue to scan the environment for unanticipated outcomes, and update the plan as necessary. Leaders should resist the urge to make dramatic changes in a plan before it has been fully implemented and the results measured. However, there should be no hesitancy to make modifications when factors do change, and it is obvious that a modification of the plan is necessary.

Monitoring and constantly seeking improvement is consistent with advice that organizational consultants often give managers to seek a culture of continuous improvement. The old adage, "if it ain't broke, don't fix it," is usually not true in today's environment. A technique widely used in government agencies, as well as the private sector, is **total quality management (TQM)**. TQM is a strategy to constantly review operations, with the goals of continuous improvement in all an organization does. Simonsen and Arnold, in writing about the importance of TQM to correctional agencies, note that the "constant striving to make improvements in incremental steps is the heart and soul of TQM."[25]

An excellent example of implementing TQM in a correctional agency is the Ohio Department of Rehabilitation and Correction (ODRC), the state agency that oversees the operation of the state's prisons and parole functions.[26] The ODRC began to focus on the concept of total quality management in 1992 when then-Governor George Voinovich required implementation of TQM in all state agencies. ODRC Director Reginald A. Wilkinson was committed to the concept, appointed a coordinator for its implementation in the agency, and began to train staff in the focus and activities required of TQM. The goal of this inclusion of TQM in the management of the ODRC was to empower staff to continuously look for ways to improve the agency's efficiency. This effort has succeeded, and the Ohio correctional system is recognized throughout the United States as a model for TQM and staff involvement.

Another approach to monitoring an agency's performance is through the implementation of **performance-based measures.** Performance-based measures provide an agency with a mechanism for assessing what they do and how well they are doing it. All agencies, government and private alike, get overly encumbered with processes, the repetitive functions that staff repeat on a regular basis. As a result, sometimes forgotten is what was to be accomplished. This becomes a serious problem if the focus on the processes, rather than the outcome, begins to drive organizational decisions. Implementation of performance-based measures can maintain the organization's emphasis on measuring results, rather than merely counting activities.

A successful correctional example is the American Probation and Parole Association, which in 1990 received a grant from the National Institute of Justice to develop performance-based measures for community corrections. Their work resulted in a monograph entitled *Results-Driven Management: Implementing Performance-Based Measures in Community Corrections.*[27] In the monograph, the authors developed six goals for a hypothetical agency and demonstrated how performance-based measures could be developed for each. The six goals examined are to assist decision makers, enforce court/parole board ordered sanctions, protect the community, assist offenders to change, support crime victims, and coordinate and promote the use of community services. Similar to TQM, incorporating performance-based measures is an excellent method to ensure an agency accomplishes its mission in a quality manner.

STRATEGIC MANAGEMENT AND LEADERSHIP

A useful approach to examining the functions of a public organization and how its leadership works to carry out its mission is through **strategic management.** Strategic management is a process carried out at the top of the organization, which provides guidance, direction, and boundaries for all aspects of operational management. Strategic management differs from strategic planning, because strategic management exists when organizations move beyond planning to develop mechanisms for implementation of strategies. The emphasis of strategic management is on organizational adaptation to environmental demands and opportunities. It requires the connection of organizational capacities of managerial capability, culture, leadership, and organization structure.

Strategic management emphasizes the linkage of scanning and understanding the ever-changing environment, creating opportunities to move an organization forward, and implementing change in response to needs. It can be useful to analyze how leaders guide their agencies through challenges and opportunities, create support for their strategies and goals, and effectively motivate staff to implement change.

The Strategic Management Triangle

Professor Mark H. Moore of the Kennedy School of Government at Harvard University has presented a conceptual framework developed by faculty at the Kennedy School to help public sector managers assess their potential and actively pursue initiatives.[28] In the framework, called the strategic management triangle, the three points of the triangle define particular calculations that managers must make in deciding whether an enterprise is worth pursuing and the particular activities that they must undertake to ensure the success of their venture.

The first aspect is to determine whether there is *public value* in the results desired or imagined by the manager. Correctional administrators often take for granted that what they do has public value or that it is important to the taxpayers and citizens that corrections serves. Obviously, protecting citizens from crime has public value. It is more difficult to determine which programs and operations have value, or are worth the resources in time and money that are required to carry them out. Should an intensive probation supervision program be implemented? Should a literacy program be established in a county jail? Should serious juvenile offenders be bound over to adult courts and correctional agencies? Should amenities in prisons, such as weights, college programs, and recreational activities, be reduced? At point 1 of the strategic triangle, the question to ask is whether making the change or implementing the program has value. In other words, is the correctional agency better able to accomplish its mission by implementing the change, to the point that it is worth the organizational resources required?

The second point of the strategic management triangle is to determine whether a goal or initiative will be *politically and legally supported*. Moore suggests "managing upward," toward political leaders, to invest the agency purpose with legitimacy and support. This is particularly true in corrections, where many elected officials respond to the public and political rhetoric. This rhetoric too often results in emotion rather than fact becoming the determining factor as to whether political leaders will support a correctional initiative. It is the responsibility of correctional leadership to educate both the public and elected officials regarding the merits and value of a correctional program or initiative.

The final point of the strategic management triangle is to determine whether implementation of an initiative is *administratively and operationally feasible*. This point of the triangle is to "manage downward," toward improving the organization's capabilities for achieving the desired purposes. Strategic management assumes a changing political and task environment, and, therefore, implementation strategies must take into account an ever-changing landscape. Too often, public administrators take this step for granted, believing that by issuing policy changes, modifications in line staff behavior will follow. As noted in the previous discussion of the sometimes unsuccessful implementation of the outcomes of strategic planning, to ensure that a change in policy results in compliance and changing behavior on the part of employees requires careful and consistent follow-up.

SUMMARY

In this chapter, we examined how a public agency creates a forward-looking approach to its management and the accomplishment of its mission. Through a vision of how the agency sees its own future, staff can understand the subjective values and direction that the organization holds as important. Organizational culture is extremely important to success, and leaders must promote a positive organizational culture that supports the vision of the agency. Equally important is how an agency develops its plans for the future, using strategic planning to involve staff, identify future challenges, and create and implement programs and strategies to move beyond these challenges.

Finally, this chapter has gone beyond strategic planning and introduced the concept of strategic management. With strategic management, an agency can determine activities that are valuable to accomplish its mission, focus on gaining support of external political leadership, and work to successfully initiate the change throughout the internal organization. Whereas strategic planning guides staff in the creation of the agency practices and procedures in response to future challenges, strategic management goes even further by helping staff envision the bigger picture of how public policy is made outside the agency boundaries.

The first section of this textbook has presented the challenges facing correctional administration in the new millennium, examined the roles of leaders and managers within their organizations, and demonstrated the process of strategic planning for developing an agency's agenda. In the next sections, there is an examination of the basic functions of a correctional organization, from security to treatment, from human resources to budgeting, and from supervision to carrying out specific tasks. In this examination, we come to realize the key elements to a complete correctional organization, and how an administrator must balance and control each to have an effective correctional agency.

ENDNOTES

1. Rodney Gibbons and Frank Pisciotta, "Corrections in the Twenty-First Century," *Corrections Today* (July 1999): 62.
2. James M. Kouzes and Barry Z. Posner, *The Leadership Challenge*, (San Francisco: Jossey-Bass, 1987), p. 85.
3. Peter Block, *The Empowered Manager: Positive Political Skills at Work*, (San Francisco; Jossey-Bass, 1987) 103.
4. Warren Bennis and Burt Nanus, *Leaders: The Strategies for Taking Charge*, (New York: Harper & Row, 1986), p. 89
5. Douglas C. Eadie, "Strategic Management by Design," in *Strategic Planning for Local Government: A Handbook for Officials and Citizens*, edited by Roger L. Kemp (Jefferson, NC: McFarland & Company, 1993), p. 85.
6. Robert M. Freeman, *Correctional Organization and Management: Public Policy Challenges, Behavior, and Structure*, (Boston, MA: Butterworth-Heinemann, 1999), p. 32.
7. U.S. Department of Justice, *State of the Bureau: Accomplishments and Goals—1997* (Washington, DC: Federal Bureau of Prisons, 1997), p. 5.
8. Federal Correctional Institution, Greenville, Illinois, *1998 Strategic Plans: FCI Greenville*, unpublished document (Greenville, IL: Federal Bureau of Prisons, 1998), p. 1.
9. Ibid.
10. U.S. Department of Justice, p. 2.
11. Kouzes and Posner, p. 81.
12. Bennis and Nanus, p. 89.
13. Richard P. Seiter, "The Leadership and Empowerment Triangle, *Corrections Management Quarterly*, 3 no. 1 (1999); 4.
14. William R. King and David I. Cleland, *Strategic Planning and Policy*, (New York: Von Nostrand Reinhold, 1978), p. 45.
15. Ibid., p. 133.
16. Ibid., p. 134.
17. R. N. Antony, J. Dearden, and R. F. Vancil, *Management Control Systems* (Homewood, IL, Irwin, 1965), p. 4.
18. King and Cleland, p. 7.
19. James Q. Wilson, *Bureaucracy: What Government Agencies Do and Why They Do It* (New York: Basic Books, 1989), p. 91.
20. King and Cleland, p. 274.

21. U.S. Department of Justice, *State of the Bureau: Accomplishments and Goals—1997* (Washington, DC: Federal Bureau of Prisons, 1997), p. 5.

22. Donna L. Sorkin, Nancy B. Ferris, and James Hudak, *Strategies for Cities and Counties: A Strategic Planning Guide* (Washington, DC: Public Technology, Inc. 1984).

23. King and Cleland, p. 45.

24. Robert B. Denhardt, "Strategic Planning in State and Local Government," *State and Local Government Review* 17 no. 1 (1985): 175.

25. Clifford E. Simonsen and Douglas G. Arnold, "Is Corrections Ready for TQM?" *Corrections Today* 56 no. 4 (July 1994): 168.

26. For a detailed description of the application and process Ohio used regarding TQM, see State of Ohio, Department of Rehabilitation and Correction, "Commitment to Quality" (Columbus: State of Ohio, 1993), an unpublished document available through the National Institute of Correction Information Center, Longmont, Colorado

27. Harry N. Boone, Jr. and Betsy Fulton, *Results-Driven Management: Implementing Performance-Based Measures in Community Corrections* (Lexington, KY: American Probation and Parole Association, The Council of State Governments, 1995).

28. Mark H. Moore, *Creating Public Value: Strategic Management in Government* (Cambridge, MA: Harvard University Press, 1995).

▰ KEY TERMS

vision	strategic planning
mission	culture
objectives	end objective in a planning process
strategies	total quality management (TQM)
programs	performance-based measures
goals	strategic management

▰ YOU'RE THE CORRECTIONAL ADMINISTRATOR

1. You are the director of a community halfway house. You know the challenges facing community correctional agencies, and you believe you and the staff of the halfway house should begin to do some planning for the future. You decide to begin by discussing with the staff a "vision" for the halfway house. Anticipate some of the discussion that would result, and develop with a vision for the halfway house. Write the vision, and highlight some of the key discussion points that influenced the selection of the vision by the staff. List five statements that were made by staff that had general agreement and were important to the vision statement.

2. You, as director of the halfway house, now want to begin a strategic planning process. You plan to follow the outline of the process illustrated in this chapter. The first decisions, however, you must make are who to invite to the planning session and what type of information should be collected before the

session begins. First, list the groups you would invite to the session and the reasons they should be represented. Second, list the types of information you want to have in hand before you begin the strategic planning process. Also, describe where this information is found and how it can be collected.

WEB LINK EXERCISES

American Probation and Parole Association (APPA) www.appa-net.org

Go to the Web site for the APPA; read some background information on the organization, and find their mission statement. After you read the mission statement, describe how you would develop a strategic plan to implement the mission. Include the steps you would take to involve members and the activities you would use to accomplish the mission.

PART

II

Managing Offenders

CHAPTER

4

Punishment and Other Correctional Goals

INTRODUCTION

Historically, corrections has had many goals. Over time, different goals were emphasized to varying degrees. However, the most predominant correctional goal over time has been punishment. Every society, regardless of how advanced their culture, technology, and economy, uses punishment to reinforce behavior that the society deems inappropriate. Throughout history, children have been punished for bad behavior, whether it be physical (for example, a slap or even a blow in more primitive times), psychological (for example, being deprived of a valued possession or opportunity such as dessert or television), or shaming (for example, having to stand in a corner). The emphasis was on letting children know that the behaviors for which they were being punished were not acceptable and on conditioning a response to prevent those behaviors in the future.

Early offenders violating society's norms or laws were punished in a fashion similar to children. They may have been physically punished (whipped, beaten, or tortured), been deprived of a possession (money in the form of a fine), or been subjected to shame (wearing a scarlet letter). Punishment is embedded into our psyche as an appropriate response to misbehavior. With punishment as an acceptable practice by society, there must be formal societal organizations authorized to carry it out. This responsibility falls on correctional administrators. Although it might seem relatively simple for correctional administrators to simply carry out the sanctions prescribed by criminal courts, the actual administration of punishment is extremely complex.

Allowable punishment is created by legislative action, and our court systems determine its acceptability. Correctional organizations and correctional administrators do not determine what is to be the punitive sanction; however, they are authorized to impose or carry out the sanction. Although punishment is the predominant goal in our criminal justice system, deterrence, incapacitation, and rehabilitation are also recognized correctional goals. The challenge for correctional administrators is to create organizational entities that carry out prescribed punishments in a just and fair manner, yet also incorporate the other "goals" of corrections in a balanced approach. Although the punitive sanctions are often spelled out through legislative action and court imposition, the other goals are not clarified through any formal or official government action. In this chapter, we describe the often conflicting goals of corrections and discuss the importance of balancing these goals through professional operations of correctional agencies.

PUNISHMENT AND OTHER CORRECTIONAL GOALS

As noted, punishment, deterrence, incapacitation, and rehabilitation are the four basic goals of corrections. Each of these goals may be referred to using other terms, or there may be minor derivations in how the goal is referenced. Similar terminology with fairly similar meanings are *punishment* and *retribution, deterrence* and *prevention, incapacitation* and *control,* and *rehabilitation* and *restoration.* Other goals sometimes suggested as within the purview of corrections include protection of society, reintegration, selective incapacitation, and restitution. This section defines and explains the primary goals of corrections.

Although some of the following information may seem basic and may have been discussed in other criminal justice or correctional classes, the material is presented in this textbook to set the stage for the actions that must be taken and roles that must be played by correctional administrators. Correctional administrators must understand the sanctions, the legal and historical implications, and how their administrator's actions influence the extent to which any goal is actualized by an offender population. After presenting some of the key concepts in the four correctional goals, this chapter goes on to discuss the role of correctional administrators in balancing these goals.

Punishment

It is easily argued that **punishment** is the first and most essential goal. Without punishment, deterrence and rehabilitation are not possible. Punishment has many aspects, elements, and purposes, and is often defined in varying ways. Greenwalt defines criminal punishment as the imposition by persons who possess authority of "designedly unpleasant consequences upon, and express . . . condemnation of, other persons who are capable of choice and who have breached established standards of behavior."[1] Greenwalt concludes that this definition has five important elements:

> (1) The person being punished must be *responsible* for the behavior. Those who are too immature or mentally incompetent to understand what they are doing may be controlled by other formal controls, but they cannot be punished. (2) The punishment is intended to be *painful* in some sense; it is a negative sanction that most ra-

tional persons would wish to avoid. (3) The pain inflicted is preceded by a judgment of *condemnation;* the person being punished is explicitly blamed for the act. (4) Punishment is imposed only by those who have the legal *authority* over the responsible actor and for the implementation of the law or standard in question. Even persons who feel directly injured cannot impose criminal punishment informally. Only those who hold formal office and are charged with determining guilt and imposing punishment can impose it. (5) Punishment follows a "legally demonstrated breach of established rules of *behavior. . . .*"[2]

How a state or other jurisdiction determines what is an appropriate criminal punishment is interesting. Consider what an appropriate sanction for any crime is. How does anyone come to a conclusion that a certain crime is worthy of a certain punishment? Legislatures always begin with the current level of sanction for a given offense. Unfortunately, notorious events often cause an emotional reconsideration of a criminal punishment. Instead of objectively examining the necessary level of punishment to respond to and prevent future crime, there is a perception that the current sanction must not be severe enough. Therefore, any change must be in a direction of enhancing the punishment.

The U.S. Supreme Court has at least twice addressed appropriate sanctions for crimes. In *Bell v. Wolfish,* the Court established the "punitive intent standard."[3] The case dealt with conditions and practices at a federal jail for short-term offenders (many not yet convicted of a crime) in New York City. The jail was newly constructed yet already overcrowded, resulting in "double-bunking" at the time of the inmate complaints leading to this decision. Also challenged by inmates were the practices of prohibiting them from receiving hardback books not mailed directly from a publisher, disallowing them to observe searches of their cells, and requiring them to submit to visual searches of body cavities after visits with family members or friends. The inmate suit alleged a violation of the Eighth Amendment of the Constitution, which states; "Excessive bail shall not be required, nor excessive fines imposed, nor cruel and unusual punishment inflicted." The Court ruled that the case should turn only on whether the practices in question violated detainees' right to be free from punishment, using a standard of whether the individual restrictions were punitive or merely regulatory restraints; whether the practice was reasonably related to a legitimate goal other than punishment, and whether it appeared to be excessive in relation to that alternative purpose.

In another case, the Court developed the **test of proportionality.** The Court, in the 1983 case of *Solem v. Helm,* declared

> [W]e hold as a matter of principle that a criminal sentence must be proportionate to the crime for which the defendant has been convicted. . . . In sum, a court's proportionality analysis . . . should be guided by objective criteria, including (i) the gravity of the offense and the harshness of the penalty; (ii) the sentences imposed on other criminals in the same jurisdiction; and (iii) the sentences imposed for commission of the same crime in other jurisdictions.[4]

At times, the term *retribution* is used in place of punishment as a goal of corrections. However, it is more correct to cite retribution as a reason for punishment, because retribution is the need for society to see an offender punished. The purpose, or more appropriately stated, the result of retribution, is the maintenance of the moral order of society, with the focus on society rather than on the individual who committed the crime. When offenders violate the law, they are brought to justice by the state, acting for society. It is the duty of society to punish offenders, because through punishment society can maintain order and show fairness to those who do not violate the law. Some think of retribution as a catharsis, a way for society to "feel OK" about the punishment doled out to the offender. However, the retributive theories are much more complex than that, because they attempt to preserve the moral order.

Deterrence

Offenders are punished as a **deterrent,** both for specific offenders, to prevent them from committing further crimes, and for people in general in society, who may consider the commission of a similar act. Even today, legislators create punishments in order to deter and prevent crimes. Correctional administrators are often urged to carry out sanctions, especially those of imprisonment, in a harsh enough manner to be sure offenders "feel punishment" and are, therefore, deterred from committing future crimes. The theories of Jeremy Bentham, an early advocate of deterrence as the primary reason for punishment, are still popular today. In his 1789 concept of **hedonistic calculus,** Bentham argued that if the sanction for committing a crime inflicted a greater amount of pain than the pleasure resulting from the offense, crime would be prevented.

Although there are many reasons this simple calculation does not work effectively in modern society, it still has credibility in the development of sentencing decisions throughout the history of the United States. Bentham's calculus assumes that rational individuals will consider the pleasure–pain aspects of their act and that the system will catch and speedily punish criminal offenders. We know that the probability of offenders being caught is low, because police clearance rates (the percentage of all crimes that result in an arrest or for which the offender is known) are usually less than 20 percent, and punishment often takes several months or even years to be carried out.

Why is the consideration of deterrence and Bentham's hedonistic calculus important to contemporary study of correctional administration? It is important because correctional administrators receive subtle, and sometimes formal, pressure to formulate their agency's policies and practices to emphasize punishment and enhance the deterrent effect of the criminal sanction. It is easy for correctional administrators to fall prey to this pressure. It is difficult to formulate a balance of all correctional goals and maximize the long-range impact of the sanction. Some of the situations that face administrators in this regard are discussed later in this chapter and are addressed in later chapters of this text.

Incapacitation

There are two ways to view the correctional goal of **incapacitation.** The first is a broad definition whereby the opportunity for offenders to commit further criminal law violations is reduced, and the second is a narrower definition that relates to imprisonment. In the first definition of incapacitation, there are many community, as well as institutional, sanctions that focus on the reduction of opportunities for an offender to commit further crimes against victims in the community. Sentences of imprisonment do maximize incapacitation, because confinement in a physically secure facility makes it almost impossible to commit new crimes against community victims. However, community sanctions can also reduce the likelihood of further criminality through supervision and control. For instance, house arrest using electronic monitoring to ensure an offender remains at home at prescribed times reduces the opportunity for criminal activity. Even regular probation supervision reduces the opportunity (in a limited manner) for offenders to commit crimes, because they must spend some portion of their time with a probation officer or in a program supervised by probation or other community staff.

However, being in prison does not make it impossible to commit further crimes against victims. Seldom discussed are crimes of assault by offenders against other inmates, perhaps because the other inmates are no longer considered potential victims, because their own behavior has placed them in prison and subjected them to added risks of victimization. Offenders in prison can still use or sell drugs, and society as a victim of their use and distribution feels the same impact as if they were not in prison. Prison staff can also become victims of crimes by inmates. Simply because they are on their job and recognize they are at risk does not immune prison staff from becoming victims of incarcerated offenders. Inmates do commit criminal acts against prison staff. There are also cases of prison inmates assaulting their visitors or prison volunteers, who must be considered community victims. Therefore, even imprisonment is not a perfect sanction to fully incapacitate, or stop the commission of future crimes.

The second way to consider incapacitation is in reference to "the crimes averted in the general society by isolation of the identified offenders during periods of incarceration."[5] In this manner, incapacitation is intended to reduce crime by focusing on the offender who is incapacitated or imprisoned, but only during that time that they are under control of the authorities carrying out the punishment. Incapacitation is based on the belief that most criminals commit several crimes throughout their lifetimes, and therefore, during the time of their incarceration, crime is prevented by their reduced opportunity. Blumstein notes that incapacitation operates on the assumption that "punishment can take a slice out of an individual criminal career."[6]

Incapacitation is based on reducing future criminal behavior, through the belief that most offenders will continue to commit crimes if not imprisoned, and through the accurate prediction of which offenders will commit further crimes. The first part of this statement is generally accepted to be true; however, the latter part is fraught with possible errors. Several studies have documented the fact that most offenders do commit more than one crime, and a small group of offenders commit a large percentage of crimes. In a review, it was found that

> Career criminals, though few in number account for most crime. Even though chronic repeat offenders (those with five or more arrests by age 18) make up a relatively small proportion of all offenders, they commit a very high proportion of all crimes. . . . In Wolfgang's Philadelphia study, chronic offenders accounted for 23 percent of all male offenders in the study, but they had committed 61 percent of all crimes. Of all crimes by all members of the group studied, chronic offenders

committed: 61 percent of all homicides; 76 percent of all rapes; 73 percent of all robberies; and 65 percent of all aggravated assaults.[7]

Unfortunately, the problem is in predicting which offenders have the highest chance of continuing their criminality after arrest and need imprisonment to prevent them from further victimizing society. Such predictions have not proven to be very accurate, because we have no "sure fire" way to identify the future involvement in crime of offenders. Therefore, authorities responsible for sentencing must make a difficult decision—should this person be imprisoned to prevent crime, even though there is no guarantee that crime will continue? Or should offenders be allowed to remain in the community, even though there is no surety that they will not commit additional crimes? Not every criminal can receive a prison sentence, and every one should not. Therefore, sanctions and sentencing decisions must take into account the best available approaches to predicting the impact of incapacitation toward avoiding further commission of crimes.

Selective Incapacitation

In the 1980s, the concept of selective incapacitation began to receive attention and debate. Recognizing that prison cells were an expensive and, therefore, scarce resource, the Rand Corporation examined this issue and developed the term **selective incapacitation.** Greenwood argued that in order to maximize the incapacitating result (preventing future crimes) of imprisonment, scarce prison and jail space should be reserved for the most dangerous, violent, and repeat offenders.[8] Earlier, Miller and others, studying crime rates in Columbus, Ohio, concluded that if selected offenders who commit repetitive crimes were imprisoned and incapacitated for a three- or even five-year period of time, significantly fewer crimes would have been committed.[9] Forst has also argued that selective incapacitation could reduce prison populations through the effect of incapacitation and by using alternative punishments for those who were not high-rate offenders.[10]

Selective incapacitation remains a hotly debated topic. The methodological approach and resultant conclusions of the Rand studies have been challenged by Gottfredson and Hirschi.[11] Issues have also been raised regarding the problem of "false positives." Because we do not have the predictive technology to determine which offenders are truly the highest risk for further criminality, a policy of selective incapacitation would raise ethical and practical questions. As noted by Allen and Simonsen, "the evidence is that we would probably incarcerate numerous noneligible (a "false positive" problem) persons and release to lesser confinement many of those eligible (a "false negative" problem) persons. Whatever benefits might accrue to this sentencing doctrine have thus far eluded corrections."[12]

Rehabilitation

The final goal of corrections is to rehabilitate offenders by providing programs that make them less likely to commit further crimes. Rehabilitation can result from linking punishment with treatment programs, the realization by offenders that life is better without crime; or the improvement of offenders through programs that enhance skills in education, vocational training, or work habits. **Rehabilitation** itself means, "returning someone to a prior state." For offenders, one may wonder what prior state they should be returned to, but it is assumed that means their life before they began to commit crimes. However, for most offenders, rehabilitation does not really mean returning to a state before they turned to crime. It means moving offenders to a new and better state, one in which they are self-restrained, do not have an interest in committing crime, and have the skills and self-confidence to be productive and law-abiding citizens.

From the late 1940s to the early 1970s, corrections followed the **medical model** of rehabilitation, in which offenders were believed to be "sick." Medical terms were interspersed into the correctional processes, and offenders were diagnosed to determine the problems that required treatment. Most offenders were committed to prison with indeterminate sentences, and release decisions were made by professionals (a parole board) who reviewed cases and determined whether offenders were adequately treated to move them to an aftercare setting in the community. Offenders would then receive additional casework therapy by parole officers, who would further analyze their status, and make recommendations to the parole board for final release when it was determined they were rehabilitated.

In the 1960s, parole and indeterminate sentences were still used in almost every state and by the federal government. However, a variation of the medical model became prominent. Correctional administrators recognized that there was a tremendous gap as offenders moved from the very structured life of prison to freedom in the community. Many programs to reduce the transition from prison to the community were initiated, and the **reintegration model** complemented the medical model. Offenders are a product of their community, and without careful guidance and supervision as they move from prison to the community, it was believed that most positive results from prison rehabilitative programs would be lost. The use of halfway houses expanded, special treatment programs were developed to supplement traditional parole supervision, and there were even "three-quarter" way houses for parolees who were failing and needed additional reprogramming to avoid a return to prison.

Challenges to Rehabilitation

Over the past 30 years, there have been many challenges to rehabilitation as an effective correctional goal. Questions have been raised regarding the role of offenders in the rehabilitative process, the effectiveness of rehabilitative programming, and public support for rehabilitation as a goal. Even when rehabilitation was strongly supported as a correctional goal in the 1960s and early 1970s, there were questions about how it should be carried out with offenders in prison or under community supervision. If rehabilitative programming were to be fully effective, it was argued, it had to be carried out in a noncoercive fashion. Even though many correctional programs were considered voluntary, parole release decisions considered the efforts toward rehabilitation put forth by offenders, judged primarily by the number of programs that were completed. Even release from parole supervision in the community considered offenders' efforts toward rehabilitation. Psychiatrist

Seymour Halleck argued that it was almost impossible to distinguish between fully voluntary and coercive treatment participation, especially in a correctional setting in which decisions affecting offenders considered such participation.[13]

As this argument and how it should be reflected in the implementation of correctional programming raged on, Norval Morris in *The Future of Imprisonment*, convincingly asserted that although rehabilitation is valuable as a correctional goal, it could not be effective if it was believed to be coercive in the eyes of offenders, or if they saw it as an element of the punishment they were receiving for their criminal offenses.[14] Morris was convincing not only because of his arguments but also because of his engaging personality and outstanding ability to deliver a lecture on the topic. He was highly respected, considered at one time to be the director of the Department of Justice's Law Enforcement Assistance Administration, and a member of many correctional groups, such as the National Institute of Corrections Advisory Board. His arguments made such a point with Norman A. Carlson, director of the Federal Bureau of Prisons during much of the 1960s and all of the 1970s, that a new federal prison in Butner, North Carolina, was to be opened and designed to operate totally on Morris' principles of fully voluntary programming.[15]

The second challenge to rehabilitation resulted from questioning the effectiveness of correctional treatment programs. An article appearing in *The Public Interest* questioned the success of correctional rehabilitation, effectively ended the medical model of corrections and initiated the decline in the use of parole and indeterminate sentences.[16] In this article, "What Works? Questions and Answers About Prison Reform," Robert Martinson reviewed 231 studies of correctional treatment programs. Although he noted that most were poorly conducted, he found that those with satisfactory research methodology were the least likely to result in positive results.[17] This article came to be known as the "Nothing Works!" finding and was popularly cited by those who believed corrections should stop spending money on efforts to treat criminals and instead, resort to punishment, incapacitation, and deterrence as primary goals. In the early 1970s, before states began to question the medical model and the use of indeterminate sentences and parole, more than 70 percent of prisoners were released via a parole decision. Fourteen states and the federal government have now implemented determinate sentencing and eliminated parole, and more than 20 other states have implemented parole guidelines to reduce the discretion of parole boards and to make decision making more "determinate." These changes have resulted in less than 30 percent of inmates being released on discretionary parole.

The "nothing works" finding gave impetus to the third challenge to rehabilitation, a public attitude shift toward making corrections more punishment oriented. Until the 1980s, the public and most elected officials accepted the importance of rehabilitation and the need for a positive, treatment-oriented environment in prisons in which to carry it out. However, as the Martinson article began to move sentiment away from this philosophy, rising crime rates, senseless drive-by shootings, and an epidemic of drug use on the streets created a public fear of violence and crime. These factors pushed the "get tough on crime" public attitude that continues to this day.

The key to public support of any correctional goal, sanction, or program is the extent to which the public believes it protects them from crime.[18] The public expects and demands that criminals receive punishment, with public safety first and foremost in importance. It is interesting to note, however, that although the public expects to be protected, they are tolerant of rehabilitative programs designed to transform offenders into law-abiding citizens. Innes notes that once offenders are incarcerated, the public feels safe, and thereafter supports the attempt to rehabilitate through prison programs.[19]

Results from the National Opinion Survey of Crime and Justice illustrate these points. When the survey questioned the public support regarding community versus prison sanctions, 53 percent of those surveyed during 1996 either "strongly agree or agree" that community corrections are evidence of leniency in the criminal justice system.[20] An even stronger result came from asking if it was a good idea to refuse parole to a prisoner who had been paroled before for a serious crime, with 75 percent of the 1995 respondents indicating that refusing parole was a good idea.[21] However, respondents from the same survey also indicate support for rehabilitative programs: 93 percent support prisoners learning a skill or trade, and 94 percent support requiring offenders to be able to read and write before release from prison. Similarly, 88 percent support inmate work programs to construct buildings, make products, or perform services.[22]

Even with public support for rehabilitative programs, elected officials believe that punishment should be the key result of imprisonment and that prison amenities should be minimized. As U.S. Senator Mike DeWine noted, "The common perception is that prisoners are sitting in a very comfortable place, watching cable television, eating three meals a day, and living off the taxpayers. We have to break through that perception, make sure prisoners give something back, *and* then make sure that we let the public know what is really going on."[23] Although rehabilitative programs in prisons and in community correctional settings continue, there are still challenges regarding funding and provision of resources. Correctional administrators must respond to these challenges by educating elected officials on the effectiveness of rehabilitative programs, as well as by arguing for the value of a balanced emphasis on all correctional goals.

CORRECTIONAL GOALS AND CRIMINAL SANCTIONS

If the criminal justice system is organized in a logical manner, the goals noted previously are all considered in the development of the range of sanctions or penalties for each type of law violation. Certain correctional goals are better met by certain criminal sanctions. For instance, rehabilitation is perhaps more effective when a sanction allows an offender to spend part of his or her time in the community rather than in prison. Treatment programs in the community deal with offenders' issues in real-life situations, whereas similar programs in prison do not allow offenders to test the skills they have gained or their strength to say no to the types of behaviors that get them in trouble.

Similarly, it can also be argued that the goal of incapacitation is most effective by removing offenders from the community, because this limits their opportunities to further victimize society. It seems logical that the punishment of losing one's freedom through incarceration is greater than the punishment of supervision in the community. As such, the deterrent effect of a prison sentence is reasonably expected to be greater than the deterrent effect resulting from a community sanction.

These arguments that certain sanctions better achieve certain correctional goals are rational and will not be rebutted in this textbook. However, the point of view suggested in this textbook is that all correctional goals are accomplished to a point by all sanctions. There is some incapacitating impact of any supervision in the community, because it does limit the opportunity for further criminality by offenders. There can be effective treatment and rehabilitative programs offered in prisons. In fact, there is an increasing amount of data to indicate this, and as a result, there is a renewed interest in these types of programs by correctional administrators.[24] And finally, every criminal sanction includes some level of punishment, whether it is financial, a restriction to an offender's freedom through community supervision, embarrassment and public shame, or incarceration. Therefore, every level of punishment carries with it some deterrent effect.

The way to maximize the cost effectiveness of criminal sanctioning is to match the appropriate level of punishment and deterrence to each individual offender. In the following sections, various sanctions are discussed and the impact on correctional goals is illustrated. Correctional administrators should be considered the "experts" regarding how to match offenders to various sanctions, and, as parole and probation officials, are called on to make specific recommendations to sentencing courts. It is, therefore, critical to fully understand and be able to articulate the potential of various sanctions on correctional goals.

Economic Sanctions

Most people only think of fines when considering economic sanctions for crimes and usually consider only small dollar amounts of fines for minor offenses. However, there are a wide variety of economic sanctions, including fines, compensation to victims, repaying society for the injury caused by the offense, forfeiture of assets, and even community service. In addition, fines and forfeiture of assets can be of very large amounts. For instance, during the 1980s, junk bond king Michael Milken defrauded investors of what was estimated to be hundreds of millions of dollars. He amassed such a fortune from his criminal activities that his criminal fine was set at $600 million, although it was believed to be far less than he made from his illegal trading.

Fines are simply a requirement that an offender pay some dollar amount to the court as punishment for committing an offense. Fines can be a set amount for every offender that commits a certain crime and are often sanctioned that way for minor misdemeanors or minor violations such as traffic offenses. However, fines for felonies can be more creative, and reflect the individual situation of each offense and offender. Courts usually consider both the seriousness of the offense and the economic gain by the offender to determine the amount of a fine. It may be a very appropriate sanction for a white-collar offender, with little risk of future criminality and little need for rehabilitative programs. The sanction should focus on pure punishment and deterrence, especially if the offender has received personal income from the crime.

Offenders Doing Public Service Work. Public service has become very popular, because offenders pay back society for their crimes. Here, offenders are picking up trash along a highway. (Courtesy of the Georgia Department of Corrections)

As noted, fines are usually paid to the court, and used for whatever purposes the court deems fit. Another type of economic sanction is **offender restitution,** requiring the offender to repay society for the harm created by the offense. Restitution can take several forms. In **victim compensation,** the offender must repay the victim for loss and harm caused by the offense. The federal courts and many state courts allow victims to submit victimization statements, which detail the amount of loss they incurred from the crime. Sentencing judges consider these losses when sentencing offenders, and they often use the submitted amount for assigning a level of victim compensation. Another way offenders provide restitution is through **community service.** With community service, offenders must give their personal time to perform tasks that are valued to the community. Tasks can range from cleaning up trash along a street or highway to counseling teenagers about the negative results of drug use. Community service is included here as an economic sanction for two reasons. First, it is often used when offenders do not have funds from which to pay a fine or make restitution. Second, it is often referred to as a "fine on their time," because time often has economic benefit to the offender. This is particularly true of a white-collar offender who has good earning potential but will obviously have to give up some potential earnings to perform community service.

Perhaps the most effective economic sanction to be used as a sanction in the past 30 years is **asset forfeiture,** or the authorized seizure by the government of money, negotiable instruments, securities, or other things of value that were obtained through illegal activities. With asset forfeiture, courts are able to punish offenders by taking away the assets they accumulated as a result of their criminal activity and, in a sense, "make crime not pay." The first use of asset forfeiture was in the RICO (Racketeer Influenced and Corrupt Organization) statute, a part of the federal Organized Crime Control Act of 1970. The RICO statutes were designed to aid law enforcement in investigating and prosecuting organized crime figures, specifying that it is unlawful for anyone involved in a pattern of racketeering to derive any income or proceeds from that activity, and allowing the government to seize anything of value that can be shown to have been acquired through the racketeering activity.

Asset forfeiture is also authorized and regularly used in the prosecution of drug offenders. Since the 1980s, when the federal government expanded their powers and more aggressively targeted the arrest and prosecution of drug offenders, asset forfeiture has been a valuable strategy. As assets are seized, if property, they are auctioned off, and the proceeds, or money, is divided among the federal and the local law enforcement agencies who participated in the investigation and prosecution. With these funds, local law enforcement has been able to enhance their own capabilities to target drug crimes, which has led to even more arrests and prosecution.

Probation

Probation is legally a sentence of imprisonment suspended on the condition that the offender follows certain prescribed rules and does not commit further crimes. **Probation** as a criminal sanction has suffered from a perception of being "soft on crime" over the past two decades, when the public and legislative bodies have demanded tougher sanctions for criminal offenses. However, every offender cannot be sent to prison, and therefore, probation is still a sanction regularly used in the United States. In fact, since 1975, the number of offenders under community supervision has risen from less than one million to more than three million in 1995.[25] However, the use of probation has changed dramatically since 1975. Several programs to enhance supervision, increase effectiveness, and increasingly limit offenders' freedom have been implemented. These include intensive probation supervision, house arrest, boot camps, and shock probation.

The use of probation as a sanction without some type of enhancement has been questioned as to its ability to effectively deter offenders and protect society from future crimes. A review of 79,000 felons sentenced to probation in 32 counties across 17 states in 1986 found that within three years of sentencing, while still on probation, 43 percent were rearrested for a felony.[26] In another study critical of probation, Petersilia followed 1,672 felony probationers from two counties in California for 40 months and found that more than 67 percent were rearrested and 51 percent were convicted for a new offense.[27] Although these studies question the effectiveness of probation, the driving force behind its continued use has been its low cost compared to other sanctions. An estimate of the cost of constructing a maximum-security prison is approximately $80,000 per bed, and the annual cost of maintaining and housing an inmate is approximately $19,000.[28] Therefore, correctional administrators continue to look for ways to increase the effectiveness of probation to protect society and deter crime.

Intensive probation supervision (IPS) has been used since the 1970s to increase the amount of supervision that is provided to selected felony probationers. Since the initial program in Georgia in 1974, IPS programs are now actively used in every state. The intent of IPS is to identify offenders who need more supervision than is available through regular probation, yet who are not such a risk to the community that they need to be in prison. Offenders placed in an IPS program are supervised by probation officers who have smaller caseloads and who provide more frequent contacts through a combination of reporting by offenders and home and work visits by the officer. The "intensity" of supervision allows for enhancing the goal of incapacitation, because the additional contacts reduce the opportunity offenders to slip into criminal behavior. IPS is also more of a punishment and deterrence, because the amount of contacts required disrupts the daily lives of offenders. Equally, it can enhance rehabilitation, as officers with smaller caseloads can provide or follow up on treatment plans for offenders they supervise.

An even greater level of supervision for sanctioned offenders who remain in the community is **house arrest.** With house arrest, offenders avoid a prison sentence, yet they must be detained or incapacitated in their own homes. They may remain employed to earn an income and support their families, as well as pay for their own upkeep and usually the cost of supervision for their house arrest. With house arrest, offenders live at home, and must be at home except for times they are to be at work or participating in other activities approved by their probation officer. House arrest has the potential benefits of being economical, imposing severe restrictions on offender's freedom and opportunity to commit crimes, and allowing for the participation in community-based treatment programs for the offenders.

Although it is not always necessary, house arrest is commonly used in conjunction with **electronic monitoring,** or the use of technology to track an offender's location. Electronic monitoring requires offenders wear a tamper-proof bracelet around their ankles. The bracelet acts as a receiver for a radio wave sent by a transmitter that is placed in the offenders home. There are two types of systems: active and passive, both of which are monitored from a central location. With active systems, the central location maintains a computerized schedule of when offenders should be in their homes, and automatically "alarms," or sends a notice, when the signal is not communicated between the transmitter and receiver during those times. This indicates to the monitor or probation officer that an offender is violating the conditions of the house arrest, and someone will be dispatched to check on or arrest the offender. The passive system requires random telephone calls during times the offender should be in the home. When a monitoring telephone call is received, offenders have a certain amount of time to place the receiver against the transmitter, proving they are in the home as required.

Electronic monitoring is not a criminal sanction, it is a method of supervision. The use of electronic monitoring has increased greatly throughout the United States, with the first systems being activated in 1986, more than 40,000 units in use by 1992, and continued growth in their use throughout the 1990s.[29] Generally, house arrest using electronic monitoring is considered effective. Evaluations of programs in Illinois[30] and Texas[31] reveal good results, and a 1989 survey on telemonitoring of offenders noted that, "There were no significant differences in successful terminations among probationers, offenders on parole, or those in community corrections. All had successful terminations rates ranging between 74 and 86 percent."[32]

An interesting development since the mid-1980s as a correctional sanction is shock incarceration or **boot camp.** The first boot camps were initiated in Georgia in

1983 and Oklahoma in 1984. Quickly gaining in popularity, boot camps were initiated in many states over the next 10 years. This development is interesting as regards the accomplishment of correctional goals, because boot camps were created to hold offenders accountable for their crimes, with a harsh punishment and deterrent effect. Operated similarly to a military boot camp, offenders are required to wear their hair short, shine their shoes, wear uniforms, do extensive physical exercise, and perform hard physical labor. At times, these requirements are complemented with educational or drug programming, but the major components of boot camps are military regimentation, discipline, exercise, and hard work. Boot camps appeal to liberals and conservatives, because they focus on being tough on crime and tough on the offender, but they are also an alternative to regular imprisonment. If offenders do well and complete boot camp, they receive a shorter sentence than if they had received a traditional prison sentence.

Boot camps are usually reserved for young, first-time prisoners who are deemed to be able to benefit from structure and discipline while gaining self-control with the rigorous daily routine. However, boot camps have been criticized for a lack of success and the high cost of the programs. Boot camps are expensive to operate, because they require a high ratio of staff to inmates, especially compared to minimum-security prisons, where most of the boot camp offenders would otherwise be incarcerated. Recent findings have been very critical of the impact of boot camps at reducing recidivism.[33] As a result of such findings, several states are questioning their efficacy and reconsidering the concept, and New Hampshire, Connecticut, and Arizona have all closed their boot camp operations.[34]

A final probation application is **shock probation,** a short period of imprisonment to "shock" the offender, with a return to the community within a few weeks to continue supervision on probation. The concept originated in Ohio with the passage of legislation in 1965. The statute allowed sentencing judges to reconsider their sentence of imprisonment after offenders served between 90 to 130 days in prison. If the offender met the criteria (a nonviolent offense with no prior offense history) and the judge believed that the punitive and, therefore, deterrent value of the sentence had already been met, the sentence could be modified to regular probation. This sanction is based on the specific deterrence model; the shock of entering prison was intended to show offenders the type of punishment they would receive from additional crimes. Several other states subsequently adopted this program. After evaluating the effectiveness of shock probation, Vito concluded

1. The shock experience should not be limited to first-time offenders; eligibility should properly include those with prior records, as deemed eligible by the judge.
2. The length of incarceration necessary to secure the deterrent effect could be much shorter, probably 30 days or less.
3. Reincarceration rates have never exceeded 26 percent and, in Ohio, have been as low as 10 percent. The level of these rates clearly indicates that the program has potential for reintegration.
4. Shock probation has considerable potential to reduce institutional overcrowding characteristics of contemporary corrections.[35]

Incarceration

The final discussion involves the sanction of incarceration in a prison. Since the 1980s, when the public sentiment toward toughening sentences was initiated, imprisonment has been seen as the most punitive sanction, and most effective in deterring crime and enhancing the goal of incapacitation. Since the mid-1980s, there has been an unprecedented level of building prisons and an unprecedented increase in the number of inmates in state and federal prisons. In 1980, after 200 years of using prisons as a criminal sanction, there were only 315,974 sentenced prisoners under state or federal jurisdiction. In one-tenth of that time, the 20-year period from 1980 to 2000, this number multiplied by almost 500 percent, to more than 1.5 million inmates. This dramatic increase resulted for many reasons, including the plethora of tough on crime legislation lengthening sentences, the war on drugs resulting in mandatory prison sentences for even first-time drug offenders, the elimination of parole, and the prosecution of serious juvenile offenders as adults. The increase in the use of incarceration has continued throughout this period, even though most index crime rates have actually declined each year since 1993.

It is reasonable to believe that punishment, deterrence, and incapacitation are maximized by a sentence of imprisonment, and that rehabilitation can be effective within a prison environment. Therefore, if the only argument were how to maximize all correctional goals, it would seem reasonable that imprisonment is the best sanction. However, the average state and federal cost to imprison one inmate per day in 1997 was $55.51, or $20,261 per year.[36] This has increased more than 15 percent since 1990 and will continue to rise each year. As a result, jurisdictions continue to look for safe and effective alternatives to incarceration.

Correctional Administration and Balancing Correctional Goals

What is the role of a correctional administrator in balancing correctional goals, even within any specific criminal sanction? Many would argue that trying to balance or blend goals within a correctional sanction is not the responsibility of correctional officials and that their function is only the fiduciary role of carrying out the sanctions imposed by the courts. This argument is similar to the continuing discussion regarding the role of other public administrators. Traditional public administration theory suggests that in a representative democracy, elected officials develop policies and determine direction for administrators. The role of public administrators is, therefore, to carry out the policies rather than to try to influence or make policy themselves. A more modern view of public administration recognizes an essential role of public administrators to play a role in making policy and influencing political decision makers.

However, the discussion of the role of correctional officials in balancing goals is more practical than political. When a legislative body creates the range of allowable sanctions for specific crimes, they consider the importance of punishment, deterrence, incapacitation, and rehabilitation. When judges sentence offenders within these ranges, they further consider the importance of these four goals for each individual offender. For instance, if a judge sentences an offender to four years in prison for commission of an armed robbery, the judge believes that punishment is necessary to incapacitate the offender and hopefully deter him or her from further criminal offenses. The judge may have in mind certain rehabilitative activities that will take place in prison during the sentence, and in some jurisdictions, may even be able to suggest or mandate program participation such as drug abuse counseling. In this regard, it may seem that correctional administrators have little to do to try to balance correctional goals.

However, the balancing of these goals can vary greatly from one prison to another, not only in the activities that are encompassed within the prison's routine but also in the institutional climate that exists. Even prisons that perform the exact same functions can take on an extremely punitive atmosphere or a positive, rehabilitative atmosphere. The strictness and harshness surrounding inmate discipline, the level and type of staff-inmate interaction, the emphasis on humaneness and personal dignity, and the amount of control over inmate activities by staff all set a tone that can make a tremendous difference in which goals dominate the prison environment.

As early as 1961, Erving Goffman wrote regarding the impact of an institutional enjoinment on those housed within the institution. In *Asylums: Essays on the Social Situation of Mental Patients and Other Inmates,* Goffman described the "total institution" as a setting that isolates people from the rest of society and unnecessarily manipulates them through the actions of the administrative staff.[37] Goffman describes three characteristics of total institutions: Staff members supervise all spheres of daily life, such as where inmates eat, work, and sleep; the environment is highly standardized, with one set of activities for everyone; and rules and schedules dictate how inmates perform all aspects of their daily routine. All of these prison characteristics are expected to "resocialize" inmates to a more law-abiding lifestyle by separating them from society, reducing their autonomy and changing their identity, and rebuilding their selves through rewards and punishments. Goffman, however, warns that although institutions can bring about the desired change in some inmates, others may become confused, hostile, and bitter, and that extended periods of institutional living can actually reduce an individual's capacity for independent living.

Goffman's presentation of the concept of a total institution makes clear how correctional administrators can create an environment that favors one goal over another. He describes the impact on inmates of making new inmates publicly strip, wearing degrading stripped uniforms, or having to shave their heads. Although these practices are seldom still carried out in modern prisons, the old traditions contributed to making prisons oriented toward the goal of punishment. However, the result was that this environment made positive resocialization difficult at best.

Even today, there are some subtle remnants of punitive atmospheres within prisons. The most obvious results from the type of interactions that are fostered among staff and inmates. If staff, through consistent enforcement of rules and maintenance of control, encourage positive interaction by showing courtesy and respect to inmates, the environment will be one that balances punishment and rehabilitation. However, if staff only talk to inmates to correct behavior or to carry out discipline for rule infractions, the environment will favor punishment to the detriment of rehabilitation.

The classic examination of how staff can tend to become authoritative in their interactions with inmates is apparent in the work of Zimbardo.[38] Zimbardo wanted to test the idea that prisons change human behavior. He constructed a mock-prison in the basement of a building at Stanford University, and he selected 24 mentally healthy young men to play randomly selected roles as either guards or prisoners. The prisoners were to spend two weeks in the "Stanford County Prison," with guards responsible for their well-being. The experiment resulted in guards and prisoners becoming hostile to each other; the guards humiliated and yelled at the prisoners, and the prisoners resisted and insulted the guards. After the first week, the situation had gotten so bad that Zimbardo canceled the remaining week of the experiment. Zimbardo noted how "some boys (guards) treat others as if they were despicable animals. Taking pleasure in cruelty, while other boys (prisoners) became servile, dehumanized robots who thought only of escape, of their own individual survival and of their mounting hatred for the guards."[39] Zimbardo's work provided the foundation for correctional agencies to concentrate on the important interactions of staff and inmates in creating a prison environment, and drawing a fine line between staff maintaining authority and dehumanizing inmates is a key challenge to correctional administrators.

Can correctional administrators' leadership reduce the likelihood of the development of attitudes by correctional workers that resulted in the Stanford study? It is generally believed that the leadership exhibited in a correctional environment is critical in setting a tone and creating an environment in which there is a balance between punishment and rehabilitation. DiIulio, in his classic examination of management and leadership within three state correctional agencies, noted, "It is the leaders of corrections agencies who are most responsible for articulating and institutionalizing a vision of how prisons ought to be governed."[40] Correctional administrators can set the tone as to what is expected regarding behavior and communications by correctional staff. By their own actions, by how they respond to unacceptable behavior, and by how they hold supervisors accountable for the actions of line staff, correctional administrators can create and mold a correctional setting into a positive environment with mutual respect among staff and inmates.

It may seem difficult to create a non-punitive atmosphere within the current tough-on-crime public climate. Correctional administrators should not feel they are fighting a losing battle in trying to encourage positive interaction within a prison. A recent study illustrated that, even with an ideological shift to a more punitive attitude in policy and practice toward crime and criminal offender, most correctional officers have not changed their attitudes to mirror this shift. This study examined the orientation of correctional officers toward inmates and found that despite the more punitive sentiment among the public and policy makers, officers still do not express a punitive attitude and support rehabilitation programs toward inmates.[41]

Although it is rewarding to know that correctional officers do not wantonly mirror punitive attitudes that exist by some in the general public, correctional administrators must remain vigilant in developing an organizational culture and guiding the attitude of staff regarding offenders. During the 1990s, there has been an increasing visibility of excessive force used by police officers against alleged offenders, such as in the Rodney King beating by Los Angeles police. In addition, a videotape was made and found its way to the news media that depicted staff of a private prison in Texas using attack dogs and beating Missouri inmates who were housed there under contract. These examples illustrate the danger of staff developing a punitive attitude and the critical importance of correctional administrators working to avoid it.

The case study in Chapter 3 describe a prison warden's efforts to use staff involvement to set a vision for the institution. This case study is continued in the accompanying Practical Perspectives to illustrate how important it is to tend to staff and inmate interaction and the impact this interaction can have on the overall prison environment.

PRACTICAL PERSPECTIVES

The Importance of Staff and Inmate Interaction

After the riot, the warden observed that staff were taking a much more authoritative approach in their interactions with inmates. More staff elevated their voices and took on a tone of discipline when talking to inmates, and statements by staff to direct an inmate to change a behavior became more like "barking orders" than reminders of the rules. Although these types of interactions are necessary in certain situations and with certain noncompliant inmates, when they become the regular rather than infrequent method of interaction, it sets a climate of tension and hostility that can make the environment more stressful and less stable for both staff and inmates. The warden believed that this behavior was the result of the riot; staff had witnessed a few inmates destroying property and assaulting other staff members. As a result, the staff began to treat all inmates as violent and dangerous, probably out of fear, and became more tense and disrespectful in their communications. The warden, in conjunction with her top staff, set out an agenda to change this interaction into one more relaxed and positive when possible. First, she initiated activities to directly respond to staff's fear of further victimization by inmates. This included "hardening" the prison by replacing wooden with metal doors and putting bars over windows to create "safe havens" for staff if another dangerous situation broke out. Staff were further trained in disturbance control, boosting their confidence that they could handle a violent situation if one occurred. Discipline and additional prosecution of inmates who were involved in the riot was publicized among inmates and staff, illustrating those inmates would be held accountable for these types of actions.

After these actions were completed and staff felt more comfortable with their personal safety, the warden set out to improve the positive communications between staff and inmates. She did several things. First, additional training was provided to staff regarding positive interactions and proper interpersonal communications. Second, a videotape was made of the warden discussing the importance of positive staff–inmate interactions and shown to all staff. On the video, the warden explained the reasons for such positive inter-action, emphasizing staff were not being to "soft" on inmates, but that this ap-proach in effect would enhance the security and safety of the institution. As well as reducing tension and lessening the likelihood of an inmate sponta-neously responding with violence in a confrontational situation with staff, pos-itive communications opened the door to inmates sharing important "intelli-gence" with staff about planned inmate misconduct or potential inmate gang activities. Third, supervisors were asked to immediately correct communica-tions by line staff that did not comply with this approach and to use this as a key discussion point in all staff evaluations. Finally, the warden appealed to line staff to recognize the problems that inappropriate communications caused and to correct their fellow employees who destabilized the environment and made it more dangerous for everyone else.

The results were that these targeted activities worked over time. Fewer and fewer staff used harsh and authoritative tones of voice unnecessarily. More staff began to repeat the importance of positive communications and to pride themselves on their ability to gain inmate compliance without having to "bark orders" and make demands. As staff discovered that they more effec-tively maintained order by treating inmates with courtesy and respect, while still consistently and fairly enforcing rules, their skill and success increased. The overall climate of the institution returned to one of positive staff and in-mate interaction, in a relaxed and less stressful environment, with a reduced level of disciplinary infractions for failure to follow orders or insubordination by inmates.

This case study represents a good example of the role of correctional adminis-trators in working with staff to keep all four correctional goals in balance. It is often very difficult for staff to be totally objective in their own work and keep their per-sonal attitudes about offenders from influencing how they perform their roles. Par-ticularly in these "tough on crime" times, when public sentiment seems to favor pun-ishment above all else, correctional staff may incorporate this attitude as their own philosophy. That is why it is critical for correctional administrators to be leaders and set the tone for professionalism.

Although punishment is the basis for many of the other correctional goals, it does not justify abusing offenders rights or treating them in a degrading or dehu-manizing manner. Correctional administrators must carry out multiple goals, even when they sometimes seem to be in conflict with one another. How do you punish offenders and rehabilitate them at the same time? Within a prison, this becomes even more difficult when there are dangerous inmates who will not hesitate to as-sault staff or other inmates. Prison administrators first create a secure and safe envi-ronment for staff and inmates, and then use this safety to carry out rehabilitative programs. Later chapters discuss security, safe environments, and the other methods of meeting the expected mission of prisons.

SUMMARY

This chapter describes the development of the four goals of corrections: punishment, deterrence, incapacitation, and rehabilitation. From the earliest written proscriptions of types of behavior within a society, there were punishments specified for those who violated societal codes, which in turn deterred offenders from future violations and deterred other citizens who realized they too would be held accountable if they violated the code. As criminal sanctions were formalized and sentencing became more sophisticated, the understanding of the linkage of the current correctional goals of punishment, deterrence, incapacitation, and rehabilitation evolved. Each criminal sanction attempts to put these goals into perspective based on the severity and need to "correct" the offender.

It is interesting to note that we use the term *corrections* in labeling the role of agencies to carry out the criminal sanctions ordered by the courts. Corrections can be thought of as a broad term that encompasses all of the goals, with a forward-looking emphasis on changing offenders' behaviors to what is deemed "correct" by society. Punishment corrects behavior. Deterrence corrects behavior. Incapacitation corrects behavior. And, rehabilitation corrects behavior. However, the process of "correction" is maximized when all four of these goals are simultaneously accomplished over the period of the criminal sentence.

Throughout this chapter, there have been discussions of these correctional goals, how they can result from a wide variety of criminal sanctions, and how a correctional administrator can influence their accomplishment. It is easy to underestimate the importance of correctional administration in shaping the implementation of criminal sanctions. Those with limited knowledge of correctional leadership and management would think their role is somewhat limited to efficiently executing the sanctions imposed by the court. This narrow interpretation of administration, however, does not do justice to the skills required by correctional administrators, nor does it allow for a thoughtful discussion of the impact that administrators can have on their agencies.

It is critical for future correctional administrators to recognize the role and impact that they, as leaders within correctional agencies, can have on the tone and environment in which they work. This tone goes well beyond an organization that, through security and strict supervision, maximizes safety for staff and inmates. The tone can be developed that promotes all of the four correctional goals simultaneously. A sanction even as restrictive and potentially dangerous as imprisonment can be implemented with a tone that emphasizes preparing offenders to return to the community rehabilitated, or better prepared for success without resorting to crime.

With the foundation that has now been presented, students are prepared to move forward in their own study and development. The next chapter elaborates on the role of rehabilitation and describes specific programs that are used in both prisons and community correctional settings. In the final chapter of this section, we examine how risk assessment of individual inmates facilitates more focused and personalized plan to carry out a criminal sentence to maximize all four correctional goals. Correctional administrators must thoughtfully and professionally guide all of these activities in order to protect the public and improve the likelihood of success by offenders after their release from correctional supervision.

ENDNOTES

1. Kent Greenwalt, "Punishment," *Journal of Criminal Law and Criminology* 74 (summer 1983): 343–344.
2. Ibid., p. 345.
3. *Bell v. Wolfish,* 441 US 520 (1979).
4. *Solem v. Helm,* 463 US 277 (1983).
5. Alfred Blumstein, "Selective Incapacitation as a Means of Crime-Control," *American Behavioral Scientist* 27 no.1 (1983): 93.
6. Ibid., p. 94
7. Marianne W. Zawitz, ed., *Report to the Nation on Crime and Justice* (Washington, DC: U.S. Department of Justice, Bureau of Justice Statistics, U.S. Government Printing Officer, 1983), p. 35.
8. Peter Greenwood, *Selective Incapacitation* (Santa Monica, CA: Rand Corporation, 1983).
9. Stuart Miller, Simon Dinitz, and John Conrad, *Careers of the Violent* (Lexington, MA: Lexington Books, 1982).
10. Brian Forst, "Selective Incapacitation—An Idea Whose Time Has Come," *Federal Probation* 47 no. 3 (1983): 21.
11. Michael R. Gottfredson and Travis Hirschi, "The Methodological Adequacy of Longitudinal Research on Crime," *Criminology* 25 (1987): 581–614.
12. Harry E. Allen and Clifford E. Simonsen, *Corrections in America: An Introduction,* 8th ed. (Upper Saddle River, NJ: Prentice Hall, 1998), p. 58.
13. Seymour Halleck, *The Politics of Therapy* (New York: Science House, 1971).
14. Norval Morris, *The Future of Imprisonment* (Chicago, IL: University of Chicago Press, 1974).
15. The plan to open the Federal Treatment Center at Butner, North Carolina, fully following the principles espoused by Norval Morris did not occur. The mission of the prison was changed to treat inmates with psychiatric problems, and because of much internal disagreement within the ranks of the Bureau of Prisons officials, the Butner, North Carolina prison reverted to the standard program implementation in other federal prisons.
16. Robert Martinson, "What Works? Questions and Answers About Prison Reform," *The Public Interest* 35 (1974): 22–54.
17. The "What Works?" article was followed by a full report submitted to the state of New York Special Committee on Criminal Offenders, which had commissioned the review. Douglas Lipton, Robert Martinson, and Judith Wilks, *The Effectiveness of Correctional Treatment* (New York: Praeger, 1975).
18. See Timothy J. Flanagan, "Reform or Punish: Americans" Views of the Correctional System," in *Americans View Crime and Justice,* edited by Timothy J. Flanagan and Dennis R. Longmire (Thousand Oaks, CA: Sage, 1996).

19. Chris A. Innes, "Recent Public Opinion in the United States Toward Punishment and Corrections," *The Prison Journal* 73 (1993): 220–36.

20. Barbara A. Sims, "Questions of Corrections: Public Attitudes Toward Prison and Community-Based Programs," *Corrections Management Quarterly* 1(no. 1) (1997): 55.

21. Ibid., p. 52.

22. Ibid., p. 52.

23. Mike DeWine, "Public Opinion and Corrections: A Need to be Proactive," *Corrections Management Quarterly* 1(no. 3) (1997): 8.

24. Richard P. Seiter, "The Rebirth of Rehabilitation: The Responsibility Model," *Corrections Management Quarterly* 2(no. 1) (1998): 89–92.

25. Todd R. Clear and A. A. Braga, "Community Corrections," in *Crime*, edited by James Q. Wilson and Joan Petersilia (San Francisco, CA: ICS Press, 1995).

26. Bureau of Justice Statistics National Update (Washington, DC: U.S. Department of Justice, 1994), p. 10.

27. Joan Petersilia, "Probation and Felony Offenders, " *Federal Probation* 49 no.2 (1985): 4–9.

28. George Camp and Camille Camp, *The Corrections Yearbook, 1994: Adult Corrections* (South Salem, NY: The Criminal Justice Institute, 1995), pp. 43, 51.

29. Voncile Gowdy, *Intermediate Sanctions* (Washington, DC: U.S. Department of Justice, 1993), p. 6. For a more recent update on the use of electronic monitoring, see Randy R. Gainey and Brian K. Payne, "Understanding the Experience of House Arrest with Electronic Monitoring: An Analysis of Quantitative and Qualitative Data," *International Journal of Offender Therapy and Comparative Criminology* 44 (1 February 2000): 84–96.

30. Michael Brown and Preston Elrod, "Electronic House Arrest: An Examination of Citizen Attitudes," *Crime and Delinquency* 41 no. 3 (1995): 332–346.

31. Richard Enor, Clifford Block, James Quinn, et al., *Alternative Sentencing: Electronically Monitored Correctional Supervision* (Bristol, IN: Wyndham Hall, 1992).

32. Gowdy, pp. 6–7.

33. For an overview of evaluative findings regarding boot camps, see Jeanne B. Stinchcomb, "Recovering from the Shocking Reality of Shock Incarceration— What Correctional Administrators Can Learn from Boot Camp Failures," *Corrections Management Quarterly*, 3 (no. 4) (1999): 43–52.

34. Stinchcomb, p. 45

35. Gennaro Vito, "Developments in Shock Probation: A Review of Research Findings and Policy Implications," *Federal Probation* 50 no.1 (1985): 23–25.

36. Camille Graham Camp and George M. Camp, *The Corrections Yearbook: 1998* (Middletown, CT: The Criminal Justice Institute, 1999), pp. 90–91.

37. Erving Goffman, *Asylums: Essays on the Social Situation of Mental Patients and Other Inmates* (Garden City, NY: Anchor Books, 1961).

38. Phillip G. Zimbardo, "Pathology of Imprisonment," *Society* 9 (April 1972): 4–8.

39. Ibid., p. 4.

40. John J. DiIulio, Jr., *Governing Prisons: A Comparative Study of Correctional Management* (New York: The Free Press, 1987), p. 187.
41. M. A. Farkas, "Correctional Officer Attitudes Toward Inmates and Working with Inmates in a 'Get Tough' Era," *Journal of Criminal Justice* 27 no. 6 (November–December 1999): 495–506.

KEY TERMS

punishment	offender restitution
test of proportionality	victim compensation
deterrent	community service
hedonistic calculus	asset forfeiture
incapacitation	probation
selective incapacitation	intensive probation supervision
rehabilitation	house arrest
medical model	electronic monitoring
reintegration model	boot camp
fines	shock probation

YOU'RE THE CORRECTIONAL ADMINISTRATOR

1. You are the warden of a state prison. The prison has an excellent record of operations, with few security breaches, high staff and inmate morale, and many active and successful rehabilitative programs. There was recently a nice background piece on the local television news discussing one of the counseling programs at the prison. A powerful state legislator and the chair of the corrections oversight committee, however, contacted you and complained about how the prison was being operated. The legislator thinks the prison is not consistent with public sentiment toward criminal sentencing, believes that the prison is too program oriented, and that inmates aren't "punished" by serving their sentence in the prison. What do you do? Do you try to make a case for continuing the current operations or do you begin to change the operation to be more in line with the legislator's and public's thinking? Which of the two approaches do you follow, and what steps do you take to implement your decision?

2. You are the chief of probation for a large, urban county. Probation as a correctional sanction has increasingly come under criticism, and recent surveys of county citizens reveal that they believe probation it is too soft a sanction and that more criminals should be sent to prison. Whenever there is a crime committed by a probationer, it makes the news. Your judges are becoming more conservative in their sentencing, and in the past few months, the percentage of offenders going to prison instead of receiving probation has increased, even though the types of offenders are the same. What action can or should you take? You are not being pushed to do anything. If you decide you should take some action, what would you do, and how would you implement your decision?

WEB LINK EXERCISES

Correctional Boot Camps: A Tough Intermediate Sanction
www.ncjrs.org/bcamps.htm

Go to the Web site for the National Criminal Justice Reference Service and the publication *Correctional Boot Camps*. Read Chapter 19, "Conclusion: The Future of Boot Camps." In this chapter, there are several reasons why boot camps will (or will not) expand in number in the future. List these, and then come to your own conclusion as to their future. Then, note the most important reasons for expansion, or not, which you relied on to come to your conclusion.

CHAPTER

5

Programs and Services

◼ INTRODUCTION

This chapter discusses programs for offenders in an institutional and a community setting, including educational and vocational preparation, drug and alcohol abuse, self-improvement programs, and prison industries and other work programs. In Chapter 4, the varying philosophies of corrections were presented, and the purposes of rehabilitation were discussed. Although the support for rehabilitation as a primary goal has varied over the history of corrections, it has always been important to both the public and to correctional administrators. Even the earliest prisons had a goal of reformation for the offender, hence, the term *penitentiary* to signify the importance of "doing penance."

Rehabilitation as a goal reached its peak during the 1960s and early 1970s, when the medical model was predominant in corrections. Under the medical model, crime was believed to result from an underlying pathology of offenders, which could be diagnosed and treated. Offenders were thought of as "sick" and in need of treatment in order to successfully return to the community as productive and law-abiding citizens. Society was blamed for many of the afflictions of offenders, and the lack of education, widespread unemployment, the disintegration of social institutions, poverty, discrimination, and drug addiction were often believed to be the core causes of criminality. Offenders were seen almost as "victims" of the system, unable to avoid their involvement in criminal behavior. As a result, corrections focused on implementing a variety of treatment programs to improve offenders and to provide them with the tools necessary to be successful members of society.

Over the past two decades, there has been a major change in the way society views offenders and criminality. Today, correctional philosophy has reverted to Darwinism and the "classical model," whereby offenders are believed to be rational individuals with free will who chose to commit, and are personally accountable for, their crimes. Swift, certain, and severe sanctions are thought to be effective crime prevention strategies. Punishment and deterrence are the dominant goals of corrections. Even in this era focused on holding offenders accountable, society has not given up on the importance of rehabilitation and providing offenders opportunities and tools to change.

Rehabilitative programs continue in prison and community corrections settings, although terms such as *rehabilitation* and *treatment* are less likely to be used to describe the purpose of such programs. Correctional "programming" is now provided for many practical reasons: to keep offenders productively occupied, to upgrade skills, or to deal with drug abuse or psychological disorders. In this regard, offenders themselves must commit to program involvement and are responsible for successfully completing and benefiting from participation. In this respect, correctional agencies do not "treat" offenders, they offer programs to provide them the opportunity to change.

REHABILITATIVE PROGRAMS

As noted, rehabilitation is not a term used regularly by correctional agencies, or by their legislative or executive branch overseers, to describe the category of activities designed to improve offenders, or at least to keep them from deteriorating during the service of their criminal sentence. More contemporary terminology includes *programs, activities,* and *correctional interventions.* The avoidance of "rehabilitation" stems from disenchantment with the medical model, whereby offenders were provided an excuse for their criminal behavior, and the state assumed some responsibility for their crime. In the current era of accountability, offenders must take responsibility for their criminal acts, and although there is recognition of the need for self-improvement of offenders, this recognition does not ameliorate offenders' accountability for their crimes.

However, for purposes of this textbook, the term **rehabilitation** will continue to be used. This is not to discredit the importance of offenders taking responsibility for their crimes. It is merely the continued use of a term that has been a part of correctional history for the past 100 years. Rehabilitation, itself, means, "to return to a previous form." Most would agree that "returning offenders to their prior lives of criminality" is not a desirable outcome. However, the goal of rehabilitation by correctional agencies was to provide treatment programs that offered offenders the opportunity to identify their needs and weaknesses, and to attempt to strengthen those weaknesses and improve their abilities to meet future challenges.

Senese and Kalinich define rehabilitation as "a programmed effort to alter attitudes and behaviors of inmates, which is focused on the elimination of their future criminal behaviors."[1] Most treatment programs are designed to modify individual behavior, even though most correctional programs are provided to groups of offenders, with little use of individual counseling or psychotherapy. Whether the emphasis is on improving the individual offender or providing activities to groups of inmates that make prisons easier to manage, there is general agreement that programs for offenders are important.

Even the most "get tough on crime" advocates realize that almost all offenders will leave prison or be released from their period of community supervision. Therefore, it would be deficient public policy if correctional supervision were so intense and restrictive that offenders were less prepared to deal with the challenges of society on release than they were when they began supervision. It has long been acknowledged that "warehousing" of prisoners (holding them in prison with no productive activities) is counterproductive to long-term crime reduction. In the past, authors wrote of **institutionalization,** whereby offenders became so accustomed to the rigid routine of a prison that they could not easily make the transition to a free life in the community. Although institutionalization is seldom discussed in contemporary corrections, prison programs are useful for prison management and control.

Programs are highly regarded because they provide variety, activity, and interest, even when they are not focused on long-lasting changes in behavior. Prison programs result in less idleness, disruption, and violence.[2] It is further suggested that, "the rehabilitative paradigm requires that government invest in lawbreakers. The goal is to improve offenders both as an end in itself and as a means of reducing recidivism and of protecting society."[3] Overall, although rehabilitation as a goal has waxed and waned throughout correctional history, it has always been, and still remains, an important part of correctional administration.

PUBLIC SUPPORT FOR REHABILITATION

As noted, in the 1950s and 1960s, Americans had a very liberal view of social programs, including how criminals should be handled. Crime was believed to be a social problem, and offenders were players in a complex system that needed assistance in order to fully participate in U.S. society. When President Lyndon Johnson appointed the prestigious Commission on Law Enforcement and the Administration of Justice in 1966, it was believed that the neglect of our inner cities had undermined the opportunity for residents to compete in legitimate ways, and, therefore, they ended up resorting to crime to meet their economic and family needs. The commission stated that the most important objective that the nation should pursue was to "seek to prevent crime before it happens by assuring all Americans a stake in the benefits and responsibilities of American life."[4] Furthermore, the commission focused its attention on the failings of government, the criminal justice system, and, specifically, corrections to provide sufficient programming for the needs of inmates and to prepare them for life after release. The commission noted a need for "substantial upgrading" of the correctional system and its reorientation "toward integration of offenders into community life."[5]

The turning point for strong support of rehabilitation in the United States seems to be the early 1970s release of the "Martinson nothing works" article, which stated that "with few and isolated exceptions, the rehabilitative efforts that have been reported so far have had no appreciable effect on recidivism."[6] In a study of 231 correctional treatment programs, Martinson and his co-authors found no common themes as the correctional interventions that consistently reduce recidivism.[7] As the idea that nothing works gained momentum, was widely reported by the media, and widely cited by conservative elected officials, the public's support for correctional treatment declined.

In its place, support for incapacitation as a means to protect society increased, sentences were extended for almost all crimes, and the prison population began its rapid ascent from less than 300,000 in 1975 to more than 1.5 million by the year 2000. Blumstein suggested, "the loss of confidence in rehabilitation has contributed significantly to the growth in prison population."[8]

During the quarter of a century since the Martinson report, the public continued to support programs for prisoners, even though they believed that criminals should be punished and that incapacitation was more effective than rehabilitation as a crime control measure. The public seems to want *criminals* punished, but are accepting of providing rehabilitation programs to *inmates*. Innes observed the distinction of attitudes of U.S. citizens: The public wants to be protected and believes that when criminals are imprisoned, the "social defense" function of the criminal justice system is satisfied, and it is then appropriate to train and educate inmates. Innes found that "there is no evidence in the available survey data that the general public shares the view that there is any necessary incompatibility among the goals of justice in society, punishment of criminals, and teaching or training programs for inmates."[9]

In reporting the results of the National Opinion Survey on Crime and Justice—1995 (NOSCJ), Flanagan notes that, "Despite the primacy of the punitive sentencing goal, however, nearly one fifth of the U.S. adults favored rehabilitation as the principal goal of sentencing, and one fourth favored deterrence and incapacitation as the most important goals."[10] Flanagan continues with an indicator of U.S. citizens' judgments on the prospect of rehabilitating offenders, because three-fifths of the respondents to the NOSCJ responded *most* or *some* to the question, "Thinking of criminals who commit violent crimes, do you think most, some, only a few, or none of them can be rehabilitated given early intervention with the right program?"[11] Therefore, even during a period of strong tough on crime sentiments by the public, there is substantial support for correctional programs and a belief that offenders can change their behavior.

◼ EXISTING CORRECTIONAL PROGRAMS

Today, there are a wide variety of programs offered both in prisons and in community correctional settings. The importance of rehabilitative programs continues for many reasons. First, it is recognized that most offenders do have problems that need to be addressed. Few are well educated, have marketable vocational skills or successful work histories. Approximately 70 percent of offenders have a history of alcohol or drug abuse. Many offenders suffer from low self-concepts, do not deal well with frustration or control their anger, and have an assortment of other interpersonal or emotional problems. Although many offenders are parents, they often have suffered from abuse and neglect as children, and do not know how to be appropriate role models and parents for their own children. And very few take responsibility for the situations that got them in trouble or learn how to avoid these situations in the future.

Second, there are an increasing number of programs that have been evaluated and are showing a positive impact on recidivism.[12] Although there are no panaceas of programs that work with everyone to reduce their likelihood of future criminality, certain programs have been found to work with certain offenders. Although correctional administrators cannot predict future success for participants, knowing that program offerings will make a difference with some offenders almost requires that they be continued. It only takes a small number of successes, resulting in a reduction of crimes and victims, a financial savings for processing through the criminal justice system, and an increase in the productivity and societal contribution by ex-offenders, to make program efforts worthwhile. And, quite frankly, even if there is no assurance that a program will result in changed behavior by even a small group of offenders, it seems almost unethical to give up and accept only supervision and warehousing as the goal of corrections.

Finally, it is important to provide programs to inmates and offenders supervised in the community, because involvement in positive programs reduces idleness and gives hope to offenders. We have to only look at the idleness that resulted in U.S. prisons during the 1940s and 1950s, because the large prisons designed for factory operations had to drastically reduce prison work as a result of complaints by labor unions and passage of anti-prison labor bills by the U.S. Congress. Resultant idleness and an increasing emphasis on security and control to try to manage large inmate populations created tensions and led to prison unrest and disturbances. Productive programs are a key tool for prison administrators to manage inmates who face increasingly long sentences, with reduced prison amenities and an ever-hardening public attitude regarding offenders and crime.

In the following section, various types of programs for offenders are discussed. The effectiveness of such programs and issues and challenges concerning continued quality programming is reviewed. The discussion includes educational and vocational training for offenders, self-help programs, drug and alcohol abuse counseling, work and prison industries, and other miscellaneous programs such as religious offerings and recreation and leisure time activities.

Educational and Vocational Programs

In describing the educational and vocational programs available to offenders, it is important to first consider the value of educational and vocational training in reducing adult incarceration. The United States is unique, in that all children, regardless of race, ethnic background, or economic status, are provided the opportunity for free education at the primary and secondary levels. Therefore, it would be reasonable to believe that most children receive the benefits of education and are equally prepared for the opportunities and challenges as adults of making a living. Unfortunately, this is not the case. Although 83 percent of whites graduate from high school, only 74 percent of African Americans, and 53 percent of Latinos graduate from high school.[13] Many young people still drop out of school and are ill equipped for the world of work. Currently, about 11 percent of young adults

Correctional Education Instructor in the Classroom. Inmates receive the same course of study as public schools, so they can be released from prison with the literacy skills required in contemporary society. (Courtesy of the Federal Bureau of Prisons)

between the ages of 16 and 24 have dropped out of school, with the rate the lowest among whites (7.3 percent), greater among African Americans (13 percent), and the highest among Hispanics (29 percent).[14]

There is also a correlation between high school experience and the likelihood of adult incarceration. In a study of high school experience and the risk of adult incarceration, Arum and Beattie concluded that

> high school educational experience has a lasting effect on an individual's risk of incarceration. . . . The risk of incarceration is lowered by individual-level attachment to school activities. . . . Our results suggest that occupational course work has a role in developing socially well-adapted and productive citizenry.[15]

❷The completion of high school is an important deterrent to future criminal behavior, and education is a part of every prison and many community correctional programs. Yet, the importance of education cannot be underestimated in programming for offenders. There should never be a question of funding for educational programs or of requiring offenders who have not completed school to be enrolled in a program of basic literacy.

Education is valued in our society. Because we have a democratic system of government, requiring participation of all adults in the process of governance, the United States must have an educated populace. In addition, our society is also a "meritocracy," in that individuals are rewarded for what they achieve and produce. Again, in order for this basic tenant of society to work successfully, we need an educated and informed citizenry. However, we know that not all groups in society receive an equal level of education, and we know that those without strong literacy skills will have trouble competing and being productive members of society. Criminal offenders fall into this category. Offenders are usually poor, unskilled, and underemployed. Therefore, it is critical that when offenders come under the jurisdiction of a correctional agency, any deficiencies in education and vocational training are addressed.

Correctional education has more than a century of history. Zebulan R. Brockway first advocated it at the American Prison Association conference in Cincinnati, Ohio, in 1870. Brockway argued that law-abiding behavior was attainable through legitimate industry and education. As a result, almost all prisons have complete educational and vocational training opportunities, and community corrections agencies usually direct offenders with needs to programs within the community. The American Correctional Association has adopted the following as a standard for correctional educational programs:

> written policy, procedure, and practice provide for a comprehensive education program, available to all inmates who are eligible, that includes the following: educational philosophy and goals, communications skills, general education, basic academic skills, GED preparation, special education, vocational education, postsecondary education, and other education programs as dictated by the needs of the institutional population.[16]

When inmates enter a prison, there is usually a record of their educational and vocational history. Presentence investigations document the level of education completed, any specific vocational training, and actual work histories. Although this comprises the beginning of a plan for an inmate's educational program, academic competency is usually also tested to determine the inmate's actual literacy level. Offenders, like the general population of nonoffenders, usually perform at a level of literacy below the grade level actually completed. Therefore, the most important information for planning educational needs is the actual performance level of an inmate.

Once they are tested, offenders will be assigned to a certain educational program. Although most prison educational programs are voluntary, many states and the Federal Bureau of Prisons (BOP) now have a requirement of **mandatory prison educational programs.** In 1983, the BOP was the first agency to implement a mandatory literacy program for inmates who functioned at less than a sixth-grade educational level. This was increased to an eighth-grade level in 1986, and in 1991, the *Crime Control Act of 1990* (Public Law 101-647) directed the BOP to have a mandatory functional literacy program for all mentally capable inmates, and the BOP raised their educational standard to the twelfth grade. Any inmate without either a General Education Development (GED) completion or a high school diploma is required to enroll and participate in the Adult Basic Education (ABE) program for at least 120 days. After that time, the inmate may opt out. However, there are incentives (such as better job assignments) for inmates who do meet the basic literacy standard. The BOP has found that the mandatory requirement has been quite effective. Not only has it increased the number of inmates enrolled in ABE programs but also thousands of federal inmates have gone on to complete their requirements and receive GEDs, which are recognized certificates of completion of a high school literacy level.

Because offenders lack vocational skill as well as education, most prisons offer programs beyond basic literacy, which focus on improving inmates' employability,

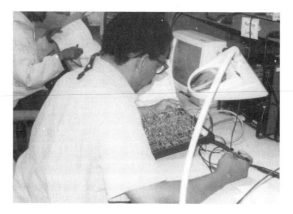

Inmates Receive Vocational Training. Inmates participate in vocational training programs to prepare them for work in the community. Some of the traditional prison programs include welding, whereas more modern programs include electronic circuit board training. (Courtesy of the Federal Bureau of Prisons and Ohio Department of Rehabilitation and Correction)

job readiness, and vocational skill. Job readiness, or **prerelease programs,** are provided in most prisons and are more general programs designed to help inmates prepare for entering the world of work. Topics may include how to fill out a job application, how to respond in a job interview, and how to follow a supervisor's directives and work with other people. **Vocational training,** however, is much more specific, and results in training inmates in a specific vocation, such as carpentry, electronics, welding, office equipment and word processing, food service, or horticulture and landscaping. These programs usually meet the same requirements as a vocational school, and offenders receive a certificate of completion of the same curriculum that other nonprison students receive. Students that complete the training are qualified for entry-level positions in the vocational area they have chosen.

Vocational training has been shown to be effective in reducing recidivism. In two studies, recidivism was found to be significantly lower for those offenders who complete vocational training programs. In a study that examined the impact of industrial work experience and vocational or apprenticeship training in federal prisons, Saylor and Gaes found that "prison programs can have an effect on post-release employment and post-release arrest in the short run and recommitment in the long run."[17] Specifically, the authors found that the study group of inmates who had either industrial work, vocational training, or apprenticeship training were "more likely to be employed than comparison group members. By the twelfth month, study group members were 14 percent more likely (71.7 percent versus 63.1 percent) to be employed."[18] As regards long-term recidivism, "those who participated in either vocational or apprenticeship training were 33 percent less likely to recidivate through the observation period,"[19] which was as long as 12 years and as few as 8 years.

In a second study, Lattimore, Witte, and Baker also found a reduction in recidivism rates by vocational training participants.[20] The authors evaluated the effectiveness of vocational rehabilitation programs offered at two North Carolina prisons for young offenders. The vocational program included working individually with inmates to identify vocational interests and aptitudes, developing individual plans of study for improving vocational skills, providing vocational training, and helping inmates secure postrelease employment. The evaluation of the Vocational Delivery System (VDS) was unusual, in that a true experimental design was used to randomly assign subjects to experimental and control groups that differed in their exposure to the VDS program. Findings were that the inmates who participated in the VDS program were less likely (36 percent) to be arrested following release from prison than the control groups (46 percent). The results of these two studies indicate that vocational training for inmates does effectively reduce recidivism, and lend support to correctional administrators' efforts, to continue or expand funding for such programs.

Drug and Alcohol Abuse Programs

Perhaps the most visible and accepted programs for offenders are those that address alcohol and drug abuse. The general public recognizes there is a link between substance abuse and crime, and believe correctional agencies have a responsibility to offer programs to address these problems. In reality, explaining the relationship between substance abuse and crime is complex and lacks a cohesive conclusion. The *National Household Survey on Drug Abuse (NHSDA)* has tracked patterns of licit and illicit drug use among the general U.S. population since 1971. Findings indicate that illegal drug use, as measured by the number of people using an illicit drug in the previous month, has steadily declined from 1979 to 1992, with a leveling off of the decline at that time.[21] Although this seems to indicate that drug abuse is substantially less of a problem than it was two decades ago, research has consistently shown a high degree of correlation between drug use and criminal behavior. The U.S. Department of Justice has found "extensive evidence of a strong relationship between drug use and crime," as summarized in the following three points.

▌ Drug users report greater involvement in crime and are more likely than nonusers to have criminal records.

▌ Persons with criminal records are much more likely than ones without criminal records to report being drug users.

▌ Crimes rise in number as drug use increases.[22]

At all stages of the criminal justice process (arrest, jail, prison), offenders report a high level of drug use. The **Drug Use Forecasting (DUF)** program of the National Institute of Justice interviews arrested offenders in 24 cities across the United States, and asks them to provide voluntary urine specimens to test for drug use. An amazingly high number (90 percent) agree to be interviewed, and 80 percent of those agree to provide urine specimens. DUF data for 1996 show that in 20 of the 33 sites where measurements were taken, more than 60 percent of arrestees tested positive for at least one illicit drug other than alcohol, leading to the conclusion that drug use continues to be a serious problem with persons coming into contact with the criminal justice system.[23] Interviewed jail inmates also report extensive drug use related to their offense.

▌ Forty-four percent used illegal drugs in the month before the offense for which they were arrested.

▌ Thirty percent used illegal drugs daily in the month before the offense.

▌ Twenty-seven percent used illegal drugs at the time of the offense, and

▌ cocaine and crack cocaine were the drugs most commonly abused by inmates.[24]

In addition, state prison inmates also report a considerable history of drug use, as 50 percent report having been under the influence of alcohol or drugs at the time of their offense.[25] Unfortunately, prison inmates often do not end their drug use once incarcerated. Tests of inmates at male adult prisons show that at least 1 percent tested positive for cocaine and heroin, 2 percent tested positive for metamphetamines, and almost 6 percent tested positive for marijuana.[26]

This information makes it clear that alcohol and drug abuse programs must be a part of all correctional programs. Most agencies recognize that many offenders abuse both alcohol and drugs, and provide a combined "substance" abuse treatment program. Such programs can vary in intensity from residential programs, with a total environment directed toward dealing with the addictions, to outpatient counseling as an element of an offender's community supervision. The following examples illustrate the substance abuse treatment programs for the Correctional Services of Canada (CSC), the drug abuse treatment program for the Federal Bureau of Prisons (BOP), and a community-based drug abuse program operated by the New York City Department of Probation.

The CSC approach is a multifaceted assessment and treatment model, which recognizes that offenders who abuse drugs and alcohol are a heterogeneous group with respect to their abuse problems.[27] CSC assesses and classifies offenders according to the prevalence and seriousness of the abuse, with about one-third identified as having a serious problem, one-third having low-severity problems, and one-third having no significant problems warranting treatment. Therefore, CSC provides a differential treatment model to match offender's need with the type of treatment program. These programs are based on a principle of **harm reduction,** which not only considers total abstinence as the only positive outcome but also the reduction of high-risk behaviors as a valid indicator of success.

After assessment of each offender's substance abuse problem, a treatment program is developed. There is no lengthy or costly therapeutic community. Rather the initial treatment is delivered in a focused and time-limited manner, and is oriented toward developing skills, modeling, role-playing, and practicing. The intensive phase is followed by ongoing maintenance sessions to expand and reinforce the principles delivered during the initial stage. The model for treatment is based on social learning theory that acknowledges the role of a variety of genetic and physiological predisposing factors. The program, therefore, incorporates a range of behavioral and cognitive-behavioral intervention modalities, and includes development of skills to teach participants about the relapse process and how to handle urges, cravings, and high-risk situations. CSC offers an inventory of various treatment programs at institutions that build on the comprehensive model previously described and allows inmates the opportunity to build on the skills developed and share experiences with other offenders.

The Federal Bureau of Prisons' Drug Abuse Programs (DAP) differ from those of the CSC. Each of the DAP units have the same staffing, structure, and length of treatment, and each offers similar programs. The philosophy underlying these programs in that offenders must assume personal responsibility for their behavior, and, despite the influence of environmental conditions and circumstances, the individual must make a conscious decision to avoid engaging in drugtaking and criminal behavior. The treatment model is bio-psycho-social and emphasizes comprehensive lifestyle change, with issues of physical well-being, family relationships, and criminality all targeted for change while acquiring positive life skills as a vehicle to avoid future drug use.[28]

The BOP employs a five-part treatment strategy that includes (1) orientation screening and referral, (2) drug abuse education, (3) nonresidential drug abuse treatment services, (4) residential drug abuse treatment, and (5) transitional services. The residential treatment is a 500-hour program, during which inmates reside in a treatment unit separate from the prison general inmate population. Treatment is typically delivered no less than four hours a day, five days a week. The remainder of the treatment day is spent in education, work skills training, recreation, or other complementary programs, such as disease prevention and health promotion instruction. A doctoral-level psychologist and treatment staff who carry a caseload of no more than 24 inmates supervise treatment.

The BOP, in conjunction with the National Institute of Drug Abuse, conducts an ongoing evaluation of the effectiveness of the program. At the institutional level, findings indicate that in high-security prisons, misconduct among inmates who complete the residential drug abuse treatment program was reduced by 50 percent. For the first six months after release from custody

1. Inmates who completed the residential drug abuse treatment program were 73 percent less likely to be rearrested for a new offense than those who did not participate in a residential drug abuse treatment program.

2. Inmates who completed the residential drug abuse treatment programs were 44 percent less likely to use drugs or alcohol than those who did not participate in a residential drug abuse treatment program.[29]

The New York City Department of Probation manages probationers with a history of drug abuse using a combination of specialized supervision units and outpatient treatment programs. The specialized units have smaller caseloads than regular units, supervising about 65 probationers rather than approximately 175. They supervised high-risk drug abusers (about one-half cocaine abusers) and had strong linkages with community-based drug treatment programs. The community contracted treatment programs were contracted by the department's Central Placement Unit (CPU) to provide a 12-month course of outpatient treatment, including intake and treatment services for offenders and extensive reporting to the probation unit about the offenders' performance. Probationers received mandatory urinalysis within the first two weeks of entry to the program, a second urinalysis within another two weeks, and regular testing thereafter.

The results of the program indicated that it was effective; "drug treatment was related to significant reductions in recidivism among clients referred through the CPU, with the greatest reduction in recidivism among those CPU clients who were appropriately matched to outpatient drug treatment on the basis of the severity of their drug use.[30] The findings indicate that it was important to identify the level of need for probationers and match that need to a treatment plan. Approximately two-thirds of the probationers only needed random urinalysis as effective treatment, whereas the remainder could benefit from services ranging from outpatient to residential. Findings also indicated that recidivism rates were significantly lower for those probationers who stayed in the program more than 90 days than those who dropped out earlier; "about half of the probationers who stayed in treatment less than three months were rearrested, while only about one-quarter of those who stayed longer were rearrested."[31]

It is acknowledged that substance abuse is a serious problem among criminal offenders. However, there is no conclusive evidence that indicates that abuse of alcohol and drugs leads to criminal behavior. Many experts believe that a more general theory of deviance applies, because individuals who commit one deviant act (substance abuse) are likely to commit another (criminal behavior). However, evaluation of substance abuse programs that indicate reductions of rearrest and other measures of recidivism lead one to believe that such programs are effective in transforming deviant into law-abiding behavior. Although not all types of programs are effective with different types of abusers, there is positive evidence of success. In a recent meta-analysis of a variety of drug abuse programs, the evaluators found that therapeutic communities are effective in reducing recidivism, whereas boot camp and group counseling programs did not show consistently good results.[32] It is the recommendation of the National Task Force on Corrections Substance Abuse Strategies that correctional agencies, "Provide a range of quality programs to meet offenders' control, supervision, and treatment needs."[33] Although there is still much to be learned regarding the effect of substance abuse programs in reducing recidivism, it is believed that effective treatment should continue to motivate correctional agencies to maintain and expand their substance abuse programs.

Self-Help and Professional Treatment Programs

Correctional agencies offer a wide variety of self-help and professional treatment programs. For purposes of distinction, **self-help programs** are those most often coordinated and directed by the participants or clients. The most well known programs are Alcoholics Anonymous (AA) and Narcotics Anonymous (NA). In these programs, clients themselves lead the discussion without much formal leadership or direction. Those who participate in self-help groups (even when staff are paid) are usually reformed or recovering clients who participate as treatment for themselves rather than as treatment for others. **Professional treatment groups** are those designed, administered, and directed by a professional, trained leader or staff member. Examples include psychological groups or individual counseling sessions. They can range from self-esteem groups to parenting classes to life skills instruction, or any other issue or problem that correctional staff believe can be addressed by a treatment program.

Psychological and Psychiatric Programs

Prisons employ staff psychologists to provide both group and individual therapy for inmates, and many contract for part-time psychiatric services to service inmates with more serious mental health problems. On admission to prison, inmates are administered a variety of psychological tests to evaluate their needs for mental health services. Using the results of these tests, individual program plans are developed for inmates with mental health needs. Services can range from a residential setting with psychiatric counseling and the prescription of **psychotropic medications** to outpatient participation in group counseling conducted by psychological services staff.

Inmates who actually have a mental illness are under the care of physicians with psychiatric specialties and, through the prescription of psychotropic medications, can usually remain in a regular prison under treatment. Psychotropic medications are used to help maintain patients in a stable condition and allow them to function within the general population of a prison. The same drugs, since their inception in the 1950s, have allowed individuals with mental illnesses to stay at home in the community rather than being admitted to mental institutions. As a result of the use of such medications, the mental health field experienced a period of "deinstitutionalization" in the 1970s, and the mental hospital population is now less than 100,000 (down from 550,000). It is not unusual to have 2 to 5 percent of a prison population under such care, taking psychotropic medication. If their mental illness requires more intensive care or control, they may be placed in a prison with a special mental health unit.

A much larger percentage of inmates do not suffer from serious mental illness yet have personality disorders, are unable to manage their anger, are potentially suicidal, or simply cannot deal with life's daily stresses and responsibilities. For these inmates, prison psychological staff provide counseling and treatment. This is sometimes provided on an individual basis, but more often it is given in groups counseling sessions, because the number of psychology staff usually cannot provide individual treatment to all the inmates who might benefit from it. Group counseling programs can use psychiatric social workers or other specially trained counselors, working under the supervision of a staff psychologist. Following are some advantages of group therapy for offender populations:

1. It is more economical than individual treatment.
2. It can provide immediate peer pressure, feedback, and information.
3. Challenges from peers are harder for offenders to deny or rationalize.
4. It helps to relieve everyday tension from the prison environment and provides a better way to deal with conflicts.
5. It can help to address the prisoner subculture.
6. It can help communication between staff and offenders.
7. It is helpful for problem solving.
8. It provides reinforcement for positive values.
9. Lay group leaders do not need extensive training.
10. Many different treatment modalities can be adapted to the group process.[34]

Group counseling uses a variety of approaches, such as **transactional analysis.** In transactional analysis, the personality is acknowledged to have three parts: the parent, the adult, and the child. Through some malfunction, many people have one of these parts dominate their personality, and group counseling assists them in understanding this and keeping their personality balanced. The communication within the group is a valuable learning mechanism for the participants, and group members point out to each other how certain behaviors and actions illustrate an "out-of-balance" personality. Participants (lead by a trained staff member) help each other recognize when one personality part dominates and can result in individuals being better able to understand, and, therefore, change, behavior to more appropriate personality proportions.

Family issues are often included in group counseling sessions. An extremely high percentage of offenders (both in prison and under community supervision) have had poor familiar experiences, no good models of stable family relationships, and poor parenting skills. A smaller percentage of men, yet almost three-fourths of women offenders, have children and plan to live with them following release from prison or supervision. Some correctional agencies even have formal "parenting programs" and work on improving an offender's role as a spouse and parent. Family counseling programs can include role-playing, communication patterns, and education about issues regarding dysfunctional families to help individuals increase their knowledge and improve their skills in dealing with difficult family situations. Most prisons have very limited visiting opportunities and very sterile environments for children to visit their parents. Therefore, some parenting programs create opportunities for visiting children for an extended period of time or in a relaxed and comfortable setting.

Residential Treatment Programs

Many times, prisons create special housing units to house a certain group of offenders and provide a total treatment experience around the housing and living arrangements of the inmates in the unit. Just as described in relation to the BOP's drug treatment program, residential programs are organized so that all the prisoners that live in a housing area are program participants, and the program modality includes the entire living experience. Besides substance abuse, residential programs are used for sex offenders, developmentally disabled offenders, violent offenders, or almost any other group of offenders that can be programmed in a group housing setting.

The earliest residential programs were often set up as token economies. In a **token economy,** the focus is on operant conditioning: Rewards reinforce good behavior, and elimination of rewards deter undesirable behavior. The Federal District Court cases of *Wyatt v. Stickney* (M.D. Alabama, 1971) and *Morales v. Turman* (E.D. Texas, 1973) resulted in the holding that basic rights, such as food, mattresses, and privacy, cannot be used as tokens, given or taken away based on behavior. The difficulty with effectively implementing a token economy is that the environment has to be totally controlled. Rewards can be given only by staff to reinforce behavior; inmates cannot be able to manipulate staff or receive rewards from sources outside the economy. Today, few such token economies exist in prisons. Although there are housing areas, called honor blocks, that provide inmates some extended privileges based on their continued good behavior, they do not try to regulate each individual reward based on specific actions or inactions of inmates.

Another model that was used in prisons extensively when the medical model for corrections was popular was the **therapeutic community.** This model originated as a method to help World War II combat veterans reenter society. It was an alternative to the typical hospital environment.[35] With this model, the patients became partners in the treatment process, rather than being "treated" by others. Patients, therefore, had to take more responsibility for their own recovery. In the prison setting, the "community" acts as a group and creates some of their own processes and rules for operation. Although prison settings have been successful in creating an atmosphere of positivism and self-worth among inmates, they present the difficulty of giving one prisoner power in any way over other prisoners. Therefore, modified therapeutic communities, with the benefits of the total treatment environment, but with staff in control, have been found to be useful in treating drug abuse or other serious prisoner psychological problems.

The accompanying case study of a program designed to change inmate "basic values" represents an example of a successful residential prison program.

PRACTICAL PERSPECTIVES

Creating a Residential Values Program

A residential program initiated at the Federal Correctional Institution in Greenville, Illinois, in 1995 is the Residential Values Program (RVP). The RVP is perceived to have produced excellent results within the institution, because it improved relations between staff and inmates and reduced the number of incident reports of negative inmate behavior.

Continued

The Federal Correctional Institution (FCI) in Greenville, Illinois, was opened in 1994 as a 750-bed medium security institution with a 250-bed minimum security satellite camp. The institution has four separate units. During activation, institution management decided that one of these units should have a specialized program focus. They believed this important program would add productive activities to keep inmates busy and, at the same time, create a culture of positive programming and professional staff–inmate interaction. The Federal Bureau of Prisons (BOP) had developed a short, 20-hour program (called "Living Free"), which focused on the four basic values of honesty, tolerance, respect, and responsibility. The Greenville staff believed these values were a good foundation for the type of program they desired and expanded the 20-hour Living Free program into a six-month, residential-based program. The RVP was based on the understanding that healthy living is comprised of positive values, physical health, and an individual sense of purpose. By reinforcing such qualities, the RVP serves to develop the safety and security of the institution.

No funds or staff positions were available to the institution to start the RVP. Therefore, the plan was to use existing staff from a variety of departments to teach/coach in the program and recruit community volunteers to contribute with special presentations and with small group programming. The unit manager responsible for the unit in which the RVP is located is responsible for the operation of the unit, and the program coordinator, a staff psychologist, is responsible for overseeing the delivery of the program content.

The original 20-hour Living Free program is first presented to acclimate the participants to the lifestyle of prosocial living. Courses address such topics as the costs and benefits of criminality, an examination of personal values, the identification of destructive thinking patterns, an introduction to changing personal habits, a review of the relapse process, the influence of family and values, and effective goal setting. A unique health promotion and disease prevention element provides inmates with an understanding of how to develop healthy living practices. Participants undergo a health evaluation at the beginning and end of the program, and determine improvements in cholesterol levels, heart rate, muscular endurance and fitness, and body fat composition.

The curriculum also includes classes in anger management, financial responsibility, and decision making based on values and morals. The Personal Power program designed by Anthony Robbins exposes participants to the primary motivators that can create long lasting change and ways to develop peak performance. Inmate participants can also teach topics of interest on items such as travel and foreign culture, both for general interest and for inmates to be fully involved in the program design and delivery.

The 300-hour program takes approximately six months to complete. Inmates attend classes for a half day and go to a work assignment the other half of the day. Inmates also are required to become involved in other institutional programs in addition to the RVP curriculum. As the program concludes, inmates review the information presented over the previous few months and are given new issues and ideas to enhance prosocial living. A formal graduation ceremony for current and past RVP graduates brings an end to the 300-hour program.

The RVP is considered to be an excellent program at FCI Greenville. Staff enjoy working in the unit and believe inmates in the program take more responsibility for their behavior. RVP inmates have fewer misconduct violations than other Greenville inmates. And, the inclusion of community volunteers builds positive relations with citizens and develops support for rehabilitative programs. Since its inception, the RVP has become acclaimed throughout the BOP, and many other federal prisons have modeled after it, creating similar residential programs. Additionally, in 2000, the RVP unit manager received one of the highest awards in the BOP, the Assistant Director Award for Correctional Programs, for her work in supervising the RVP. The program has become the positive and successful program that its originators desired.

PRISON WORK PROGRAMS

Inmate work programs have been a part of prison operations since the Walnut Street Jail was opened in 1790 in Philadelphia. The Quakers, founders of the Walnut Street Jail, believed in hard work, and, therefore, it was natural that work by prisoners became a key component of the operation of the first prison in the United States. The creation of an operational approach for the first U.S. penitentiaries under the Pennsylvania system of prisons emphasized hard work as a part of the reformative process. Inmates were expected to labor in individual cells at spinning wheels, small textile looms, and shoemaking.[36] The failure of the Pennsylvania system and the major advantage of the Auburn system of prisons was that it allowed inmates to work in settings that were more productive for the manufacture of goods that could be sold. Champion notes that a "feature of the Auburn system was that prisoners helped defray a portion of their housing and food costs through their labor. . . . prison industry was gradually recognized to be a mutually beneficial enterprise—prison officials could interpret prisoner labor as worthwhile and rehabilitative, and they could also contemplate the possibilities of profits from prison-manufactured goods."[37] Early prison labor benefited the state by helping prisons to be self-sufficient, rather than benefiting the inmate with rehabilitation.

In the effort to use prison labor, state prisons in the early 1800s leased prisons to the private sector. The company winning a bid for the lease would essentially become the leaseholder and have control of the prison and its labor. The leaseholder could work the inmates in their industrial operations, spending as little as possible to house and feed the inmates, and try to earn as much as possible through the unpaid inmate work. The use of inmate labor by the private sector continued into the twentieth century, when abuses of the lease system caused most of them to end, and states returned to operating their own prison industries to both keep inmates busy and create a profit from the production and sale of goods.

Prison operators recognized the importance of prison labor and the opportunity for profits. During the first 40 years of the twentieth century, the prison population grew by 174 percent.[38] To house this increase, large Auburn style prisons were built with large areas for industrial operations, and the main function of the prison became the production of goods. Unfortunately, these prison industries became so efficient that organized labor began to complain about the unfair competition resulting from free prison labor's production of goods. Lobbying before the U.S. Congress resulted in the passage of the Hawes-Cooper Act in 1929, which required that prison products be subject to the laws of any state to which they were shipped. Subsequent legislation, the Ashurst-Sumners Act of 1935, required that prison products be clearly marked as prison-made goods. This act was amended in 1940 to fully prohibit the interstate shipment of prison goods. This series of legislation effectively ended the sale of prison products on the open market.

Prison industries, therefore, began to produce goods that could be used by the state and federal governments. With the "state-use" system, prison industries began to produce products such as inmate clothing and furniture, for use in the prisons; to grow food for their own consumption; and to produce office furniture and products for other state agencies. The U.S. Congress established the Federal Prison Industries (FPI) in 1934 as a wholly owned government corporation that operated the prison industries in the federal prisons. FPI became heavily involved in producing goods for the military, especially during World War II. Today, FPI is a major producer of goods for the U.S. government, producing and selling almost $500 million worth of products a year.

Although they have gone through several transitions over the past 200 years, in many ways, today's prison work programs are essentially the same as they were in the first U.S. prisons. Although many inmates work in prison industrial settings, the majority of prisoners work in other areas of prison operations. Most states and the Federal Bureau of Prisons require inmates to be assigned a job and work, unless they are enrolled in educational or other self-improvement programs. The general public does not want inmates idle, or spending their days exercising or leisurely watching television. Public sentiment also supports prisoners doing whatever they can to defray the cost of incarceration. Therefore, there is support for prison work programs and for prison industries.

There are several reasons for active work programs in prisons. Work benefits inmates as a rehabilitative instrument. Inmates learn to work for a supervisor, follow instructions, and develop positive work habits. Work programs benefit prison administrators. Inmates keep busy and assist in maintaining control of the prison environment. Finally, work programs benefit the public by making available prison products and performing other work to keep down the cost of incarceration. The following represents the variety of prison work assignments.

Work to Support Prison Operations

The largest percentage of inmates work in assignments that are critical to operating the prison and providing services to the inmate population. This includes the operation of prison laundries, food services, and maintenance departments; cutting grass and maintaining the grounds; and cleaning and doing janitorial services for the general sanitation of the prison. In addition, prisoners work in almost every other aspect of prison operations, including assisting staff in recreation services, typing

Prison Industries: Textile Factory at the U.S. Penitentiary, Leavenworth, Kansas, 1936. In the early to mid-1900s, industries thrived in the U.S. prisons. Not only did these industries employ hundreds of inmates in some prisons but they were also profitable and helped fund the cost of operations. (Courtesy of the Federal Bureau of Prisons)

and doing clerical work, tutoring in educational classes, and even working in the prison law library.

The largest portion of inmates work in service areas of the prison, including laundry, food service, and maintenance. Most people unfamiliar with prisons are not aware that inmates do most of the work to operate prisons, under the supervision and guidance of staff. Every prison has a **laundry,** washing the tons of sheets, blankets, and inmate clothing on a daily basis. These are usually unskilled jobs, such as sorting laundry, loading washing machines, transferring clean laundry to dryers, and folding and preparing laundry to be returned to the inmate population. One or two staff oversee the operation of a laundry, know how to operate the large commercial laundry equipment, and know how to maintain control of clothing and other items being laundered. Almost anything in a prison can be of value to inmates. Inmates wanting to have extra clothes beyond their assigned amount can be a nuisance and costly. Extra sheets or blankets can create a security issue, because they can be used as ropes to assist in an escape attempt. Therefore, laundry staff have to be alert to inmates stealing items from the laundry.

Food service operations require many inmates. As in the laundry, inmates work under the supervision of staff to store food, prepare it for cooking, read recipes and cook food, serve food to the inmate population, and clean dishes and cooking equipment for the next meal. A prison with 1,000 inmates will have to serve three meals per day, 365 days per year, for a total of more than one million meals per year. This requires a tremendous amount of labor, and it would not be unusual to have 25 percent of the inmates assigned to the food service operation in a prison of this size. Most inmates do not like to work in food service, and, therefore, most prisons

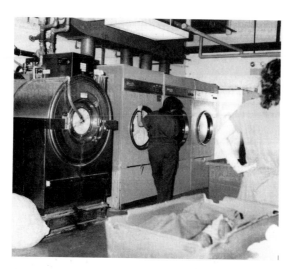

Prison Laundry. Prisons have an enormous amount of laundry to be cleaned. Sheets, blankets and inmate clothing must be regularly laundered, creating many jobs for inmate workers. (Courtesy of the Federal Bureau of Prisons)

require that all new inmates be assigned to the food service department for a period of time.

Inmates often begin their food service assignment with the most unskilled jobs, such as washing dishes, cleaning tables, and performing other janitorial services. Other inmates are assigned to serve food, usually under the close supervision of staff to discourage serving extra portions or portions that are smaller than prescribed. Food service in a prison must meet all usual restaurant requirements for sanitation and the prevention of food contamination by keeping food at proper temperatures during service. Inmates must wear serving gloves, appropriate headgear, and clean clothing when handling food. Not only is this a health requirement but also inmates receiving the food can become very angry when food is not prepared or handled in a sanitary fashion.

Some inmates enjoy food service, and recognize the potential for postrelease jobs in the food industry. Many prisons even have vocational training programs in food service, and inmates who complete the training may be assigned in the food service department as cooks. They learn to read recipes, prepare food, and present it in an attractive and efficient manner. These inmates become very valuable to a food service department, because their knowledge of food preparation can reduce the requirement of close supervision and guidance by staff.

A prison food service department usually begins with breakfast, serving it as early as 6:00 A.M., and finishes with dinner served at 5:00 P.M. This makes for a long day of food preparation and cleaning, and it requires two full shifts of inmates. Combine this with the need for meals seven days per week, and it is obvious why it requires such a large inmate workforce to cover the 80-plus hours per week of food service operation.

Another service area in a prison requiring inmate labor is the **maintenance department.** Inmates do plumbing, electrical maintenance, heating and air conditioning upkeep, carpentry, and general maintenance of a prison. Just as in the other work areas, staff supervise inmate crews assigned to each of these areas. If they are fortunate, staff supervisors will find inmates skilled in these areas. Often, however, staff are assigned unskilled workers and must train the inmates to do these jobs. Maintenance departments do routine work, such as changing light bulbs and unclogging toilets, as well as more complex jobs, such as building complete structures or renovating entire areas of the prison. Inmate workers may lay brick and concrete blocks, install electrical wiring, and run heating ducts.

Prisons, like most commercial use buildings, are projected to have a life of 50 years. However, few prisons ever go out of service before they are more than 100 years old. The residents are not necessarily motivated to take good care of the building and facilities; however, the maintenance of the prison is critical. It can both keep inmates busy in real work activities and save the state money by having inmates perform preventative maintenance that extends the life of the structure. Inmates usually like this type of work, consider it enjoyable, and recognize that it can lead to a job after release.

Agricultural Work Activities

Historically, most prisons were located in rural areas and operated farms to produce food, which reduced the cost of food purchases. The image of large numbers of inmates working in fields using hand tools was common during the early history of corrections. The general public believed that most prisons used chain gangs of inmates to work in the fields and grow food products under the eye of armed correctional officers on horseback. Several states did operate farms in this manner. But most prisons used minimum security inmates, who were not chained together or supervised by armed guards, to work farm operations.

As urban development crept toward prisons, the surrounding agricultural land became more valuable. Agriculture production became more mechanized, and expensive equipment requirements made agricultural operations capital intensive and not cost effective for prisons to continue to operate. Also very few inmates will work in agriculture after release, so it has little value for community reintegration. Therefore, most states reduced or discontinued agricultural programs for prisons, thus curtailing or eliminating the need for inmate agricultural work.

In 1992, however, the American Correctional Association reported that there were still 29 states with prison agricultural programs.[39] The largest of these are Texas and California, which produce beef, swine, milk, and vegetables for consumption by the prison inmate population. Although Texas employed almost 7,000 inmates in agricultural jobs,[40] most states have less than a few hundred.

Inmate agricultural assignments are still believed to be as a way to keep a small number of inmates busy, and many minimum security prisons with enough available land start small vegetable gardens to supplement the food menu for a prison. The gardens can provide fresh fruit and vegetables at little cost. In addition, these programs do not require large numbers of staff to oversee and operate the farms. The

Federal Bureau of Prisons stopped almost all of their agricultural programs in the mid-1970s, when they found that the cost to purchase and maintain equipment and to assign staff to farm programs did not warrant the savings in food costs from the farm output. Many federal prisons that once operated large-scale farms, today, only have these small vegetable gardens.

Prison Industries

Even with the restrictions placed on the sale in the open market of prison-made goods, inmate work activities in prison industries continue to be an important element in prison operations. Prison industries has several benefits for the institution, its management, and the inmates:

1. Industrial work assignments that are similar to private sector operations provide inmates realistic work experience and instill positive work habits.
2. Work experience can provide valuable training and skill development that inmates can use after release.
3. Inmate earnings can be used to support families, pay fines and restitution, and provide inmates with money to purchase personal items allowed in prison.
4. Earnings by the industry can be used to offset the cost of incarceration.
5. Industrial work assignments are a positive way to reduce idleness, and they serve as an incentive for good behavior, which is valuable for inmate management.

Every state prison, and many local jails, operate **prison industries.** These include a wide variety of products and activities, and some states even include services for themselves (food service, agriculture, and laundry) as a prison industry. Industry work assignments differ from other prison work programs in that the "fruits of the industry" (products or services) are sold, and the industry creates income to cover the cost of operations, staff salaries, and (in almost every state) minimal reimbursement for inmate workers. Most states have **state-use laws,** whereby products and services are sold only to other government agencies in the state or political jurisdiction. For most prison industries, the corrections department is the largest customer.

Prison industry programs account for a significant amount of work done in prisons. As of January 1, 1998, there were 76,080 inmates (6.7 percent of the total) assigned to prison industries in the 50 states, the District of Columbia, and the Federal Bureau of Prisons. In 1997, prison industries operated by the correctional agencies had sales of nearly $5 billion and profits of over $39 million. There were 7,679 agency staff working in prison industries. Wages to staff and inmates by the government agency exceeded $100 million. Forty-seven industries produced wood products and furniture, and almost as many produced paper products and printing (43), garments and textiles (42), and metal products (37).[41]

In addition to the state-use programs of prison industries, Congress expanded the available markets for goods in 1979 when it passed the Private Sector Prison Industry Enhancement Certification Program, referred to as the PIE Program. Under the **PIE Program,** if states meet several conditions they can be certified to sell their goods on the open market. These requirements include

Prison Industries—Textile Factory at an Ohio Prison, 2000.
Currently, prison industries is an important prison program, although not to the extent of the early 1900s. Garment factories are still a favored industry, because many inmates can be employed in a labor-intensive manner. (Courtesy of the Ohio Department of Rehabilitation and Correction)

1. Paying the inmates wages comparable to similar jobs in the community.
2. Consulting with representatives of private industry and organized labor.
3. Certifying that the PIE industry does not displace employed workers in the community.
4. Collecting funds for a victim assistance program.
5. Providing inmates with benefits in the event of injury in the course of employment.
6. Ensuring that inmate participation is voluntary.
7. Providing a substantial role for the private sector.[42]

PIE programs are operated by private companies that organize industrial operations in prisons. The private organizations fund the purchase of equipment and pay the salaries of their staff and the inmates they hire. As noted, one requirement is that the private company pay inmates wages comparable to what they pay for similar jobs in the community. As of January 1, 1998, the agency-operated prison industry paid an inmate on average from a low of $1.60 to a high of $7.06 per day, whereas the privately operated industry paid an inmate on average from a low of $24.27 to a high of $38.23 per day.[43]

Although the PIE programs seemed like excellent opportunities to sell products on the open market and expand the use of prison industries, they have not been as successful as hoped. The Bureau of Justice Assistance reported that 36 states had active PIE programs in 1995 but that they employed just more than 5,000 inmates in these public–private partnerships.[44] Because they are required to pay comparable wages, the private company does not receive the benefit of cheap prison labor.

Although the comparable wage requirement is, in many ways, a very positive element of the program, it severely limits its the growth. Companies quickly discover that it is difficult and inefficient to operate within prison security restrictions. Even with inmate workers putting forth maximum effort, the PIE companies usually are not as productive as similar operations outside a prison.

One positive result of the PIE provision for comparable wages is the requirement that there be withholdings from inmates' salaries for fines, victim compensation, room and board, and family support. From the beginning of the PIE Program until June 1995 there was more than $23 million withheld from pay and distributed for these purposes, of which 44 percent was given to the state to pay for room and board, 26 percent for taxes, 15 percent for victim restitution, and 15 percent for family support.[45]

OTHER PRISON PROGRAMS

Because prisons are, in a sense, microcosms of the larger society and operate similar to a small city, they must provide a wide variety of programs and activities. These often include religious programming, recreation, and other leisure time activities. Prisons were created as places for religious reformation, so it is not surprising that religious programs within prisons have always been important to administrators and inmates. Providing religious programs for any group or individual that wants to worship as they truly believe is much more difficult than would be imagined. Although most inmates are Muslim, Jewish, Protestant, or Catholic, there are dozens of other religious sects and worship groups. Prisons attempt to allow inmates to worship in whatever manner is a valid tenet of their religious belief, if it does not undermine security.

To oversee religious programming, prisons usually employ one or two full-time chaplains and contract with a variety of other ministers to hold services and provide religious guidance for prisoners. In addition to regular services, this usually includes such activities as Bible study or religious discussion groups. At any prison, the chaplain's calendar is usually very full, with services throughout the week and two or three groups meeting on any given night. Volunteers are an important part of religious programming; they visit the prison to participate in or lead discussion and study groups.

Even though religious activity has always been an important part of prison operations, the issue of what type of practices should be allowed caused considerable judicial intervention. In the 1871 decision of *Ruffin v. the Commonwealth of Virginia*,[46] the U.S. Supreme Court enunciated the Slave of the State Doctrine. This case held that inmates were, for all intents and purposes, slaves of the state and had no rights that were not granted them by the state. In this decision, the Court created the **hands-off policy,** whereby they determined to avoid getting involved in prison rights issues. This policy was based on (1) the fact that the Court had no expertise in corrections and showed deference to the judgment of prison administrators (2) the need for separation of powers between the judicial and the executive branches of government, and (3) the concern that accepting prisoner rights cases would open the floodgates to further litigation.

Full House in the Prison Chapel. Although there is seldom a religious service as well attended as the one illustrated here, religious programming is a basic and critical part of every prison. (Courtesy of the Federal Bureau of Prisons)

However, in the 1964 landmark case of *Cooper v. Pate*,[47] the Court decided to hear a case regarding religious freedom in prison. Black Muslim inmates were not being allowed to congregate, eat their prescribed religious diet, or wear distinctive items of clothing. The Supreme Court recognized the Black Muslim faith as constituting an established religion and determined that Black Muslims, therefore, could follow the prescribed practices of that religion. The only proscription to practice of accepted religious tenets was clear and present danger to the security and orderly running of a prison.

This decision did open the floodgates for further prison litigation, but it also gave direction to allowing the practice of religion within a correctional institution. Today, the courts allow restrictions when there is a "reasonable and substantial justification," but they often put the burden of proof on correctional administrators to show they cannot make accommodations and to prove why the administrators must impose restrictions.[48]

Another area of prison programming involves recreation. Currently the public believes that prisons are not tough enough and that prisons allow inmates too much idle time to watch color television and lift weights. This perception is not true, and recreation is an important part of prison operations. Idle time is a prison administrator's worst enemy, and wardens continuously challenge recreation staff to create and supervise activities that engage and keep a large proportion of the inmate population busy. Most prison systems require inmates to work approximately six hours per day, around security counts and meals, five days per week. Most prison jobs (such as food service) require inmates to work beyond the standard 8:00 A.M. to 5:00 P.M. workday and often on Saturday and Sunday. When they are not working, inmates may participate in evening programs, such as psychological counseling or religious activities. However, these activities still leave many hours of idleness if the time is not absorbed with productive leisure time programs.

A Full Prison Recreation Yard. Prison recreation programs are important to keep inmates busy, relieve tension, and build teamwork. (Courtesy of the Federal Bureau of Prisons)

To reduce the amount of available idle time, prisons have recreation programs, including outside sports, such as soccer, basketball, or softball; less active recreation, such as table games, card playing, billiards, or ping pong; arts and craft activities, such as painting; and fitness programs, such as running or calisthenics. Although some in the public may question the benefits of these programs, they are a valuable aid to prison management. Organized athletic activities, with intramural teams, require inmates to work together, participate in team efforts, and learn how to follow rules and procedures. Recreational activities are an incentive for good behavior for inmates. Other leisure time programs can create interest in positive activities that offenders never would have participated in otherwise. As such, these are much better activities than others in which these individuals may have spent their idle time, such as hanging out with friends or using drugs.

Perhaps the most controversial recreational activity is weight lifting. There is both a philosophical and practical opposition to weight lifting that has resulted in many state prisons and local jails eliminating all weight-lifting equipment. Philosophically, the public does not like the image of people who have victimized others spending their time working out with weights and getting stronger. The public believes that inmates with time to lift weights and participate in body building activities is indicative of the stereotypes of leisurely prison life, which is not a punishment. Practically, it can be argued that inmates who get stronger represent a danger to correctional and law enforcement officials.

Weight bars and plates have been used as weapons against inmates and staff. For example, in 1993, at the Southern Ohio Correctional Facility in Lucasville, Ohio, rioting inmates used weight-lifting equipment to break into an area and take staff hostages. The area was supposed to be a safe haven, physically reinforced and secure, where staff could go for protection during just such a situation. As a result of this incident, the first effort to ban weight lifting in prisons was the initiative of an Ohio congresswoman, who heard about the incident and believed eliminating weights would protect staff from harm.

However, there are relatively few correctional agencies or officials who are against the use of weight equipment in a prison setting. Although they understand the political sensitivity, they have not seen many instances in which an inmate used brute strength to overpower staff. Staff are trained not to attempt to break up fights and not to get into physical confrontations in situations in which they do not have a definite physical advantage or in which staff do not greatly outnumber inmates. Also, prison staff readily note that inmates who are serious weight lifters seldom get into trouble, because those inmates are usually disciplined and self-controlled. These inmates also do not want to lose the privilege and opportunity to continue to exercise.

Recently, prison administrators have initiated recreation programs designed with education about health and diet to develop healthy lifestyles for inmates. Criminal offenders often have histories of limited medical care, poor nutrition and eating habits, and a lack of understanding about the need for exercise and aerobic activities to reduce fat and improve heart functioning. These health improvement and disease prevention programs can be of great benefit to the inmates and to the correctional agency. Inmates are serving much longer sentences than they did for similar offenses 20 years ago. As prison stays increase, the cost of medical care for aging inmates geometrically increases. An investment in healthy living training can pay health dividends for inmates and save money for the agency.

DOES CORRECTIONAL TREATMENT WORK?

This chapter describes many current correctional programs designed to improve the likelihood of offenders returning to society as productive and law-abiding citizens. There are many excellent programs offered both in prisons and in community correctional settings. These programs have a variety of goals. First, they reduce idleness and keep offenders positively engaged. Second, they create opportunities for inmates to learn how to work in a group and open channels for communications with staff. Third, they can increase the confidence and self-esteem of offenders, and encourage them to accept challenges and strive for success. And, finally, these programs can increase the skills of inmates (through education, vocational training, work experiences) that can be used as they compete for jobs and success in the community.

However, the key question is whether these programs effectively reduce recidivism. In a recent article in *Corrections Management Quarterly* regarding the importance of evaluating correctional programs, Latessa and Holsinger argue for measuring the quality of programs, yet point out that "Recidivism cannot be ignored."[49] Although the public supports rehabilitative programs for offenders, there is the expectation that such programs will have a cost-effective outcome of reducing crime and recidivism. If not, corrections is merely repeating the rehabilitative era of the 1960s and early 1970s, which ended with the conclusion that nothing works.

What is different today from the early 1970s when it was believed that correctional treatment did not work? Robert Martinson, whose earlier study initiated the concern with prison rehabilitation, did a further review of 555 studies of correctional programs and reconsidered the conclusion that nothing worked. He found evidence of effective treatments, noting that correctional interventions have differential effects, and concluded that "those treatments that are helpful must be carefully discerned and increased, those that are harmful or impotent eliminated."[50]

Over the past decade, there has been a renewed interest in reviewing evaluations of correctional treatment interventions, and there have been many assessments of what is known regarding the effectiveness of such intervention.[51] In a 1992 publication, Lipsey reviewed 443 correctional programs and found that 64 percent of the studies indicated an effective reduction of recidivism for program participants.[52] In what was referred to as the Carleton University Meta-Analysis, Andrews, Zinger, and others reviewed 124 studies of correctional interventions, and the difference in recidivism between the control and treatment group. Overall, they found that these interventions reduced recidivism an average of 15 percent.[53]

Although this reduction in recidivism is significant, it is even more impressive to review the further analyses of these studies. The authors categorized studies using three principles: risk, need and responsivity. They wanted to determine first, whether the treatment provided was appropriate, unspecified, or inappropriate for the learning styles of offenders. Second, they wanted to determine whether the treatment impacted intermediate targets (changing antisocial attitudes, promoting familial affection, or increasing self-control). In the 54 studies identified as providing "appropriate" treatment, there was a 30 percent reduction in recidivism.[54] In contrast, this study also included 30 studies of the impact of enhanced criminal sanctions, and found that "more versus" less punishment actually increased recidivism by 7 percent.[55]

In another review of correctional rehabilitative programs, Gibbons first describes many studies completed over the past decade that indicate positive outcomes; then he deliberates the question of what we have learned over the past 30 years in developing and delivering rehabilitative programs. Gibbons expresses surprise on the volume of material that has been developed regarding correctional treatment. He summarizes his review by noting

> However, although still fairly weak, there are signs of reviewed interest on the part of both politicians and ordinary citizens in correctional treatment and intervention or, in other words, positive efforts to divert delinquents and criminals away from law-breaking paths.[56]

These findings bode well for the future of rehabilitation. In today's emphasis on the bottom line for corrections, there must be an outcome that seems cost effective compared to the cost of the rehabilitative intervention. From the findings previously noted, simply enhancing criminal sanctions by increasing punishment does not reduce recidivism. However, correctly matching offenders with the type of treatment interventions that have shown the best promise for achieving intermediate goals does result in a significant reduction in recidivism. These findings also hold significant importance for correctional administrators who recognize the value of providing positive programs that maintain hope and keep offenders busy. Administrators can argue for the maintenance of rehabilitative programs not only for their benefits of offender management but also for the reduction of crime.

SUMMARY

This chapter has presented an overview of the reasons for and operations of rehabilitative programs. Even in the current era with a demand for punishment, retribution, and offender accountability, there is still a critical need for continued treatment and skill-building correctional programs. These programs benefit inmates and community offenders. They benefit correctional administrators, who struggle with how to supervise offenders and keep inmates productively occupied. And, they benefit the general public, because there is significant evidence that they can reduce recidivism. All of these reasons lead to cost-effective outcomes in providing programs for offenders.

In prisons, programs such as counseling, religious activities, recreation, and work all help create an environment of productivity and, even more importantly, hope. Prisons can easily have a dire and depressing climate, impacting negatively on staff and inmates. Such circumstances can lead to tension and inmate unrest, as is discussed in later chapters. However, prisons can actively promote and provide programs, and build an atmosphere of optimism for the future, without undermining punishment and deterrence. The end result will be a much better situation for taxpayers as well as offenders and the staff who must govern prisons.

ENDNOTES

1. J. Senese and David B. Kalinich, "Activities and Rehabilitation Programs for Offenders," in *Corrections: An Introduction*, edited by S. Stojkovic and R. Lovell (Cincinnati, OH: Anderson, 1992), p. 223.
2. John Irwin, "The Changing Social Structure of the Men's Prison," in *Corrections and Punishment*, edited by D. Greenberg (Beverly Hills, University of California Press, 1977).
3. Francis T. Cullen and Brandon K. Applegate, editors, *Offender Rehabilitation: Effective Correctional Intervention* (Dartmouth: Ashgate, 1998), p. xiv.
4. President's Commission on Law Enforcement and the Administration of Justice, *The Challenge of Crime in a Free Society*, (Washington, DC: U.S. Government Printing Office, 1967), p. vi.
5. Ibid. p. 183.
6. Robert Martinson, "What Works? Questions and Answers about Prison Reform," *The Public Interest* 35 (1974): 25.
7. Douglas Lipton, Robert Martinson and Judith Wilks, *The Effectiveness of Correctional Treatment* (New York: Praeger, 1975).
8. Alfred Blumstein, "Prisons," in *Crime*, edited by James Q. Wilson and Joan Petersilia (San Francisco: ICS, 1995), p. 396.

9. Christopher A. Innes, "Recent Public Opinion in the United States Toward Punishment and Corrections," *The Prison Journal* 73, (1993): 232.

10. Timothy J. Flanagan, "Reform or Punish: Americans' View of the Correctional System," in *Americans View Crime and Justice: A National Public Opinion Survey*, edited by Timothy J. Flanagan and Dennis R. Longmire (Thousand Oaks, CA: Sage 1996), p. 78.

11. Ibid., p. 78.

12. For a recent summary of several evaluations of correctional treatment programs, see Gerald G. Gaes, Timothy J. Flanagan, Laurence L. Motiuk, and Lynn Sterart, "Adult Correctional Treatment," in *Prisons*, edited by Michael Tonry and Joan Petersilia (Chicago: The University of Chicago Press, 1999), pp. 361–426.

13. U.S. Bureau of the Census, *Educational Attainment in the United States: March 1996 (Update)*, Current Population Reports, (Washington, DC: U.S. Government Printing Office, 1997), pp. 20–493.

14. U.S. National Center for Education Statistics, *Digest of Education Statistics 1997*, (Washington, DC: U.S. Government Printing Office, 1997).

15. Richard Arum and Irene R. Beattie, "High School Experience and the Risk of Adult Incarceration," *Criminology* 37 no. 3 (1999): 532–533.

16. Commission on Accreditation for Corrections, "Comprehensive Education Program, Standard 3-4410," in *Standards for Adult Correctional Institutions*, (College Park, MD: The American Correctional Association, 1990), p. 141.

17. William G. Saylor and Gerald G. Gaes, "Training Inmates Through Industrial Work Participation and Vocational and Apprenticeship Instruction," *Corrections Management Quarterly* 1 no. 2, (1997): 42.

18. Ibid., p. 40.

19. Ibid., p. 42.

20. Pamela K. Lattimore, Ann Dryden Witte, and Joanna R. Baker, " Experimental Assessment of the Effect of Vocational Training on Youthful Property Offenders," *Evaluation Review* 14 no. 2 (1990): 115–133.

21. Substance Abuse and Mental Health Services Administration, *National Household Survey on Drug Abuse, 1995*, (Washington, DC: U.S. Government Printing Office, 1996).

22. Bureau of Justice Statistics, *Drugs, Crime and the Justice System*, (Washington, DC: U.S. Government Printing Office, 1992), p. 2.

23. National Institute of Justice, *Drug Use Forecasting 1996: Annual Report on Adult and Juvenile Arrestees*, (Washington, DC: National Institute of Justice, December, 1997).

24. Bureau of Justice Statistics, *Drug and Crime Facts, 1993* (Washington, DC: U.S. Department of Justice, 1994), pp. 4–5.

25. Ibid., p. 6.

26. Caroline Wolf Beck, *Drug Enforcement and Treatment in Prison, 1990* (Washington, DC: U.S. Department of Justice, 1992), p. 1.

27. Correctional Services of Canada, "Substance Abuse Treatment: Canada's Approach," in *Best Practices: Excellence in Corrections*, edited by Edward E. Rhine (Lanham, MD: American Correctional Association, 1998), pp. 420–426.

28. Federal Bureau of Prisons, "Drug Treatment Programs in Federal Prisons, in *Best Practices: Excellence in Corrections,* edited by Edward E. Rhine (Lanham, MD: American Correctional Association, 1998), pp. 427–430.

29. Ibid., p. 429.

30. Gregory P. Falkin, Sheila Strauss, and Timothy Bohen, "Matching Drug-Involved Probationers to Appropriate Drug Interventions: A Strategy for Reducing Recidivism," *Federal Probation* (June 1999): 4.

31. Ibid., p. 5.

32. Frank S. Pearson and Douglas S. Lipton, "A Meta-Analytic Review of the Effectiveness of Correctional-Based Treatments for Drug Abuse," *The Prison Journal* 79 no. 4 (1999): 384–410.

33. The National Task Force on Correctional Substance Abuse Strategies, "Intervening with Substance-Abusing Offenders: A Framework for Action," (Washington, DC: U.S. Department of Justice, National Institute of Correction, June 1991), p. 27.

34. R. Masters, *Counseling Criminal Justice Offenders* (Thousand Oaks, CA: Sage, 1994).

35. See Maxwell Jones, *Beyond the Therapeutic Community* (New Haven: Yale University Press, 1968).

36. For a description of the work programs in early prisons, see Enoch C. Wines and T. W. Dwight, *Report on the Prisons and Reformatories of the United States and Canada,* (Albany, NY: Van Benthuysen & Sons, 1973).

37. Dean J. Champion, *Corrections in the United States: A Contemporary Perspective,* 2nd ed. (Upper Saddle River, NJ: Prentice Hall, 1998), p. 240.

38. Margaret Calahan, *Historical Corrections Statistics in the United States: 1850–1984* (Washington, DC: U.S. Department of Justice, 1986), p. 36.

39. American Correctional Association, *Correctional Industries Information: Correctional Industries Survey Final Report* (Laurel, MD: American Correctional Association, 1992).

40. Texas Department of Criminal Justice, *Annual Report of 1993* (Austin: Texas Department of Criminal Justice, 1993).

41. George M. Camp and Camile Graham Camp, *The Corrections Yearbook, 1998* (Middletown, CT: Criminal Justice Institute, 1998), pp. 96–113.

42. National Institute of Justice, *Developing Private Sector Prison Industries: From Concept to Start Up* (Washington, DC: Government Printing Office, 1990), p. 22.

43. Ibid., p. 110.

44. Bureau of Justice Assistance, *Prison Industries Fact Sheet* (Rockville, MD: Bureau of Justice Assistance Clearinghouse, 1995)

45. Ibid.

46. *Ruffin v. Commonwealth of Virginia,* 62 Va (21 Gratt.) 790, 796 (1871).

47. *Cooper v. Pate,* 378 U.S. 546 (1964).

48. The standard for correctional institutions limiting religious practices was modified to "reasonable and substantial justification" in *Brown v. Johnson,* 743 F.2d 408 (6th Cir. 1985).

49. Edward J. Latessa and Alexander Holsinger, "The Importance of Evaluating Correctional Programs: Assessing Outcome and Quality," *Corrections Management Quarterly,* 2 no.4 (1998): p. 28.

50. Robert Martinson, "Reaffirming Rehabilitation, New Findings, New Views: A Note of Caution regarding sentencing Reform," in *Offender Rehabilitation: Effective Correctional Intervention,* edited by Francis T. Cullen and Brandon K. Applegate (Dartmouth: Ashgate, 1998), p. 90.

51. See D. A. Andrews and J. Bonta, *The Psychology of Criminal Conduct,* (Cincinnati, OH: Anderson, 1994) Paul Gendreau, "The Principles of Effective Intervention with Offenders," in *Choosing Correctional Options That Work: Defining the Demand and Evaluating the Supply,* edited by A. Harland (Thousand Oaks, CA: Sage, 1996), pp. 117–130.

52. M. W. Lipsey, "Juvenile Delinquency Treatment: A Meta-Analytic Inquiry into the Variability of Effects," in *Meta-Analysis for Explanation, edited by* T. D. Cook, H. Cooper, D. S. Cordray, H. Hartmann, L. V. Hedges, R. J. Light, T. A. Louis, and F. Mosteller, (New York: Russell Sage, 1992), pp. 83–127.

53. D.S. Andrews, I. Zinger, R. D. Hoge, J. Bonta, P. Gendreau, and F. T. Cullen, "Does Correctional Treatment Work? A Psychologically Informed Meta-Analysis," *Criminology* 28 (1990): 369–404.

54. Ibid., p. 382.

55. Ibid., p. 398.

56. Don C. Gibbons, "Review Essay: Changing Lawbreakers—What Have We Learned Since the 1950s?" *Crime and Delinquency* 45, no. 2 (April, 1999): 272.

KEY TERMS

rehabilitation	token economy
institutionalization	therapeutic community
mandatory prison educational programs	laundry
pre-release programs	food service
vocational training	maintenance department
Drug Use Forecasting (DUF)	prison industries
harm reduction	state-use laws
self-help programs	PIE Program
psychotropic medication	hands-off policy
transactional analysis	

YOU'RE THE CORRECTIONAL ADMINISTRATOR

1. You are the warden at a medium security prison with 1,000 inmates. The director of the department of corrections has decided it would benefit the department, and corrections nationally, if the state had a few "model" prison programs that could be shown to meet offender needs, be cost effective, and reduce recidivism. The director has asked you to create a model program at your prison, any type of program. You cannot increase staff; you must reassign current staff to meet any staffing needs. What program would you pick, how would you build it, and how would you make it as successful as possible? Describe why you decided to create this model program.

2. You are the chief budget analyst for a state department of corrections. The state legislature wants to cut the budget for the department and suggests reducing by 50 percent all funding for community and prison treatment programs. Create an argument that is as convincing as possible that this money should not be cut from the department budget.

WEB LINK EXERCISES

Correctional Industries Association: www.correctionalindustries.org

Go to the site for the Correctional Industries Association (CIA). Identify what the CIA is and the role it plays. Then, find information on the Prison Industries Enhancement (PIE) Program and identify the requirements for a private company and a correctional industry to enter the PIE program. Which requirements provide the major impediments to forming a successful PIE partnership.

6

Offender Classification and Risk Assessment

INTRODUCTION

What is offender classification, and how does risk assessment contribute to it? What does it have to do with correctional administration? And, how do each of these assist in the management of offenders and of correctional agencies? These questions are answered in this chapter. Both of these concepts are defined and presented in detail in this chapter. In general terms, **classification** is a process that is used throughout the criminal justice decision-making process to identify and match offender needs with correctional resources, resulting in the assignment of offenders into groups of individuals with similar traits or characteristics. **Risk assessment,** to some extent, is a subcomponent of offender classification. Risk assessment is an attempt to predict an offender's future behavior, especially the potential for or likelihood of future criminal violations. Therefore, risk assessment provides information useful to offender classification decisions and helps guide the placement of offenders into homogeneous management categories.

Classification is a technique that has been used by correctional administrators for several years. The earliest classification of prisoners was the separation of women from men, and of youths from adults. Systems and groupings have become extremely sophisticated, and a variety of approaches are available for correctional administrators to categorize offender groups for housing, program assignments, security, and management purposes. Margaret Pugh, previously the commissioner of the Alaska Department of Corrections, notes, "I still believe in that old correctional ideal that classification is the cornerstone of good management."[1] Classification is used in almost every type of correctional setting and, as Pugh notes, is the beginning of policy and practices for how to staff, fund, and manage a particular group of offenders.

Early uses of classification helped identify treatment needs in response to the medical model of corrections. Over the years, however, classification has evolved in response to the changing priorities for correctional goals. As the medical model lost support and public sentiment began to favor offender accountability and public safety, classification models began to change focus from treatment purposes to predicting the potential for escapes, violence, and recidivism. This chapter includes the historical evolution of risk assessment as an aid to classification, its purposes and practical uses, and its applications for the administration of correctional agencies.

Actually, risk assessment is not a new development; it has been used by correctional administrators since John Augustus, the father of probation, began bailing criminals out of jail who indicated a willingness to change their ways and commit no further crimes. Historically, risk assessment was a subjective or, later, clinical, appraisal of how likely an offender was to commit crimes after release or to create a risk for violence or escape while in prison. Over the past few decades, risk assessment has become increasingly objective, using actuarial methods. **Actuarial methods** involve identifying factors that are linked to future behavior and determining the strength of the relationship between those factors and behavioral outcomes of past offenders to create formulas to predict an offender's expected future behavior. As correctional administrators have become fearful of negative publicity around criminal acts by offenders under their supervision, they have turned to these actuarial risk assessment instruments to aid in decision making regarding prison assignment, release on parole, and level of supervision while in the community.

In this chapter, you examine the many uses of classification for correctional administrators. Classification is used for making decisions about sentences and placement of offenders in community or institutional settings, to determine the level of supervision required to monitor an offender's behavior, and to decide on the types of programs or services needed by a group of offenders. You also review risk prediction as a refinement to and a philosophical change in classifying offenders. The actual process for classifying offenders is described for both prison inmates and offenders in the community. Finally, you consider some of the issues surrounding risk assessment and classification, including the impact of changing sentences and the relationship of race and gender with classification and risk assessment.

CURRENT USES OF CLASSIFICATION SYSTEMS

Most people with little knowledge of correctional processes have a fairly limited idea of how classification systems are used by correctional administrators. Some uses of classification systems have not changed throughout the history of corrections. However, the development of actuarial risk assessment methods to aid classification decisions has expanded the potential use of this information for correctional administrators. The following illustrate some of the most common uses of classification and risk assessment.

1. To ensure that the high-risk offenders supervised in the community receive an appropriate level of supervision and treatment services. Historically, offenders in the community under parole or probation supervision were assessed using a clinical model. With this approach, an experienced officer interviewed the offender and used professional judgment to determine the best level of supervision and any required treatment. Although the clinical model of assessment is still popular, risk assessment using actuarial methods has been implemented in many jurisdictions throughout the 1990s. The actuarial predictive models have become popular among probation and parole officers both to set supervision levels and to add monitoring through intensive supervision or electronic monitoring. Although some studies indicate that actuarial methods are superior to clinical methods,[2] many practitioners believe the best results are achieved through a combination of the two approaches.

2. To determine the appropriate security level of a prison to which an inmate should be assigned.   Most states now use some level of actuarial risk assessment to determine an inmate's initial assignment to a prison. Many states have a reception center, where newly received inmates are processed into the correctional system, and decisions are made regarding their prison placement and treatment needs. One of these reviews is to determine their initial classification to a certain security-level prison. This initial classification is based predominantly on offense history and sentence length. The goal of the initial assignment is to ensure that inmates are placed in institutions with an appropriate level of physical security to prevent escapes and provide them a safe and controlled environment.

Prison security levels range from minimum to maximum. According to the *Corrections Yearbook*, as of January 1, 1998, 11.7 percent of all prison inmates were assigned to maximum security prisons, 13.3 percent were assigned to close/high security prisons, 34.6 percent were assigned to medium security prisons, 30.6 percent were assigned to minimum security prisons, 4.1 percent were assigned to community security prisons, and 5.7 percent were unclassified.[3] It is interesting to note how classification assignments to certain security prisons have changed over time. In 1978, 51 percent of prisoners were in maximum security, 38 percent in medium, and 11 percent in minimum security prisons.[4] Using clinical rather than modern actuarial classification methods resulted in a tendency to overclassify inmates, taking a conservative approach in assuming dangerousness and propensity for escape unless there was some evidence that they do not exist. In reporting on this tendency, which results in lower-security inmates being assigned to higher-security prisons, Duffee notes that, "Few correctional administrators would admit that this distribution is consistent with the security rating of the inmates. . . . prison administrators try to accommodate this situation by creating more desirable subunits within an otherwise undesirable fortress-prison."[5] The new inmate classification system based on actuarial methods rather than clinical approaches is called an **objective classification system.**

A major benefit of using objective classification systems is the realistic matching of an inmate's need for security to available physical security of a prison. There is no need to have minimum security inmates housed in a maximum security prison. Maximum security prison beds are expensive to build and operate, and it is wasteful to overclassify and assign inmates to this level of prison when their security needs do not require it. With objective classification systems providing actuarial information to staff who assign inmates to prisons, it is much less likely that overclassification will occur, and the system can make better use of its expensive high-security bed space. Much of the downward trend in classification (comparing 1978, when 51 percent of inmates were in maximum security prisons to 1998 when less than 25 percent were in maximum or close/high security prisons) can be credited to the implementation of risk assessment and objective classification systems.

3. To determine which type of housing assignment within a prison (internal management classification) is most suitable for each inmate. Once they have been assigned to an institution, inmates must then be placed in an appropriate housing situation. This decision is important for two reasons. First, many prisons have a variety of housing areas for inmates, which may be either individual or multiperson cells or dormitory style housing with several (possibly hundreds) inmates in an open area without physical security to separate them from each other or from staff. Second, certain housing areas may be designated for particular groups of offenders (the mentally ill, sex offenders, aggressive and violent offenders). As reported in 1994, only 10 states and the Federal Bureau of Prisons have implemented a formal **internal classification system,** independent from the external classification used for initial prison assignment.[6] Internal classification systems are tools to assign inmates to housing or programs after they are placed in a particular prison. Most agencies still make these decisions based on "clinical" judgments, or they make housing assignments based primarily on the availability of space.

The most widely used internal classification system is the Adult Internal Management System (AIMS) developed by Dr. Herbert Quay. AIMS classifies inmates based on two inventories: the analysis of life history records and a correctional adjustment checklist. The resultant classification identifies the likelihood that inmates will be violent and aggressive, or whether they are likely to be victimized, and it allows staff to separate likely victims from likely aggressors. Different states have designed their own systems. Illinois, for example, uses an internal classification system to make assignments within its maximum security prisons. The Illinois system uses some of the criteria regarding past criminal behavior from the external classification system, but adds prison disciplinary conduct and history of gang activities to predict a level of institutional aggression, which becomes the basis for assignments of housing, work and inmate programs.

4. To guide interinstitutional transfers because of security or treatment purposes. Once offenders are assigned to particular institutions, they usually will not stay at that prison during their entire term of incarceration. Over their time served, inmates' risk of violence and escape and their program needs almost always change. Therefore, correctional agencies regularly move them to other (higher- or lower-security level) prisons based on these changes. The two factors most often used to determine changes are time served on the current sentence (often calculated in percentage of sentence served) and institutional conduct.

As inmates serve a portion of their sentence, it is natural to assume that they will adjust and be less likely to attempt escape. Correlations of time served to risk of escape have proven to be positive, because inmates, after serving significant portions of their sentence, understand that the chance of escape is low and the risk of an attempt usually results in additional prosecution and time added to a sentence. Therefore, inmates who have served a large part of their sentence usually decide to get out of prison the legal way, by finishing their sentence. In addition, past prison conduct is a valid predictor of future prison behavior, and using an inmate's disciplinary record as an added score to the external classification instrument indicates whether there is a need for changing the security level. Inmates with serious or violent misconduct receive scores that add to their security needs, and they are likely to be transferred to higher-security prisons. Inmates who serve a portion of their sentence with little or no misconduct reduce their security need scores and are likely to be reassigned to a less secure prison.

5. To match offenders to appropriate treatment and services.   Matching offenders to appropriate treatment and services, sometimes using risk assessment, is valuable for both community and institutional placements. Although it is more commonly expected to be used in a clinical classification process under the medical model of corrections, contemporary objective classification systems also contribute to this purpose. This can occur in two ways. First, through the process of determining security needs of offenders, objective classification instruments also help align appropriate program and service activities. In each prison, there are some programs and services that are unique to the security level of facilities. For instance, in extremely high security prisons (sometimes called "supermax"), in which inmates spend most of their time in their cells, many educational or self-improvement programs are presented via video tape presentation in the inmates' cells, without the need for an instructor or group settings. In minimum security prisons, there are often community service programs whereby inmates can assist the community by cleaning up of community areas such as parks or highways. These programs are not available for high-security inmates.

Just as the security level dictates types of programs, it is common to find like program needs clustered around inmates with like security requirements. Inmates serving long periods of time are more likely to be in high-security prisons. Also, inmates serving long periods of time have needs for basic education, active recreation programs, and psychological counseling. Inmates serving short sentences, who are usually assigned to minimum or low security institutions, are more in need of prerelease preparation, substance abuse counseling, and work-related training. Therefore, as inmates are matched to required security levels, programs and services are likely to be matched to prisons that serve a certain security level of inmate.

6. To begin the process of positive interaction between staff and offenders.
Just as any new relationship is uncomfortable until common ground is found for discussion, the relationship among offenders and staff charged with their supervision and management can be uncomfortable to a heightened degree. However, the classification process facilitates the beginning of a process of positive interaction. With both clinical and actuarial approaches to classification, inmates and staff participate in an interview and discussion to clarify certain background factors and identify present needs. The requirement of a structured discussion to determine these issues forces inmates to be honest with staff and gives staff the opportunity to explain the process and how information will be used.

With objective classification instruments, the process "depersonalizes" the staff member's judgment of the inmate. First, staff do not make professional judgments regarding the inmate's placement that are, perhaps, difficult for them to explain and the inmate to understand. The staff member can share the objective scoring sheet with the inmate, illustrating how factors are weighted and how the final score is determined. With the possibility of later reassignment and a move from one security level to another, staff can even show an inmate how (and sometimes when) certain factors will be reduced if the inmate's behavior is good, thereby facilitating the inmate's placement in a lower-security prison. The processes are also depersonalized, because staff do not have to threaten any type of action. Inmates do not have to try to convince staff that they have been doing a good job and deserve special treatment. The staff member simply explains how the system works, how certain factors and behaviors are weighted, and what will occur if an inmate behaves in a good or bad way.

The initial classification process also usually includes a discussion of an offender's needs for certain programs. As the staff and offender discuss these needs, they agree on goals and program assignments that are designed to benefit the offender. These discussions exhibit a concern by staff for offenders to resolve issues and improve the inmates' chances for success both while under supervision and after release. The program plan developed serves as the road map for monitoring the offender's progress throughout the period of incarceration or community supervision.

7. To match assignment of staff and financial resources to offender security and program needs. There is a significant difference in the numbers and categories of staff required to manage an offender population at various security levels, both in an institutional and in a community setting. As noted previously, it is possible to identify certain program needs (and related staff resources) of offenders based on a security classification system. Security classification systems also identify the need for supervision and control that offenders require, whether in an institution or in the community. These requirements for supervision and programs dictate the corresponding requirements for staff as well.

In a prison, inmates always outnumber staff. The key to controlling the inmate population is to have the right number of staff available to supervise inmates. For staff safety reasons, one would never want to have too few staff. Yet, for cost reasons, it would be expensive to have too many. A typical minimum security prison for 1,000 inmates may have a staff complement of 250, whereas a maximum security prison for the same number of inmates would have double the number of staff. Although costs for food and clothing would be the same for inmates in the two facilities, the staff costs (estimating $40,000 for salaries and benefits) would require an additional $10 million per year in personnel costs. A probation officer supervising an intensive caseload may be responsible for 25 probationers, while an officer supervising a regular caseload may be responsible for over 100 probationers. These examples indicates how much cost is linked to staff salaries and how critical it is to have the right amount and type of staff for prison operations or for supervision in the community.

8. To use in planning for future prison bed space needs. In the 10-year period from 1986 to 1996, the number of prisoners in adult state correctional facilities in the United States grew from just more than 500,000 to more than one million inmates. Housing these 500,000 new inmates required almost 500 new prisons to be designed, constructed, and opened. The first requirement in planning a new prison is to determine the security level of the prison. As noted previously, the level of security has a dramatic effect on staff numbers and operational costs. In addition, the cost of construction varies greatly by security level. As reported in the *1998 Corrections Yearbook*, the average construction cost per bed by security level for prisons under construction in 1998 was $70,909 for maximum security, $49,853 for medium security, and $29,311 for minimum security.[7]

These costs indicate how critical it is to correctly plan bed space needs by security level. Under the clinical approach to classification, it is much more difficult to anticipate the need for security level of the required expansion. However, objective classification systems can predict the future needs for bed space at each security level. The increase in prisoners is because of two factors. First, sentenced inmates are serving longer periods of time in prison. Second, as a result of increased law enforcement and court prosecution emphasis on certain crimes (drug offenses, for example), more offenders are entering prison. Predicting the growth in the number of inmates has become a fine art; however, most states have become very accurate in the process. The state agency planners use past break downs of the percentages of inmates who were assigned to various security levels to predict incoming inmates' security needs. Objective classification systems have increased the accuracy of these predictions, and, as a result, have saved states millions of dollars by not building higher-security prisons than will be necessary.

HISTORY OF RISK ASSESSMENT IN CLASSIFYING OFFENDERS

As noted previously, classification has been a critical element of corrections for many years. In a 1947 document published by the American Prison Association (the precursor to the American Correctional Association), it is noted that, "Classification is a term that has been used with increasing frequency in the field of correctional administration during the past two decades. . . .The field of criminal treatment is in the stage of development. Classification methods and techniques are in their formative stages."[8]

The report on classification also included a discussion of the purposes of classification: "Increasing emphasis [is] given to the concept that the fundamental purpose of prisons is the protection of the public welfare," and "Not all offenders needed all of the constructive services which were being developed. Not all required vocational training or academic education or psychiatric treatment."[9] The earliest uses of classification were to determine what programs were needed and what inmates needed treatments. Although public safety has always been considered a critical goal of correctional institutions, at the time of this report, it was believed that the public could best be protected by effectively treating and preparing offenders for release. The report noted, "the necessity for an institution program which will have a constructive effect upon prisoners is based upon the inescapable fact that over 95 percent of all prisoners committed to prison are sooner or later returned to the community."[10]

In the earliest days of corrections and prisons, offenders were classified by a team of correctional officials who interviewed the offenders and discussed their needs for housing and program assignments. An interesting side note was the methods used to identify inmates prior to fingerprinting and even DNA testing. Prisons used the "Bertillon" method, which was named after its creator, Alphonse Bertillon. With this method, illustrated by the accompanying 1905 Bertillon information sheets for a federal prison inmate, a photograph and specific body measurements were the primary means of criminal offender identification.

Prison Classification Team in the 1940s. Prior to the use of risk assessment instruments and objective classification, a team of several professionals met with each inmate to determine their needs and create a treatment plan.
(Courtesy of the Federal Bureau of Prisons)

As the medical model became more widely accepted and practiced by correctional administrators during the 1950s and 1960s, clinical decisions by trained professional staff were more extensively used for classification decisions. Diagnoses of offenders' problems using psychological and medical examinations, social investigations, and educational and vocational studies were made. After data were collected on an offender, a staff conference would be held to discuss the case and develop a treatment and training program. The treatment team ensured that the offender's program was carried out, and the team would observe the offender's progress as a result of program participation and make changes in the program as necessary. The entire classification process is based on the way medical personnel diagnose and staff a case, carry out treatment, monitor progress, and make changes and adjustments as necessary. Decisions were subjective by using the professional judgment of treatment team members and no formula to weight factors.

Little changed in the classification process until the mid-1970s, when correctional agencies began to reexamine the subjective methods they used to classify offenders. As a result of a changing public view of the goals of corrections, which emphasized accountability and public safety, correctional administrators reconsidered the purposes of the classification process, and looked to research for identifying factors predictive of success and failure of criminal offenders. As described in earlier chapters, with the Martinson report indicating nothing works, the movement away from the medical model of corrections and toward a repositioning of the use of risk assessments for classifying inmates in order to reduce their risk of reoffending began.[11]

At the same time the medical model was being questioned, several alternative correctional approaches and philosophies began to emerge that impacted the classification and risk predictions of offenders. For one, Fogel suggested the "justice

Bertillon Method of Identifying Inmates. Prior to the use of fingerprinting, prison staff took exact measurements of inmates' bodies, noting scars, marks, and moles for purposes of identification. This method is demonstrated in the 1905 Bertillon method of inmate John Arnold at the U.S. Penitentiary in Atlanta, Georgia. (Courtesy of the Federal Bureau of Prisons)

model," with less emphasis on rehabilitation, elimination of discretionary parole board decision making, and surveillance of offenders after release by law enforcement rather than parole officials.[12] Andrew von Hirsch also argued against the continued use of discretionary parole release, suggesting that sentencing should be simple and consistent for offenders committing the same types of crimes. He advocated a "just deserts" form of sentencing, with rehabilitation irrelevant to the parole deci-

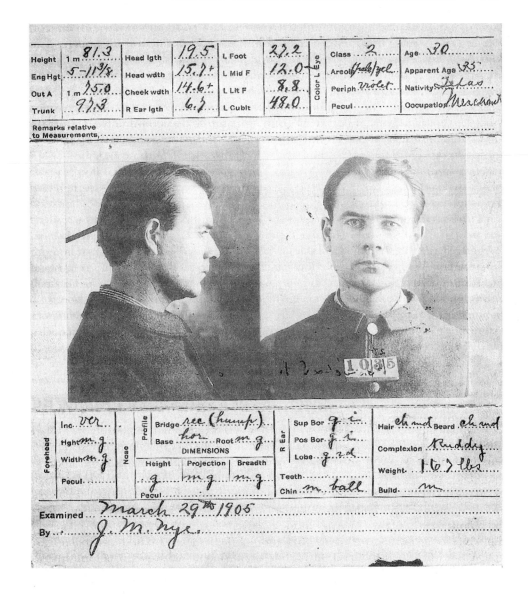

Height	1 m *81.3*	Head lgth	*19.5*	L Foot	*27.2*	Class	*2*	Age *30*
EngHgt	*5-11 3/8*	Head wdth	*15.7+*	L Mid F	*12.0*	Areol *pale/yel*	Apparent Age *35*
Out A	1 m *75.0*	Cheek wdth	*14.6+*	L Lit F	*8.8*	Periph *violet*	Nativity *Texas*
Trunk	*97.3*	R Ear lgth	*6.7*	L Cubit	*48.0*	Pecul	Occupation *Merchant*

Remarks relative to Measurements,

Forehead	Inc *ver*		Nose	Profile	Bridge *rec (hump)*		R Ear	Sup Bor *g. i.*	Hair *ch md*	Beard *ch md*
	Hght *m. g*				Base *hor* Root *m. g*			Pos Bor *g. i.*	Complexion *Ruddy*
	Width *m. g*				DIMENSIONS			Lobe *g. 2d*	
					Height / Projection / Breadth				Weight *167 lbs*
	Pecul				*g* / *m g* / *m g*			Teeth	
					Pecul			Chin *m ball*	Build *m*

Examined *March 29th 1905*
By *J. M. Nye.*

sion, substituting instead a determinate sentence based on the severity of the crime.[13] Noted criminologist James Q. Wilson maintained that without scientific evidence to support the medical model, sentencing should consider deterrence and incapacitation as primary goals. In arguing for isolation and punishment, he noted that society must protect itself from dangerous offenders, because "society really does not know how to do much else."[14]

These arguments against the continued use of the medical model helped to push the emphasis of corrections away from rehabilitation and toward punishment, deterrence, and incapacitation. Protection of society became the most important function of the criminal justice system, and methods and mechanisms to implement this policy change began to develop. The predictive capabilities of certain traits in criminals had been identified as early as the 1920s, but they were used little by prison officials to classify offenders or by parole boards to consider release decisions. Although the medical model and offenders' readiness for release were the dominant approaches in corrections, expert clinical judgments about treatment, management, and release of offenders was believed to be most important. As rehabilitation lost support and the public lost confidence in correctional officials' ability to treat and manage offenders, it was only a matter of time before more objective measures were developed for predictive purposes. According to Daniel Glaser,

> An accelerating rate of acceptance of statistical tables for risk classification has occurred during the 1970s and 1980s because of a change in stance by researchers. They began to present their prediction tables as purely advisory information and in many cases designed tables to deal with other problems besides classification for risk. But most important for the acceptance of these tables, the officials who would use them were involved in designing the tables."[15]

In addition to the use of classification systems for separating inmates within correctional facilities, there have been three other developments using risk prediction since the 1970s. Each of these developments was prompted by a changing public philosophy regarding the role of corrections. Public mood and expectation became less accepting of the importance of treatment and more in favor of the importance of surveillance of offenders in order to prevent further criminal behavior. First, predictions of risk concerned release decision making by parole boards was initiated. Risk prediction also began to be used to identify the level and intensity of community supervision required for parolees and probationers. Finally, risk prediction provided a foundation for the use of sentencing guidelines by courts in determining appropriate criminal sanctions.

Risk Assessment in Prison Classification

In response to the philosophical developments, the Federal Bureau of Prisons (BOP) in 1977 asked a team of specialists to design an objective classification system. The BOP was the first correctional agency to implement such a system. They began with 96 factors that were considered important for classification purposes and sought the opinion of correctional professionals across the United States on these factors. The original list was initially pared down to 47 and then to 6, including: history of escape or attempted escape, detainees, types of prior commitments, history of violence, severity of offense, and length of sentence. "Instead of assigning offenders to certain security levels based on gut reaction and subjective discussion, this new system provided an orderly and objective way of separating violent from nonviolent inmates."[16] The objective classification system focused on public risk, using many factors that occur before sentencing. Brennan suggests that these security classifications emphasize "legal variables, history of criminality, seriousness of current offense, and past escape attempts."[17] Brennan also lists prior criminal behavior, age, socioeconomic status, unemployment, and drug and alcohol use as factors useful for predicting dangerous recidivism.[18]

The objective classification system is used primarily to assign inmates to the proper institution security level. The BOP's current security levels of prisons are minimum, low, medium, and high. Just after sentencing, a staff person responsible

INMATE LOAD AND SECURITY DESIGNATION FORM - MALE (BP-337)				
INMATE LOAD DATA	1. REG NO		2. LAST NAME	
3. FIRST NAME		4. MIDDLE		5. SUFFIX
6. RACE	7. SEX	8. ETHNIC ORIGIN	9. DATE OF BIRTH	
10. OFFENSE/SENTENCE				
11. FBI NUMBER		12. SOCIAL SECURITY NUMBER		
13. STATE OF BIRTH		14. OR COUNTRY OF BIRTH		15. CITIZENSHIP
16. ADDRESS - STREET			17. CITY	
18. STATE		19. ZIP CODE	20. OR FOREIGN COUNTRY	
21. HEIGHT - FT: IN:		22. WEIGHT	23. HAIR	24. EYES
25. ARS ASSIGNMENT				

SECURITY DESIGNATION DATA ///

1. PUBLIC SAFETY FACTORS A - NONE B - DISRUPTIVE GROUP C - GREATEST SEVERITY OFFENSE	F - SEX OFFENDER G - THREAT GOVT OFFICIAL H - DEPORTABLE ALIEN	I - SENTENCE LENGTH L - SERIOUS ESCAPE M - PRISON DISTURBANCE	
2. USM OFFICE	3. JUDGE	4. REC FACILITY	5. REC PROGRAM
6. TYPE OF DETAINER	0 - NONE 1 - LOWEST/LOW MODERATE	3 - MODERATE 5 - HIGH	7 - GREATEST
7. SEVERITY OF CURRENT OFFENSE	0 - LOWEST 1 - LOW MODERATE	3 - MODERATE 5 - HIGH	7 - GREATEST
8. MONTHS TO RELEASE _____			
9. TYPE OF PRIOR COMMITMENT	0 = NONE	1 = MINOR	3 = SERIOUS

10. HISTORY OF ESCAPE OR ATTEMPTS		NONE	>15 YEARS	10-15 YEARS	5-10 YEARS	<5 YEARS
	MINOR	0	1	1	2	3
	SERIOUS	0	3 (S)	3 (S)	3 (S)	3 (S)

11. HISTORY OF VIOLENCE		NONE	>15 YEARS	10-15 YEARS	5-10 YEARS	<5 YEARS
	MINOR	0	1	1	3	5
	SERIOUS	0	2	4	6	7

12. PRECOMMITMENT STATUS 0=NOT APPLICABLE -3 (R)=OWN RECOGNIZANCE -3 (V)=VOLUNTARY SURRENDER	
13. VOLUNTARY SURRENDER DATE	14. VOLUNTARY SURRENDER LOCATION
15. CRIM HX PTS _____	16. SECURITY POINT TOTAL
17. OMDT REFER (Y/N) _____	
18. REMARKS	

FIGURE 6-1
Inmate load and security designation form (BP-337) for scoring placement in a specific prison security level. Source: Federal Bureau of Prisons, *Security Designation and Custody Classification Manual* (Washington, DC: U.S. Department of Justice, 1999), Chapter 5, p. 17.

for inmate designations reviews the background of the offender and assigns a score for each of the six areas. Figure 6–1 shows the form used to determine security designations for each inmate. An offender's security point total is then the basis for assignment to a federal prison. As indicated in Table 6–1, there is a range of point

■ TABLE 6–1

Security Designation Table for Determining Placement in a Specific Security Level of Federal Prison for Male Inmates

Classification Score	Public Safety Factors	Inmate Security Level
0–5	**No public safety factors**	**Minimum**
	Deportable alien	Low
	Greatest severity offense	Low
	Sex offender	Low
	Threat to government officials	Low
	Sentence Length	
	Time remaining > 10 years	Low
	Time remaining > 20 years	Medium
	Time remaining > 30 years	High
	(includes non-parolable life or death penalty cases)	
	Serious escape	Medium
	Disruptive group	High
	Prison disturbance	High
6–8	**No public safety factors**	**Low**
	Serious Escape	Medium
	Sentence Length	
	Time remaining > 20 years	Medium
	Time remaining > 30 years	High
	(includes non-parolable life or death penalty cases)	
	Disruptive group	High
	Prison disturbance	High
9–14	**No public safety factors**	**Medium**
	Disruptive group	High
	Prison disturbance	High
	Sentence length	
	Time remaining > 30 years	High
	(includes non-parolable life or death penalty cases)	
15+		**High**

Source: Federal Bureau of Prisons, *Security Designation and Custody Classification Manual* (Washington, DC: U.S. Department of Justice, 1999), Chapter 7, p. 7.

totals that determines the security assignment when there is no public safety factor. **Public safety factors,** such as being a member of a disruptive group (prison gang) or a sex offender, are special factors the BOP uses to override the standard security-level assignment and usually result in placement in a higher-security-level prison. With no public safety factor, as noted in Table 6–1, the following security point to-tals result in placement in the corresponding security level of federal prison:

Security Point Totals	Prison Security Level
0–5	Minimum
6–8	Low
9–14	Medium
15+	High

Since its adoption by the BOP, many states have developed their own objective classification systems to predict the need for specific levels of prison security for inmates. Adoption of objective classification systems requires a change in philosophy and a careful process of implementation. Because installing such a system has proved complicated, many states have sought the assistance and guidance of the **National Institute of Corrections (NIC).** NIC is an agency within the U.S. Department of Justice, and with only limited funding from Congress, it is a great resource for local and state correctional agencies in identifying and adopting emerging policies and procedures that can aid their operations. NIC provides small grants to these agencies to bring in experts who can help design and implement new approaches that meet the needs of the local agency. The accompanying case study presents a good example of how a state received assistance from NIC to move from a subjective to an objective classification system.

PRACTICAL PERSPECTIVES

Creating an Objective Classification System

In the early 1980s, a new director of corrections had been appointed to lead a fairly large state prison system, a system that was considered outdated in terms of modern professional correctional practices. The director was chosen from outside the state, partly because of his experience, but also because he had worked in other jurisdictions and had had the opportunity to witness the most current developments in correctional management and practices throughout the United States.

On arrival in the state and beginning his new job as director, he began to identify the areas that needed upgrading and change. In terms of classification, the state still used a model of inmate classification and assignment to institutions from the 1950s. The state had approximately 10 prisons: one maximum security prison, one female institution, one for youthful offenders, and the rest medium security with small minimum security satellite prisons. While offenders were still in reception status, a central office classification committee reviewed the cases and assigned them to one of the prisons. The most serious offenders were sent to maximum security, females were sent to the female prison, those under 25 were sent to the youthful offender prison, and everyone else was distributed to whichever prison had bed space available.

Continued

After arrival at the designated prison, an inmate would meet with the "classification committee," which was composed of the assistant warden of treatment, the chief psychologist, and the head of social services. Their job was to discuss the needs and problems of the inmate and to create a treatment plan for the inmate. The committee would meet regularly to review the inmate's progress to determine whether new programs were needed or whether the inmate could be reassigned to the satellite minimum security facility (or, in the case of a maximum security prison, to a medium security prison). There was very little movement between facilities, because each prison was very much the same in terms of security and programs, and females and youths, of course, stayed at their respective assigned prisons. All decisions were subjective and reflected the culmination of expertise of the committee members, who knew best how to handle offenders.

The new director was aware of the expanding use of objective classification systems, and the benefits that could result. Not only could inmates be better separated by risk of escape and risk of violence but also they could be moved up or down in security as time went on and as their behavior and length of sentence served would warrant a move down (or up) in security level. Inmates would be aware of the factors in this decision, and the system would seem fairer and more consistent to them. Staff and other resources could be appropriately assigned to institutions based on the types of inmates the facility housed. And with a statewide problem of prison overcrowding, objective classification based on risk factors could maximize the efficient use of bed space.

Another interesting benefit of an objective classification system was the ability to explain inmates' assignments to certain prisons. The director found that he was getting requests from advocates of certain inmates to consider moving them from one prison to another, often for ease of visitation with their families. Although it was easy to explain that there were different security levels of prisons, it was difficult to explain the factors that go into deciding the security level of an inmate or when an inmate would be considered eligible for a security reduction. In an objective classification system, inmates and their families knew why they were placed at one institution, what an inmate could do to earn a security reduction (such as good behavior), and at what point in the sentence risk factors were reduced.

The director asked the National Institute of Corrections to support the review of an objective classification system to determine whether it would be good to implement such a system in the state. If the decision were made to implement, NIC would then fund two national experts to come to the state and guide the staff in its implementation. NIC funded state staff to travel to another similar state that had an objective classification system. Visiting staff liked the approach, and on return to their home state, recommended implementation of such a system. Two national experts (Dr. Robert Levinson, who had developed the system for the BOP, and Dr. Allen Ault, a national expert on inmate man-

Continued

agement and previously the director of corrections in three different states) were recruited to help the state implement an objective classification system.

The first step was to conduct a research study of the state's inmates to identify factors (similar to those noted in the BOP system previously discussed) that were predictive of risk of violence and risk of escape. This resulted in many of the same factors being used. Staff were trained on how to use the classification system and how to rate the predictive factors. Inmates were given written notice of how the system would work and how their behavior contributed to their institutional assignments. Rating forms were printed and distributed throughout the institutions. Institutions were realigned in security levels from minimum, medium, and maximum to a four-level system of minimum, medium, close, and maximum security. This four-level system better facilitated separation of inmates by risk and efficient use of bed space.

The new system was implemented and used successfully for more than 10 years. After that time, another review of the factors was completed, adjustments were made, and the system continues today, almost 20 years later. It was determined to be more fair by staff and inmates; it allowed for better utilization of bed space; institutions were realigned by security level, and staff and resources were assigned based on security needs; and it provided much better background checking, data gathering, and follow-up on success than the previous subjective system. Overall, the implementation was deemed a success and an important management advancement by the state.

Risk Assessment in Parole Decision Making

Parole was coming under attack in the 1970s and 1980s, and there was a public outcry for reform and reduction of the seemingly total discretion of parole boards. As a result, 14 states and the federal government abolished parole as a release mechanism, opting instead for a determinate sentence structure. Other states, to counter the arguments against using discretionary decision making, began to use formal risk prediction instruments, or **parole guidelines,** to help structure and make consistent parole decisions. Parole guidelines are predictive devices to identify the potential for recidivism based on the offender's criminal background.

Similar to objective classification instruments, parole guidelines have certain "salient" factors, which are predictive of success or failure after release. These factors are weighted and then added together to create a "seriousness score" for each offender. The higher the score of the offender, the greater the likelihood of reoffense, and the less the likelihood they will be paroled early in their sentence. The use of these objective instruments has been shown to be accurate in predicting the range of risks for reoffending by inmates released on parole.[19] The use of parole guidelines has become extremely popular; one-half of the United States now use a formal risk assessment instrument for the parole decision process.[20]

Missouri is one state that uses parole guidelines. The state parole board created the guidelines in order to "establish a uniform parole policy, promote consistent

■ **TABLE 6–2**

Missouri Board of Probation and Parole Salient Factor Scoring

Salient Factor	Assigned Score
1. Conviction and Confinement Measures	

A.   No prior convictions = 2
          One prior conviction = 1
          Two or more prior convictions = 0
	_____

B.   No prior incarcerations = 2
          One prior incarceration = 1
          Two or more prior incarcerations = 0
	_____

C. Total prior incarceration time does not exceed five years = 1 Prior incarceration time exceeds five years = 0	_____
2. Stability Measures	

A.   Age at first commitment
          18 or older = 1
          17 or younger = 0
	_____

B. No history of alcohol or drug abuse = 1 Alcohol or drug abuse history = 0	_____
C. Five years conviction free prior to present offense = 1 Conviction within previous five years = 0	_____
3. Performance and Behavior Measures	
A. Has never had parole, probation, or conditional release revoked = 1 Has had parole, probation, or conditional release revoked = 0	_____
B. Has never escaped or attempted to escape = 1 Has escaped or attempted to escape = 0	_____
C. Has no prior conviction for burglary = 1 Has had prior conviction for burglary = 0	_____
Total Score	_____

Source: Board of Probation and Parole, Department of Corrections, *Rules and Regulations Governing the Granting of Paroles, Conditional Releases and Related Procedures* (Jefferson City, MO: State of Missouri, 1992), pp. 21–23.

exercise of discretion and equitable decision making, without removing individual case consideration."[21] The Missouri procedures include the calculation of a **salient factor score,** which combines offense seriousness, offender characteristics, and sentence length to assign a risk of reoffending to each offender. Table 6–2 illustrates the salient factor scoring sheet.

In Missouri, felonies are classified by severity from A (most severe) to D (least severe). The crimes carry an increasing penalty of prison sentences; C and D crimes are punished by a sentence of seven years or less in prison, and A and B crimes are punishable by five years or more in prison. After determination of the salient factor scores for inmates, the parole board uses Table 6–3 as a guideline as to when inmates should be paroled. The time guideline correlates the salient factor score with the seriousness of offense and sentence length. For instance, in Table 6–3, a Missouri in-

▬ **TABLE 6–3**

Time to Be Served Under the Missouri Guidelines for Parole

Offense	Sentence	11–9	8–6	5–3	2–0
		Excellent	Good	Fair	Poor
		Salient Factor Score (time ranges shown in months)			
Classes C and D	2	4	5–6	8–10	10–16
	3	5–7	8–9	12–15	15–24
	4	7–9	10–12	20–24	24–32
	5	9–11	12–15	25–30	30–40
	6	11–13	14–18	30–36	36–38
	7	13–15	17–21	35–42	42–56
Classes A and B	5	20–25	25–30	30–35	35–40
	6	24–30	30–36	36–42	42–48
	7	28–35	35–42	42–49	49–56
	8	32–40	40–48	48–56	56–64
	9	36–45	45–54	54–63	63–72
	10	40–50	50–60	60–70	70–84
	11	44–55	55–66	66–77	77–96
	12	48–60	60–72	72–84	84–108
	13	52–64	64–76	76–88	88–120
	14	56–68	68–80	80–92	92–132
	15	60–72	72–84	84–96	96–144
	16	64–76	76–88	88–100	100–132
	17	68–80	80–92	92–104	104–144
	18	72–84	84–96	96–108	108–156
	19	76–88	88–100	100–112	112–168
	20	80–92	92–104	104–116	116–180
	21	84–96	96–108	108–120	120–192
	22	88–100	100–112	112–124	124–204
	23	92–104	104–116	116–128	128–216
	24	96–108	108–120	120–132	132–228
	25	100–112	112–124	124–136	136–240
	26	104–116	116–128	128–140	140–252
	27	108–120	120–132	132–144	144–264
	28	112–124	124–136	136–148	148–276
	29	116–128	128–140	140–152	152–288
	30	120–132	132–144	144–156	156–300

Source: Board of Probation and Parole, Department of Corrections, *Rules and Regulations Governing the Granting of Paroles, Conditional Releases and Related Procedures* (Jefferson City, MO: State of Missouri, 1992), pp. 20–21.

mate committing a Class A or B felony, serving a 10-year sentence, with a salient factor score of 7, would be normally considered for parole after serving between 50 and 60 months in prison. These guideline times assume the inmate has good institutional adjustment and program progress. Mitigating and aggravating circumstances surrounding the offense may warrant the parole board making a decision outside the guideline time frame, and the board will state their reasons for going outside the guidelines in the notice of decision to the inmate.

As can be seen from this Missouri example, parole guidelines combine risk of reoffending and chance for successful rehabilitation to identify a uniform time in which inmates will usually be considered for release. These guidelines make clear to inmates what they can expect if they maintain good institutional adjustment and actively participate in rehabilitative programs. Also, the public is aware that parole guidelines take into account, first and foremost, the risk to the community. Those offenders who indicate the highest risk (those with the lowest salient factor scores) will serve significantly more time in prison before release than offenders who have committed the same offense but present less risk for committing further crimes.

Risk Assessment in Community Supervision

Another development in the use of predictive instruments assisted in classifying offenders under probation and parole supervision. It made sense that if factors could be identified to predict the risk of reoffending and were being used for prison classification and parole release decisions, they could also be useful for supervising offenders in the community. The use of such instruments became popular during the 1980s,[22] although risk assessment for case management of community supervision was originally developed in Wisconsin in 1975. The Wisconsin Client Management Classification (CMC) system helped to identify the required level of surveillance for each offender and also determined the specific needs of the offender and the resources that would be needed by the offender. The NIC then suggested the Wisconsin system as a model, and it was adopted in many jurisdictions throughout the United States.

Parole and probation classification systems work similar to the classification systems previously described. The factors that are identified as most predictive of success while under supervision are scored. Figures 6–2 and 6–3 illustrate of the current Missouri model used to determine levels of community supervision. When a parole or probation officer is first assigned a case, the officer completes the Client Analysis Scale-Risk for the offender (Figure 6–2). Each case is scored on the number of prior convictions, employment status, age, present offense, and whether the present offense is a Class A felony. The total of these scores becomes the permanent risk score and is used to determine the classified level of risk and intensity of supervision. After the initial classification of risk, each offender is rescored on the Monthly Supervision Report (Figure 6–3) to determine needs for additional programs or supervision. If the offender has a risk score of 10 or more and a need score of 11 or more, the offender is automatically screened to participate in intensive supervision or another special supervision caseload. Not only can the use of risk assessment be useful in the supervision process but it can also aid judges and parole boards who must decide whether an offender has performed at a level of success during the period of supervision to warrant release from supervision and a formal end to the parole or probation status.

Risk Assessment in Sentencing

The final development in the use of risk assessment concerns sentencing guidelines. **Sentencing guidelines** are procedures designed to structure sentencing decisions based on measures of offense severity and criminal history. Minnesota was one of

STATE OF MISSOURI
DEPARTMENT OF CORRECTIONS
CLIENT ANALYSIS SCALE-RISK

OFFICER CODE

NAME	NUMBER	DATE

PRIOR CONVICTIONS (ADULT-FELONY, MISDEMEANOR, CRIMINAL ORDINANCE INCLUDING SIS)

☐ 1	☐ 2	☐ 3
NONE	1 OR 2 PRIORS	3 OR MORE

EMPL0YMENT/VACATION

☐ 0	☐ 1	☐ 0
FULL TIME WORK	PART TIME WORK	UNEMPLOYED

AGE (AT ASSIGNMENT)

☐ 0	☐ 1	☐ 2
30 YEARS OR OVER	22 TO 29 YEARS	21 YEARS OR YOUNGER

PRESENT OFFENSE (CHARGE FOR WHICH CONVICTED) (ROBBERY, BURGLARY, STEALING, FORGERY, SEXUAL ASSAULT AS PER RSMO 589 015)

☐ 0	☐ 2
NO	YES

PRESENT OFFENSE A FELONY (OFFICIAL CHARGE)

☐ 1	☐ 2
NO	YES

RISK SCORE

FIGURE 6–2
Missouri client analysis scale-risk for probationers and parolees. Source:
Missouri Department of Corrections, (Jefferson City, MO: State of Missouri, 1991).

STATE OF MISSOURI
DEPARTMENT OF CORRECTIONS
BOARD OF PROBATION AND PAROLE
MONTHLY SUPERVISION REPORT

OFFICE USE ONLY
☐ INITIAL SCALE
☐ ENTER

OFFICER NAME AND NUMBER

SUPERVISION NUMBER

NAME

PHONE NUMBER

ADDRESS   (CITY)   (STATE)   (ZIP CODE)

WITH WHOM DO YOU LIVE? (NAME AND RELATIONSHIP)

YOUR SOCIAL SECURITY NUMBER

NAME OF PRESENT EMPLOYER, ADDRESS, CITY, ZIP CODE

EMPLOYER'S PHONE NUMBER

NAME OF SUPERVISOR   IS EMPLOYER AWARE OF PROBATION/PAROLE? ☐ YES ☐ NO

TOTAL INCOME FOR PAST 30 DAYS

DO YOU OWN A VEHICLE? ☐ YES ☐ NO   MODEL   YEAR   MAKE

DESCRIPTION/COLOR   LICENSE NUMBER

HAVE YOU BEEN ARRESTED DURING PAST 30 DAYS? ☐ YES ☐ NO   IF YES, DATE OF ARREST _____

ARRESTING DEPARTMENT   CHARGE

SIGNATURE   ACCEPTED BY   DATE   TIME   ☐ A.M.   ☐ P.M.

DO NOT WRITE BELOW THIS LINE

_____ **EMPLOYMENT/EDUCATIONAL VOCATIONAL**
0 - FULL-TIME FOR PAST 3 MONTHS
1 - PART-TIME; SCHOOL; TRAINING; FULL-TIME LESS
    THAN 3 MONTHS; UNEMPLOYMENT COMPENSATION
2 - UNEMPLOYED
    DATE EMPLOYED _____

_____ **LEGAL (EXCLUDES PRESENT OFFENSE)**
1 - NO ARRESTS IN THE PAST 3 MONTHS
2 - NO CONVICTIONS, 1 ARREST IN PAST 3 MONTHS
3 - 2 OR MORE ARRESTS, PENDING CHARGE, OR
    CONVICTION IN PAST 3 MONTHS
    DATE OF ARREST/CONVICTION _____

_____ **TECHNICAL VIOLATIONS**
1 - NO TECHNICAL VIOLATION REPORT IN PAST 6 MONTHS
2 - TECHNICAL VIOLATION REPORT IN PAST 6 MONTHS
3 - TECHNICAL VIOLATION IN PAST 3 MONTHS OR
    PENDING REVOCATION
    DATE OF LAST TECHNICAL VLTN. RPT. _____
    CONDITIONS CITED _____

_____ **SUBSTANCE ABUSE**
1 - NO DRUG USE/ALCOHOL ABUSE WITHIN 6 MONTHS
2 - DRUG USE/ALCOHOL ABUSE IN PAST 4-6 MONTHS
3 - DRUG USE/ALCOHOL ABUSE IN PAST 3 MONTHS
    DATE OF LAST USE/PROBLEM _____

PROBLEM CODES: 1=NO PROBLEM   2=IDENTIFIED HISTORY
3= PROBLEM PAST 4-6 MOS   4= PROBLEM PAST 3 MOS

_____ **SOCIAL**
0 - NO PROBLEM
1 - PROBLEM NOT REQUIRING INTERVENTION
2 - PROBLEM REQUIRING INTERVENTION
    DATE OF LAST OCCURENCE _____

_____ **SUBSTANCE ABUSE**   _____ # UA'S   _____ # POSITIVE
_____ ALCOHOL
_____ MARIJ/HASHISH   _____ STIM/COCAINE   _____ INHALENTS/SOLVENTS
_____ OPIATES   _____ DEPRESSANTS   _____ HALLUCINOGENS
SOCIAL
_____ MENTAL PROBLEMS   _____ FINANCIAL   _____ PHYSICAL
_____ FAMILY PROBLEMS   _____ ASSAULT/AGGRESSIVE   _____ REPORTING

RISK SCORE _____   NEED SCORE _____   _____

ISP/EMP/RF SCREEN FOR REPLACEMENT IF RISK
IS 10 OR NEED IS 11 OR MORE

SCORE OVER-RIDES (If scored minimum; check only most serious one)

LEVEL OF SUPERVISION

SPECIAL CONDITIONS

_____ SEXUAL OFFENDER   _____ FINANCIAL   _____ COMMUNITY SERVICE

MONTHLY ACTIVITIES

FIGURE 6–3
Missouri probation and parole monthly supervision report. Source: Board of Probation and Parole, Department of Corrections, (Jefferson City, MO: State of Missouri, 1991).

Severity levels of conviction offense		Criminal History Score						
		0	**1**	**2**	**3**	**4**	**5**	**6** or more
• Unauthorized use of motor vehicle • Possession of marijuana	I	12	12	12	15	18	21	24 *23-25*
• Theft-related crimes ($150–$2,500) • Sale of marijuana	II	12	12	14	17	20	23	27 *25-29*
• Theft crimes ($150–$2,500)	III	12	13	16	19	22 *21-23*	27 *25-29*	32 *30-34*
• Burglary-felony intent • Receiving stolen goods ($150–$2,500)	IV	12	15	18	21	25 *24-26*	32 *30-34*	41 *37-45*
• Simple robbery	V	18	23	27	30 *29-31*	38 *36-40*	46 *43-49*	54 *50-58*
• Assault, 2nd degree	VI	21	26	30	34 *33-35*	44 *42-46*	54 *50-58*	65 *60-70*
• Aggravated robbery	VII	24 *23-25*	32 *30-34*	41 *38-44*	49 *45-53*	65 *60-70*	81 *75-87*	97 *90-104*
• Assault, 1st degree • Criminal sexual conduct, 1st degree	VIII	43 *41-45*	54 *50-58*	65 *60-70*	76 *71-81*	95 *89-101*	113 *106-120*	132 *124-140*
• Murder, 3rd degree	IX	97 *94-100*	119 *116-122*	127 *124-130*	149 *143-155*	176 *168-184*	205 *195-215*	230 *218-242*
• Murder, 2nd degree	X	116 *111-121*	140 *133-147*	162 *153-171*	203 *192-214*	243 *231-255*	284 *270-298*	324 *309-339*

Italicized numbers within the lighter boxes denote the range within which a judge may sentence without the sentence being deemed a departure. First-degree murder is excluded from the guidelines by law and is punished by life imprisonment.

FIGURE 6–4
Minnesota sentencing guidelines grid. Source: Minnesota Sentencing Guidelines Commission, *Report to the Legislature,* (St. Paul, MN: Minnesota Sentencing Guidelines Commission, 1983), p. 14.

the first states to implement a sentencing guidelines process in the early 1980s. Figure 6–4 illustrates the Minnesota sentencing guideline grid used at that time. There are several reasons that states adopt sentencing guidelines. First, because of a get-tough attitude by the public and state legislatures, it was believed that judges might not be harsh enough on certain criminals. Sentencing guidelines take away much of the discretion of judicial sentencing. Second, sentencing guidelines create consistency within a jurisdiction, ensuring that offenders who commit similar crimes receive similar sentences. And finally, sentencing guidelines provide planners (using projections of crime rates) a better estimate of the number of inmates in prison or offenders under probation supervision in the future.

Guidelines are adopted by the state legislature and passed on to the courts. There is usually some limited discretion allowed to sentencing judges, but they often must include their reasons for varying from the guidelines if warranted. The guidelines provide a narrow range of sentences for each type of offense, increasing the sentence with the severity. Many, such as the Minnesota model, also include a prediction of risk for the offender to be factored into the sentencing decision. Factors, such as the number of prior convictions, history of incarceration, absconding from community supervision or escape from prison, history of violent offenses, or age at first arrest, are often included as risk predictors. Once the score for these items is developed using information from the presentence investigation, the offender is assigned a severity score. As in the Minnesota model, the higher the score across the top of the grid, the more serious risk the offender. Down the side of the grid is the list of offenses rated in increasing severity. By finding the intersecting block of the offense and the offender's severity score, the judge has a guideline to use for sentencing.

As noted previously, risk assessment has become an important part of the criminal justice system and particularly the correction system. Many correctional agencies use risk assessment in some capacity, substituting actuarial tables for professional judgments. It is possible that correctional agencies have gone too far in this regard, and that the loss of discretion and the judgment of experts makes the system too insensitive to individual situations, disallowing innovation in sentencing and handling of offenders. While it is arguable that subjective decision making was not proven to be successful, and actuarial risk assessment may be a notable improvement, there is room for both predictive instruments and professional judgments in correctional administration. Those agencies that acknowledge this, and create procedures that encourage and allow for both, have the best of both worlds. Predictive instruments can provide information and be guidelines useful to knowledgeable professionals in the formulation of their judgments and decisions.

THE CLASSIFICATION PROCESS

After a jurisdiction has adopted a classification system (whether a more modern actuarial based system or a clinical system), a process and statement of procedures is established for its use. For inmates, this process includes reception and initial classification, reclassification or interim classification, and prerelease classification. For community-supervised offenders, it includes an initial assessment and assignment of risk level, regular reviews and modifications, and review for termination from supervision. For both inmates and community offenders, classification is considered a continuous process of reviewing current behavior and adjusting the need for security and supervision. The next sections describe the process for classifying prisoners as well as community offenders.

Classification of Prison Inmates

When an offender is sentenced to prison, one of the first activities of the correctional system is the **initial classification** to determine to which prison the offender will be assigned. Most states have prison reception centers, where all inmates are initially placed until their security and program needs are determined. Shortly after they are sentenced, offenders are transferred to the state reception center for processing. During this time, they may take psychological, educational, or vocational tests; their records are reviewed, and any previously unknown information is collected. The reception process can take from 60 to 90 days. However, because of overcrowding at the prison where the inmate will be assigned, an inmate may have to wait in reception until space is available, even after completing the classification process.

Some states and the Federal Bureau of Prisons do these assessments right after sentencing, while the offender is in jail or on bond pending the beginning of a sentence. On sentencing, the correctional agency is formally notified and given a copy of the sentence order, and it begins the classification process. The sentencing court is then notified (usually within a matter of days) of the prison assignment, and the court makes arrangements for the inmate to be transferred to the prison by jail staff, or (if they pose a very low security risk and are on bond) an offender may be allowed to report independently to the assigned prison on the date the sentence is to begin. In both situations, the presentence investigation (PSI) is the key document for determining risk and program needs. If there is information required that is not in the PSI, correctional staff may need to conduct interviews with the offender at the reception center or the local jail. On occasion, correctional staff will have to collect some information themselves, either because there is no PSI or because it does not have all the elements required by the correctional agency. When a PSI is not available, a **postsentence investigation** is completed, which then becomes the basis for the initial classification process.

Correctional staff use their existing clarification grids to rate the offender as to security level. As noted in Figure 6–1, much of this information is based on past criminal conduct, length of sentence, and history of violence. Points are totaled, and the offender is assigned to the corresponding security level. For instance, using the classification instrument in Figure 6–1, if an inmate has a total of 9 to 14 points, he or she will be assigned to a medium security prison. Assignment to a prison is primarily for security purposes, to match an offender's risk for violence and escape with physical security, and to supervise and control the offender. However, program needs, mental health, and medical condition are also considered in the initial placement. Once assigned, the inmate is transferred to the designated prison and remains there until a reassignment is warranted.

As noted previously, the purpose of a classification system includes coordinating offenders with institutions that have the physical security and staff complement to prevent escapes and control inmates' behavior. Objective classification systems are useful to prevent overclassification, which results in assigning an expensive, higher-security bed space when a less expensive, lower-security assignment will meet the need. For correctional agencies that have multiple institutions at varying security levels (and, therefore, varying costs of operation), there is an effort to continuously

Razor Ribbon. The top of a security fence is covered by a tightly woven fabric to prevent escape. Inmate classification is important to match the inmate's potential for escape with the physical security of the prison assigned. (Courtesy of the King County (Washington) Department of Corrections)

review inmates' progress and move them to a different security level when their needs warrant a change. Therefore, a **reclassification** review is scheduled at regular intervals (often three or six months) to modify the original classification and possibly reassign the inmate to a different prison. Reclassification has three basic purposes: (1) to consider changes in program needs, mental health, or medical condition; (2) as an incentive for good behavior by dropping the security level of inmates who conform and follow prison rules; and (3) to identify the need to increase inmates security level because of misconduct and resultant disciplinary action.

At the regular reclassification review, staff and the inmate interact, reviewing the progress toward intended program goals in preparation for release. These goals can include educational participation, substance abuse programming, or psychological counseling. Because various prisons have different program offerings, an inmate may need to be transferred to a prison whose programs better match the inmate's needs. There is also a review of mental health and medical status. Any change in these conditions could warrant a transfer to another prison better equipped to deal with the inmate's condition. Between regular reviews, if an inmate's mental health or medical condition suddenly and unexpectedly changes, there will be an immediate consideration of the need to transfer to another prison.

The reclassification is also an incentive for good behavior. At the reclassification review, an inmate's behavior and the percentage of the sentence served is combined into the classification score system. If behavior is good, and as the inmate reaches certain stages in the sentence (so many months served or a certain percentage of the sentence completed), it may result in a lowering of the security score and resultant prison assignment. Because most prison systems want to use their highest security bed space in the most efficient manner, it is cost effective to move an inmate who warrants a lower classification to a less secure (and less costly) prison. Inmates become well aware of the scoring system and know what will make them eligible for reassignment to a lower-security prison. Less security generally increases an inmate's privileges and results in a less stressful and less dangerous environment. Therefore, inmates strive to reach these levels and to be considered for a reduced security level.

Reclassification can also be initiated by serious inmate misconduct, illustrating that the inmate cannot be controlled in the current security level and must be placed at a higher level (such as moving from medium to maximum security). When an inmate commits a serious disciplinary infraction or continues to commit minor infractions, the inmate receives extra points on the security instrument, which may warrant an upgrade to a higher-security-level prison. With increased security come fewer privileges, more control, less freedom of movement, often fewer program opportunities, and housing with other inmates who have shown a propensity for misconduct.

Although it is often dealt with informally rather than as a discrete stage in the classification process, **prerelease classification** is usually conducted within the last year of an inmate's incarceration, and it can serve three functions. First, as staff begin to prepare the inmate for transition to the community, they may reexamine program needs and create a continuum of suggested services that can be found in the community. Inmates will be monitored by a parole or other postrelease supervision officer after release from prison. Many institutions conduct a specific prerelease program to educate inmates on services available to them on release and the requirements of any mandatory supervision.

The second function of prerelease classification is to use some of the same criteria used in the security classification process for the parole or other type of discretionary release decision. Parole boards often use actuarial guidelines to assist in their decision making, and parole staff may review this material and prepare guideline recommendations prior to the formal parole board deliberation. Third, a prerelease classification may be used to determine whether the inmate is in need of a residential transition from the prison to the community.

Every state and the Federal Prison System uses halfway houses to transition some inmates to the community. Prison staff often weigh the need for assistance against the risk to the community. Not all inmates have a need for a placement in a halfway house, but those with no definite place to live and few financial resources are usually considered candidates for halfway houses. Even if inmates have little need, if there is a high likelihood to recidivate, they may also be placed in halfway houses to maximize the level of supervision and restrictions on the offender's movements. Prison officials, during the prerelease classification process, weight the combination of needs and risk to determine whether and for how long inmates will receive a halfway house placement. For most jurisdictions, halfway house placements last from 60 to 180 days.

Classification of Offenders in the Community

As described previously, classification and risk assessments are also used to match offenders under parole or probation to the level of supervision that they require. Similar to institutional classifications systems, community classification identifies offender risks and matches appropriate supervision in order to maximize the distribution of resources and to focus on public safety. In the mid-1970s, models of risk assessment were being developed for probation supervision. In an early review of such methods, the U.S. Comptroller General tested the predictive power of risk-prediction models, and concluded that

> probation prediction models could improve probation systems operations by allocating resources to offenders who most need help. . . . Model sources appeared to be useful in determining supervision levels and more successfully selected probationers for early release.[23]

Although it expressed some of the problems inherent in the use of such models, a National Institute of Corrections report entitled *Directions for Community Corrections in the 1990s* noted, "In general, one effective way to increase decision reliability is to make visible the criteria for decisions. For that reason, we advocate the use of statistically based devises to classify offenders according to relative risk."[24]

Offenders receiving probation or released from prison on parole, if under the supervision of an agency using statistical risk assessment, are scored based on their offense background and personal characteristics. Again, similar to institutional classification, community classification can be described as initial, reclassification, and prerelease classification. At the initial classification, once scored for risk, offenders are assigned a supervision level. Usually, the higher the risk score the greater the level of supervision. The highest level is called **intensive supervision.** Intensive supervision offenders are classified as posing a significant risk of committing a new offense and are assigned to a small caseload (usually about 25). They must report at least once a week to the supervising officer, and they are visited two to three times per month at home or at work. There may also be additional random contacts as the officer believes necessary.

Those offenders not posing as serious or immediate a risk to the public, yet who require substantial to moderate levels of supervision and have significant problems needing assistance, are assigned to **regular supervision.** Under regular supervision, officers supervise approximately 50 offenders. Officers serve the dual function of monitoring behavior and assisting offenders through substance abuse programs or employment counseling. Most jurisdictions also have specialized caseloads, whereby an officer's entire caseload is made up of offenders with a particular type of problem, such as substance abuse or a history of sex offenses. Such specialization allows the officer to become knowledgeable and proficient in dealing with this particular problem.

Finally, offenders who pose little risk to the community may be placed on **minimum supervision,** with caseloads as high as 300 offenders. These offenders often have contact only every few months and are basically responsible themselves for following the conditions of their supervision. These offenders have few needs and are likely to have committed white-collar crimes. They are aware that their community supervision can be revoked and that they can be sent to prison. That threat is enough of a deterrent for them to follow supervision conditions and avoid further criminal acts. Some jurisdictions also have a category called **administrative supervision.** Offenders under administrative supervision have no contact with a parole or probation officer. However, they are still under conditional release, and if they commit another crime, their original parole or probation will be revoked. Administrative supervision is not likely to be used on initial classification. However, after low-risk offenders demonstrate a good adjustment to supervision, this status may be assigned.

Just as in the prison classification scheme, after an initial classification, there are regular reviews of status, and a reclassification, in which the risk factors are rescored based on behavior and time spent under supervision. The purpose of reclassification is to ensure proper matching of resources and placement of offenders at a supervision level. As supervision time goes on without a violation, it becomes evident that an offender is at a reduced risk, and a lower level of supervision is usually warranted sufficient to monitor behavior and meet offender needs.

Finally, risk prediction can be useful for consideration of early termination from supervision, a form of prerelease classification. Almost every jurisdiction provides offenders the opportunity to be released from community supervision before the maximum period, if their behavior has been good and they have met all of the special conditions of their supervision. Although there are usually no formal criteria for an early release from probation or parole supervision, risk assessments provide guidance regarding the likelihood of the offender reoffending. Offenders with high scores usually continue under supervision, whereas those with low risk scores may receive an early termination.

ISSUES IN RISK ASSESSMENT AND CLASSIFICATION

There are many issues that result from the use of risk assessment and objective classification systems. Some of these issues are being addressed and improved. However, many others continue as potential problems. The problematic issues include the use of classification in jails; the impact of longer sentences on early objective classification systems; the influence of race, gender, and age on offender classification; the effect of prison overcrowding on classification; and the lack of resources devoted to classification and risk assessment.

Jail Classification Systems

Although prison systems have historically used some type of classification, the use of classification in jails is relatively recent. Even now, many jails still only classify (in reality, separate) males from females, adults from juveniles, and sentenced from non-sentenced prisoners. There are very few jails that use more sophisticated systems to separate inmates by risk or dangerousness. However, over the past decade, the National Institute of Corrections has been assisting jails to implement objective classification systems.[25] To date, however, it is usually only the largest jails that have implemented such systems.

There are several problems and operational restraints that confront the implementation of classification systems in jails. First, jails hold a very diverse population, such as offenders in every pretrial stage, offenders serving short sentences, offenders being held or detained for another jurisdiction, and those sentenced and awaiting transfer to a prison system. Second, jails have limited information regarding offenders on which to base classification decisions. Jails receive offenders immediately after arrest, and the only verified information available is the crime for which they are charged. Jail staff conduct interviews with offenders to collect self-reported information, such as medical histories, suicide potential, and the need for separation from other inmates in the jail. And, because most jail inmates are released within 72 hours of confinement, there is little time to collect any official criminal history. Third, jails (in comparison to prisons) have an extremely large number of admissions, and without a large staff, it would be overwhelming to attempt to do as thorough a classification as is done in prisons.

In addition to these operational constraints, Brennan suggests that jail classification has "suffered from benign neglect. Unlike prison administrators, jail administrators traditionally have not accorded classification a central role in management."[26] It is not unusual for jail inmates, who have little criminal history and have been arrested for minor crimes, to be assaulted by other inmates who have lengthy and violent criminal histories. In these cases, it is now common for assaulted inmates to sue the jail for failure to separate and protect them from higher-risk inmates. The increasing number of legal challenges from jail inmates for failure to protect them from more dangerous offenders is forcing additional jails to implement some form of basic classification system.

Changing Sentence Structures and Classification

Over the past two decades, the United States has been experiencing a more punitive approach to sentencing. As a result, there have been several changes in sentences, including the implementation of mandatory minimum sentences, the lengthening of sentences, three strikes legislation, and truth-in-sentencing laws. **Mandatory minimum sentences** limit judicial discretion and require a set minimum sentence in prison for certain crimes. **Three strikes legislation** is similar to prior "habitual offender" statutes, requiring that offenders who are convicted of three felonies (in some jurisdictions, violent felonies) serve a long sentence, usually life without parole. Finally, **truth-in-sentencing** laws are a federal initiative passed in the 1994 Federal Omnibus Crime Bill to reward states that move to determinant sentences and require offenders to serve 85 percent of their sentences prior to release. The initiative started as a result of prosecutors and other public officials complaining of parole of inmates well before their mandatory maximum sentence. If a criminal received a sentence range of 3 to 10 years, the officials believed that the public expected the offender would serve close to 10 years. As a reward for implementing the truth-in-sentencing, the federal government gives states financial grants to build new prisons in order to house the increases in the prison population as a result of the truth-in-sentencing laws.

The result of these changes in sentencing laws is that the makeup of the inmate population within a prison system changes, because a larger proportion of the inmate population is serving long sentences. With objective classification systems weighing heavily on the length of the sentence and time left to serve to predict risk, there is an upward movement in terms of the percentage of inmates requiring placement at medium- and high-security institutions. As these inmates serve longer sentences, they age and their propensity for violence is reduced, balancing out the importance of the length of sentence. As noted by Austin, "unless these and other states take steps to adjust their instruments and policies, inmates will be over classified and the types of facilities being constructed will not mirror the security needs of an older and less aggressive inmate population."[27] Austin suggests that states rework their classification systems to take these new factors into account or conduct an "administrative override" and reduce the level of security that results from changes in criminal statutes.

The Influence of Race, Gender, and Age on Classification

Race, gender, and age are three characteristics of offenders that are not considered by most objective classification systems. Yet all seem to have some definitive correlation and influence the classification process in some manner. Race, in itself, is not thought to be a predictor of criminal behavior or a predictor of risk to reoffend. However, almost one-half of all inmates in state and federal prisons as of January 1, 1999, are African American,[28] approximately four times the percentage of the general population of the United States.

Many factors (low economic status, lack of education, low availability of jobs, high concentration of drug use in low-economic status) are most often mentioned as the cause of high rates of crime among African American citizens. Although some studies have found little evidence to support systematic discrimination against African Americans,[29] the fact is that African Americans are arrested, prosecuted, convicted, and incarcerated in numbers far disproportionate to their percentage in the population. High crime rates and the fact that typical African American offenders have a more extensive history of crime and violence than white offenders cause African Americans to be more concentrated in high- than low-security prisons. Therefore, there is a high correlation between risk and race.[30] Even with an understanding of the apparent overclassification of security level for African American offenders, there have been no efforts to date to try to adjust for this factor.

Concerning gender, some jurisdictions are reexamining and making adjustments in their objective classification systems. In the late 1980s, the Federal Bureau of Prisons (BOP) reviewed their classification system and made adjustments based on gender. The BOP found that female inmates, when classified using the same instrument as male inmates, were being placed at a much higher level of physical security prisons than their risk to escape or tendency for violence warranted. To correct the problem, the BOP administratively reduced the number of points assigned for certain types of crimes (such as crimes of violence or use of a weapon during the offense). They found that, in most cases, women were accomplices with men, and the male offenders were the ones who actually handled the weapons or resorted to violence. In addition, the BOP realized that female inmates often had children and close ties in the community, factors important in predicting escape. By making adjustments, the BOP was able to move a high percentage of their female inmate population to less secure, and less expensive to build and operate, prisons.

Finally, age is another factor that is correlated with risk of escape and violence, and risk to reoffend, and results in youthful offenders being placed in high-security prisons.[31] As noted earlier, as sentence lengths increase, the average age of prisoners also increases. The implementation of mandatory minimum sentences and the

Women Inmates Work Outside the Prison on a Community Work Project. Women inmates usually require a less secure prison than comparable male offenders. Classification instruments are often adjusted to place women offenders in minimum or low-security prisons, which are less expensive to build and operate. (Courtesy of the Maricopa County (Arizona) Sheriff's Department)

use of sentencing guidelines also require judges to sentence elderly criminals to prison without considering their age. Therefore, there is an aging population in prison, which result in some prisons resembling nursing homes more than correctional institutions. In the largest maximum security prison in the United States, the Louisiana State Prison in Angola, it is estimated that more than 80 percent of the prisoners will die before they are released. About one-half of the inmates are serving life sentences and not eligible for parole, and another one-third of the prisoners have such long sentences that they are not likely to survive.[32]

Most states now have prisons for older inmates and, to a point, ignore the objective risk assessments, using instead common sense to determine who should be assigned to them. It makes no sense to place feeble and elderly inmates in a high-security prison, with the latest technology and secure fences around the perimeter. Most of these inmates do not have the physical capabilities to climb a fence or run away from staff while trying to escape. Age is also negatively correlated with recidivism: The older an offender is at release, the lower the rate of recidivism. Therefore, risk assessments to determine community supervision levels also must be adjusted to take age into account in determining intensity of supervision.

Prison Overcrowding and Classification

One obstacle in the use of risk assessments and objective classification is the ability to maintain effective classification systems in times of severe prison overcrowding. Throughout correctional jurisdictions in the United States, the higher the security of the prison, the higher the degree of overcrowding. Many high-security inmates

Older Inmates in a Low-Security Prison. Older inmates, with less physical mobility, can often be placed in a lower-security prison than the risk assessment (based on history of crime) would suggest. (Courtesy of the Ohio Department of Rehabilitation and Correction)

get held over in a reception center until an appropriate security-level bed is available, "or they may be placed in any bed that's open. This can create security risks, not to mention a host of other problems throughout the system."[33]

There is no simple solution to this problem. Although reception centers are usually designed to house high-security inmates, they are not designed to house offenders for a long period of time, and the lack of programs and recreational opportunities can cause tension among an inmate population "held in limbo." Placing offenders in a lower-security prison than their classification warrants is an even greater risk, because without the physical security and staff ratio to supervise and control inmates, the probability of escape and violence greatly increases.

The most common solution to the lack of available high-security space is to resort to the old clinical model and make administrative "overrides" of the classification system. As noted previously, age and gender are related to risk. Classification teams may be asked to take these factors into account and identify inmates who they believe can be successfully placed in a less secure prison. The classification teams are sometimes directed to review circumstances around the use of a weapon during the offense or the manner in which violence was involved in the offense. Both of these factors drive up the security designation, yet, the circumstances in many cases, do not indicate a pattern of violence that warrants the high level of security resulting from the objective classification process. When an agency requests staff to review cases and make these judgments, the efforts usually do reduce security levels of inmates waiting assignment and temporarily relieve the problem of overcrowding by placing inmates in lower-security prisons that are not experiencing a crowding problem. If the overcrowding in higher-security prisons persists, some agencies allow for clinical judgments and administrative overrides to be built into the classification instrument on a permanent basis.

Resources Committed to Classification

The final issue regarding classification of offenders is the general lack of resources devoted to the process. No correctional agencies ever seem to have as many staff as they need to complete their mission in the manner the agency leadership would like. When having to make a decision on how to extend staff in times of increasing demand, so-called "staff" rather than "line" positions are reduced or not increased. Line positions include those persons who directly deliver services, such as probation or correctional officers. Staff positions include those people who complete administrative functions, such as those who complete the classification process or determine when the classification system needs revision or updating. As a result, shortcuts in the classification process often occur, and continuous tests of relevancy and predictive value of certain criteria are not performed. The lack of these activities can undermine the effectiveness of a classification system and relegate such a system to a paper process, rather than as a predictor of behavior to match correctional resources with offender risk. Again, there is no simple solution to a lack of resources. Correctional administrators must be cautious of the dangers in ignoring staff functions, particularly those associated with a failure to monitor and revise a classification system as necessary. These are dangers of overspending and overclassifying rather than dangers of undermining safety and security. However, they are the errors of omission that trained leaders must avoid.

SUMMARY

Prison classification has been recognized as important for more than 100 years. However, sophisticated risk assessments to predict risks to public safety have only of late been implemented in prisons and community supervision. These objective classification instruments can be extremely useful to correctional administrators, because they help increase the safety of staff and inmates and help appropriately assign scarce resources where they are most needed. Currently, most states do use objective classification for prisons, and a growing number are implementing such systems for community supervision.

However, as far advanced as these systems have become, and as recognized as their benefits are, there remain many issues and concerns that must be addressed. Objective classification systems and actuarial methods are only successful if they reflect the changing population and demographics of the offenders they are supposed to evaluate. Although many prisons use systems developed by the National Institute of Corrections (NIC) and other agencies, they must still train staff in system use, application, and underlying principles. As changes occur in sentencing laws, the makeup of the offender population, and offender characteristics, staff must make adjustments to keep the system current and functioning effectively. When the objective systems fail to meet agency needs, staff must resort to clinical and professional judgment to ensure that the system works efficiently and that offenders are placed under appropriate security and supervision levels.

ENDNOTES

1. Mary Dallao, "Keeping Classification Current," *Corrections Today* 59 no. 4 (July 1997): 86.
2. See R. M. Dawes, D. Faust, and P. E. Meehl, 1989, "Clinical Versus Actuarial Judgment," *Science* 243 (1989): 1668–1674. Also, C. E. Goggin, *Clinical Versus Actuarial Prediction: A Meta-Analysis,* unpublished manuscript (University of New Brunswick, Saint John, New Brunswick, 1994).
3. Camille Graham Camp and George M. Camp, *The Corrections Yearbook: 1998* (Middletown, CT, Criminal Justice Institute, Inc., 1998), pp. 18–19.
4. Joan Mullen, *American Prisons and Jails,* Volume I: Summary and Policy Implications of a National Survey (Washington DC: U.S. Department of Justice) 1980, p. 57.
5. David E. Duffee, *Corrections: Practice and Policy* (New York: Random House, 1989), p. 334.
6. James Austin and Luiza Chan, "Survey Report on Internal Offender Classification System" (San Francisco: National Council on Crime and Delinquency, April 1994).
7. Camp and Camp, p. 79.
8. The Committee on Classification and Case Work of the American Prison Association, *Handbook on Classification in Correctional Institutions* (New York: American Prison Association, 1947), p. iii.
9. The Committee, p. 1.
10. The Committee, p. 1.
11. Douglas Lipton, Robert Martinson, and Judith Wilks, *The Effectiveness of Correctional Treatment and What Works: A Survey of Treatment Evaluation Studies* (New York: Praeger, 1975).
12. David Fogel, *We Are the Living Proof* (Cincinnati, OH: Anderson, 1975).
13. Andrew von Hirsch, *Doing Justice: The Choice of Punishments* (New York: Hill and Wang, 1976).
14. James Q. Wilson, *Thinking About Crime* (New York: Basic Books, 1985).
15. Daniel Glaser, "Classification for Risk," in *Prediction and Classification: Criminal Justice Decision Making,* edited by Don M. Gottfredson and Michael Tonry (Chicago: University of Chicago Press, 1987), pp. 266–267.
16. Dallao, p. 87.
17. Tim Brennan, "Classification for Control in Jails and Prisons," in *Prediction and Classification: Criminal Justice Decision Making,* edited by Don M. Gottfredson and Michael Tonry (Chicago: University of Chicago Press, 1987), p. 343.
18. Ibid., pp. 343–4.
19. Norman Holt, "The Current State of Parole in America," in *Community Corrections: Probation, Parole, and Intermediate Sanctions,* edited by Joan Petersilia (New York: Oxford University Press, 1998), pp. 28–41.
20. John Runda, Edward Rhine, and Robert Wetter, "The Practice of Parole Boards" (Lexington, KY: Association of Paroling Authorities, International, 1994).

21. Board of Probation and Parole, Department of Corrections, *Rules and Regulations Governing the Granting of Paroles, Conditional Releases and Related Procedures* (Jefferson City, MO: State of Missouri, 1992), p. 18.

22. Todd R. Clear and K. W. Gallagher, "Probation and Parole Supervision: A Review of Current Classification Practices," *Crime and Delinquency* 31 (1985): 423–444.

23. General Accounting Officer, Report of Congress, *State and County Probation: Systems in Crisis* (Washington, DC: U.S. Government Printing Office, 1976), p. 53.

24. Vincent O'Leary and Todd R. Clear, *Directions for Community Corrections in the 1990s* (Washington, DC: U.S. Department of Justice, June, 1984), p. 11.

25. See National Institute of Corrections, *Objective Jail Classification Orientation Workshop* (Longmont, CO: National Institute of Corrections, 1990).

26. Tim Brennan, "Implementing Organizational Change in Criminal Justice: Some Lessons from Jail Classification Systems," *Corrections Management Quarterly* 3 no. 2 (1999): 14.

27. James Austin, "The Impact of Truth in Sentencing on Prison Classification Systems," *Corrections Management Quarterly* 1 no. 3 (1997): 55.

28. Camp and Camp, p. 13.

29. M. DeLisi and B. Regoli, "Race, Conventional Crime, and Criminal Justice: The Declining Importance of Skin Color," *Journal of Criminal Justice* 27 no. 6 November–December, 1999: 549–557.

30. Stephen D. Gottfredson and G. Roger Jarjoura, "Race, Gender, and Guidelines-Based Decision Making," *Journal of Research in Crime and Delinquency* 33 no. 1 (1996): 49–70

31. Ibid.

32. Jurgen Neffe, "The Old Folk's Slammer: Aging Prison Population in the U.S.," *World Press Review* 44 no. 6 (June 1997): 30–2, reprinted from *Der Spiegel* (10, March 1997).

33. Dallao, p. 86.

▨ KEY TERMS

classification	postsentence investigation
risk assessment	reclassification
actuarial method	prerelease classification
objective classification system	intensive supervision
internal classification system	regular supervision
public safety factor	minimum supervision
National Institute of Corrections (NIC)	administrative supervision
parole guidelines	mandatory minimum sentences
salient factor score	three strikes legislation
sentencing guidelines	truth-in-sentencing
initial classification	

YOU'RE THE CORRECTIONAL ADMINISTRATOR

1. You are the chief of classification for a large prison system that has had an objective classification system in place for almost 20 years. You are experiencing extreme overcrowding in the high-security prisons. The director of corrections has asked you to assess the situation. Where do you start? What questions do you want answered? How would you go about identifying whether the classification system is doing what it should be or adding to the overcrowding problem.

2. You are the chief of probation in a county with more than 5,000 offenders on probation. You do not use any type of classification system. Everyone that is placed on probation starts under regular probation supervision, and each probation officer can recommend a reduction in an offender's supervision level. You also have an intensive probation supervision (IPS) and an electronic monitoring house arrest program, both of which offenders can be assigned to with the recommendation of probation officers. Your probation caseload sizes have been increasing, and you cannot get support from the courts or county commissioners for any new positions. What can you do to stretch your current resources to meet the growth needs?

WEB LINK EXERCISES

National Institute of Corrections (NIC): www.nicic.org

Go to the Web site for the National Institute of Corrections. Read the general mission and role that NIC plays for adult correctional agencies. One of the principle activities of NIC is to provide technical assistance. Describe what technical assistance is, the issues it can be used to address, the types of assistance available, and the process for applying for technical assistance. Then, identify one issue in correctional administration that would benefit from receiving technical assistance.

PART

III

Managing the Environment— The Prison Setting

CHAPTER 7

Staff Organization and Functions

INTRODUCTION

What should now be apparent to readers of this textbook is that corrections and the administration of prisons has become very complex; its mission has broadened in scope, and, therefore, the functions that must be performed by staff have increased. First, the operations of a prison have become intricate, extending well beyond past years' emphasis on "lock them up, work them, and feed them." Expansion of inmate rights, rehabilitative programs, and many more prison service options have broadened the internal management puzzle for administrators to piece together. Second, the external environment of dealing with the public, the media, and government agencies has increased the number of activities to which prison administrators must attend. Finally, the political and public interest of corrections puts additional demands on administrators, both on their time and on their sensitivity as to what they do and how they do it. In order to respond to these increased activities, the organization of prisons has become very complicated.

Prison organization and management has changed dramatically as a result of prisons moving from "closed systems" to "open systems." Historically, from their inception in the late 1800s until approximately the 1960s, prisons were closed systems. Closed systems consisted of only the internal environment, and for prisons, that meant what happened within the walls or fences, under the direct control of the wardens. The organization of a closed system, often with autocratic leadership, was usually very simple, and the mission and goals of the organization were determined, and compliance was enforced, by the leader.

The civil rights movement, the Vietnam conflict, and an era of prison riots changed the way society perceived prisons. Several external forces began to impact prison management, and open systems soon replaced the closed systems of prisons.

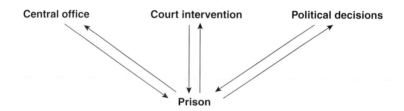

Snarr described the open system of prison management as having numerous inputs and outputs with external government units.[1] This evolution is presented in the accompanying diagram, which illustrates how external factors now influence the activities within a prison. Three groups that exert influence are the corrections central office, the courts, and political decision makers. An open system is the result of frequent interactions of an organization with other groups in order to obtain resources, gain support, and accomplish goals.

How are staff organized to carry out the expanded mission of a prison? What are the various functions that must be accomplished by prison staff? What are the different levels of prison staff, and what is the chain of command? What organizational entities have been created to respond to the external demands on prison administrators? How are staff supplemented by volunteers or contractors to carry out their functions? All of these questions are addressed in this chapter. Included are sample agency and prison organizational charts, with presentations of how various sections, divisions, and departments all work together to complete tasks both internal and external to the management of prisons.

CORRECTIONAL ORGANIZATIONS

Over the past several years, the organization of correctional agencies has experienced a somewhat slow, but deliberate, transformation. In contemporary prisons, the bureaucratic model and the centralization of authority have greatly influenced the organization and operation of prisons. As internal operations of prisons became more complex, prisons became more bureaucratic. Freeman characterizes this development as the **era of bureaucratic wardens,** in which wardens take responsibility for maintaining a safe, secure, and humane prison environment in accordance with accepted standards (the U.S. Constitution, sound management practices, applicable court decisions, etc.). In this regard, Freeman suggests many specific activities for the bureaucratic warden:

1. Development of the mission statement for the organization.
2. Coordination of the budget process.
3. Strategic evaluation and emergency planning.
4. Management of daily activities.
5. Management of labor relations.
6. The formulation of policy.
7. The supervision and professional development of staff.[2]

Another way to describe the development of a bureaucratic approach to prison management and organization is by its linkage of mission and goals to written policy and procedures. Mann notes that a bureaucracy is "an organization whose structure and operation are governed to a high degree by written rules."[3] Prisons began to organize around their mission by developing written policy and procedure to complete goals that would contribute to the mission. Goals were assigned to specific organizational entities, such as departments or divisions, to accomplish.

The centralization of authority also greatly influenced how prisons were organized and managed. With pressures and influences from many external forces (courts, politicians, and the media), it was imperative that there be consistency between prisons within the same governmental jurisdiction. During the first half of the twentieth century, many wardens of state prisons were appointed by governors, and there was often not even a cabinet-level agency that oversaw prison operations. Prisons were organizationally within an umbrella agency that may include other law enforcement agencies or perhaps other social service agencies. With the increasing intervention of courts, and as prisons became more in the public eye, many states formed departments specifically to oversee the state prisons. Riveland notes, "Today, 32 states are organized with separate Departments of Corrections reporting to the Executive; 11 as separate departments reporting to boards or commissions; 5 under a Department of Public Safety umbrella, and 1 under a social services umbrella. Twenty-four of the separate departments have been so organized since 1979."[4]

PRINCIPLES OF ORGANIZATIONS

Before examining actual organizational structures of a few correctional agencies, it is important to understand some terminology, basic principles, and the function and operation of a correctional agency. There are many basic principles of good management and organization that can be applied to corrections. However, correctional agencies, apart from other private or public organizations, experience certain pressures and influences that impact these principles. The following discussion considers such issues as how centralized an agency should be and whether there should be regional divisions to oversee field operations. How should work be divided, and what organizational divisions or departments should be created in prisons and headquarters? How much authority should various levels of the organization have and how should authority be aligned with responsibility? And finally, what is the chain of command and span of control?

Centralization and Regionalization

Centralization usually has two meanings when it is discussed in terms of management and correctional agencies. First, the typical definition of **centralization** has to do with the degree to which control and decision making is consolidated in one person in an organization. For instance, can prison staff make a decision without first consulting the warden? Can wardens make adjustments in how they operate their prisons without getting the approval of headquarters? Autocratic organizations usually have much power vested in one person: the leader. Traditionally, that was the way prisons operated, and there are still vestiges of that approach in corrections today. The degree of centralization of authority, today, usually has more to do with the personality of the leader, and his or her willingness to trust staff and share decision making.

The second definition of centralization for a correctional agency involves the degree to which a headquarter's office provides oversight and control over field operations. As is discussed later in the chapter, with the increase in complexities and of political and public interest in correctional operations, central headquarters have broadened their role and function regarding prisons and other field activities. Today, most correctional agencies have a rather large headquarter's staff that develops budgets, manages human resource issues, creates policy, deals with external interest groups, and directs field operations. Although central office staff provide services that assist prisons in managing inmates and carrying out the agency mission, most wardens would suggest the reach of the central office goes well beyond a service function to the point in which they often dictate activities at the field level.

Regionalization involves geographically breaking down field operations into smaller and, therefore, more manageable components. Because the number of inmates and prisons has grown in nearly every jurisdiction, it has become almost impossible for one supervisor to stay abreast of all the activities taking place in the prisons. As a result, many correctional agencies have created regions to oversee prisons and other field operations in a particular geographic area. These regions then create additional layers of staff to support and coordinate activities of the prisons. Regional supervisors must have service staff to assist them in directing and guiding the budget, human resources, policy, and operations of the prisons. Therefore, correctional agencies that regionalize end up with three levels of organization with parallel, and oftentimes overlapping, functions. The true challenge for an organization that has a strong centralized headquarters, as well as regions to supervise prisons, is to avoid duplication of staff and services, which can result in inefficiency and micromanagement of prisons.

Division of Labor and Departmentalization

The first principle that must be considered in organizing an agency is **division of labor,** or specialization of work. There are many tasks that must be accomplished in a correctional environment, such as tracking gang members, classifying inmates, conducting security checks, and providing medical treatment. These tasks are broken down into steps that can be carried out by one person, and the tasks are then grouped into job specifications for each position. For example, a headquarter's gang management specialist will collect information from prisons on inmate gang activities, review and approve recommendations to validate an inmate as a gang member, and issue reports on the latest gang activities and threats. A prison nurse will conduct medical screenings of new inmates, do a triage examination of inmates reporting for sick call, and instruct inmates on prescribed medication or rehabilitative exercises. A correctional officer assigned to a housing unit will inspect all windows for signs of attempted escape, conduct inmate counts, and search cells for contraband.

The division of labor results in like tasks being assigned to individuals who can be trained to perform them.

Once a group of specialists is identified by division of labor, they are usually organized into a coordinated group assigned like duties. The group may be made up of several individuals who do the same functions, such as correctional officers. Or, it may be made up of individuals doing similar functions that support one another. For example, medical staff may have a nurse assigned to screen inmates at sick call and schedule them to see a physician, the physician does an examination and prescribes treatment, and a pharmacist prepares and delivers the medication to the inmates. This grouping is called **departmentalization.** It allows for like activities to be coordinated in a way to efficiently carry out the required work, and is usually facilitated and supervised by a single manager. In a prison, examples of departments include security, medical services, mental health, food services, and the business office.

Responsibility and Authority

One of the most important principles of management is that like responsibility and authority must be assigned for every role or position. **Responsibility** is the expectation and obligation to carry out assigned duties. In a prison, the warden is responsible for managing the prison and meeting its mission of a safe, secure, and humane environment. Likewise, correctional officers are held responsible for carrying out their assigned functions, such as conducting security checks, searching inmate cells, or counting inmates. When tasks are assigned, it is essential that staff take responsibility to complete these tasks in the prescribed manner. **Authority** is the right of workers to give orders and expectation that those receiving the orders will comply. In the private sector, and in most public sector agencies, authority usually is only vested in management and supervisory-level employees. However, in a prison, all staff members supervise inmates and must have the authority to get compliance when they issue orders.

How do responsibility and authority coincide? For each task assigned to an individual, there are certain actions that must be carried out to complete the task. When correctional officers conduct counts, they must ensure that inmates are in the proper cell during the count. Imagine inmates not being in their cells, the officer ordering them to the proper cells, and the inmates responding, "The unit manager said we did not have to be counted in our cells." If line correctional officers do not have the authority to require that counts be conducted in the prescribed manner, they cannot be responsible if the count is not right. Similarly, a manager who is responsible for installing another security fence in the prison must also be given the authority to purchase supplies, move inmate activities away from the work zone, and request additional staff to guard equipment used during construction.

Chain of Command and Span of Control

Chain of command and unity of command are critical to every organization, especially a "paramilitary" organization such as a correctional agency. The **chain of command** is most familiar to military operations, where ranks of individuals (private, sergeant, captain) relate to their position in the chain of command. Chain of command is the vertical hierarchy in an organization, identified in terms of authority. Persons receive orders from the person immediately above them, who issues orders to the people immediately below them. The accompanying diagram illustrates a simplified prison chain of command from a warden to a correctional officer.

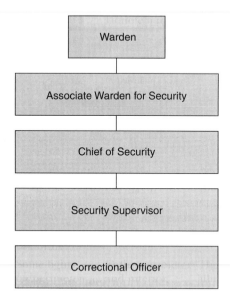

Unity of command involves the principle that a subordinate should report to only one supervisor. For a worker to take orders from more than one person can not only be inefficient but also can lead to conflict and chaos. Obviously, a worker may receive orders from someone in their chain of command who is not their immediate supervisor. A warden may see a security concern that needs attention (a door unlocked that should be locked), tell a correctional officer to take care of it (immediately lock the door), and there is usually no need to channel the order back through the chain of command. However, if the security concern is a broader issue, such as a change in procedures or need to reinforce current procedures (e.g., too many inmates moving across the compound during nonmovement times in a prison that uses "controlled movement"), the warden would officially issue the order through the chain of command; the order (to limit inmate movement during nonmovement times) may be passed through the chain of command so that all in the chain, and all correctional officers, are made aware of the change.

Span of control is the reverse of unity of command. Just as subordinates should only report to one supervisor, supervisors should only supervise the number of staff they can effectively direct. The designated span of control for an organization dictates the number of vertical levels in the organizational hierarchy, and the number of managers and supervisors needed to carry out the organizational objectives. There is no magic number of persons a supervisor can effectively direct. It depends on the complexity of the functions and tasks and how much direction the workers need. A prison warden may determine that a security supervisor can effectively direct 20 correctional officers, and still give them guidance and intermittently observe the performance of their duties. However, the prison warden may also determine that the span of control for a manager of the inmate classification section can only effectively direct the work of eight classification specialists, reviewing their work, updating them on changes in regulations, and responding to appeals from inmates about their classification status.

These management principles are key to understanding how correctional agencies are organized. In the following sections, both the table of organization for a central headquarters and a prison are examined and explained. To illustrate the function and influences driving the organizational structure, each division and department is described in terms of organization and function.

■ CENTRALIZED HEADQUARTERS ORGANIZATION

As noted, state prisons are organizationally located under a centralized agency that supervises all the prisons and often community correctional programs under state jurisdiction. The most common organizational structure (used in 24 states) has the director, commissioner, or secretary of corrections appointed by and reporting directly to the governor. This framework seems to have many positive advantages, especially by giving governors direct authority to operate the state prisons as they see fit. With crime and corrections often an issue in statewide political elections, candidates for governor usually take a policy position on correctional issues, and want to be in a position to influence the correctional agencies in a direct and immediate manner. This framework, however, often results in a change in correctional leadership with each new governor.

At the federal level, the Bureau of Prisons (BOP) is an agency of the U.S. Department of Justice, and the director is appointed by and reports to the Attorney General. Because of the size of the federal government, corrections is not as important politically as it is at the state level of government. Presidential candidates seldom campaign around an issue regarding the operation of federal prisons. However, with the BOP director reporting to a presidential cabinet secretary, the desires of the chief executive (the president) can easily be implemented. Historically, there has seldom been a change in the director of the BOP as a result of a political change of leadership. However, many people believe that this may change as corrections continues to become a larger federal budget item and a more important domestic policy issue.

In the 11 agencies in which the corrections chief reports to a board or commission, the nexus between politics and correctional policy is not quite clear. The corrections boards or commissions have members appointed by the governor. However, they usually consist of individuals from different political parties (usually equal numbers of Republicans and Democrats) and serve overlapping terms. Therefore, a governor would not be able to immediately replace the board or commission with his or her appointees and would have to wait until terms run out to make replacements.

Figure 7–1 illustrates three models of reporting by correctional agencies. In the first, the corrections director reports directly to the governor. In the second, the director reports to a board or commission. And, in the third, the federal model, the BOP director is appointed by and reports to the attorney general.

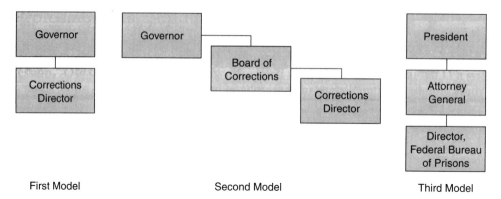

First Model　　　　　　　　Second Model　　　　　　　Third Model

FIGURE 7-1　Three models of correctional agency relationships to the chief executive.

The benefit of boards and commissions is that they somewhat insulate the corrections agency from political influence. This is believed to have at least two advantages. First, as noted previously, there is more likelihood of continuity of leadership in the correctional agency. In those states in which the corrections director serves at the direct pleasure of the governor, it is not unusual to have a new director appointed at each turnover of governor, regardless of how good a job the director did or how issue-free the department was. Second, there is likely to be continuity of policy and less political pressure to adopt politically popular, but poor, public policy. Even though the board or commission is a result of a political appointment, the members serve a fairly long term and become educated about the operations of a corrections agency. They are, therefore, able to make informed judgments about the value of a specific policy and weigh it against the political positions regarding the policy. The following case study is a good example of the conflict of policy and politics.

PRACTICAL PERSPECTIVES

When Policy Confronts Politics

The following case study describes the situation around a very experienced director of corrections having to deal with the political implications of implementing certain "tough on crime" correctional policies. The director began working in state government in 1962, became the warden of a maximum security prison in 1971, and progressed to director of corrections in that state. He served in that position on two occasions, leaving most recently in 1996. He was also director of corrections in two other states, chairman of the criminal justice department at a large state university, and president of a private planning and design firm that did consulting in forty-four different states. As is obvious, he was well qualified to lead a major state department of corrections.

He became the director of corrections for his home state for the second time in the early 1990s. In the state, as in many other states, the politics of corrections drastically changed after the 1994 elections. The director, however, felt very comfortable in this position as director, working directly for the governor. The governor had worked in corrections, taught public policy at a university, and understood the nuances of correctional policies. However, the public was stirred up by the rhetoric of the 1994 campaign, and the governor listened to the public. There was a public cry for a harsher prison system, with fewer amenities, and policies that made it appear that inmates were being punished and would not enjoy their period of confinement. One poll had the public 85 percent in favor of chain gangs in the state.

The governor was listening to the voters and was very politically astute. He suggested that the director put some of these politically popular programs in place. However, the director was focusing on other things than implementing popular correctional policy, such as trying to implement effective programs to reduce the 39 percent recidivism rate in the state. He believed that if the corrections department was really going to safeguard the public, this needed to be done. He knew the state had good discipline, control and a safe system, and was ready to move forward with the next step in program development. When the director did not implement the programs the public wanted, the governor sent the director a letter that was also for public consumption which outlined steps to reduce privileges and programs, and to make state prisons a harsher environment. In essence, the governor was making the director look bad publically, and was showing the public he was forcing the department of corrections to make changes in their operations. The director chose to resign instead of implement the tough on crime policies in which he did not believe. The governor then appointed a former state legislator, with no experience whatsoever in corrections, to be the director of corrections.

The former director admitted that in retrospect, he was listening to the public, but did not react appropriately. He did not do the necessary market research to subsequently develop a program that made policy sense, and could offer the governor operations that would appear to meet the goals of public safety. The director does not feel that correctional leaders should cave in and implement correctional programs that are unsafe and destructive. But they need to be innovative enough to develop a package that is both effective and politically saleable. He stated that no corrections director can win a fight that forces the governor to choose between him and the public sentiment. He still believes in the things that the department was doing, but recognizes they were not acceptable at that point in time to the public and by the voters. The advice the director would give to others in his position would be to be proactive, and read the concerns of the public and political leaders. He would put some programs in place that did appear to be tough on inmates, yet not undermine the most important functions of a safe and secure prison. In that way, correctional agencies can be both professional in implementing effective policy, and wise politically.

Even with the advantages of the board and commission format, most directors of corrections favor working directly for the elected official. They believe they are capable and persuasive enough to educate the governor and the governor's staff about correctional policy, so that their professional input will be sought on policies that could impact prison operations. By working directly for the governor, the directors find they are better able to get the support of the executive branch agencies for positions and finances needed to meet a continually growing client demand. Even with corrections becoming a very political issue, most governors support good public policy once they are elected and become responsible for the operations of an agency. It is not unusual for gubernatorial candidates to modify their positions regarding correctional policy, if they find their positions have some negative consequences.

The growth of corrections over the past 20 years,[5] as well as the growing interest of politics, have been the primary factors encouraging the creation of cabinet-level departments of corrections within state governments. The interest and involvement of external factors (politics, legislative oversight committees, the media, public interest groups) on correctional operations has a direct impact on the organization of the centralized agency. Most agencies find that there are great demands for information from the governor's staff, the media, and the legislature. To meet these demands, agencies create organizational entities to respond to requests and keep external interest groups informed of changes in correctional policy.

The Organization of the Central Office

The central organization that oversees the state and federal prisons is often called the "central office" or "headquarters." These organizations have grown dramatically with the increasing number of inmates, and the increasing demand for central control and consistency among prisons. As an example, Ohio created a cabinet-level correction agency (the Department of Rehabilitation and Correction) in 1971. Prior to that the oversight of state prisons was part of the Department of Mental Hygiene and Corrections. There were only six prisons and less than 20 corrections staff in the department's central office. There was little opportunity for strong leadership, guidance for the state prisons, or central policy coming from the headquarters.

Currently, Ohio is the sixth-largest correctional agency in the United States. The five largest (in order of size) are California, Texas, the Federal Bureau of Prisons, New York, and Florida. By the end of the year 2000, Ohio had 34 state prisons and approximately 200 staff working in the headquarters office in the state capital of Columbus. The table of organization of the central office of the Ohio Department of Rehabilitation and Correction (Figure 7–2) represents the complexity required to run an agency with an annual budget of $1.8 billion, approximately 16,000 staff, 46,500 inmates, and the responsibility of supervising 27,500 offenders in the community.

As noted, the Federal Bureau of Prisons is the third-largest correctional agency in the United States, with approximately 140,000 inmates in more than 100 prisons in the year 2000. Unlike Ohio, the BOP does not supervise probationers or released offenders under community supervision. They do, however, have certain cooperative agreements to assist the U.S. Marshal's Service by housing detention inmates awaiting trial, as well as the Immigration and Naturalization Service by housing

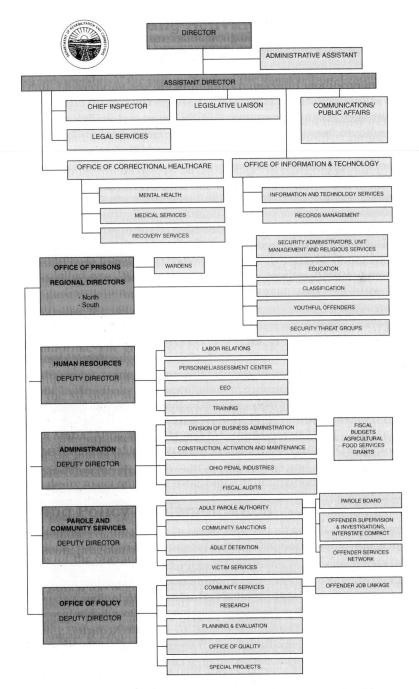

FIGURE 7-2 Table of organization for the central office of the Ohio Department of Rehabilitation and Correction.

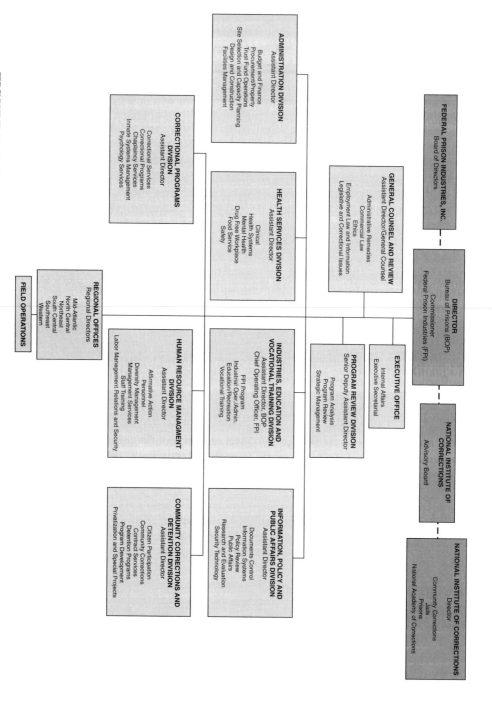

FIGURE 7-3 Table of organization for the central office of the Federal Bureau of Prisons.

aliens who have entered the country illegally. These additional missions complicate the organization of the BOP. Figure 7–3 represents the central officer table of organization for the Federal Bureau of Prisons.

The table of organization of these two headquarters are representative of some of the responsibilities of a large and complex correctional agency. Some of the similarities and unique organizational issues are presented in the following paragraphs.

Office of the director. Most central correctional agencies organizationally locate the external management functions close to the director, and they report to the director. Correctional agencies have found that external issues are so sensitive and can so quickly become political or media crises that there should be immediate access and no screening of the issues between the staff dealing with the issues and the director. The worst thing that can happen to a correctional agency is for an issue that is potentially sensitive (for example, weight equipment in prisons as discussed in Chapter 6) to be misrepresented by lower-level staff who have not been provided input from the person in charge of the agency. Directors of correctional agencies most often lose the confidence of their elected supervisor and lose their jobs because of the agency policies of handling of these types of issues, rather than a failure in the internal management of the agency. Therefore, directors of corrections do not want any surprises when it comes to developments around sensitive external communications.

Common organizational entities in the office of the director include public or media affairs, legislative liaison, legal advisors, and internal affairs. As one of the largest state agencies, there is a tremendous demand on correctional agencies for public information and responding to the media. When minor items are of media interest at a prison, staff at that location will usually handle the media requests. However, if a policy issue, a major incident, or something that has statewide interest is involved, the media will contact the headquarters for a response from the director or a senior official. An office of public affairs also oversees the preparation of standard reports, such as an annual review of the department and its status or information regarding a program or project in which there is much public interest.

Because state correctional agencies use a large percentage of the state budget, the legislature is always interested in operations, and legislative members may have particular questions about a prison in their district or from a constituent. Therefore, there is usually an office of legislative affairs, which tries to be responsive to legislative requests and to build support for the department regarding resources and programs. The objective is to get a member of the legislature an answer to any question very quickly. Also, staff of the office of legislative affairs regularly brief staff from legislative offices and committees as to the purposes of programs and so as not to be surprised by media reports or bills submitted by the department. A valuable guideline for dealing with the legislature is that your first meeting with a member or the member's staff should not involve asking for support. It is important to visit and get to know key legislative members, find out their interests, and share information with them proactively. Then, when support is needed, it is much more likely to be forthcoming.

Legal divisions for correctional agencies often report to the director of corrections. An average size state corrections agency will have four to six attorneys and about the same number of support staff in the legal division. The legal work falls into three general categories: (1) responding to inmate lawsuits; (2) reviewing policy for its legal impact; and (3) general advice regarding the implementation of programs that are in line with past legal decisions. With the demise of the hands off doctrine by federal courts, inmate litigation surged. In 1997, there were more than 30,000 lawsuits filed against adult correctional agencies.[6] Although most claims end up being frivolous, each requires some processing and the filing of a response. Legal staff at correctional agencies regularly review all changes in policy to determine whether there are any legal concerns.

Legal staff not only become familiar with cases decided regarding the department but also those regarding other correctional agencies. Therefore, they know the types of issues on which a court has taken a position, and a precedent may exist that could impact the department's operations. As changes in operations and procedure or new program implementation are discussed, legal staff offer advice on how the courts are likely to consider the new operation or program in light of the legal precedents. Correctional agencies have found that it is far better to be aware of prior case law, and consider it in decision making, than to have to defend a change in operations or a new program in court at a later time.

Finally, the office of the director usually has an inspector or internal affairs division as a part of the organization. Ethics in government is a high priority, and the opportunity for unethical, or even illegal, behavior is great when staff are in daily contact with manipulative inmates. Staff may be enticed to bring contraband into the prison, or they may be physically abusive to inmates. Whenever there is a complaint of staff misconduct by anyone (inmates, other staff, inmate families, or the general public), the allegation is investigated. An objective look by trained investigators is the best defense for staff against untrue allegations. Correctional staff know that inmates are likely to be unhappy with staff, and inmates will allege misconduct. Knowing that it will be investigated and, if not sustained, the staff member will be cleared is a comfort to correctional staff. However, staff know that if they do become involved in unethical behavior it will likely be reported and investigated. If sustained, they also know there will be discipline or criminal charges filed against them. This reminder is a deterrent to staff who may be tempted to violate the agency's standards of ethics.

Administration division. The two major areas of the administrative division of a corrections central office are budget development and new prison construction. These are two areas that do not have parallel departments in the prison, although prison business offices do provide budget needs that are used to compile the overall agency budget request for each fiscal year. The administration division collects information from all the prisons, other divisions, and the governor's office to create a budget that represents desired programs, growth, and continued operations. Once approved by the governor's office, the administration division begins to educate and explain the budget request to the legislative budget committee, which reviews the request and makes a recommendation for funding to the full legislative body. Corrections agencies are expensive. In budget year 1998, the 50 states, District of Columbia, and Federal Bureau of Prisons had operating budgets totaling more than $28 billion.[7] After a budget is approved, the administrative division maintains accountability of funds and keeps current on spending levels so that the agency does not exceed their allocated amount.

Usually included in a budget request are funds to construct new prisons. During the 1990s, there was unprecedented levels of prison construction by the state and federal governments. In 1997, there were 31 new prisons opened in the United States at a cost of $1.16 billion; there were 60 new prisons under construction and 130 existing ones expanding capacity for a cost of $3.8 billion; and funding for capital construction for budget year 1998 was $2.6 billion.[8] The administrative division is usually charged with overseeing design and construction of the new and renovated facilities. This includes hiring architects, coordinating their design with the department correctional experts, overseeing construction, and preparing to activate the new facilities.

Correctional programs division. A correctional agency will usually have a central office division that oversees the operation of correctional programs, such as security, education, religion, mental health, and unit management. In the Ohio state headquarters table of organization (Figure 7–2), the supervision of the prisons is divided into the North and South geographic regions. Each of these regions has staff who develop policy, monitor operations, and advise prison staff in these functional areas. In the Federal Bureau of Prisons example (Figure 7–3), these functions come under two divisions: the Correctional Programs Division, and the Industries, Education and Vocational Training Division.

Medical or health care division. One of the most complicated and expensive functions within a prison is health care. As a result, there is a central office division that develops policy, does quality assurance, and looks for ways to make more efficient and less expensive health care to inmates. Correctional health care has developed into a specialty within itself, unique because it deals with the practice of medicine and because it deals with a high-risk, incarcerated population. As such, it is critical to recruit staff for this division who understand both health care and prison medical services.

Human resource management division. Included under the human resource management division are the usual personnel functions of recruitment, hiring, evaluations, and retirement. In addition, most correctional agencies have groups to deal with affirmative action or equal employment opportunity (EEO), as well as labor relations. Workforce diversity is important for correctional agencies, particularly because of a high percentage of minority (African American and Hispanic) inmates and a growing number of women inmates. Most states have a unionized correctional workforce, and negotiating contracts and management of labor issues is very time consuming. Therefore, the central office usually has staff with expertise in labor relations who do the negotiations and advise prison managers on labor contract issues. Finally, these divisions are usually responsible for staff training. Some training is done locally at each prison. However, almost all states now operate a central training academy for new prison staff to prepare them for their duties.

Field operations division. Finally, central offices have a division (or sometimes two or more regions) that directly supervise prison and other field operations. In addition to prisons, correctional agencies may have parole or postrelease supervision of offenders, may operate community-based facilities such as halfway houses, and may have some responsibility for local jail inspections. In the Ohio example, there are two field regions to supervise the prisons and another division to supervise parole and other community service functions. In the Federal Bureau of Prisons, there are six regional offices (each with a regional director) that supervise all field operations within their geographic jurisdiction. A third model for central offices (usually in states with 10 or fewer prisons) has a deputy director who supervises all the prisons and wardens as direct subordinates.

The role of the central office, particularly during times of intense scrutiny, has increasingly become one of dealing with external interest groups and ensuring consistency in the operation of prisons. Carlson notes, "The critical and dangerous task of running prisons requires uniformity within each specific facility (fairness and equity—the perception that all inmates receive the same treatment) and precision of control."[9] With this in mind, we turn to the organization of individual prisons.

THE ORGANIZATION OF PRISONS

Considering that the mission of most prisons is to "provide a safe and secure environment for staff and inmates, while providing offenders an opportunity for program participation that can assist them after release," how are prisons organized to accomplish the mission? As described by Clear and Cole, "The formal administrative structure of a prison is a hierarchy of staff positions, each with its own duties and responsibilities, each linked to the others in a logical chain of command."[10] These authors continue with a description of how this hierarchy has changed over time.

> The traditional prison had custody and perhaps industry or agriculture as its goals. Given this orientation, it was run as an autocracy, with the warden dominating the guard force. Discipline of employees was often as unbending as that imposed on the inmates. With the coming of rehabilitation as a goal of the criminal sanction, treatment and education programs were incorporated into the organization, and a separate structure for programs, often headed by a deputy warden, was added.[11]

Today, the organization of prisons is as complicated as that of the central headquarters. Although the mission of prisons has changed little over the past 50 years, the organizational structure has changed considerably. Organizational entities that internally control the internal management of staff and inmates is very much the same, but functional entities have been added to respond to external management needs. Take, for example, the 1998 table of organization for the Lebanon (Ohio) Correctional Institution (Figure 7–4). Attached to the warden's office are an inspector of institutional services, an institutional investigator, labor relations, and a management analyst supervisor, who also serves as EEO chairperson. None of these functions were part of a prison table of organization a few decades ago.

The inspector of institutional services and the institutional investigator deal with inmate complaints against staff. Each Ohio prison, since the passage of a collective bargaining bill by the state legislature in the mid-1980s, now has a full-time position to coordinate compliance with labor contracts and provide a first-line communication link with prison union officers. There is constantly a need for information, and to review the effectiveness of prison programs and services. The management analyst supervisor collects and provides this information to central headquarters. In the Greenville federal prison, the warden's staff also includes a computer services manager to maintain the extensive reliance on management information systems within

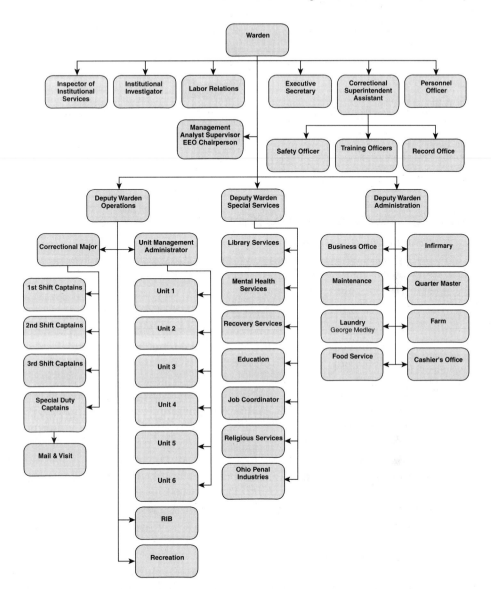

FIGURE 7–4 Table of organization for the Lebanon (Ohio) Correctional Institution.

the BOP. As mentioned in the discussion of central office organization, equal employment opportunity and affirmative action for staff are critically important and visible in contemporary prisons.

The table of organization for the warden's staff at the Federal Correctional Institution in Greenville, Illinois (Figure 7–5), illustrates some additional functions, including an attorney advisor. Many federal prisons have full-time attorneys or paralegals as a part of the prison staff, and some larger or higher-security federal prisons

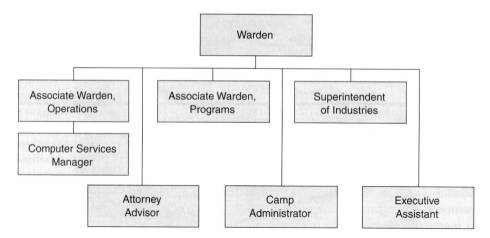

FIGURE 7–5 Table of organization for the warden's staff at the Federal Correctional Institution in Greenville, Illinois.

may have a legal staff of two or three people. Their role is to handle the volume of information needed by headquarter's legal staff and offices of U.S. attorneys, who provide legal representation for federal prison staff sued by inmates.

Also reporting to the warden are deputy (Ohio) or associate (federal) wardens. These individuals supervise the operational departments within each prison. In the Lebanon, Ohio, table of organization, the three deputy wardens are for operations, special services, and administration. The deputy warden for operations supervises correctional security (correctional supervisors and officers), unit management, the inmate disciplinary committee (Rules Infraction Board [RIB]), and recreation. The deputy warden for special services supervises the library, mental health, recovery services (alcohol and drug abuse), education, prison job assignments, religious services, and prison industries (Ohio Penal Industries [OPI]). The deputy warden for administration supervises the business office, prison maintenance, laundry, food service, the infirmary (medical services), quartermaster (issuer of clothing), the farm, and the cashier.

In the Greenville, Illinois, federal prison, there are only two associate wardens (AWs), one for operations and the other for programs. The AW for operations (see Figure 7–6) is similar to the Ohio deputy warden for administration and supervises food service, health services, facilities (maintenance), and finances (the business office). In addition, this AW also supervises human resources, safety, and employee development (training). The AW for programs supervises many of the same functions as the Ohio deputy wardens for operations and special services. These include (see Figure 7–7) unit management, psychology (mental health), correctional services (security), chaplain (religious services), teacher supervisor (education), and inmate systems (records). Although the titles of organization differ somewhat, these represent the basic functions required to operate and meet the mission of a prison. Several of these operational departments are thoroughly described in Chapter 10. Following is a summary of the organization of other departments within a prison.

FIGURE 7–6 Table of organization for departments reporting to the associate warden for operations at the Federal Correctional Institution in Greenville, Illinois.

Correctional services/security. The correctional services/security department supervises all of the security activities within a prison. This includes not only the duties of all of the security staff but also such functions as the special housing unit (SHU), inmate transportation, and the inmate disciplinary process. Correctional services are the most paramilitary within a prison, and most states and the Federal Bureau of Prisons still use ranks for correctional staff. In addition, security staff wear uniforms that are similar to military uniforms. A major is usually the highest ranking uniformed personnel and supervises this department. Captains run each eight-hour shift and coordinate security operations during that period. Lieutenants often are responsible for an area of the prison, such as recreation or the SHU, and sergeants are supervisory correctional staff who either supervise smaller areas than lieutenants or are senior correctional officers assigned to the most difficult posts.

Correctional services is the largest department (in number of staff) in a prison, ranging from 50 to almost 70 percent of all staff, depending on the state. It is interesting to consider the ratio of line correctional officers to inmates. The 1998 *Corrections Yearbook* illustrates the ratio of inmates to correctional officers, all uniformed staff (correctional supervisors such as lieutenants and captains), and total institution

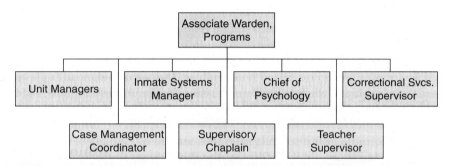

FIGURE 7–7 Table of organization for departments reporting to the associate warden for programs at the Federal Correctional Institution in Greenville, Illinois.

staff. As of January 1, 1998, the average for state and federal prisons is 5.6 inmates per correctional officer, ranging from the highest (worst) ratio in Oklahoma with 12.3 inmates for every officer to the lowest (best) ratio in New Mexico and Vermont, with only 3.2 inmates for each officer.[12]

Although these ratios may at first seem like there are many correctional officers in a prison, that is the average of all correctional officers, not the number of officers on duty at any given time. In a prison with the average of 5.6 inmates per officer, it would not be unusual to have one correctional officer assigned to a housing unit with 100 inmates, so the practical ratio would be one officer for 100 inmates. In many state and federal prisons, there are no correctional officers assigned to certain areas of the prison, such as education or prison industries. The nonuniformed staff who work in those areas (such as teachers and industrial specialists) carry out the security functions as well as their specialty functions. This all-encompassing model is more fully examined in Chapter 11.

Unit management. Unit management was first established by the Federal Bureau of Prisons at the National Training School for Boys in 1966, and it was expanded throughout most federal prisons by the early 1970s. Since that time, almost every state has adopted **unit management** to assist in controlling their prisons. The BOP defines a unit as a "small, self-contained, inmate living and staff office area that operates semi-autonomously within the larger institution.[13] The purpose of establishing unit management was twofold. First, it decentralized the management of the prison, and second, it enhanced communication among staff and between staff and inmates.[14]

The average size of prisons has grown over the past three decades; there are few prisons designed to hold fewer than 1,000 inmates, and many hold 3,000 inmates or more. Recognizing that effective centralized management of such large prisons would be difficult, unit management breaks the prison into more manageable units based on housing assignments; assignment of staff to a particular unit; and giving the staff adequate authority to make decisions, manage the unit, and deal directly with inmates. Units usually comprise 200 to 300 inmates. The second advantage of unit management is that it enhances communication. Staff are not only assigned to units but also their offices are located in the housing unit, making them accessible to inmates and providing staff the opportunity to monitor inmate activities and behavior on a daily basis. Accessibility of staff provides, "each [unit] with a sense of group identity, and increases the frequency of employee–staff contacts [with inmates] so that small problems can be addressed before they become large problems."[15]

In addition to enhancing staff and inmate communication, unit management improves communications among staff from various departments. As illustrated in Figure 7–8, a table of organization for a functional unit includes staff from many disciplines and departments. A unit is directed by a unit manager. In most jurisdictions, unit managers are selected from a variety of disciplines, which may include security, case management, education, or psychology. The rest of the unit staff make up the "unit team," which jointly reviews inmates' backgrounds, evaluates needs, and determines program and job assignments. On arrival, new inmates meet with their team to outline their program activities and usually meet with their team every six months thereafter.

Directly reporting to the unit manager are case managers and correctional counselors. **Case managers** (sometimes called social workers, or case workers in

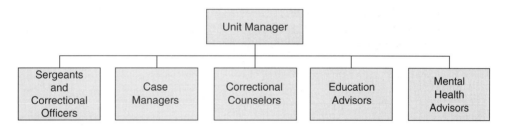

FIGURE 7–8   Table of organization for a unit in the Federal Bureau of Prisons.

some states) have a caseload of from 100 to 150 inmates. They are responsible for developing the program of work and rehabilitation for each inmate, and writing progress reports that can be used by release (parole) authorities or classification staff when considering an inmate for a program or transfer to another prison. **Correctional counselors** are selected from the ranks of correctional officers and wear officer uniforms. Their role is to work with inmates on the daily issues that confront inmates while in prison, such as creating a visiting or telephone list, correcting an error on their account of finances held by the prison, learning how to find a prison job, or getting along with other inmates. The wearing of a uniform reduces the perception that all security personnel do regarding inmates is enforce rules and give orders. Counselors assist inmates, and inmates begin to see that every staff who wears a uniform is not out to harass them.

Less clear is the supervision of correctional staff (sergeants and officers) who work in the housing unit. In some jurisdictions, these staff report to and are evaluated

A Unit Management Team Meets with an Inmate. Unit management is beneficial for several reasons. One of these is the opportunity to have interdisciplinary input regarding an inmate in a relaxed setting. (Courtesy of the Federal Bureau of Prisons)

by the unit manager. In others, they still report to their security supervisors, but the unit manager provides input on their performance for their evaluation. Although they are not a direct reporting link, yet a part of the unit team, are educational and mental health specialists. These staff evaluate inmates and provide the unit team with information to help create a program of education, vocational training, substance abuse counseling, or psychological assistance that best fits the inmates needs. They may actually attend unit team meetings regarding inmates, or they may simply issue reports and recommendations to the team for each inmate.

Education departments. In most prisons, the education department operates the academic teaching, vocational training, library services, and sometimes recreation programs for inmates. Types of prison education programs are described in Chapter 5 (Programs and Services). Organizationally, an educational department is managed similarly to a community elementary or high school. In fact, in a few states, the prison system is actually an accredited "school district", teaching supervisors must be certified as school principles, and teachers must be certified the same as their community counterparts. Teachers in prisons must be certified even in states where the educational department is not a school district and cannot graduate students, yet provides GED (general equivalency diploma) testing to recognize a student completing basic high school requirements.

Teaching supervisors in a prison have a faculty that teaches all subject matters required by the state department of education or a part of the GED test. At a minimum, this includes math, English, science, and reading. The number of teachers depends on the number of inmates assigned to participate in educational programs. A classroom teacher in a prison usually has a class of from 15 to 20 inmates. Vocational training is often offered in addition to academic training. Traditional vocational programs provided in prison include carpentry or general building maintenance, landscape or horticulture, food service, and office skills. Vocational instructors also report to the teaching supervisor (principal), and both the instructor and curriculum must be certified by the state board of education. Therefore, the quality of both academic and vocational training in a prison is similar to that in the community.

Library services, including leisure reading and legal libraries, are under the supervision of the educational department. As with the teaching staff, prison libraries usually must have licensed school librarians in order to be eligible for state funds or to use interlibrary services. In many states and in the Federal Bureau of Prisons, recreation is a part of the educational department. In Ohio, as shown in the Lebanon Correctional Institution example (Figure 7–4), recreation is a separate department and even reports to a different deputy warden than does education. The standard organization has several (5 to 10) recreational specialists reporting to a recreational supervisor. Recreational facilities are usually open seven days a week, approximately 10 hours per day. Staff are assigned to areas, such as the gymnasium or the recreation yard; they not only supervise the area but also plan and schedule leisure time activities to try to involve the largest possible number of inmates.

Penal industries. Prison industries is often a unique organization, with direct reporting to the warden, but with some technical supervision coming from the central headquarters. In many states and in the Federal Bureau of Prisons, prison industries is legislatively chartered, and there is often a requirement that the industry be self-supporting or operate from funds generated by the sale of products. In 1997, prison industries across the United States reported approximately $1.5 billion in sales; 41 agencies had profits of $42.9 million; and four agencies had losses of $3.2 million.[16] Prison industries are usually chartered as separate government corporations, administered by a board of directors appointed by the governor (the president with the BOP), and have a corporate structure under the umbrella organization of the correctional headquarters agency.

As an example, Federal Prison Industries, operating under the trade name of **Unicor,** was created by an act of Congress in the 1930s. It is governed by a seven-person board of directors. The director of the BOP is the chief executive officer and an assistant director is the chief operating officer. All operations must be supported by Unicor funds, because no tax dollars can be used. This includes funds for staff salaries, purchase of materials, and production and marketing costs. Because governments usually do not allow any "mixing" of funds (using some prison industry dollars and some tax dollars), a rather strict chain of command with industry personnel is usually required.

In most states, this means that the highest ranking prison industry manager at a prison reports to an industrial manager in the central headquarters, and the warden is advised of operations and issues. In a few states and the BOP, the prison industry manager reports to the warden for day-to-day activities, but production orders and industrial and budgetary issues are directed by the central headquarters staff. Prison industries are large operations nationally. On January 1, 1998, there were 7,679 staff members working in prison industry programs.[17]

Within the prison, the chief industrial manager may report to the warden (as in the Greenville, Illinois, federal prison) or to one of the deputy wardens (as in the Lebanon, Ohio, state prison). A typical prison industrial table of organization is presented in Figure 7–9. The superintendent of industries supervises staff responsible for production, quality assurance, and financial activities. The production staff is led by a factory manager, who is responsible for several production supervisors. The supervisors are assigned inmates who work in certain areas of production or assembly. In a clothing sewing factory, these areas may include fabric cutting, assembly of parts

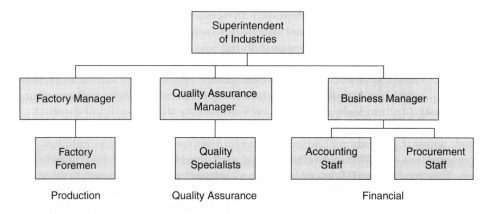

FIGURE 7–9   Table of organization for prison industries.

(such as collars and pockets), sewing the body of the clothing, assembly (attaching the parts to the body), and packaging and shipping. Production staff may also include supervisors responsible for equipment maintenance.

Quality assurance is critical in a private sector or prison industry production operation. In prison industries, there will be a quality assurance (QA) manager, who develops the quality program, the types of inspections, and the way a product is finally inspected to ensure customer satisfaction. There may be quality specialists who supervise inmates who actually do the inspections according to customer specifications. Finally, the industrial program has a business office, supervised by a business manager. The two major delineations are accounting (to keep financial records of costs and sales) and procurement (to purchase the materials needed for production). Each area has staff with expertise in these business functions who supervise inmates who assist in collecting and assembling financial reports.

These descriptions of several departments in the organization of a prison cover many of the main departmental functions. As noted, some program departments were addressed in Chapter 5, Programs and Services. Other operational departments are examined in Chapter 10. Finally, human resource and staff development organizations and activities are presented in Chapter 11. In addition to formal staff organizations, prisons often use volunteers, or even private contractors, to supplement staff activities.

VOLUNTEERS AND CONTRACTOR SERVICES

Volunteers and contract staff play a critical role in delivery of services and operations of correctional institutions. For purposes of this discussion, volunteers are defined as nonpaid and intermittent providers of a service to the prison or inmates. In contrast, contract staff are paid, regularly scheduled providers of service to the prison or inmates. Even though contract staff are paid, their contracts are usually much less expensive than full time staff. They receive no agency paid benefits, such as sick and annual leave, health insurance, or retirement. Also, contract staff usually work considerably fewer hours than full-time staff. There are three reasons that prisons would use volunteers and contract staff. First, to expand the volume of services that can be provided to inmates. Second, to provide specialized services that staff are not qualified to provide. And finally, to involve the community in the operation of the prison.

As discussed in earlier chapters, correctional budgets are becoming more and more stretched, with increasing numbers of inmates without comparable increases in staff and financial resources. To provide services that are deemed important, yet cannot be afforded with the available budget, prisons use volunteers and sometimes contract staff. Religious service departments use volunteers to facilitate discussion groups, or assist with religious services. Most prisons also contract with ministers to provide for the specific needs of faith groups with small numbers of inmates (such as Muslims, Jews, or Buddhists) or when they are unable to hire a full time chaplain. Similarly, volunteers or contract staff may provide substance abuse counseling, facilitating programs such as Alcoholics Anonymous or Narcotics Anonymous. Recreation and hobby craft programs often make use of volunteers and contract staff to teach painting or music classes, instruct inmates on diet and healthy lifestyles, and even to provide competition for inmates' sports teams.

Contract staff can provide specialty services that are not available with staff or that are not needed full time. Examples include medical specialists, such as surgeons, dermatologists, or physical therapists. As is further discussed in Chapter 10, prison medical departments are similar to family practice medical offices and cover general illnesses and injuries. Any medical condition requiring a specialist is referred to a contract physician or medical person. Other contract staff may teach a special discipline in the prison educational department, such as English as a second language or reading for inmates with learning disabilities.

Finally, volunteers are an excellent way to involve the community in the prison, and mobilize support and understanding for its operations. Community service clubs are sometimes invited to form chapters within the prison, both to provide leisure time activities for inmates and to link the community to the prison. Toastmasters International and the Jaycees are good examples of service clubs that often have chapters in prisons. At times, church congregations offer to assist in prisons. Church congregations are often asked to assist inmate visitors with transportation or accommodations when the visitors come to the prison from long distances to visit inmate family members or friends.

In general, volunteers and contract staff can be, and have been, used in almost any department within the prison. They can be of excellent assistance but they must also be carefully organized and monitored to ensure effectiveness. Ogburn suggests the following steps in establishing and maintaining an effective volunteer program:

1. Evaluate needs.
2. Develop goals and job descriptions.

A Volunteer Counseling an Offender. Volunteers can be a valuable asset to prisons, because there are many talented individuals willing to offer their time to assist in providing offender programs. (Courtesy of the Federal Bureau of Prisons)

3. Involve staff in planning and implementation of the volunteer program.
4. Actively recruit volunteers.
5. Educate volunteers about inmates and the potential for manipulation.
6. Explain security needs to volunteers.
7. Give volunteers the big picture about the prison mission and the volunteers'roles in accomplishing it.
8. Evaluate volunteer program effectiveness.
9. Recognize volunteers' contributions.[18]

Most of these guidelines hold true for contract staff as well as volunteers. By following these guidelines, the volunteer and contract services are likely to be effective and successful.

SUMMARY

This chapter has illustrated how the organization of correctional agencies and prisons has evolved and changed as influences and demands on them have evolved and changed. A few decades ago, correctional central headquarters and prisons were almost totally concerned with internal management, and there was little requirement for accountability, little need for consistency between prisons, and little interest from outside the organization. The functional organizational hierarchy was very simple and reflected the need for control and clarity in the chain of command without organizational entities to manage functions such as labor relations, affirmative action, legislative liaison, legal services, or media relations.

Today, there are several staff devoted to these functions, and wardens spend as much of their time dealing with external as they do internal management activities. Organizational functions within a prison even have staff and assigned duties that are focused on responding to external management requirements. These include media relations, investigators for inmate complaints against staff, and legal coordinators. At the same time, the internal functions of prisons have become more complex, and the organizational hierarchies have evolved in response.

Prison are much like other public establishments: Their organization is designed to most effectively complete tasks and carry out their mission. For prisons to provide safe and secure environments, with rehabilitative program opportunities for inmates, they must have several departments, clustered under the supervision of associate or deputy wardens. Each department has goals and objectives that contribute to the overall prison mission. Staff within each department are similarly organized, with each job completing tasks that help to accomplish the departmental goals and objectives.

Just as the prison organizations of 50 years ago were very different from contemporary organizations, the prisons of 50 years from now may well be very different from today. As is presented in the final chapter of this book, it is time for corrections to look for a new paradigm and new models for operations. It appears that all that is occurring today is incarcerating more offenders for longer periods of time, with little impact on crime or recidivism rates. As new models of correctional operations develop, they will demand new models of prison and headquarters organization.

ENDNOTES

1. Richard W. Snarr, *Introduction to Corrections,* 3rd ed. (Madison, WI: Brown & Benchmark Publishers, 1996), p. 179.
2. Robert Freeman, "Management and Administrative Issues," in *Prisons: Today and Tomorrow,* edited by Jocelyn M. Pollock (Gaithersburg, MD: Aspen Publishers, 1997), p. 279.
3. Michael Mann, *The International Encyclopedia of Sociology,* (New York: Continuum, 1984), p. 28.
4. Chase Riveland, "The Correctional Leader and Public Policy Skills," *Corrections Management Quarterly* 1 no. 3 (1997): 23
5. During the 1990s alone, there has been almost a doubling in the number of adult offenders in prison. According to the *Corrections Yearbook* (Camille Graham Camp and George M. Camp, *The Corrections Yearbook:* 1998 [Middletown, CT: The Criminal Justice Institute, 1998], p. 5), the population on January 1, 1990, was 750,000, and on January 1, 1998, it was 1,390,000.
6. Camp and Camp, p. 87.
7. Ibid., p. 64.
8. Ibid., pp. 74, 76, and 87.
9. Peter M. Carlson, "The Organization of the Institution," in *Prison and Jail Administration: Practice and Theory,* edited by Peter M. Carlson and Judith Simon Garrett (Gaithersburg, MD: Aspen, 1999), p. 28.
10. Todd R. Clear and George F. Cole, *American Corrections,* 3rd ed., (Belmont, CA: Wadsworth, 1993), p. 312.
11. Ibid., p. 320.
12. Camp and Camp, p. 155.
13. United States Bureau of Prisons, *Unit Management Manual,* (Washington, DC: U.S. Bureau of Prisons, 1977), p. 6.
14. For a discussion of the history of unit management within the Federal Bureau of Prisons, see Robert Levinson and Roy Gerard, "Functional Units: A Different Correctional Approach," *Federal Probation* Vol. 37, No. 4 (1973): 8–16.
15. Freeman, p. 300.
16. Camp and Camp, p. 107.
17. Camp and Camp, p. 112.
18. Kevin R. Ogburn, "Volunteer Program Guide," *Corrections Today* 55, no. 5 (1993): 66.

KEY TERMS

era of bureaucratic wardens	unity of command
centralization	span of control
regionalization	unit management
division of labor	case managers
departmentalization	correctional counselors

responsibility
authority
chain of command

Unicor
quality assurance

YOU'RE THE CORRECTIONAL ADMINISTRATOR

1. You are the chief of program services in the central office of a medium size state correctional agency. Your agency has not implemented unit management in the state prisons. The state director of corrections has asked you to review unit management and make a recommendation as to whether the state should adopt it as a management approach. Do not make a recommendation, but describe the process you would go through to consider whether it should be adopted. What are the key factors that you would look at within your state in your analysis? What are the key pieces of information you would like to find out from states who have implemented unit management? How would you blend these two types of information into a recommendation to the director?

2. You are the human resource manager for a state prison organized similar to the Lebanon (Ohio) Correctional Institution. The warden has asked you to do an analysis of the organization and consider any need for a reorganization, with various departments reporting to different associate or deputy wardens, or reducing or increasing the number of associate or deputy wardens. Describe the process you would go through to analyze the most efficient organization you would recommend for the prison. What type of information would be important, and how would you get the information?

WEB LINK EXERCISES

Ohio Department of Rehabilitation and Correction: www.drc.state.us

Go to the site for the Ohio Department of Rehabilitation and Corrections (ODRC). Find the community corrections components of ODRC, and identify how those components are organized. Based on this chapter's discussion of the principles of organizations, analyze how the community corrections components deal with centralization and regionalization, division of labor and departmentalization, and chain of command and span of control.

8

Creating a Safe and Secure Environment

What, in a prison, can be more basic and essential than creating a safe and secure environment? An often stated saying in a prison is, "24–7," referring to the fact that prisons are operational 24 hours per day, 7 days per week. Inmates and staff note and relate to the idea of 24–7. Inmates must live in the prison and endure the environment 24 hours per day, 7 days per week. Staff usually work only 40 hours per week, but they understand that the environment during the time they are there is impacted by events that occur in the prison at any other time. If there is a breakdown in security or a conflict between two inmate groups on a Sunday at 8:00 P.M., the staff working the "day-watch" on Monday may have to deal with the results of that breakdown or conflict. In every sense, creating a safe and secure environment is a 24–7 responsibility.

▬▬▬▬ INTRODUCTION

What are the key essentials for a safe and secure environment? Even more basic than this question is, "What is a safe and secure environment?" Is it a prison without any assaults by inmates on other inmates or staff? Is it a prison without escapes? Or, is it a prison in which staff and inmates feel safe in their environment? Once defined, how is a safe and secure environment established? What does a correctional administrator have to do to create and oversee the continuation of a prison that has a positive record for safe and secure operations? All of these questions are addressed in this chapter.

There are no simple solutions to creating a safe and secure environment. And, it is getting more difficult to provide such a setting. Inmates are serving longer sentences, often have little hope for quick release, and may have few incentives for positive behavior. Long sentences can also create frustration and a sense of bitterness and unfair treatment on the part of inmates toward staff. The increasing percentage of the inmate population that are youthful, impulsive, and gang affiliated heightens the likelihood of violence. Violence in prisons continues to be a serious problem,[1] and an expanded level of violence and fighting by inmates not only undermines a safe environment but also contributes to the development of a violent inmate subculture, which thereafter continues a downward spiral of fear and danger for staff and inmates.[2]

Maintaining a safe and secure prison involves the integration of several elements within the prison. As noted in a 1999 document of the National Institute of Corrections (NIC), "Good sight lines, integrated with sound security hardware and reliable technology have become the hallmarks of efficient, safe, secure, and humane correctional housing and they serve to balance cost effectiveness, ease of maintenance, and efficient use of staff resources."[3] Yet, this alone is not enough to ensure a successful security program. The NIC document continues,

> The most innovative design and advanced technology cannot substitute for well-trained staff and good security practices that are based in comprehensive security policies, procedures, regulations, and rules that are clearly written, standardized, and fully implemented. And even then, without a well-planned, comprehensive monitoring program, effective security practices cannot be sustained over the long term.[4]

In this chapter, there is extensive discussion of the integrated elements necessary for a successful program of prison safety and security. It is first essential to identify the security and escape risk for inmates using a contemporary system of *inmate classification*. A second element is the *physical security* provided by the prison, which involves matching inmate classification of risk with the physical security level of the prison. There is a massive amount of technology available to prisons, which, if it is used properly, may contribute to the overall enhancement of security. Third, prisons must have appropriate written *policies and procedures* that are fully implemented and monitored. Fourth, *inmate accountability* involves knowing where inmates are supposed to be at any given time of the day and ensuring they are where they are supposed to be. Next, there must be *control of contraband*, those items that pose a risk for escape or undermine prison security. Another key element is *professional staff* performing their duties as directed by policy, thoroughly and conscientiously. Finally, there are many *basics of prison operations* (such as effective food service and medical care) as well as issues of prison crowding that must be addressed for a safe and secure environment. Unfortunately, there are inmates who will, no matter what the consequences, violate rules, often with violent acting out. Just as these elements are key to a proactive approach to prison security, there must be effective reactive approaches for inmates. The activities for managing violent and disruptive inmates are examined in the next chapter.

For the uninformed, creating a safe and secure prison environment sounds like a simple thing to do in a prison. Simply lock inmates in cells by themselves, and how can the environment be anything but safe and secure? Locking inmates in cells for long periods of time, however, is not how contemporary prisons are operated. In most prisons, inmates are out of their cells almost 18 hours a day. They work, interact with other inmates and staff, participate in recreation, receive medical care, and take part in educational and other rehabilitative programs. With all this movement and activity, there are continuous opportunities for inmates to violate rules and undermine the safe and secure operation of a prison. Creating and maintaining a safe and secure environment is one of the most difficult tasks for staff and administrators, and it is one that requires constant effort and diligence.

CLASSIFICATION OF INMATES

In Chapter 5, risk assessment and classification of inmates was discussed. **Classification** is a continuous process used to identify and match offender needs with correctional resources, and it results in the assignment of individuals into groups with individuals of similar traits or characteristics. Correctional classification uses risk assessment to assign offenders to homogeneous categories for management purposes, to promote custody and security needs in a prison. In addition, classification of offenders provides opportunities to identify the need for varying approaches and treatment programs for inmates. For purposes of safety and security, classification matches inmates' risk for violence and escape to the appropriate physical security of a prison.

Classification to determine risk of violence and escape requires a multistep process. First, inmates' backgrounds must be searched for elements predictive of future behavior. Second, these background elements are scored and matched to a security level. Third, prisons are assigned a security level based on the physical security available. One common mistake involves trying to "fit" inmates into the security level of existing prisons instead of planning prison security around the risk needs of inmates. It is critical for states to continuously review the security levels of the current and projected inmate population and make any necessary adjustments to ensure the right "mix" of prison security space matches the need.

On the "macro" level, state prison systems identify the percentage of inmates that will be assigned to each security level. Prison security levels usually range from minimum to maximum, based on the inmate's risk for violence and escape. As of January 1, 1998, 11.7 percent of all prison inmates were assigned to maximum security, 13.3 percent were assigned to close/high security, 34.6 percent were assigned to medium security, 30.6 percent were assigned to minimum security, 4.1 percent were assigned to community security, and 5.7 percent were unclassified.[5] If this were the population makeup for any single state, that state would (after identifying their own guidelines of physical security for minimum through maximum security) try to ensure, or make adjustments so they would have, approximately 11.7 percent maximum security beds, 13.3 percent close/high security, 34.6 percent medium security, and 30.6 percent minimum security bed space available.

Predicting Risk of Violence and Escape

State correctional agencies first attempt to identify those factors in an inmate's background and prison behavior that are predictive of violence or escape. **Objective classification systems** have been developed since the late 1970s; they assign weighted scores to various background, sentence, and behavioral factors. The first objective classification systems were developed by the Federal Bureau of Prisons, California, and New York. The National Institute of Corrections then developed a model system of classification.[6] Most states adopted or modified one of these systems for their own use. These objective classification systems use such factors as offense severity, length of sentence, prior criminal history, family and other social stability, and prior institutional behavior to determine the risk for violence and escape during the prison sentence. These factors contribute to the predictive strength of a classification instrument, with length of sentence often having the most influence on determining an inmate's custody level.[7]

Figure 8–1 shows the classification score sheet for the California Department of Corrections, completed at a reception center for new commitments or parole violators who have received a new sentence term. This sheet is scored and determines the placement of inmates into various custody levels of California prisons. A major factor for calculation of the score is the term of incarceration. From the presentence investigation, prison reception staff identify and score background factors, including stability and prior escapes. Factors that determine the stability score include age, marital status, education, employment, and military service. The escape score includes whether there was an escape from a secure prison (a prison with a perimeter fence instead of a minimum security camp) and whether force was used in the escape.

If the inmate has served a prior sentence of incarceration of more than 31 days, behavior in jail or prison is included in the classification scoring. Unfavorable behavior factors include serious disciplinary infractions, escapes, assaults on staff or inmates, drug trafficking, possession of weapons, or inciting disturbances. There are also "favorable" behavior factors such as avoiding disciplinary infractions, completing a period of time at minimum custody, and performance in prison programs. Factors such as special medical needs or having a **detainer** (a warrant or hold for prosecution from a jurisdiction other than the offense for which the current offense was received) are also considered and scored.

All of these factors are combined, and inmates receive a score that represents the security level of the prison to which they are assigned. In California, instead of minimum through maximum, there is a four-level system of prison security. Using more common terminology, level I is similar to minimum security and, in California, includes facilities and camps that consist of primarily open dormitories with a low-security perimeter. Level II is similar to low security and includes facilities that consist primarily of open dormitories with a secure perimeter, which may include armed coverage. Level III is similar to a medium security prison, with a secure perimeter with armed coverage, and housing units with cells adjacent to exterior walls. Level IV facilities are maximum security, with a secure perimeter with internal and external armed coverage, and housing units as in level III facilities or cell block housing with cells nonadjacent to exterior walls.[8] Inmates who receive the following number of points on the classification score sheet are assigned to the matching level of prison:

0 to 18 points	Level I
19 to 27 points	Level II
28 to 51 points	Level III
52 or more points	Level IV

After inmates are assigned to a prison, their behavior continues to be monitored, and they may be reassigned to another prison based on either good or bad conduct. Figure 8–2 represents the California Department of Corrections reclassification score sheet. Unfavorable and favorable behavior scores are combined to recalculate an inmates classification score. Unfavorable factors include serious rule

Form 839 (7/88)

CDC Classification Score Sheet

STATE OF CALIFORNIA
DEPARTMENT OF CORRECTIONS

I.   IDENTIFYING INFORMATION

C. RECEPTION CENTER

D. RACE/ETHNIC STATUS
WHI = White   ASI = Asian/Pacific
HIS = Hispanic   OTH = Other
BLA = Black
AME = American Indian

F. YEAR OF BIRTH

F. DATE RECEIVED CDC
mo   day   year

G. COUNTY OF COMMITMENT

H. BASE OFFENSE

I. BASE OFFENSE
CODE   NUMBER

II. CALCULATION OF SCORE

A.   BACKGROUND FACTORS

1. Current Term of Incarceration
   a) Length of term   (   ) (   )
      years   months
   b) Term in years, minus 1 (   ) (   ) x 3 = (   )
      years   months
   c) Enter total term points (not to exceed 50) = ___ 44

2. Personal
   a) Under 26 years at reception + 2 = ___ 46
   b) Never married or marriage/common law not intact for
      12 months prior to reception + 2 = ___ 47
   c) Not high school graduate of GED + 2 = ___ 48
   d) Not more than 6 months with one employer, and not
      primary role maintaining household + 2 = ___ 49
   e) No military service or not honorable discharge + 2 = ___ 50

3. Prior Escapes
   a) Number of walkaways/minimum custody escapes
      dates: ___ x 4 = ___ 51
   b) Number of broached perimeter/medium custody
      escapes, dates: ___ x 6 = ___ 53
   c) Number of escapes with force
      dates: ___ x 16 = ___ 55

4. TOTAL BACKGROUND FACTORS SCORE + ___

PRIOR INCARCERATION OF 31 DAYS OR MORE, SKIP THE ITEMS BELOW; ENTER TOTAL
BACKGROUND FACTORS SCORE IN BOX FOR TOTAL SCORE (Sec. III, Item A.8)

B.   PRIOR INCARCERATION BEHAVIOR

1. Unfavorable Behavior
   a) Number of serious disciplinaries llast incarcerated
      year, dates: ___ x 4 = ___ 57
   b) Number of escapes in last incarceration or escape is
      committment offense, dates: ___ x 6 = ___ 59
   c) Number of physical assaults on staff
      dates: ___ x 6 = ___ 61
   d) Number of physical assaults on inmates
      dates: ___ x 4 = ___ 63
   e) Number of smuggling/trafficking drugs
      dates: ___ x 4 = ___ 65
   f) Number of deadly weapon possessions (Double-
      weight if within last 5 years), dates: ___ x 4 = ___ 67
   g) Number of inciting disturbance
      dates: ___ x 4 = ___ 69
   h) Number of assaults that caused serious injury
      dates ___ x 16 = ___ 71

2. TOTAL UNFAVORABLE POINTS + ___

3. Favorable behavior
   a) No serious disciplinaries in last 12 months of incarcerations – 4 = ___ 73
   b) Successfully completed at least 12 months of minimum
      custody in last incarceration(s) – 6 =
      OR   ___ 74
      Successfully completed at least 4 months of minimum custody,
      or 4 months of dormatory living during last incarcerations – 4 =
   c) Average or above performance in work, school, or voca-
      tional program for last incarceration year – 4 = ___ 75

4. TOTAL FAVORABLE CREDITS – ___
   POINTS ASSESSED IN ITEMS 8, 1-4 ABOVE SKIP ITEM B.5

5. Undocumented Prior Incarceration Behavior
   a) Records of incarceration behavior inadequate to assess
      unfavorable or favorable points (limit to 3 priors) ___ x 4 = ___ 76 x

6. TOTAL PRIOR INCARCERATION BEHAVIOR SCORE ___

III. PLACEMENT

A.   SPECIAL CASE FACTORS

1. Medical Restriction
   (If not camp eligible enter FULL duty but not camp;
   RESTricted or light duty, or UNASsigned medically) ___ 77

2. Holds, Detainers, and Warrants
   (enter A for Active or P for Potential)
   a) Felony Hold ___ 81
   b) Immigration and Naturalization Hold ___ 82

3. Restricted Custody Suffix Required (enter R) ___ 83

4. Category or Special Housing Recommendation
   (enter appropriate letter) ___ 84

5. Other Placement Concerns
   a)   85   b)   88   c)   91

6. Work Skills ___ 94

7. Caseworkers
   a) Counselor ___ 101
   Last name   FI
   b) Supervisor ___ 110
   Last name   FI

8. TOTAL CLASSIFICATION SCORE ___ 119
   (Combine from Section II, A.4 Total Background Factors
   Score and B.6 Total Prior Incarceration Behavior Score)

B.   CLASSIFICATION STAFF REPRESENTATIVE ACTION

1. Classification Staff Representative ___ 122
   Last name

2. Date of CSR Action ___ — ___ — ___ 130
   mo   day   year

3. Administrative Determinants
   a) PRIMARY   136   b)   139   c)   142

4. Category/Special Housing ___ 145

5. Institution Approved ___ — ___ 146

6. Reason for Administrative or Irregular Placement ___ 153

A. CDC NUMBER   B. INMATE'S LAST NAME

FIGURE 8–1   California classification score sheet.

STATE OF CALIFORNIA   **CDC Reclassification Score Sheet**   DEPARTMENT OF CORRECTIONS

II. RECALCULATION OF SCORE

A. UNFAVORABLE BEHAVIOR SINCE LAST REVIEW

Last Review Date

☐ ☐ — ☐ ☐ — ☐ ☐   24

mo   day   year

1. Number of serious disciplinaries
   dates: _____   _____ x 6 = ☐ ☐   30

2. Number of escapes during current period
   date: _____ x 8 = ☐ ☐   32

3. Number of physical assaults on staff
   date: _____ x 8 = ☐ ☐   34

4. Number of physical assaults on inmates
   date: _____ x 4 = ☐ ☐   36

5. Number of smuggling/trafficking in drugs
   date: _____ x 4 = ☐ ☐   38

6. Number of deadly weapon possessions
   date: _____ x 16 = ☐ ☐   40

7. Number of inciting disturbance
   date: _____ x 4 = ☐ ☐   42

8. Number of assaults that caused serious injury
   date: _____ x 16 = ☐ ☐   44

9. TOTAL UNFAVORABLE POINTS = + _____

B. FAVORABLE BEHAVIOR SINCE LAST REVIEW

Number of Six Month Periods

1. Continuous minimum custody
   _____ x 4 = ☐ ☐   46

2. Continuous dorm living
   _____ x 2 = ☐ ☐   48

3. No serious 115's
   _____ x 2 = ☐ ☐   50

4. Average or above performance in work, school, or vocational program
   _____ x 2 = ☐ ☐   52

5. TOTAL FAVORABLE CREDITS = – _____

C. COMPUTATION OF CLASSIFICATION SCORE

1. Prior Classification Score = ☐ ☐ ☐   54

2. Net Change in Behavior Score (A.9 minus B.5) = ☐ ☐ ☐   57
   (+ or –)

3. Change in term points = ☐ ☐ ☐   60
   (+ or –)

4. Current Classification Score = ☐ ☐ ☐   63

III. PLACEMENT

A. SPECIAL CASE FACTORS

1. Placement Concerns
   a) Hold (enter A, P, or #)   b) Restricted Custody Suffix (enter R or •)   c) Medical Restriction (enter FULL, REST, UNAS, or •)
   Felony INS
   ☐ 66 ☐ 67 ☐ 68 ☐ ☐ ☐ ☐ 69

2. Other Placement Concerns
   a) (•) ☐ ☐ ☐ ☐ 73   b) (•) ☐ ☐ ☐ ☐ 77

3. Caseworkers
   a) Counselor ☐ ☐ ☐ ☐ ☐ ☐ ☐ ☐ 81
   Last Name   FI

   b) Supervisor ☐ ☐ ☐ ☐ ☐ ☐ ☐ ☐ 90
   Last Name   FI

4. Current Custody ☐ ☐ ☐ — ☐ — ☐ 99

5. Current Institution and Facility ☐ ☐ ☐ ☐ — ☐ ☐ ☐ ☐ 107

B. CLASSIFICATION STAFF REPRESENTATIVE ACTION

1. Classification Staff Representative ☐ ☐ ☐ ☐ ☐ ☐ ☐ 114
   Last Name

2. Date of CSR Action ☐ ☐ — ☐ ☐ — ☐ ☐ 122
   mo   day   year

3. Administrative Determinants
   a) (•) PRIMARY ☐ ☐ ☐ 128
   b) (•) ☐ ☐ ☐ 132   c) (•) ☐ ☐ ☐ 136

4. Placement Approved   a) Cat. ☐
   b) Institution and Facility ☐ ☐ ☐ ☐ — ☐ ☐ ☐ ☐ 141

5. Reason for Administrative or Irregular Placement ☐ ☐ ☐ 148

I. IDENTIFYING INFORMATION

A. CDC NUMBER ☐ ☐ ☐ ☐ ☐ ☐ ☐ 1

B. INMATE'S LAST NAME ☐ ☐ ☐ ☐ ☐ ☐ ☐ 7

C. Date of Current Review ☐ ☐ — ☐ ☐ — ☐ ☐ 15 —
   mo   day   year

D. PAROLE VIOLATOR ADMISSION TYPE (enter RTC or WNT) ☐ ☐ ☐ 21

FIGURE 8–2 California reclassification score sheet.

violations, escapes, assaults on staff or inmates, drug smuggling, weapon possession, or inciting a disturbance. Favorable behaviors include maintenance of minimum custody, continuous living in dormitory type housing, no serious rule violations, and good program performance. For reclassification purposes, inmates are usually reassessed every six months or when there is a serious rule violation that may trigger an increase in the number of security level points.

Each new point total on a reclassification replaces the initial or prior reclassification, and the new point total is then used to determine whether there should be a reassignment and transfer of the inmate to a higher- or lower-security prison. In this sense, the security classification process is continual and takes into consideration the most recent behavior, either good or bad. The overall goal is to maintain homogeneity of inmates by risk and stability and to ensure they are placed in prison facilities that are physically designed to meet their potential for violence and escape. Housing high-security inmates in a facility that is low or minimum security only invites escape, predatory behavior, violence, and other management problems. Yet housing inmates with low or minimum security classifications in high-security prisons has equally serious, yet not so obvious, results. Placing lower-security inmates in danger of violence and intimidation is a waste of correctional resources. It cost three to four times as much to build and operate a high-security than a minimum security prison, and these costs are not necessary for the risks associated with low-security inmates. In the next section, we examine the physical security issues that coincide with the risk factors presented by various security levels of inmates.

PHYSICAL SECURITY OF PRISONS

Prison security results from the conscious design of certain physical features within a prison that makes it easy to visually supervise inmates, and use materials that are difficult to compromise. Prisons have layers of barriers between the inmate population and freedom. Correctional administrators and architects who design prisons generally think of physical security from the "outside in," meaning they begin with the perimeter, and then consider the various layers of security working in that are necessary for each institution.

The most outer layer is referred to as the **perimeter security;** it is the wall or fence that surrounds the prison. The perimeter must be monitored, and staff must address attempts to escape by breech the fence. This is often accomplished with the existence and operation of **towers** along the perimeter, from which armed correctional officers can watch inmate movement and respond to escape attempts. When towers do not exist, there are usually **mobile patrols,** or officers in vehicles that continuously drive around the perimeter and can respond to escape attempts. Another key issue of perimeter security is whether there is some type of **electronic detection device** on the perimeter to alert staff of attempts to compromise the perimeter in case they do not visually see the attempt. When there is an attempt to compromise the perimeter, detection devices set off an alarm in a central control room where staff monitor communications and electrical components of the prison. Sometimes the mobile patrols have electronic detection devices as well. The alarms are triggered by any attempt to climb or cut a fence. Some detection devices are

A Guard Tower on the Perimeter Fence of the U.S. Penitentiary in Marion, Illinois. At high-security prisons, guard towers to monitor the fence are still regularly used. These towers are staffed 24 hours per day, and staff are armed and authorized to shoot any escaping inmate. (Courtesy of the Federal Bureau of Prisons)

underground or at ground level inside the fence and are triggered if there is any movement encroaching the fence.

The next layer of security in many prisons in an **internal perimeter**, which may be either a physical barrier or simply an area in which inmates are not allowed. The internal perimeters for high or maximum security prisons often use interior fencing with razor ribbon and a detection device to physically make it difficult for inmates to go outside the internal perimeter. For medium or low security prisons, the internal perimeter acts more like a boundary, with "slow down" fences that are not physically imposing or difficult to cross. When an inmate attempts to climb the fence or wall, there is no question that the inmate intends to violate rules or attempt an escape.

Finally, prison housing buildings for inmates include a **secure envelop**, which is designed to hold inmates in a building or cell, both to make escape difficult and to isolate them from other inmates or staff during certain periods of the day. Housing is either **dormitory style**, with several beds (often double bunk beds) lined up in one room, or small cells in which one or two inmates may live. Cells can be either "outside" or "inside." **Outside cells** are adjacent to the exterior wall of the housing unit and have a window on the outside wall. With an outside cell design, there is only one physical barrier between the inmate and the outside of the housing unit. **Inside cells** are not adjacent to an exterior wall, and inmates therefore have both the cell wall and the housing unit wall between themselves and the outside of the housing building.

In addition to the layering of physical security, other security considerations for a prison include the type and amount of lighting after dark, the type of building materials that make up walls and other barriers, whether there are interior corridors for inmate movement or whether inmates move freely in an outside area, the location

Electronic Detection Device on a Prison Perimeter Fence. At many prisons, fences usually have electronic detection devices to alert staff that an inmate is trying to climb or cut the fence. Such systems can eliminate the need for towers at medium- or low-security prisons. (Courtesy of the Ohio Department of Rehabilitation and Correction)

"Inside" Cell Arrangement in a Prison Housing Unit. Inside cells have no exterior wall, and therefore have a double layer of security for an inmate trying to escape—just to get out of the housing unit. (Courtesy of the New York City Department of Correction)

███████ **TABLE 8-1**

Typical Design Features of Facility Security					
Security Levels	**I**	**II**	**III**	**IV**	**V**
Perimeter	None	Single fence	Double fence and/or unarmed "posts"	Double fence Secure entrance/ exits	Same as IV and/or wall and secure entry/exits
Towers[1]	None	None[1]	Combination	Combination of intermittent tower and/ or patrol surveillance	Same as IV with tower and/or patrol surveillance
External patrol	None	Intermittent	Yes	Yes	Yes
Detection devices	None	Optional	Yes, at least one type	Yes, more than one type	Yes, extensive
Housing	Single rooms and/or multiple rooms or dorms	Single rooms and/or multiple rooms or dorms	Single cells or rooms	Single outside or inside cells	Single inside cells
Lighting	Minimal	Some lights on perimeter and interior	Entire perimeter and interior compound illuminated	High-intensity illumination of all perimeter and interior areas	High-intensity illumination of all perimeter and interior areas

[1]Towers may be used for control of traffic and/or pedestrian movement.

and design of posts for staff supervision, and how technology (such as camera detection or electronic cell and other door opening devices) is integrated into the physical design of the prison. Table 8–1 illustrates the coordination of various elements of physical security to security levels assigned to prisons.[9]

Technology is a valuable element of physical security. Selecting technology suitable for each prison, including its physical security and the level of inmates, is difficult because of the vast amount of technology that is available. There are high-tech systems that use global positioning satellite (GPS) systems and can identify where all inmates in a prison are at any time. There are systems that conduct retina scans to ensure proper identification of inmates or staff. There are also electrified fences that deliver a lethal charge of current to anyone coming in contact with the fence. All of California's high-security prisons use this type of perimeter fence to help reduce escape attempts.

Perhaps the most commonly used and useful technology is the integration of camera surveillance with inmate movement, the design of buildings, and the availability of staff supervision. Camera surveillance can aid in the supervision and monitoring of sensitive and high-risk areas of the prison, such as the pharmacy, special housing units, and entrance and exit gates. Cameras may also be used to assist in surveillance of high-density inmate activity, such as the recreation yard, dining room,

Cameras Monitor Inmate Movement. Camera monitoring of inmate movement is an excellent security measure within prisons. Not only can staff watch remote locations but videotapes are also usually made of the camera views, aiding in identifying or prosecuting inmates who commit violent acts. (Courtesy of the Ohio Department of Rehabilitation and Correction)

or housing units. When continuous videotaping is a part of the camera surveillance system, the videotapes can be reviewed to identify inmates and help investigate particular incidents. If there was an assault in the recreation yard, the videotape may identify both the assailant(s) and potential inmate witnesses.

Physical Security by Level of Prison

Using the five levels of security noted in Table 8–1, it is possible to describe the security aspects for various levels. No state is exactly the same in their definition of security level or in their specific guidelines as to what physical security should be used with each level, but the following examples indicate some common approaches. Terminology of security levels varies, and some states will have as few as three or as many as six categories of security. For purposes of illustration, the following five categories are used: level I (minimum), level II (low), level III (medium), level IV (close), and level V (maximum).

Level I, or **minimum security**, prisons are used to house those offenders who pose no serious risk for violence or escape; if they do escape (walk away), there is little risk to or concern by the community about their being at large. These are usually nonviolent, first offenders, white-collar offenders, or those who have spent most of their sentence at a higher-security level with good behavior. As such, they have an "investment" on their sentences and they would not choose to escape and face additional charges and an additional sentence. Therefore, at level I prisons there is usually no perimeter fence of any kind; the only thing keeping inmates in the prison is their knowledge that violating the privilege of being in minimum security will cause an additional sentence or movement to a higher-security prison.

Without a concern for escape, physical security is almost totally absent, because it would be inefficient to spend much money on expensive and secure construction. Walls, even in housing units, are of commercial or residential construction to keep costs down. Housing styles are usually multiple room or open dormitories, which are much less expensive to construct than cells. There is little use of security, and if there are cameras, they are to monitor traffic, and sometimes to keep "outsiders" from entering the prison grounds. The most significant risk at this level of prison is the likelihood that inmates will have someone bring prohibited substances (such as drugs or alcohol) into the prison.

Level II, or **low security**, prisons hold inmates who have committed more serious crimes and who may have a minor history of violence. Like minimum security, there may also be inmates who have demonstrated good behavior at a higher-security prison or those who have violated the rules at a minimum security facility and have been reassigned to low. This level of security will have a single, or sometimes double, fence, sometimes with a detection device and mobile patrols. The perimeter security is often not enough to prevent serious and well-planned escape attempts but is enough to avoid the impulsive act of walking away that can occur at minimum security prisons. Housing in low security prisons is usually either dormitory or multiple-occupancy rooms similar to minimum security. The walls of the housing units may use security construction features such as reinforced concrete and windows with bars.

Level III, or **medium security**, prisons are those that house inmates who are violent and escape risks. In many states and the federal correctional system, inmates in medium security prisons may be serving average sentences of 10 to 12 years and often may have prior sentences of incarceration. The perimeter security at medium prisons is designed to stop escape attempts or at least make them very difficult. The standard perimeter has two 12-foot-high fences with several rolls of **razor ribbon** hanging from the fences and stacked between the fences. Razor ribbon can be described as high-technology barbed wire made of stainless steel in a ribbon design with sharp barbs at frequent intervals along the ribbon. When rolled into approximate 24-inch circles and stacked or hung on a fence, individuals who come in contact with razor ribbon will receive many cuts and often their clothes or even their skin becomes entangled in the barbs. Inmates have quickly learned to avoid razor ribbon, knowing the peril of coming in contact with it. There are detection devices along the perimeter, and mobile patrols and (in some states) towers to monitor the perimeter.

Housing for medium security is usually external cells, adjacent to the outside wall of the housing unit. There is always a preference to have single cells, but many states accept multiple-occupancy cells for medium security prisons. Construction of the housing unit uses reinforced concrete and barred windows, making escape through walls or windows difficult without tools to cut bars or chip away concrete. Cameras are often used to enhance supervision of inmates and monitor areas of the prison that are more important for the overall security operation. Inmate movement is usually across an open area (rather than in corridors), but movement is limited and steel doors keep buildings locked when there is no scheduled movement of inmates.

Level IV, or **close security**, prisons are for the more dangerous and escape prone inmates. The physical security aspects of a close security prison are often the same as a maximum security facility, but it allows for a larger inmate population and, therefore, a greater economy of scale. The larger the population, the more danger

Razor Ribbon on a Perimeter Fence. Razor ribbon acts as a very effective deterrent to inmates trying to get through a security fence. (Courtesy of the Ohio Department of Rehabilitation and Correction)

there is that a riot could get out of control and the more staff that would be assigned to monitor and supervise inmates. Therefore, only the smallest percentage of the most dangerous and violent inmates are reserved for **maximum security** prisons. The perimeters for both close and maximum will have double fences or walls, with armed gun towers, continuously staffed to monitor movement and prevent escapes. There are often also mobile patrols and extensive detection devices on the perimeter in case one is not working or inmates are able to avoid detection.

Housing at both levels are single cells. Close security might use external cells, whereas maximum security always has internal cells for an extra physical barrier to prevent escape. These security-level prisons may have remote officer stations that are protected and separated from inmates with bars and glass. From these isolated posts, staff observe inmate movement and control electronic door opening and closing. In 5 to 10 states, some of these inside secure posts are armed, and staff are instructed to use deadly force if violence erupts that threatens staff or other inmates. Inmate movement is often through corridors with several grill gates at intervals along the corridor that can be closed electronically if there is a disturbance. These corridors reduce the freedom of movement by inmates, and if there is a riot, the gates help isolate small groups of inmates who can then be brought under control. Cameras and other high-technology systems are extensively used to monitor inmates. Cameras often have continuous videotaping of activities, so that any rule violations or violence can be reviewed on tape to aid in identifying involved inmates and assisting with prosecution or inmate discipline for the violations or crimes.

As is obvious, physical security is designed to match the risk of violence and escape, and the highest security prisons use extensive layers of physical security to prevent escapes and keep staff and other inmates safe from violent predators. This level of security is very expensive, however, and should not be provided to those inmates who do not need it. In addition, as extensive as some of the physical security may seem, it alone is not enough to create a safe and secure prison environment. There must also be well-developed policies and procedures that are consistently followed and enforced by professional correctional staff.

SECURITY POLICY AND PROCEDURE

Most individuals, when they think of a secure prison, mainly consider the "steel and concrete" or the physical security of prisons. Yet no matter how expensive, how high-tech, or how overlapping the layers of physical security, they can all be compromised if they are not properly used and monitored. That is where the value of well-written, clearly communicated, and consistently enforced security policies and procedures becomes evident. Inmates can overcome or break through any physical security if given the time and tools. They can find ways to get dangerous and prohibited items (such as weapons and drugs) into a prison if there are not satisfactory checks of packages and individuals who enter a prison. And they can threaten, intimidate, and coerce other inmates if there are not adequate procedures for inmate accountability and control by staff.

For policy and procedure to contribute fully to a safe and secure prison environment, three elements are key. First, policies must be consistent with professional standards, and be written and authorized by the prison administration. The American Correctional Association (ACA) is the major professional organization for corrections in the United States, and it publishes manuals of standards for all types of correctional practices that have been reviewed and approved by national correctional experts. Similar to the American Medical Association or the American Bar Association, the ACA standards are created by practicing professionals in the field, and they are used for guidance and evaluation of acceptable models of operation. Not only are these standards professionally accepted but they are also recognized and used by state legislatures for funding purposes, and federal courts for determining issues of humane treatment of inmates.

Some ACA standards that pertain to prison security include the operation of an armory (where weapons and chemical agents are maintained), control of keys and tools, transportation of inmates, use of force, searches of inmates and areas, and handling inmate visitors. Although ACA standards provide guidance and examples of professionally accepted security procedures, there is no requirement that any state prison or local jail follow them. It is the responsibility of the prison or jail to establish their own policy and procedure manual of operations. The manual should consider the professional standards but adapt them to the specific situation and facility. It seems almost trite to note that policies and procedures should be written, yet written policy manuals were not universal in corrections even 20 years ago, and today many practices are passed on by word-of-mouth or informal memos. However, it is critically important to formalize policy in writing, and have an official sign and authorize the policy for implementation throughout the facility. By formalizing policy in this manner, it begins the process of communicating it to staff and inmates and facilitates training and discipline of staff and inmates.

The second element of effective policy and procedure is that it should be clearly communicated to staff and inmates. Some policy or procedures within a prison (including almost all security policies) are only available for staff. For instance, inmates should not know the tactics staff will use to respond to a disturbance or a riot. However, most nonsecurity policies are made available to inmates, so they know what is expected of them and of staff. A failure in policy implementation often occurs when it is assumed that once a policy is adopted, written, and authorized, it will be followed by staff. However, in any organization, change and modification of past routines is difficult, and there is an organizational momentum to continue present practices. This requires there be a major effort to communicate new security policies to staff through briefings and training.

The third element of effective security policy is to ensure procedures are consistently carried out. For instance, many prisons have policies prohibiting smoking in common areas, such as in television rooms. If one correctional officer lets inmates smoke in the television room, it makes enforcement of the policy much more difficult for those who do not allow smoking. It can also cause tensions and fights between inmates who want to smoke and those who do not want to be bothered by smoke. Security policies often relate to issues where inmates should not have a choice, and staff have to make a decision and enforce it. In the smoking example, if staff let inmates decide whether there will be smoking in the television area, the strongest or most violent inmates would always get their way.

Inmates realize the need for security, and they welcome the opportunity to live in a safe environment. They recognize that they may not like the infringement on their freedoms resulting from security policies. Yet, they also recognize that if these policies are not consistently implemented, or staff are not diligent in their monitoring and enforcement, some inmates will take advantage of the complacency and violate the policies. In effect, the overall safe environment for inmates as well as staff can be undermined. It is acknowledged that in a prison, inmates will accept and begin to follow any reasonable policy that is consistently enforced. However, if there is inconsistency, they are likely to not accept or follow the policy, and they may continue to test the limits and attempt to avoid compliance. This creates a tension among staff and inmates that can result in violence or inmate disturbances.

Monitoring Policy Implementation

The method most commonly used to monitor security policy implementation is through an active program of "security audits," the process that determines the extent to which policy is effectively carried out and contributes to the safe and secure prison environment. There are three types of audits of correctional facilities to monitor security operations: an audit of ACA standards, a policy audit, and a security operations audit.[10] ACA provides audits of correctional facilities to determine whether ACA will "accredit" a facility. A team of objective ACA-trained auditors comes to the prison, reviews written policy, and observes procedures. If all standards identified as "life safety" and 90 percent of others are met, ACA will accredit the prison, meaning that it meets standards of professional operations. However, the ACA audit covers the entire operation of the prison and does not provide an in-depth or intense focus on security within the prison.

The second type of audit is a policy audit, which ascertains whether broad agency policy is in place at the prison. In most states, the central headquarters of a correctional agency will dictate broad policy that must be complied with by each prison in the state. An example of a statewide security policy is that "all vehicles, carts, and equipment must be throughly inspected before being allowed to enter or exit a prison." The policy audit would match all the agency-required policy with local prison policy to determine whether there is a like policy in place at the prison to address each agency policy. A policy audit is valuable to begin an overall review of security operations, but it only identifies whether there are the required scope of written, authorized, and mandated policies at the prison. It does not determine compliance with implementation, consistency in practice, or thoroughness of procedures.

That type of intensive review is the role of the third type of audit, the security audit. The security audit identifies whether the policies are actually and consistently being carried out by correctional staff. Whereas the policy audit is a review of written documents, the security audit is a review of actual operations. It is usually completed by a team of knowledgeable security professionals who can observe the methods by which correctional staff carry out their assignments and identify if there is any lack of compliance with established policy. Even though staff are aware their behavior is being observed during a security audit, such an audit procedure can identify those weaknesses in compliance resulting from failure to train staff, use of improper procedures, or misunderstandings about the policy requirements.

A good program of policy and procedure will meet acceptable professional standards, such as those pronounced by ACA, will clearly communicate policy to staff and train them in its implementation, and will audit procedures on a regular basis to ensure compliance. To reiterate, policy and procedure should be well written, clearly communicated, and consistently carried out. With these elements in place, policy and procedure are an integral part of creating a safe and secure prison environment.

■ INMATE ACCOUNTABILITY

Like many other elements critical to effective security in a prison environment, **inmate accountability** is one that requires an understanding of day-to-day functions in a prison. With inmates out of their cells almost 18 hours in a normal day, and without movements during which all inmates are closely watched, it is essential to have systems to maintain accountability of where inmates are supposed to be and to confirm that they are there. Inmate accountability is often defined in fairly narrow terms. In *Guidelines for the Development of a Security Program*, the authors write, "Inmate accountability, the staff's ability to locate and identify inmates at any point in time, is the very heart of institution security, from minimum-security camps to maximum-security penitentiaries."[11] For this textbook, inmate accountability will be more broadly defined, with several categories of activities:

■ A routine schedule of activities that is followed on a regular basis.
■ The availability of program and work opportunities and a process to assign inmates to these opportunities in order to have them under the supervision of staff responsible for that program or work activity.
■ A system of movement that reduces the likelihood that inmates may go to other than their assigned locations.

▪ Both casual and direct inmate supervision during all out-of-cell times.

▪ Inmate counts at regular and random times to ensure the correct number is in custody and in the location within the prison as assigned.

A Daily Routine

A normal day of prison activities has many routine functions that should occur daily at exactly the same time and in the same manner. As an example, on a weekday, inmates may be awakened between 5:30 A.M. and 6:00 A.M. and released from their cells at 6:00 A.M. to shower and prepare for the workday. Doors to the housing unit open and inmates may go to the dining hall for breakfast from 6:30 to 7:00; they must return to their housing unit by 7:15 A.M. There will often be a "work call," at 7:30 A.M., when the work and program day begins, and inmates move to their assigned jobs or programs, such as educational or vocational training. Inmates remain at their assignment until 10:30, when they are to return to their housing unit, and then be released to move to the dining hall (usually one unit at a time) to eat lunch from 11:00 until 12:00 noon.

After return to the unit from lunch, there will be an afternoon work call at 12:30, and inmates will remain at their assignments until 3:30 P.M. They again return to the housing unit, and release to dinner (as with lunch) begins at 4:45 P.M. Once dinner is served, evening programs and unstructured (any inmates who are not working or in a program may participate) recreation begins. At 8:30 P.M., inmates return for the final time of the day to their housing unit. They may watch television, play table games, or use telephones to call family or friends in the housing unit until 11:30 P.M., when they are locked in their cells. The next day, the same routine begins again.

This type of routine is very important, because it serves as the foundation for inmate accountability. Staff and inmates know the schedule and routine, and they prepare to follow it. For instance, a few minutes before the 7:30 A.M. work call, inmates will gather inside the housing unit door and wait for the unit correctional officer to unlock the door when work call begins at 7:30. Although they are not that excited or anxious to go to work, they know the routine and out of habit and for ease in movement, gather at the door. It is similar to how airplane passengers begin to move to the gateway to board an airplane when they know the gate personnel are preparing to begin boarding. Even though they have an assigned seat and everyone is going to be boarded, human nature is to prepare for an activity one knows is about to happen. In the prison situation, inmates who do not make the movement or go to their assignments at the scheduled time are quickly identified as "out of place," not where they are supposed to be.

Program and Work Assignments

In Chapter 6, there was extensive discussion of the importance of active and productive inmate programs within a prison. In addition to the rehabilitative potential of these programs, they also aid in security by keeping inmates active, which limits the time inmates might otherwise direct toward planning an escape or violating rules; providing opportunities for positive interaction between staff and inmates; and helping to pass the time. However, the most important security outcome of an ample amount of inmate assignments is that it is supervised by staff and inmates are kept under watch, without the unsettling feeling of a lack of privacy.

In most prisons, all inmates must have an assignment of program or work five days per week. Some work activities (such as food service) involve work on the weekends and may not follow the normal work schedule outlined in the example. However, most assignments do fall into this schedule. Each work and program assignment is supervised by a staff member. As an example, an inmate assigned to participate in an educational program will be assigned to the classroom of a specific teacher, who checks the inmate in at the beginning of the activity, and is responsible for them until the end of the assignment. Similarly, inmates working in the plumbing shop of the maintenance department are assigned to the staff in charge of that shop, and the inmates remain under his or her supervision until the assignment ends for the day. The benefit for inmate accountability is that there are specific correctional staff responsible for inmates who are assigned to them; the staff maintains continuous supervision of the inmates during that period of time.

Inmate Movements

As is obvious from the routine schedule, prison inmates do not stay in one location throughout the day. They move in large groups from their housing units to work, to meals, or to educational or recreation programs. As an alternative to total individual movement or unregulated mass movement, many institutions use a "controlled" system of inmate moves. This is true in minimum security institutions as well as higher-security prisons. **Controlled movement** is based on the daily schedule and provides for all inmates to move at the specified time. For example, when the 7:30 A.M. work call is announced, the doors to the housing unit and the program work activity areas will be concurrently unlocked, staff who unlock the doors stand at the doors and watch inmates come and go, and inmates have a certain amount of time (usually 10 minutes) to go from one location to another. At the end of the 10 minutes, the doors are all relocked; inmates must be at their designated and assigned area or are subject to disciplinary action.

The advantage of a controlled movement system is that it limits the times that inmates may be moving or walking around the prison and when they must be monitored. With everyone moving at once, security doors within the prison can remain locked most of the time, allowing for inmates to be isolated in smaller groups if a disturbance breaks out. With a relatively short period of time for a move, inmates cannot stand and talk to other inmates (perhaps to organize gang activities or pass information), and they do not have time to go to an unauthorized area and still get to their designated location. A prison that has an effective controlled movement system is a model of efficiency; doors are unlocked and locked exactly on time. Inmates know they cannot move slowly and miss the movement without getting in trouble for violating a rule. Efficient controlled movement gives staff both real and perceived control over inmates, because they, through subtle and relaxed means, require inmate compliance and obedience to rules.

There are instances when inmates must move individually and may not be able to move at the exact time of a mass movement. They may have a visit from family or perhaps their attorney, they may have an appointment with the prison or a contract physician, or they may be required to meet with a staff member who is not their work or program supervisor. These individual movements can also be controlled in a variety of ways. Usually, prisons require these institutional appointments, such as the physician appointment or an interview with a staff member, to be scheduled at least a day in advance. A "call out" schedule is prepared and distributed to staff with a schedule of all inmates who have times they are authorized to move to a location other than their usual assignment.

A call out system, with staff monitoring the individual movement, is usually sufficient for inmate accountability. However, some institutions also use a "pass system" as an alternative or even double-check of the authorized movement. A prison **pass system** is similar to that used in many high schools: an inmate is issued a pass by the work or program supervisor to go to the scheduled appointment. The pass indicates the time an inmate leaves the supervision of the releasing staff, and it is signed by the receiving staff who notes the time the inmate arrives and leaves the appointment. On return to the work or program supervisor, the pass is returned to the staff member, who completes the process by noting the return time. Staff are aware of the time it takes to move from one area of the prison to another and quickly recognize any discrepancy in the times noted on the pass. Staff who see inmates moving should ask to see if they have a pass allowing the movement, proving they are authorized to go where they are headed.

Through both controlled mass movements and using call-outs or a pass system to monitor individual movement, staff can easily control inmates going from one prison location to another without having to escort them. A well-coordinated system of daily schedules and inmate movements is valuable to a successful system of inmate accountability. In addition, schedules and timely movements enhance the opportunity for staff to monitor and supervise inmates.

Casual and Direct Supervision of Inmates

Another element of inmate accountability is the casual and direct supervision of inmates. As expected, staff work and program supervisors are responsible for inmates during the times they are assigned to a particular activity, and correctional officers in the housing units are responsible for their supervision when they are locked in the units. However, inmate accountability can be enhanced through casual, as well as direct, supervision. **Casual supervision** is supervision by staff who are not responsible for the inmate but still have the opportunity to monitor movement and activity. Well-designed prisons take the need for casual supervision into account in the construction of the facility. The location of staff offices and windows, and the use of windows in walls between areas of the prison, allow staff to watch inmates as they perform other duties.

The design of a prison educational area is an example of how casual supervision works. Educational administrators have offices with windows that view the prison center yard or compound area, across which inmates move from one location to another. The windows facilitate the viewing of inmates during movements. The administrators also have large windows into adjacent classrooms or the library area, so they may casually supervise inmates in those locations and support the supervising staff, in case there are any confrontations. Classrooms have large windows from the classroom to the interior corridor, adjacent classrooms, and the outside of the building. Teaching staff can watch other inmates, and other staff can see if the teachers are in trouble and need assistance. This ability to see in and out keeps staff from feeling isolated and insecure, as well as providing opportunities for casual supervision of inmates throughout the prison.

Inmate Counts

The final "piece of the puzzle" for inmate accountability is a procedure of counting inmates at varying locations and times of the day. There are three types of **prison counts:** regular, census, and random. Regular counts are the scheduled counting of inmates to ensure that all inmates in the prison are still there and have not escaped. Because counting is done several times during the day, inmates know they will be quickly discovered missing. ACA standards require a minimum of one count per eight-hour correctional shift; however, most agencies have at least five scheduled counts during a day. These counts usually take place at midnight and 3:00 A.M. when inmates are asleep in their cells, before work call at approximately 7:00 A.M., after return from work for the day (approximately 4:00 P.M.), and when inmates are required to return to their housing units after evening programs or recreation (approximately 9:00 P.M.). These counts not only note the number of inmates to ensure all are present but also identify the inmates (sometimes using cards with pictures of the inmates during the count).

In addition, census counts are less formal counts, conducted by work and program supervisors as well as correctional officers. They are held at the beginning and end of each work period to ensure that each work or program detail has the right amount of inmates assigned there. Random counts can be done at any time. Because inmates know when the regular and census counts are held, random counts "keep them honest," so they cannot plan on trying to leave their assigned area right after a count, because a random count may occur at any time.

As noted at the beginning of this section, inmate accountability is at the heart of institution security. As can be seen by the interwoven elements of accountability, these procedures provide prisons a method to have relaxed and staff-efficient inmate movements, without compromising security. If inmates were allowed to go wherever they desired at any time in the prison, they could participate in all types of behavior, which could undermine the safe and secure environment for staff and other inmates.

CONTROL OF CONTRABAND

Another essential element of prison security is to control contraband. **Contraband** is broadly described as any item that inmates are not allowed to possess. Contraband includes those items that can assist in an escape (ladders or ropes), are dangerous (weapons or drugs), can sabotage or subvert prison physical security (chewing gum that can damage locking devices or wire cutters that can cut a security fence), or nuisance items that can promote unhealthy or unsanitary conditions (clothing beyond the issued amount or unsealed food that could spoil in an inmate's cell). All of these categories of contraband can undermine the maintenance of a safe and secure prison environment. Many prison policies and procedures and much staff time is directed toward the control of contraband.

All prisons have policies that identify contraband items that are not allowed in an inmate's possession, or those items that are allowed in certain amounts and the limits for an inmate's possession (e.g., one pair of personally owned athletic shoes or five sets of prison-issued work clothing). In addition, the policies often categorize the risk of certain contraband items, and how they should be handled and stored. Tools used in the maintenance and repair of the prison are often included in such categories. One guideline suggests using a minimum of two categories:

▌ Class A tools are those, such as files, knives, saw blades, ladders, ropes, extension cords, lift devices, grinders, and others, presenting inherent safety or security risks. Class A tools should be used only under the direct supervision of staff and are always placed in a secure tool storage area when not in use. Poisonous chemicals, dangerous drugs, acids, and hypodermic needles should be controlled with the Class A methods.

▌ Class B tools, such as light pliers, short power cords, and others, constitute a lower-level of risk. They may be stored, issued, and used under less stringent conditions, but the institution or department still must account for them.[12]

Institution policy also identifies procedures to keep inmates from possessing contraband items and methods to search for contraband. Contraband may end up in the possession of inmates in many ways. First, they may receive prohibited items through the usual mail and package procedures. Second, visitors may bring items into the prison. Third, items that are in the prison, but that should not be in the possession of inmates without staff supervision, may be smuggled by inmates out of the area of use or storage. And finally, unethical staff may provide inmates with prohibited items.

Controlling Contraband Through Searching. One critical way of preventing prisoners from obtaining contraband involves an active program for searching inmates and their housing areas. Here, a correctional officer is performing a "pat down" search on an inmate, and a correctional officer is searching the property of an inmate cell. (Courtesy of the Federal Bureau of Prisons)

Prisons encourage correspondence by inmates with family and friends, and inmates may usually send and receive an unlimited number of letters. Prisons require inmates to pay for their own postage, unless they are indigent, in which case they will be provided with a small number of stamps per month. Mail received in a prison is not read, but it is opened and searched for contraband items. This process takes a tremendous amount of staff time, yet it is critical to keep small items such as drugs from being mailed to a prison. Many prisons prohibit receiving packages (with food or personal clothing items) from family or friends, because items cannot be searched well enough to find anything that could be concealed in them. Hardback books and magazines may only be ordered and mailed to the inmate directly from the publisher, reducing the opportunity for anyone to hide a small item in the publication.

The visiting area is highest in risk for introducing contraband into a prison setting. Visiting is considered by prison officials as important in order to maintain inmates's ties to their community contacts and in order to accomplish successful reintegration on release. The visiting room is designed to allow as relaxed as possible contact and conversation between inmates and visitors. Only inmates who have proven to be a serious risk for escape or committing violent acts are not accorded contact visiting. Therefore, in the usual visiting setting, it is difficult to control the introduction of contraband such as drugs. Visitors have been known to put drugs in small balloons and pass them to the inmate who swallows the balloon. At a later time, the inmate retrieves the drugs in the balloon when they defecate. As unthinkable as this seems, the value of drugs in a prison make this a method that inmates are willing to endure.

Prisons initially require inmates to list the persons they want to include on their visiting list, and if a proposed visitor has a criminal record, they may be denied the right to visit. Visitors must pass through a metal detector on entry to the prison, and they are permitted to take only limited personal items into the visiting room, such as money and unopened packages of cigarettes. The prisons provide lockers for storage of other personal items such as purses. During the visit, correctional staff (often using camera surveillance for assistance) watch the visiting room and the conduct of inmates and visitors. When the visit is over, inmates are "strip searched" before reentering the prison area. When all visiting is over, the visiting room is searched before any more inmates enter the area.

In local jails and for violent and escape-prone inmates, visiting is "noncontact" and is afforded through glass and telephones. Even in these situations, drugs have been smuggled in, often by inserting a drug-filled straw through the hole where the telephone handset cord enters the wall. A relatively new technology to avoid this is video visitation, allowing inmates to converse with visitors without leaving their cells.[13] In these circumstances in which noncontact visiting is acceptable practice, video visitation reduces the smuggling of drugs and other small items. Video visiting can also reduce staff time. "Prior to the installation of video visitation, Brevard County (Florida) Jail was using four staff members to conduct visitation. Today, only one staff member is assigned to that task."[14]

Inmates often attempt to smuggle items already in the prison out of the allowed area of supervision. An example of contraband that can cause health and sanitation problems is food that is served in the dining room. Inmates may try to get extra food, sell it to others, or keep it for their own use at a later time. More serious contraband includes tools, such as those described as Class A, that are a serious risk to safety and security. Inmates who work in food service often must be issued knives to prepare food. Those who work in a maintenance shop may sometimes be issued pliers that can cut wires. Prison procedures call for several actions to reduce the chance of tools that can aid in escapes or be used in violent acts from falling into an inmate's unauthorized possession.

Class A tools are usually hung on a "shadow board," a light colored background with the outline of the tool painted on it. It is quickly obvious to staff when the tool is missing. When they are issued to inmates, there is a record of what staff issued what tool and the inmate to whom it was given. As a double check, inmates who work in these areas often have "chits," or small metal or plastic tokens with their names engraved on them, and the chits are hung on the shadow board in place of the tool when it is checked out. Before the end of the work period, all tools must be accounted for and back on the shadow board before allowing inmates to leave. And finally, before inmates are released from a work area with these type of tools, they are searched and may have to walk through a metal detector.

Unfortunately, there are a very small percentage of staff who will bring contraband items to inmates. Some will do it for money, because inmates will arrange payment to the staff member by someone in the community if they bring drugs or, possibly, weapons into the prison. Other naive staff may do it "to be nice," bringing an inmate only nuisance items such as food or cigarettes, which an inmate cannot get in prison. However, in these situations, the staff member does not realize the "trap" into which they have fallen. Manipulative inmates will threaten to tell prison officials about the staff actions, knowing the staff will receive disciplinary action, such as suspension without pay or even job loss. The inmates then blackmail the staff into bringing more serious and dangerous contraband into the prison in exchange for their silence. Once in this situation, the staff member is totally at the mercy of the inmate, and they usually end up resigning to avoid the inmate pressure or getting caught and either terminated from employment or prosecuted for their illegal actions of bringing contraband into a prison.

Most prisons do not search or require their staff to walk through metal detectors as they come to work. Practically, because the staff knows the process and search procedures, it would be simple to avoid detection. In principle, agencies want to indicate to staff that they are trusted and try to share the responsibility of identifying staff who may be smuggling items with line staff as well as administrators. Every prison training program for new staff includes a discussion of how smuggling items to inmates undermines the safety of fellow staff and the manipulative process that inmates go through to trap staff, as illustrated in the preceding example. Even so, there are some staff who make the mistake or intentionally decide to assist inmates in smuggling items into the prison.

■ THE ROLE OF PROFESSIONAL STAFF

As might be expected, the way that staff do their jobs can have a tremendous impact on the creation of a safe and secure environment within a prison setting. First, staff must carry out their assigned duties in a thorough and effective manner. Second, if staff communicate with inmates in a respectful and courteous manner, it has a positive impact on reducing tension and encourages discussion about inmate concerns or grievances. Positive interaction between staff and inmates opens lines of communication that can lead to inmates providing staff advance warning about plans to escape, assault of another inmate, or a riot. Particularly in crowded institutions, with the potential for an increased level of tension and frustration, communications between staff and inmates is critical. George and Camile Camp, in discussing the importance of staff and inmate communications in crowded prisons, note

> Lack of effective communication can lead to frustration. Impatience within the system can cause discontentment, disenchantment and even disturbances. Keeping staff and inmates informed of the administration's concerns and plans for dealing with crowding becomes extremely important. Communication is a valuable means of ensuring stability and providing opportunity for feedback before implementation of specific programs.[15]

As was previously noted, it is critical for staff to consistently carry out security procedures in order to create a routine and ensure regular compliance of rules by inmates. However, the quality and style of communications is also critical, because each individual interaction between a staff member and an inmate contributes to the overall culture of a prison and can establish a relaxed environment. The accompanying case study offers an illustration.

PRACTICAL PERSPECTIVES

The Importance of Respect

Robert Dillion, a new correctional officer at Alpha State Prison, wants to establish himself as tough and unwilling to take anything from inmates. He is assigned as a "yard officer," and, as such, he watches inmates move across the prison compound from one building to another. As a part of his duties, he is to randomly "pat search" inmates. A pat search is the same as a frisking by the police. Officers move their hands over inmates to search for concealed weapons, drugs, or other contraband under their clothing. When Dillion sees an inmate (Jones) he wants to pat search, he calls out, "Hey, you come over here," to the identified inmate, and tells him, "Hold your arms out for a pat down," in a brusk and terse manner. When finished and finding nothing prohibited, he orders the inmate, "OK, keep moving."

Jones realizes he will be searched from time to time but doesn't like the attitude of disrespect he believes that Dillion presented. He is angry about it, and when he arrives at his work area, he is confronted by his work supervisor who wants to discuss his recent poor performance with him. Jones is not a very responsible or mature person and reluctantly begins the conversation with his supervisor. When the supervisor asks why he did not complete a task assigned the previous day, Jones angrily responds, "You guys are just looking for me to screw up, and this is a bunch of bull." The supervisor tries to calm him down, but Jones only seems to get madder and starts yelling at the supervisor. Soon, other correctional staff have to intervene, and while trying to move Jones away, Jones strikes one of them. He is forced to the ground by staff, handcuffed, and taken to the special housing unit (used to separate inmates who are unruly or violate rules).

This incident can happen almost anytime with Jones because of his lack of maturity and responsibility. However, when correctional officer Peter Meeks is working as the yard officer, there are fewer such problems. Meeks's style is different from Dillion's. Meeks would handle the pat searches as such. When Jones approaches, and Meeks decides to pat him down, he looks at Jones and states, "Mr. Jones, could you step over here, I need to pat you down." When Meeks finishes the search without discovering anything, he says, "That's it, Mr. Jones, thank you." Jones is not thrilled with being searched, but goes on feeling that Meeks respects him through his courtesy. Both Dillion and Meeks accomplish their tasks equally effective, yet both created an outcome (Dillion's bad, and Meeks's good) as a result of how they did their job.

This simple example is all too common in some prisons. It does not take too many Dillions to create a tense and angry atmosphere, leading to the likelihood of violence and undermining the safety of staff and inmates. But how does a correctional administrator create a culture of respect and courtesy in an environment with hostile inmates, many of whom have a history of violence and impulsiveness? Staff must carry out their duties and maintain control, and they do not want to be seen as "weak" by inmates or fellow staff members. The case study in Chapter 4, in which the warden recognized the need to modify the communications between staff and inmates is a good example. The warden took leadership by clarifying expected behavior, involving staff in explaining to others the important reasons for professional communications, and involving supervisors and holding them accountable in correcting such improper behavior. Without such decisive action, a negative and hostile culture can easily develop and become both hard to change and a danger to the overall safe and secure environment for staff and inmates.

DOING THE BASICS

Most correctional administrators would argue that the most important activity for maintaining a safe and secure prison environment is to "take care of the basics." This means not only having an effective security policy but also providing services required and expected by inmates in a professional and competent manner. One of the results of incarceration is that inmates do not have the right to choose many services they receive, such as food service, medical care, clothing and laundry service, and the purchase of personal items. They eat whatever is served in the dining room at meals.

They receive medical care from prison medical staff or contracted medical personnel. They wear the clothing that is issued, and they may not alter or personalize it to fit their own taste or cultural style. And, although they are allowed to buy limited personal items such as athletic clothing and shoes, snack foods, and toiletries, they must buy the brands and pay the prices offered at the prison commissary.

There are, no doubt, many citizens and public officials who would argue that these services are too good for inmates. They note that people who do not commit crimes have to use their own money to buy food and clothing, and to receive medical care. The issue in prison, however, is that inmates do not have a choice of what they eat, the medical professionals they see, the clothing they wear, or the personal items they buy. When people do not have a choice, they naturally have complaints about the quality and timely delivery of service. Therefore, it is important that prison staff provide these basic services professionally and ensure the services meet acceptable community standards.

From a safety and security standpoint, failure to do so increases tension and inmate frustration within a prison. If inmates believe staff are negligent or insensitive in delivery of these services (whether true or not), it heightens anxiety and reduces feelings of respect and trust between inmates and staff. A situation filled with these emotions is ripe for rash acts of violence. This condition creates a dangerous precipitating situation, in which a minor act or incident can spark a riot or inmate disturbance.

Although there may be legitimate arguments as to the type and scope of services that should be offered in prisons, once an expectation for a certain level of service is established, it must be maintained. If prison policy dictates that services will be provided in a certain manner, and inmates perceive the policy is not being met, that failure undermines security and safety. The condition that most likely results in a problem is creating expectation through a policy or past levels of service and then failing to continue at that level or to meet that policy. Correctional administrators understand that inmates will accept almost any conditions, if they are meeting policy, are clearly communicated, staff perform professionally and show empathy, and there is consistency in providing services. Inmates know they are in prison, and if staff are honest and do their best to do their jobs, inmates accept that as the status quo.

▰▰▰ SUMMARY

This chapter described the proactive activities that are critical to creating a safe and secure environment in prisons. The overlapping and integration of certain security elements (layers of physical security, use of technology, methods of inmate accountability) seems very complex. Yet, there are many basics to effective prison security (good communications, doing what you say you will do, consistency in practices) that seem rather simple. In reality, creating a safe and secure environment is a combination of some very complex and some very simple components. The more simple task for an administrator is to construct the needed concepts in the creation of a safe and secure environment. The most difficult task is to maintain them at a consistent and acceptable level of performance.

Professional life in the public sector, especially the public sector in which the activity is dealing with people, is a very tenuous experience. Even when all the proactive systems of security are implemented in perfect fashion, and everything is going smoothly in a prison, the one thing that is sure is that *things will change.* People are different and act differently from day to day. The racial makeup of inmates or the number of gang members can cause conflicts that disrupt stability. Factors outside the prison (legislative adoption of new laws or emotional situations, such as the Rodney King assault by the Los Angeles police) can change the mood of the inmate population. At any time, a situation can create change in the usual operation of a prison, and correctional administrators must be able to quickly respond to the change.

This chapter addressed the important activities of managing inmates in usual situations using standard approaches to prison security. However, all situations within a prison are not usual, and the day-to-day activities of prison administration are not enough when the risk of violence or escape increases. Correctional administrators must be equipped to deal with these extreme cases, to manage prison gangs, and to react to prison riots and emergencies. The next chapter addresses many of the actions necessary by correctional administrators to manage violent inmates.

ENDNOTES

1. R. Montgomery, "American Prison Riots: 1774–1991," in *Prison Violence in America,* 2nd ed., edited by M. Braswell, R. Montgomery, and L. Lombardo. (Cincinnati, OH: Anderson Publishing, 1994), pp. 224–252.
2. M. Silberman, "Violence as Social Control in Prison," *Virginia Review of Sociology* (1992): 77–97. Another good overview of violence in prisons is found in Matthew Silberman, *A World of Violence: Corrections in America* (Belmont, CA: Wadsworth, 1995).
3. No author, "The Security Audit Program: A 'How To' Guide and Model Instrument for Adaptation to Local Standards, Policies, and Procedures," a work in progress document by the National Institute of Corrections (Washington, DC: U.S. Department of Justice, November, 1999), p. 1.
4. Ibid.
5. Camile Graham Camp and George M. Camp, *The Corrections Yearbook: 1998* (Middletown, CT, Criminal Justice Institute, Inc., 1998), pp. 18–19.
6. For a review of these models, see James Austin, "Special Edition: Prison Classification Systems" in *Crime and Delinquency* (Beverly Hills, CA: Sage, 1986).
7. N. Holt, *Inmate Classification: A Validation Study of the California System* (Sacramento, CA: California Department of Corrections, June, 1996).
8. These definitions are taken from the classification manual of the California Department of Corrections (Sacramento, CA: California Department of Corrections, 1998).
9. James D. Henderson, W. Hardy Rauch, and Richard L. Phillips, *Guidelines for the Development of a Security Program,* 2nd ed. (Lanham, MD: American Correctional Association, 1997), p. 21.
10. "The Security Audit Program," p. 2.

11. Henderson et al., p. 65.
12. Henderson et al., pp. 143–144.
13. Harry S. Sands Jr. and Anthony H. Johnson, "Visitation in Absentia: New Technology Allows Inmates to Receive Visitor Without Leaving Cells," *Corrections Today* 59 no.2 (April 1997): 96–98.
14. Ibid., p. 97
15. George M. Camp and Camile G. Camp, *Management of Crowded Prisons* (Washington, DC: U.S. Department of Justice, 1989), p. 51.

▧ KEY TERMS

classification	low security
objective classification systems	medium security
detainer	razor ribbon
perimeter security	close security
towers	maximum security
mobile patrols	inmate accountability
electronic detection device	controlled movement
internal perimeter	pass system
secure envelop	casual supervision
dormitory style housing	prison counts
outside cells	contraband
inside cells	minimum security

▧ YOU'RE THE CORRECTIONAL ADMINISTRATOR

1. You are the new warden at a close security prison that has been fraught with several security lapses, resulting in two escapes, several assaults by inmates on other inmates, and a serious assault on a staff member. There have not been audits to determine what security problems actually exist and why these events occurred. However, morale of both inmates and staff is very low, and you were told to "get in there and straighten things out." What do you do? How do you begin? What priorities would you take to create a safe and secure environment within this prison?

2. You are the warden at a well-operated, low-security prison. However, the state has been experiencing rapid increases in inmates, and the prisons are very overcrowded. The department has done an analysis of the new inmates and determined that longer sentences have resulted in an increasing number of higher-security inmates. You have been told that your prison needs to be converted to a medium security prison and that you will begin to receive medium security inmates in six months. You must prepare both the facility and the staff for this transition. What do you do? What analyses do you need? What types of changes in physical security, policy and procedures, and other security operations do you need to make? Prepare an action plan for the transition to a medium security prison.

WEB LINK EXERCISES

Federal Bureau of Prisons (BOP): www.bop.gov

Go to the Web site for the Federal Bureau of Prisons. Find the Quick Facts section, and identify the percentage of inmates currently in the BOP by security level, gender, race, and ethnicity. Find any of these facts that differs considerably from the average figures for all state and federal prisons in the United States as indicated in this text. Based on your search of the Web site of the BOP, identify reasons that the BOP percentages may be considerably different from the national averages.

9

Managing Violent and Disruptive Inmates

INTRODUCTION

In Chapter 8, several elements essential to creating a safe and secure prison environment were addressed. It was suggested that a correctional administrator must juggle several balls in order to try to keep all of these elements at a highly effective level and, at the same time, respond to continually changing situations. However successful an administrator is at managing, molding, and maintaining a positive prison environment, there are always incidents that occur to "stir the pot" and undermine the desired stability. On returning home from work and being asked by a spouse or child, "How was work?" it is almost comical for prison wardens to answer, "It was great; a wonderfully boring and routine day."

Unfortunately, too many days in a prison are not routine and boring. The state legislature may be considering a bill to limit recreation for inmates. The governor's office may have called for a 2 percent budget cut through the remainder of the fiscal year. A new agency sick leave policy may have the labor union representing correctional officers upset and threatening a "blue flu." A group of foreign judges may want to tour the facility and spend time discussing international correctional practices. An employee may be having financial difficulties, and creditors want help in collecting debts. The type of incident that most often disrupts the stability of the daily routine results from inmate actions, such as tensions between rival gangs, anxiety as a result of changed security procedures, a serious assault, or rumors of a food strike.

Unfortunately, violence in prisons has been rising over the past few years. After a decline in deaths of prison inmates in the late 1980s, such violence increased steadily from 1992 through 1995 (see Figure 9–1). Why are there so many violent acts in prisons, and are there actions that administrators can take to prevent or reduce the likelihood of violence? There has been considerable research examining violence in prisons and the potential reasons for such violence, including overcrowding;[1] tension

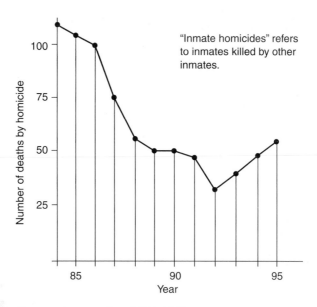

FIGURE 9-1 Inmate homicides 1984–1995. Source: Adapted from *Corrections Compendium*, JUNE, 1996.

between inmate gangs;[2] the powerlessness, boredom, and sexual frustration of inmates;[3] and the importation of street cultures of "face to face rivalries, retaliation, machismo, disrespect, and drunkenness."[4] Interestingly, the overall conclusion is that prisons hold violent people who will continue to act out in violent ways and that the prison culture and environment adds to the tension and threat of violence by inmates.

In *Prison Violence in America*, Braswell, Montgomery, and Lombardo distinguish between interpersonal violence and collective violence.[5] **Interpersonal violence** is that which occurs between two or more individual inmates, but the reason for the violence is a personal issue between the individuals. Collective violence includes prison riots and disturbances that are initiated by one group against another, usually by inmates against prison staff and administration. However, large-scale gang conflicts (sometimes even referred to as "wars") could also fall into this category. **Collective violence** stems from the fundamental difference in values and positions of the two groups, rather than an individual conflict.

This chapter covers the types of actions that correctional administrators take to respond to interpersonal violent or collective inmate activities. Prisons need an effective inmate disciplinary system to hold inmates accountable for their misbehavior, coupled with a method to separate or isolate inmates who must be removed from the general inmate population. Gang management strategies must identify and deal with prison gang activities. Policies must be in place regarding the management of inmates who present the most serious risk for escape or violence, and some agencies have created special prisons only for that purpose. There must also be preparation for emergency situations, such as riots, work or food strikes, or other dangerous group actions by inmates.

INMATE DISCIPLINARY SYSTEMS

What does a prison administrator do to encourage inmates to follow the rules? Although it may seem easy to suggest that staff simply "make them do it," this issue requires a complicated system of enforcing discipline among an inmate population. An **inmate disciplinary system** is the process by which correctional staff, once they become aware of violations of prison rules by inmates, respond. The process includes an accusation of the violation, investigation of the incident, a hearing to determine guilt, and the pronouncement of a sanction if guilt is determined. The following are components of a successful inmate discipline system: (1) a written policy documenting prohibited behavior, which is provided to all inmates; (2) a fair and equitable set of corresponding sanctions increasing with the severity of the rule violation, and a process to appeal those sanctions; (3) a way to separate inmates accused of rule violations from the general inmate population when the security of the prison could be threatened; and (4) opportunities for long term separation or special security handling for inmates who continuously threaten institutional security or against whom a serious threat of violence exists.

Inmate disciplinary processes and policies are guided by the Fourteenth Amendment to the U.S. Constitution, which provides that, "No State shall make or enforce any law which shall abridge the privileges or immunities of citizens of the United States; nor shall any State deprive any person of life, liberty, or property, without due process of law, nor deny any person within its jurisdiction the equal protection of the laws." For inmates, the 1974 case of *Wolff v. McDonnell*[6] dealt with a claim that the state of Nebraska's disciplinary processes were unconstitutional. The Supreme Court, while differentiating between due process required by a defendant at trial and that of a prison inmate, identified the following as required prisoner due process rights:

▮ The right to receive advanced written notice of the alleged infraction.
▮ The right to have sufficient time (at least 24 hours) to prepare a defense.
▮ The right to present documentary evidence and to call witnesses on his or her behalf, unless permitting this would be unduly hazardous.
▮ The right to have assistance (by an inmate or staff representative) when the circumstances of the case are complex or if the prisoner is illiterate.
▮ The right to a written statement of the findings of an impartial disciplinary committee of the evidence relied on to support the finding of fact and the reasons the disciplinary action was taken.

Inmate Discipline Policy and Process

The first component of an inmate disciplinary system is a written policy that documents the specific behavior that is prohibited. This documentation usually explains the process for considering guilt and determining punishments, and the range of punishments that usually result from rule violations. The purpose and scope of the Federal Bureau of Prisons' policy regarding inmate discipline is stated as follows:

> So that inmates may live in a safe and orderly environment, it is necessary for institution authorities to impose discipline on those inmates whose behavior is not in compliance with Bureau of Prisons rules. The provisions of this rule apply to all per-

sons committed to the care, custody, and control (direct or constructive) of the Bureau of Prisons.[7]

The policy lists all prohibited acts by inmates, such as assaulting any person, escaping from custody, possession of weapons, introduction or possession of any narcotic or drug, stealing, and a general statement prohibiting any conduct that disrupts the secure running of an institution. A copy of the policy is provided to every inmate on arrival at a prison, and in most correctional agencies, the inmates sign it indicating that they have received, read, and understood the policy. If the inmate is illiterate or does not speak or read English, the policy is translated. Because many correctional agencies have a large number of Spanish-speaking inmates, inmate disciplinary policies are usually also available in Spanish. The purpose of providing and having inmates sign the policy is to send a clear message that they are responsible for their actions and that sanctions will be taken against rule violators. The fact that inmates were fully informed of prohibited acts also reduces the potential for successful appeals of inmate disciplinary actions before a federal court.

In most correctional systems, the prohibited acts are categorized by severity. In the Federal Bureau of Prisons policy, there are four categories of prohibited acts: greatest, high, moderate, and low moderate.[8] A specific range of sanctions is authorized for each category if the inmate is found to have committed the prohibited act. There is a two-stage disciplinary process, allowing minor violations to be handled in a less formal manner. The policy process also spells out the time frames associated with each step, so inmates know the time available for collecting evidence or seeking assistance (see Figure 9–2).

In the Federal Bureau of Prisons policy, once staff become aware of the inmates' involvement in the violation, staff have 24 hours to give the inmate written notice (an incident report) of the charges. During this period, there is an investigation of the incident. If, during the investigation, it becomes likely that the incident may result in criminal prosecution for the act, the prison's investigation is suspended, and law enforcement officials are notified to complete the investigation, providing the inmate full due process rights as a criminal offender. When the infraction is minor, the bureau and many other jurisdictions allow correctional officials to use an informal resolution, such as assigning the inmate extra work. On completion of the assignment, the incident report is expunged, and there is no mention of the infraction on the inmate's prison record.

If the incident report is issued to the inmate, there must be an initial hearing within three work days. At this hearing, if the infraction is not serious, the hearing panel (referred to as the Unit Disciplinary Committee [UDC]) can determine guilt and impose minor sanctions, such as a loss of privileges. The inmate may be present during the hearing (except during deliberations), may make a statement, and may present documentary evidence. If the violation is more serious and could result in other than minor sanctions (such as a loss of good time, therefore, lengthening the overall time served in prison, disciplinary transfer to another prison, or disciplinary isolation from the general inmate population), the UDC will refer the case to an upper-level hearing panel, a Discipline Hearing Officer (DHO) in the Bureau of Prisons.[9] The DHO is usually not a staff member of the prison in which the incident took place and, therefore, is believed to be more impartial than prison staff would be.

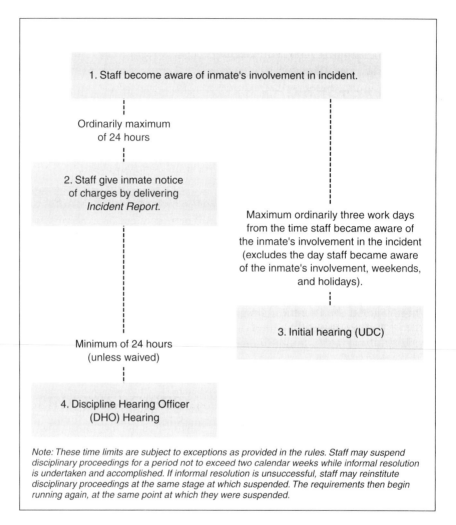

FIGURE 9–2   Time limits in the disciplinary process.

On referral to the DHO, the UDC advises inmates of the rights they will be afforded, based on the limited due process rights spelled out in *Wolff v. McDonnell*. A 1995 U.S. Supreme Court case clarified and gave new guidance to circumstances requiring due process. In *Sandin v. Conner*,[10] the Court acknowledged that the purpose of prison disciplinary action is to maintain good prison management and achieve prisoner rehabilitative goals. The Court determined that disciplinary actions in pursuit of those goals, which do not add on to the sentence being served or change the conditions contemplated in the sentence being served, do not create a liberty interest and do not require due process. Thus, under *Sandin*, placement in disciplinary segregation for a temporary period does not trigger the need for due process, whereas loss of good time extending the sentence does. However, even after the *Sandin* decision, most prisons continued to provide the full *Wolff* due process rights for handling inmate discipline.

Inmates are provided a written finding of the UDC referring the incident to the DHO. Prisons do not allow inmates to use attorneys to assist them in disciplinary hearings but will provide a staff representative to ensure that the inmate understands the process and their rights. Staff also may assist in gathering evidence or speaking to witnesses.[11] The inmate may be present for the hearing, request witnesses who have information directly relevant to the charges, and present evidence.

The DHO considers all evidence presented at the hearing and may find that the inmate either committed or did not commit the prohibited act. A record is made of the proceedings, including the advisement of the inmate rights, the findings, the decision and evidence relied on in the decision, and a statement of the reasons for the sanctions imposed. The inmate is given a copy of the decision shortly after the hearing. The sanctions imposed, if there is a finding of guilt, are carried out immediately, even if the inmate appeals the decision. It would be overly burdensome to delay a sanction of disciplinary segregation or transfer simply because an inmate indicated a plan to appeal. The next section describes the types of punishments available for various degrees of disciplinary infractions.

Punishing Inmates for Rule Violations

To enforce rules and provide a disincentive for commission of prohibited acts, prisons have several sanctions that may be taken against misbehaving inmates. Sanctions can be minor, such as restriction from privileges, or may be serious, such as transfer to a "supermax" prison in which inmates have no freedom of movement and very limited time out of their cells. Table 9–1 lists types of sanctions (in increasing levels of severity) that are often used to discipline inmates.

■■■■ TABLE 9–1

Possible Sanctions
Warning
Reprimand
Assignment of extra duty
Restriction to quarters
Impounding of personal property
Loss of job
Removal from program or group activity
Change of quarters
Loss of privileges (recreation or commissary)
Monetary restitution
Withholding good time
Disciplinary segregation
Disciplinary transfer
Placement in supermax prison

Warning. Warnings are usually issued as a part of an informal sanction but may also be used as a sanction for a minor rule violation. Some jurisdictions allow a temporary "suspension" of disciplinary action, with an inmate receiving a warning. If there are no further violations during the period of suspension, the warning is sufficient, and the rule violation may even be expunged from the inmate's record.

Reprimand. A reprimand is one level more serious than a warning, and some jurisdictions may combine the two and issue a "warning and reprimand." A reprimand is simply a written admonishment against the behavior with no other sanction or punishment and is usually coupled with a warning that another violation will result in a more serious sanction.

Assignment of extra duty. Prisons always have extra work that needs to be done, and they sometimes save certain jobs for "extra duty" inmates. Assignments are usually for a specific number of hours (e.g., eight hours of extra duty) and can be carried out in one or two ways. The inmate may be assigned a specific job, such as picking up cigarette butts from the inner yard of the prison for two hours each night for the next four nights. Or, the inmate may be told to report to a certain staff member for the next four evenings at 6:00 P.M. for assignment of two hours of extra duty work.

Restriction to quarters. A rather common punishment is restriction to quarters, which simply means that the inmate must remain in the quarter's location for a specific period of time (e.g., one week) whenever they are not at work, meals, or an assigned program. Correctional officers working a housing unit have a list of inmates on restriction and will randomly check to be sure they have not left the building.

Impounding of personal property. Inmates may have personal property that is not allowed in the prison, or they may have a greater amount than is allowed (e.g., five personal books are allowed and an inmate has eight). A sanction is to confiscate or impound something, and either hold it or require the inmate to pay to send it out of the prison.

Loss of job. Inmates must work while they are in prison, and they strive to get a job they like or that pays well. As a punishment (usually only when the infraction has something to do with the job assignment), they may lose their job and have to find or be assigned another, less favored job.

Removal from program or group activity. Similar to the loss of a job, if the infraction is linked to a program or group activity, the inmate may be removed. As an example, if the inmate is disruptive in a voluntary educational program, he or she may be removed. Removal may be permanent, or the inmate may be allowed to reapply to the program after a specific period of time.

Change of quarters. Inmates may be required to move from one housing unit to another. This sanction may be used if an inmate is verbally abusive to a staff member in the unit, or if it is a privileged housing assignment and the inmate fails to meet required sanitation standards.

Loss of privileges. Effective punishments include restricting inmates from participation in recreation or the loss of the use of the prison commissary. Recreation is very important to inmates, as is the opportunity to buy personal items (snack foods or toiletry items). This sanction is usually for a specific period of time.

Monetary restitution. If the infraction included damaging government or another inmate's property, the violating inmate may be required to pay for the damage. This sanction has a dual benefit: It forces inmates to accept responsibility for their actions by paying for their damage, and during the time it takes them to pay (inmates usually have limited funds and restitution is deducted from their prison job earnings until completed), they have little money to spend on commissary products they would like to buy.

Withholding good time. Prison sentences allow inmates to earn a certain number of days off their sentence for each month of good behavior. When good time is not granted, it actually lengthens the sentence and eliminates the inmate's freedom. Therefore, this sanction can usually only be eliminated or withheld by the DHO or other second-tier hearing disciplinary panel, when the inmate is provided all the *Wolff v. McDonnell* rights.

Disciplinary segregation. Disciplinary segregation is actually a "jail within the prison." Covered in more detail in the next section, inmates serve a sentence in segregation, in a separate facility from the general inmate population, with little time out of their cells, no participation in programs, and very limited (if any) personal property.

Disciplinary transfer. Inmates who continuously violate prison rules or commit serious violations can be transferred to another prison as punishment. The receiving prison is usually a higher-security level, and therefore, the inmate has less freedom and fewer privileges.

Placement in a supermax prison. Supermax prisons are a relatively new phenomena in the world of corrections, and they are discussed in detail later in this chapter. Supermax prisons are designed to house the most violent and dangerous inmates, and all operations are based on safety and security. Placement in such a prison is usually very undesirable for inmates. In some correctional systems, another panel separate from the disciplinary hearing officer or panel must review and approve transfer to a supermax prison.

Once there is a finding of guilt and imposition of a sanction, the inmate has the opportunity to appeal the disposition. Correctional agencies usually provide an **administrative appeals process,** and federal courts often require inmates to exhaust their administrative remedies before filing for consideration before the court. These administrative appeals are usually at least two levels: The first is for a reconsideration before the warden, and if the inmate is not successful, a second level of review is available at the headquarters or central office level of the agency. Because inmates are seldom accepting of any disciplinary sanction and because the appeal procedure is simple and not burdensome, most serious disciplinary sanctions are appealed by inmates.

In most correctional agencies, the appeal cannot dispute a finding of fact and is limited to a complaint regarding the procedure and due process rights. Inmates have a time limit to appeal, usually 30 days after notice of the decision. In describing the review process, Cripe provides the following description:

> The records (the disciplinary offense report, the investigation report, and the written report of the hearing officer or committee) are examined, to be sure that the procedures required by the agency's disciplinary policy have been followed. The facts of the case and the sanction imposed are summarily reviewed. There must be

some evidence to support the finding of the disciplinary authority. The reviewer ensures that the sanction imposed is within the range of punishments authorized for that offense. There is a legal requirement that the hearing officer or committee record the evidence relied on to support the conclusion reached, and that the reasons for the sanction(s) imposed be given.[12]

Although few disciplinary decisions are overturned in the review process, this process is important to maintain credibility and fairness in the system. In some cases, federal courts will review the appeal process and ensure that appeals are examined as suggested. The courts may examine if, in those instances in which the prison staff did not provide appropriate due process or have sufficient evidence to support the finding of guilt, the appeal process does overturn the decision. If the appeals do not overturn decisions in which there are errors, the courts are likely to accept inmate appeals for consideration. An impartial appeal process promotes acceptance by inmates and prevents expensive and burdensome reviews of disciplinary decisions by federal courts. It also provides an avenue to relieve inmate frustrations and tensions.

Special Housing Units of a Prison

An essential tool for a prison administrator is the ability to temporarily separate inmates believed to be a danger to prison security, or in danger themselves, from the general inmate population. Therefore, prisons have a separate housing area, often referred to as a **special housing unit (SHU),** which serves a similar function to jails in the community. Like a jail, an SHU holds inmates in two general situations: when they are under investigation as a result of an incident or potential incident (administrative detention) and when they are serving a sentence for violating prison rules (disciplinary segregation). An SHU should only be a temporary housing assignment, even though the length of stay could be as long as 12 months. If there is a need for a longer separation from a prison's inmate population, the inmate will usually be moved to another prison.

Administrative detention is a "non-punitive confinement used to house inmates whose continued presence in the general population may pose a serious threat to life, property, self, staff, or other inmates, or to the security or orderly running of the institution."[13] Before inmates can be placed in administrative detention, they must be provided notice of the reasons for placement, with a reasonable degree of detail to facilitate their understanding of those reasons. There are at least three specific categories of placement in administrative detention.

First, inmates may be charged with violating serious rules in the prison, and allowing the inmates to remain in the general prison population threatens prison security or order. Consider this status similar to not awarding someone bail pending the outcome of criminal charges and requiring him or her to remain in jail. An inmate may have had an altercation with another inmate, and both need to be separated to determine whether the problem behind the altercation is over or if it is likely to cause continued fighting or spread to other inmates. In addition, if the violation is severe enough that it is expected that a punishment of disciplinary segregation may result, the inmate is usually held in detention status.

Second, there may not yet be a charge of a rule violation against any specific inmate, yet prison staff know some incident occurred, such as a fight or assault without a firm identification of participants. If staff have a reasonable suspicion that an inmate

Standard SHU Cell. A SHU cell is very secure, with a steel toilet, a sink, a mirror, and a metal bed bolted to the wall and floor. The floors are usually bare concrete. (Courtesy of the Ohio Department of Rehabilitation and Correction)

was involved in the incident, they will hold that inmate in administrative detention until the investigation is completed and more information is collected to determine who was involved. An example is a fight between two inmates in the recreation yard, with several other inmates around, and staff see that some type of altercation is occurring but cannot respond quickly enough to identify the inmate fighters. Staff would call for support from other staff, keep all the inmates in the general area, then examine each inmate for evidence of a fight—scraps or swelling on a hand from throwing a punch or cuts or bruises on their face consistent with being punched. Inmates with these marks would be placed in detention, and the investigation would begin. If there was camera surveillance, the videotapes would be checked. Other inmates in the area would be interviewed to determine whether they witnessed and can identify the fighters. The inmates held would be interviewed to see if they admit to fighting. Once the investigation was complete, the inmates would either be charged with a rule violation and maintained in administrative detention or released if believed not to have been involved.

Third, inmates may be placed in administrative detention for their own safety. If an inmate believes she or he is being threatened or at risk of being assaulted in the prison, the inmate may come to staff and seek protection. For example, an inmate may have seen a codefendant against whom testimony was provided, and the prison staff were not aware of the testimony. The inmate will be placed in administrative detention, and an investigation as to any risk of their remaining in the population will begin. In this situation, the prosecutor will be contacted to confirm whether testimony was provided, and if so, one of the inmates will be transferred to another prison. The inmate who will be transferred remains in administrative detention until moved to the other facility.

The other SHU placement is for **disciplinary segregation.** This is a punitive status, as a result of the finding of guilt for a serious prison rule violation. Disciplinary segregation is for a set amount of time established by the disciplinary officer or committee, and inmates cannot be held in this status beyond the time specified. In the Bureau of Prisons disciplinary policy, infractions of "greatest" severity can result in disciplinary segregation of up to 60 days, infractions of "high" severity can result in up to 30 days, and those of "moderate" severity can result in up to 15 days.[14]

Both administrative detention and disciplinary segregation are in the same SHU building within a prison, and the design of the cells is usually the same. Because there is some difference in status and privileges allowed, the two are in separate locations within the SHU building. Cells are very secure, with metal doors and metal furnishings. The furnishings consist of a stainless steel toilet and sink, a bed, and a writing table (both bolted to the floor or walls). Although single celling of inmates is preferred, most prisons must double-cell inmates because of space needs. Adjacent to the SHU is a fenced recreation area, with concrete floors, located visually separate from other inmate areas.

The privileges in SHU also vary between the two statuses. Administrative detention is to be nonpunitive, and, therefore, inmates have all the privileges afforded the general inmate population. This includes access to their property and the opportunity to continue with program participation. Because inmates cannot be allowed out of the SHU to go to school or attend drug abuse classes, prison staff provide materials and allow inmates to work on these program activities in their SHU cells. Disciplinary segregation is punitive, and inmates are not allowed personal property or participation in programs. In many other operational ways, the two statuses are the same.

In both administrative detention and disciplinary segregation, inmates only come out of their cells when handcuffed and escorted by staff. They have only limited access to recreation, usually five to ten hours per week; they are escorted to the fenced recreation areas in small groups or possibly even individually if they could be assaulted by (or assault) others. Food is the same as that provided to the general inmate population, but it is brought to each cell and inmates eat in their cells. Medical staff make rounds in the SHU several times daily to deliver medication and check on inmates' medical needs. There is usually an examination room in the SHU, which is used when an inmate must be examined by medical staff. All SHU inmates have access to correspondence, limited reading material, and visiting privileges.

There are some inmates whose behavior in a prison is extremely violent and some who attempt to escape. For these inmates it is determined that they cannot remain in a regular prison (even high or maximum security) without being a threat to security. In these cases, the usual inmate disciplinary system is ineffective, and even continued SHU placement for disciplinary segregation may not change behavior. As a result, it becomes apparent that a special placement in an even more secure physical setting is necessary. For these inmates, several states and the Federal Bureau of Prisons have developed "supermax" prisons.

SUPERMAX PRISONS

As prisons across America began to receive a higher proportion of violent and long-term inmates, as well as a greater number of gang-involved inmates, there was a growing concern about how to control and prevent violence. Prison administrators looked for ways to protect staff and other inmates from dangerous, predatory inmates. One solution seemed to be supermax prisons. These ultrahigh-security institutions are designed for maximum inmate control, with few treatment programs and inmate privileges.

During the crime wave that swept across the United States during the Great Depression of the 1930s, correctional administrators were first challenged with how to handle a "new breed" of offenders with serious criminal histories of violence. The answer came with the 1934 opening of Alcatraz Island as a federal prison, the most supermaximum prison ever created in the United States. Sitting literally on a rock, surrounded by water in the San Francisco Bay, Alcatraz was designated to handle the most notorious and dangerous criminals of the era with strict regimens of control and tight security.

However, Alcatraz was very expensive to operate. It had no fresh water wells, and the only transportation system was ferries from San Francisco. Alcatraz was closed in 1963, due in part to these reasons. The closing created new problems and concerns among prison administrators. The replacement for Alcatraz was the U.S. Penitentiary (USP) in Marion, Illinois. Although USP, Marion, did take some of the Alcatraz prisoners, many of the problem prisoners were dispersed throughout the federal system with the intent of rehabilitation, because this had become the dominant correctional rationale of the 1960s. However, after the Attica prison uprising in 1971, the isolation and control methods used at Alcatraz were soon missed.[15]

In 1979, the prison at Marion began reconcentrating high-security inmates, most of whom had been violent or disruptive in other federal prisons, in new long-term units and matriculating them into the systematic Control and Rehabilitation Effort (CARE).[16] Marion was designated as the only "level-six" federal prison. Level six meant higher security and the highest staff-to-inmate ratio in the federal system.[17]

With the new restrictions and higher security, prisoners began coordinating food and work strikes. After a long 1980 work strike, the Bureau of Prisons permanently closed Marion's prison factory and terminated all classes. Tensions increased between prison officials and inmates, and on October 22, 1983, two inmates separately killed

"The Rock," the U.S. Penitentiary on Alcatraz Island, California. Alcatraz was opened as the first supermax prison to house the extremely violent, dangerous, and escape-prone inmates of the 1930s. (Courtesy of the Federal Bureau of Prisons)

"Broadway," the Main Corridor in a Cell House at Alcatraz. Alcatraz had many famous places and created great interest among citizens. "Broadway" was the main corridor of the largest cell house, with rows of cells on each side of the corridor. (Courtesy of the Federal Bureau of Prisons)

two correctional officers. Four days later, a prisoner was found murdered in his cell. On October 28, Warden Harold Miller established the entire prison as in a state of emergency and implemented a 24-hour lockdown of prisoners in solitary cells.[18]

After several weeks of total **lockdown,** Marion settled in as a permanent lockdown institution, with inmates allowed out of their cells only for five hours per week for recreation, showers, and visits with family members. Inmate programs were eliminated, except those provided by video on in-cell television sets or by program staff (such as chaplains) coming to the inmates in their cells. In 1985, inmates challenged the lockdown. In the case of *Bruscino v. Carlson,* a federal judge denied their motion stating, "the Court is of the firm conviction that this litigation was conceived by a small group of hard-core inmates who are bent on the disruption of the prison system in general and of USP–Marion in particular."[19] The U.S. Court of Appeals upheld that decision in 1988, claiming that the conditions were not a violation of the Constitution, and in 1989 the U.S. Supreme Court let that decision stand. Since then, Marion has served as the supermax prison model that has been followed by many states, eliminating the use of rehabilitation and linking control to every aspect of the inmates' lives.

The move to supermax prisons is a change in operational philosophy from a "dispersion" to a "concentration" method of handling troublesome inmates. Traditionally, correctional agencies would disperse, or spread out, their troublemakers throughout the system to prevent them from uniting and gaining strength and power in the institution in which they were housed. Unfortunately, prison officials found that the problems often seemed to multiply with the dispersal method, because the troublemakers created havoc at every institutional placement. Therefore, prison administrators moved to the concentration approach of creating special units to handle these inmates and isolating them from other inmates, which made the institution less violent and more manageable. Today, more than 30 states have separate facilities used for this purpose, and almost every state has identified a unit designated to control the most troublesome inmates.

Definition, Mission, and Goals

Although each supermax prison may have different policies and procedures, the **supermax prison** is generally defined as

> A free-standing facility, or distinct unit within a facility, that provides for the management and secure control of inmates who have been officially designated as exhibiting violent or seriously disruptive behavior while incarcerated. Such inmates have been determined to be a threat to safety and security in traditional high-security facilities, and their behavior can be controlled by separation, restricted movement, and limited access to staff and other inmates.[20]

Most prisons in the United States have segregation cells for short-term disciplinary or protective custody. However, the supermax prison was designed for housing offenders known to be violent, assaultive, major escape risks, or likely to promote disturbances in a general population prison for an extended period of time. Therefore, the criteria for admission to and release from such a facility is explicit and narrow.

The concerns and critique of the justice system by the American public is ongoing, and over the past 30 years, public perceptions of the correctional system have wavered. The criminal justice system is continually attacked for being soft on crime, and as a result, new criminal codes have been enacted that result in admitting more and more offenders into the prison system. To accommodate the increasing number of offenders, more prisons have had to be built, including more supermax prisons, because as much as there is an interest in housing more offenders, so too, has there been an increase in the desire to make the prisons "tougher."[21]

Prison Operations

Security is the dominant feature of the supermax prison. All aspects of maintaining the prison, including structure of the building, education and programs, human contact, medical services, food service, property, and policies and procedures, revolve around proper security measures. Since the evolution of Marion into a supermax prison, more supermax prisons have been built. Consequently, each prison is somewhat different in its structure, but each is designed to have 24-hour lockdown, using cutting-edge technology to ensure the best security. For example, at the new federal Administrative Maximum Prison (ADX) in Florence, Colorado, the building is surrounded by double 20-foot fences interwoven with 10 rows of razor wire. Two perimeter roads, 8,000-watt lights, microwave sensors, escape wires, and six sniper towers separate the ADX from the other facilities.[22] The new Illinois supermax prison in Tamms, Illinois, is designed with inmate housing pods to minimize inmate movement. Each pod has its own medical room, outdoor recreation enclosures, and library. Inmates are only allowed to be in any of these out-of-cell areas one at a time. The cells are also designed for security purposes, containing simply a concrete bed, a wall-mounted writing surface and shelf, a steel sink and toilet, and a steel mirror.[23]

Most supermax prisons provide some limited program activities. Education is provided in a variety of ways depending on the facility. Some allow televisions in the cells to provide education through cable or video. Others have instructors that provide education on a one-on-one basis. Programs, such as substance abuse treatment and vocational programs, are provided only through television, a one-on-one meeting with a counselor, or reading materials. Religious programs are usually provided through individual meetings between an inmate and a chaplain.[24]

Human contact in a supermax prison is very limited. Inmates may have contact with medical staff, clergy, or a counselor on a cell visit. Physical contact is usually limited to touch through a security door by a correctional officer while an inmate is being put in restraints or having them removed. The majority of verbal communication is over an intercom system. Approved visitors are allowed into the facilities, but they are only permitted in no-contact visiting areas.[25]

One of the complications in a supermax facility is providing medical services, because inmates must be escorted at all times. To help eliminate this complication, most facilities have cell visits by medical staff and provide small examination rooms within the housing unit. More advanced medical care requires the transfer of an inmate to the prison's central medical clinic, or even to another facility. This can only be done by two to three correctional officers escorting the inmate. To reduce the movement of inmates from supermax prisons to be seen by medical specialists, technological advancements of telemedicine is provided in some facilities. Using video cameras and monitors, medical staff are able to perform medical examinations from a different site, which eliminates the need for inmate transport and can reduce the costs of staff security.[26]

Meals are delivered to the cells and the inmates must eat in solitude. The food is eaten behind sliding doors of perforated steel plates.[27] Every facility provides adequate, nutritionally balanced meals, and great care is taken in the preparation, distribution, and cleanup of the food.

Ohio Supermax Prison Cell. Cells within a supermax prison are very secure, almost indestructible. Note how this cell has a stainless steel sink and toilet, a steel seat and writing surface, and a concrete bed. (Courtesy of the Ohio Department of Rehabilitation and Correction)

Another issue in any prison is how much of an inmate's personal property is allowed in a cell. This is an even bigger problem within supermax facilities, because most of the inmates are placed within the control unit for acts of violence and aggression. Some personal property such as radios and reading material may be allowed so inmates can cope with the lack of other stimuli. However, these materials also create opportunities for more contraband and cause difficulty during searches. Hence, prison officials must evaluate each prisoner and the piece of property to make a decision of what may be allowed. Items such as razors and matches that are a threat to security are also given special attention.

The supermax prison is operated under specific policies and procedures to ensure the safety of inmates and staff. Each staff member is well trained to help eliminate any errors that may occur. Every detail of how a supermax prison is maintained, from the transfer of an inmate to the delivery of a meal, is prescribed and is known and followed by every staff member, thereby ensuring that there are no questions as to how something should be handled. One of the most important policy and procedural issues that every inmate and staff should be aware of is the use of force, which is inevitable in a supermax prison. As Riveland asserts

> critical to use-of-force planning or evaluation are policies and procedures that clearly articulate what level of authority is required for each level of force used, the steps taken to reduce or eliminate the need for using force, the type of force to be used, and the steps to be taken once the force had been applied. Operational policies should require . . . thorough documentation . . . videotaping . . . examination of practices . . . regular review of all use-of-force incidents by facility administrators and . . . mandated review of documentation and videotapes.[28]

Some facilities are now installing panoramic video cameras in the housing units to eliminate any discrepancies that may occur in a use-of-force situation.

Issues and Controversies

Despite the declaration of the *Bruscino* decision that the treatment of inmates at Marion was constitutional, the conditions within the supermax prisons are still a controversial issue. Proponents point out that the presence of such prisons is an incentive for good behavior, because inmates want to avoid being sent to lockdown confinement. Also, the general population institutions are more peaceful and orderly without the inmates who end up in a supermax.

Activists against supermax prisons declare that there are many human rights violations within such control units. They argue that the lack of human contact, the absence of work, and the deficiency of intellectual stimulation have negative consequences on an individual. In addition, they argue that physical violence toward the inmates may be common in such a controlled atmosphere. There is also a question of the impact on staff working in such a rigid and secure facility over long periods of time. Over their career, staff may in actuality spend more time in a supermax prison than inmates, and the impact of this controlled environment creates serious challenges for line staff and administrators.

Supermax prisons are extremely expensive to build and operate. The requirement for high-security building materials and components, elaborate electrical and technical systems, and the overlay of physical security drives construction costs up to almost double what a normal medium security prison would be. The increased staff-to-inmate ratio, the need to take services to inmates in a lockdown status, and the absence of inmate workers to carry out many functions also drives up the day-to-day operational costs.

Debate as to whether the rigidity of supermax prisons is more harmful toward inmates poses new questions and concerns for the effectiveness of the supermax prison. The supermax prison was designed with the hope of reducing physical violence within the prison systems. Administrators point out that this has certainly been the case. However, there have been no well-designed research studies that prove this is true. There is no question that supermax prisons effectively control the behavior of inmates assigned to them. However, continued research of supermax prisons is necessary to determine the cost–benefit, long-term effect on staff and inmates, and the overall system reduction of violence in other prisons as a result of their operation.

MANAGING PRISON GANGS

Prison gangs came to attention of correctional officials in the early 1960s, when California prison personnel realized they were having problems with violence, intimidation of staff and inmates, and the introduction of drugs by groups of organized inmates. In reporting on this development of gang activities in the California Department of Corrections, a U.S. Department of Justice publication notes, "Their organization was so firmly entrenched before authorities understood the danger confronting them that control of the institution was seriously threatened. This phenomenon has been repeated in numerous jurisdictions as the presence and influence of gangs has spread throughout the country."[29]

Since that time, prison gang activities have received a tremendous amount of attention; and much more is known about their operations, membership, and organization. Historically, prison gangs developed from street gangs, when such groups as Bloods and Crips found that many of their street gang members ended up in prison together. It was only natural that they continue their street activities of developing and maintaining turf, recruiting membership, intimidation, and drug dealing in prison. However, gangs such as the Mexican Mafia and Black Guerilla Family originated in prison, because individuals with like ethnic or racial backgrounds began to band together for strength and support, and they soon found that, through good organization, they could control other prisoners and many activities in the prison. As some ethnic and racial gangs began to show their strength, others organized, almost in self-defense, and began to challenge the earlier gangs for control and power.

Gangs have become very sophisticated; some have extensive membership and money available to them, they have clear and understood linkages to the street gang, and they plan and communicate in a way that would make a Fortune 500 company jealous. Correctional administrators must implement and maintain a number of strategies to keep the influence and control by prison gangs to a minimum. These strategies include early detection of gang activities, identification of leaders and members, surveillance of gang activity, denial of gang turf or wearing of gang colors and symbols, and a variety of gang control tactics.

Early Detection of Gang Activities

The most important action that prison administrators can take to begin a process of gang control is to educate and train staff about the gangs, organization, approaches, and known membership at the prison. Some of the major national gangs include the following:

The Aryan Brotherhood. The Aryan Brotherhood, or AB, is limited to Caucasians and is a Nazi-oriented, anti-African American, gang that dislikes authority and adheres to violence to gain prestige. They do not hesitate to kill to keep their membership and organization secure. In the early stages of gang organization, it was said prospective members had to kill someone to show their worth and to die to get out of the gang. They are closely aligned with many street motorcycle gangs and have extensive networks for dealing drugs.

The Black Guerilla Family. The Black Guerilla Family, or BGF, started in San Quentin (California) Prison, and its first leader was George Jackson, the Black Panther who was killed in a 1971 escape attempt. They follow a revolutionary philosophy, intent on destruction of the "white establishment" and overthrow of the government, with a goal to control the destiny of African American inmates.

La Nuestra Familia (NF). The NF recruits only Chicanos and is primarily based in northern California. The gang takes priority over all else, and they use violence to gain control and power. It is said that rank or position in the gang is achieved by the number of killings accomplished for the gang. They are enemies of the Aryan Brotherhood and the Mexican Mafia (another Hispanic gang), yet members will form alliances when it suits their purposes with the Black Guerilla Family.

The Mexican Mafia. Also called MM or EME, the Mexican Mafia gang excludes non-Hispanics, and members take an oath of "blood in, blood out." This means prospective members must make an assault to prove themselves and are badly beaten or even killed if they desire to get out of the gang. Since its origination in the Deuel Vocational Institution (California) in 1958, it has become one of the most powerful prison gangs in the United States. It has no underlying political views and is only focused on crime, both inside and outside the prison. Leaders control both prison and community criminal activities and often rob banks to gain funds to support their prison activities.

The Texas Syndicate. The Texas Syndicate (TS) is another California-originated prison gang, which was begun by prisoners who migrated from Texas and wanted to maintaxin their heritage rather than associate with one of the other two Hispanic gangs. On release from California prisons, members returned to Texas and established the gang in Texas prisons, as well as many other southwestern states and the Federal Bureau of Prisons. They have a reputation for violence, and have quickly become feared by other general population inmates.

Early detection of potential gang affiliation and activity can occur by watching the behavior of groups of inmates who regularly associate together. Gangs like to "mark their turf," wear gang colors, have tattoos, draw graffiti, and use hand signals. When staff see these activities, they should identify the individuals involved and report the occurrences to the prison staff unit responsible for intelligence gathering. If gang activities can be detected early, before the numbers or influence grows too large, it is much easier to manage and prevent expanded gang behavior. If gangs are organizing in a prison, there is likely to be an increase in disruptive behavior among inmates, particularly assaults on other inmates. Assaults establish power and intimidation, or they may be a part of taking or maintaining control of drug trade within a prison.

Identification of Gang Leaders and Members

In the early development of gangs, they liked to be visible to staff and inmates, to brazenly show their power and strength. Today, they try to avoid staff detection to hide their illegal activities. Most correctional agencies today maintain detailed records of gang membership, often divided into three categories: leaders; hard-core members; and marginal members.[30] Other terminology of categories include members, associates, and suspect. Agencies often use a validation process to place individuals into these categories and to confirm their membership and participation.

Staff are trained to look for and identify certain items that can be used to validate inmates as a member of a prison gang. Through staff surveillance, past records, and even self-admission, intelligence is collected on individual inmates. Before inmates are identified as full-fledged members of a gang, there must be multiple sources of evidence that they involved in a gang. There are several ways to collect intelligence, which can be used to validate an inmate as a gang member:

▌ Self-admission: An inmate may admit to being a gang member. This inmate should be asked to sign a self-admission statement. Self-admission should not be the sole source of membership validation, because an inmate may lie in order to intimidate others or for personal advantage.

▌ Presentence investigation report: This document may contain information about an inmate's street gang affiliation and activities.

▌ Staff information: An inmate's central file may include staff reports that substantiate gang affiliation.

▌ Confiscated gang-related documents: These materials may provide membership lists or notes and letters from confirmed gang members. An inmate may also possess items (e.g., photographs, insignias, correspondence) that establish gang membership.

▌ Disciplinary records: An inmate's disciplinary file may reveal involvement in illegal activities associated with prison gangs (e.g., drug trafficking, gambling, homicide). Such involvement may substantiate gang affiliation.

▌ Records of previous incarceration: Facilities operated by the federal government, county jails, or other states may have information pertaining to an inmate's gang affiliation or activities.

▌ Known associates: Gang members typically associate only with one another. An inmate who fraternizes with known or suspected gang members or who was a codefendant with confirmed members may also be a gang member.[31]

Correctional agencies use a tabulation of these items and usually require five or six different items to validate an inmate as a member. Three or four items may substantiate an inmate as an associate, and one or two identify an inmate as a suspect.

These validations are important, because they are often the basis of classification or assignment to one of the gang control strategies presented later in the chapter. Some of the strategies take away inmates' freedom or movement or affiliation, and therefore, for these actions to be legally defensible, there must be an elaborate and reasonable method of validation.

Surveillance of Gang Activities

Once gang members are identified, their activities are closely monitored. First, agencies keep complete lists of validated gang members and are able to monitor the number of members at each prison. Prison staff next keep a record of incidents and activities that are initiated or participated in by gang members. By doing this, prison staff can identify patterns of behavior by specific gangs and determine whether there are any upward or downward trends of activity. In prior examination of gang activities, there appeared to be certain prescribed patterns:

> Loyalty to the gang and allegiance to its members is accompanied by a code of secrecy, an outwardly cooperative attitude to prison authority who in reality are resented. This posture reflects the gang members' basic position which is placing himself where he can dominate and control others, and in particular to run the prison rackets—primarily the drug traffic within the institution. To intimidate and to be feared by other inmates and staff is the model role for all gang members.[32]

The importance of gang surveillance cannot be overstated. Not only does it allow prison staff to gain intelligence on activities and members of gangs but also staff can anticipate the type of expected endeavors that gangs will undertake, knowing the general philosophies and approaches by the gangs and in what they have been currently involved. In this way, staff can understand and attempt to maintain the balance among gang members. It has been shown that in situations in which one gang is considerably stronger (usually because of numbers of hard-core members) than others, the gang becomes more aggressive and uses more tactics of intimidation. When gang numbers are more comparable, one gang will not risk "disrespecting" another gang in a way that could cause violence to erupt between the two. Although gangs do not hesitate to use violence and intimidation when it helps their cause, they do not like to use it for other than "business" reasons, because it draws attention to them and may cause the prison administration to put a number of gang members in administrative detention.

To have an effective gang monitoring plan, the National Major Gang Task Force of the U.S. Department of Justice recommends the following actions:

1. **Posted picture file:** Require all staff to review a centralized photo and data file on significant gang members, suspects, and associates who pose a unique threat to staff or other inmates.
2. **Confidential reports:** Housing unit officers should be fully familiar with the need to report gang related grouping activity on the daily confidential reports from the housing units.
3. **SIS (intelligence) hotfiles:** The intelligence office should make a concentrated effort to ensure the institution hotfile (list of active gang members) is current,

accurate, and reconciled with an agency master hotfile system. This will help ensure the correct inmates are being monitored.

4. Gang communications: A high priority should be assigned to efforts to intercept notes passed between gang members, either directly or through mail drops in the community. Efforts should also be made to identify visitors who attempt to visit inmates at multiple institutions in an effort to pass along gang information and "hit contracts." Telephone calls of known gang leaders and significant members should be monitored.

5. General: All staff, regardless of area, should watch for efforts by gangs to dominate any physical area of the institution, efforts to control access to any inmate program, or clearly inappropriate conversions of an authorized activity into a gang activity (such as a talent show, athletic event, cultural awareness activity, and so on).[33]

Denial of Signs of Influence

Another important activity in prison is to keep gangs from showing their power and strength to the rest of the inmate population. When this is allowed, it aids the gang in recruitment of new members and encourages gang members to be more aggressive and violent to show their strength. Gangs like to tout themselves as being in control, tough, and willing to take violent actions against enemies. Gangs will try to flaunt colors, handsigns, symbols, and stake out turf to seem larger than their actual numbers. The prisons take many precautions to prevent gangs from promoting themselves.

Colors mean certain things to different gangs. For instance, the Bloods and the La Neustra Familia favor red, whereas Crips and the Mexican Mafia favor blue. Prisons try to avoid providing clothing that may have these colors and try to not sell items in the commissary that use these colors. In addition, there are many common brands that signify certain gangs. National Football League or National Basketball Association teams have been adopted by certain gangs to represent something about them, and members try to wear that team's clothing. The Chicago Bulls clothing is preferred by the Bloods, because "BULLS" means *B*loods *U*sually *L*ive *L*onger and *S*marter. The Latin Kings, a Chicago-based gang favors the Los Angeles Kings team clothing. The People, another Chicago-based gang, favor the Dallas Cowboys clothing, because the five-point star represents the People's Nation.

Inmates will also try to give each other tattoos while in prison that represent the gang. The Mexican Mafia likes to use a large letter *M*, and the Aryan Brotherhood prefers two parallel lightning bolts or the number *666*. Inmates also have specific haircuts that identify them as gang members, such as an image of lightning bolts cut into their hair or hash marks on their left or right eyebrow (left representing Folks and right representing People). Even the way inmates wear clothing can identify them as a gang. Some Chicago gangs will roll up a specific pant leg, or wear caps on a certain side of their heads. The Crips and Bloods like to "rag and sag," by wearing their trousers very low on their hips and often partially open.

Gangs also regularly try to stake out an area of the prison as their turf. They often do this in a certain area of the recreation yard, where the members gather and other inmates avoid. The gang may try to use the weight room during a certain time, declaring it as their own and discouraging other inmates from using the facility during "their" time. They even try to take over an educational library table or religious activity as a show of solidarity and to tout their strength. These actions of grouping and declaring turf are often more difficult for staff to recognize than the showing of colors, because gangs often do them quietly, without showing their colors or using graffiti. The gang lets other inmates know by forcing them out of the area, but it may not be obvious to staff unless an inmate complains, which is unlikely.

Gang Control Strategies

Gang identification and validation activities assist in sorting out members when it comes to implementing gang control strategies. In a 1985 review of state strategies to deal with prison gangs, collecting information and identifying members and leaders was believed to be an important strategy. Since that time, intelligence gathering has become a common operation in prisons, and strategies have been designed to control and manage gang members. The 1985 survey by Camp and Camp received input from 33 states who noted a significant problem with gangs in their prisons. Table 9–2 illustrates the number of states that use a particular strategy for dealing with prison gangs.

The 1985 survey of gang strategies then conducted site visits of nine states that had the most concern about gang activity in their prisons. Administrators of those states were asked to rate the value or importance of a specific strategy used to control gangs. The rating score is illustrated in Table 9–3.

TABLE 9–2

Gang Control Strategies Used by State Agencies

Technique	Agency Use
Move or transfer	27
Use informers and prevent events	21
Segregation of gang members	20
Lock up leaders	20
Lockdown	18
Prosecute	16
Intercept communications	16
Identify and track	14
Deal with situations case by case	13
Refuse to acknowledge	9
Put different gangs in particular institutions	5
Infiltration	5
Co-opt inmates to control	3

Source: George M. Camp and Camille Graham Camp, *Prison Gangs: Their Extent, Nature, and Impact on Prisons* (Washington, DC: U.S. Department of Justice, Office of Legal Policy, Federal Justice Research Program, July 1985), p. 64.

TABLE 9–3

Rating of the Value of Gang Strategies by States

Strategy	Rating Score
Separate and isolate leaders	37
Identify gang members	33
Good communication with inmates	30
Lock up members	30
Prosecute	20
Interstate transfer	20
Transfer within the agency	19
Intelligence	18
Attend to job and housing assignments	15

Source: George M. Camp and Camille Graham Camp, *Prison Gangs: Their Extent, Nature, and Impact on Prisons* (Washington, DC: U.S. Department of Justice, Office of Legal Policy, Federal Justice Research Program, July 1985), p. 65.

The 1991 National Institute of Corrections publication lists management strategies for prison gangs as follows: out-of-state transfers, use of separate facilities, isolation of gang leaders, targeting individual gang members, control of inmate programs and jobs, and prosecution of gang related activities.[34] Acknowledging that once gangs are entrenched in an institution, the goal is more likely control than elimination. The following strategies are viewed to be effective, and most agencies use many of these strategies in combination.

Out-of-state transfers. If gangs are not yet firmly developed or entrenched in a prison, it is sometimes valuable to move leaders and known members out of state. State correctional agencies usually have interstate agreements to allow this kind of transfer, often agreeing to trade one state's gang leaders for another's. When the leaders moved do not have significant numbers of members in that state, they find themselves powerless. When a gang is already well established in a state, moving a leader out of state creates a power vacuum that may allow prison staff to eliminate some prestige, and possibly power, from a gang. However, this strategy is believed by some administrators to be negative, because it can lead to the spread of gangs to the receiving state and result in a nationally organizing gang.

Use of separate facilities and isolating gang leaders. When gang membership is not large, it is possible to move all known members to a high-security prison. The Federal Bureau of Prisons policy requires that validated members (not associates or suspects) be assigned to a maximum security prison. Connecticut was one of the first states (beginning in the early 1990s) to not only move members and leaders to a high-security prison but also to place them in a lockdown status similar to disciplinary segregation as described previously. The only way for members to get out of the lockdown situation is to refute their membership and **debrief,** or tell, correctional officials everything they know about the gang's operations and membership. Once inmates debrief, they can never be accepted back into the gang, and, in fact, they become enemies of the gang. California uses a similar strategy, because all gang leaders are placed in the supermax prison at Pelican Bay, kept in single-person cells, and recreate by themselves. Until they agree to debrief, gang members do not leave Pelican Bay.

Targeting individual gang members. Some jurisdictions try to identify gang members who may be vulnerable. Gang members may want to leave the gang or give information to staff about the gang activities. If a prison has good intelligence, it may know of gang members who have become alienated or fallen out of favor with gang leadership. At times, a gang member "disrespects" a member of another gang with whom the gang has an alliance. When this occurs, the gang will often discipline the member, rather than allowing the other gang to do it and perhaps cause some tension with the alliance. This discipline usually involves a serious beating by fellow gang members. Some gang members decide they do not want to endure the beating to regain favor and are, therefore, a good prospect for defection and providing information to staff.

Control of inmate programs and jobs. Gangs like to try to group together in jobs and program assignments, and then take control and use the job or program for their own benefit. They may "sell" a chance to participate in a program or work in a job to other inmates. They may use the job or program to deal in drugs. Or they may use the job or program for recruiting new members. Prisons must monitor job and program assignments by gang members and not let groupings occur.

Prosecution of gang-related activity. Many violations of inmate rules in a prison can also be criminal acts. Assault, possession or sale of drugs, attempted escape, or bribing a staff member are all crimes. However, these are usually handled administratively within the prison, rather than attempting to prosecute and add another criminal sentence to an inmate's present term. Local prosecutors in a county in which a prison is located are usually too busy to take the large number of prison cases that could be handled criminally. However, when gang members are involved, these situations are sometimes referred for prosecution. Some states (New York and Wisconsin) provide financial resources to local prosecutors to handle prison cases. Others (Arizona and Texas) have special gang units to prosecute criminal actions by members. Aggressive prosecution increases the risk of being a gang member and discourages membership and gang activity.

PREPARING FOR PRISON EMERGENCIES

Unfortunately, all of the effort to create a safe and secure environment, and all the strategies to manage violent and dangerous inmates are not always effective. Prisons do experience emergency situations, which include inmate disturbances and riots, escapes, hostage taking, and nonviolent food or work strikes. It is important to recognize and address situations that can increase the likelihood of inmate-created emergencies, develop plans for response, and have staff trained to take the critical roles as hostage negotiators or tactical response teams. In reality, prison emergency situations can be other than those created by inmates. Floods, the threat of hurricanes or tornados, a hazardous chemical spill near the prison, or even a work action

A Burned-Out U.S. Penitentiary in Atlanta, Georgia, 1987. In 1987, Cuban detainees took control of the U.S. Penitentiary in Atlanta and held hostages for several days. By the time the government regained control, the Cubans had destroyed almost the entire prison and completely burned down the prison factory. (Courtesy of the Federal Bureau of Prisons)

by employees create emergencies that require planning and staff preparation. This chapter, however, deals only with inmate-precipitated emergency circumstances.

Inmate disturbances have a devastating impact on a prison, the inmates, and the staff. Over the past 30 years, there have been several serious riots, each one causing correctional officials to reconsider what they do and the circumstances within the agency prisons. Perhaps the most serious riot, and one that first captured the interest of the American public, was the 1971 riot in Attica, New York.[35] Attica held predominantly African American inmates from New York City, and it was staffed predominantly by Caucasians from rural, upstate New York. Civil rights, the Vietnam War, and many other outside influences created tension in prisons throughout the United States, especially when there seemed to be such a gap in understanding and communication between staff and inmates. In September 1971, inmates took control of a large section of the prison and held several staff members hostage. After four days, the New York governor and director of corrections decided to end the siege and sent the state police into the prison with authorization to use deadly force to regain control. They did, but in the aftermath, there were 43 deaths, including 32 inmates and 11 staff. Of the deaths, 39 were killed by the state police during the retaking of the prison.

In the 1980s, another riot resulted in many deaths. In February 1980, prisoners took over the entire prison in Santa Fe, New Mexico, held 12 staff hostage, controlled the prison for 36 hours, and incurred more than $100 million in damages.[36] During this time, inmates got into inmate records and found documentation of inmates who had acted as informants. The rioting inmates found these informants, tortured them, and killed 33 of their fellow inmates.

In the early 1990s, prisoners took over one cell block of the Southern Ohio Correctional Facility in Lucasville, Ohio. Following is a good representation of the impact of a riot on an entire correctional agency:

> On Easter Sunday 1993, inmates returning to L-block from recreation at the maximum security Southern Ohio Correctional Facility in rural Lucasville assaulted the entry officer. Minutes later, L-block was overrun, and the longest prison siege in U.S. history where lives were lost was underway. Eleven days later the riot ended. Corrections Officer Robert Vallandingham and nine inmates had been murdered. Thirteen corrections officers had been taken hostage. Five were held for the duration of the disturbance. L-block was virtually destroyed. As the more than 200 media reporters packed up their cameras and satellite dishes, Ohioans breathed a collective sigh of relief that the carnage was over. But for the 11,000 employees of the Ohio Department of Rehabilitation and Correction, the end of the riot signaled fundamental changes at every level of the operation.[37]

Causes of Inmate Actions

Most inmate disturbances or hostage situations are not fully planned and initiated by inmate leaders. When emergency situations occur, there are usually **environmental factors** that create tension and an underlying unrest among inmates, as well as a **precipitating event,** which is the "spark in the haystack" that sets off the inmate action. There is often no single environmental factor but rather several interrelated factors that create a condition ripe for a prison disturbance. At times, these factors are beyond the control of prison administrators. Hot weather, reduction in budgets for recreation equipment, prison crowding, and outside legislative action are all factors that can cause unrest and cannot be tended to by prison staff.

However, there are many preventative actions that prison administrators can take to reduce inmate unrest and the chance of inmate-prompted emergencies. Henderson, Rauch, and Phillips list the following:

- The importance to both staff and inmates of managerial visibility and approachability.
- Effective security auditing that uncovers security deficiencies so they can be corrected before inmates exploit them.
- Consistently enforcing all rules and regulations.
- Effective communication between inmates and staff, among staff, and particularly between line and supervisory personnel.
- The need to provide appropriate programs and services of all types (food, medical care, and so forth).
- Management systems, such as sanitation, safety and security inspections, contraband deterrence and detection, tool and key control, and inmate accountability.
- Sensitivity to changes in inmate actions or the institution atmosphere.
- A risk-assessment program to identify possible trouble spots and correct them as soon as possible. Such systems may include objective indicators (tests, review of incident data, sick call data) or subjective elements (staff and inmate interviews) to assign levels of risk to a situation or institution.[38]

The following case study of the Federal Correctional Institution in Greenville, Illinois, is a good example of the factors that can contribute to an environment of unrest and a precipitating event that can set off a riot.

PRACTICAL PERSPECTIVES

Greenville, Illinois (October 1995)

The Federal Correctional Institution in Greenville, Illinois, was one of the new federal prisons funded by the U.S. Congress after rewriting drug laws, abolishing parole, and moving to a determinate sentencing structure. These changes caused the inmate population of the Federal Bureau of Prisons to grow rapidly from little more than 30,000 in the early 1980s to more than 80,000 by the early 1990s. The prison was constructed as a standard medium security federal prison and first accepted inmates in early 1994. As is common practice in federal prisons, some experienced staff were transferred to the new prison, but the majority were hired locally and, for most, it was their first job in a prison.

There was a rapid increase of inmates at the prison, which had approximately 500 cells. By the middle of 1995, there were more than 1,000 inmates in the prison; every cell had two inmates, and some had three inmates. Procedures were new, and some were still changing and developing. The newly hired correctional officers and other staff were learning to deal with medium security inmates; almost all were transferred from other prisons and knew how to try to take advantage of new staff and untried procedures. Because the Midwest had the lowest crowding level of the Federal Bureau of Prisons and a new medium security prison had just opened in northern Illinois, Greenville presented available bed space for the more overcrowded Southeast and West Coast federal prisons. Many inmates were transferred from those regions to Greenville; they were moved away from their families and friends, and did not want to be in southern Illinois.

During most of 1995, there was considerable public discussion about changing the federal drug laws regarding crack cocaine. There was a ten-to-one ratio of crack to powder cocaine, meaning that to receive a mandatory 10 year prison sentence, drug offenders only had to possess one-tenth the grams of crack cocaine as powder cocaine offenders. Because crack cocaine was primarily used in African American communities, more than 95 percent of the crack cocaine offenders at Greenville were African American. This became an issue of racial injustice and was being considered by the U.S. Sentencing Commission (Commission). In fact, in the summer of 1995, the Commission recommended to Congress that the two drugs be equalized in their weight and corresponding sentence. Through rumor, African American inmates convicted of crack cocaine trafficking believed that a change would be made, it would be retroactive, and that many would receive a reduction of their sentences as a result.

In the fall of 1995, a report was issued by the U.S. Department of Justice, Bureau of Justice Statistics, that noted the much higher percentage of African American men between the ages of 19 and 30 who were incarcerated than their percentage in the overall U.S. population. This also became a rallying cry for racial injustice. During the summer and fall of 1995, much media attention was given to a call for a "Million Man March" by Minister Louis Farrakhan, leader of the Nation of Islam, who was often controversial and was believed to be calling for revolution against the white-dominated power structure in the United States. The Million Man March was a tremendous success, in both positive and negative ways. It called attention to the need for African American men to take responsibility for their families. Yet, it also called attention to many instances of racial injustice, and the crack and powder cocaine disparity was mentioned in many speeches.

The Million Man March occurred on Monday of the third week of October. On Wednesday evening of the same week, the U.S. Congress rejected the recommendation by the Commission to reduce the disparity between crack and powder cocaine sentences. The next morning, a riot broke out in a federal prison in Alabama, followed the same day by one in Tennessee and another in Pennsylvania. There was national media coverage of the fires and destruction from these riots, and inmates in Greenville were aware of these events.

On Friday of that week, the Federal Bureau of Prisons decided to take peremptory action to prevent more riots and called for a national lockdown of all the prisons. At Greenville, inmates were called back to their housing units at about 3:00 P.M., about one hour before usual. Once they arrived, they were told to go into their cells to be locked down. Inmates suspected a lockdown and rebelled. In two of the four housing units, inmates refused to go into their cells and began assaulting staff who were trying to encourage their compliance. Thirteen staff were injured and two housing units had massive destruction. All federal prisons were locked down for more than 30 days, and during this time there were smaller disturbances at four to five others.

The environmental factors in the case study are obvious, with new staff and new procedures. There was no consistency and routine in the prison's practices, nor had a level of professional communication developed between experienced staff and inmates. Many inmates were unhappy at Greenville, having been taken against their will from prisons closer to their homes. There were feelings of racial injustice and expectations that "wrongs would be righted." The Million Man March increased feelings that injustices should not be tolerated. And the congressional action to maintain current sentences was unexpected by prison officials and was disappointing to inmates. The precipitating event was the attempted lockdown, when tensions were high, and inmates were being told to do something (be locked in their cells for an unknown amount of time) they did not want to do and did not believe they deserved.

Planning and Responding to Emergencies

Knowing that emergencies will occur, prisons develop "contingency," or "emergency," plans that identify steps and activities to be taken when an emergency occurs. These plans become very detailed and include everything from preventing a disturbance to conducting postemergency activities. Plans usually include responding to media interest, identification of the chain of command or authority, and the availability of weapons and chemical agents. Henderson, Rauch, and Phillips list the following categories for an emergency plan:

1. Prevention
2. Initial reaction and notification
3. Command issues and command center operations
4. Resources assembly and post assignments
5. Accounting for staff and inmates
6. Firearms and ordinances
7. Physical plant and utilities
8. Equipment
9. Media relations
10. Reporting
11. Postemergency action
12. Training
13. Other specific plan information, including relevant backup materials.[39]

The detail of an **emergency plan** is critical, because it acts as the guide for actions at a time when emotions are high, staff and inmates may be in danger or already injured, everything seems chaotic and out of control, and it may be the first time in this type of emergency for the person in charge or all the staff. A detailed plan provides order to the thought process, allowing staff to rationally consider the steps to take. Also, plans are not only to be read but to be practiced. Prisons train staff and practice drills for a variety of emergencies, so when the "real thing" occurs, staff are aware of required responses and they have some experience performing the necessary actions. In a review of the aftermath of riots, Boin and Van Duin note, "As prison authorities find themselves confronted with a riot, . . [they] will have to take some sort of action in order to cope with the threat and restore a state of normalcy. It is in this stage that the actions of prison authorities may make the difference between a food strike in an isolated cell block (a riot you will never hear about) and the overtaking of an entire institution (a riot you might never forget)."[40]

When an emergency situation, such as a riot, does break out, there are several actions that must be taken. Although correctional agencies may not agree entirely on the order of activities, the following represents a general guideline to be followed. Many of the functions are carried out simultaneously. First, notify all staff in the prison about what is happening and initiate the emergency plans. If the disturbance begins when the warden and other executives are not at the prison, they should be immediately contacted to come to the prison. If the emergency seems serious, most prisons have procedures for quickly summoning all staff not on duty. Automatic dialing systems with recorded messages ("there is a major disturbance at the prison, report immediately to the designated assembly area") or phone trees may be set up so staff can quickly be called to work.

Second, ensure the security of the perimeter and the most "at-risk" areas of the prison. During a riot, many inmates will use the chaos to attempt escape, and correctional staff must first ensure they contain the inmates in the prison. Extra staff are often sent to the towers or stationed along the fence line to prevent escapes. There are some other areas within the prison that must be protected. These include the medical area where drugs are maintained, the maintenance shops where cutting torches and tools that could be used as weapons or to assist in escape are stored, and areas that contain confidential records such as gang memberships or lists of informants.

Third, lock down the institution in an attempt to contain the disturbance to as small an area as possible and with participation by as few inmates as possible. This step is extremely important. There are many precipitating events (inmate fight, assault of staff, attempted escape) that could cause a disturbance that could spread across the institution. If inmates are separated and cannot join in during the few seconds of the most heated confrontation, these events usually are quickly calmed and do not spread. If a large group of inmates gathers around the event, a gang mentality begins, and it is likely that other inmates may become involved.

Fourth, account for staff and inmates and ensure they are safe. As soon as possible, prison staff should call for a count of inmates (often in the area where the staff member is) to determine who and how many inmates are involved in the disturbance. It is important to account for staff to ensure their safety and to be sure they are not injured or taken as hostages. If staff are in danger, it is important to try to remove them from the danger immediately. That would seem obvious, because no one wishes staff to be injured. But it is critical for a broader reason. An inmate disturbance with staff hostages is much more difficult and complex to respond to than one in which there are no staff hostages.

Fifth, assemble and organize staff into the response teams that can, in an organized fashion and with the appropriate amount of force, react to the disturbance. Most prisons have at least three types of formal and preselected teams: disturbance control, special operations, and hostage negotiations. While on duty staff are accomplishing these activities, the teams are assembling and preparing for response as needed. At the same time, predesignated community resources are notified and called to assist as needed. Community help can include the local fire department, an emergency medical squad, state and local police, and perhaps other prisons with response teams in case the prison's own teams are not enough.

Sixth, notify local officials, media, and agency headquarters. All of these other groups usually have actions they too must take in the event of a disturbance. The agency headquarters can coordinate collecting other resources that may be necessary. Local officials need to approve some responses by local law enforcement and medical resources. And the media can notify the community in case of an escape so the community may report any sightings of inmates. In addition, from a postemergency public relations position, local citizens are very upset if they are not notified of dangerous situations, because they believe they should be kept informed of circumstances that could affect their personal and family safety.

At this point, most of the preliminary actions are in place, and the tactical responses to the disturbance can begin. The next section identifies the role of each team, and the types of responses they take under certain conditions.

Emergency Response Teams

As noted previously, prisons usually have at least three major teams that coincide with the three major options available in a crisis situation: "negotiation, the option involving the least amount of force, is the preferred option when time permits; DCTs (Disturbance Control Teams) using less than lethal options such as chemical agents and distraction devices; and the use of deadly force through intervention by a tactical team."[41] Correctional administrators in an emergency situation must think through the conditions of the disturbance and dispatch the proper team to carry out the option that is chosen. In any emergency, it is possible for all three options to be implemented at some point in time.

When a team assembles and prepares to be dispatched to the situation, they develop their own plan, which they recommend to the correctional official (the warden once he or she is on the scene) in charge of the facility. The warden, or other person in charge, stays in a preordained location (a command center) where communications, intelligence, and information necessary for decision making are close by. The on-scene commander considers the proposed plan and must approve it, but the team leaders develop the plan as they review the situation and their capabilities to respond to it. The following description of emergency response teams includes an explanation of their tactical use and the potential changes in a situation that calls for a change in strategy.

The **disturbance control team (DCT)** has a permanent membership of 25 to 30 staff, but additional staff can be added to supplement the ranks as needed. This team's primary mission is to control inmate riot situations, using defensive tactics and equipment. The team is outfitted with jumpsuits, helmets with protective shields, ballistic-resistant vests, baseball catcher–style shin guards, batons, gas masks, handcuffs, chemical agents such as tear and pepper gas, and other ordinances such as smoke grenades, stun and flash-rounds, and stingball grenades.

Disturbance Control Team Member. DCT members wear full protective gear, including helmets with face shields. They also carry riot batons and often use body shields, such as those next to the DCT member. (Courtesy of the New York City Department of Corrections)

The DCT is the first response to a disturbance. The team gathers, puts on their equipment, and plans a response. The DCT serves several purposes. They are a "show of force"; their organization and equipment appears threatening to inmates, who often give up without a confrontation simply by seeing the team. The DCT moves groups of inmates into locations that provide prison staff a tactical advantage. The team, using chemical agents, batons, and handcuffs, take control of rioting inmates and then move them individually to a secure location (often the SHU). Finally, the DCT may support a hostage or special operations team, the tactical team that is used if deadly force is necessary.

Following is an example of a response by the DCT. A group of inmates in the recreation yard have begun to riot, arm themselves with recreation equipment, and refuse staff orders to put down the weapons and return to their housing units. The DCT is deployed, and moves to the recreation yard. They march in formation, batons at the ready, calling out cadence. This show of force illustrates their readiness to the rioting inmates. The plan is first to again order inmates to drop their weapons and lay on the ground. If the inmates do not comply, the DCT will form a line and move slowly and methodically with riot batons at the ready position toward the inmates to move them away from the entrance to the recreation yard. This prevents inmates from leaving the yard and spreading the riot to other areas of the prison. Inmates will again be given a chance to give up, and those who do not want to be involved are given the opportunity to move to another location in the recreation yard to avoid the confrontation. If all this fails, the DCT may throw tear or pepper gas grenades to disable inmates and again order them to lie on the ground. In almost all cases, this will work, because the gas makes it impossible for inmates to see or respond. Pepper gas makes individuals feel unable to breath, and their lungs begin to burn. The DCT, with their gas masks in place, can then move to the group, handcuff each inmate, and move them individually to a backup group of staff who take them to SHU.

The most difficult and stressful emergency situation in a prison is when there are staff or other non-inmate hostages. Inmates may be taken hostage by other inmates, but this usually does not occur, because inmates do not think inmate hostages will have much negotiating value. When hostages are taken, it may be appropriate to quickly respond with force (such as a DCT or even simply an assembled group of staff) to quickly free the hostages before the inmates build physical barriers and get organized. This, however, is very risky, and moving to a negotiation strategy is often preferred and considered more likely to be successful. With this option, a trained **hostage negotiation team (HNT)** is called on to respond.

The HNT is a group of eight to ten prison employees who have excellent communication skills, handle themselves well under stress, and for whom inmates may not have any particular negative feelings. For this reason, prison psychologists or counselors are often used on the teams. Only one person negotiates at a time, but if the situation continues for some time, other team members can relieve the negotiator, because it is a stressful and tiring activity. Other team members play roles of recorders, advisors to the negotiator, and liaisons with the command center and other tactical teams.

The purpose of the negotiating team is to preserve life and regain control of the prison and inmates. Their goals are to "open communications lines, reducing stress and tension with the hostage takers, build rapport, obtain intelligence, stall for time, allow hostage takers to express emotion and ventilate, and establish a problem-solving atmosphere."[42] Team members are the only persons who should talk to hostage takers, never anyone in command or with decision-making authority, and never the media, family, or friends of hostage takers. Negotiations take time, and with time rapport builds between the negotiators and the hostage takers. The Stockholm Syndrome develops, which is a psychological state in which hostages and captors begin to identify with each other, and the hostage takers begin to develop positive feelings toward their hostages. As the Stockholm Syndrome sets in, it is less likely that captors will physically harm or kill their hostages. Additionally, over time, intelligence may be gathered, tactical teams can prepare if an assault is needed, and hostage takers become tired and hungry.

As the negotiations continue, tensions are reduced, and the hostage takers begin to think more rationally and less emotionally. They consider their real options and realize that prison officials are not going to negotiate for release, reduced sentences, or weapons. The hostage takers expectations are reduced, and they realize that they may only be successful at getting grievances or concerns heard by officials. Exchanges of minor things, such as a chance to talk to hostages or check their medical conditions for food or drink, creates a mentality of agreement. As this continues, captors begin to move toward a peaceful solution to the hostage taking, and situations are usually resolved without violence.

Unfortunately, there are hostage situations that end with a forceful retaking of control by prison staff. In these cases, prison officials call on a **special emergency response team (SERT).** A SERT uses lethal force when all else fails to resolve an emergency situation. In most cases, this is a hostage situation, because if inmates are contained in an area without the risk of escape, there is usually no need to rush or risk using lethal force to resolve a situation.

SERTs are similar to police SWAT teams in that they are trained in a variety of weapons, entry procedures, and the use of snipers. SERTs use snipers when sniper fire can successfully save a hostage or resolve a situation quickly and successfully. Snipers also protect the rest of the team if the team is called on to assault, because a critical principle in bringing weapons into a prison is to cover and protect the weapons so they cannot fall into hands of inmates. If a hostage situation is breaking down and hostage takers are becoming unstable and it is determined that hostages are in imminent danger, the SERT may be ordered to assault and attempt to rescue the hostages. The SERT should never be deployed until they have a fully prepared and approved plan, including how to enter, knowledge of the location and identity of hostages, and whether the hostage takers are armed.

The hardest decision a person in command of a prison hostage situation must make is to commit to the use of a SERT assault with deadly weapons. There are many times in a hostage situation in which captors give deadlines and threaten to kill hostages if their demands are not met. The best strategy is to have the negotiating team try to talk hostage takers past deadlines, instead of ordering an assault. However, hostage takers may get to a point where they are about to kill or injure hostages, and an assault must begin. The SERT will have prepared a plan, received approval, be in position, and be ready to begin the entry and assault on receiving orders.

The SERT will first have an entry plan. They may have to scale a wall, rappel down from a roof and enter a window, or use explosives to blow open a door. They will usually use some type of diversionary tactic before they enter to confuse hostage takers and shield their entry. Diversionary tactics may include tear or pepper gas, loud "concussion grenades" that stun and deafen anyone close by, or bright lights to blind hostage takers. The SERT will have the best intelligence available as to the location of hostages and will quickly move to the hostages to protect them from harm from their captors. The SERT will try to avoid using their weapons, but if they or the hostages are in danger, they will have the authority to use deadly force. Key principles are that if force is necessary, it must be overwhelming, but only in the amount necessary to restore order, and prison officials should only commit to a tactical action that assures total control of the inmates as the final outcome, so inmates cannot take the weapons and get SERT members as more hostages.

Prison officials have many tools available if a disturbance breaks out. However, tactical teams must be well trained and prepared. Decision makers must know their capabilities and the type of situations they can most effectively handle. All prison staff must know and be trained in their roles in a disturbance or hostage situation. And staff must be aware of the risk of working in a prison and discuss this risk and the types of responses available to prison officials with their families. In this way, families can understand what is happening if their family member is taken hostage. Although inmate disturbances are dangerous and can cause great property damage, proper preparation by prison staff greatly increases the chance to regain control while minimizing the likelihood of harm to persons or destruction of property.

SUMMARY

Prisons protect society by incarcerating offenders judged to need separation from law-abiding citizens. Many offenders are violent and dangerous. It is likely that when many violent and dangerous people are consolidated in one small location, there will be incidents of violence and noncompliance of prison rules. Offenders who have a long history of failure to respect authority and the rights of others, and of reacting to frustration with anger and violence are likely to continue their past habits of behavior. Therefore, prison administrators must create policies, procedures, and plans for responding to such situations.

Inmate disciplinary systems hold inmates accountable for their actions and provide punishments as disincentives for misbehavior. Disciplinary systems must provide reasonable due process and be considered fair and consistent by inmates. They must also allow for separating problem inmates from the general inmate population if they pose a risk to safety and security. For the most violent and escape-prone inmates, many correctional agencies have developed supermax prisons, which are focused on control and safety. Prison gangs have grown tremendously during the past decades and actively seek to further their own power and control. Only through aggressive strategies that identify and manage prison gang members can correctional officials keep their activities in check. And finally, inmate collective actions, such as riots and hostage taking, can occur because of conditions at a prison or conditions totally out of the control of prison administrators. Although administrators try to balance and maintain effective programs and operations as well as security, the potential of violence by inmates must never be underestimated, and preparation by staff must never be shortchanged.

ENDNOTES

1. Ekland-Olson, S. "Crowding, Social Control, and Prison Violence: Evidence from the Post-*Ruiz* Years in Texas," *Law and Society Review* 20(no. 3); (1986): 289–421. See also G. G. Gaes and W. J. McGuire, "Prison Violence: The Contribution of Crowding Versus Other Determinants of Prison Assault Rates," *Journal of Research in Crime and Delinquency* 22(no. 1) (1985): 41–65.
2. J. Irwin. *Prisons in Turmoil.* (Boston, MA: Little, Brown and Co., 1980).
3. J. B. Jacobs, *Statesville. A Penitentiary in Mass Society* (Chicago, IL: The University of Chicago Press, (1977).
4. Mark S. Fleisher, *Warehousing Violence* (Newbury Park, CA: Sage, 1989), p. 198.
5. Michael C. Braswell, Reid H. Montgomery, Lucien X. Lombardo, *Prison Violence in America*, 2nd ed. (Cincinnati, OH: Anderson Publishing, 1994).
6. *Wolff v. McDonnell*, 418 US 539, 94 S.Ct. 2963, 41 L.Ed.2d 935, 71 O.O.2d 336 (1974).
7. Federal Bureau of Prisons, policy statement number 5270.07, "Inmate Discipline and Special Housing Units" (Washington, DC: U.S. Department of Justice, Chapter 1, 29 December 1987), p. 1.
8. Ibid., Chapter 4, p. 4.
9. Ibid., Chapter 2, p. 3.
10. *Sandin v. Conner*, 515 US 472 (1995).
11. In *Baxter v. Pahnigiano*, 425 US 308 (1976), the United States Supreme Court reiterated its ruling that inmates are not entitled to attorneys in the disciplinary process.
12. Clair A. Cripe, "Inmate Disciplinary Procedures," Chapter 29, in *Prison and Jail Administration: Practice and Theory*, edited by Peter M. Carlson and Judith Simon Garrett (Gaithersburg, MD: Aspen Publishers, 1999), p. 214.
13. James D. Henderson, W. Hardy Rauch, and Richard L. Phillips, *Guidelines for the Development of a Security Program*, 2nd ed. (Lanham, MD: American Correctional Association, 1997), p. 129.
14. Federal Bureau of Prisons, Chapter 4, pp. 4–10.
15. Robert Perkinson, "Shackled Justice: Florence Federal Penitentiary and the New Politics of Punishment," *Social Justice* 21 no. 3 (1994): 118.
16. Ibid., p. 119.
17. Cisco Lassiter, "Roboprison," *Mother Jones* (September/October 1990); 76.
18. Perkinson, p. 119.
19. Lassiter, p. 79.
20. Chase Riveland, *Supermax Prisons: Overview and General Considerations* (Washington, DC: National Institute of Corrections, January 1999), p. 3.
21. Rodney J. Henningsen, Wesley Johnson, and Terry Wells, "Supermax Prisons: Panacea or Desperation?" *Corrections Management Quarterly* (Spring 1999): 54.
22. Perkinson, pp. 124–125.

23. A. Shepperd, Jeffrey R. Geiger, and George Welborn, "Closed Maximum Security: The Illinois Supermax," *Corrections Today* (July 1996): 86.
24. Riveland, pp. 9–10.
25. Ibid., p. 11.
26. Ibid.
27. Shepperd, Geiger, and Welborn, p. 87.
28. Riveland, p. 15.
29. National Institute of Corrections, *Management Strategies in Disturbances and with Gangs/Disruptive Groups* (Washington, DC: U.S. Department of Justice, 1991), p. 2.
30. Ibid., p. 2.
31. Ibid., pp. 5–6.
32. George M. Camp and Camille Graham Camp, *Prison Gangs: Their Extent, Nature, and Impact on Prisons* (Washington, DC: U.S. Department of Justice, Office of Legal Policy, Federal Justice Research Program, July 1985), p. 38.
33. Intelligence Section, Federal Bureau of Prisons, "Gang Interdiction Strategies, Briefing Guide" (Washington, DC: U.S. Department of Justice [unpublished document], 29 April 1996), p. 17.
34. National Institute of Corrections, pp. 9–12.
35. For an excellent discussion of the Attica riot, see Tom Wicker, *A Time to Die* (New York: Quadrangel/The New York Times Book Company, 1975). See also Reid H. Montgomery, Jr., and Gordon A. Crews, *A History of Correctional Violence: An Examination of Reported Causes of Riots and Disturbances* (Lanham, MD: American Correctional Association, 1998), pp. 59–60.
36. Attorney General's Office, *Report of the Attorney General on the February 2 and 3, 1980 Riot at the Penitentiary of New Mexico* (Santa Fe: State of New Mexico, Office of the Attorney General, 1980).
37. Reginald A. Wilkinson and Thomas J. Stickrath, "After the Storm: Anatomy of a Riot's Aftermath," *Corrections Management Quarterly* 1 (no. 1) (1997): 16.
38. Henderson, Rauch, and Phillips, pp. 180–181.
39. Ibid., p. 180.
40. R. Arjen Boin and Menno J. Van Duin, "Prison Riots as Organizational Failures: A Managerial Perspective," *The Prison Journal* 75 no. 3 (September 1995): 365.
41. Earnest A. Stepp, "Preparing for Chaos: Emergency Management," in Carlson and Garrett, p. 371.
42. Gothriel Lafleur, Louis Stender, and Jim Lyons, "Hostage Situations in Correctional Facilities," in Carlson and Garrett, p. 376.

KEY TERMS

interpersonal violence	supermax prisons
collective violence	debrief
inmate disciplinary system	environmental factors
administrative appeals process	precipitating event
special housing unit (SHU)	emergency plan

administrative detention

disciplinary segregation

lockdown

disturbance control team (DCT)

hostage negotiation team (HNT)

special emergency response team (SERT)

▰▰ YOU'RE THE CORRECTIONAL ADMINISTRATOR

1. You are the chief of the gang intelligence section of a large, maximum security prison. The prison has experienced several serious inmate-on-inmate assaults, and little information has been received about the causes or reasons for the assaults. You believe the assaults are the result of some rival gangs trying to show force and intimidate other inmates. You were called to the warden's office and confronted about not knowing what was going on and not suggesting how to prevent further assaults. You have to collect more information before you can come up with a strategy of how to stop the assaults. Develop a plan to collect gang intelligence, which will lead to some strategies for controlling the gang activities.

2. You now have the intelligence to show that a recent influx of gang members of two rival gangs has caused the fighting for power. Most of the assaults have been gang to gang, but some other nongang inmates have been caught up in the violence as well. Develop a strategy to control the two gangs. List five steps you would take to control the gang activities, and describe how you would implement each of them.

▰▰ WEB LINK EXERCISES

Florida Department of Corrections   www.dc.state.fl.us

Go to the Florida Department of Corrections Web site, and find the section regarding gangs. In this section, there is a "learn more" topic. Go to it, and find the information on the gangs described, including identifiers, alliances, philosophy, and leaders. Based on this information, describe how you would develop a specific plan for staff to monitor and control the activities of a particular gang in a prison. Include specific information you would provide to your staff about watching for identifiers and the types of activities your staff should expect from the gang members.

The Basics: Food, Housing, and Medical Care

INTRODUCTION

In looking at contemporary prison operations in this section of the textbook, you have examined how prisons are organized to accomplish their tasks, how safe and secure prison environments are created, and how violent inmates are managed. In earlier chapters, programs available both for prison inmates and community offenders were presented. In this final chapter of the section on the prison setting, you will review the basics of prison operations, including how prisons are designed, and the operational areas of medical care and food service.

As noted in the chapter on staff organization and functions, many prisons separate their activities into custody or security programs and "operations." These operational areas are described as "basic" because there are certain requirements that must be carried out in a prison. Obviously, this includes the provision of food, shelter, and medical care. This chapter describes the development of prison architecture and how the design of a prison influences its management style, the complexities of providing medical care to an incarcerated population, and the critical activities in providing nutritious and appealing food in a prison setting.

THE DESIGN OF PRISONS

The importance of the architectural design of prisons cannot be overstated. When planning the architecture for a new prison, the management philosophy of the correctional agency should dictate the way the prison is designed. Once the prison is built, correctional administrators have to manage in a way consistent with the layout of the prison. Although some minor modifications may be possible, the type or design of housing units, the location of the buildings within the secure perimeter, and even the perimeter itself mandates certain operational and staffing patterns.

Prison architecture has evolved slowly over the past 150 years. There have been few major changes since the first prisons were built in the United States in the early 1800s. The first U.S. prison was the Walnut Street Jail in Philadelphia, Pennsylvania, which was not designed as a prison. An existing wing of the jail was converted to house the first offenders receiving a term of incarceration as punishment for their crimes. The philosophy of the Walnut Street Jail was toward prisoner reformation, and the main activities were for inmates to read the Bible, work, and reflect on their behavior, all done alone in their cells. In fact, the Walnut Street Jail maintained a totally **separate system**, with single cells and total isolation of prisoners from one another. Therefore, the design and operation of the facility was focused on preventing contact between prisoners.

This emphasis on a "separate system" continued as Pennsylvania built the Western State Penitentiary in Pittsburgh, which opened in 1826. In planning for the facility, there was to be little movement out of cells by prisoners; cells were very small and designed on the "inside" of the cell blocks so that inmates would not face each other. However, the small and dark inside cells were quickly found lacking, because inmates could perform little work. The state legislature quickly modified the operational plan and approved changes to allow inmates to perform labor. The original cells were torn down in 1833 and replaced with larger "outside" cells.

Figure 10–1 illustrates the difference between inside and outside cell arrangements. In the early days of prison design, both inside and outside cell designs were "linear"; the cells were arranged in a row along a corridor. With inside cell design, the cells back up to one another, and the corridor is around the cells, between the cell fronts and the cell block walls. With **outside cells,** the corridor is between the

Inside Cell in the Federal Penitentiary on McNeil Island, Washington (c. 1909). These early inside cells had little light, and were very small for two inmates. (Courtesy of the Federal Bureau of Prisons)

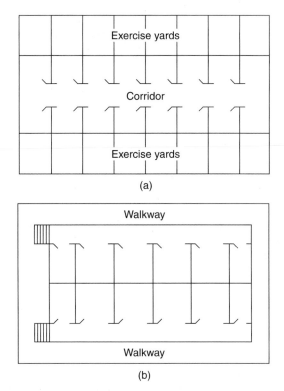

(a)

(b)

FIGURE 10-1   Comparison of "outside" (top) and "inside" (bottom) cell arrangements. Source: Harry E. Allen and Clifford E. Simonsen, *Corrections in America: An Introduction,* 9th ed., (Upper Saddle River, NJ: Prentice Hall, 2001), p. 34.

two rows of cells, which face each other and are abutted to the wall. Cell block walls usually have windows to allow for natural light. The **inside cells** are considered more secure, because inmates attempting escape would have to both get out of their cells and get through the cell block walls. With outside cell arrangements, each cell usually has its own window, and there is only one barrier between the inmate and breaking out of the cell block.

Learning from the mistakes of the Western Penitentiary, Pennsylvania later built the Eastern Penitentiary outside of Philadelphia. The design included larger outside cells, so inmates could perform work in their cells, yet the separate system with no communication between inmates was maintained. The Eastern Penitentiary was constructed using the **radial design,** in which the cell blocks extended from a central hub, although there was still a linear array of cells within the blocks.

The state of New York, in planning its own construction and operation of prisons, was impressed with the reported success of the Pennsylvania system of separate confinement. In 1816, the state legislature authorized the construction of a prison in Auburn, New York, based on the Pennsylvania design and operations. When

View of Cells at the Federal Penitentiary on McNeil Island, Washington (c. 1909). This view of the inside cells illustrates how the ranges are stacked on one another and steel grills that were used as doors. (Courtesy of the Federal Bureau of Prisons)

Auburn opened in 1819, administrators experimented with the Pennsylvania approach and kept prisoners both silent and separate. However, the experiment was marked by inmate idleness, sickness, insanity, and suicide, and it was quickly determined a failure. By 1822, the Auburn administrators created a new approach to operations. Inmates remained in their cells at night, but during the day, they worked with other inmates in common areas. They continued the emphasis on silence to prevent contamination between inmates, however, and enforced strict discipline through use of the whip and solitary confinement. The **congregate system** of the Auburn prison became the model for many other states; it was copied by almost 30 prisons built and opened before 1850.

Types of Prison Design

Throughout the history of prison construction, there have been basically four models of prison layout: the radial design, the telephone-pole design, the courtyard style, and the campus style.[1] (See Figure 10–2.) The first two models are linear designs with cells aligned in rows down the cell blocks. In the radial design (the Eastern Penitentiary of Pennsylvania), the cell blocks and program buildings extend from a central hub. It has not been copied in prisons built over the past 75 years. The main disadvantage is that all inmate traffic and movement comes to one point in the prison. The congestion that results presents a dangerous situation, particularly in high-security prisons. The other linear design is the telephone-pole, which was used extensively between the 1920s and the 1970s. Inmates and staff move along a main corridor down the center (the pole), and the cell blocks and program buildings extend from that corridor. It was popular, because it was easy

         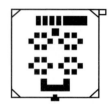

(a) Radial design   (b) Telephone-pole design   (c) Courtyard style   (d) Campus style

FIGURE 10–2   Four designs of prison architecture. Source: Todd R. Clear and George R. Cole, *American Corrections*, 5th ed. (Belmont, CA: Wadsworth Publishing Company, 2000), p. 235.

The Walled U.S. Penitentiary in Lewisburg, Pennsylvania. This prison had a high wall and a telephone-pole style design. Cell houses extend out on both sides from the middle of the prison. (Courtesy of the Federal Bureau of Prisons)

to erect barred grills across the "pole," and close them to isolate smaller groups of offenders in case of a riot or disturbance. These telephone-pole prisons were designed to control prison violence and were built as fortresslike structures that appeared quite secure from outside the prison. However, on the inside, there were numerous hard-to-monitor corners and places that were ideal for stabbing, beatings, and other types of violence.

The final two designs have been used in more recent prison construction. Campus style prisons were initiated by the Federal Bureau of Prisons and were first used at the Federal Correctional Institutions in Morgantown, West Virginia; Pleasanton (now called Dublin), California; and Miami, Florida. In the early campus designs, all of the buildings were separated and spread out over several acres within the secure perimeter. It is believed that forcing inmates to move from one building to another, walking outside instead of within a corridor, has a positive effect on the environment of the prison. Also, with the decentralized location of the buildings, there is little inmate congestion as they move through the prison, reducing the likelihood of tension.

As the benefits of the campus style of prisons became better known, this model was adopted by several states and continued in use by the Federal Bureau of Prisons. However, it was sometimes believed to be less secure, not providing the physical control over inmates important to prison operations. The following case study is an excellent description of an administrator's challenge in progressing to the campus style design, to incorporate the benefits, and have prison design consistent with the desired operational philosophy.

PRACTICAL PERSPECTIVES

In with the New, Out with the Old

In the early 1980s, a new director of corrections was appointed by the recently elected governor in a fairly large state. The Department of Corrections was facing many challenges, among them a rapidly growing inmate population and the need for significant prison expansion. The state legislature had approved a $550 million prison construction program, and the outgoing administration had hired architects and initiated designs for the first two prisons.

The state had not built a new prison in almost 20 years, and the last prison (a maximum security prison) was a telephone-pole design with a linear array of cells in the cell blocks. When the new director arrived at the department, she was quickly visited by the architects for the first prison, which was a 1,250-bed, medium security prison with a budget of $60 million. This new facility had already been designed in a telephone-pole style, very much like the last prison constructed in the state. The state was very traditional and conservative in their style of prison management, and every prison in the state was a telephone-pole design. The director wanted to change to a campus style design, but in meetings with the architects, was told how they could not make the modifications to the design work that was already completed. She was told that the design work (with a $2 million fee) was almost complete. The dilemma was how to get the type of design consistent with the management approach that the director wanted to instill in the department without wasting the $2 million already spent on design work.

The director sought the advise of associates who had designed campus style prisons in other states and the Federal Bureau of Prisons. She asked these associates if they thought the completed design could be modified, and what the additional design and construction costs might be. She was told that a change from the current design to campus style would be almost impossible, and the changes still would not have the overall benefit of campus style management she desired. So the director asked the associates for their cost estimates for design and construction if the entire plan was started from scratch, incorporating a campus style.

The rough estimates were that the design costs would again be close to $2 million, but the prison could probably be constructed for $54 million. Even with starting over, the total cost would be approximately $58 million, which included the original $2 million for the first design, the second design of another $2 million, and construction of $54 million. Although it was both a financial (depending on whether bids were received to construct the prison for $54 million) and public relations risk, the new director decided to scrap the first design and commission a new design for a campus style prison. The original architects were committed to the telephone-pole design (the same architects also designed the last prison built in the state) and were not supportive of the decision. They even complained to friends in the governor's office and state legislature about the director's decision to "throw out $2 million of design fees."

However, the director was determined and convinced the governor to let her proceed with the new design. In the end, the new prison was built for $54 million, both saving money and resulting in the style of prison consistent with direct supervision and unit management as was planned to be implemented by the new director. When the decision was final, the entire department staff welcomed it, knowing that the new director could handle pressure from politically influential groups and that the campus design would allow for progressive changes in how the state managed their prisons. The remainder of the new prisons were built based on this campus model. Fifteen years later, the Department of Corrections considers this change in design and philosophy a turning point in their administration and management, from a very traditional to a more progressive and professional style.

As the campus design was used more regularly, a further refinement came into being. As illustrated in Figure 10–3, the campus design was modified to take advantage of potential cost savings. Instead of each area of the prison being a separate building, some buildings are put together to use common walls and a common roof. An example of this style of architecture is the Federal Correctional Institution (FCI) in Greenville, Illinois. At FCI Greenville, one large programs and operations building includes space for maintenance, food/inmate services, vocational training, education, Unicor (industries), and passive recreation. As the "footprint" of FCI Greenville illustrates, the prison is still a campus style, even with these several activities sharing a common roof and walls.

The fourth model of prison design is the courtyard style. This model was developed to take advantage of the benefits available from both the telephone-pole and campus designs, and it is most often used in high-security prisons. With the courtyard style, buildings are attached to a corridor that runs around the prison, leaving a courtyard in the middle. The corridor can be used for inmate movement during much of the day, allowing prison administrators to contain and isolate inmates in the corridor by closing grills across the corridor. The recreation yard is in the middle of the courtyard, and it also facilitates inmate movement across the courtyard into building entrances off the courtyard rather than via the corridor. This provides prison administrators the flexibility of keeping inmate movement within the corridor or across the courtyard, as well as some advantages of outside movement similar to those in the campus design. The courtyard style also provides improved supervision of inmates in the middle recreation yard, and always keeps inmates within the inner perimeter of the prison.

The Federal Correctional Institution (FCI), Otisville, New York. FCI Otisville is a good illustration of a campus design. Note the triangle-shaped housing units. (Courtesy of the Federal Bureau of Prisons)

The State Prison in Lucasville, Ohio. The state prison in Lucasville is an excellent contrast to the campus design commonly used today. This prison usually holds more than 2,000 inmates. One can imagine the congestion when all these inmates move at one time through the central corridors that make up the "pole" of the telephone-pole design. (Courtesy of the Ohio Department of Rehabilitation and Correction)

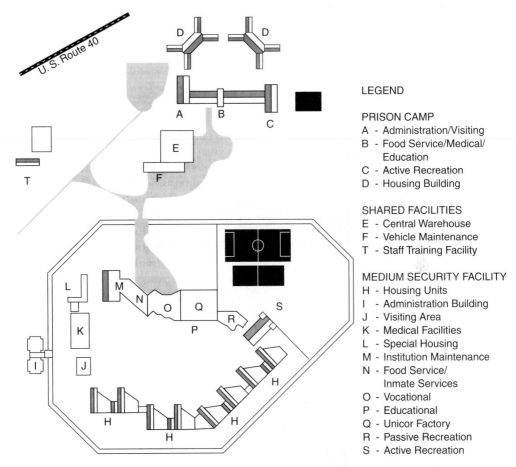

FIGURE 10–3   A "footprint" location of buildings at the Federal Correctional Institution in Greenville, Illinois.   Source: Federal Bureau of Prisons, *Greenville Federal Correctional Institution* (WASHINGTON, DC: U.S. DEPARTMENT OF JUSTICE, NO DATE) p. 3.

Direct Inmate Supervision

Another development in the design of prisons in the use of **direct supervision** in inmate housing buildings. Direct supervision is both *physical*, in that it improves the lines of site for inmate monitoring, and *philosophical*, in that it puts staff in direct contact with inmates during most of the day. Direct supervision is often created through the use of a "triangle" design of housing buildings. Two triangles are often connected by central staff offices and record storage areas, creating a "bow tie," as illustrated in the housing building in Figure 10–4.

In a direct supervision design, inmate cells are situated around the outside of the building, with staff offices, showers, and quiet recreation rooms interspersed among the cells. During the day, cell doors are kept unlocked, and inmates may

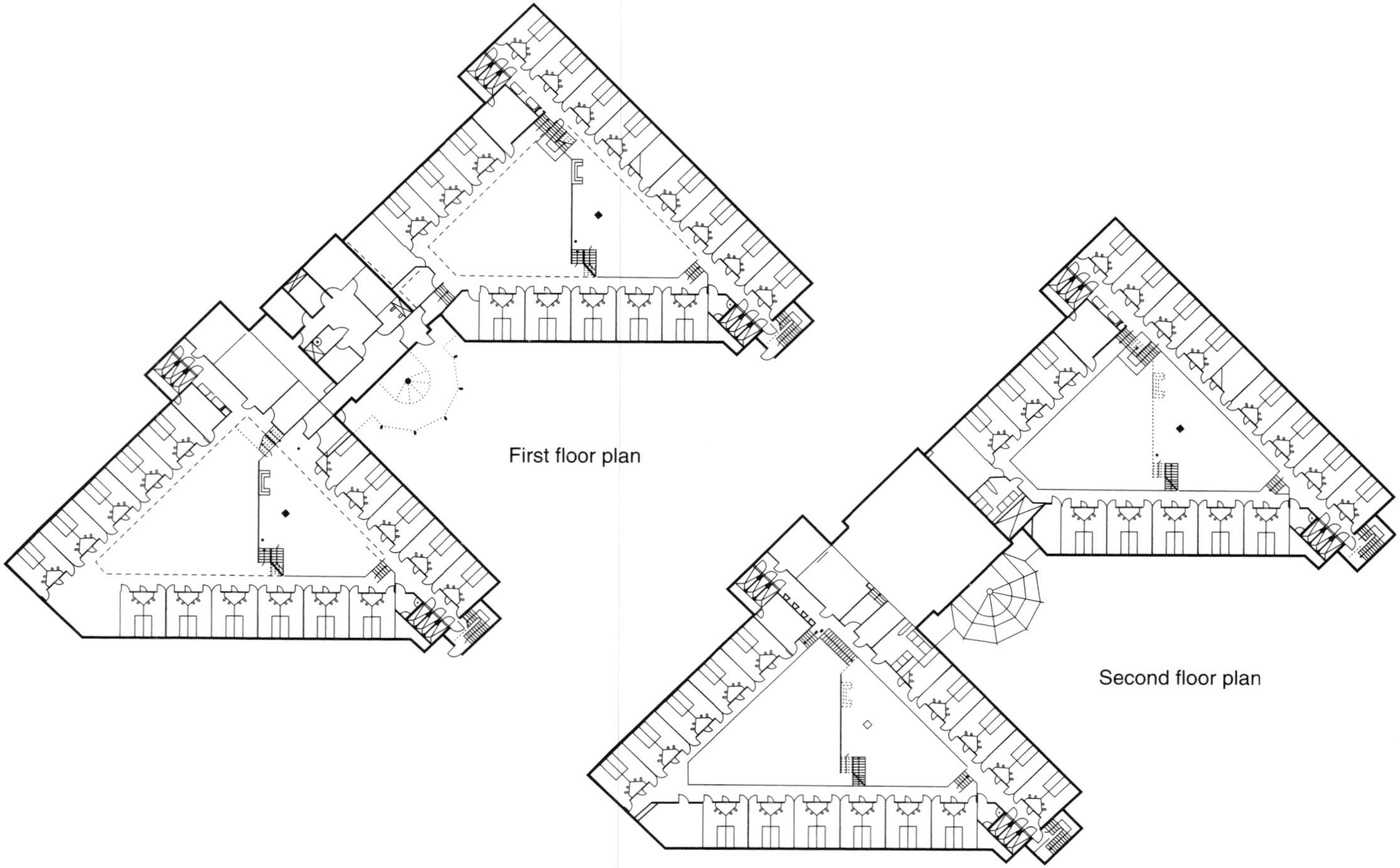

First floor plan

Second floor plan

FIGURE 10–4 Housing building at FCI Greenville. Source: Federal Bureau of Prisons, *Greenville Federal Correctional Institution* (Washington, DC: U.S. Department of Justice, no date) p. 8.

Housing Unit at the Federal Correctional Institution (FCI), Phoenix, Arizona. The housing unit at FCI Phoenix illustrates direct supervision, with an open day room with cells around it. Correctional officers working in the unit move freely among inmates who are out of their cells and in the day room much of the day. The officers can easily see all of the cell doors from the center of the unit. (Courtesy of the Federal Bureau of Prisons)

move from their cells into the open, central day room space where there may be televisions, tables for writing, and cards or other games. Correctional officers move freely with inmates in the day room and can easily see into cells. The cells seldom are more than two tiers high to facilitate supervision and inmate movement. This design is ideal for unit management, because staff offices are located among the cell locations and make staff easily accessible to inmates.

The design of a prison greatly contributes to the management style desired by administrators. Most contemporary prisons use the campus style of design, because it is compatible with unit management and disperses inmates across a large area within the secure perimeter. Once administrators have decided on the architecture of a new prison, they can then create programs and operations that compliment the design and contribute to the secure and safe management of the prison.

MEDICAL CARE FOR INMATES

Most prison administrators would agree that the most challenging operation within a prison is the delivery of medical care. There are very few prison administrators with backgrounds in medicine. They have difficulty sorting out the complex medical issues that arise, and they must rely on the substantive expertise of their medical staff. The courts have become very involved in delivery of medical care, and there is no area of prison management that has more inmate lawsuits filed. The problems of delivery of quality medical care in prisons continues to increase.

An aging inmate population, an increasing number of AIDS infected inmates, and an increasing number of women offenders has challenged the resources typically devoted to prisoner health care.

At the same time, there are unanswered philosophical questions about the quality and quantity of medical care that should be provided to incarcerated felons. Costs of inmate health care continue to rise, and there is constant pressure on administrators to reduce medical spending. Prisons have never been an attractive recruiting ground for medical personnel, and competition for providers has intensified over the past decade. All of these issues require prison administrators to look for new ways to solve serious problems. Yet there are few states that would suggest they have found the answers, and are comfortable with the cost and quality of the medical care provided in their prisons.

There are many new medical approaches being tested to determine whether they hold promise for the future. Some states have looked at the private sector approach of "managed care" to determine whether they can limit the delivery of nonessential health care. Prisons are now contracting with private providers to deliver medical care in prisons, and although some appear very successful, others are questionable. The use of technology may provide some answers to improved health services, but advances in technology are often difficult for prison administrators to evaluate, and there is limited information to use in determining their success and cost savings. Finally, prison administrators are trying to be more proactive, by providing health promotion and disease prevention programs that may reduce the long-term medical needs of inmates, large proportion of whom are serving extremely long or even life sentences.

Background of Prison Medical Care

During the first 150 years of the United States, there was little concern about the quality of medical care provided to inmates. Prisons delivered limited medical care to inmates, and few trained medical personnel were part of the staff. In many cases, inmates themselves even delivered what little care was provided. However, beginning in the late 1960s, the need for improved medical care in prisons came to the public eye. Federal courts began to accept prisoner complaints about inadequate treatment. In addition, the uprisings in many prisons during the 1970s brought attention to the dilemmas of prison health care administration.

When 43 inmates and staff lost their lives in the riot at New York's Attica Correctional Facility, many of the problems in the nation's prisons became apparent. One of the reasons attributed for the riot was the administration's failure to address a variety of longstanding inmates grievances, including medical care.[2] This lack of adequate medical care was not only a problem in New York. As suggested by Prout and Ross, "In the 1970s, . . . 95 percent of the inmates of most prisons needed medical attention, two-thirds had never had a medical examination in their lives, more than one-half were drug abusers, and at least 15 percent had diagnosable psychiatric disturbances.[3]

This lack of medical care forced the federal courts to consider these issues. Prior to the 1960s, the U.S. Supreme Court had accepted a "hands-off" doctrine regarding prison operations. Under the doctrine, the Court recognized it had no expertise in corrections and should show deference to prison administrators, while worrying that accepting prison cases would "open the floodgates" to further litigation.[4] It was not until the 1964 case of *Cooper v. Pate* that the Court changed its policy and agreed to hear a case regarding religious freedom in prison.[5] In the 1970 case of *Holt v. Sarver*, the court looked at conditions throughout the Arkansas prison system, including medical care, and created a **test of cruel and unusual punishment** within the Eighth Amendment. Instead of only including the concept of torture or physical punishment, the Court found that if people of reasonable sensitivity found the treatment shocking or disgusting, it would also be considered cruel and unusual.[6]

After the *Holt* decision, there were many other significant Supreme Court decisions that clarified the constitutional standards for the delivery of prison medical care. In *Estelle v. Gamble*, the Court determined that because inmates are dependent on prison authorities to provide treatment for their medical needs, the authorities have a duty to provide that treatment. As such, the Court prohibited **"deliberate indifference,"** in that neither the medical staff in responding to needs, nor correctional staff in denying, interfering with, or delaying access to medical care can be deliberately indifferent to such needs without the unnecessary or wanton infliction of pain.[7] The Court went further in *Ramos v. Lamm* when it suggested that deliberate indifference can also result from "repeated examples of negligent acts which disclose a pattern of conduct" by the correctional and medical staff.[8] And in *Fernandez v. United States*, the court established that medical care in prisons must be "reasonably commensurate with modern medical science and of a quality acceptable within prudent professional standards.[9] During the past decade, these cases continue to be cited in legal challenges by inmates alleging a lack of, or poor quality of, medical care in prisons.

The Development of Professional Standards for Prison Medicine

These legal cases provided guidelines for the required level and quality of medical care for incarcerated offenders. At the same time, corrections as a discipline was becoming more professional, and the American Correctional Association (ACA), the American Bar Association (ABA), and other professional organizations were developing standards for the operation of prisons and jails in the United States.[10] In the ACA standard's document, a justification for provision of proper medical care is included:

> The delivery of medical and health care is expensive. However, compensatory costs for employees and inmates injured, disabled or killed far exceed the cost of an adequate health care program. Recent judicial rulings and jury awards in health care related cases often have been staggering blows to the financial plans for correctional agencies. For these reasons, coupled with the universal concern to alleviate suffering, all correctional programmers must direct increasing attention toward the management, planning and supervision of the health care program.[11]

In the most recent update of correctional standards regarding health care by the ACA, there are 54 standards,[12] under the stated principle that, "The institution provides comprehensive health care services by qualified personnel to protect the health and well-being of inmates.[13] ACA standards are valuable for many reasons. One of the first things that a federal court considers when an inmate claims inadequate medical care is whether the prison is "accredited"[14] by the ACA or meets other professional standards for health care delivery. In addition, with correctional administrators lacking substantive knowledge of medical care, they can use these standards as a barometer of the quality of prison medical services. Many prisons, in fact, make the ACA standards available in the library, so that inmates can see the standards and expectations accepted by the prison for health care. When inmates compare, and recognize that the prison is meeting these standards, they often, although reluctantly, acknowledge that the level of care provided is adequate. However, they may still believe they personally have not received the services that their illness or injury warrants.

Another association that has developed standards and assisted correctional agencies in improving their delivery of health care is the National Commission on Correctional Health Care (NCCHC). Having roots within the American Medical Association, the NCCHC was initiated in 1983 to improve correctional health care. The NCCHC created a series of standards and "is the only accrediting agency that uses medical, dental, and mental health professionals to maintain its accreditation program.[15] NCCHC is recognized and supported by both the ACA and the American Jail Association (AJA) for their work with correctional agencies and correctional medical staff.

Since the 1970s, the delivery of prison health care has improved dramatically. Health care is still an area of prison operations that results in many inmate complaints and lawsuits, and there remain many significant challenges in the delivery of quality care. However, most correctional agencies believe they meet a level of care consistent with "community standards," the term used to describe the level of care established in the *Fernandez* decision. In describing this progress, McDonald writes

> Since the intervention of the federal courts and the emergence of professional standards pertaining to medical care, correctional authorities have moved away from relying on untrained inmates and unlicenced physicians for primary care. Now, primary care is generally delivered by medical professionals, principally physicians, physicians' assistants, nurses, and pharmacists.[16]

Issues in the Delivery of Correctional Health Care

As noted previously, there are many issues that challenge the effective delivery of quality medical care in a prison. Moore suggests that, "Problems in providing care to the incarcerated fall into two broad categories: health status of the inmate population and deficiencies in the delivery of medical care."[17] Moore also identifies six factors inherent in correctional settings that hamper the provision of health services:

1. not a priority of the correctional institution;
2. limited financial resources;
3. difficulties in staff recruitment;
4. absence of a current manual of health care policies and procedures;
5. isolation of the institution from community health care; and
6. lack of a constituency for inmate health services.[18]

Several issues that complicate the delivery of health care in prisons are presented and discussed in the next section. The first issue is to determine the quality and quantity of care that should be provided. In order to contain costs, the use of HMOs and managed care programs in the private sector are techniques to reasonably limit how much care is provided for specific illnesses. These approaches are controversial issues for private citizens and there are even more complicating factors regarding inmate health care. Inmate medical problems are getting more serious, with an aging prison population suffering from years of unhealthy life experiences. Cost for medical care continues to increase. The problem of infectious diseases has reached epidemic proportions in certain instances, and inmates historically have a higher rate of these diseases than the general population of citizens in the community. And it remains a problem to recruit and retain qualified medical staff to work in prisons.

How Much Medical Care Should Be Provided?

A common complaint among citizens is that inmates get more extensive and better medical care than many law-abiding citizens, especially the millions of Americans who are without medical insurance. This complaint often pressures state legislatures and correctional agencies to try to limit the availability of care provided. Studies that have examined the amount of health care services by inmates are inconclusive, even though they do document a relatively high level of service.[19] Inmates have little ability to get over-the-counter medications and treat themselves, because they are more reliant on medical professionals than are citizens in the community.

The courts have prescribed the minimum levels of care to be provided to incarcerated inmates, but there are no guidelines for maximum levels. Questions persist. Should death row inmates receive organ transplants? Should AIDS infected inmates receive some of the very expensive medication, even though there is no sound evidence that it cures the disease? Should cosmetic surgery be performed when it is believed that it will make a significant difference in the inmates self-esteem and chance of future success. It is difficult to create limits on what type of care should be delivered, and inmates become very difficult to manage when they believe they are not being adequately treated for obvious ailments. In the community, there are health care providers; patients rights groups; and governmental agencies who inspect, license, certify, and regulate the type of care provided. However, in the prison setting, inmate patients have no powerful voice and cannot bargain for improvements or guidelines. Without some limits and guidelines on quality and quantity of care, it is almost impossible for correctional agencies to both keep up with health care demands of inmate populations and contain costs in any viable manner.

Inmates Have Extensive Medical Needs

It is generally acknowledged that prison inmates have a higher level of medical needs than the general population of free citizens, and it is expected that these needs will increase over the next decade. However, there have been few research studies that compare the needs of long-term prison inmates with community citizens. A 1975 study of inmates admitted to New York City jails did not find that these inmates had more health problems than private citizens but concluded that "prisoners are not a healthy population, but have a high frequency of medical complaints, problems and prior hospitalizations, largely associated with substance abuse, psychiatric disorder, and trauma."[20]

It is believed that inmates present more difficult health problems than the non-incarcerated because of increases in the length of sentences and exposure of inmates for longer periods of time to the stress and dangers inherent in prison, the rising proportion of elderly offenders in prison, and the relatively high number of offenders with infectious diseases. Silverman has noted that, "The number of inmates age 55 years and older more than doubled from 1981 to 1990, . . . and a 1988 Federal Bureau of Prisons analysis estimated that the percentage of federal inmates 50 years and older will increase from 11.7 percent to 16 percent by the year 2005.[21] Other authors estimate that, "Inmates over the age of 50 will comprise 33 percent of the total prison population by the year 2010. . . . Inmates are serving more mandatory sentences and longer terms, and release policies are becoming more restrictive."[22]

Inmates are more likely to have infectious diseases, requiring extensive medical care and the prescription of expensive drugs. One infectious disease more prevalent in the population of prison inmates than in the community is tuberculosis (TB). A 1996 Centers for Disease Control study found the rate of prison inmates with TB to be six times that of the general population.[23] An even more deadly, expensive, and serious management problem in prisons is HIV/AIDS. MacDougall writes,

> Prisons and jails contain perhaps the highest concentrations of persons infected with HIV and those at greatest risk of acquiring HIV by injection drug use and sexual contact. According to a report by the U.S. Bureau of Justice Statistics, the rate of confirmed AIDS cases is more than six times higher in state and federal prisons than in the general population. About 2.3 percent of all persons incarcerated in the U.S. in 1995 were HIV-seropositive, and about 0.51 percent had confirmed AIDS.[24]

The increase in elderly offenders, longer sentences, and a large number of prison inmates with infectious diseases causes significant problems for correctional health care providers and prison administrators. These problems are complicated by the increasing cost of health care and the countervailing pressure to reduce the cost of operating prisons.

The Cost of Inmate Health Care

Health care for inmates is one of the largest expenditures (other than staff salaries and benefits) in the operation of prisons. The average per capita cost per day for federal and state prison health care was $4.68 in 1990, and the cost increased by almost 50 percent to $6.97 per day, or $2,500 per year, per inmate in 1997.[25] In 1997, federal and state prisons spent $3.4 billion for inmate medical needs. In a 1996 review of the prison health care costs, the *Corrections Compendium* reported that although states attempt to maintain increases in the cost of inmate health care consistent with the increases in the overall cost of confinement, the growth in the inmate population and increased specialized medical needs threatens to increase health care costs at a much greater rate.[26]

What can prison administrators do to try to keep down the increasing cost of inmate health care? There are some promising alternatives, and later in this section, you will examine some of the options, such as managed care and contracting with the private sector. One question involves whether it is possible to simply reduce the level of health care provided to inmates because of a lack of financial resources. To some extent, this question has already been answered. The federal courts will not accept limited budgets as an excuse for reducing the level of inmate health care provided. In *Jackson v. Bishop,* Judge Blackman writes, "Humane considerations and constitutional requirements are not to be measured or limited by dollar considerations."[27] There are many problems that complicate cost containment strategies in providing medical care for inmates. One is the fact that it is difficult to recruit quality health care providers to prisons, and institutions often have to pay a premium price to induce specialty physicians and other providers to treat inmates. Another problem is the fact that most prisons are located in rural areas, and there is very little (if any) competition in contracting for hospitalization or specialty treatment to keep prices low. Finally, it is likely that inmates do have more complicated and serious medical problems than a comparable age group of nonoffenders. As these offenders continue to serve longer sentences and rely on prisons for the provision of their health care needs, per capita medical costs for prisons are likely to continue to rise.

Recruiting and Retaining Medical Staff

Although the perceptions may not be true, most uniformed medical professionals believe that the working conditions in a prison would be unpleasant and do not consider prison health care as a career choice. In describing staffing challenges, McDonald writes:

> But there are a number of difficulties in recruiting well-trained professionals, including physicians, because of the prisons' remote locations and generally unappealing conditions, the absence of formally organized health care systems distinct from other functional divisions, inadequate facilities, and inadequate medical record-keeping systems.[28]

There are many reasons medical staff hesitate to consider employment in a correctional institution. First, they believe that the facilities are inadequate. Most people have a perception of prisons as dark, dungeonlike buildings and a prison hospital as little more than a dreary room with an examination table. Second, there are concerns that inmates are difficult patients who sue the medical staff for any care that the inmates believe is inadequate. Prisoners are often difficult patients, but this is understandable because, as prisoners they do not have a choice of health providers. And prisoners have a perception that prison medical staff must be poorly trained, or "why would they work in a prison."

Thirdly, prison routines and security precautions can be frustrating to medical personnel who do not want to be burdened with the inflexible schedules and security procedures necessary to prison operations. In addition, some medical personnel do not consider prison work because they fear for their safety, and there is a potential (although it seldom occurs) for assault by an inmate. Finally, it is probably a fact that the salaries for public sector medical persons is lower than many options available to health care providers in the community. However, with today's emphasis on managed care and efficiency in treating patients, the gap in pay and working conditions between a prison and the community is closing.

Prison administrators must work hard to counter the negative image that medical staff have about prisons. In reality, there are many benefits to working in a prison environment. The facilities are often new and are certainly comparable to that in any physicians' office or community clinic. Prison physicians usually do not have to carry malpractice insurance, because they are government employees and are not personally liable (the government agency has to cover legal fees and lost claims) if they practice according to accepted professional standards. Some medical personnel find prison medical care fascinating work, because they see a wide variety of medical problems in a population of prisoners. And pay and benefits (especially retirement) are not as bad as most people perceive. As government agencies found that they could not compete for medical staff, many adjusted their pay scales to be able to hire and retain medical staff.

Current Medical Operations in a Prison Setting

Medical care for prisoners is usually provided with a combination of prison and community resources. Care is typically provided through four levels: the standard prison infirmary, contracts with community specialists, the use of community hospitals for serious problems or surgical needs, and prison hospitals for inmates with long-term or continuous medical needs. Correctional agencies have their own staff of full-time medical personnel and have part-time contracts with specialty providers. Individual prisons usually have contracts with many local hospitals to meet the more serious needs that cannot be met at the prison. The next sections describe these four levels of prison medical care.

Prison Infirmaries

The first level of medical needs within a prison is for the day-to-day minor illnesses and injuries, similar to the needs of the general public who go to a family practice physician's office. Inmates with colds, influenza, sprained ankles, and other routine medical conditions are seen and treated at the **prison infirmary.** The infirmaries are a combination doctors office, dentists office, and pharmacy. There is usually staff coverage of the infirmary 24 hours every day, and physicians are typically in the infirmary on week days. Most prison infirmaries have an x-ray machine, a laboratory, and an emergency or trauma room for injuries and illnesses requiring immediate attention.

Most inmate medical needs are met in the infirmary, including preliminary medical screening when inmates are received at a prison, daily sick call, referrals to specialists, and continuity of care for inmates with chronic illnesses. At the preliminary screening, inmates receive a physical examination, there is an inquiry into current illnesses and health problems (which include dental and mental health needs), and a treatment plan is developed for meeting these needs during the period of imprisonment. Every day, prisons hold **sick call,** at which inmates with a medical need

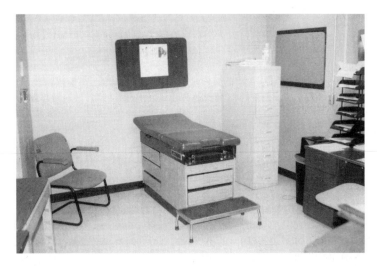

Typical Examination Room in a Prison Infirmary. Inmates are seen by medical personnel in examination rooms that are very similar to those in a community physician's office. (Courtesy of Ohio Department of Rehabilitation and Correction)

can come to the infirmary and be examined by a nurse, who can either provide necessary treatment or schedule the inmate for an appointment with the physician. If the physician prescribes medication, the prescription is given to the prison pharmacy to fill. Inmates are not allowed to have prescription drugs in their possession, because they may not take them as prescribed or may abuse them in some way. Therefore, they must come to the "pill line," which is held several times per day, and receive and take their dosage. Pill line is simply that. Inmates line up at the pharmacy window or counter, are given their dosage of medication, and must take it in front of a medical staff member. Most over-the-counter medicine may be kept by inmates, and although some prisons provide it, others require inmates to purchase these medicines at the inmate commissary.

If the prison physician determines that an illness or injury must be referred to a specialist, the referral is made and an appointment scheduled by prison medical staff. Many inmates have chronic medical problems that require long-term treatment plans. If the plans do not require hospitalization, the inmate may stay at the prison under the care of the prison physician or a contract specialist. The treatment plans may include certain exercises, a special diet, physical therapy, and regular doctor visits and checkups. All of these activities can be provided in most prisons, and the medical staff coordinate exercise or dietary requirements with other departments within the prison.

Specialty Medical Care

The standard staffing pattern for a prison infirmary includes one or two physicians, a dentist and dental assistant, several nurses, and a pharmacist. If an inmate suffers from medical needs that cannot be met by the full-time staff, they are referred to a

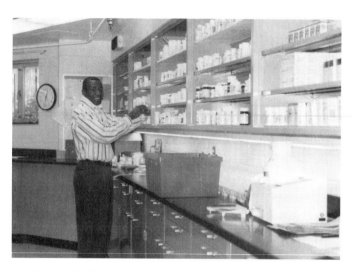

A Pharmacy in a Prison Infirmary. Inmates who require prescription medication have the prescription filled by a pharmacist on the staff of the prison infirmary. (Courtesy of the Ohio Department of Rehabilitation and Correction)

community medical specialist. Prisons usually contract with special medical providers in the community, including orthopedic surgeons, heart specialists, psychiatrists, dermatologists, and eye care providers. This care is delivered in one of two ways. The method preferred by the prison administration is to have the specialist visit the prison and see patients for as many hours per month as required. Most infirmaries are equipped to provide examination areas for these specialists to see and treat patients. If there is a need for specialized testing, inmates may be transported to the physicians office or a hospital for the testing.

If the contracted medical specialist cannot or will not come to the prison infirmary to see patients, the inmates will be transported to the hospital or physicians' office for examination and treatment. This requires extensive security precautions, including escort by two or three armed correctional officers, restraining the inmate with handcuffs and leg irons (chains), and secrecy regarding the time and route of transportation so that the inmate will not know the exact time or location of the appointment. Because of the security and staffing requirements, transporting an inmate to a local hospital or physician's office for a visit ends up being expensive.

Local Hospitalization of Inmates

When an inmate requires surgery or other treatment that must be provided in a hospital, the prison usually uses a local hospital through a contract for services. Each prison establishes a contract with local hospitals to provide services that are beyond the scope of care available at the infirmary but that do not require transfer to the state prison hospital. The process for admitting an inmate is no different than that for community citizens. A physician admits the inmate for hospitalization and performs the tests, treatment, or surgery during the hospital stay. After completion of

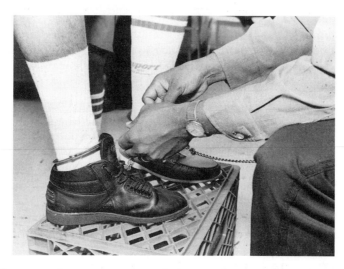

Leg Irons. Security of inmates in outside hospitals is always a problem. Whenever inmates leave a prison, they are placed in leg irons. When they are in a hospital, one of the ends of the leg iron is attached to a secure place on the hospital bed. (Courtesy of the Ohio Department of Rehabilitation and Correction)

treatment, inmates stay in the hospital long enough for recovery and to be seen by the attending physician. Once the physician discharges an inmate from the hospital, the inmate returns to the prison and receives any follow-up care by prison medical staff or further visits with the specialist.

Security of the inmate is always difficult during hospital stays. Even though the inmate is sick and the chance of escape is reduced, the prison administrators must take all available security precautions. Depending on the security level of the inmate and potential for violence or escape, there will be from one to three armed correctional officers constantly guarding the inmate. Officers usually work eight-hour shifts, and then another group of officers relieve them in the hospital. Inmates are not handcuffed while they are in the hospital, but they usually do have leg irons (cuffs for the ankles) attached to one leg and to the hospital bed. Inmates are not allowed visits from family or friends while they are in the hospital, because there are no facilities to ensure that visitors do not bring weapons or drugs to the inmate. Movement of inmates to a hospital is a dangerous situation for staff. A few years ago, correctional officers from the U.S. Penitentiary in Lewisburg, Pennsylvania, were escorting an inmate to a local hospital. Associates of the inmate found out about the time of the hospital trip, ambushed the escort team in an escape attempt, and murdered one of the officers.

Prison Hospitals

Every state and the Federal Bureau of Prisons operate at least one **prison hospital.** The role of these hospitals it to house and treat inmates with chronic care needs over a long period of incarceration, or whose medical problems are so serious that they cannot be met in a regular prison infirmary. Prison hospitals are used instead of local contract community hospitals when the length of stay in a hospital makes it more cost efficient to transport the inmate to the prison hospital. These prison hospitals are a combination of standard prison housing and in-patient hospital beds. The dual role of prison and hospital is illustrated by the mission statement of the Federal Medical Center at Lexington, Kentucky.

> The mission of the Federal Medical Center, Lexington, Kentucky, is to protect society through providing confinement services to committed offenders. In carrying out the judgements of the Federal Courts, we provide a safe, secure, and humane environment with encouragement and opportunity for positive change. In addition, as a Federal Medical Center, we provide extensive medical services, mental health care, and drug treatment to the inmate population.[29]

Some inmates with serious medical needs, but who do not have to continuously live in the hospital, are assigned to a regular housing status in a prison hospital. They can receive out-patient treatment, using the more extensive medical capabilities available in a prison hospital rather than at a normal prison infirmary. Inmates with in-patient needs are housed in the actual hospital beds at the prison, with medical staffing and equipment similar to any community hospital. When these inmates are able to be released from the hospital, they may be returned to a regular prison, or stay in the regular housing status at the prison hospital.

Historically, these prison hospitals have provided all types of treatment, to include complicated surgeries. However, most states have found that they cannot afford to keep up with modern technology and equipment required for such surgical procedures, nor can they recruit surgeons as full-time staff. Therefore, current prison hospitals more commonly use local community hospitals and contract surgeons, performing required surgical procedures in the community. Following the surgery, inmates are housed at the prison hospital for postoperative treatment and recovery.

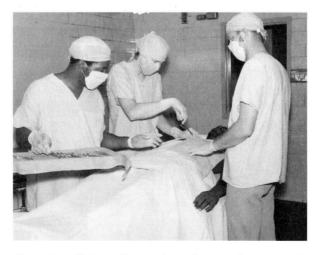

The Operating Room in a Prison. Few prison doctors do surgery in prison hospitals today. However, until the 1960s, this was common practice. (Courtesy of the Ohio Department of Rehabilitation and Correction)

Future Approaches to Providing Medical Care for Inmates

There is no question that the delivery of health care to prison inmates has improved dramatically over the past few decades. The involvement of federal courts and the implementation of correctional health care standards are two factors that have most influenced this improvement. However, there are still many issues regarding increasing need for inmate care and the resulting cost of care that must be addressed. Therefore, correctional administrators are experimenting with a variety of new approaches for the delivery of medical care for inmates. These include cost containment initiatives, such as requiring inmate copayment for services, and the implementation of managed care procedures, contracting with the private sector, the increased use of available technology, and inmate health educational programs.

Cost Containment Initiatives

One of the ways correctional agencies are trying to contain cost increases for prison health care is through managed care strategies, similar to those implemented in the community. The major components of community **managed care** include universal access, limited scope of services, limited choice of providers, minimal copayments, selective contracts with a network of providers for specialized treatment, and the use of negotiated fixed fees for service providers. All of these practices are usually associated with health maintenance organizations (HMOs). Although there is controversy about the decisions and cost-saving measures regarding HMOs, they have shown success in containing the cost of health care delivery.

It has been suggested that correctional agencies provide favorable settings for this type of managed care, and several agencies have been using it for some time. Clark writes that, "many in correctional health care have been practicing managed care for the past 15 years, in that inmates have universal access to care, the scope of services is limited, there is no choice of provider, inmate co-payment fees are widely used, and contracting for health services has been commonplace in many correctional institutions across the country."[30] Although this statement is true, there are many factors that have worked against prisons using these components to the fullest to contain cost.

With the rural location of most prisons and lack of competition among prospective medical providers, prisons usually cannot develop networks or medical contracts using fixed costs for services. In many cases, prison managers believe they are fortunate to get anyone to provide medical services, even if it costs a premium. Security, not cost-efficiency, concerns must also be the dominate decision making factor in the delivery of medical care. McDonald identifies three strategies that can be used by correctional agencies to implement managed care principles and contain costs, including "reducing the costs of purchased goods and services, containing costs by limiting or dissuading prisoners' use of services, and contracting with full-service firms to deliver health care."[31]

Reducing the costs of purchased goods and services is possible through creative approaches to government contracting, such as combining a prison need for services with the needs of other prisons or other similar agencies. In some jurisdictions, prisons are beginning to combine their contract needs with mental health institutions, Veterans Administration hospitals, or other nearby prisons to increase their contract levels and, therefore, improve their competitive positions. Some states have found it beneficial to consider using their state university medical schools as a resource for providing health services to inmates.

The issue of limiting services for inmates is difficult, but certainly possible, if it does not reduce the level of care below constitutional standards. Court decisions have required that inmates receive adequate levels of care, consistent with community standards. Because there is no clear definition of community standards, correctional agencies try to declare that they will perform "necessary" rather than "elective" medical problems, although even this delineation varies in the minds of physicians. Other correctional agencies decide they will not perform services, such as cosmetic procedures, yet removing tattoos from gang members who want to leave the gang is believed to be valuable in the offender's rehabilitation. The department of corrections in California uses "Medi-Cal standards" as a guide to the types of services they will provide.[32]

One of the most interesting approaches in delivery of prison medical care has been the requirement of a copayment from inmates. Camp and Camp report that as of January 1, 1998, 32 state correctional agencies (and many more county jails) charged inmates a copayment from $2.00 to $5.00 per visit to the infirmary.[33] Some assume that inmates come to sick call when it is not medically required. This unnecessary use drives up the overall cost of providing prison health care and diverts staff resources from where they can better be used. In order to make copay fair, without denying access to medical care, the California Medical Association's Corrections and Detention Committee developed guidelines for its use. These guidelines include the communication of the policy and fee schedules to inmates, a possibility to waive fees for indigent inmates, a grievance process for inmates to challenge a billed service, and the importance of evaluating the effectiveness of a copay system.[34] Most correctional agencies believe that their copay policies have been effective. As an example, an Alabama jail director of nursing reports that the jail had cut its sick call to see a nurse, doctor, or dentist by 50 percent.[35]

A rapidly growing approach to providing health care to inmates is through contracting for its delivery with the private sector. Moore describes the state of private sector involvement in prison health care as follows:

> The first jail system to contract for a wholly provided inmate health system by a private vendor was Rikers Island in June of 1973. . . . Today, there are 14 private sector firms that provide inmate health care on a national or regional basis, and 20 states have privatized all or part of their inmate health care services.[36]

Under a full-service contract, the private vendor operates the prison infirmary and provides all health care and prescription medications to inmates. The private vendor hires and pays the salaries of all the medical staff, contracts for specialty services or hospitalization in the community, and makes medical decisions regarding inmate needs. The contract with the private provider usually lists the types of services that must be provided, such as initial health screening, daily sick call, specialty care clinics, radiology services, physical therapy, and treatment of infectious diseases such as TB and HIV/AIDS. Contracts are usually a fixed price for each inmate per day, although they may specify a maximum spent on any one inmate per year.

There are many advantages and disadvantages of contracting with a private provider (see Table 10–1). One of the concerns regarding contracted medical care is identified by Moore, who suggests that "too often the existence of appropriate policies on paper may not translate into quality health care."[37] Contracts with private providers must be closely monitored and evaluated. The government agency cannot contract its overall responsibility for the delivery and overall quality of the health care, and still be liable for failure to provide adequate health care for inmates.

The Use of Technology

The most widely used technology to respond to current challenges in the delivery of prison health care has been the use of "telemedicine." Simply stated, **telemedicine** is "the use of telecommunications technologies to offer health care, or clinical information, across geographic, time or cultural barriers."[38] For most correctional institutions, however, "telemedicine was used increasingly to refer to interactive video conferencing, in which information is exchanged through video and audio systems, with clarity close to broadcast capability. This is the telemedicine that correctional institutions are using with increasing frequency and ease."[39]

Telemedicine works by using live video conferencing that enables a health care provider at another location to examine an inmate. A medical staff member with the inmate "presents" the patient, summarizing the medical history and current problem. The camera illustrates the symptoms, and the physician at the remote location can ask questions of the patient and request other camera views of the affliction. It is also possible to use a "document" camera to share medical information and data

▦ TABLE 10–1

Advantages and Disadvantages of Privatization of Inmate Medical Needs

Advantages	Disadvantages
Liability/risk transfer	Liability for contractor's decisions
Lower cost	Strong profit motive
Cost containment measures (i.e., utilization review, clinical pathways, formulary)	Possibility of delay in scheduling off-site consults and services
Improved quality of service delivery	Financial risk of underbidding contract
Provision of adequate equipment and supplies	Use of lobbyist to obtain contracts
Recruitment of health care staff	Union resistance
Central control and accountability	Lack of budgetary control
Fewer time demands on warden or jail administrator	Potential for conflicts with security staff

Source: Jacqueline M. Moore, "Privatization of Inmate Health Care: A New Approach to an Old Problem, *Corrections Management Quarterly* 2 (no.2) (1998): 51.

such as x-rays and EKG results. With this technology, many specialty examinations can be completed without the physician being at the same location as the patient.

Telemedicine can help solve many of the problems facing correctional health care. As noted, with the rural location of many prisons, there are few specialty providers who are available or willing to see inmates. Because telemedicine does not require the specialist to be located near the facility, the availability of specialty clinics is expanded and contracting can become more competitive. In addition, the high cost for security to take inmates outside the prison for examinations is eliminated. No extra staff cost is incurred, because inmates simply report to the prison infirmary for video conferencing examinations. There are costs for the video conferencing equipment and transmission, but they are much lower than costs for inmate transport outside the prison.

Health Educational Programs

One of the most promising strategies for reducing the demand for health care for inmates is the implementation of health promotion and disease prevention programs in prisons. Prison administrators, recognizing that they will have custody of many offenders for long periods of time, have realized the potential financial and service-avoidance benefits of such programs. Few offenders have lived a very healthy lifestyle prior to their incarceration. Although there is not verifiable evidence, it is assumed that improved habits in diet and exercise, along with reducing high-risk activities, such as intravenous drug use or homosexual activities, can reduce the frequency of inmate illnesses in the future.

Although most of the **health educational programs** are preventative, some also educate inmates in better managing current illnesses, thereby lessening the severity of the problem and the need for medical care. For instance, inmates with lower-back problems are educated about the importance of stretching before exercise, how to perform their own physical therapy, and activities to avoid. This conservative treatment can reduce pain, allow inmates to continue their normal activities, and lessen the potential need for back surgery. Similarly, inmates with diabetes or heart disease receive education on the benefits of proper diet and exercise, which can reduce the potential for a heart attack or death. Almost every prison educates inmates on the danger of infectious diseases, such as HIV/AIDS or TB, and how to avoid activities that can lead to infection of these diseases.

Other areas often included in health educational programs are changes in recreation and diet by inmates. Instead of offering only traditional recreation programs targeting young and healthy inmates, many prisons are now providing moderate exercise programs for all segments of the population (including the elderly or handicapped) to encourage them to increase their activity and improve their long-range health. And prison medical staff work closely with food service staff to offer heart healthy meals. In the year 2000, the Federal Bureau of Prisons announced they will even provide a "meatless" diet for interested inmates. All of these activities are believed to provide excellent opportunities to reduce the long-term health problems of incarcerated offenders.

As has been illustrated, medical services to inmates represent a difficult problem for prison administrators: Costs for medical care are rising dramatically, it is difficult to recruit qualified staff, inmates regularly sue prison administrators for failure to provide adequate medical care, and offenders with long prison terms are aging and have even more medical needs. However, prison administrators are experimenting with a variety of new approaches to meet these challenges. Although many cost reduction and disease prevention strategies are expected to prove successful, there are still many controversial issues in the use of private providers to deliver medical care. The next decade should prove whether these strategies are successful.

FOOD SERVICE PROGRAMS IN PRISONS

The history of food service in prisons in many ways mirrors the history of prison medical care. In the early years of prison operations, food was poorly prepared, met few nutritional standards, and was not served in a professional or attractive style. The vision of "slopping" unrecognizable food on a tray for inmates was not too far from reality in the 1800s and early 1900s. However, just as with medical care, another causal factor behind many prison riots (including Attica) in the 1970s was poor food service operations. Federal courts also started looking into food service and other areas of prison operations. As a result, prison administrators turned to organizations such as the ACA for guidance in the development of professional standards.

In the ACA *Standards for Adult Correctional Institutions,* the principle guiding food service standards is that, "Meals are nutritionally balanced, well-planned, and prepared and served in a manner that meets established governmental health and safety codes."[40] The standards that follow this principle include the need to plan food menus well in advance to meet nutritional needs, maintain stored and prepared foods at appropriate temperatures to avoid food-borne illnesses, and serve food in a relaxed and normal cafeteria setting whenever possible. Another organization that works to assure quality prison food service operations is the American Correctional Food Service Association (ACFSA). The ACFSA was formed in 1969 to "enhance, represent, and promote the correctional segment of the food service industry . . . and encourage standards of excellence and professionalism among its members to enhance food service operations in prisons."[41]

Food service in a correctional institution is extremely important to inmates, and there are few other services that impact the morale and undermine control quicker than poor food service. Much of this has to do with the fact that, unlike citizens in the community, inmates have limited choices in what is available to eat. In most prisons, inmates can buy a few snack items in the commissary. However, prisons do not want inmates eating exclusively from commissary purchases, and, therefore, the amount and selection is limited. With three meals each day, food service is experienced by all inmates at every meal, and it plays a key role in their daily routine. Therefore, it is understandable why some authors suggest that prison food service "is no doubt the most personal service provided in a correctional setting . . . if personnel do not do their jobs correctly and on time, negative reactions from the inmate population are likely to occur."[42]

The challenge is to provide tasty and nutritional meals at a reasonable cost. In 1997 the average state and federal prison spent only $3.54 per inmate per day for food costs.[43] There are several measures used by prisons to keep these costs relatively low. First, state prisons often combine their food ordering needs, and because they purchase extremely large quantities of food, they often get a very good price. In addition, many correctional agencies operate farms and can provide for some of their own food needs. Food is prepared by inmates, and, therefore, labor costs for food preparation and serving are very low. However, even with these advantages, it is a continuous challenge for menu planners and food administrators to provide good food service and stay within the relatively low food service budgets.

Food Service Operations

There are several key areas of prison food service, including menu planning, food preparation, serving options, and special diets. For an idea of the challenges of correctional food service, the following description in the California Department of Corrections is enlightening.

> Imagine you're the team of California Department of Corrections' (CDC) food managers. It's Thanksgiving Day, and 150,000-plus inmates are wondering, "Where's the turkey?" What do you do? For starters, you order 77,000 pounds of turkey. Then stuff the turkeys with 51,000 pounds of dressing, and start them baking. Next, whip up 38,000 pounds of salad, 51,000 pounds each of potatoes and yams, and top it off with 300,000 dinner rolls. That's a Traditional Thanksgiving, CDC-style. And that's pretty typical for a holiday menu in a California prison. While this is more sumptuous than on average days, inmates receive heart-healthy, well-balanced, tasty meals three times a day, seven days a week, 52 weeks a year. "As your food service program goes, so goes your institution," said CDC Food Administrator Don Barker.[44]

The first key for prison food service administrators is menu planning. Most correctional agencies develop agencywide menus that can be modified and supplemented by each prison. The menu is developed by a food dietitian to ensure that the meals are well-balanced and meet daily health needs and requirements. In California, the meals add up to about 3,200 calories a day for men and 2,900 calories a day for women.[45] With the menu providing the prison food administrator the types of food combinations and portions to meet nutritional needs, the local prison staff can then mix the serving order and supplement the menu to meet the specific needs and likes of their inmate population, as long as they stay within their budget allowances.

The next key to successful food service is preparation and service. Prisons usually keep a 30-day food products supply, just to ensure they do not run out because of unexpected problems with wholesale sellers or transportation of food products. To prepare food, prisons employ a core of staff who supervise inmates in preparation and cooking. The inmate cooks follow standard recipes, such as the Armed Forces Recipe Cards, that are designed for food preparation for large numbers of people. Once prepared, there are several ways in which food is served to the inmate population, including cafeteria style and feeding on the units.

"Old Style" Inmate Dining Room in the Ohio Penitentiary (c. 1950). This style of dining room was used in prisons until the 1970s, when most prisons redesigned for a more relaxed and less congested space for dining. (Courtesy of the Ohio Department of Rehabilitation and Correction)

Cafeteria style feeding is done in two ways. The first is the "open line," similar to buffet restaurants in the community, where customers take a tray and move along a line of foods, selecting those they want to purchase. In a prison cafeteria, inmates come to the dining room in groups, either from housing units or from their work assignments. They form a line and move along the serving line with their trays. With the open line style, inmate servers put food on the trays, or inmates may be allowed to serve themselves certain items (perhaps potatoes or bread) if there is no limit on serving portions. Some prisons use "blind lines" in which inmates cannot see who is serving, and servers cannot see who will receive the tray. This reduces complaints of the size of portions inmates receive, because they simply get the next full tray on the line. Unlike a community cafeteria restaurant, inmates have few choices from the prison menu, but they can choose not to take an item on the menu. There are, however, usually religious or medical diet options, such as nonpork options for Muslims, or nonsalt servings for medical reasons.

When they reach the end of the food line, most prisons allow inmates to sit wherever they want in the dining room. Dining rooms are usually large and optimally seat about one-third of the entire prison population at a time. Inmates are allowed to talk to friends at the table, but they are not usually allowed to move around the dining room to talk to other inmates. Allowing inmates to move around the dining room from table to table creates a minor security concern, because large numbers of inmates are together in one location. However, the more important concern is the need to quickly move inmates through the dining room, so that all inmates can be fed in a reasonably short (usually one hour) period of time.

The second food service option is to bring the food to the inmates in the unit in which they are housed. With **unit dining,** the food is prepared in a central kitchen and then transported in hot and cold carts or in insulated trays (to maintain proper food temperatures) to the units. Unit dining is primarily used in jails or detention facilities, or in prison special housing units (SHUs) in which the inmates seldom leave their cells. If the institution uses insulated trays, the food is put on the trays ahead of time and delivered to each inmate in the cell or in a small unit dining area. If the food comes in a bulk hot/cold cart, it is usually placed on the trays at the housing unit by inmate servers under the supervision of staff to maintain portion control.

California prisons use a "cook chill" process for feeding. In the cook chill process, food is prepared in a central kitchen, and quickly chilled to 34 degrees, just above freezing, and maintained in walk-in coolers for up to three days. For serving, it is delivered to satellite kitchens near the housing units in the institution, where it is "rethermed," or heated to the proper temperature for serving. California has found this to be a convenient and efficient method of preparing and serving food. Many of the California prisons house more than 4,000 inmates, and it would be impossible to bring that many inmates to a central dining area.

Food service operations in a prison are a key to inmate morale and order. Food service staff must be knowledgeable of nutritional requirements, food purchasing, cost containment, food preparation, health and safety issues, and attractive service practices. Many correctional administrators believe food service staff have one of the most challenging jobs in a prison. They must supervise a large inmate workforce; they must maintain security of food, equipment, and utensils; and they must ensure tasty and nutritional meals are prepared and served three times every day. And unfortunately, as Scott Fisher, a regional food administrator for the Federal Bureau of Prisons, says, "You are only as good as your last meal."

SUMMARY

Part 2 of this text, discussed managing offenders through corrections' focus on punishment and deterrence, the use of risk assessments, and programs to aid in rehabilitation. In Part 3, the focus was narrowed to a more operational emphasis, by examining how correctional goals and philosophies are carried out in a prison setting. Not only was the manner in which prisons are organized discussed, but also approaches to creating a safe and secure environment, and managing violent inmates were discussed.

The focus then turned to the study of some of the operational areas within a prison. Prison design, medical services, and food services are considered the three basic and extremely important areas of prison operations. In Chapter 10, we examined how prison architecture reflects (or even mandates) the management style of a prison. This chapter included the evolution of prison architecture, from a design emphasizing isolation and repentance, to a design maximizing the relaxed movement of inmates to work and program activities. Decisions made early in the design process can impact the way a prison is managed and the culture that develops for the future.

Two basic services in a prison are medical care and food service. Both share a not-too-proud history, one in which the provision of these services was done poorly and unprofessionally. Unfortunately, it took prison riots and the intervention of the federal courts to bring attention to the need for upgrading these areas. However, prison staff who manage these areas in modern prisons should be commended for the excellent jobs they do in very difficult situations. There are many challenges to the delivery of high-quality, yet cost-effective, prison health care and food service. Yet these managers are creating new techniques and experimenting with new procedures that provide promise for a much brighter future.

In the next section, you begin to examine staff, rather than offender issues, and the critical importance of managing staff as a resource. Corrections is a "people business," and the most important key for success is having qualified and well-trained staff. The issues in human resource management of a correctional agency and the challenge of supervising and empowering staff are examined. Also considered are the roles of many correctional workers who perform the entry-level jobs, which are most likely to be sought by recent graduates of two- or four-year college programs in criminal justice or correctional administration.

ENDNOTES

1. For a description of the four models, see Todd R. Clear and George R. Cole, *American Corrections,* 5th ed. (Belmont, CA: Wadsworth Publishing Company, 2000), pp. 234–235.
2. John DiIulio, *Governing Prisons* (New York: The Free Press, 1987), p. 29.
3. Curtis Prout and Robert Ross, *Care and Punishment,* (Pittsburgh: Pittsburgh Press, 1988), p. 5.
4. See *Ruffin v. Commonwealth of Virginia,* 62 Va (21 Gratt.) 790, 796 (1871).
5. *Cooper v. Pate,* 378 US 546 (1964).
6. *Holt v. Sarver,* 309 F. Supp. 362 [E.D. Ark. 1970], *aff'd* 442 F.2d 304 98th Cir. (1971).
7. *Estelle v. Gamble,* 429 US 97 (1976).
8. *Ramos v. Lamm,* 639 F.2d 559, 576 (10th Cir., 1980).
9. *Fernandez v. United States,* 941 F.2d 1488 (11th Cir. 1991).
10. For a review of the earlier developed standards for correctional facilities, see American Correctional Association, *Sample Guidelines for the Development of Policies and Procedures for Use in Adult Correctional Institutions and Adult Local Detention Facilities* (College Park, MD: American Correctional Association, 1987); American Bar Association, *Medical and Health Care in Jails, Prisons, and Other Correctional Facilities: A Compilation of Standards and Materials* (Washington, DC: American Bar Association, 1974); and American Public Health Association, *Standards for Health Services in Correctional Institutions* (Washington, DC: American Public Health Association, 1976).
11. American Correctional Association, p. 277.
12. American Correctional Association, *Standards for Adult Correctional Institutions: Third Edition* (Lanham, MD: American Correctional Association, 1990), pp. 109–128.
13. Ibid., p. 109.
14. The ACA (through the Commission on Accreditation for Corrections) has a process whereby prisons can be inspected by independent correctional

professionals to determine whether they meet the standards at a level that allows them to be "accredited" and recognized as meeting the professional standards for operating a prison.

15. Kenneth E. Kerle, *American Jails: Looking to the Future* (Boston, MA: Butterworth-Heinemann, 1988), p. 121.
16. Douglas C. McDonald, "Medical Care in Prisons," in *Prisons*, edited by Michael Tonry and Joan Petersilia (Chicago: University of Chicago Press, 1999), p. 428.
17. Jacqueline M. Moore, "Privatization of Inmate Health Care: A New Approach to an Old Problem," *Corrections Management Quarterly* 2(no.2) (1998): 46.
18. Ibid., p. 47.
19. For a summary of the question of whether inmates receive too much medical care, see McDonald, pp. 445–446.
20. Lloyd R. Novick, R. Della Penna, M. S. Schwartz, E. Remmlinger, and R. Lowenstein, "Health Status of the New York City Prison Population," *Medical Care* 15 (no.3) (1977): 215.
21. Charles Silverman, "Geriatric Inmates—Design and Health Care Considerations," *The State of Corrections: Proceedings of the ACA Annual Conferences in 1993* (Lanham, MD: American Correctional Association, 1994), p. 145.
22. Connie L. Neeley, Laura Addison, and Delores Craig-Moreland, "Addressing the Needs of Elderly Offenders," *Corrections Today* 59, no. 5 (August 1997): 120.
23. Centers for Disease Control, *Reported Tuberculosis in the United States, 1996* (Atlanta, GA: Centers for Disease Control, 1997), p. 19.
24. David S. MacDougall, "HIV/AIDS Behind Bars: Incarceration Provides a Valuable Opportunity to Implement HIV/AIDS Treatment and Prevention Strategies in a High-Risk Population," *Journal of the International Association of Physicians in AIDS Care* (April 1998).
25. Camille Graham Camp and George M. Camp, *The Corrections Yearbook: 1998* (Middletown, CT: The Criminal Justice Institute, 1998), p. 92.
26. G. Wess, "Inmate Healthcare Part I: As New Commitments Climb, Healthcare Budgets Follow," *Corrections Compendium* 10 no. 2 (1996): 6–9.
27. *Jackson v. Bishop*, 404 F.2d 572 CA (1968).
28. McDonald, p. 438.
29. Mission Statement of the Federal Medical Center (Lexington, KY: U.S. Bureau of Prisons, 1995), unpublished report.
30. John Clark, "Providing Correctional Health Care Services," in *Prison and Jail Administration: Practice and Theory*, edited by Peter M. Carlson and Judith Simon Garrett (Gaithersburg, MD: Aspen Publishers, 1999), p. 103.
31. McDonald, pp. 459–471.
32. Ibid., pp. 464–465.
33. Camp and Camp, pp. 90–91.
34. For a full description of the California guidelines, see John Clark, "Guidelines for Implementing Inmate Medical Fees," *Corrections Today* 59 no. 6 (October 1997): 106–107.
35. Kerle, p. 130.

36. Moore, p. 48.

37. Ibid., p. 56.

38. Michelle Gailiun, "Telemedicine Takes Off: Correctional Systems Across Country Embrace Cost-Saving Technology," *Corrections Today* 59 no. 4 (July 1997): 68.

39. Ibid., p. 68.

40. American Correctional Association, p. 99.

41. American Correctional Food Service Association, Web site: www.acfsa.org. February 2001.

42. Lavinia Johnson, "Correctional Food Service," in Carlson and Garrett, p. 134.

43. Camp and Camp, p. 92.

44. California Department of Corrections, "Corrections' Dedicated Food Service Team Plans Menus a Year in Advance" (Sacramento: California Department of Corrections, 1997), unpublished document, p. 1.

45. Ibid.

KEY TERMS

separate system	prison infirmary
outside cells	sick call
inside cells	prison hospital
radial design	managed care
congregate system	telemedicine
direct supervision	health educational programs
test of cruel and unusual punishment	cafeteria style feeding
deliberate indifference	unit dining

YOU'RE THE CORRECTIONAL ADMINISTRATOR

1. You are the chief of prison design for a large state correctional agency. The state has not built a prison for more than 20 years, but a new prison construction bill has just been passed that authorizes and funds the construction of seven new prisons. You are charged with determining the type of prisons (security level, location, etc.) that are needed and the style in which they will be designed. How do you go about the process of making these decisions? What information do you seek? Who do you involve in the process? How do you test and confirm your decisions are right before they are literally "set in stone"?

2. You are the chief of medical services for the state department of corrections. The department budget planners have come to you for advice. They show you figures on how the medical services budget has increased by almost 18 percent a year for the past four years. They are concerned because the budget is getting tighter, the number of inmates is increasing, and you have been projecting that certain developments within the department may increase medical costs by an even greater percentage. They ask you to estimate the increase and come up with several solutions that can be implemented to

reduce costs or at least slow the increases. What are some of the types of issues that must be considered when calculating medical costs for prisoners, and how do you first identify issues? Also, what are some techniques that you can implement statewide to reduce the cost of medical care, and what steps do you take to implement these techniques?

WEB LINK EXERCISES

National Commission on Correctional Health Care (NCCHC): www.ncchc.org

Go to the Web site for the NCCHC. You will find a discussion of certification for individuals who work in correctional health care. Process description, eligibility, and cost are included in the discussion. Read this section, and identify what you think are the benefits of becoming certified by NCCHC. Then, recommend whether you think the cost and time required to become certified make it worthwhile.

PART IV

Managing Correctional Staff

CHAPTER

11

Human Resource Management for Corrections

■■■■ INTRODUCTION

The resources of a correctional agency include prisons and office space, budgets, equipment, and staff. It is generally agreed that staff make up the most important resource, with a large percentage of agency budgets going to staff salaries. Nearly 85 percent of annual operating funds of a prison is required to cover the salaries and benefits for employees. In probation and parole organizations, the percentage may be even higher. This "human resource" must be created, cultivated, and continually supported. The challenge for these activities rests with the staff working in human resource departments of correctional agencies.

Human resource department staff have many significant challenges as corrections moves into the new millennium. First and foremost is the challenge resulting from the tremendous growth of correctional agencies. The increase in the number of prison inmates receives the most attention. However, the number of offenders under probation and postprison supervision has also grown considerably. Seldom discussed outside of correctional agencies is the collateral growth in the number of staff required to supervise and manage the offender increases. In most prisons, there is approximately one staff member for every three inmates. Therefore, as the inmate population grows, the number of staff also grows by about one-third of that number. Human resource departments must recruit and hire this large increase in the number of staff to keep up with the growth in the number of offenders.

After they are hired, new staff must be trained and prepared for taking over very difficult and potentially dangerous assignments. Staff must be developed in a faster-than-normal pace, in order to be prepared to quickly assume supervisory and management functions. Correctional agencies must have effective performance evaluation systems to identify and improve staff weaknesses. There must be employee recognition programs to reward outstanding performance and motivate employees to excellence. And there must be systems to fairly discipline staff for unethical behavior or inability to perform duties at an acceptable level.

Human resource departments also administer collective bargaining programs within correctional agencies. Although the percentage of manufacturing workers who are members of labor unions has been steadily declining, the percentage of public employees who are union members has been on the increase. Much of this increase is the result of the growth of criminal justice employees whose work environment is both stressful and dangerous. Other areas of responsibility for human resource departments involve maintaining diversity in the workforce and overseeing affirmative action and equal employment opportunity programs. The scope of activities in human resource departments is very broad, and the complexity of this work is increasing. This chapter presents the many facets and challenges facing correctional agencies as they recruit, hire, train, and develop their staff.

AN OVERVIEW OF THE GROWTH IN CORRECTIONAL STAFF

The number of offenders supervised by correctional agencies continues to grow. By the beginning of the twenty-first century, there were more than six million offenders either in prison, in jail, or under supervision in the community. Table 11–1 illustrates the growth from 1980 until 1995, during which there was almost a 200 percent increase in the number of offenders under correctional supervision.

The number of prisons and jails has also increased; there were approximately 1,450 prisons and 3,300 jails in 2000. The most dramatic increases have come in the adult prison population. Figure 11–1 illustrates the growth during the 1980s and 1990s, in all segments of correctional populations.

TABLE 11–1

Increase in the Adult Correctional Population, 1980–1995			
	1980	1995	Percentage
Change			
Probation	1,118,097	3,090,626	176.4%
Jail	163, 994	513,122	212.9
Prison	329,821	1,126,293	241.5
Parole	220,438	700,174	217.6
Total	1,832,350	5,433,054	196.5

Source: U.S. Department of Justice, Bureau of Justice Statistics, *Prison and Jail Inmates,* 1995. U.S. Department of Justice, Bureau of Justice Statistics, Probation and Parole Populations in the United States, press release (30 June, 1996). U.S. Department of Justice Bureau of Justice Statistics, *Jail Inmates,* 1990.[1]

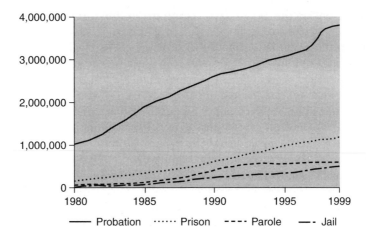

FIGURE 11-1   Adult correctional population, 1980–1999.
Source: Bureau of Justice Statistics Correctional Surveys (the National Probation Data Survey, National Prisoner Statistics, Survey of Jails, and the National Parole Data Survey) as presented in *Correctional Populations in the United States, 1996* and *Prisoners in 1999.*

The number of staff employed by correctional agencies has also increased steadily throughout the 1990s. On January 1, 1998, there were 413,318 employees in adult correctional agencies and another 57,317 employees in probation and parole agencies.[2] When jail staff are included, there is well over one-half million people employed in prisons, jails, and community correctional agencies. This large and critical resource results in a great need for thoughtful management and planning. Unfortunately, correctional agencies have rather high turnover rates (from 10 to 15 percent annually), requiring replacement of former staff, as well as recruitment of new staff because of growth.

The role of staff in correctional agencies is even more critical than the role of staff in most private sector companies, and even more critical than most other public agencies. This is because of the mission of corrections. First, correctional agencies are responsible for protecting the public, and they do so by taking away or severely limiting offenders' freedoms. These two items are a serious responsibility. If correctional staff fail to effectively perform their duties, innocent citizens may suffer the consequences of becoming victims of crime. When correctional staff supervise inmates and take away their individual freedoms, they do so under the authority of law. Staff must be aware of their legal obligations in this regard and the high ethical standards expected of this responsibility.

In some jurisdictions, correctional staff are also sworn peace officers. In 31 of the 51 state or federal correctional agencies, probation or parole officers are given **peace officer status.** This status affords correctional staff the authority to carry weapons when off duty and to make arrests. With this status comes the additional requirement to carry out these duties in a fair and impartial manner, and to do so in a manner that maintains safety for the community. Carrying a weapon is a tremendous responsibility, and it requires good judgment and respect for authority. When sworn peace officers are granted the authority of law to use deadly weapons, it is incumbent on the persons who commission this authority to ensure the individuals have both the training and mental preparation to carry out this duty responsibly.

Another point that makes the role of correctional workers difficult is that, although there are many policies and procedures, there is also considerable personal discretion that accompanies the performance of duties. Policy statements explain the agency mission, goals, and standards expected of agency operations. Procedures are standardized methods for carrying out the agency policy. However, policy and procedure cannot address every situation that a correctional staff will encounter. Staff must, therefore, use policy and procedure as guidelines or as principles to consider when they confront new situations that require the use of individual, professional judgment. It is much easier to train employees on the techniques and steps required to carry out job duties than to create an understanding of principles and the effective use of them to guide actions under a variety of unanticipated situations. And finally, correctional staff must be flexible and able to deal with change. Many forces within corrections (new types of offenders, new laws, external pressures to change policy, new technology) bring about change in operations and procedures. Correctional staff must be able to incorporate these changes into their own roles and responsibilities.

Human resource management is complicated by the growth of corrections and the many issues previously noted, which are part of the correctional environment. The human resource staff do not simply perform bureaucratic duties to recruit, hire, and fire staff. They are charged with finding high-quality individuals, encouraging them to consider corrections as a career, and developing employees to conform to the agency mission and goals. As such, they must recruit individuals with the proper background and maturity for correctional work. They must train staff to capably perform standardized procedures, and to consider agency ethics and principles as they use their own judgments to perform day-to-day activities. They must also help staff develop by increasing their skills and preparing them to take on greater responsibilities.

Correctional Systems and Subsystems

In terms of human resource management, corrections has many systems and subsystems. The two major categories of correctional agencies are institutions and community corrections. There are two types of correctional institutions: jails and prisons. The majority of jail inmates are pretrial offenders who are being held without bond until their trial. Jails also hold misdemeanor offenders and minor felons who are serving short jail terms as the punishment for their crimes. Prisons almost exclusively house more serious felons who are serving a year or more as a criminal sanction. However, both jails and prisons have similar staffing patterns and similar human resource management processes.

Community corrections includes probation and parole agencies, as well as halfway houses and other agencies that administer community sanctions, such as house arrest (often using electronic monitoring), intensive probation, community service programs, or other intermediate sanctions. Some community correctional agencies are public, whereas others are private or not-for-profit agencies. The categories of staff needed for the variety of agencies often varies considerably.

Prisons and jails both have a large portion of their workforce categorized as correctional officers. On January 1, 1998, there were 203,330 correctional officers of the total 413,318 staff (49 percent) of adult correctional agencies (prisons),[3] and almost 70 percent of jail staff are jailers or correctional officers.[4] A few decades ago, most correctional agencies used the term *guard* for the staff who primarily did security work. However, with the movement toward professionalism in correctional agencies and the realization that correctional security staff do much more than "guard" inmates, the term **correctional officer** became more commonly used. The term *correctional officer* more accurately conveys the many activities (security, interacting with inmates, monitoring standards, recommending improvements in procedures) required of correctional staff who perform security duties in a prison or jail. Today, it is considered by many who work in corrections as unprofessional, and even insulting, to refer to correctional officers as guards. However, the term *guard* is still regularly used by the media and the general public when describing prison or jail security staff.

Other staff positions used extensively in prisons and jails are treatment staff, such as mental health and counseling professionals. These groups vary in terms of the types of educational degrees required. Some of these professions require graduate degrees, yet others are entry-level positions. The *Corrections Yearbook* reports the following numbers of these staff working in adult correctional agencies as of January 1, 1998: psychologists (2,331), social workers (809), caseworkers (1,541), recreation therapists (774), and counselors (3,732), totaling 9,187 or just more than 2 percent of the overall staff on this date.[5]

The greatest number of staff in community correctional agencies are probation and parole officers. There are three types of agencies that administer probation and parole functions. First, probation may be exclusively a function of a county government criminal court system. A second type is a mixed community correctional system, with the state government providing assistance to counties to provide probation supervision or conduct presentence investigations. The third type is a state-administered community correctional system. Parole supervision is almost exclusively administered by state governments, and in some jurisdictions, the state governments also oversee the probation services for the entire state. Of the 57,317 total staff working in state probation and parole agencies on January 1, 1998, 27,490 (48 percent) were probation and parole officers.[6]

Parole and probation officers play a variety of roles for their agencies. First and foremost, they supervise offenders in the community, ensuring that offenders meet the requirements of their supervision. Second, they conduct investigations. Probation officers do presentence investigations for the sentencing courts, and parole officers investigate prospective release plans for inmates. Finally, officers assist in the operation of other community correctional programs. They may supervise intensive probation or parole caseloads, or they may be assigned special caseloads, consisting only of offenders with drug abuse problems, mental problems, or those with a history of sex offenses. Parole and probation officers are also often responsible for collecting financial sanctions, such as offender restitution and victim compensation. They may also be required to monitor offenders under house arrest and sometimes using electronic monitoring.

Professionalism and Corrections

As previously noted, over the past several decades, corrections has taken many steps to be recognized as a profession by incorporating several facets ascribed to a "profession." Organizational components associated with a profession include (1) a systematic body of theoretical knowledge acquired through lengthy academic study and not possessed by those outside the profession, (2) community interests rather than self-interest as a motivator of professional behavior, (3) self-regulation, and (4) a system of rewards.[7] The corrections profession has made many progressive strides to be recognized as meeting these components.

Although not all jobs within correctional agencies require "lengthy academic study," corrections certainly does have its own body of theoretical knowledge that is acquired through either experience or academic study. There are many positions in correctional agencies that do require an undergraduate or even graduate degree. As an example, to qualify for a position as a correctional officer for the Federal Bureau of Prisons, candidates must have either a bachelors degree or two years experience working in a correctional or law enforcement setting. In addition, there have been some attempts to "certify" wardens, correctional psychologists, and other correctional positions. This certification usually requires a combination of education and years of experience.

There has been a developing body of knowledge for the field of corrections. The **American Correctional Association (ACA)** has been instrumental in assisting in this development. ACA is the major correctional professional organization, with more than 20,000 members internationally. The ACA publishes many professional manuals regarding corrections and is a valuable source of information regarding policy, procedure, and professional standards for corrections. Over the past 30 years, there have been a number of professional journals, research reports, and monographs published regarding the practice of corrections. In describing the development of a body of knowledge for corrections, Williamson writes, "The support provided by the Law Enforcement Assistance Administration (LEAA), which began in 1968, was a primary contributor to a significant increase in research and expansion of the theoretical knowledge base."[8]

There is no question that correctional staff operate for "community" rather than "self" interest. Salaries for correctional workers are often less than for positions requiring like-experience or education. Correctional work is stressful and can be dangerous. Therefore, correctional staff must be motivated by public service, or by work in a helping profession, rather than by personal financial gain. Researchers have found that correctional staff are similar to other law enforcement personnel, who want to help their fellow citizens, and do work that is difficult, yet they recognize that it contributes to the public good.[9] With the continued growth and visibility in corrections, more staff not ordinarily interested in correctional work (psychologists, teachers, medical personnel, attorneys, and the clergy) have opted for correctional employment.

In the early 1970s, corrections also made a strong push to improve its ability to self-regulate and be considered a profession. Standards for operations were developed by the ACA, and the Commission of Accreditation for Corrections (CAC) was formed. Agencies may apply for consideration and, after extensive auditing and on-site visits, may be accredited by the CAC. The first accreditation audits were completed in 1978. Through the development of standards and self-review of compliance, correctional agencies meet the component of being "self-regulating." According to the ACA, the purpose of this process is

> to promote improvement in the management of correctional agencies through the administration of a voluntary accreditation program and the ongoing development and revision of relevant, useful standards. . . . The recognized benefits from such a process include improved management, a defense against lawsuits through documentation and the demonstration of a "good faith" effort to improve conditions of confinement, increased accountability and enhanced public credibility for administrative and line staff, a safer and more human environment for personnel and offenders, and the establishment of measurable criteria for upgrading programs, personnel, and physical plant on a continuing basis.[10]

Part of being self-regulating involves having a professional code of ethics. The ACA adopted a code of ethics at the 105th Congress of Corrections in 1975. The ACA Code of Ethics (Figure 11–2) is a guideline for correctional professionals in terms of accepted behavior. However, unlike other associations (the American Medical Association or the American Bar Association), which certify individuals and can take sanctions against them for violating the professional standards, the ACA neither certifies nor may take sanctions. Discipline for unprofessional conduct (discussed later in this chapter) is the prerogative of the agency that employs the staff member.

Finally, professions provide a system of rewards. Without an organization that "certifies" individual correctional professionals, there is no recognition for reaching certain levels of competence as there is in the legal and medical professions. However, there is recognition of correctional agencies and organizations through the accreditation process. Agencies that meet the accreditation standards often use this recognition as a defense to inmate lawsuits, and find accreditation helpful in explaining to their political oversight groups and legislative funding committees, why certain functions and operations are important. In the year 2000, ACA listed 78 affiliated professional organizations (see Figure 11–3).[11] These organizations also recognize and give awards to agencies and individuals for noteworthy performance.

The movement to professionalize corrections is important to the focus and goals of human resource management. Employees should "join" the profession and commit to it as their life's work. Through the entire process of human resource management (recruitment, staff development, retention, rewards, and recognition), there is an emphasis on hiring staff committed to a career in corrections and developing them to contribute fully to the enhancement of their chosen profession. Critical to success is the fact that staff must believe they have ownership in their careers. Ownership can be developed through four important steps:

1. Allow people to work on important issues.
2. Trust their judgment and provide them with the freedom to do their jobs.
3. Give praise and recognition.
4. Build relationships for people, connecting them to sources of power and resources and to opportunities to learn and develop.[12]

The American Correctional Association expects of its members unfailing honesty, respect for the dignity and individuality of human beings, and a commitment to professional and compassionate service. To this end we subscribe to the following principles.

Relationships with clients/colleagues/other professions/the public—

- Members will respect and protect the civil and legal rights of all clients.
- Members will serve each case with appropriate concern for the client's welfare and with no purpose of personal gain.
- Relationships with colleagues will be of such character to promote mutual respect within the profession and improvement of its quality of service.
- Statements critical of colleagues or their agencies will be made only as these are verifiable and constructive in purpose.
- Members will respect the importance of all elements of the criminal justice system and cultivate a professional cooperation with each segment.
- Subject to the client's right of privacy, members will respect the public's right to know, and will share information with the public with openness and candor.
- Members will respect and protect the right of the public to be safeguarded from criminal activity.

Professional conduct/practices—

- No member will use his or her official position to secure special privileges or advantages.
- No member, while acting in an official capacity, will allow personal interest to impair objectivity in the performance of duty.
- No member will use his or her official position to promote any partisan political purposes.
- No member will accept any gift or favor of such nature to imply an obligation that is inconsistent with the free and objective exercise of professional responsibilities.
- In any public statement, members will clearly distinguish between those that are personal views and those that are statements and positions on behalf of an agency.
- Members will be diligent in their responsibility to record and make available to review any and all case information which could contribute to sound decisions affecting a client or the public safety.
- Each member will report, without reservation, any corrupt or unethical behavior which could affect either a client or the integrity of the organization.
- Members will not discriminate against any client, employee, or prospective employee on the basis of race, sex, creed, or national origin.
- Members will maintain the integrity of private information, they will neither seek personal data beyond that needed to perform their responsibilities, nor reveal case information to anyone not having proper professional use for such.
- Any member who is responsible for agency personnel actions will make all appointments, promotions, or dismissals only on the basis of merit and not in furtherance of partisan political interests.

(Adopted August 1975 at the 105th Congress of Correction)

FIGURE 11–2   Code of ethics. Source: Reprinted with permission of The American Correctional Association.

Dual Membership Chapters (DMC)

Arizona Probation, Parole and Corrections
  Association
Colorado Correctional Association
Connecticut Criminal Justice Association
Correctional Association of Massachusetts
Hawaii Criminal Justice Association
Illinois Correctional Association
Indiana Correctional Association
Kansas Correctional Association
Louisiana Correctional Association
Maryland Criminal Justice Association
Michigan Corrections Association
Missouri Corrections Association
Nebraska Correctional Association
Nevada Association of Criminal Justice Professionals
New Jersey Chapter
New Mexico Correctional Association
New York Corrections and Youth Services Association
North Carolina Correctional Association
Ohio Correctional and Court Services Association
Oklahoma Correctional Association
South Carolina Correctional Association
Virginia Correctional Association
Washington Correctional Association
Wisconsin Correctional Association

State and Regional Organization (SAF/RAF)

Alabama Council on Crime and Delinquency
Central States Corrections Association
Florida Council on Crime and Delinquency
Iowa Correctional Association
Kentucky Council on Crime and Delinquency
Middle Atlantic States Correctional Association
Minnesota Corrections Association
Oregon Criminal Justice Association
Pennsylvania Association on Probation, Parole and
  Corrections
Southern States Correctional Association
Tennessee Corrections Association
Texas Corrections Association
Utah Correctional Association
Western Correctional Association

Professional Affiliates (PAF)

Alston Wilkes Society

American Association for Correctional Psychology
American Correctional Chaplains Association
American Correctional Food Service Association
American Correctional Health Services Association
American Institute of Architects
American Jail Association
American Probation and Parole Association
Association for Correctional Research and Information
  Management
Association of Paroling Authorities
Association of Women Executives in Corrections
International Association of State Correctional
  Administrators
Association on Programs for Female Offenders
Correctional Accreditation Managers Association
Correctional Education Association
Correctional Industries Association
Family and Corrections Network
International Association of Correctional Training
  Personnel
International Association of Correctional Officers
International Community Corrections Association
International Correctional Arts Network
Juvenile Justice Trainers Association
National Association of Adult and Juvenile State
  Corrections Mental Health Directors
National Association of Blacks in Criminal Justice
National Association of Juvenile Correctional
  Agencies
National Association of Probation Executives
National Coalition for Mental and Health Substance
  Abuse Care in the Justice System
National Correctional Recreation Association
National Council on Crime and Delinquency
National Council Juvenile Correctional Administrators
National Juvenile Detention Association
North American Association of Wardens and
  Superintendents
Parole and Probation Compact Administrators
  Association
Prison Fellowship
The Salvation Army Volunteers of America

FIGURE 11-3   State and regional chapters, and affiliate organizations of ACA.
Source: ACA Web Site: http://www.corrections.com/aca/membership/chapters.html October 12,
2000.

The following sections of this chapter illustrate how human resource management attempts to guide staff through their careers, while building ownership, commitment, and competence.

RECRUITMENT, HIRING, AND RETENTION OF CORRECTIONAL STAFF

Recruiting is the "lifeblood" of corrections. Any effort toward professionalism and excellence in managing correctional agencies is impossible to accomplish if newly recruited staff do not have the requisite experience, education, attitude, motivation, and commitment to work in the difficult environment of institutional or community corrections. In a 1996 study of how correctional agencies manage staff, employees of four state correctional agencies were surveyed, and some questions were directed toward recruitment practices. The authors report:

> Among the management and line employees in the four states surveyed, there was general agreement on one fact—corrections as a profession is not for everyone. The basic unsuitability of some individuals to work in a corrections environment was consistently cited as a major factor contributing to high turnover rates. . . . The managers interviewed acknowledged that the recent nationwide expansion of correctional facilities has resulted in an unprecedented hiring of new recruits. The anemic external job market has also made available a more qualified pool of applicants than in the past, but the sheer number of new positions being filled is taxing agencies' ability to screen for professional suitability as well as sample qualifications.[13]

Every person who expresses an interest in corrections is not suitable for this type of work. It is the responsibility of human resource management staff to recruit employees, usually by targeting populations that have the potential for turning up interested and suitable candidates. Recruitment of staff has progressed considerably over the past 30 years. Previously, correctional agency recruitment was all too often like the following situation:

> Massachusetts in the 1970s had a depressed economy with high unemployment. At the same time, the Massachusetts prison system had a high turnover rate among officers and a chronic need for new officers. Yet the Massachusetts Department of Correction was hard pressed to fill each new training class with recruits. The waiting list of applicants to police and fire departments were years long, while corrections with its similar salary and benefits was in reality a "walk-in" job. Screening and selection were largely limited to investigation of possible criminal records of applicants. So haphazard was the system that the correction officer exam was not even given for six years. The prison officer recruit was largely self-selected.[14]

In the Massachusetts description, there was little actual recruitment occurring. The most common way a new employee was recruited was through encouragement by relatives or friends who were already employed, and "recruitment in these cases was often casual in nature."[15] There was no plan by which characteristics of successful employees were identified, organizational needs considered, and an aggressive recruitment effort implemented. As a result, most correctional agencies ended up hiring new employees with little experience, academic training, or diversity. As the review of Massachusetts correctional hiring reported, "Most of the Massachusetts recruits who were a part of this study were young, white men who had no formal education beyond high school and who had a history of blue-collar employment.[16]

Recruitment by correctional agencies has now become much more sophisticated. Prompted by problems of high turnover and the challenge of a growing workforce, correctional agencies began to invest in quality recruitment material, make targeted recruitment trips and participate in job fairs, and screen candidates against the qualities identified as desirable for employees. Corrections, first and foremost, needs individuals with excellent interpersonal skills, and an ability and interest in working with others. Even entry-level staff must make numerous decisions during a daily shift, and therefore, good judgment and decision-making skills are critical. Finally, although staff should not be overly empathetic to the problems of offenders, they should not have a bias against offenders, minorities, or people with different backgrounds from their own.

Correctional agencies have become very successful in recruiting from a variety of sources. First, they recruit from other government and criminal justice agencies. Individuals leaving the military, especially if they have law enforcement or corrections experience, have often been found to make outstanding correctional officers. Their history of working in large organizations, with a variety of individuals, and with an understanding of criminal justice, makes the career transition to corrections fairly easy. Second, correctional agencies recruit from both public and private social service agencies. Many staff with this type of work background have knowledge of community resources and have worked with disadvantaged clients with a variety of needs.

A Job Fair for a New Prison. Although recruiting the right people is sometimes a challenge, getting large numbers of applicants seldom is a challenge. As new prisons open in rural communities with little other employment opportunities, it is not unusual to get large numbers of people turn out to fill out an application for employment. (Courtesy of the Ohio Department of Rehabilitation and Correction)

Finally, correctional agencies recruit from community and four-year colleges. Many colleges currently have criminal justice (and sometimes corrections specific) courses of study, and graduates, therefore, understand the way correctional systems are organized to meet their mission and roles. Probation and parole agencies regularly recruit candidates for parole and probation officer positions from college campuses. Prisons now recruit college graduates for entry-level correctional officer jobs. Some college graduates have the perception that correctional officer jobs are "below" their educational accomplishments. However, as they learn more during the recruitment process, they often understand how working as a correctional officer is excellent experience for developing skills in security and managing inmates. These proficiencies are an important foundation for success in other corrections jobs that the individual may later acquire.

The Hiring Process

The goal of recruiting is to generate a large pool of qualified applicants. From this pool, human resource staff then screen applicants to find those best qualified and suited for correctional employment. Agencies identify the characteristics important to success and then create a screening process to rate applicants' abilities on these areas. For instance, following are examples of skills needed to be a successful correctional officer.

- Good interpersonal skills (both oral and written)
- Ability to make sound decisions
- Lack of prejudice toward criminal offenders
- Understanding of the need to treat each client and inmate in a fair and consistent manner
- Ability to "think on one's feet"
- Ability to supervise others
- Good presentation of self

To identify applicants' abilities in these areas, several screening and rating mechanisms have been instituted. First, a candidate for employment must complete a fairly extensive application, which includes past educational, military, and job experience. In some agencies, the previously listed skills are included on the application, and candidates are requested to provide examples of past experiences that are indicative of these abilities and traits. Government correctional agencies are required to use a **competitive hiring process.** To ensure all candidates receive equal consideration, their applications are scored anonymously, and the candidates with the highest scores are considered first for employment.

Many public agencies require hiring through a process called the **rule of three.** The hiring organization (a state prison, for instance) will receive the names of the three highest rated candidates. They then complete the interview and screening process on these three, and hire the one they determine best meets their needs. They will not even be allowed to consider other than these three applicants unless one is later determined to be "unqualified," rather than simply "not liked." The rule of three assists in providing fairness and objectivity in hiring. If an organization was allowed to consider anyone who met minimum standards, preferential treatment would more likely result, and agencies might end up hiring less qualified candidates. The rule of three ensures that the most qualified candidates receive the best opportunities for employment.

After identifying the best group of candidates from their applications, screening usually includes a personal interview, review of a writing sample, and an interview to determine integrity concerns. In the personal interview, interviewers ask candidates questions that allow them to be rated on each of the important skills. Interviewers often try to put candidates in stressful situations to see how they approach and handle a correctional situation. As an example, interviewers may ask candidates if they would tell their supervisor if another staff member was showing preferential treatment toward one inmate. Candidates are often required to provide a writing sample, which is scored on both ability to communicate in writing and on the judgment shown in the situation they have to describe.

The **integrity interview** is a relatively new process in correctional agency screening of candidates. Staff who work in corrections are continually confronted with the opportunity to benefit personally from giving offenders favored treatment, either by allowing them something they should not have or by granting them additional privileges. Integrity interviews seek information such as financial difficulty, current drug or alcohol abuse, or other conditions that could put a correctional worker into a compromising situation. Agencies follow guidelines for the types of integrity issues (recent drug use, arrests for a felony, recent termination from another job, financial problems) that disqualify a candidate for employment.

After these screening processes, the candidate rated the highest is usually offered employment, although it is usually a "conditional offer," contingent on their passing a physical examination, passing a test for drug use, or completing mandatory training. Over the past decade, more agencies are requiring candidates for employment to take a test to determine recent drug use. In 1998, eleven agencies reported performing drug tests on all employee applicants, and 34 agencies reported performing drug tests on correctional officer applicants.[17] If candidates pass the physical exam and the drug screening, they are officially hired and a date is set to begin their employment.

Problems of Retention

Turnover of staff is a problem for correctional agencies. The *Corrections Yearbook* indicates turnover rates for correctional officers from a low of 9.6 percent to a high of 14.9 percent over an eight-year period (1990 to 1997).[18] Wright has examined correctional turnover problems, and notes that, "Prisons experience high rates of turnover among employees, averaging 16 percent nationwide and reaching more than 40 percent in some settings.[19]

Obviously, one of the reasons for a high turnover rate is the stressful and dangerous nature of the jobs. Both institution and community correctional workers must work with difficult clients and (even though the incidents are infrequent) risk assault and potential serious injury. However, a study of why dissatisfied prison staff leave their jobs identified two reasons (the poor quality of the work environment and the lack of opportunity to influence prison policy) as even more important in their decision than safety or difficult clients.[20]

Salary is also often cited as a reason for high correctional turnover. Whether salary is a significant consideration for retention usually depends on the employee's motivation for entering corrections in the first place. In this regard, Shannon found that 59 percent of those working in corrections chose the field because of economic necessity, and only 22 percent chose the field as their first choice of careers.[21] Public service pay is usually less than pay for comparable private sector work. Although difficult to compare, in 1998 the average starting salary for state and federal prison correctional officers was $21,246, and the average maximum salary for a correctional officer was $34,004. As the economy improved and correctional agencies became more competitive in order to attract quality workers, the starting salary for correctional officers increased 21 percent, from an average of $17,521 in 1990, to an average of $21,246 by 1998.[22]

Human resource staff do many things to respond to retention issues and to improve retention levels for correctional staff. First, they collect information on comparable salaries and turnover rates, and this information is presented to legislatures and budget agencies to lobby for increases in pay when appropriate. Second, they can work with correctional administrators to develop programs for improved staff safety. All correctional agencies teach self-defense, disturbance control, and stress management. Many have recently added training in interpersonal communications and for diffusing potentially dangerous situations (sometimes called "verbal judo"). With these skills, correctional staff usually believe they can protect themselves if assaulted and can better avoid the likelihood of assault.

Most importantly, human resource staff often encourage correctional administrators to involve employees in policy making and decisions involving their welfare. Some of this is accomplished through the collective bargaining process. However, even more important is the change in organizational management styles to empower employees. The aspects of moving to an empowering environment are discussed in Chapter 12. Prison employees want control and influence over their daily work activities, and they want the opportunity to be challenged and to grow professionally.[23]

TRAINING AND DEVELOPING CORRECTIONAL STAFF

As new employees are hired by correctional agencies, the first and perhaps most critical activity is to provide them with "basic" training and to prepare them to perform their assigned duties. Basic training is designed to accomplish two major goals: to develop skills needed to effectively do the job for which they were hired, and to instill the organization culture and expectations into them. Neither of these goals is a simple task. Correctional workers perform such a diverse range of functions, that basic training must be very broad to cover all the types of required activities. Correctional workers also come from various backgrounds, and melding them into a unit with an understanding of purpose and culture is a difficult challenge.

Staff training continues throughout the careers of employees. Even if employees never change jobs, there are changing techniques, legal requirements, changing offender population, and external pressures that require staff skills and knowledge be continuously upgraded. Very few, however, correctional workers stay in the same job throughout their careers. Most receive promotions, and move up in their organization by accepting more responsibility or becoming supervisors. Others change job roles and move from one function to another (e.g., prison security to casework or probation officer to administrator). These career progressions also require retraining and the development of new skills.

Correctional training takes many forms. Basic training takes place within the first few months of hiring (during the employees probationary period) and is designed to provide the basic skills necessary for correctional work. In-service training takes place on the job and is designed to improve skills in the particular work area assigned to the employee. Developmental training can occur at any time in an employee's career in corrections and prepares the employee to progress into another function or area of responsibility. Specialty training can add to an employee's skills, either in general correctional practices, or in very specific duties performed in addition to the employee's regular duties. The following sections describe all four of these areas of correctional training.

Basic Correctional Training

As noted, **basic training** both develops skills for job performance and instills the organizational culture in new employees. Required basic skills are both technical and human, and include the need to understand the agency culture and mission. Whether hired into a probation or correctional officer role, certain technical skills are required. Figure 11–4 lists the curriculum for the Federal Bureau of Prisons basic training provided at the Federal Law Enforcement Training Center in Glynco, Georgia. After a one- to two-week institution familiarization training period, new employees attend the Introduction to Correctional Techniques training for three weeks at Glynco. These two training courses cover *technical* skills as diverse as firearms use, emergency communication devices, controlling inmate use of tools, and supervising inmate visits. There are also several topics of study that help develop the *human* skills necessary in a prison environment. These include stress management, communication skills for correctional workers, and avoiding problems with routine orders and requests. Finally, there are courses that help instill the agency *culture* into new recruits, which cover the mission of the Bureau of Prisons, the history of the Bureau of Prisons, and managing diversity.

The Bureau of Prisons, and many states take a general view of basic training focused on developing "correctional workers." The **correctional worker concept** goes well beyond the provision of basic training. Essentially, organizations that embrace employees as correctional workers, recognize all employees as the same, regardless of their job specialty as correctional officer, secretary, nurse, plumber, or other role. They recognize that all correctional workers perform basic functions of security, inmate supervision, self-defense, and disturbance control. As such, all staff complete the same basic training and are trained in how to search an area or inmate, how to control contraband, how to enforce the inmate disciplinary system, and how to manage a hostile and aggressive inmate. With the correctional worker concept, there is

Institution Familiarization Topics	Hours	Institution Familiarization Topics	Hours
Administrative processing	6 $1/2$	Escorting inmates	$1/2$
Affirmative action	$1/2$	Controlling inmate use of tools	$1/2$
Introduction to the Bureau of Prisons (BOP)	1	Correctional officers and the control center	$1/2$
Mission of the BOP	1	Control center observation	$1/2$
Legal and ethical issues	1	Orientation to religious services	1
Employee conduct and responsibility	1	Self-study test	1 $1/2$
Role of the employees' club	$1/2$	Identifying and accounting for contraband	2
Tour of prison	2	Drug and alcohol testing and phone monitoring	1 $1/2$
Glynco preparation	1	Metal detection devices	1
Organization of institutions	1	Administering the pass system	1 $1/2$
Inmate programs	2	BOP hostage policy	1
On-the-job training (OJT)	8 $1/2$	Incident reports performance tests	1
Individual personal protection	1	Self-study	1
Logs, memos, and incident reports	1	Managing diversity	1
Daily safety and security checks	1	Employee assistance program and suicide prevention	1
Emergency communication devices	1	Orientation to prison industries	1
Review of disturbance plan	1	Orientation to the labor union	1
Disturbance control program	2	Communicable diseases	1
Use of fire extinguisher and hoses	1	Basic first aid	1 $1/2$
Use of restraints	3 $1/2$	CPR training	1 $1/2$
Key control and use	1 $1/2$	Conducting pat searches	1
Staff library	1	Conducting visual searches	1
Use of force	1 $1/2$	Conducting area searches	2
Monitoring inmate mail	1	Inmate counts and accountability	3
OJT—living unit	1	OJT—observing count	1
Supervisor's responsibility	1	Computer training	3

FIGURE 11–4   Topics and hours in the Federal Bureau of Prisons Institution familiarization and introduction to correctional techniques.

no separation of staff into treatment, operations, or custody. All staff recognize they perform some functions in all of these areas.

Some states focus most of their basic training on their correctional officers, and in other states, correctional officers are the only work group that receives extensive basic training. These agencies believe that correctional officers have the most inmate contact and are primarily responsible for the security of the prison and enforcement of institution rules. Other staff may receive an overview of or familiarization with the prison but often receive their training on their job. Often, new correctional staff have a period of "probation." During probation a new employee is

Firearms Training as a Part of Basic Training. Although correctional staff seldom have to use a weapon, they must be very familiar and proficient with a variety of firearms. Here, new recruits are practicing firing the pistol. (Courtesy of the Federal Bureau of Prisons)

Self-Defense Training as a Part of Basic Training. All staff should have training in self-defense, whether they will work as a probation officer, correctional officer, counselor, or secretary. (Courtesy of the Ohio Department of Rehabilitation and Correction)

evaluated and can be removed without having violated any work rules. If organization managers do not believe the employee is "right" for correctional work, or if the new employee seems to be having difficulty performing duties effectively, he or she may be terminated from employment without cause during the probationary period.

Introductory or basic training ranges from 40 hours to 400 or more hours, with an average of 232 hours of introductory training among the 42 state and federal correctional agencies included in a recent survey.[24] The introductory training includes both classroom and on-the-job training. The difference between those states with the lowest hours of introductory and those with the highest hours is usually a philosophy of when the employee is believed to be ready to perform correctional duties. The lower number of hours accepts the employees' familiarization with duties and then assigns them to a correctional post to do the job as they continue to learn and become proficient with their duties. These employees often receive closer supervision during the first few weeks on the job. The agencies with the highest number of hours do not assign employees to a post until they become proficient with duties to be performed.

Training for probation and parole officers is similar in that it may be a combination of classroom and on-the-job training. In some cases, the training for probation and parole officers is very similar to basic training for prison staff, because the human relations requirements and skills are very similar, and the need for self-defense and dealing with hostile clients is necessary in the community as well as in prison. Figure 11–5 presents an outline of a basic curriculum for the Missouri Board of Probation and Parole. The first two weeks (phase I) are provided jointly to prison and community corrections employees and covers topics such as an overview of the criminal justice system, the profession of corrections, stress management, conflict resolution, managing diversity, verbal judo, and constitutional law. Phase II is specifically for new probation and parole officers, providing them skills in interview and assessment, presentence investigations, supervision and community tracking, managing substance abusers, violating offenders, writing reports, and time management. In Missouri and several other states, probation and parole officers may elect to carry

Graduation from Basic Training. Once staff complete basic training, they are prepared to begin their careers. (Courtesy of the Pennsylvania Department of Corrections)

a weapon, but they are not required to do so. Every new officer receives a 30-minute overview about carrying firearms, and those who will carry weapons receive an additional one-week of training (phase III) on both firearms safety and physical safety skills.

Missouri currently provides their new probation and parole officers with 200 hours of training (240 hours for those officers who elect to carry a weapon), which is just under the average for other states combining probation and parole (243 hours required) but above the average for those who have separate probation and parole agencies and training programs (101 hours for probation-only agencies and 146 for parole-only agencies).[25] Even though the combined agencies have almost twice the number of average hours of training for their officers, there is really no reason that this combined training should require more time.

In-Service Training

As noted, corrections is a rapidly changing enterprise, and staff need to be continually updated on developments and new procedures or programs. Each year brings new legal cases, new information regarding inmate and street gangs, new technologies, and new legislation impacting correctional practices. To keep staff aware of changes, correctional agencies offer **in-service training.** In-service training is provided to employees on an annual basis and can last from a few days to more than a week.

There are many reasons that in-service training is important for correctional agencies. First, there are many technical skills that require practice and "refresher" training. Some of these activities are essential to correctional work (self-defense and disturbance control tactics) but may not be used often, which can result in an erosion of skills. In-service training provides an opportunity to practice these skills and be reeducated regarding the philosophy and approach to be considered when confronted with a need to use these skills. Second, in-service training is used to update employees in changes in laws, rules, policies, and procedures impacting the agency.

Finally, agencies use in-service training to emphasize an existing practice or concern that may be a problem and requires a reminder to staff of the problems that can result if they are not sensitive to the concern. For instance, if an agency has had a "rash" of incidents in which staff developed sexual relationships with inmates or offenders supervised in the community, in-service training can be a reminder of how these relationships can develop (for instance, if an employee is vulnerable as a result of personal problems), and the severe criminal and administrative penalties that result from such conduct. If agencies discover that inmates are trying to mail drugs into the prison using a newly discovered technique, in-service training can be used to remind staff of the importance of thorough searching using mandated procedures.

Developmental Training

As staff progress in their careers, they often consider changing career specialties, seek a promotion, or even move to another prison or community region to broaden

Phase I: Taught to all Missouri Department of Corrections employees

	Course	Hours
Week 1	Overview of the criminal justice system	4
	The profession of corrections	8
	Restorative justice	4
	MoDOC response to substance abuse	4
	Stress management	3
	Conflict resolution through communication	4
	Gender and sexual harassment issues	6
Week 2	Managing diversity	6
	Verbal judo	16
	Infectious diseases	2
	Constitutional law in corrections	10

Phase II: Taught only to probation and parole staff (a separate training program is available for all other MoDOC employees)

Week 3	Vision, values, and principles	1
	Offender rights and restrictions	3
	Confidentiality	1
	Cognitive restructuring	4
	Reality therapy	12
	Sex offender	12
Week 4	Interview and assessment process	6
	Presentence investigation	8
	Supervision strategies and community corrections tracking	4
	Substance abuse	12
	Education, vocation, and employment	4
Week 5	Domestic violence	6
	Case summary	4
	Mental health	4
	Violation process	8
	Interstate compact	2
	Parole policy	6
	Institutional reports	3
	Time management	1

Phase III: Safety Training (for probation and parole officers who choose to carry a weapon)

Week 6	Use of force	8
	Safety awareness	4
	Pepper spray	2
	Physical safety skills	16
	*Introduction to firearms	30 minutes

Developed for correctional service trainees (CST), the entry-level position for probation and parole officers, this class provides information regarding carrying a weapon

FIGURE 11–5   Training topics for probation and parole officers hired by the Missouri Department of Corrections (MoDOC). Source: Eastern Regional Human Resource Center, Missouri Department of Corrections (Park Hill, Missouri, August 2000).

their experience. To aid staff in making decisions about career choices and to prepare them for taking on jobs with additional responsibilities, agencies often provide **developmental training** for staff. Developmental training can often be accomplished in two ways: by providing staff cross-training in another correctional job specialty or by appointing staff to an "acting" promotional assignment.

Cross-training involves assigning a staff member to work in an area other than their job specialty in order to experience a different type of work and to identify the staff member's skills and aptitude for a new type of work. For instance, correctional officers who are interested in being counselors or case managers may be designated to work in that job specialty area for a short time to fill a vacancy or cover for another staff member who is on sick or vacation leave. By doing this, the correctional officer receives some experience and can decide if he or she wants to pursue that type of work in the future. Case managers or counselor supervisors also get the opportunity to see how well the correctional officer performs and the potential they have for success in that role.

Vacancies also exist (in between appointments or for leave purposes) in supervisory and management positions. Line staff may be temporarily appointed as "acting" in a supervisory or management position, with all the authority and responsibility they would have under a permanent appointment. As an example, a case manager may be appointed to "act" as the unit manager, or a senior correctional officer may be appointed to "act" as a lieutenant or other correctional supervisor. The acting position is usually in the same job category in which the employee already works, but in a higher-level or supervisory position. Acting assignments provide excellent training for staff to experience the more challenging role and to develop their own skills in supervision or performing different tasks.

In addition to the two primary ways that staff develop and move from their own discipline, correctional staff must also be kept up-to-date in developments in their own specialty area. Chaplains, medical personnel, psychologists, and educators are only a few of the staff who must stay apprised of new knowledge or findings in their professions. Most correctional agencies fund travel and training costs for these purposes. The ACA also promotes these activities through their accreditation standards, one of which states

> The institution encourages and provides administrative leave and/or reimbursement for employees attending approved professional meetings, seminars, and similar work-related activities. The institution should encourage participation in outside training and educational programs, including membership in local, state, and national professional organizations. Adequate funds for this purpose should be included in the budget.[26]

Specialty Training

The final area of training provided for correctional staff is **specialty training.** Specialty training is some skill that will add to an employee's contribution to the agency, either in general correctional practices or in very specific duties. Three common types of specialty training are supervision training, training for newly appointed management positions, and training to develop a special technical skill required by the agency. An example of training in supervision is the correctional officer who has just been promoted to a supervisory correctional position or a food service employee who becomes the assistant food service manager. These staff now need general supervisory training to understand the responsibilities and practices of a supervisor. They must learn how to change their job behaviors from "doing" to "supervising." This type of training usually includes completion of supervision surveys so individuals understand their own styles and supervisory preferences, procedures to complete employee performance appraisals and counsel employees regarding their performance, and management of a budget.

Most agencies also provide specialty training to staff newly selected to perform a specific managerial job function. As an example, the Federal Bureau of Prisons has specialty training for newly selected lieutenants (correctional supervisors) and newly selected unit mangers. In each of these, staff are trained in how to perform the key duties of their new job specialty. Lieutenants will learn how to calculate staff leave ratios and schedule correctional shift assignments, how to investigate inmate disciplinary incidents, and how to respond to a riot as the most senior person in the prison. A new unit manager will learn about objective inmate classification systems, cooperating with other department heads, and time management.

The skills necessary for effective supervision and management in a correctional agency are diverse. Williamson suggests

> The primary obligations of correctional administrators are to exercise leadership in reconciling diverse forces and to formulate rational correctional policies that respond humanely and realistically to present and future demands of specified populations in an efficient and effective manner. These all-encompassing obligations require special skills (both political and administrative), deep commitment, high education achievement, refined personal skills, and the ability to "see the big picture" (conceptual skills) and function effectively in ambiguous environments.[27]

Finally, correctional agencies use their own staff to perform very special roles, often as a "collateral duty." Staff maintain and perform their own job but also perform a specialty role when the need arises. Examples of specialty roles may include a self-defense trainer, a supervisor of the urine analysis program for probationers, or a disturbance control squad leader. Because each prison or parole or probation office may only need one person to perform the specific duty, the prison or office will either have to wait until the state agency provides training for many prisons or offices, or find a training program outside the state that the staff member can attend. The training and assignment of the collateral duty increases the skill base for the individual and provides the prison or office with a specialty that they need.

All four types of training (basic, in-service, developmental, and specialty) contribute to the creation of a professional and competent correctional staff. In such a challenging, rapidly changing, and dangerous work environment, it is essential that agencies invest in their staff by providing extensive and well-rounded training opportunities. By doing so, the agencies provide staff with the abilities needed to perform their duties both now and in the future. As would be expected, the state and local correctional agencies that have the best reputations for management excellence are usually those that take training seriously and commit financial and time resources to build staff competencies and capabilities.

PERFORMANCE APPRAISAL AND RECOGNITION SYSTEMS

Performance appraisal and recognition systems are important in the management of human resources for many reasons. First, these systems provide the formal opportunity for staff and their supervisors to discuss their performance. As noted in Chapter 12, discussions about an employee's performance are not easy, unless the employee is one of the very, very few who has no faults and no need to improve their performance. No one likes to hear that they are not doing as well as they could, even when the criticism is offered constructively, with the primary intention of helping the employee. A formal performance appraisal system provides a process and creates the expectation that certain elements important to job performance will be discussed and suggestions made for improvement. This process makes evaluations less "personal," and more businesslike.

Second, performance appraisal systems are targeted toward improving employees, not criticizing them. If they are done well, staff evaluations spend little time discussing the past and most of the time discussing how performance can be improved in the future. Evaluations allow both the supervisor and employee to jointly discuss and agree on a plan for improvement. This plan may include additional training, more regular review and feedback on employee performance, or informal mentoring and coaching to discuss job issues and problems. When they include these aspects, performance appraisals provide both employees and supervisors a road map that can lead to improvement and the chance for successful careers.

Third, an evaluation system is a motivator for staff. If staff believe the evaluation process is fair and consistent, they are motivated to perform well and receive a high rating on their evaluation. Most people do want to perform well and please their supervisors. Everyone wants to be successful, and the evaluation process allows positive feedback and a reaffirmation of successful work. Also, every agency considers evaluations for promotions or other assignments. It is usually believed that employees who cannot perform their current jobs well should not be promoted or given expanded responsibility. Likewise, employees who do perform well prove they are ready for a greater level of responsibility. In the formal, competitive process used to determine who gets promoted in most public agencies, evaluations may often count for up to one-third of the consideration of employees readiness for advancement.

Finally, a recognition system is a way to reward staff who consistently perform at a high level. Every agency has a disciplinary process (discussed in the next section) to respond to unprofessional conduct or poor performance. Truly exceptional agencies have just as sophisticated and meaningful a recognition program to identify and reward those staff who are professional and demonstrate job excellence. Agencies have a variety of recognition programs. Public agencies do not give "bonuses" as does the private sector. However, the formal evaluation system in public agencies will often result in a pay increase or cash award. Agencies often have a pool or "merit pay increases," which are awarded at a greater amount or percentage to employees with the highest performance ratings. In addition, correctional agencies usually have awards such as "employee of the month," or more specialized forms of recognition such as "correctional (or probation) officer of the month." Although the recognition of a job well done is enough for many outstanding employees, there is usually a small monetary award that accompanies this recognition.

The overall value of appraisal and recognition systems is that they differentiate high-performing from low-performing staff, giving attention to those who need encouragement and improvement, and recognizing those who deserve to be rewarded. As important a resource as staff are to accomplish the correctional mission, a meaningful and well-administered performance appraisal and reward system is critical.

DISCIPLINING STAFF

Most correctional staff perform at expected levels and act professionally. Unfortunately, not all staff do so; therefore, agencies must have a disciplinary system to respond to poor performance or inappropriate behavior. A comprehensive and well-understood disciplinary process is extremely important for a correctional agency. Correctional agencies supervise law breakers. As clients, offenders often complain about staff, some of which is justified and some of which is not. These clients also regularly try to compromise staff by tricking or bribing staff to provide them favorable treatment. This section explains how important a fair disciplinary system is to an organization, and especially a correctional agency.

An employee disciplinary system encompasses many facets and is not the same thing as "punishment." An **employee disciplinary system** is designed to inform employees of unacceptable behavior and provide a fair process to address the unacceptable behavior. By clarifying unacceptable behavior and developing a process for dealing with it, unethical behavior will likely be avoided or reduced. It could be argued that the disciplinary system has failed when it actually results in punishment. This proactive approach is captured in the following:

> The term *discipline* essentially encompasses three interrelated factors:
>
> 1. The framework of policies, rules, and procedures established by the organization.
> 2. The employee's and supervisor's attitude toward, and degree of compliance with, this framework.
> 3. The leadership process—example, instruction, training, and so on—exercised by the supervisor that largely determines the employee's attitude and compliance.
>
> In other words, *discipline* might be described as orderly conduct based on definite standards catalyzed by effective leadership.[28]

Although there is nothing wrong with punishment as a motivator for compliance with agency policy, all supervisors seek to instill *positive* rather than *negative* discipline. Positive discipline is the self-control that most people have that drives them to succeed, to do their jobs well, and to please their supervisors and themselves. Both human resources staff and supervisors have a role to play in positive discipline. Human resources staff must ensure that there are punishments for poor performance and rewards for good performance. Supervisors must show employees how the employees and the organization benefits from their compliance with expected performance.

Negative discipline is used as a last resort, when a positive, informal approach for gaining compliance has not worked, and the agency and supervisor must resort to punishment to change the employee's behavior. This approach, if administered with certainty and uniformity, can achieve compliance. However, it can also achieve only the minimum compliance necessary to avoid discipline and penalties without encouraging employees to perform at their fullest. Although no supervisor enjoys using negative discipline to gain compliance, it must be practiced when necessary in order to differentiate between positively and negatively performing staff.

There are several keys to an effective disciplinary system:

- Clarifying expectations for acceptable behavior and punishments for noncompliance.
- Training staff in the disciplinary process.
- Training supervisors in the disciplinary process.
- Separating the review of performance from decision making regarding punishment.
- Administering the disciplinary process in an impartial, timely, and consistent manner.
- Allowing for appeals from the disciplinary process.

Agencies clarify expectations by publishing a list of prohibited behavior and the range of punishments that coincide with each type of behavior. No circumstance is exactly the same, and agencies usually provide a wide range of punishments for each type of misbehavior. This allows the decision maker broad discretion in considering mitigating and aggravating circumstances. All staff must be trained and must understand the disciplinary process. They must know there will be consequences when agency rules are violated. Staff should never be surprised that poor conduct results in discipline. They should have been given a list of prohibited acts and punishments, and the topic should be covered each year during in-service training. Supervisors play a key role in identifying inappropriate conduct, especially when it has to do with failure to perform duties, and they must be sure to follow the process as prescribed. Dowling and Syles suggest the following for supervisors administering discipline.

> Timing . . . the supervisor shouldn't procrastinate in administering discipline. The longer he postpones reproof or punishment after he has observed the violation, the more likely he is to get a 'who—me?' Follow-through . . . Once he (the supervisor) has disciplined a subordinate, it's crucial that he treat him as he did before his reproof. Consistency . . . Obviously, it's unfair when one supervisor, all other things being equal, imposes a penalty harsher than that imposed by another supervisor.[29]

The best way to reduce inconsistency is to separate the decision making regarding punishment from first-line supervisors. This also encourages supervisors to instill positive discipline. In fact, most legal reviews of staff disciplinary processes require this separation. The process usually requires that a first-line supervisor or department manager states the violation and proposes discipline, an objective third party investigates the incident, and an upper-level manager decides on guilt and imposes discipline. One advantage of this approach is that it limits the number of individuals who actually impose punishment and, therefore, there is likely to be more consistency of punishments.

The disciplinary process should be administered in an impartial, timely, and consistent manner. The most difficult dilemma for an administrator is to have to impose discipline on an employee who has a history of dedication and following the rules. However, if the administrator gives the good employee "too much of a break," it becomes almost mandatory to give the same break to a poorer employee who commits the same violation. The imposition of discipline must be impartial. A like act deserves a like penalty, and although prior discipline can be considered, prior performance and commitment usually cannot. Staff must believe that the system is fair and equitable. If they believe that the decision maker "plays favorites" and shows partiality, the credibility of the system is undermined.

Finally, the system must provide for appeals for disciplinary actions. A fair process for appeal adds credibility to a system. Also, disciplinary actions almost always are seen as personal, because employees feel like victims, and their supervisors and managers feel betrayed. Knowing there is an appeal process reduces personalizing the process to a certain extent, and it forces decision makers to step back and consider how the punishment will be viewed in other's eyes.

Negative discipline is never preferable to positive discipline. However, there will always be a failure by some staff to fully comply with standards of conduct for correctional agencies. When this occurs, it is imperative that the agency has a fair and equitable process to investigate and administer discipline. Corrections is a profession that must have public trust, allow for redress of wrongs against inmates and offenders, and prove itself to be above reproach. The type of disciplinary system described is very important to accomplishing these requirements.

COLLECTIVE BARGAINING IN CORRECTIONAL AGENCIES

Collective bargaining is relatively new to corrections, although a few states (Connecticut in the 1940s, and New York and Washington in the 1960s) have had public employee unions for some time. For other states, collective bargaining among public employees started in the East and moved to the South and to the West. In the 1970s, more than 20 states formally authorized collective bargaining by public employees, and by the end of the twentieth century, most states had some recognition of labor organizations to represent public employees. The first time that collective bargaining was a part of the ACA program agenda was in 1977, when at least one-third of the states had collective bargaining agreements covering correctional agencies.[30] The movement to collective bargaining has, perhaps, had even more of an impact on corrections than on most public agencies, because of the mission of security and public protection, and the interaction among line staff and their unions, management, and inmates.

There were several historical developments in corrections that spurred the emergence of unions. First, corrections and especially prisons, had unpleasant working conditions, low pay, and low job prestige. Second, the advent of prisoner reha-bilitation during the late 1950s and 1960s clouded the security mission of prisons and threatened correctional officers with a loss of discipline and control over in-mates. The move to professionalize corrections, pushing for increased educational requirements for staff and bringing treatment and program staff into prisons, also threatened the traditional strong role of correctional officers. Finally, during the 1960s and early 1970s, prisons experienced a number of riots, and violence against staff increased. Staff had less confidence in the administration to provide for their personal safety, and they sought help from unions to argue for policies to protect them and reclaim their lost authority.

In general, **collective bargaining** is the formal recognition of employees, along with their right to negotiate with management regarding issues in the workplace. The purposes of collective bargaining lead one to question why anyone would op-pose it. Collective bargaining includes the right

- To establish and protect employees' rights.
- To improve working conditions and benefits.
- To establish and maintain more harmonious employer–employee relationships.
- To establish a participative role for employees in management decisions that affect employees.[31]

However, in the early days after authorization of collective bargaining, many correctional administrators feared it would diminish management authority and undermine staff discipline and prison security. It was also believed that unioniza-tion would bring more emphasis on **seniority** of staff in post assignment and pro-motion. Seniority allows the employees who have been employed the longest their choices of work assignments, days off, or shift schedules. At times, it is even considered for promotions. The administrative concern is that correctional man-agers need the utmost discretion in placing staff with unique abilities in the po-sitions that require these strengths. At the same time, managers do not want to have to place inexperienced staff, or those with certain weaknesses, in critical po-sitions. There is no question that correctional administrators prefer the maxi-mum flexibility to make decisions with no guidelines and without challenge. However, over the years that collective bargaining has been in place with correc-tional agencies, the early fears have not materialized, and the benefits of "shared governance" by line staff and management has led to better decisions and higher morale.

The Collective Bargaining Process in Corrections

When a state or local government authorizes public employees to organize and en-gage in collective bargaining, the first step is for the employees to select a labor or-ganization to represent them. A major decision that must be made early in the col-lective bargaining process is how to align employee groups for representation. Seldom are all correctional employees a part of the same bargaining unit that ne-gotiates for their working conditions. For instance, all correctional employees may be represented by one labor organization, or employees may be clustered into logical groups (all correctional officers, all trade employees, all treatment staff) to be represented by a union. After the employees are grouped for representation, the group votes to elect the labor organization that will represent them in negotiations and contract management.

There are many national labor organizations that represent public sector and correctional employees. These include the American Federation of Labor and Congress of Industrial Organizations (AFL-CIO), the American Federation of State, Federal and Municipal Employees (AFSFME), and even the International Brotherhood of Teamsters. Several organizations can vie for representation of correctional employees. The election process can be extremely difficult for both management and employees. The elections are often very highly contested, and the competing unions seek to find issues and convince staff they can best represent their interests.

After a labor organization is elected to represent employees, the parties prepare for negotiations. Most of the issues involve pay and benefits for the public employees, and they are usually negotiated statewide or countywide, including non-corrections as well as corrections employees. However, there will also be separate issues in negotiations regarding correctional employees about the role of seniority. Unions always want seniority to be the determining factor in many decisions. For instance, the labor position for promotions is that the most senior person is selected from all candidates found to be "qualified." Management wants to be able to select the "most qualified" person, and be able to consider affirmative action and other management needs. Unions also want seniority for "job bidding," or allowing correctional officers by seniority to pick the post they want to work.[32] Negotiations will also include many issues specific to correctional employees, such as how staff are selected for overtime, the type of clothing provided to staff by the agency, and possibly the coverage by correctional officers in areas such as educational programs and the medical clinic.

After the contract is negotiated, each prison or community corrections office must implement and administer it. Unfortunately, there are always questions that come into dispute about the true meaning of the contract. In these instances, management can make a decision, and the union can file a grievance to argue it. A **grievance** is a formal complaint that the decision is not within the language or intent of the labor contract as negotiated, and the grievance must go through a formal process for resolution. The grievance is usually reviewed by the next level of agency and union officials to see if they can resolve it. If not, it may go to a labor mediator to assist in its resolution, or the parties may have agreed to "binding arbitration." With binding arbitration, the parties have previously agreed that any grievance will go to arbitration, and the decision is final; it may not be further appealed by either party. One thing is clear in a collective bargaining environment: If either or both parties want to be confrontational and argue almost every minor contract issue, they will spend a tremendous amount of time and money to resolve their disputes.

The following case study describes the stages of collective bargaining in one state correctional agency during the early 1980s.

PRACTICAL PERSPECTIVES

Implementing Collective Bargaining in a Correctional Agency

A state in the central United States had an "ugly" history of collective bargaining. There had been some unofficial and non-statutory negotiations between the department of corrections in the 1960s, which resulted in agreements with several labor groups which represented small numbers of correctional employees. The result was constant friction among the unions and between labor and management. A walk out of correctional officers occurred at several prisons, and inmates rioted and several escaped from a high-security prison during one of the strikes. As a result, the conservative governor stopped all negotiations, and had the unions disband. Since that time, the state legislature several times passed a statewide collective bargaining bill, but the governor vetoed the bill. After a new governor was elected with the support of labor, he signed a collective bargaining bill passed by the legislature. The department of corrections, with the history they had, was very hesitant to move forward and implement the new law. The director describes the events and stages of the next several months as follows.

The first stage was the organizing and election process for correctional staff to select the labor union that would represent them. It was horrible. We are a large state, and our employees would end up being several thousand union members. I thought management had a really good relationship with staff, and I personally spent a lot of time with line staff whenever I visited the prisons. I know they appreciated it and respected me for my concern and leadership. All of a sudden, the three national unions vying to represent them were campaigning and trying to find issues to get employee attention. Since there really were no major issues regarding safety or prison management, they had to make things up. It was a personal affront to me with some of the things they came up with. I couldn't believe some of the nefarious schemes they came up with to suggest why we made certain decisions. Fortunately, the least professional and most untruthful of the labor groups quickly lost credibility. I was glad to see our employees elected the union I felt was the most sophisticated and professional during this campaign period.

The next step was the statewide negotiations. We, even though a large agency in state government, did not have a lot of say at the table, since it was a negotiations with all state employee organizations. The key issue our employee union wanted was "pick a post." This means that correctional officers could "bid" on the job or post assignment in the prison they wanted by seniority. We drew the line in the sand, and would not negotiate it at all. So, we had to go to arbitration before a third party. I remember to this day the testimony I gave,

Continued

and the experts that the union brought in from other states to say why pick a post would work. I worked hard with our attorneys to research and prepare my testimony, and made the point that pick a post could result in the more junior correctional officers with the most difficult assignments or security jobs in the SHU or high security housing areas. We won the arbitration, but the union continued to fight for seniority to be recognized in other ways.

In some of the prisons, they took a really hard stance in their interpretation of what the contract actually said, and it seems we almost had to do individual prison re-negotiations on several of the issues we thought had been addressed. I remember a few prisons, where we had really difficult union leadership and really stubborn management staff. It seems all we did was respond to grievances, and use staff resources to answer complaints by union stewards. I admit, we were as much at fault as the union, but we just couldn't get an understanding of what the contract meant with all parties. It probably took three to four years before everyone found a comfortable communications point, and things began to level off. Today, the union and management really work well together, and collective bargaining does serve everyone well. But, for a long while, I questioned the whole process, and whether it would ever work in our department. I guess the history of the 1960s left too many scars that had to be forgotten before we could start over again, and approach collective bargaining for the positive, shared interest and communications it could provide.

Collective Bargaining Implications for Corrections

Collective bargaining is now well entrenched in prisons and other correctional agency operations, and it will continue to have an impact on policy and practice. There is, however, much dispute about the implications of collective bargaining. Those who oppose it argue that collective bargaining interferes with management's rights and need for flexibility, and undermines the historical solidarity that is important for prison staff working in a stressful and dangerous environment. Those who favor collective bargaining suggest that the sharing of power in a correctional setting between management and staff benefits all parties, and labor unions can even be a strong voice to the legislature for additional staff and financial resources.

One significant issue involves the impact of collective bargaining on staff solidarity. Historically, prison wardens were autocratic rulers who could hire, promote, discipline, and fire at will, and who demanded allegiance to those in command. As unfair as this may seem, this allegiance resulted in solidarity of staff, because they pulled together to maintain prison security. Collective bargaining has changed that, resulting in a clear distinction between line staff and management. Managers are no longer seen as looking out for line staff, because union leadership promotes their own version of staff advocacy and downplays management efforts as self-serving. Jacobs and Crotty suggest, "It [collective bargaining] has redefined the prison organization in adversary terms so that wardens are bosses and complaints are grievances."[33]

A second major issue involves the "right to strike." Most public safety organizations are not allowed to strike, taking away a major tactic to getting the government to accept labor's demands during negotiations. One can only imagine, however, the crises that would occur if police and correctional officers were allowed to strike. However, unions representing these groups sometimes sanction informal job actions (known as "blue flu," for the blue uniforms traditionally worn by the police) to get the attention of management and force them to consider the union positions. There have also been illegal strikes by correctional officers. In New York state, the Taylor Law sets penalties whereby strikers lose two days' salary for each day they are on strike.[34] However, this did not deter a 1979 strike by New York state correctional officers. A study of this strike found that officers believed they had lost status and authority, and racial tensions had mounted within the officer workforce as well as between officers and inmates. An analysis of the strike found that collective bargaining was not well suited to resolve these types of problems and may have even aggravated them.[35]

Another concern regarding collective bargaining is its impact on correctional policy and efforts toward rehabilitation. As previously noted, the rehabilitative movement spurred concern by officers and unionization within prisons. In the late 1980s and 1990s, rehabilitation was replaced by a renewed emphasis on inmate accountability and prison security and control. Some argue that prison unions, stressing staff safety issues, may subtlety lobby against any reemphasis of rehabilitation, fearing it could lead to the perceived loss of authority officers felt in the 1960s. Others suggest that interests of prisoners and officers are intertwined, and as one group benefits, so does the other. Improved working conditions for staff must also include improved living conditions for inmates. Also, rehabilitative programs that improve inmate morale, reduce idleness, and enhance security result in benefits to the staff who work in a prison.

Overall, it is not the allowance or the process of collective bargaining that seems to have negative or positive implications for corrections, it is the attitude of agency administrators and union leaders, and the relationships that they develop, that signals the type of impact that collective bargaining has on correctional operations. If both parties communicate with and listen to each other, show mutual respect, and are reasonable in their positions, collective bargaining can have a very positive effect on a correctional organization. However, if the parties let the issues get personal, and become overly adversarial in the relationship, collective bargaining results in few positive and many negative outcomes.

THE IMPORTANCE OF DIVERSITY IN CORRECTIONS

Throughout its early history, correctional organizations have made little effort to emphasize diversity in their workforces. Prisons were usually located in rural areas and had predominantly white, male staff. Community correctional agencies, such as halfway houses and probation and parole offices, were located in urban areas and had a greater proportion of minority and women staff. However, there was little recognition of the value of a diverse workforce. It was also believed that women correctional officers could not work in male prisons, and similarly, that male correctional officers could not work in female prisons. The disastrous riot at the state prison in Attica, New York (discussed in Chapter 9), brought attention to the problems that result when the prison staff do not reflect the diversity of the inmate population.

Table 11–2 illustrates the makeup of offender populations (prison, probation, and parole) as of January 1, 1998. Of the 1.25 million inmates on that date, only 6.4 percent were female. The percentage of female offenders under community supervision is somewhat greater, ranging from 20.1 percent supervised by probation-only agencies to 10.4 percent supervised by parole-only agencies. The ethnic composition of offender groups is much more diverse. African American inmates make up almost one-half (47.4 percent) of the prison population, and approximately one-half of the offenders supervised on probation and parole. In prisons, 17 percent of the inmates are of Hispanic heritage. Approximately 12 percent of offenders on probation or parole are Hispanic.

As correctional agencies began to consider the importance of staff diversity in the 1970s, they recognized that staff did not mirror the gender and ethnic makeup of offenders. Two developments resulted from this examination. First, correctional agencies initiated affirmative action programs in order to hire, develop, and promote a greater number of minority staff. With an offender population that is close to one-half nonwhite, correctional agencies strive for as high a percentage as possible of minority staff. Second, prisons opened the door to women correctional officers working in male prisons and (more hesitantly) for male correctional officers to work in female prisons.

Most public agencies have aggressive affirmative action and equal employment opportunity (EEO) programs. The goals are often to have the workforce reflect the makeup of the citizens in the area or district represented by the government agency.

TABLE 11–2

Gender, Race, and Ethnic Composition of Offender Populations on January 1, 1998

	Total Number	Male	Female	Black	White	Asian Pacific Islander	Native American Native Alaskan	Other[1]	Hispanic[2]
Prison	1,243,271	93.6%	6.4%	47.4%	43.3%	0.7%	1.0%	7.6%	17.0%
Probation only	1,979,088	79.9	20.1	30.0	55.6	0.7	0.9	12.8	10.3
Parole only	493,933	89.6	10.4	42.7	46.7	0.4	0.5	9.7	22.1
Probation and parole[3]	132,644	78.2	21.8	13.5	80.2	1.7	2.3	2.4	6.4

[1]Other is nonwhite.

[2]Ethnicity and race are in separate categories, so inmates of Hispanic ethnicity are counted in other columns as well as in the Hispanic column.

[3]Probation and parole combined include those agencies that supervise both groups and do not separate in offender characteristics.

Source: Adapted from Camille Graham Camp and George M. Camp, *Corrections Yearbook: 1998* (Middletown, CT: Criminal Justice Institute, 1998); pp. 13, 164–166.

For instance, federal agencies often have a goal of approximately 14 percent African American employees, because the population of the United States has approximately that percentage of African American citizens. However, correctional agencies not only take into account the overall makeup of the population but also the makeup of the clients they serve. Therefore, it is not unusual for a correctional agency to have a goal much higher for African American staff, with such a large percentage of African American offenders under supervision.

There are several reasons for staff affirmative action programs in corrections. First, as public agencies, there are affirmative action laws that mandate efforts for aggressive recruitment of minorities. Second, public agencies have personnel or human resources offices that are charged with overseeing the processes required by the affirmative action and EEO programs. But also, in addition to the *legal* and *personnel* reasons for affirmative action, correctional agencies pursue cultural diversity as a *management necessity*.

Effective management of correctional offenders requires more than physical security and more than intense community supervision. Offender management is most successful when there is interaction and communications between staff and inmates or community offenders. Although this does not mean that white staff cannot communicate with African American offenders, the perception of racial discrimination and, therefore, tension is reduced when the workforce and client group are similarly represented. In discussing the prison workplace, Carlson suggests, "The staff must 'look like' the inmates; the ideal is to have the same proportions of Caucasians, African Americans, and Hispanics in staff and inmate ranks."[36]

Similarly, opening opportunities for women to work as correctional officers in male prisons began as a legal and personnel requirement, yet it quickly became valuable for management purposes. There were several reasons that women were barred from working as correctional officers in male prisons. First, there was concern that women could not physically respond to violence or protect themselves against inmate assault. There was even concern that the presence of women working in solitary situations may spur a sexual attack by predatory inmates. Second, it was believed that having opposite sex correctional officers working in housing units or other remote areas of prisons would result in an increase in romantic involvements of staff with inmates. And finally, there was a question about how to deal with the privacy concerns of inmates, because correctional officers must supervise all areas of a prison, including bathrooms, showers, and sleeping rooms.[37]

Because of these concerns, women were not allowed to work as correctional officers in male prisons until the 1970s.[38] And, when they were employed, they found that a bias against their being in the prison environment continued. A study of gender relationship in San Quentin (California) Prison found gender conflicts, competition, divisions among workers, and an uneasy social order in the prison.[39] Another California prison study found that male officers and male inmates perceived that women were less effective in responding to violent situations requiring physical strength. However, the study (when analyzing actual performance instead of perceptions) found that women actually performed their jobs as well as male officers.[40]

More recent studies have found that some perceptions continue. A 1998 study of Minnesota prison staff perceptions found that the historical concerns by male staff about women correctional officers' acceptance, safety, and job performance continued, but the resistance to women in the workplace was not as great as in past studies.[41] Overall, correctional agencies believe that gender is not a factor in officers performance and that the presence of females in a male prison "softens" the environment. Male inmates are less likely to become hostile and aggressive with female than male officers, because they seem almost "unmanly" if they become confrontational with a woman. Although they still face some resistance, women are now fully integrated into the correctional workplace.

Table 11–3 illustrates the gender, race, and ethnicity of adult correctional agency (prison) staff and probation and parole agency staff as of January 1, 1998. There has been progress in the increase of minorities and women employed in correctional agencies. In both prisons and community corrections, African American employees comprise more than 20 percent of overall staff. The percentage of women employed in community corrections is significant, because women represent more than one-half of all employees in parole and probation agencies. Females make up 32.2 percent of all state and federal prison employees. However, women comprise only 21.7 percent of all correctional officers. The percentage of female correctional officers has increased from 16.5 percent in 1990 to 21.7 percent in 1998, and this percentage is expected to continue to increase.

Workforce diversity is an important factor in correctional agencies, and significant effort and improvements have been made in the past 25 years. Although public agencies espouse diversity as fair, good public policy, and a legal requirement, correctional agencies embrace diversity as a management necessity. Having a diverse workforce to supervise and manage a diverse offender population improves communications, eases tensions, and builds trust and respect among staff and offenders.

TABLE 11–3

Gender, Race, and Ethnicity of Correctional Staff (in percentages) on January 1, 1998

	Number of Staff	Male	Female	Black	White	Asian Pacific Islander	Native American Native Alaskan	Other[1]	Hispanic[2]
All prison staff	413,318	67.8%	32.2%	20.4%	70.5%	1.0%	0.7%	7.5%	7.7%
Corrections officers	203,330	78.3	21.7	24.1	68.7	0.6	0.6	6.0	6.4
Probation staff	26,014	46.5	53.5	15.1	76.4	1.4	0.5	6.6	6.8
Parole staff	10,336	48.3	51.7	29.2	57.7	1.6	0.2	11.3	12.9
Probation and parole staff[3]	20,967	47.0	53.0	21.1	71.4	0.9	0.6	6.0	6.3

[1]Other is nonwhite.

[2]Ethnicity and race are in separate categories, so staff of Hispanic ethnicity are counted in other columns as well as in the Hispanic column.

[3]Probation and parole agencies include those who supervise both types of offenders.

Source: Adapted from Camille Graham Camp and George M. Camp, *Corrections Yearbook: 1998* (Middletown, CT: Criminal Justice Institute, 1998), pp. 130, 134, 196–197.

Although it is unfortunate that prison disturbances, such as the 1971 Attica, New York, riot, which ended in several deaths, were necessary to the understanding of the value of staff diversity, it is fortunate that the growth in correctional populations and increase in number of staff have presented an opportunity to quickly add minorities and women to correctional workplaces and increase diversity.

SUMMARY

Human resources are the key to the successful operation of a correctional agency. When considering correctional institutions, most people think of the facility, the concrete and the bars. However, the quality of the facility is insignificant in comparison to the quality of the staff. In this chapter, we examined the administrative activities and challenges that go into recruiting, developing, and training staff, and the importance of evaluating staff performance, collective bargaining, and workforce diversity in accomplishing correctional missions.

The management of human resources is an ever-evolving and never-ending undertaking. Outstanding correctional agencies (every organization, for that matter) are those that invest in these activities and pay particular attention to maintaining the best staff possible. In good economic times, well-qualified recruits do not apply for correctional jobs without some urging. Even the best-qualified, new staff need to be provided adequate technical skills, and they need to understand the culture and guiding principles of their organization. Correctional staff need training to prepare for supervision and management, and other positions of increasing responsibility. Performance appraisal and recognition systems are key to continuing to motivate staff to perform at their highest level. And when staff fail, or behave in less than a professional manner, they must be fairly and impartially disciplined in order to maintain high ethical standards.

In the following two chapters, we look more in depth at some of the "people" issues of corrections. Chapter 12 presents the key function of supervising people in correctional organizations, and the critical activities that effective supervisors must undertake. In Chapter 13, we examine more fully the actual work of some entry-level positions in correctional agencies, identifying not only what they do, but the skills and traits necessary to be successful. Because it is widely recognized that corrections is a "people" business, it is important that the key elements of administrating human resources are covered and explained in this text.

ENDNOTES

1. Information from this table was adapted from James Austin, "An Overview of the Nation's Jails," *Corrections Management Quarterly* 3 no. 2 (1999); 2.
2. Camille Graham Camp and George M. Camp, *The Corrections Yearbook: 1998* (Middletown, CT: Criminal Justice Institute, 1998), pp. 131, 196, and 197.
3. Ibid., pp. 130–135.
4. Ibid., p. 268.
5. Ibid., pp. 156–157.
6. Ibid., pp. 199–200.

7. E. C. Hughes, "Professions," in *The Professions in America* edited by Kenneth S. Lynn, (Boston, MA: Houghton-Mifflin, 1965), p. 4.

8. Harold E. Williamson, *The Corrections Profession* (Newbury Park, CA: Sage, 1990), p. 77.

9. C. Cherniss and J. S. Kane, "Public Sector Professionals: Job Characteristics, Satisfaction, and Aspirations for Intrinsic Fulfillment Through Work," *Human Relations* 40 (March 1987): 125–136.

10. American Correctional Association, *Standards for Adult Correctional Institutions*, 3rd ed. (Laurel, MD: American Correctional Association, 1990), p. vii.

11. American Correctional Association Web site: http://www.corrections.com/aca/membership/chapters.html (21 July, 2000).

12. Rosabeth M. Kanter, *The Change Masters: Innovation for Productivity in the American Corporation* (New York: Simon and Schuster, 1983).

13. George M. Camp, Camille G. Camp, and Michael V. Fair, *Managing Staff: Corrections' Most Valuable Resource* (Washington, DC: U.S. Department of Justice, National Institute of Corrections, 1996), p. 38.

14. Kelsey Kauffman, *Prison Officers and Their World* (Cambridge, MA: Harvard University Press, 1988), p. 167.

15. Ibid., p. 168.

16. Ibid., p. 167.

17. Camp and Camp, p. 154.

18. Camp and Camp, p. 151.

19. Kevin N. Wright, *Effective Prison Leadership* (Binghamton, NY: William Neil Publishing, 1994), p. 47.

20. Nancy C. Jurik and Russell Winn, "Describing Correctional-Security Dropouts and Rejects—An Individual and Organizational Profile," *Criminal Justice and Behavior* 14 (1987): 5–25.

21. M. J. Shannon, "Officer Training: Is Enough Being Done?" *Corrections Today* 49 (April 1987): 172–175.

22. Camp and Camp, p. 149.

23. See, Jurik and Winn.

24. Camp and Camp, p. 147.

25. Camp and Camp, p. 201.

26. American Correctional Association, p. 27.

27. Williamson, p. 141.

28. Robert W. Eckles, Ronald L. Carmichael, Bernard R. Sarchet, *Essentials of Management and First-Line Supervision* (New York: Wiley, 1974), pp. 494–495.

29. William F. Dowling, Jr., and Leonard R. Sayles, *How Managers Motivate: The Imperatives of Supervision* (New York: McGraw-Hill, 1971), pp. 129–131.

30. John M. Wynne, Jr., "Unions and Bargaining Among Employees of State Prisons," *Monthly Labor Review* (March 1978): 10–16.

31. M. Robert Montilla, *Prison Employee Unionism: Management Guide for Correctional Administrators* (Washington, DC: U.S. Department of Justice, National Institute of Law Enforcement and Criminal Justice, 1978), p. 2.

32. For an overview of the positions regarding seniority in correctional negotiation, see Lynn Zimmer, "Seniority Job Bidding in the Prisons," Society

for the Study of Social Problems, association paper 85S17096, Sociological Abstracts, Inc., 1985.

33. James B. Jacobs and Norma Meacham Crotty, *Guard Unions and the Future of Prisons* (Ithaca, NY: Institute of Public Employment, 1978), p. 41.

34. Andrew A. Peterson, "Deterring Strikes by Public Employees: New York's Two-for-One Salary Penalty and the 1979 Prison Guard Strike," *Industrial and Labor Relations Review* 34 no. 4 (July 1981): 545–562.

35. Lynn Zimmer and James B. Jacobs, "Challenging the Taylor Law: Prison Guards on Strike," *Industrial Labor Relations Review* 43 no. 4 (July 1981): 531–544.

36. Peter M. Carlson, "Correctional Officers Today: The Changing Face of the Workforce," in *Prison and Jail Administration: Practice and Theory*, edited by Peter M. Carlson and Judith Simon Garrett (Gaithersburg, MD: Aspen Publishers, Inc., 1999), p. 185.

37. For a review of the constitutional bases for inmate privacy and equal employment opportunity for women, see Susan L. Reisner, "Balancing Inmates' Right to Privacy with Equal Employment for Prison Guards," *Women's Rights Law Reporter* 4 no. 4 (Summer 1978): 243–251.

38. J. Pollock, *Sex and Supervision: Guarding Male and Female Inmates* (New York: Greenwood Press, 1986).

39. Barbara A. Owen, "Race and Gender Relations Among Prison Workers," *Crime and Delinquency* 31 no. 1 (January 1985): 147–159.

40. H. Holeman and B. Krepps-Hess, "Women Correctional Officers in the California Department of Corrections" (Sacramento: California Department of Corrections, 1983).

41. Richard Lawrence and Sue Mahan, "Women Correctional Officers in Men's Prisons: Acceptance and Perceived Job Performance," *Women and Criminal Justice* 9 no. 3 (1998): 63–86.

KEY TERMS

peace officer status
correctional officer
American Correctional
  Association (ACA)
competitive hiring process
rule of three
integrity interview
basic training
correctional worker concept

in-service training
developmental training
specialty training
performance appraisal and
  recognition systems
employee disciplinary system
collective bargaining
seniority
grievance

YOU'RE THE CORRECTIONAL ADMINISTRATOR

1. You are the newly appointed manager of human resources for a rural prison. The prison has a history of hiring relatives of current employees who reside in the local area. This has resulted in a lack of diversity in prison staff, some

problems of potential nepotism, and the need to avoid assigning relatives to work for other relatives. The staff believe this system is fine, however, and that their relatives deserve an opportunity to be hired before "outsiders." This trend is now causing problems in quality of staff, a lack of staff diversity reflective of the inmate diversity, and administrative problems because "everyone is related to each other." How do you go about changing this situation? First, address the types of recruitment and hiring processes you want to implement. Then, address the process you would go through to convince staff that changing the current practice of hiring relatives is a good idea.

2. You are the chief of labor relations for the state correctional agency. You have been asked by the local prison to mediate a dispute they are having that is not addressed in the local or state labor contract. The local union members want to have "pick-a-post" by seniority: They want the most senior correctional officers to have first choice to work their preferred correctional assignment. There are many posts, including security/fence towers, outside the prison security, educational building, food service, control center, front desk processing of visitors, inmate housing units, and inside compound security. The prison administration wants to avoid "pick-a-post," arguing that the best and most senior correctional officers will select jobs with little or no inmate contact and the most junior and inexperienced staff will have to work in the housing units, in which an error of judgment can cause serious problems. Also, the administration argues that there are some more technical and highly sensitive jobs that involve a risk of undermining the overall security of the prison if the wrong staff member is assigned there. Your first step is to objectively list some of the issues that the two sides will agree on and some that they will dispute on this topic. Then, suggest a process that they can use to reduce their disagreements before you attempt to mediate the dispute. Finally, list the arguments you assume the two sides will present to you as mediator. Although a mediator does not make decisions, list the decisions you would make to resolve this dispute if you had the authority to do so.

WEB LINK EXERCISES

AFSFME Chapter in Wisconsin for Correctional Workers:
www.geocities.com/researchtriangle/2789

Go to the Web site for the Wisconsin state chapter of AFSFME. Look at the Master Contract between the state and AFSFME. As noted in this chapter, even after a contract has been negotiated, there can be many problems and differences of opinion regarding its implementation. Pick any section of the contract (overtime, scheduling of work, grievance procedure, etc.), and identify how it could be interpreted differently by management and by labor. Then, prepare to present your arguments (three or four significant points) as a representative of management or labor to an arbitrator who will decide on the proper interpretation.

C H A P T E R

12

Supervising and Empowering Employees

▰▰ INTRODUCTION

Corrections is described as a "people business." This means that corrections staff, doing their jobs in a professional manner, are the most important resources available to a correctional agency. In Chapter 11, we discussed how an agency recruits, trains, and prepares staff to do the difficult jobs in a prison or community correctional setting. This chapter presents another key element in making sure that the people of the corrections business perform their jobs as well as they are capable. This chapter discusses **supervision** of line staff and the importance of supervision in accomplishing the correctional mission.

When casual observers think of supervision or a supervisor, they probably think of someone that simply tells employees what to do and ensures they do it. Supervision, however, is extremely difficult to carry out, and a poor job of supervising employees, particularly when it occurs in a stressful and dangerous environment, can undermine morale, efficiency, and effectiveness. Doing a good job as a supervisor is not easy, and it takes not only preparation but also an extremely thoughtful and conscientious approach. In this authors mind, supervision is the *most important element* in a correctional operation. All of the security, programs, equipment, and financial resources can be deemed inconsequential, if the supervision is not good. Supervisors guide staff in the specific duties necessary to accomplish the agency mission. Excellent supervision is where, "the rubber meets the road" in a correctional agency.

In this chapter, the role of supervision is defined, explained, and differentiated from leadership and management. The key components of supervision, including effective communications, clear expectations, delegation and directing of work, and giving feedback are also identified and discussed. Some to the challenges to effective supervision are also presented, including dealing with a problem employee, using the disciplinary process, preparing to be a supervisor, and the stressful situations that often accompany supervision. Finally, the emphasis on staff "empowerment" is introduced. Empowerment is a recent buzzword in organizational management and supervision. The process of developing an empowered workplace is not the same as developing effective supervision. And, empowerment does not replace the need for competent supervision. By the end of this chapter, readers should have a good understanding of why it is suggested that supervision is the most important element in a correctional operation.

THE SUPERVISORY ROLE

Historically, supervision has always been getting the job done through others or seeing that the work gets done. The supervisor must play many roles, including boss, manager, leader, advisor, counselor, mentor, coach, trainer, and motivator. The accompanying simple organizational chart helps in understanding and defining some functions within the organization. However, the roles listed are not as clearly delineated within most organizations as the hierarchy makes them appear. In particular, the supervisor is often seen by employees as the leader, manager, supervisor, and co-worker.

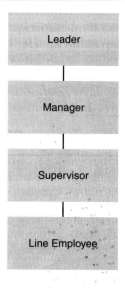

For purposes of this discussion, leaders create vision and set direction, manage the external environment, encourage and empower staff, shape organizational culture, and provide resources for the organization. Managers organize their departments, plan and develop goals and objectives, and oversee the efficient use of resources. Supervisors direct work activities, assign tasks, provide employee feedback, and serve as technical experts for the staff reporting to them. Line employees carry out the production and delivery of services. They complete tasks as assigned and suggest improvements in the process of completion of tasks. Broadwell suggests, the higher the level of management, the more time is spent on long-range planning, giving direction to the organization and working on problems that have to do with setting up the structure of the organization . . . lower down the ladder of levels we should find people concerning themselves with short-range problems, such as, directing people and checking on how well the work is done.[1]

Supervision is difficult when supervisors have to play all of these roles, sometimes simultaneously. Staff perceive supervisors as leaders. Even in a prison, where the warden is the acknowledged leader of the organization, supervisors can support or undermine the warden's leadership. Staff expect their direct supervisors to also be leaders, showing understanding, courage, and conviction in the roles they play. Supervisors are often assigned to manage a department or section, and must complete management tasks such as budget and policy development, as well as supervise other employees. And, supervisors often have to carry out functions just as line employees. Sometimes, supervisors have actual line staff duties (for instance, correctional sergeants in a prison) that must be accomplished at the same time they supervise correctional officers. Supervisors usually have more technical expertise in their area, and while supervising employees they often take on the most difficult assignments themselves.

It is sometimes suggested that supervisors have to wear two hats: those of both worker and supervisor, or as a "functional specialist" and "management generalist." Phillips and McConnell describe the functional specialist as "the worker who is responsible for doing some of the basic work of the department . . . the specialist is ordinarily concerned with some function that is unique or nearly unique to that department. The management generalist, on the other hand, is concerned with activities that are common to many departments and to most situations in which someone must guide and direct the work of others."[2] Line employees are almost always functional specialists. In large departments, the manager is almost always a management generalist. However, the supervisor's role falls between the two, and often, particularly in a department with a small number of staff, must perform both specialist and generalist roles.

Although the following discussion presents the key elements of the supervisory role, supervision does not have a distinct role, which presents another difficulty in performing the role. Perhaps more than any other level within a formal organization, supervisors are "all things to all people." They seem to never have the luxury of not performing at their best. Employees are always seeking direction and feedback. Supervisors are very visible, and they are constantly watched and modeled for leadership style. They have to balance completion of tasks with available resources. Bartollas and Miller aptly describe the challenge of supervision.

> Supervisors have one of the most demanding positions in correctional institutions. They are cast in the role of interpreting top management's policies and must do so in a manner convincing to their subordinates. They must be able to coordinate the activities of many below them who may not agree with the philosophy of top management. Middle managers, perhaps even more than top executives, are responsible for developing effective communication networks throughout the organization. Supervisors must be generalists and systems managers in much the same manner as their superiors. Even though they do not make policy decisions, they should be aware of how broad policy decisions affect their actions. They should also know how personnel above, under, and on their same level do their jobs.[3]

As pointed out, supervision can be very difficult. Yet, it can also be very rewarding. Before moving on to further discussions of various aspects of supervision, the accompanying illustration of a few hours in the life of a correctional (security) supervisor in a prison gives the reader some idea of supervision in a correctional environment.

PRACTICAL PERSPECTIVES

Second Shift—Federal Maximum Security Prison

Lieutenant Melody Rodriguez is a GS-11 lieutenant at a federal maximum security prison. She has worked with the Federal Bureau of Prisons for eight years, and been in her current assignment for 18 months. As a GS-11 lieutenant, she acts as a shift supervisor. During the second shift (from 4:00 P.M. until midnight), she is usually the highest ranking staff member at the prison. She has 23 correctional officers assigned to the shift, with one GS-9 activities lieutenant, who works until 9:00 P.M. and covers the recreation yard, commissary, and other high-activity areas during the shift. In addition to the correctional services staff, there are also a few unit management staff, and four education and recreation staff who work until 9:00 P.M.

"Lieutenant Rod," as she is called by other staff, is thought of as a good lieutenant. She gets out of the office, visits most of the areas and posts where officers are assigned nightly, is direct yet pleasant with officers, and accessible to inmates. Her day usually begins by 3:00 P.M., because she likes to get to work early, talk to the day-shift lieutenants, get the feel for the institution, and be sure she has coverage for all posts if anyone has called in sick or there are special activities that require additional coverage.

A few minutes before 4:00, she holds a role call for officers, briefing them on the activities of the day and what to expect during the evening. She also covers any special functions (e.g.,volunteers in for a religious program) that are happening that evening. Today was pretty typical, with no unusual incidents or tensions among inmate groups. At 4:00 P.M. the most important institution count of inmates takes place because they have not been counted since early morning. It is also important to do it quickly, because inmates are anxious to go to dinner and begin evening recreation and educational activities.

A new officer in one of the units seems to be having trouble with the count and has called in a wrong number. Lieutenant Rod suspects the new officer has simply missed someone and asks the activities lieutenant to go support the officer and help if he is having problems with the count procedure. The next count is accurate, because the officer simply needed a reminder to make sure all inmates are out of bed and standing in easy view of the door of the cell. Inmates are then released to dinner, and Lieutenant Rod goes to the dining room to watch the meal.

She realizes that there are only three correctional officers in the dining room during the feeding of more than 1,000 inmates and uses the radio to ask available unit management, educational, and recreation staff to come to the dining room for additional support. That's a good move, because during the meal two inmates got into a shoving match, but they are quickly separated. Lieutenant Rod has the inmates handcuffed and instructs one officer and a recreation staff member to take one of the inmates to SHU, and another officer and a case manager to take the other one to the lieutenant's office. She wants them to be separate, in case emotions get hot again. She also instructs the officers to find out from the inmates what the problem was about and to inform her right away if it seems like more than simply a dispute between two individual inmates.

After the meal, Lieutenant Rod begins to go through paperwork in her office. There are overtime approval slips to sign and a memo noting it is time to conduct an audit of the SHU procedures for recreating inmates in the evening. She decides to do the audit tonight, because with only one special activity (the religious volunteers) she knows she can use a senior correctional officer who is working the main compound to conduct the audit. The senior officer has a lot of ability and wants to be a lieutenant someday. Conducting the audit will be an excellent learning opportunity for him. She radios him to tell him he will be doing it and to meet her at 7:00 at SHU, where she will give him the format and instructions to do the audit.

At 6:15 P.M., Lieutenant Rod visits the recreation yard, which usually has 350 to 400 inmates jogging, playing basketball, or lifting weights on a nice evening. She talks to recreation staff, as well as the correctional officers working the yard. She notices a group of inmates recognized as members of the Mexikanemi, a Hispanic prison gang. She instructs the officers to keep an eye on them, list any inmates they recognize in the group, and submit a memo with the names at the end of the shift. On the way to SHU, an inmate stops her and explains he is being pressured to bring drugs into the institution by a group of inmates and is fearful for his safety if he does not do it. Lieutenant Rod tells the inmate she will arrange to have him placed on the "call out" to receive some legal material at the inmate records office in the next few days. One of the investigative lieutenants will meet him there and interview him in private, so that no attention will be drawn to the inmate talking to staff.

When she arrives at SHU, she delegates the audit to the senior officer, makes sure he knows how to do the job, understands the purpose, and explains that it is an excellent training opportunity for him. She tells him where she will be in case he has any questions and tells the SHU staff the senior officer will be doing the audit and to cooperate in any way necessary for him to get it done. She then decides to go to Unit 1 to talk to Officer Brady. Brady was 10 minutes late tonight and that is the second tardiness in the past week.

She gets to the unit and chats with Brady, suggesting they walk through the unit as is usual when she makes her rounds. This makes it appear there is nothing out of the ordinary to inmates and that she is not "calling Brady on the carpet." She asks Brady about the tardiness and gets a poor excuse.

Continued

Therefore, she informs Brady of the importance of being on time and how she cannot let it continue without taking some type of formal disciplinary action. She informs Brady that this should be considered an informal counseling session and that no formal action will be taken unless the tardiness continues.

It is now 8:00 P.M., and Lieutenant Rod's shift is half over. She goes to the officer's lounge to eat, so she is not far from her office or anyone who needs her. This 15 minutes to relax and reflect is all the break she gets. She thinks about the past four hours, feels good that all has gone well, thinks about how much she likes her job, and then heads out on the compound to be visible when the inmates are called to return to the units at 8:30 P.M.

The case study represents a typical four hours for a correctional supervisor in a prison. Lieutenant Rodriguez has done even more than it seems. She has checked to see that she has adequate staff resources to operate the shift safely and securely and found replacements for those officers who will be absent. She has provided information to her staff, so they know what to expect during their shift. She has responded quickly to a potential problem (the wrong inmate count), without overreacting. Her sending the activities lieutenant as support was a learning opportunity for the new officer without making the officer feel incompetent and without everyone realizing the count was being conducted incorrectly. She makes a good decision in handling the shoving match in the dining room, taking assertive action, and thinking ahead to keep the problem from escalating further.

Lieutenant Rod also decides that the audit can be done immediately, not putting it off until later. She does a good job of delegating the audit task as a learning experience to a senior officer, who has the interest and potential to become a lieutenant at some point. She uses her knowledge of the inmates to monitor the Mexikanemi activity and finds a way to get information from the inmate being pressured without putting him in danger. She also, in a direct, yet nonthreateningly manner, advises Brady to get to work on time. Even when taking her break, Lieutenant Rod thinks about her job, her staff, and the next four hours.

KEY ELEMENTS IN SUPERVISION

What does it take to be a good supervisor? What are the activities that must be performed for supervision to be as effective as possible? The following sections present many of the activities commonly acknowledged to be important in supervising employees, including

1. Communications
2. Clarifying expectations
3. Delegating and giving directions
4. Understanding behavior

5. Training and coaching
6. Giving feedback

Each of these elements are important to supervision, yet there is no required method to carry them out in the most effective way possible. No two people are the same, and no two supervisors do their jobs exactly the same way. The key is to understand each element and to blend each to one's own personality and supervision style.

Communications

Why are communications a key element to supervision? Because the only way that managers and supervisors get things done is through others. As noted earlier, supervision is about getting work done through others. A supervisor must constantly communicate by seeking input, by giving direction, by listening to what others have to say, and by transmitting information. In the case study of Lieutenant Rod, it is obvious that she communicates on almost a continuous basis. She asks questions, she listens to concerns, she gives instructions, and she makes clear the outcome of failure to comply with directions. The higher up the organizational ladder one climbs, the more the job depends on communications. A rather dated, but still accurate, study discovered that first-line supervisors spend 74 percent of their time communicating, second-level supervisors spend 81 percent, and third-level supervisors spend 87 percent of their time communicating.[4]

Directions of Supervisory Communications

Supervisors communicate with everyone and in every direction. Not only do they communicate downward with the employees who work directly for them but they also must communicate upward with their supervisors, the managers and executives within an organization. Information most often flows downward in an organization. In a correctional organization, it is critical that information be transferred quickly to line staff so they are prepared to deal with incidents that may occur. One of the first things Lieutenant Rod did when the shift started was to give a shift briefing. If information had been obtained that day from a confidential informant (inmate) that there was trouble brewing between the Mexikanemi (EMI) and the Texas Syndicate (two Hispanic gangs often at odds in prison), the grouping of the EMI on the recreation yard would possibly have much more meaning than it would otherwise.

Supervisors also communicate horizontally with other supervisors and with other departments. In corrections, a complex task can seldom be accomplished with only one person or with only one division or department involved. As simple a task as Lieutenant Rod trying to get more staff into the dining room during the evening meal needed horizontal communications. Few correctional officers can leave their assigned posts, because they must stay in that position to monitor inmates and security. More likely able to come to another location are other departmental staff, such as the unit management and education or recreation staff. Lieutenant Rod cannot simply issue an order for them to come to the dining room; these staff do not work for her. However, she may explain to them the need for additional people in the dining room, and she would probably expect cooperation. If the lack of staff in the dining room was a continuing problem, Lieutenant Rod should communicate the concern to her supervisors, who can put a policy or procedure in place to ensure adequate staff are available, rather than force the lieutenant on duty to deal with this problem every evening.

In most correctional organizations, supervisors also communicate with labor unions and stewards. A large percentage of government line employees are members of labor unions, and as discussed in Chapter 11, have a negotiated contract that provides rules for the workplace. Although it is hoped that these rules provide clarity in acceptable relationships between supervisors and employees, there are always questions that arise and concerns that need to be communicated. Officer Brady may not like the fact that Lieutenant Rod said that no more tardiness would be tolerated and that formal disciplinary action could follow. If Brady complained to a union steward, the steward may ask Lieutenant Rod for some background regarding Brady's tardiness. Perhaps the steward may note that the contract requires that Lieutenant Rod give Brady a written memo of the discussion. Supervisor and union steward communication are usually not adversarial, and it can be useful in reminding all parties of information in the contract, so a later controversy may be avoided. In this case, if Lieutenant Rod had been approached by a union steward, she may have told the steward that Brady had been tardy twice this week. More than likely, the steward would support Lieutenant Rod and remind Brady of the responsibility to be on time.

Finally, supervisors may also communicate with external sources. Prison staff often communicate and share information with other law enforcement agencies, or even the general public. Lieutenant Rod may be asked to give a speech to a community organization explaining how the prison operates and the importance of security and programs. Lieutenant Rod may also be asked to visit the "gang task force" of the state police, which monitors and keeps information on criminal gang activities that occur outside the prison. It is usually beneficial to share communications about gang activities and tensions from parties both inside and outside the prison. This information can help prevent gang conflicts in the prison.

Figure 12–1 presents a simple illustration of the directional flow of information between the supervisor and other groups within the organization. As is obvious, it is important for supervisors to communicate upward, downward, and horizontally. Communications are two-way and requires the supervisor both to speak and to listen. The next section deals with the supervisor–employee relationship and the critical skills required for effective communications.

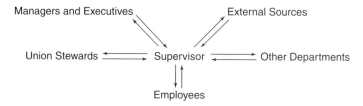

FIGURE 12–1   Information Flow Within an Organization

Communication: A Two-Way Street

Although it seems unnecessary to remind people that communications is a two-way street, one-way communications still happen all too often. Sometimes, supervisors seem too busy and rushed to make communications flow in both directions. Some supervisors are insecure in themselves and their position, and do not want feedback. And sometimes, supervisors in a paramilitary organization simply develop bad habits and are not even aware their communications have evolved into a one-way pattern. There are even times when one-way communications are acceptable and effective, such as during a crisis. During a prison riot, staff expect to hear one-way directions and orders. There has been much training and planning for this type of situation, and staff know the range of orders to expect in an emergency. In these cases, it is not necessary to open the door for two-way communications. However, the situations in which this is acceptable are very few.

In a later section, the importance of listening is discussed. Even before supervisors can practice good listening skills, they must create an environment that shows they desire feedback and want communications to be two-way. Many times employees, when receiving directions, do not understand and have to ask a question to clarify the order. However, if supervisors make snide remarks, frown, or use body language that shows they think the question shows a lack of understanding on the part of the employee, employees will quickly learn not to ask questions. The employee then has to guess or ask a co-worker how the supervisor wants the job done, which wastes other's time and often ends up with the task being performed in an unsatisfactory manner.

Some supervisors may also discourage feedback from employees about the effectiveness of a policy or procedure. When receiving an order, an employee may know that there is a better way to carry out the assignment. However, if supervisors give the impression they do not want feedback, staff will quickly learn to not give it and will simply do the job the way the supervisor wants it done. Again, this results in inefficiency and a failure to ever improve on processes and procedures. It is the responsibility of the supervisor to create an atmosphere where communications are truly "two-way." Good supervisors will even set the tone for feedback by asking, "Have you done that task before, and do you know how it is to be performed?" Or, they may even seek feedback by requesting, "Do you have any suggestions on a good way to accomplish that task?"

Positive Verbal Communications

In supervisory communications, many things are transmitted, including facts, opinions, feelings, and importance of the message. It is critical that supervisors think about what they want to communicate and how they want employees to hear it. The following steps can help supervisors avoid confusion resulting from their communications.

1. Know the subject.
2. Make sure the facts are complete and correct.
3. Organize remarks.
4. Know the background of the message recipient.
5. Use language the receiver understands.
6. Avoid generalities by being specific.
7. Consider the situation in which the message is delivered.
8. Communicate the purpose and importance of the message.
9. Seek feedback.

Supervisors are expected to know what they are talking about, but unfortunately, they sometimes do not. Lieutenant Rod may not have known anything about the requirement of a regular audit of SHU or how that audit was to be performed. She could still have decided to delegate responsibility to do the audit, which, in this situation, would have meant delegating responsibility to determine the requirements of the audit. If supervisors try to communicate something they do not understand, the communication will often end up being unclear, particularly if the supervisor wants to give the false impression they do understand. Supervisors should know what they are talking about before they try to deliver a message, both for the sake of understanding and for their own credibility.

A related key step to communications involves getting the facts before communicating. When a person is uncertain about what needs to be communicated, it usually means there are unknown facts or information. If there is tension between two prison gangs, and a supervisor wants correctional officers to be aware of this and look for unusual activities, it is valuable to share what has caused the tension or what evidence of tension has been detected. Instead of a simple, "Watch for any signs of tension between the Mexikanemi and Texas Syndicate," the listener of the message gets much more understanding of what to do if the supervisor includes facts and information. The following would be much more helpful, "There was a fight between a Mexikanemi (EMI) and Texas Syndicate member yesterday. At lunch today, there seemed to be a lot of grouping of the gangs and movement between tables to pass messages. A credible inmate has said that there will be a meeting of the EMI tonight in the recreation yard to decide if they want to retaliate. Watch for groupings anywhere, the recreation yard, dining room, or library, and report them to the Lieutenant's Office immediately."

We all speak "off the cuff," without much thought or preparation of our message. However, the more important the communication, the more important it is to organize one's thoughts. In the preceding example about gang tension, the supervisor would have thought through the information to be conveyed, including the background, what to watch for, and how to report any findings. Organizing thoughts about simple messages usually does not take much time or require written notes. However, if the message is complex, and if it is important to communicate many facts and be specific with information, it may require more preparation and making of notes to use in communication.

It is also important for the communicator to consider the receiver of the message. Who will receive the message—what is their background, will they understand certain terms I use? A new correctional officer will need a more extensive explanation than an experienced one. A staff member from other than the correctional services department may not understand slang or security terms familiar to correctional officers. Supervisors must consider the recipient of the information, and use language and terminology the receiver understands. Many employees will not ask questions about the meaning of terms, thinking they might look "stupid" in front of their boss or co-workers if they do.

When they are in a hurry, or if they are not fully aware of the facts, supervisors may simply communicate generalities rather than the specifics of an assignment or information to be communicated. When Lieutenant Rod asked the senior officer to conduct the SHU audit, she took the time to go over the assignment rather than simply asking the officer to conduct the audit. Specifics include what is to be done, what guidelines to use, what authority the receiver will have, when the task is to be completed, and what outcome is expected. Generalities of communications leave all of these elements to chance, and supervisors cannot be upset with employees who fail to carry out an assignment in the desired way if the supervisors did not communicate the specifics when giving the assignment.

The situation also dictates how communications are delivered and received. Is it in the midst of a prison riot? Are inmates listening? Is it a part of an employee evaluation? Or, can the failure to follow through have dire consequences for the person or the organization? Supervisors must also share the importance of the communications. When Lieutenant Rod told Brady that repeated tardiness would not be tolerated, she made it clear that formal disciplinary action would be taken if there was another incident of tardiness. That point should be a "red flag" to Brady, indicating that tardiness was unacceptable and would be personally costly if not corrected.

Finally, good communications should seek feedback. Supervisors can tell from the look on an employee's face or from body language whether the employee understands a message. Supervisors should also sincerely ask, "Are there any questions?" and give employees time to respond at the end of each communication. A message delivered without the opportunity for feedback is an incomplete message. It may have been misunderstood, some critical facts may have been left out, or the employee may not be aware of the authority and responsibility that go along with the assignment or message. It is the supervisors' responsibility to seek feedback and then move to the listening stage of the communications process.

The Listening Process

Often neglected in communications is effective listening. After verbally communicating a message, supervisors should move to a listening stage to complete the two-way communication. Unfortunately, some supervisors have a weakness when it comes to listening. They may think it is a threat to their authority if they allow feedback from employees, or they may not have prepared fully and fear their lack of information will be discovered and they will look foolish. However, it is important to supervisors' own needs to be good listeners. Supervisors are ultimately held responsible for completion of tasks by their staff. If supervisors fail to make clear an assignment and it is done incompletely or unsatisfactorily, the supervisors not only have to take more time to correct it but will also be held accountable for the failure to complete it.

Sometimes people hear but do not listen. They may be distracted, be thinking of something else, or be mentally preparing what they want to say instead of really listening. When the feedback is not what someone wants to hear, they often "turn off" their listening skills and begin to think negatively of the person speaking, wondering, "why does this person always make it difficult to give him (or her) an assignment." The American Correctional Association has published a series of workbooks to promote professionalism and improve leadership skills in the workplace. In their supervision handbook, they identify seven steps to effective listening:

1. **Ask questions.** If something is unclear or seems to contradict your own personal sense of logic, ask questions. Asking questions shows that you're interested in understanding what's being said.

2. **Concentrate.** Don't let your mind wander. People think at the rate of about 500 words per minute, but people talk at a rate of only about 150 words per minute. Stay focused on what is being said, or you will risk missing key points.

3. **Listen for the main idea(s).** It's not uncommon for people to develop ideas as they talk, to be somewhat vague when discussing sensitive issues, or to have trouble coming to the point. Make sure that you determine what the person's key issues are. Restate the other person's main ideas in your own words and ask him or her if you've understood correctly.

4. **Listen for the rationale behind what the other person is saying.** This is especially important if what he or she is saying doesn't seem to make sense to you. A staff member may be making a request on the basis of erroneous information about the organization. Be sensitive and make sure that you understand why the person is saying what he or she is saying.

5. **Listen for key words.** Key words can become your own internal cue or memory stimulator to help you retain what you hear.

6. **Organize what you hear in your own mind in a way that is logical for you.** Your way of organizing information may differ from the way the information was presented, but it is critical for you to use what you hear.

7. **Take notes if the issue or request is complex.** It is worthwhile to get your thoughts down in writing.[5]

Clarifying Expectations

A very important function of supervision is to set expectations for the acceptable quality of work performed. Supervisors give feedback to employees about how well they have done a job. As they do this, they are communicating a level of expectations. In discussing the need to set standards, Wright suggests the following:

> If the overarching goal is a safe, humane, and productive prison, then one must have an idea of what standards of safety, humanity, and productivity he or she aspires to achieve. These standards must be realistic. Over time, as staff make improvements, standards may be elevated . . . after an institution sets a standard, then it must be someone's responsibility to see that expectations are met. . . . Staff must understand that being responsible involves more than simply being accountable. Responsibility carries with it commitment to achieving the standard.[6]

Two important principles are believed by many correctional managers. First, staff will perform to the level of expectation. Among the roles of supervisors are setting high standards (they must be a reachable standards, however) and encouraging staff to perform at those levels. Second, any time a lower level of performance is accepted, it lowers the standard for the future. Consistency in demanding high standards is also important, because the standard soon becomes the lowest noted level of performance, not the highest. Following are examples of these two principles.

One function of a correctional supervisor in a prison is to do "quality assurance" checks of how well correctional officers perform their jobs. Lieutenant Rod, in making her rounds to the various posts, may stop to spend time with a housing unit officer. The officer is to perform many security checks during the shift, including checking windows for tampering, searching areas where contraband may be hidden, making sure all doors are locked, and "tapping" bars to make sure they have not been cut. Lieutenant Rod has the officer go through each of the checks with her, both as a review of the officer's technique and also to confirm it is being accomplished as required. Lieutenant Rod notices that the officer only "taps" every other bar. When questioned about it, the officer states that another officer told him this was acceptable practice, because it saved time and all the bars would be tapped over a few days. Lieutenant Rod can accept this (it seems reasonable), but instead she informs the officer that the post orders require tapping *every* bar, every night, and nothing less is acceptable. She may take time to explain why this is important, but what she has communicated is that nothing less than full compliance with post orders is acceptable. If correctional officers get in the habit of making what they see as acceptable compromises, then this practice will spread to many other tasks. However, if staff understand the standard will not be compromised, they will get into the habit of performing at that level, and an organizational culture will develop for doing jobs at full compliance.

An illustration of the second principle is the following example. Lieutenant Rod is making rounds in the housing unit. There is a prohibition against smoking in the television rooms, because smoking is only permitted in inmate cells. Lieutenant Rod goes into a television room, and there are cigarette butts and the smell of smoke, but no inmates are there to indicate who has been smoking. If Lieutenant Rod does not say anything, the officer will accept that the rule against smoking in the television rooms is "not that important." However, Lieutenant Rod knows that the warden has emphasized enforcing this rule and stated that any evidence of smoking will result in the television rooms being closed for the day. She also knows this message has been communicated to inmates. She, therefore, instructs the officer to lock the television rooms, tells inmates that she ordered the locking because of the smoking policy violation, and that television rooms will be closed every time there is a violation. This takes the pressure off the correctional officer and confirms the high standard of no smoking in the television rooms. When this is understood by officers and inmates, it is much easier to enforce.

Supervisors set standards and expectations by every action they take (or do not take). No action sets a standard. Never bending or compromising on the required duties sets a standard. Supervisors must always understand that they are not being a "good guy or gal" by letting less than full compliance with policy or procedure pass as acceptable. In fact, by accepting less than full compliance, they make it unlikely to ever occur. Also, accepting less than full compliance by staff and inmates makes it more difficult (if not impossible) for another supervisor who tries to enforce the rules and maintain the expected standard.

Delegating and Giving Directions

Much of what supervisors communicate are orders or delegation of duties. **Delegation** is the assignment of a task to someone. In a correctional setting, most activities are routine and staff are trained in their duties required to be completed on a regular basis. However, many times, supervisors have special projects or unusual duties that need to be assigned to a staff member (such as the audit that Lieutenant Rod assigned to the senior officer). Delegation in an effective manner is the key to successful completion of a project. When performance of assigned duties or special projects has in an unsatisfactory result, in most cases, it is at least partially caused by poor delegation on the part of the supervisor.

Why do supervisors delegate, and who benefits from such delegation? There are three reasons and three primary beneficiaries. First, supervisors delegate for themselves. They cannot possibly do all the work that passes down the chain of command and becomes their responsibility. Therefore, they delegate to get others to do the work, yet they continue to maintain control over the work to ensure it is done in a timely and quality manner. Second, supervisors delegate for organizational efficiency. Tasks should be assigned to staff best suited to complete them. Matching tasks with employees who have time and skill to effectively perform the duties results in a good product, therefore, benefiting the agency. Finally, supervisors delegate to benefit employees. By assigning employees special projects or unusual duties, the staff improve their skills and become better prepared for promotion and advancement. Most public correctional agencies promote staff on a competitive basis, and proving competence at a task improves their competitive score and chance for promotion. In fact, it is not unusual to have correctional employees complain that they have not been assigned enough projects to make them equally competitive for promotion with their peers.

An important part of delegation is the clear transfer of authority and responsibility. These items must be attached to the delegation. **Authority** involves the recognition by the organization and other employees that a particular employee has been delegated a task, and that employee can use agency resources and call on others to cooperate in or support the assignment. When supervisors delegate, they should give employees an adequate level of authority to get the job done. In the assignment of the senior officer to conduct the SHU audit, Lieutenant Rod informed the staff working in SHU of the senior officer's assignment. This created credibility in the senior officer's authority to ask for their cooperation.

Somewhat different, but often confused with authority, is responsibility. **Responsibility** means that the delegation has passed to another the obligation to complete the work. Persons who are delegated assignments understand they have become responsible for its completion. If an assignment is not completed, they can legitimately be blamed for the lack of performance. Supervisors do not delegate to pass the blame for failure. However, it is important for employees who are delegated an assignment to realize that they are accountable for the completion of the task.

The Delegation Process

There are several key steps to effective delegation. Some supervisors believe that simply because they have told someone to do something, they have effectively delegated the assignment. In their mind, they believe they have delegated the task, and perhaps even in the mind of the employee, they have received the delegation.

However, effective delegation involves much more than merely telling someone to do something. The following steps are essential to effective delegation, which results in a task being completed as expected.

1. Select, define, clarify, and organize the task.
2. Select the person for the delegation.
3. Instruct and motivate the person.
4. Gain consent for the delegation.
5. Establish limits of authority.
6. Maintain control and monitor the project.

The following is further clarification and explanation of the steps in delegating assignments.

1. Select, define, clarify, and organize the task. A supervisor must determine what tasks should be delegated. The audit of SHU could have been completed by Lieutenant Rod, but she decided to delegate it. A supervisor cannot delegate every task but must delegate some. In determining which tasks should be delegated, supervisors consider the importance, need for any special skill, learning opportunity for staff, and time frame for accomplishing a task. If they decide to delegate it, they must clarify and define the task. As an example, a probation supervisor wants a report of the percentage of drug use by probationers compared to the amount of time under supervision and decides to ask a probation officer to compile the report. The delegation should include a definition of "use," such as testing positive on a urine analysis. In addition, there should be a clarification of how to examine the number of months during supervision. For instance, the time may be per month or it may be categorized into three- or six-month intervals.

2. Select the person for the delegation. A delegation is doomed to failure if the supervisor does not think through the selection of the right person for a job. Phillips and McConnell suggest, "Pick the employee you will delegate to by matching the qualifications of available employees with the requirements of the task to be delegated."[7] The supervisor should consider several things: (1) Does the employee have the time, or can that employee's regular duties be reassigned to others to create the time; (2) does the employee have the skill and background necessary to complete the task; (3) have other employees of like status been given assignments so that developmental opportunities are equally shared; and (4) will there be ample opportunity to monitor and check on the assignment with this employee?

3. Instruct and motivate the person. Some of the important considerations in giving instructions for delegation are the same ones noted previously under positive verbal communications. The directions should be complete, organized, and specific. The time frame for accomplishing the task should be provided, as should the authority delegated to the employee. The supervisor should emphasize the importance of the delegation, and communicate its purpose and value to the organization. When Lieutenant Rod asked the senior officer to conduct the SHU audit, she should have explained the audit program, how it is used to maintain security, and how critical security is in the daily operations of a SHU. Supervisors delegating assignments should also make clear that they are available for questions. Finally, persons receiving a delegation should be informed of possible positive and negative consequences of failing to complete the assignment. In the SHU audit example, the senior officer should be informed that this assignment is excellent training in SHU security and the audit procedure, items that are often considered for promotion to lieutenant.

4. Gain consent for the delegation. Even though supervisors have the authority to delegate tasks to their employees, it is important to gain the employee's consent for the assignment. An employee may not believe he or she is capable of completing a task, or the employee may already have an assignment that prohibits him or her from accepting another. The employee may not want to take on any extra work, even if there is a potential benefit. If the employee does not want to accept the delegation, the supervisor has to decide whether to force the employee to accept it or to find someone else to whom to assign the task.

5. Establish limits of authority. When authority is vaguely defined, it can be abused, misrepresented, or resented by other employees. The supervisor should communicate with other employees the authority delegated for completion of the task, so employees understand and cooperate as necessary with the person assigned the task. It should be clarified that when the task is complete, the delegated authority ends. Although few employees will take advantage of or abuse authority, clearly establishing limits avoids any potential for problems.

6. Maintain control and monitor the project. Even when a project is delegated, it is important for supervisors to check on the progress of the project. Black suggests;

> The superhighway to disaster is to delegate and forget. It is foolish to assume that work is being done satisfactorily simply because you told someone to do it. An effective system of controls keeps you informed on progress and tells you whether or not projects are moving forward satisfactorily. Reports (oral and written) and visual inspection are a protection against mistakes.[8]

During a delegation, employees should be informed of the type of feedback the supervisor expects. For instance, a supervisor may state, "Give me an update on your progress every Wednesday afternoon." This motivates the employee to keep on schedule and also allows for the opportunity to make adjustments, if the direction or method of completing the project is different than the supervisor expected. It is also valuable to visually inspect progress. Employees are not always candid in reporting on their progress, and supervisors should visit the work site to see for themselves what is being accomplished. If they do not, supervisors will, all too often, find that progress is not exactly as has been verbally reported.

Delegation of tasks is an extremely critical function for supervisors, and it can benefit supervisors, employees, and organizations. However, effective delegation requires thorough planning, good communications, and follow up. When delegation is done poorly, it wastes time and results in frustration by supervisors and employees. However, well-delegated assignments and successful outcomes are positive motivators for employees, provide encouragement for staff to take on extra tasks, and increase potential for future promotional opportunities.

Understanding Behavior

Most articles and books regarding supervision extensively describe the process, systems, and steps for effective supervision. However, few present the "human" side of the job. It is important to understand that supervision involves the human side of an organization. Production companies have assembly lines and manufacturing equipment. High-tech companies have computers and the Internet. Correctional agencies have offenders and policies and procedures. But every organization has people who work for, and with, other people. The key elements of supervision are critical to the supervisory function. However, understanding the human side of supervision cannot be underestimated in its importance in making supervisors and their employees effective.

The value of understanding behavior, as it relates to the supervision process is not new. In a book on supervision published more than 30 years ago, the authors write;

> Recognizing that there is a cause behind each act is the first basic step toward understanding human behavior. It is also a fundamental principle for intelligent motivation of others. When the supervisor really knows the worker and when he explores and analyzes each situation and reaction, he is on the way to understanding the cause responsible for the reaction or behavior. He is then in a better position to know what will happen when an order is given and to understand the reason for what may appear to be insubordination or just plain stubbornness.[9]

The first step in understanding the behavior of others is to understand one's own behavior. Although we all want to think we are "close to perfect," we do our jobs well, and we are supportive of our employees, there is a nagging feeling when we are wrong or have not done a good job. It is valuable for supervisors to recognize their technical job skills and weaknesses, their personality strengths and faults, and their tendencies to become stubborn and refuse to listen to good advice. Humans are not perfect, and understanding how these imperfections impact one's ability to supervise others increases the potential for effective supervision.

The second step is to consider the employee, including personality and behavior, and the type of supervision to which the employee best responds. Some supervisors believe that employees should adjust to the supervisor's style. They believe that if they are brash and curt, "so what, let them get used to it." Employees must recognize that supervisors are different and have various styles, and the employees should make some adjustments to accommodate their supervisors. However, supervisors are responsible for getting tasks accomplished. If they consider the characteristics of their employees (both as a group and as individuals) and try to tailor communications and style around these characteristics, it usually improves moral, saves time, and enhances performance.

As an example, consider the situation of Lieutenant Rod counseling Brady about being tardy. If she knows Brady is a hard working employee who tries to do the best job possible, she will probably spend more time trying to determine whether there is an issue or problem behind the tardiness, and she may try to help resolve the problem. However, if she knows Brady is not very dedicated and committed to the organization, shirks responsibility whenever possible, and seems to respond more to avoid disciplinary action than to seek encouragement, she will probably be more direct, ask if there is a problem, accept no excuse, and get quickly to the bottom line, "If tardiness continues, there will be formal action taken."

Training and Coaching

The process of training staff to work in the field of corrections was covered in detail in Chapter 11. However, in addition to formal training, a supervisor is constantly, informally training employees. This on-the-job training most often takes place without a lesson plan, is not in a classroom, and usually occurs without any official documentation. Supervisors also coach, which sometimes means the same as training. However, for purposes of this discussion, these two terms are defined differently. **On-the-job training** involves demonstrating to an employee the correct way to do a job. When the activities lieutenant visited the unit with an inaccurate count, he showed the new officer how to ensure he saw and counted all inmates. **Coaching,** however, is less active than on-the-job training and involves guiding, preparing, mentoring, or prompting. Supervisors coach employees constantly. When discussing the SHU audit with the senior officer, Lieutenant Rod probably did considerable coaching. She probably told him of her experience in using the audit checklist and how it takes less time if you audit physical areas within SHU rather than following the numbers on the checklist. She could have coached him regarding how to handle a lack of cooperation by other departments or in different ways of dealing with certain individuals.

Whatever it is called, good supervisors spend an enormous amount of time training and coaching staff. Less effective supervisors often believe they do not have the time to train or coach, or that employees will learn more and remember things longer if they have to discover things relating to their job through trial and error. Sometimes, supervisors learned that way. However, that does not mean learning a job through trial and error should be continued. Good supervisors recognize that, in the long run, training and coaching saves both their time and employees' time, tasks are more likely to have better results, employees will probably have a better experience, and staff will look forward to the next assignment with enthusiasm.

Why do supervisors train and coach? The bottom line is that they want their employees to accomplish the job the way it is expected to be done. When expectations are not met, the problem is not that employees do not want to please their supervisors. A survey of 4,000 managers asked, "Why don't subordinates do what they are supposed to do?" The responses were as follows:

1. They don't know what they are supposed to do.
2. They don't know how to do it.
3. They don't know why they should.
4. There are obstacles beyond their control.
5. They don't think it will work.
6. They think their way is better.
7. Not motivated—poor attitude.
8. Personally incapable of doing it (personal limits).
9. Not enough time for them to do it.
10. They are working on wrong priority items.
11. They think they are doing it (no feedback).
12. Poor management.
13. Personal problems.[10]

For item 8, "personally incapable of doing it," the supervisor should refer the employee to the training department to receive remedial training. However, all the other reasons on the list can be improved by the supervisor acting as a trainer or coach. Sometimes, supervisors have to convince staff they can do a job, that it is worth doing, or that the procedure suggested is the best way to accomplish the task. Sometimes, supervisors have to counsel employees on how to manage their time or what tasks have the most priority. Other times, supervisors have to support employees by removing obstacles or coopting other managers. And at times (particularly when dealing with employees with poor attitudes), supervisors have to be direct, make clear that employees are to do the task, and complete it the way the organization expects it to be done. Always, supervisors must provide feedback, inform employees of how they are doing, and tell them whether they are accomplishing what is expected.

Giving Feedback

Feedback provides employees with an idea of how well they are doing a job, whether through a formal evaluation process or through informal verbal response. Supervisors cannot expect employees to perform as desired if the employees are not told how they are doing. Giving feedback may be as simple as telling employees they did a good job or giving constructive criticism regarding how do a job better the next time. It may also be more complex, using agency evaluations, and influence decisions regarding retention, pay, and promotion. No matter how formal or informal it may be, giving feedback is a critical element of effective supervision.

As prudent as this seems, many supervisors do a poor job of providing feedback to their employees. Some say, "they will know if I am not happy with their performance." Others are uncomfortable telling employees how they are performing and find it hard to give praise or provide constructive criticism. Some supervisors may not be familiar with the procedures of the formal evaluation process and avoid it because they don't understand it. Others think anything negative they tell employees will result in a complaint to the union. But supervisors who give regular feedback (a pat on the back, immediate correction of errors, and performance evaluations that are fair and follow the agency guidelines) find that their effectiveness as supervisors increases significantly.

Positive feedback is the easiest and most pleasant for supervisors to give. It is satisfying to tell people that they did a good job and that their efforts are appreciated. It can be argued that there is nothing that has a better impact on morale than positive feedback. The most negative impact on morale is no feedback, or giving the same feedback to all staff, including those who perform at a high level and those who perform at a low level. A good analogy is how some parents never pay attention to their children except to discipline them. Children crave attention and, therefore, misbehave simply to get some recognition. Similarly, good employees who get no feedback may question why they are working so hard and may end up performing at a lower level, or even performing poorly simply to get some feedback. When supervisors do not differentiate between good and poor employees, by failing to give praise, by failing to give constructive criticism, or by giving everyone the same evaluation, employees find little reason to maintain good performance.

Correcting behavior or performance is also key in supervision. As noted in the survey of managers as to why employees do not perform as they are supposed to, one reply was, "They don't know how to do it." Supervisors should immediately correct an employee who is incorrectly performing a task or one who is using the wrong procedures to accomplish a job. A regular function of correctional officers is to pat search inmates (explained in Chapter 8). Supervisors who note a correctional officer's failure to properly or thoroughly search an inmate should immediately correct him or her. Doing the pat search wrong will soon become a habit and will be noticed by inmates. Inmates will determine that they can hide drugs or other contraband because of the poor searching techniques by an officer.

Every agency has a formal evaluation procedure. The supervisor's role in the process is perhaps the most important.[11] Supervisors write evaluations and discuss them with employees. The evaluation process is delicate for both employees and supervisors; it is designed to encourage improved performance. However, if it is not done well, the evaluation process leaves no one satisfied, can have a negative affect on morale, and can have the opposite effect on performance. Following are tips for supervisors regarding their role in evaluating employees:

▮ Take the evaluation process seriously. If a supervisor gives the impression that the evaluation is not important, it will not serve as an incentive for employees to maintain good or improve bad performance.

▮ Give all employees the level of evaluation they deserve. By failing to differentiate between good and bad employees, the process has no credibility and will be ineffective.

▮ Do not "inflate" evaluation levels. Some supervisors do not want to hurt any employees' feelings, so they rate everyone highly. When good employees see poor employees get above adequate ratings, the good employees' own ratings mean less to them.

▮ Be candid in discussing performance. If a supervisor is not comfortable being direct and is not candid about the need for improvement by employees, the evaluation will not help them to improve.

▮ Spend the proportionate amount of time praising as well as correcting employees as they deserve. Many supervisors may not tell a good employee all the things they do right. They say, "You are doing a really good job, but I would like to see you improve on these items." If a supervisor thinks an employee is doing 90 percent of the job well, the evaluation discussion should reflect that, and the supervisor should spend 90 percent of the time saying how much he or she appreciates the way the employee performs certain tasks.

EMPOWERING EMPLOYEES: THE WAVE OF THE FUTURE

Empowerment is, in contemporary leadership and management, considered the "right" way to manage people. During the past two decades, in order to make organizations better able to respond to change, while taking full advantage of the skills of employees, corporations began to adopt principles of total quality management

(TQM). TQM essentially involves employees in finding solutions to problems, using work groups or teams who best understand the problems and who can, therefore, best devise appropriate solutions. Involving employees in the TQM process prompted a further movement away from rigid, bureaucratic management toward empowering employees, giving them authority to find and implement solutions to problems.[12]

What is empowerment, and is there something different in today's organizational environment that makes it the right thing to do? Real employee empowerment is not easy to implement, although many managers believe they do it. Empowerment is especially difficult to implement in correctional agencies, in which issues such as escapes and riots are feared by both agency and political leadership. Correctional leaders and managers often believe they have to personally attend to the activities in a prison or community correctional program in order to avoid problems and risk embarrassment.

In its pure sense, **empowerment** is a change in the overall culture of an organization. It is not simply extensive delegation. It is more than asking employees their opinions about policies and procedures. It extends beyond involving employees in creating solutions to problems. Empowerment involves pushing decision making down to the lowest possible level, not only involving employees but also letting them manage and make decisions. Empowerment involves giving employees the authority to create new approaches when they believe a new way improves the old. Empowerment involves providing employees with the principles and values of the organization, along with the desired outcomes (vision and mission), and allowing them to make decisions and respond to situations that are consistent with the principles and values, and move toward the desired outcomes. Foy describes empowerment as follows:

> In empowering organizations, people know what the organization expects from them, and how well they are meeting their targets. More than that, in the ultimate empowering, they are able to help develop the objectives, and their experience feeds into the development of credible strategies. That kind of organization will be good for its members, and they will be good for the organization.[13]

Empowerment of employees and organizations is important in today's public and private organizations for several reasons. First, change is so rapid that organizations have difficulty developing routine procedures that can be counted on to work over time. Second, rapid change results in situations that have never before been encountered. Third, employees are better educated today than they were in the past and have grown up in an environment of rapid change. Therefore, these employees are prepared to meet never-before confronted challenges. Finally, today's employees demand to be involved in the organization and cringe at a rigid bureaucracy in which they are only expected to follow orders and carry out prescribed functions. They do not tolerate the old adages of "we have always done it this way" or "if it ain't broke, don't fix it." If they know a better way to carry out their duties, they expect the authority to implement it.

The need to embrace empowerment is important in a correctional environment. Change is rapid, because new inmates, new technology, and abrupt growth constantly require new approaches to maintain control within a correctional agency.

Correctional administrators cannot themselves stay ahead of all the changes, and they must rely more on their staff, who deal daily with the environment, better understand it, and are best able to respond to issues or emergencies in appropriate ways. The warden used to be the person within a prison who confronted every possible situation and was aware of the "tried and true" remedies for each problem. Unfortunately, that is no longer the case, because each day brings new dilemmas.

Contemporary correctional staff are professional, experienced, trained, and educated. They have grown up in a computer and information age, learned how to face new challenges, and are comfortable without routine, prescribed methods and procedures. The generation X workforce does not accept orders without wanting to know why. They want to understand how the organization developed a specific response to a situation. These staff are more committed to an organization outcome or procedure that they helped to create. Prison staff, in noting reasons why they terminated their employment, listed two issues: the quality of the work environment and the inability to influence prison policy.[14] In a study of prison climate, with more than 3,000 staff responses, it was found that staff with greater input into decision making had higher job satisfaction and believed they were more effective in their roles.[15]

Empowerment is not only acceptable but it is also mandatory for managing a correctional agency. The question is not whether to empower staff, it is how to empower staff without giving up authority and without failing to provide leadership. It may seem that empowerment is an acceptance that employees will learn by making mistakes. However, in a correctional organization, where mistakes can mean injury or death to someone, it is not acceptable for leadership to simply take a "laissez-faire" attitude, let staff do what they want to do, and experiment with a variety of procedures. By involving staff, forewarning them of information about offenders and offender groups, and training them about the risks and potential dangers regarding responses to problems, staff should be expected to use sound professional judgment to make decisions. This is not "trial and error." It is using informed, professional judgment at all staff levels within a correctional organization. If correctional administrators understand empowerment and use acceptable practices to empower staff, employees grow and mature in a way that they make excellent decisions and perform effectively. The next few sections present the practices and processes to reach these results.

The Empowerment Process

Just as with making any change, correctional administrators must plan an implementation strategy for creating an empowered environment. However, it is never simple to change "how we manage." It is much easier to change "what is managed." Steps to implement an organization with empowered employees include the following:

1. Tell staff they are going to be empowered.
2. Explain what empowerment means.
3. Generate commitment by top managers.
4. Realign responsibilities.

5. Provide staff direction and a vision for guidance.
6. Involve staff in the creation of a strategic plan, including empowerment strategies.
7. Simplify the organization, and remove any unnecessary levels.
8. Create a focus on performance and outcome.
9. Establish a communications strategy.
10. Initiate a mechanism for feedback.

The following further explains the key activities instrumental to implementing on empowering overcriticized culture.

1. Tell staff they are going to be empowered. The first step is to tell staff they are going to be empowered. Although this seems obvious, organizational leaders must advise staff that there is going to be a change in the way the organization is managed. Staff hear about change in organizations all the time, to the point that they often tend to ignore changes until the changes affect how staff do their day-to-day jobs. By telling staff of plans for empowerment, correctional administrators commit to the change, or they put their credibility at risk. Staff know this, and respect leaders who are willing to take this risk. Also, announcing the plan begins the process of staff understanding that they must accept some responsibility in return.

2. Explain what empowerment means. The next step is to educate staff on what empowerment means and what will be expected of them. Staff at first will think, "Oh, great, I won't have a boss looking over my shoulder at everything I do from now on." However, once they realize that a tremendous amount of responsibility comes with empowerment, it will be threatening to them. The biggest change with empowerment is that staff can't simply do their jobs and avoid taking responsibility for improving processes. Instead of only being concerned with "process," every staff member becomes responsible for "outcome." Staff must continually look for ways to improve both themselves and the organization.

3. Generate commitment by top managers. Perhaps most hesitant to accept empowerment of employees are mid- and upper-level managers in an organization. They believe they are losing the most, and they are in many ways. For narrow-minded managers, who relish and protect information to maintain their organizational importance, providing information to employees, with little concern for rigidly following the chain of command, is threatening. Sometimes, these managers must themselves be convinced that empowerment is right for the organization. It is critical for correctional administrators to tend to the concerns, fears, and needs of these managers by explaining their new roles as mentors and coaches for line staff. Unless these managers also support this philosophy, a move to empowerment will be unsuccessful.

4. Realign responsibilities. To implement an empowering environment, almost everyone in the organization must change what they do and how much time they spend on various functions. In Chapter 2, there was a presentation of the leadership and empowerment triangle. The triangle described the roles the three levels of staff should play in an empowered organization. Leaders should focus on four activities: (1) creating a vision and setting a direction for the organization, (2) creating an empowering environment, (3) identifying areas of challenges for the future, and

(4) building (or reinforcing) the organization culture and character. Managers change their focus to set goals and objectives, refine and improve policies and procedures, develop staff through training and mentoring, and continually reinforce the agency mission in employees' minds. Line employees are empowered to respond to situations and make decisions in a manner consistent with the culture, principles, ethics, and values desirable within the organization.

5. Provide staff direction and a vision for guidance. For staff to be successful in an empowered environment, they must know what the organization values, wants to be, and the types of behaviors that contribute to this outcome. These elements are captured in an organization's vision. As staff understand the vision, they can perform in a manner consistent with it. In Chapter 3, the vision of the federal prison in Greenville, Illinois, was presented as, "We envision FCI Greenville as a safe, pleasant, and empowered workplace." In addition, a process for establishing a vision statement was presented. Empowerment begins with a vision statement to convey to staff the values, principles, and expected outcomes of the organization. Staff use this vision as guidance and direction for their behavior.

6. Involve staff in the creation of a strategic plan, including empowerment strategies. The next step is to plan to implement empowerment strategies. Key strategies focus on communications, performance and outcome, and continuous feedback. However, these activities simply do not occur without considerable planning and thought. Implementation requires considerable effort by all staff until empowering activities become habit and part of the routine way of doing business. An implementation plan should be developed that identifies specific strategic activities and dates they will be implemented. Staff from all levels of the organization should be involved, and should participate as peers, rather than superiors and subordinates.

7. Simplify the organization, and remove any unnecessary levels. Many organizations, especially public agencies, become increasingly bureaucratic over time, and they create organizational layers and departments to respond to new issues and challenges. Too many levels within an organization chart becomes an obstacle to effective empowerment. For effective empowerment, it is important to simplify communications and avoid redundant layers through which information passes. While implementing empowering strategies, organizations should examine themselves to determine whether they have created unnecessary layers that exacerbate the ability to share information and empower staff. If so, the organization should eliminate unnecessary and overly bureaucratic layers of management.

8. Create a focus on performance and outcome. Too often, public organizations measure input and process, rather than output. This is primarily the result of the public budget process requiring funding for programs, number of staff, number of clients, or number of forms processed. In correctional agencies, budgets are primarily for the number of staff employed. Public budget processes do not require measurement and funding for successful outcomes, and although that may be desirable, it is usually not mandatory. In *Reinventing Government*, a book recommending a redesign of government to make it more efficient and responsive to tax payers, the authors suggest, "Organizations that measure the results of their work—even if they do not link funding or rewards to those results—find that the information transforms them."[16] As an example, a probation agency can go a long way toward empowering probation officers and improving performance by simply collecting information and rewarding staff on the number of probationers who find and maintain productive employment, rather than the number of probationers on the officers caseload.

9. Establish a communications strategy. It is extremely important to develop systems to continuously share information throughout the organization. As noted earlier, bureaucratic and strict hierarchical approaches of passing information up and down the chain of command make it difficult to have a fully empowered environment. There are few valid reasons that information must be filtered through managers and supervisors before it reaches employees. However, communication strategies must ensure that managers and supervisors are not "jumped over" with the flow of information to line staff. Therefore, it is important to develop strategies that work for the entire organization and to share information quickly and continuously. With today's technology, there are many ways that information can be immediately transmitted to all staff; it involves a process called information "immersion." Phone systems can be programmed to call all staff phones with a recorded message of breaking information. Or, there can be a "dial in" message center (with staff-only access) with a recorded message about what occurred and possible follow-up incidents of which to be aware. Computer systems can transmit "flash" messages to all staff at the same time. A certain radio code or signal on the prison loud speaker system can alert staff to use a planned system for information sharing. Although face-to-face communications remain important, it is more important to have quick and widespread access to information.

Within a prison, a combined model of chain of command and immersion can work successfully. As incidents occur and information develops (e.g., a fight in the recreation yard between two gang members that may lead to additional fights between gang members), those in possession of the information (e.g., the warden or the chief of security) can do an information immersion and then conduct a briefing for all available staff. This allows for questions, interchange of information, and even collecting ideas for strategies if further incidents occur. As other staff report for work, they can be briefed with information updates by their supervisors. There are many ways to create immediate and continuous sharing of information. Such information is critical for empowering staff, so they can make sound decisions based on the situation and the impact it will have on the overall correctional environment.

10. Initiate a mechanism for feedback. Finally, there should be opportunities for line employees to discuss their ideas, propose solutions or changes in procedures, and share proposals with correctional administrators. In most situations, staff cannot change procedures on their own without resulting in inconsistency in operations. If an employee idea for a change in procedures has merit, it should be discussed and considered for implementation throughout the organization. One way ideas have been considered in a prison was by creating a Line Staff Advisory Committee. The warden personally met with the committee and listened to ideas that had been suggested and discussed among line staff. Decisions to make changes in procedures were not made at these meetings. However, if the committee agreed an issue needed attention, committee members were assigned the responsibility to talk to other staff, identify some options for responding to the issue, and then discuss the suggestions with the responsible department head. Although this process may seem threatening to department heads, it soon became popular with both line staff and department heads. After discussion at the Line Staff Advisory Committee meeting, it was simply decided that the issue needed attention. Department heads were told that they had the authority to make any change they believed addressed the problem. Line staff had an outlet for feedback, rather than grumbling and complaining among themselves that problems were never addressed. Department heads had the authority to make decisions about procedures under their control. As both line staff and mid-level managers recognized the opportunity to make positive change in the organization, they became enthusiastic about looking for ways to improve procedures.

Empowerment of staff is important for correctional agencies, but efforts to empower must be well planned and thoroughly implemented. It is easy to say staff are empowered, but actions speak much louder than words. Staff throughout the organization must be committed to the empowerment process, and definitive steps must be taken to change both actual behavior and staff taking of responsibility for improvement. If empowerment is successfully implemented, the improvement in efficiency, morale, and operations can be dramatic.

PREPARING FOR SUPERVISION

The old adage of the "born leader" had long been believed to be true. However, today the idea of born leaders is in question, especially with the emphasis on transformational leadership. Transformational leaders communicate values and principles, they create strategies to share information, and they push authority for decision making to the lowest possible level. A transformational leader of a correctional agency noted that once the staff became empowered, they grew tremendously in their willingness and skill at taking actions consistent with the organizational goals. The administrator even joked that he had nothing to do anymore, as staff were not constantly coming to him to ask what to do.

The same is true for supervisors. The contemporary challenge for supervision is not to learn how to give orders clearly but to learn how to develop staff through training, coaching, and creating opportunities for staff to experience and learn new procedures. Organizations can implement specific activities and approaches to prepare staff for supervisory positions. Some line staff believe all they have to do is wait their turn to become supervisors. However, successful supervisors are those who have taken advantage of their time by understanding the skills needed for supervision, candidly analyzing their strengths and weaknesses, and taking initiatives to improve and prepare themselves.

What are the skills and traits necessary for supervision? The American Correctional Association handbook on supervision lists the following personality traits or characteristics to be successful as a supervisor.[17]

▮ Patience
▮ Tolerance
▮ Sensitivity

- Empathy
- Punctuality
- Decisiveness

The authors suggest prospective supervisors consider their own characteristics against this list of traits and consider how to improve their own abilities in these areas. Individuals do not have to accept that they are impatient or lack tolerance. They can recognize the need to make changes and can improve themselves in the area of valued supervisory traits.

One of the most important activities line staff can take to prepare for being supervisors is to do their current jobs well. Sometimes, staff think so much about the job they want to have, they fail to concentrate on performing at a high level in their current assignment. When staff are considered for promotion to supervisory positions, the most important factor considered is how they perform their present jobs. Staff are usually evaluated for their potential as supervisors on how well they handle the technical aspects of their current jobs.

An important trait for supervisors is effective time management. As is obvious in the case study of Lieutenant Rod, a supervisor must juggle many balls at the same time. Some people simply seem to get more done than others, and it is not clear why. Unfortunately, hard work is not the best solution. It is more important for employees to organize their workload and complete a task once it is started. In supervision, especially in a fluid correctional environment, there are many distractions that interrupt the accomplishment of an ongoing task. Effective supervisors know how to focus on a task and how to manage resources to complete assignments. Every employee has a variety of work tasks that must be organized and competed. Understanding and improving one's ability to organize work and manage time is excellent preparation for taking on supervisory responsibilities.

Another way to prepare for supervision is to develop skills to effectively manage stress. Correctional jobs by their nature are prone to a tremendous amount of stress. They can be dangerous, and fear of physical injury increases personal stress. As correctional staff climb the organizational ladder, they quickly realize they feel responsible for incidents such as fights, riots, prison escapes, or new crimes committed by probationers or parolees. Add to the usual stresses of supervising people, correcting performance, giving evaluations, or responding to bad attitudes or lack of motivation, and correctional supervision is a formula for high anxiety. Staff who do not learn how to manage stress have a difficult time as correctional supervisors. Phillips and McConnell provide the following five suggestions for supervisors to reduce job related stress.[18]

- Learn to say no, or at least to speak up, when the last request or demand (from your boss) finally becomes too much.
- Do not let work accumulate until it becomes uncontrollable.
- Delegate before the level of work gets out of control.
- Vary your pace by interspersing short, quiet tasks among the more hectic, tension-producing contacts required.
- When the going gets rough, take a few minutes to relax. There are methods to reduce the physical response to stress through stretching, breathing exercises, or walking to clear your head.

Good communications skills are essential for supervision. Supervisors must regularly communicate to individuals and to groups. They must have good verbal and good written communication skills. Staff who do not have strong skills in these areas can improve their abilities. Individuals with inadequate writing skills should take writing courses. Most correctional agencies recognize the importance of written communications and provide self-study courses to improve these skills. Similarly, there are training programs to improve verbal communications. For individuals who are uncomfortable speaking to groups of people, the best way to reduce their anxiety is for them to practice public speaking. Employees who believe their public speaking needs work should seek opportunities to speak to groups, for example, by briefing other employees or volunteering as trainers. The more one does public speaking, the easier it becomes.

Preparation for supervision includes the following. First, employees should candidly analyze their strengths and weakness. No one is perfect, and ignoring a weakness will only make it that much more of a weakness as employees increase their level of responsibility. Second, employees should develop a plan for their personal improvement. All required supervisory traits can be strengthened, and all weaknesses can be improved. Finally, employees must take initiatives to improve. Some employees make the mistake of waiting for their supervisors or the agency to recognize their training and development needs to place them in a program. However, the best and quickest way to improve and prepare for supervision is for employees to take action themselves. They should take self-study courses, enroll in college courses, avail themselves of opportunities to use and practice supervisory skills, and ask for training they believe will prepare them for supervision. As employees take these three steps, they will find they are prepared when the time comes for them to move into a supervisory role.

SUMMARY

Supervision is perhaps the most difficult, yet the most critical function within a correctional agency. Failure to effectively supervise employees can very quickly undermine the ability to operate a safe and secure prison, to efficiently manage a community corrections program, or to prepare offenders for success in the community. Correctional line employees are "where the rubber meets the road," as they carry out the day-to-day functions of corrections. Regardless of facilities, technology, or financial resources, if line staff do not do their jobs well, correctional goals will not be fulfilled. Correctional supervisors play a critical role, because they oversee and ensure line staff perform their jobs.

Poor supervision wastes resources, discredits the agency, damages morale, and undermines staff loyalty and dedication. Good communications, clarifying expectations, proper delegation (including the transfer of authority and the acceptance by staff of responsibility), understanding behavior, on-the-job training and coaching staff, and giving feedback to employees are all essential tasks for supervisors. These activities cannot be taken for granted. They require specific skills to be carried out effectively. Beyond these basic supervisory functions, contemporary supervisors must learn to empower staff, enlighten them with the organizational vision, and trust them to take responsibility and make decisions that conform to the organization's principles and values. It can be the most rewarding function for those staff who perform supervision well. It is gratifying to watch staff you have developed perform at a high level, take responsibility, and mature into effective staff who contribute to the organization.

■ ENDNOTES

1. Martin M. Broadwell, *Moving Up to Supervision* (Boston, MA: CBI Publishing Company, 1979), p. 3.
2. Richard L. Phillips and Charles R. McConnell, *The Effective Corrections Manager: Maximizing Staff Performance in Demanding Times* (Gaithersburg, MD: Aspen Publishers, 1996), p. 29.
3. Clem Bartollas and Stuart J. Miller, *Correctional Administration: Theory and Practice* (New York: McGraw-Hill Book Company, 1978), p. 143.
4. Keith Davis, *Human Relations at Work: The Dynamics of Organizational Behavior,* 3rd ed., (New York: McGraw-Hill Book Company, 1967), p. 326.
5. Bruce B. Tepper, adapted for the American Correctional Association by Ida M. Halasz, *Supervision: A Handbook for Success* (Lanham, MD: American Correctional Association, 1998), pp. 59–60.
6. Kevin N. Wright, *Effective Prison Leadership* (Binghamton, NY: William Neil Publishing, 1994), p. 18.
7. Phillips and McConnell, p. 70.
8. James Menzies Black, *The Basics of Supervisory Management: Mastering the Art of Effective Supervision* (New York: McGraw-Hill Book Company, 1975), p. 95.
9. Willard E. Parker, Robert W. Kleemeier, and Beyer V. Parker, *Front-Line Leadership* (New York: McGraw-Hill Book Company, 1969), p. 249.
10. Ferdinand F. Fournies, *Coaching for Improved Work Performance* (New York: Van Nostrand Reinhold Company, 1978), p. 77.
11. For a discussion on conducting employee evaluations, see, Scott Hutton, "How to Conduct Employee Performance Evaluations," Chapter 6 in *Staff Supervision Made Easy* (Lanham, MD: American Correctional Association, 1998), pp. 51–60.
12. For an excellent discussion of the move from the traditional bureaucratic mindset to the empowerment movement, see, Paul Block, *The Empowered Manager: Positive Political Skills at Work* (San Francisco, CA: Jossey-Bass, Inc., 1990).
13. Nancy Foy, *Empowering People at Work,* (Brookfield, VT: Gower Publishing Limited, 1994), p. 7.
14. Nancy C. Jurik and Russell Winn, "Describing Correctional Security Dropouts and Rejects—An Individual and Organizational Profile," *Criminal Justice and Behavior* 14 (1987): 5–25.
15. William G. Saylor and Kevin N. Wright, "A Comparative Study of the Relationship of Status and Longevity in Determining Perceptions of Work Environment Among Federal Employees," *Journal of Offender Rehabilitation* 17 (1992): pp. 133–160.
16. David Osborne and Ted Gaebler, *Reinventing Government: How the Entrepreneurial Spirit Is Transforming the Public Sector* (Reading, MA: Addison-Wesley, 1992), p. 146.

17. Tepper. p. 7.
18. Phillips and McConnell, pp. 108–109.

▀▀▀ KEY TERMS

supervision	on-the-job training
delegation	coaching
authority	feedback
responsibility	empowerment

▀▀▀ YOU'RE THE CORRECTIONAL ADMINISTRATOR

1. You are a unit manager in a prison, supervising two case managers, two correctional officers, two correctional counselors, and one secretary. You have a very good, dedicated team with generally positive morale. However, one of your case managers has been performing very poorly for the past three months. This case manager has missed several days of work, does not get required tasks completed on time, and regularly complains about more work than is possible to do. The other staff are becoming unhappy about the situation. They regularly have to adjust their schedules to cover in the case manager's absence. They often have to help perform tasks the case manager doesn't complete or to redo them. How do you handle this as the supervisor. Describe the steps you would take to ensure that the case manager performs at expected standards and that the rest of the team continues to perform at a high level.

2. You are a very talented probation officer who is ambitious in your desire for rapid promotion. You want to get ahead as fast as possible; you want your bosses to recognize your talent and consider you for the next probation supervisor job. You are not the most senior officer. There are at least five other officers who have more experience. What can you do to enhance your potential to receive this promotion? Be as specific as possible in creating a list of activities you could take to prepare yourself and come to the attention of the probation administrators who decide on the promotion.

▀▀▀ WEB LINK EXERCISES

National Institute of Corrections Information Center
www.nicic.org/services/info_center

Go to the Web site for the NIC Information Center. Go to the NIC publications database, and search for publications regarding "empowering." Once you get a list, find the article, "What Jail Administrators Can Learn from Community Policing," by Susan McCampbell. Read the section of the article regarding empowering staff. Identify the key obstacles to effective empowerment that McCampbell lists. Which of the other comparisons of jail administrators with community policing techniques do you think are most relevant for staff supervision and empowerment?

CHAPTER 13

The Role of Staff in Corrections

■■ INTRODUCTION

Part 4 of this text examines the critical role that correctional staff play in the functions and mission of a correctional agency. Chapter 11 presents an overview of human resource management, describing the growth in staff numbers; the types of jobs performed by correctional staff; the transition to professionalism; and the activities to recruit, train and develop, and retain staff by correctional agencies. Chapter 12 describes the supervisory functions within corrections, and how it is a difficult, yet critical role, in the management of staff as a resource. Many people think of "corrections" as bars and fences, prison cells, and violent offenders. However, based on these two chapters, students should have an understanding of some of the key activities that must occur in agencies to create the most valuable correctional resource—the staff.

There is no doubt that staff are the most valuable resource of a correctional agency. Corrections is a people business, in that the work is not accomplished by bars and fences, prison cells, or the use of electronic monitoring. The work of corrections is accomplished by people, staff supervising offenders to carry out sentencing orders of the courts, and monitoring and guiding behavior in what will hopefully be a crime free and productive completion of a criminal sentence. In Chapter 11, it was suggested that correctional agencies are responsible for protecting the public; they do so by taking away or severely limiting offenders' freedoms. These activities are critically sensitive and important, and the work of staff who must take these responsibilities requires knowledge, professionalism, training, and ethical behavior.

Students who study corrections are likely to consider a career in corrections or may already be working in corrections but seek to improve their knowledge and opportunities for advancement. Therefore, this chapter describes some of the entry-level jobs of correctional staff, including the roles of correctional officers, counselors or caseworkers, probation or parole officers, or social service workers. It is important for students of corrections to thoroughly understand what these staff do in their jobs, either to consider whether to seek such employment or to be able to effectively administer a correctional agency. As staff advance in their organizations, they are much more effective if they fully understand the role of each staff person. A football quarterback can have exceptional individuals skills, such as running or throwing a football. However, quarterbacks, even with outstanding athletic skills, will be ineffective at moving the team forward toward a touchdown, unless they know the role of every player on every play, and can adjust and modify the play as situations change and the unexpected occurs.

Therefore, this chapter thoroughly describes the actual functions of correctional staff, as well as the considerations, challenges, and stresses that are a part of the job. By the end of this chapter, you should clearly understand what it is to be a correctional officer or a halfway house counselor. You will know some of the critical issues concerning correctional staff. You will recognize the importance of agency culture and leadership in setting the tone for the daily performances of staff. And you will be able to envision some of the future needs and challenges to meet the increasing difficulty of maintaining the effectiveness and efficiency of corrections most valuable resource—correctional staff.

THE IMPORTANCE OF CORRECTIONAL STAFF

It almost goes without saying that correctional staff are important to accomplishing a correctional mission. As noted previously, corrections is a business of people interacting with people. Approximately 85 percent of a correctional agency budget is spent on staff salaries. And, especially over the past decade of the 1900s, there has been a tremendous increase in the number of correctional staff. For all these reasons, when correctional administrators think in a broad way about the profession, they think of staff.

With the public's focus on crime control, a push for stiffer sentencing practices, and the increase in length of prison terms as well as time supervised on probation and parole, the need to increase the number of staff necessary to supervise offenders has dramatically increased. As of January 1, 1998, state and federal correctional agencies employed almost 415,000 prison staff,[1] there were more than 57,000 probation and parole staff,[2] and jails that held 200 or more inmates employed another almost 70,000 staff.[3] Approximately 550,000 people working in corrections represents an unusually large work group. One of the largest industries in the United States is the auto industry. In September, 2000, the United Auto Workers reported approximately 750,000 members, and that includes its international affiliates.[4]

Historically, the role of correctional staff, especially those who worked in prisons, was very narrowly defined and did not attract the most educated or professional staff. In prisons, the custodial staff has always made up the largest group of employees. In fact, in early U.S. prisons, uniformed custodial officers made up almost the entire staff, except for a few clerks and administrators. As an illustration, the

Staff at the United States Penitentiary in Leavenworth, Kansas, c. 1895. During the early years of prisons, almost all of the staff were custodial personnel. (Courtesy of the Federal Bureau of Prisons)

accompanying picture of the staff of the United States Penitentiary in Leavenworth, Kansas in the late 1800s shows only uniformed guards.

Today, individuals who perform custodial work in a prison are called "correctional officers." Until approximately the 1970s, they were referred to as **guards,** because that term implied most of what they were hired to do. The role of guards, also referred to as "turnkeys," was to simply guard inmates, unlock and lock their cells (hence the term turnkeys) when necessary, march inmates from the cell houses to other locations for work or eating, and brutally enforce rules and discipline. Duffee writes, "In the early penitentiary, there was not a great deal of concern about goal conflict among the prison staff. Staffing patterns were rather simple, and guards played a prominent role in both guarding and supervising work."[5] Goffman, in his classic study of the harsh treatment and deleterious effect of imprisonment on inmates, described the great social distance of inmates and staff, which was formally dictated and reinforced.[6]

There was little discretion or decision making required by guards during early prison operations. Cressey even suggests about this simple role, "Most guards have nothing to do but stand guard; they do not use inmates productively any more than they themselves are used productively by prison managers."[7] In a description of the role of prison guards prior to 1970, Jacobs and Crotty write about their work in Statesville (Illinois) prison:

> In the course of a day's work, the guard stationed at the cell house gate is required to open and close the steel-barred cell house. Another guard may distribute medicine, mail, and laundry; answer telephones; and supervise maintenance activities. A third guard is positioned in an enclosed observation post in the middle of the cell house where he can see into every cell. The most important responsibility of the cell house guard is conducting the "count"—determining several times a day if all inmates are accounted for.[8]

The role of custodial staff in modern prisons has changed considerably, even to the point that it is now a misnomer to refer to them as merely "custodial" staff. The contemporary term of **correctional officer,** is more regularly used to describe the complex role of staff who carry out security functions within a prison. The changing role of custodial staff prompted the American Correctional Association (ACA) in 1993 to pass a resolution to encourage the use of the term *correctional officer* rather than guard (see Figure 13–1), because it much better describes their responsibilities of custody and control, which "require extensive interpersonal skills, special training and educations, and . . . correctional personnel are skilled professionals."[9]

Correctional officers face ambiguous and sometimes in-conflict goals, and must be intelligent and well trained. This change in the role of prison security staff evolved for many reasons. Crouch suggests three factors that have changed the work of correctional officers: (1) an increased emphasis on the goal of rehabilitation, (2) growth in the size and changes in the composition of the inmate population, and (3) judicial intervention.[10] Perhaps even more important than these three is the fact that these factors all occurred over approximately the same period of time and interacted with each other in such a way as to almost mandate a new role for correctional officers.

As noted in earlier chapters, during the 1950s and 1960s, prisons began to emphasize the importance of rehabilitation as a correctional goal. As such, many new professionals, including psychologists, educators, and administrators, were brought into the prison environment. As the emphasis on rehabilitation developed, the importance of the overall prison experience on inmates was recognized. This included the interaction of correctional officers with inmates, and officers were therefore trained in interpersonal communications, so they could take on a human service role (discussed later in this chapter) as regards to inmates. In addition, the immigration of professionals sympathetic to the plight of inmates into the prison changed the culture and communications among staff. Previously, the dominant personality

WHEREAS, the duties of correctional personnel whose primary responsibility are custody and control require extensive interpersonal skills, special training and education; and WHEREAS, correctional personnel are skilled professionals; and WHEREAS, the term "guard" produces a false and negative image; THEREFORE BE IT RESOLVED that the American Correctional Association adopt the term "correctional officer" as the official language in all Association publications, meetings, events and communications to describe custodial/security personnel; and THEREFORE BE IT FURTHER RESOLVED that the Association actively promote the use of the term "correctional officer" and discourage the use of the word "guard" by the media, general public, educational institutions and publishers.

FIGURE 13–1   ACA's resolution on the term *correctional officer.*
Source: "Resolution on the Term 'Correctional Officer.' " *Corrections Today* (April 1993): 60, 146.

style of staff was machismo and authoritarianism. Even though this style continued with many correctional officers, those who wanted to adopt a more helping style found support for their approach.

The 1980s brought the beginning of the prison construction boom, with dramatic increases in the number of prisoners, and the number of prisons and staff to operate them. As many prisons became overcrowded, officers often felt overworked, frustrated, and in fear of losing control. Totally outnumbered, the authoritarian style was less effective, and staff who were good communicators gained better compliance of inmates and maintained order while completing their responsibilities. Both the move to rehabilitation and the increase in the use of prisons as criminal sanctions created frustration and some uncertainty in the role of correctional officers, and many officers became more punitive, "to the extent that they assault or misuse disciplinary action against inmates."[11] Prison administrators, therefore, focused their hiring practices on officers with good communication skills who were comfortable working with the multiple goals of custody and rehabilitation.

With the disappearance of the hands-off doctrine, federal courts began to examine many aspects of the prison environment and the overall conditions of confinement. Judicial decisions often dictated certain requirements or practices within the operation of prisons. Many correctional officers and prison administrators believed this intervention undermined their control of prisons and overall prison security. However, the courts were not to be deterred, and judicial intervention in prison operations continued extensively into the early 1990s. The effect was that those correctional officers who could not work in an environment of judicial intervention retired or found other jobs. Newly hired officers accepted the involvement by federal courts in prison operations and found they could work comfortably in a prison setting that emphasized staff–inmate interaction and communication.

To describe the changing role of contemporary correctional officers, Johnson suggests, "In the prison, the skills that matter are human relations and human service skills. These are the skills that can be used to develop relationships and hence to reduce tension, defuse crises, and conduct daily business in a civilized (and potentially civilizing) manner."[12] Not only has the role of correctional workers changed but also college educated individuals, minorities, and women have been recruited into correctional positions in much greater numbers. All of these developments have changed the current and future outlook for corrections.

The importance of staff on the correctional environment dovetails closely with the recognition of the importance of management and leadership. Early prisons were simple to manage through strict discipline and enforcement of rules on both staff and inmates. Today, prison order is more involved with fairness and equity, leadership and empowerment, and organization and management. As suggested by DiIulio,

> The answer to be offered . . . is that the quality of prison life varies according to the quality of prison management. The evidence will lead us to the conclusion that prison management is the strategic variable, one that may be subject to change with predictable and desirable consequences.[13]

Throughout this chapter, there is an examination of the role of various correctional staff, issues affecting staffing, and the importance of management and leadership in making a difference in the future of corrections.

THE CORRECTIONAL OFFICER

The first job function to be examined is that of the correctional officer. The segment of the criminal justice system with the most rapid growth has been institutional corrections, and the largest job category in an institution is that of correctional officer. Of the 415,000 staff working for state and federal correctional agencies that operated prisons on January 1, 1998, almost 240,000 were uniformed correctional officers.[14] When jail staff are included, there are more than 330,000 correctional officers in the United States. With the increasing number of new prisons, the opening of many private prisons and jails, and the need to replace individuals who retire or find other work, a need for correctional officers is expected to remain for the foreseeable future.

Unfortunately, many individuals who receive a two- or four-year college degree do not seriously consider correctional officer positions. They often think of correctional officers as unskilled, poorly paid, and not using their education. However, as previously noted, the role of correctional officers has changed, education and good decision-making skills are important, and the pay has become more competitive in order to keep positions filled and maintain quality staff. Also, many correctional agencies have officer positions as the entry level for all employees, recognizing the value of this experience in learning security and developing skills in managing inmates. Promotions or selection of staff for other professional positions, such as caseworkers, counselors, or teachers, are often based on the current pool of correctional officers.

What Correctional Officers Do

Although the role of correctional officers has changed considerably over the past 30 years, there are still some basics that remain true about the position. Correctional officers are responsible for overseeing individuals who are detained in jail while awaiting trial or who have been convicted of a crime and are serving a sentence in prison. Their basic responsibility is to maintain order and contribute to the secure operation of the institution. As such, officers are assigned and oversee various sections of an institution, such as a housing unit, yard or compound, perimeter fence, or inmate work or program area. Prisons and jails usually have written policies and procedures (post orders) for the operations of these areas, and correctional officers' first responsibility is to carry out the prescribed duties of their post orders. Lombardo identifies seven basic roles or areas of responsibility for correctional officers:

- Living unit officers supervise inmate housing areas.
- Work detail officers oversee inmate work assignments.
- Industrial shop and school officers control and provide security to these areas.
- Yard officers supervise inmate movement and maintain accountability.

▌ Administration building assignments perform office functions.

▌ Perimeter security is maintained through armed surveillance.

▌ Relief officers fill in when others have days off.[15]

There are many tedious and detailed functions that must occur in the maintenance of security and order. For instance, officers must control doors and grills, and lock and unlock them to allow only approved inmate movement. Officers must search inmates and areas, because constant efforts to find contraband such as drugs and weapons is a key element of security. Officers must conduct "inmate counts," (described in Chapter 8), in order to maintain inmate accountability and prevent escapes. Officers ensure inmates obey rules and initiate disciplinary action when they do not. And officers must oversee inmate work crews, such as those assigned sanitation responsibilities, and ensure that the inmate crew performs the work at the accepted standard. Although some prospective officers may find these details of the job unexciting and uninteresting, they are basics that must be accomplished.

There are many other challenging roles for correctional officers. According to Carlson, Hess, and Orthmann, "The correctional officer is also a disciplinarian, link between inmates and other staff, behavioral manager, environment setter, dispute settler, educator and consultant."[16] This provides an excellent example of how an officer may feel role conflict or ambiguity. It is difficult to never show favoritism in handing out discipline or enforcing prison rules or policy. Yet, many of these roles require understanding, communications, and recognizing the individualism of every inmate. Less successful correctional officers are those who show favoritism under the guise of treating each inmate as an individual.

The responsibilities of modern-day correctional officers are broad and challenging. The challenges stem from the fact that correctional officers must maintain order and gain compliance from offenders who are incarcerated against their will

Correctional Officer Escorting Handcuffed Inmate. The first responsibility of correctional officers is to maintain the security of the prison. (Courtesy of the Federal Bureau of Prisons)

and who have a natural inclination to resent those who try to control them. Jacobs and Kraft describe the situation as "structured conflict."[17] Some uninformed about the operations of prisons have difficulty understanding why gaining compliance is not an easy task, because "inmates are in prison and have to follow the rules." However, if staff have to make inmates comply with rules, by resorting to disciplinary action or using force on a regular basis, prisons become the tense, violent, and dangerous world that these people envision. Effective correctional officers and other prison staff gain compliance by communicating expectations, fairly enforcing rules, and treating inmates with respect and dignity. Officers who constantly "write up inmates" for insubordination or failure to follow an order usually do not last long on the job, because they are not respected by either staff or inmates.

One of the responsibilities that makes the job of correctional officers difficult is contributing to the rehabilitation of offenders. As corrections moved away from the strict authoritarian management of prisons toward a setting balancing the correctional goals of punishment and treatment, there were concerns over the proper contribution of correctional officers to the treatment aspects for prisoners. Most administrators agree correctional officers play a role in treatment, but it is difficult to determine how this role should be integrated into the daily duties of officers. To resolve this issue, a few correctional agencies began to consider correctional officers as part of the treatment team and expected them to be aware of inmates' treatment programs, even, at times, to provide counseling for offenders. However, asking officers to move very far away from their traditional custody and security responsibilities was seen as a loss of control by some, and as an unworkable conflict by others.

Throughout the 1960s and 1970s, correctional officers' requirements to contribute to both the custody and treatment aspects within prisons caused confusion. This conflict in roles is described by Freeman:

> The dual roles of custody and treatment create a role conflict for the correctional officer. Although the central goal of an officer's custody role is well defined (maintaining order and security), the central goal of the treatment role (assisting in the rehabilitation of the inmate) entails flexibility, the use of discretionary justice, and the ability to secure inmate compliance through informal exchange relationships that deviate from the written rules. Knowing which rules can be bent, how far they may be bent, and under which circumstances they may be bent is not always apparent or understood by the officer.[18]

This description of officers' struggles with how far to "bend the rules" to recognize and treat inmates as individuals is not acceptable to most correctional administrators. According to correctional administrators, correctional officers should not bend the rules, because once they begin to do so, they lose their ability to maintain required rules or standards for other inmates. The conflict of custody and treatment is evident in the fact that there are dozens of situations in correctional officers' days that do not fit any rule or policy, and officers must use their own discretion in deciding how to handle them. An inmate may tell an officer he or she is depressed about something that happened at home. An officer may see two inmates in a mildly heated argument. An officer may find an inmate has nuisance contraband (property not allowed, yet not dangerous, such as too many magazines or more than the allowable number of packs of cigarettes). How to handle these issues is not always spelled out in prison policies, nor are they always addressed in a rule. In these types of situations, correctional officers must recognize their custodial roles, yet they can use their knowledge of individual inmates in deciding how to handle each situation.

Today, most correctional agencies have clarified the conflicting roles of custody and treatment by establishing a realistic and practical role for officers in the rehabilitation of inmates. This role includes three aspects: (1) contributing to an environment of control without threats and tension, (2) communicating with inmates on a professional basis, and (3) focusing on providing human services. None of these three requires the officer to be a counselor or treatment specialist. Officers contribute to the rehabilitative aspect by the manner in which they conduct themselves and do their jobs, not by trying to befriend or advise inmates about personal problems.

Perhaps more than any other staff, correctional officers impact the tone and environment of a prison. Officers contribute to the overall prison setting by carrying out their security activities, such as searches for contraband and maintaining inmate accountability, in a thorough and constant manner. By doing so, inmates realize that staff control the prison, and they do not have to be overly concerned with their personal safety or join a gang for protection. They can relax and become involved in rehabilitative programs without fear of looking weak to other inmates or appearing to be **snitches** (inmates believed by other inmates to cooperate with staff by giving them information regarding misbehavior by other inmates) because they spend time talking to staff.

The approach that officers take in communicating to inmates also contributes to the rehabilitation of inmates. Recall the case study in Chapter 8 about Officer Dillion and the type of communication he had with inmates. His style of dealing with inmates certainly set a tone in his institution, a tone that created bitterness and poor

Correctional Officer Discussing an Issue with an Inmate. Correctional officers must constantly communicate with inmates. Although they are not counselors, listening to inmate concerns and problems helps ease tension and blurs the line between custody and treatment personnel. (Courtesy of the Federal Bureau of Prisons)

communication between staff and inmates. For a prison to have effective rehabilitation programs as well as to maintain order and control, there must be an overall environment of respect for inmates as individuals. As counseling or educational staff
work with inmates to acknowledge their problems and take steps to solve them, any
progress they make can be easily undermined by an overly authoritarian style of custodial staff such as Officer Dillion.

Correctional officers' roles in offender rehabilitation involve providing "human
services." A variety of authors conclude that a human services role is beyond what is
usually expected of correctional officers,[19] and there is still a lack of clarity as to what
is expected of officers in this regard. Johnson and Toch note that providing inmates
with human services, "should not be confused with providing treatment."[20] Whereas
treatment is proactive, the officers' human service role is usually reactive. For instance, an inmate who may not be able to talk to a counselor or prison psychologist
tells a correctional officer about problems the inmate's family is experiencing. An
inmate may not have been able to get to the laundry to pick up clean sheets and
needs some help or intervention by the officer to resolve the issue over the weekend
when the laundry is not open. A correctional officer, acting in a human services role,
may contact a counselor or psychologist about the inmate experiencing family problems or may ask a supervisor if clean sheets can be provided for the inmate. These
basic, yet sympathetic, responses to real issues in the lives of inmates are considered
the appropriate human services role of correctional officers.

Although correctional officers spend their days maintaining order and providing security, the manner in which they perform their tasks and communicate with
inmates has a major impact on the overall prison environment. A brusk and harsh
manner, an unwillingness to recognize genuine inmate issues, or a lack of respect
for inmates creates an environment with constant tension between inmates and staff.
However, a fair and impartial upholding of prison rules, a pleasant personality, a respect for individual dignity, and an understanding of correctional officers' role in
prisoner rehabilitation, contribute to a relaxed environment with positive interaction between staff and inmates. The role of correctional officer has moved well beyond that of guarding inmates; it now requires knowledge, training, good interpersonal communications, and sound decision making.

Correctional Officer Pay and Requirements

Although the salary for correctional officers is still relatively low, it has increased
steadily throughout the 1990s. As reported in the *Corrections Yearbook, 1998,* the average starting salary for correctional officers on January 1, 1990, was $17,521, and it
increased to $21,088 on January 1, 1998.[21] New correctional officers usually receive
two very quick raises, one as they complete training and another as they finish probation; therefore, starting salary may increase by approximately $2,000 within the
first few months of hire.

The base salaries for correctional officers do not include what officers can usually make by working **overtime,** additional pay received for working more hours than
the typical 40 hours per week. With staff vacations, sick leave, or the need for additional staff for prisoner escorts or to respond to emergencies, most officers are required to work some overtime, and they can easily add 15 to 20 percent to their an-

nual pay level. Some officers who regularly volunteer for additional work increase their base salary by as much as 30 percent.

To be hired as a correctional officer, candidates must usually have completed high school, have some experience in law enforcement or the military, and have no criminal convictions. Even though most correctional agencies still have relatively low requirements for the position of correctional officer, these positions have become very competitive, and candidates selected usually have qualifications well beyond the minimum requirements. Advanced qualifications are also important for promotion within correctional agencies. Williamson writes that, "Though entry level requirements are still comparatively low in some places, advancement often requires higher education, commitment to professional values, and exemplary performance."[22]

During the screening of correctional officer candidates and the selection process, some agencies do psychological testing, and others do extensive interviews to determine whether there are ethical issues in the candidates background (recent drug use, financial problems, or unfavorable termination from a job) that may indicate the possibility of a candidate being compromised by inmates. Most agencies also conduct an interview to determine the candidates' interpersonal skills and decision-making abilities. Camp and Camp reported that as of January 1, 1998, 11 agencies performed drug tests on all employee applicants, and 34 agencies performed drug tests on all correctional officer applicants.[23]

As corrections has become more complex, and as more correctional agencies look toward promotion and filling of other professional jobs from the ranks of correctional officers, education at the entry level for officers has become more important. Williamson notes,

> The past 20 to 25 years of research and correctional activity has created an increasingly complex body of knowledge. Extended periods of education—for example, bachelor's and master's degrees—are becoming more important as selection criteria and/or practical requirements for promotion and professional advancement.[24]

Raising the educational requirement for hiring correctional officers is being reconsidered because the job complexity requires it and because it will result in an increase in professionalism. A recent survey identified 15 correctional agencies (14 states and the Federal Bureau of Prisons) that require some college courses or a two-year degree for consideration as a correctional officer.[25] There is usually no requirement for a specific college major, because correctional agencies believe that the exposure to higher education with any topic of study improves individuals' maturity, decision making, ability to prioritize, and understanding of diversity.

As individuals consider a career in criminal justice, they should think about the opportunity for promotion and professional advancement. There has never been a better time in the history of corrections to acquire an entry-level job and move up in an organization. Many correctional officers with two- or four-year college degrees decide they like correctional security work and apply for promotions in correctional services departments. Others seek advancement through moves to another career track, such as teachers, social workers, or casemanagers. In most state and federal prisons, there are qualified candidates for these upper-level positions already employed as correctional officers, and therefore, job vacancies are never advertised or applicants accepted outside the available prison staff.

Guard on Duty at the U.S. Penitentiary, McNeil Island, Washington, c. 1909. The role of correctional officers has changed considerably since the time when they simply watched inmates, guarded doors, and "keyed" locks. Today, correctional officer roles are complex, requiring education, training, and good interpersonal skills. (Courtesy of the Federal Bureau of Prisons)

Employment as a correctional officer is challenging and rewarding. It is an excellent opportunity for entry to a correctional career, and correctional officer work builds a foundation of knowledge and skills that will improve an individual's performance in other prison jobs. The role of correctional officers has changed considerably over the past 25 years, and agencies are responding with increased salaries and increased requirements for hiring. Recently, college graduates are realizing the excellent career opportunities that are available by becoming a correctional officer, and the number of college-educated applicants received for these positions continues to increase.

▰ THE COUNSELOR OR CASEWORKER

Another position in prisons that is often considered as an entry-level job for recent college graduates is that of a counselor or **caseworker** (also called social worker in some agencies). These are professional positions in correctional agencies that are responsible for working directly with inmates to create a plan for program and work participation throughout the period of confinement, and in preparation for release. Fox suggests,

> Casework includes professional services in (1) obtaining case histories and descriptions, (2) solving immediate problems involving family and personal relationships, (3) exploring long-range problems of social adjustment, (4) providing supportive guidance for inmates about to be released, and (5) providing supportive guidance and professional assistance to probationers and parolees.[26]

Caseworkers often work as part of a team with prison educators, mental health professionals, and substance abuse counselors to create treatment plans and monitor inmates' progress toward their goals. Some casework staff actually perform counseling, but in most state and federal prisons, their principle role is to guide inmates through all aspects of their prison sentence, including the legal sanction and expectation for release, an understanding of their individual treatment needs, and the availability of prison programs to meet these needs. Caseworkers can also act as liaisons with services outside the prison (job assistance, family counseling, or halfway house agencies) to assist inmates in their prison-to-community transition.

Casework duties usually require good interpersonal, decision making, and writing skills. Although some states do not require a college degree for casework positions, most states find that completion of college is highly beneficial. When a college degree is required, the college major varies with the specifics of casework duties. According to Williamson, "The primary determinants of educational requirements are the specific job description and the states in which they are located."[27] If caseworkers do a considerable amount of therapeutic treatment themselves, they may be required to possess a clinical degree in mental health or social work. When their work is primarily as liaisons to other resources, there may be no single major specified, although a four-year degree with a certain amount of hours in sociology or social work is usually recommended. Although the salary for most state or federal casework jobs is usually 15 to 20 percent higher than the starting pay for a correctional officer, caseworkers usually have less opportunity to earn additional overtime pay.

THE PROBATION OR PAROLE OFFICER

Probation and parole officers supervise inmates at the two ends of the sentencing continuum (incarceration being in the middle). However, the work is very similar for the two jobs. **Probation officers** supervise offenders with a suspended prison sentence, monitoring their behavior in the community, and their compliance with the conditions of their probation and suspended prison sentence. **Parole officers** supervise inmates who have been conditionally released from prison and returned to the community. Similarly, parole officers monitor released inmates' behavior and compliance with the conditions of their release. Both probation and parole officers' primary responsibility is to supervise these offenders with "conditional" placement in the community, enforce the rules governing their supervision, and report any violation to the body that authorized their community placement and placed conditions on their behavior (the court for probation, and the parole board for parole).

Even though the number of offenders in prisons has grown considerably during the past two decades of the twentieth century, probation and parole continue to play significant roles in the criminal justice system. As reported in *The Corrections Yearbook, 1998,* there were more than 2.5 million offenders under active supervision by state correctional agencies on January 1, 1998.[28] There are at least another million offenders on probation supervised by county correctional agencies. Of those supervised by state agencies, there were 1,979,088 on probation, 493,933 on parole, and

132,644 under the supervision of a state that combines probation and parole populations, in which records do not distinguish between the two statuses. The same agencies reported employing 26,014 probation staff, 10,336 parole staff, and 20,967 staff in a combined probation and parole function (a total of 57,317) on January 1, 1998.[29] During 1997, the average caseload per officer was 175 for probation, 69 for parole, and 93 for combined probation and parole.[30] These averages may be misleading, however, because the probation caseloads range from 60 in Arizona to 900 in California, whereas parole caseloads ranged from 30 in West Virginia to 144 in the District of Columbia.

Probation and parole officers usually require college degrees, and important skills include those similar to a prison caseworker, such as good interpersonal communication, decision-making skills, and writing skills. Carlson, Hess, and Orthmann note, "A significant part of a probation or parole officer's job involves understanding human nature, something that cannot be learned in a classroom."[31] Probation and parole officers serve as agents of the court or the parole board, and their decisions and recommendations can lead to the loss of offenders' freedom and placement in or return to prison. It is important for probation and parole officers to recognize the legal due process rights for offenders, and the legal nature of their jobs and their written reports support the fact that most agencies require at least an undergraduate college degree.

Probation and parole officers operate much more independently, or with less supervision, than most prison staff. Probation and parole officers are trained in the techniques for supervising offenders and then assigned a case load. Their daily activities are much less regimented than the routine of prison work, and they must manage their time and create their own work plans. They schedule their day to include meeting with offenders in the probation or parole office, contacting employers and law enforcement agencies, making home or workplace visits, and conducting urine tests for drug use. A Missouri probation officer states, "No one tells me how to spend my day. They expect me to manage my case load within the policies and guidelines of the state. I, as closely as possible, monitor the activities of my case load, and must report any violations of the conditions to the court or to the parole board."[32]

Pay for probation and parole officers also varies considerably. Entry-level pay for a probation officer in West Virginia or a parole officer in South Carolina is slightly more than $20,000 per year, with a maximum salary for a federal probation officer at more than $57,000 as of January 1, 1998.[33] Table 13–1 illustrates the entry, average, and highest salary for probation, parole, or combined probation and parole officers as of January 1, 1998.

A controversial issue regarding probation and parole officers is the carrying of firearms. Some agencies require, others permit, and still others do not allow officers to carry firearms. Officers must make home and employment visits in the neighborhoods in which offenders live. These areas are not always safe, especially for individuals who are easily identified as some type of law enforcement officer. Also, officers must often inform offenders that they will be recommending their revocation, which could result in imprisonment. It is easy to imagine how uncomfortable an officer would be in an offender's home, informing him or her of a recommendation for sending the offender to prison, or actually taking him or her into custody pending the revocation decision.

▬▬ **TABLE 13–1**

Probation and Parole Officers' Starting, Average, and Maximum Salaries, January 1, 1998			
Averages	**Entry Salary**	**Average Salary**	**Highest Salary**
Probation	$26,014	$34,396	$46,325
Parole	27,888	34,190	42,441
Combined	24,410	32,145	43,066
Average	25,821	33,318	43,795

Source: Adapted from Camille Graham Camp and George M. Camp, *Corrections Yearbook, 1998* (Middletown, CT: The Criminal Justice Institute, 1998), p. 202.

Although this scenario makes it seem obvious that officers should carry a weapon, many agencies do not want, or even allow, their officers to take offenders into custody, and the agencies advise officers how to avoid dangerous situations such as the one described. Many probation and parole agencies believe that if officers carry weapons they are perceived dramatically different than as counselors or advisors to guide offenders into treatment and self-help programs. Over the past two decades, there has been a philosophical move from casework to surveillance by officers; the caseloads include more dangerous offenders, and there is evidence (or at least a perception) that acts of violence against officers is increasing. In a 1993 study by the Federal Probation and Pretrial Officers Association, it was discovered that there was a significant number of assaults and even murders of officers in the line of duty. The survey revealed more than 2,600 violent acts against officers from 1980 to 1993. Table 13–2 lists the violent acts against officers in the line of duty.

There is no standard policy for probation and parole agencies regarding carrying weapons, and even officers themselves are not in agreement as to whether they should be armed. Champion reports that 59 percent of officers believe they should have the option to carry a firearm on the job, yet 80 percent of female and 69 percent of male officers disagree that they should be required to carry a firearm.[34] Some states classify probation and parole officers as peace officers and grant them the authority to carry a firearm both on and off duty. It seems perhaps the best policy regarding officers' carrying of weapons is that established by the American Probation and Parole Association (APPA), which in 1994, adopted a weapons "position statement." Essentially, APPA does not support or oppose officers' carrying weapons but suggests the decision should be based on the need, officer safety demands, and local laws and policies.[35]

▬▬ THE COMMUNITY RESIDENTIAL STAFF

Many offenders in the community need more than standard probation or parole supervision to avoid further criminality and to become productive citizens. For those without resources (jobs, a place to live, finances) or those who need more structured or regular supervision, residential community centers or halfway houses serve an

▦ **TABLE 13–2**

Violence Against Probation and Parole Officers, 1980–1993	
Murder or attempted murder	16
Rape or attempted rape	7
Other sexual assaults	100
Shot or wounded or attempts	32
Use or attempted use of blunt instrument or projectile	60
Slashed or stabbed or attempt	28
Car used as weapon or attempt	12
Punched, kicked, choked	1,396
Use or attempted use of caustic substances	3
Use or attempted use of incendiary device	9
Abduction or attempt	3
Attempted or actual unspecified assaults	944
Total	**2,610**

Source: Phillip J. Bigger, "Officers in Danger: Results of the Federal Probation and Pretrial Services Association's National Study on Serious Assaults," *APPA Perspectives* 17 (1993): 14–20.

important function. **Halfway houses** serve offenders on probation, parole, work release, or any other legal status. Offenders placed at halfway houses stay there from a few days to several months. The halfway house provides food, shelter, supervision, and treatment services. McCarthy lists the following as the goals of a community residential center:

▌ To assist in the reintegration of offenders.
▌ To reduce or ease overcrowding in jails or prisons.
▌ To reduce correctional costs by providing a cost-effective intermediate sanction.
▌ To provide an appropriate setting for the treatment of substance abuse problems.[36]

Community residential programs offer good opportunities for employment for individuals who want to work with offenders in the real-life setting of the community rather than in a prison. The centers usually have little physical security and are very similar in design and construction to a boarding house or a small hotel. They do, however, have around-the-clock staff who supervise the facility and perform some of the functions of correctional officers. These staff may be called program monitors or correctional assistants. These staff maintain inmate accountability by enforcing sign-in and sign-out procedures as offenders come and go from the center and conduct counts of offenders. They also search for drugs or other prohibited materials. They enforce the overall rules of the center and can initiate disciplinary action for offenders who violate the rules. Program monitors or correctional assistants are usually paraprofessionals, and do not require a significant amount of education and experience. They are often filled by part-time or temporary staff, and as such, are excellent jobs for college students to gain experience in working with offenders.

Halfway houses also employ counseling and treatment staff. The roles of these staff are extremely varied, because they deal with both the practical problems of community living and the more complex treatment needs of offenders. Halfway house counselors work with offenders to address all areas of community living, such as family counseling, job searches, transportation, and liaison to other social service agencies. They may also do counseling in substance abuse, or conduct classes regarding parenting or job interviewing skills. Although most halfway house counselors find their jobs very challenging, they usually also enjoy the jobs, because they do a variety of things and never know from day to day the types of issues they will have to confront.

The requirements for halfway house counselor positions are similar to those of a probation or parole officer or a prison caseworker, usually requiring a college degree with several curriculum hours in social work or sociology. Most halfway houses are operated by the private sector, most are nonprofit, and most had their originations with a church or religious organization. Perhaps because of their history of service, salaries are usually low, and there is considerable turnover of staff in both the paraprofessional monitors and the counselor positions. Even with the low pay and challenging work, these positions provide excellent experience, opportunities for staff to develop a variety of skills, and excellent opportunities to network with other criminal justice and social service agencies.

Group Home in the Bronx, New York. Jobs in halfway houses, or community residential centers, are challenging. There is little physical security, offenders must learn to avoid criminal behavior while living in the community, and staff play a dual role of custody and treatment. (Courtesy of the New York City Department of Juvenile Justice)

GENDER AND RACE ISSUES IN CORRECTIONAL STAFFING

This section examines the significant issues of gender and race regarding staffing of correctional agencies. Earlier in this book, the importance of staff diversity in a correctional environment was addressed. The problems resulting from a lack of staff diversity became expressly clear after the riot in the New York State Penitentiary in Attica in 1971. One of the problems identified as a cause of the riot was the guarding of urban, African American, and Hispanic inmates by rural white staff, who were separated by culture, mistrust, and a lack of communication. Soon thereafter, correctional agencies began to recruit minorities as correctional officers and other professional staff, with a goal of having a workforce more representative of the inmates or offender clients served.

It is probably not surprising to many that only within the past two decades women have been accepted as equally able to perform as men correctional officers while working with male prisoners. When they hear that women work in male prisons, many people express surprise, thinking it may be too dangerous, that male inmates would prey on women officers, and that women would be unable to effectively supervise male inmates showering and sleeping. Corrections management realized that differences in culture and race between staff and the inmate population needed to be addressed by the explosive situation at Attica. However, the pressure to bring women into the male prison environment was the result of several legal decisions and the desire of women correctional staff for equal employment and advancement opportunities.

Women as Correctional Officers

Historically, people did not believe that women could perform effectively and safely as correctional officers in male prisons. Arguments against female correctional officers included, "(1) women weren't strong enough, (2) their presence would be disruptive to prison operations (inmates would not follow their orders or would fight for their attention and (3) the privacy of male inmates would have to be violated."[37] Many prisons employed women but only in traditional roles of clerks, secretaries, and other noninmate contact positions.

With the passage of the 1964 Civil Rights Act, as amended in 1972, women received the legal right to seek employment as correctional officers in male prisons, because Title VII proscribes employment discrimination on the basis of race, religion, sex, and national origin. Thereafter, several cases were quickly filed by women with the Equal Employment Opportunity Commission (EEOC) claiming discrimination on the basis of sex by several criminal justice agencies. Most correctional agencies hesitated in hiring women into these correctional officer positions in male prisons, believing that it would be considered an acceptable exception to the act. A provision of Title VII states that some discriminatory practices might be allowed if there is "a **bona fide occupational qualification [BFOQ]** reasonably necessary to the normal operation of that particular business or enterprise."(emphasis added)[38]

This exception occurred in 1977, when the U.S. Supreme Court decided the case of *Dothard v. Rawlinson*.[39] Rawlinson was a woman who desired a position of correctional officer in an Alabama male prison, but Alabama prohibited women in prisoner contact positions with male inmates. The Court ruled that a BFOQ against women correctional officers was allowable because of the deplorable conditions of the Alabama prisons and the presence of predatory male sex offenders as inmates. However, the Court did not address the important issue of privacy for inmates. In a 1979 case (*Gunther v. Iowa*), a federal court did consider an employers claim for privacy of inmates.[40] The U.S. District Court of Iowa, in deciding the *Gunther* case, did not find the same predatory environment in a medium security Iowa prison that was believed to exist in the *Dothard* case within a maximum security Alabama prison. In addition, the court determined that inmate privacy was not a valid reason to refuse to hire women as correctional officers, and that the state could create staffing and assignment patterns to avoid infringing on inmate privacy. After the *Gunther* decision, correctional agencies had few legal grounds to challenge the hiring of female correctional officers, and many quickly moved to do so.

Although women are still underrepresented as correctional officers compared to men, their numbers have been increasing, and today they represent a significant percentage of the uniformed staff of most correctional agencies. Camp and Camp report that the percentage of female uniformed staff increased from 16.1 percent in 1990 to 19.1 percent in 1998.[41] There has historically been an assumption that women would have different attitudes and carry out their duties differently from their male counterparts. However, several studies have found no, or only minor, differences in relation to the attitudes and job performance of women compared to men.[42]

Most correctional agencies believe there are many benefits to having women as a significant portion of the correctional workforce. The greatest benefit has been the belief that female supervision style brings a calming and normalizing influence to a prison. According to Pollock,

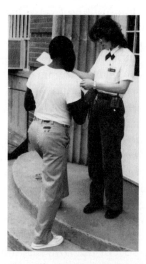

Female Correctional Officer Performing Her Duties. Although there was significant hesitancy to allow women to work as correctional officers in male prisons, women are today fully integrated into almost every correctional environment. (Courtesy of the Federal Bureau of Prisons)

Women officers tend to ask inmates to do things rather than tell them. Female correctional officers foster personal interest in the inmate and use the relationships they develop as a technique of control. This relieves some of the tension found in prisons for men and encourages male prisoners to interact with correctional officers rather than cultivating isolation and separate subcultures.[43]

Other authors agree, and even note, "Women in corrections have demonstrated their ability to meet or exceed the required levels of performance."[44] At this point, women are fully integrated into the workforce. Open-minded correctional administrators accept them as able to perform the role of correctional officers in male prisons, yet some of the stereotypes still exist, and other officers and supervisors sometimes still think the women need protection or cannot handle the more difficult assignments. Even though these perceptions are not based on fact, it may be several years before women officers are treated equally in terms of assignments and promotions, and are respected as much as their male counterparts.

Minority Correctional Staff

As noted earlier, the riot at the Attica prison brought to light the need for a diverse workforce in prisons, which to some extent mirrors the inmate population in ethnic and racial makeup. Having a diverse workforce reduces the opportunity of minority inmates to claim racism as an element to decisions made and actions taken by nonminority staff. Although staff of different ethnic or racial background can effectively communicate with inmates, the presence of large numbers of minority staff reduces tension and opens lines of communications that might not otherwise exist between staff and inmates.

The situation prior to the Attica riot, with a large percentage of white staff at most prisons, was not believed to be the result of racist hiring practices by correctional agencies. The issue resulted from a lack of understanding and sensitivity to the importance of minority staff working in the prisons, and the fact that the rural location of most prisons resulted in the pool of applicants for most prison jobs being rural and white. Historically, prisons were not desired by most communities, and were, therefore, usually located in the country where they would be seen by and offend the fewest number of citizens. In addition, the design of prisons usually requires a considerable amount of acreage, which is not often available in urban locations. With the realization of the need for more workforce diversity during the 1970s, most correctional agencies began minority recruitment efforts and attempted to expand their recruitment base to reach urban areas within a reasonable commuting distance of the rural prisons. The difficult economic times during the early 1980s made prison jobs more attractive, and most correctional agencies were able to significantly increase their number of minority staff. As of January, 1, 1998, there were 30.2 percent nonwhite, uniformed staff working in state and federal prisons.[45]

Even with the support of the administration, new minority staff hired at these rural prisons were not easily accepted. Some white staff believed that the nonwhite, urban officers were more proinmate and less trustworthy, and the white staff did not accept them easily.[46] A study in the late 1980s suggests nonwhites experience more stress than white officers and that African American officers are more likely

to quit their jobs than white officers, primarily because of conflicts with their supervisors.[47] Just as inmates become bitter and perceive many actions as racist when
the workforce is not diverse, minority staff may have some of the same feelings
when they represent a small minority of the staff and do not feel fully accepted into
their workplace.

It has been argued that the best solution to the challenge of recruiting minorities for prison work is to build prisons in urban areas rather than the traditional rural locations. However, this presents many difficulties. It is not only hard to find
enough space in urban areas to build prisons, but also neighbors to a proposed
prison site usually argue against the prison, fearing an increase in crime, danger from
escapes, and reduced property values. Although none of these factors have resulted
from locating a prison in a neighborhood, it is very difficult to get a neighborhood to
accept the risk, and when there is community opposition, most elected officials will
not try to convince their constituents to build a prison in their neighborhood.

One exception to this is the now-deceased C. J. McLin, a member of the Ohio
House of Representatives for more than 20 years from a predominantly African
American district in Dayton, Ohio. McLin, the leader of the Black Elected Democrats of Ohio (BEDO), very early recognized the importance of minority staff in a
prison. However, he also recognized the economic value of a prison to a community,
including the hiring of local residents and purchasing from local businesses. When
Ohio passed a $500 million prison construction bill in the early 1980s, McLin had
written in that many of the prisons would be located within the city limits of many
of Ohio's largest cities, including Dayton.

He then took the bold step of publicly stating he wanted the Dayton prison located in the district he represented. Even though many of his constituents disagreed
with McLin and threatened to work against him in the next election, he continued

Basic Training: Preparing to Work in Ohio Prisons. Diversity of a correctional
workforce is critical to the accomplishment of the mission. This basic training
class in Ohio reflects their success in recruiting a diverse workforce. (Courtesy of
the Ohio Department of Rehabilitation and Correction)

to speak in favor of the prison and actively encouraged his constituents to accept the prison. In the end, the Dayton Correctional Institution was built in the district represented by McLin. Soon after the prison opened, the local community recognized that McLin was right. The Dayton Correctional Institution was the first of Ohio's prisons to be accredited by the American Correctional Association. Crime rates did not increase, there have been no escapes, and property values actually increased. And, the Dayton prison hired many local residents, and more than 50 percent of its employees are minorities. Unfortunately, there are very few elected officials with the determination and commitment of Representative C. J. McLin, who will support an unpopular position and risk losing votes and potentially even losing an election, for an issue they believe is right.[48]

SETTING THE TONE: THE IMPORTANCE OF LEADERSHIP

In this section, we examine the importance of management and leadership for a correctional agency. No matter how talented, experienced, and educated the staff are, without proper leadership to set a tone and establish standards, a correctional organization's performance will deteriorate. According to Wright,

> When one enters a facility (prison) for the first time, it does not take long to determine the quality of management. An unused mop leaning against the wall in the entry way lets you know that the institution lacks administrative attention to detail . . . hallways may be dank and dark, with walls in need of painting and floors not recently shined. In poorly run prisons, inmates mill around with no particular destination or work to do. You hear shouts, insults, and incessant testing of one another. Violence occurs routinely and inmates easily acquire drugs and alcohol. Low-quality management produces depressed staff morale and low job-satisfaction. Professional pride among the staff and hope among the inmates rarely develops in poorly run prisons.[49]

What can correctional administrators do to set a tone or "show" leadership in a correctional agency? Is leadership evident when an individual manages authoritatively, making all decisions and barking orders constantly? Is leadership the ability to take charge when a riot occurs? Is leadership making staff get approval for any initiative they believe would better the prison operation? Most correctional administrators would say no, none of these examples explain fully what leadership really is in a prison or other correctional agency. In fact, most of these are poor examples of good leadership. What are the types of activities or measures of impact that leaders have on their agencies?

In *Governing Prisons,* DiIulio suggests three consequences that are affected by the quality of prison management: order, amenity, and service. Order is the absence of individual or group misconduct that threatens the safety of others. Amenity is anything that enhances the comfort of inmates, such as clean cells or good food. Service is that intended to improve the life prospects of inmates, such as treatment programs.[50] Effective correctional leaders attend to details within their environment and set high standards for order, control, good communications between staff and inmates, and excellence in professionalism.

How a leader sets a tone and how a leader carries this out is another story. There is no standard routine for successful management. In a study of how correctional leaders manage staff to get the most from their performance, the authors examined four correctional agencies, and interviewed many correctional administrators. They concluded that, "Each administrator subscribes (either formally or informally) to a particular philosophy or style of management. Accordingly, approaches to the actual task of managing the workforce differed among the administrators interviewed."[51]

One of the keys to achieving quality is to "pay attention" to the fundamental values that a leader determines are important to the agency.[52] A leader attends to fundamental values (security, sanitation, staff pride, order, etc.) in many ways. The most important is visibility or **managing by walking around (MBWA).** Good correctional administrators do not sit in their offices, they move through a prison or visit various community components of their agency, visit and talk to staff where they work, and comment on the factors that they want to encourage. Many administrators believe that the things that get staff's attention and get done are those things that the staff hear administration mention or ask about. The accompanying case study presents an interview with a correctional administrator, the director of a state department of corrections. It is an excellent example of how an administrator shows leadership, sets a tone, and attends to the fundamental values of the organization.

PRACTICAL PERSPECTIVES

An Interview with a Correctional Administrator

Q: I understand that you regularly visit the prisons in the state, and that these visits are "from dawn to dusk," covering every area and talking to every staff member in the prison. I also understand that when you are there, you do a thorough sanitation inspection, looking, as I am told, "for dust in every corner and on every ledge, for soap grime in the bathroom sinks, and at every fire extinguisher for the monthly inspection documentation." First of all, why do you make such regular and extensive visits to the prisons.

A: Well, the problem with working in a "headquarters" of an agency is that you get removed from the day-to-day working of the agency and its people. So, I do it so I do not forget what it is like, how hard the jobs are, and to hear from our staff firsthand how they are doing and what issues are on their mind. But, as much as anything, I do it because I enjoy it. This may sound pretty strange, but I really get a kick out of being in the prisons, and interacting with staff and inmates.

Q: Let's discuss that in more detail. Talk more about the danger of getting too far removed from the day-to-day operations of the prisons.

Continued

A: I see my job as primarily to make the job of those staff working in a prison easier. This means many things. First, I need to stay ahead of the issues that are confronting them, so the problems do not get to a point where they are out of control. Every prison has problems in management. That is simply the nature of the beast. Inmates are not used to following rules and complying with authority. So, every day, someone will try to avoid compliance, and staff have to deal with each situation—many will not work out as perfectly as planned. They have to take care of those issues by themselves; I can't help them with each situation. But I can understand the forces that create situations and make prison management more difficult. For instance, if we are beginning to have a newly developing friction between some competing gangs, it is important to get on top of it as soon as possible. By being in the prisons, I can get a sense of what is happening from those who have to deal with it, gather some intelligence they have picked up, and see how urgent it is to create a system wide response.

Let me stick to that point for a second. I think an extremely underacknowledged skill of administrators is their ability to understand when an issue has urgency, especially when the administrator is removed (in the prison office or in the state headquarters) from the situation and does not feel the intensity of those staff who have to react to it. Not all issues or situations (regardless of how serious they may be—for instance a murder of an inmate by another) have the same urgency for a systemwide response. Some simply need to be handled the best way staff can deal with them as they come up. Others need a deliberate and thoughtful response, and the proper response can almost "bubble up" from each sequential incident. Administrators must be careful not to do the wrong thing, or create the wrong response, simply to react to something before they really understand the cause and underlying issues. Finally, some issues do have real urgency, and staff are crying out for guidance and policy change or new direction. Let me go back to the example I started to reference about developing gang tensions. If I hear staff concern about this issue in one prison, it is worth having our staff (often call security threat groups) in headquarters survey some other prisons to determine whether they are experiencing similar situations. The fact that I heard about the issue from prison staff firsthand helped me understand the urgency and my responsibility for action. Otherwise, you may only read reports about a variety of incidents in a variety of prisons, and although you sense a link and ask staff to look into it, you do not do so with the urgency that it is critical to the safe management of the prisons. I have talked to my colleagues about issues such as this one that have gone on in a state, with staff constantly seeking help on how to deal with it. However, because the top administrators are so tied up with their own issues (budget, the legislature, the media about an escape), they don't jump on the importance of this to the prisons. I personally get a better sense of the urgency of an issue by being in the prisons and hearing staff talk about it. One final note, line staff and even wardens tend to downplay certain things when talking to their bosses—staff do not want to give the impression they can't handle it. So, they don't "sound an alarm" themselves and don't communicate a sense of urgency. That is when your own correctional experience and common sense comes into play, and you hear a sense of urgency that is not overtly communicated.

The second way I try to make the job of prison staff easier is to show them I support them, appreciate them, and respect the job they are doing. Correctional administrators can do this in a variety of ways. They can provide an adequate level of funding for employee awards programs to recognize staff who do a good job. They can urge managers to use incentive awards and can create special awards to recognize the behaviors they think are important at any particular time. They can send notes to employees they hear have done some especially good job or had a significant accomplishment. They can do media interviews and make public statements of support for staff and the jobs they do. However, there is nothing more important than giving staff your time, going to them and saying hello, shaking their hands and showing them you care about them personally. I received feedback from a prison in the town in which I grew up. In fact, it was told to my mother, which really made me feel good. She met a staff person from the local prison, a relative of a friend of hers in her church. The staff member told her that he thought I was a pretty good guy, that when many "dignitaries" visited the prison where he worked, and came into an area he was working, they often treated him as if he was invisible and did not talk to him. The dignitaries only talked to the warden or whoever was giving the tour. But the staff member told my mother that whenever I entered the area where he worked, I went straight to him, said hello, and shook his hand. This made him feel that I respected him and thought he was important. Line staff make these kinds of judgments about the administrators they work for, and those interactions are more important than creating the most effective policy and getting the most favorable budgets from the legislature. They do tough jobs, and have to know and believe that their bosses acknowledge this and acknowledge them.

Another thing I do when I go to the prisons that I enjoy, and I believe staff enjoy, is to challenge them. All staff take pride in their work and want it to be recognized. They feel even better if they have to work really hard and are still successful. When I made my first round of visits to all the state prisons, I checked every fire extinguisher for the required monthly inspections. Each one has a tag on it showing that it has been inspected every 30 days to ensure it is ready for action if needed. Every prison probably has 200 or 300 extinguishers, and it is easy to miss a few. I always found a few that had not been checked, until I went to this one prison, which had an extremely dedicated fire and safety officer. I found only one or two extinguishers that had been missed some month over the past few months that were noted on the tag. I was extremely complimentary of the fire and safety officer, and he responded that he would be sure there were none missed for my next visit. So, I returned the

Continued

challenge and assured him that I would be back. Each time I returned I looked in one new place that I thought he might have missed—like in a security tower guarding the fence or on a farm tractor. Our challenge, his attempt to be sure no fire extinguishers were missed, and my attempt to find one that was became almost legendary at the prison. Staff would follow my prison tour route by radio, trying to anticipate what new place I would look this visit. If I found one, everyone knew within minutes, and the fire and safety officer had to live with the ribbing of his fellow staff for days. If he won, he could bask in their still ribbing him about trying to please the boss. I would do the same thing with sanitation issues with all staff, looking for dirt or dust in some of the less obvious places, complimenting them when I found none, and poking fun at them when I found some. Seldom would I find much after the first couple of visits to a prison. Staff enjoyed the challenge and the fact that I pushed them to do better and appreciated them when they did.

Finally, I can make their jobs easier by creating a culture with a positive work environment. Prison jobs are tough enough without administrators second-guessing staff and the decisions they make. I can help with this by not accepting problems or mistakes, but accepting that individuals will make some. I have a saying, "be tough on the issue, but be soft on the staff." Don't accept the notion that things just happen and that nothing can be done to reduce the likelihood that problems will occur. But, don't let it be taken personally by the staff that make the error. If they blatantly disregarded policy, they will be disciplined for that. However, if staff make an error of judgment or don't deal with a situation as well as they should, look for ways to improve the likelihood that they will do better next time. This may mean a particular type of training should be provided to staff. It may mean a new policy, procedure, or response to a situation needs to be developed. It may mean causal factors need to be found and handled. But, it is wrong not to look for underlying issues, ask tough questions of responsible staff, and try to respond appropriately when possible. And, it is wrong to overreact to a staff error with discipline of that staff member and to do nothing to improve all staffs' ability to be successful the next time.

Q: That was a really interesting overview of the role of an administrator in setting a tone and helping staff do their jobs. But, you usually don't think of a director of corrections checking toilets for sanitation, checking fire extinguishers, or looking at farm tractors. Why do you spend so much of your prison tour times on these kinds of activities?

A: That's really a good question and one I am not surprised you asked. It can seem odd to do these things. But I do them for a couple of reasons. First, when you enter an area of a prison and want to interact with the staff person working in the area, there are limits on what you can focus. Many line staff working in an area rotate regularly and do not have much control over policy or operational procedures. But they do have control over sanitation. So by checking this thoroughly, you can deal with something under their control, and your few minutes with them will be focused on their work, rather than something they have no control over.

But the most important reason is for myself and for the staff to pay attention to detail. In corrections, there is a saying that, "if you pay attention to detail, the big issues will be worked out." As strange as that seems, it is very true in this environment. Prisons work on routine and consistent following of policy and procedures. Staff and inmates come to expect certain things to happen in certain ways. Inmates also watch staff who shortcut the way they do their jobs, which often result in a security breakdown that observant inmates will take advantage of. If every staff member pays attention to details and makes sure that each step of a procedure is done the right way every time, there are no security breaches or breaks in routine that can undermine the safe and secure environment you are trying to accomplish. There will be fewer resulting problems and, therefore, fewer big issues.

When staff see how much attention I pay to detail, they realize the importance of it. I don't only check sanitation, I check the details of the policy. I look at log books to see that they are used as required; I note how staff lock doors behind them, even if they know they are going to have to unlock the door 30 seconds later. I check how we control and keep inventories of syringes in the hospital. Staff expect me to look at the details of how they do their jobs, and they know these things are important to me. I have seen an improvement in their attention to detail since I have been doing this. I seldom find the same thing twice in a visit to a prison. So, I combine a concern for them personally with a challenge for them to do their jobs right each and every time. Through those two things, I send the messages I want to send, and do what I can to help establish the environment in the prisons that I think is necessary.

SUMMARY

One thing is without question: There is nothing more important to the quality operation of a correctional agency than staff and leadership. The manner in which staff understand and work toward accomplishing the agency mission, the skill and pride with which they carry out their duties, and the concern and attention of leadership all contribute to the success of a correctional agency. Correctional jobs are challenging, and they are unlikely to be successfully accomplished without highly trained staff working together for high quality and high standards. Although staff are the most important resource of a correctional agency, that resource can never be taken for granted. It must be carefully assembled, prepared, and properly led in order to meet the complex responsibilities and far-reaching goals of correctional agencies.

This chapter reviewed the types of jobs that are available in the correctional profession, including descriptions of the workplace, types of functions to be fulfilled, and challenges. Issues of pay, career opportunities, and entry-level requirements have been presented. The importance of a diverse workforce was addressed, and the movement away from a predominantly white, male correctional staff was described. The role of leadership in a correctional agency, leadership's impact on standards staff follow, and the morale of staff and commitment to their jobs were described.

In this section of the text, the broader issues regarding correctional staff were reviewed. Correctional agencies management of their human resources were identified. These management elements include the recruitment, training, and continued development of correctional staff. The importance of good supervision and the vital elements of supervision, whether they occur in a correctional, or other public or private sector, environment, were examined. At this point in the study of correctional administration, you should clearly understand the value of correctional staff and how staff must be nurtured and developed to maximize their potential. The final section of this text moves from the present to the future, and reviews the issues that will confront correctional administrators over the next decade and beyond.

ENDNOTES

1. Camille Graham Camp and George M. Camp, *The Corrections Yearbook, 1998* (Middletown, CT: Criminal Justice Institute, 1998), p. 130.
2. Ibid., pp. 196–197.
3. Ibid., pp. 262–265.
4. Web page of the United Auto Workers, <http://www.uaw.com> (April 8, 2001).
5. David E. Duffee, *Corrections: Practice and Policy* (New York: Random House, 1989), p. 388.
6. E. Goffman, *Asylums: Essays on the Social Situation of Mental Patients and Other Inmates* (Garden City, NY: Doubleday & Company, 1961).
7. Donald Cressey, "Prison Organization," in *Handbook of Organizations,* edited by J. March (New York: Rand McNally, 1965), p. 1024.
8. James B. Jacobs and Norma Meacham Crotty, *Guard Unions and the Future of the Prisons* (Ithaca, NY: Institute of Public Employment, 1978), p. 3.
9. American Correctional Association, "Resolution on the Term 'Correctional Officer'," *Corrections Today* (April 1993): 60.
10. Ben Crouch, "Guard Work in Transition," in *The Dilemmas of Corrections; Contemporary Readings,* 2nd ed. (Prospect Heights, IL: Waveland Press, 1991).
11. Michael Welch, Corrections: *A Critical Approach* (New York: McGraw-Hill, 1996), p. 138.
12. Robert Johnson, Hard Time: *Understanding and Reforming the Prison* (Belmont, CA: Wadsworth, 1996), p. 224.
13. John J. DiIulio, Jr., *Governing Prisons: A Comparative Study of Correctional Management* (New York: The Free Press, 1987), p. 95.
14. Camp and Camp, p. 132.
15. Lucien X. Lombardo, *Guards Imprisoned,* 2nd ed., (Cincinnati, OH: Anderson Publishing Company, 1989), pp. 51–57.
16. Norman A. Carlson, Karen M. Hess, and Christine M. H. Orthmann, *Corrections in the Twenty-First Century: A Practical Approach* (Belmont, CA: West/Wadsworth, 1999), pp. 433–434.

17. James B. Jacobs and Lawrence Kraft, "Integrating the Keepers: A Comparison of Black and White Prison Guards in Illinois," *Social Problems* 25 (1978): 308.

18. Robert Freeman, "Correctional Officers: Understudied and Misunderstood," in *Prisons: Today and Tomorrow,* edited by Jocelyn M. Pollock (Gaithersburg, MD: Aspen Publishers, 1997), pp. 319–320.

19. See, Robert Johnson, "Informal Helping Networks in Prison: The Shape of Grass-Roots Correctional Intervention, Journal of Criminal Justice 7(no. 1), (1979) 53–70, and Lucien X. Lombardo, *Guards Imprisoned: Correctional Officers at Work* (New York: Elsevier, 1981).

20. Robert Johnson and Hans Toch, *The Pains of Imprisonment* (Newbury Park, CA: Sage, 1982), p. 287.

21. Camp and Camp, p. 149.

22. Harold E. Williamson, *The Corrections Profession* (Newbury Park, CA: Sage, 1990), p. 89.

23. Camp and Camp, p. 154.

24. Williamson, p. 89.

25. Gary Hill, "Correctional Officer Traits and Skills," *Correctional Compendium* 22, no. 8 (August 1997): 1–12.

26. Vernon Fox, *Correctional Institutions* (Englewood Cliffs, NJ: Prentice Hall, 1983), p. 71.

27. Williamson, p. 137.

28. Camp and Camp, pp. 164–165.

29. Camp and Camp, pp. 196–197.

30. Camp and Camp, p. 172.

31. Carlson, Hess, and Orthmann, p. 448.

32. An interview by the author with a State of Missouri probation officer. (October 20, 2000).

33. Camp and Camp, p. 202.

34. Dean Champion, *Probation, Parole, and Community Corrections,* 2nd ed., (Englewood Cliffs, NJ: Prentice-Hall, 1996), pp. 429–430.

35. American Probation and Parole Association, *APPA Position Statement: Weapons,* Approved 1994.

36. Bernard J. McCarthy, "Community Residential Centers: An Intermediate Sanction for the 1990s," in *Corrections: Dilemmas and Directions,* edited by Peter J. Benekos and Alida V. Merlo (Cincinnati, OH: Anderson Publishing, 1992), p. 177.

37. Carlson, Hess, and Othmann p. 441.

38. 42 U.S.C. 2000e-2 (1976), p. 703 (e).

39. *Dothard v. Rawlinson,* 433 US 321 (1977).

40. *Gunther v. Iowa,* 612 F.2d 1079 (1980).

41. Camp and Camp, p. 133.

42. See Nancy C. Jurik and Gregory J. Halembia, "Gender, Working Conditions and the Job Satisfaction of Women in a Non-Traditional Occupation: Female Correctional Officers in Men's Prisons," *The Sociological Quarterly* 25 (1984): 551–566. Also see Lincoln J. Fry and Daniel Glaser, "Gender Differences in Work Adjustment of Prison Employees," *Journal of Offender Counseling, Services and Rehabilitation* 12 (1987): 39–52.

43. Joycelyn M. Pollock, "Women in Corrections: Custody and the 'Caring Ethic,' " in *Women, Law, and Social Control,* edited by Alida V. Merlo and Joycelyn M. Pollock (Needham Heights, MA: Allyn and Bacon, 1995), p. 111.

44. Carlson, Hess, and Othmann p. 441.

45. Camp and Camp, p. 133.

46. For a discussion of these difficulties of bringing nonwhite staff into rural prisons, see John Irwin, "The Changing Social Structure of the Men's Correctional Prison," in *Corrections and Punishment,* edited by D. Greenberg (Beverly Hills, CA: Sage 1977), pp. 21–40.

47. Susan Philliber, "Thy Brother's Keeper: A Review of the Literature on Correctional Officers, *Justice Quarterly* 4(no.1) (1987): 9–33.

48. For an interesting look at the life of C. J. McLin, see *Dad, I Served: The Autobiography of C.J. McLin, Jr.,* as told to Minnie Fells Johnson (Dayton, OH: Wright State University, 1998).

49. Kevin N. Wright, *Effective Prison Leadership* (Binghamton, NY: William Neil Publishing, 1994), p. 6.

50. DiIulio, pp. 11–12.

51. George M. Camp, Camille G. Camp, and Michael V. Fair, *Managing Staff: Corrections' Most Valuable Resource* (Washington, DC: National Institute of Corrections, 1996), p. 31.

52. Wright, p. 25.

KEY TERMS

guard	probation officer
correctional officer	parole officer
snitch	halfway house
overtime	bona fide occupational qualification (BFOQ)
caseworker	managing by walking around (MBWA)

YOU'RE THE CORRECTIONAL ADMINISTRATOR

1. You are the human resource manager of a state correctional agency that operates prisons and halfway houses, and supervises probation and parole. You know the agency is expected to increase substantially over the next five years, and it will require the addition of many new staff. You also know that the agency mission has become more complex, and your staff have identified the need for recruiting college graduates to fill these positions in the future. You are creating a recruitment campaign for two- and four-year colleges. What are the attractive features of correctional work that you want to convey to candidates for employment? Describe each and how your recruiters will present them. What are the concerns that college students will have about correctional work? Describe how they will be presented to prospective employees. In addition, describe the most effective processes and methods for recruiting college students for correctional positions.

2. You are the chief of staff development for a state correctional agency. The agency administrators have just completed a strategic plan for the agency. You have been told that the most critical function over the next 10 years is to ensure the agency has a highly skilled staff who are able to confront highly complex problems in the future. Not all of these problems can even be identified at this time, but it is expected that rapid change, a changing makeup of offenders, and increased availability of technology will continue well into the future. Design a comprehensive program to ensure you have employees who can meet these challenges of the future.

WEB LINK EXERCISES

Federal Bureau of Prisons (BOP): www.bop.gov

Go to the Web site for the Federal Bureau of Prisons (BOP). Find the employment information. Research the description of duties, requirements, and process for applying for a job as a correctional officer. From the other information available on the Web site, list the key requirements for obtaining a job as a correctional officer in the BOP.

PART

V

The Future
of Correctional
Adminstration

14

Critical Issues for Correctional Administration

▨ INTRODUCTION

In Chapter 1, several issues facing today's correctional administrator were presented. These issues were categorized into three areas: substantive, administrative, and policy and philosophy. Examples of substantive correctional issues include dealing with prison overcrowding, managing offenders serving long periods of time, controlling young and violent offenders, and prisoner transition to community supervision. Administrative issues include maintaining budget growth to meet an increasing number of offenders, recruiting an increasing number of staff and training and developing them for the future, and planning for a rapidly changing and uncertain future. Issues of policy and philosophy include the appropriate balance between punishment and rehabilitation, the appropriate use of risk assessment instruments, and whether the private sector should operate correctional programs for a profit.

These general topics seem daunting enough for even the most experienced and capable correctional administrators. However, this chapter presents several more issues that face administrators, and tax their organizations and personal abilities. Most of these issues are not new, but they have become more critical over the past few years or are expected to intensify over the next few years. Everyone has heard the comic retort when someone is asked if they have been keeping busy. "Busier than a one-armed paper hanger!" Although simple and perhaps not funny to some, one can envision this person running back and forth, trying to get paper on the wall, applying adhesive, and not ending up with total chaos. After reading about the many issues facing correctional administrators in this chapter, you will have a similar vision of an administrator running from one issue to the next, trying to keep them each from faltering, and trying to continue to move the organization forward.

Unfortunately, that image is too often the life of a correctional administrator in these times. There is seldom a boring day, never a lack of issues that need attention, and always an opportunity to create new policy and practices in response to these issues. The successful administrator is one who can juggle many balls at the same time without dropping any. For individuals who like activity and thrive under challenges, correctional administration is the career for them. For those who want a more mundane and slow-paced professional life, stay away from corrections. The pace is going to increase before it slows down.

Following are only a few of the many issues that present serious challenges for those who manage and lead correctional agencies, or those who are politically charged with setting policy or allocating budget and personnel resources. There are issues about sentencing, including prison versus community alternatives, the impact of the war on drugs, and the disproportionate representation of minorities under correctional supervision. There are issues regarding the changing makeup of offenders, such as the aging inmate, juveniles sentenced as adults, women offenders, and the mentally ill. Other issues that need to be addressed include evaluating correctional options and programs and the link between policy and effectiveness, and management decisions regarding the use of changing technology. Finally, there is the emerging dilemma of the reentry of large number of prisoners from correctional supervision back to society. Although reentry issues have been around for as long as criminal sanctions, the increase in the number of offenders that leave prison and return to their communities each year has created challenges regarding community services, offender families, victims, and the community in general. Although these challenges included in the primer reentry issue are broader than corrections, they provide examples of how correctional administrators will have to reach out and work with many of society's other components to respond to developing problems.

SENTENCING ISSUES

Over the decade of the 1990s, the one thing that was clear, both in policy and practice, was that criminal offenders were being sentenced to longer periods in prison than previously for the same crimes. Regardless of whether this is good policy, the end result is that the prison population has increased dramatically, and there is a different makeup of inmates in terms of age, length of sentence, gang affiliation, and needs, all requiring a change in approach to their management. On January 1, 1990, the nation's prisons held 750,000 inmates. This number increased steadily from 6 to 8 percent per year, until it reached 1.32 million on January 1, 1999.[1] The following sections present issues that have resulted in a change in sentencing practices and an increase in the prison population in the United States.

The Public Fear of Crime and Demand for Tougher Sentencing

Over the past two decades, the public fear of crime has increased, resulting in a demand for tougher sentencing. According to Gallup polls, in 1989, 84 percent of citizens polled believed there was more crime in the United States than the year before; only 5 percent believed there was less. Crime rates were rising during the 1980s, but in the early 1990s they began to decline, and they have decreased in almost every category of felonies every year since 1993. By 1998, the Gallup poll results revealed that 52 percent of citizens polled still believed that there was more crime than the year before.[2] Table 14–1 illustrates the results of the poll.

As crime rates continued to decrease throughout the 1990s, the public began to realize this, and the percentage of those polled who believed that there was less crime than the previous year increased. However, there was still a majority of people, even after several years of declining crime rates, that believed that the crime rate was still increasing. As a result, the public demand to get tough on crime, and be tougher on criminals continued. It really did not matter that criminal sentences had already been significantly increased, the public wanted criminals sentenced for longer periods of time, and they did not want prisons to be places where criminals could spend idle hours watching television or working out with weights.

As a result, the average length of incarceration increased from 1990 through 1996. The average length of stay for inmates released during 1990 was 23.7 months. By 1996, the average time served for inmates released was 30.0 months, an increase of more than 25 percent.[3] Every time there is a heinous crime that gets considerable media attention, or an unusual situation surrounding an offender's commission of a crime, elected officials try to respond by proposing increases in criminal sanctions for the crime or type of criminal. This leads to increased sentence lengths for offenders to serve, not in response to increasing crime rates, but in response to the fear of crime and the demand for tougher sentencing by the public.

TABLE 14–1

Attitudes Toward Crime Level in the United States: Selected Years, 1989–2000

Gallup Polling Question: "Is there more crime in the United States than there was a year ago, or less?"

	More	Less	Same[1]	No opinion
1989	84%	5%	5%	6%
1990	84	3	7	6
1992	89	3	4	4
1993	87	4	5	4
1996	71	15	8	6
1997	64	25	6	5
1998	52	35	8	5
2000 (August 29–Sept. 5)	47	41	7	5

[1]Response volunteered
Source: The Gallup Organization, Inc. *The Gallup Poll (Online),* available at
http://www.gallup.com/pol/indicators/indcrime.asp. 2 March 2001.

Partisan Politics and the Lack of Policy Alternatives

It is often argued that the length of sentences continues to increase because crime and punishment have become more of a political issue than ever before, and elected officials must show they will act to protect citizens from crime. In reality, there are very few policy choices that are available to decision makers, and in an attempt to do something, the end result is to rely on incarceration by increasing prison time. There are few political gains to be made by elected officials advocating a balanced approach to criminal sanctions, weighing the availability of prison space, the cost to build and operate more prisons, the opportunity for maintaining offenders under community sanctions, and the potential use of restorative justice models. Elected officials believe that to appear sincere about the crime problem, there must be increased use of incarceration, rather than alternative sanctions.

Over the past few decades, crime has become an important issue in the public's eye. Both Republicans and Democrats have used it as an opportunity to show how they differ from each other, and arguments about appropriate crime policy have to be put into "sound bites" in 30-second commercials, rather than thoughtful debate of substance and effectiveness. Tonry, in analyzing reasons for the increase in incarceration rates in the United States, notes that examples of the partisan political approach to crime policy include "widespread adoption of broadly defined three-strikes laws, mandatory minimum-sentence laws, sexual psychopath laws, and the federal sentencing guidelines [that] are too rigid and often result in unjustly harsh penalties."[4]

The War on Drugs

Since the 1980s, we as a society, have been led to believe that illicit drug use and trafficking have created a danger to our freedom and way of life, to the extent that we must "declare all-out war," and fight the use and availability of drugs by whatever means available. There is no question that drug use is a serious problem and that it results in high costs to society in areas difficult to quantify, such as sickness and health care for users, fragmentation of the family, lost human potential and productivity, and the cost of drug-related crime. We can, however, quantify the cost of law enforcement activities that respond to illegal drug use and trafficking, processing criminal cases, and drug treatment programs.

The U.S. Department of Justice reports, "there is extensive evidence of the strong relationship between drug use and crime."[5] This report notes that drug users report more involvement in crime, persons with criminal records are more likely than those without criminal records to report being drug users, and that crime rises as drug use increases. In *Drug Use Forecasting* studies of incarcerated populations by the National Institute of Justice, it was discovered that in 18 of 23 cities involved in the studies, more than 50 percent of those booked on criminal charges tested positive for some illicit drug.[6] Other research found that among jail inmates, 27 percent had used illegal drugs at the time of their offenses, and among jail inmates 61 percent said that they or their victims had been under the influence of drugs or alcohol at the time of their offenses.[7]

There is no doubt that the **war on drugs** has been a costly one. In 1998, the federal government drug control budget was almost $16 billion.[8] These dollars only include the costs of federal law enforcement activities, educational activities, and interdiction. They do not include the costs of prosecuting and incarcerating offenders for drug crimes. The federal criminal codes require either 5- or 10-year mandatory sentences for offenders convicted of trafficking or sale of drugs, and more than two-thirds of all inmates in Federal Bureau of Prisons institutions are currently serving sentences for drug crimes.

Johns takes the concern about the cost of the war on drugs a step further and suggests it has been "used as a mechanism for vast expansions of state power and state control. This can be seen domestically in moves to allow warrantless searches, the introduction of illegally seized evidence, asset seizures, random drug testing, the militarization of housing project, and the incarceration of pregnant women for drug use, among other measures."[9] Although this may seem like an overstatement of the issue, in 2000, evidence came to light by Rafael Perez, a veteran of the Los Angeles Police Department, about his own shooting of an innocent man and planting of evidence, and of the many other police abuses from lying, falsifying evidence, and even stealing drugs from the police evidence locker.[10] It seems that in the push for arrests and convictions in the war on drugs, some combatants may have decided to accept as true the old adage, "All is fair in love and war."

Sentencing and Race

Race and corrections is perhaps one of the most controversial topics today. There are many allusions to the disproportionate number of minorities in the criminal justice and correctional systems, but there have been few serious discussions or thorough research into the **overrepresentation of minorities** and the subsequent policy implications. Is there institutional racism in the criminal justice system? How does race (separate from social class, poverty level, drug use, and other issues) impact the discretionary decisions by police, prosecutors, judges, prison officials, and parole board members? If racism does not exist in the criminal justice process, what policy and management issues do the disproportionate percentage of minorities in the correctional system present to administrators?

A disproportionate number of minorities does exist in the correctional system. Of the 1,243,271 inmates in state and federal prisons on January 1, 1998, racial breakdowns were approximately 43 percent white, 47 percent African American, and 10 percent "other." Among all of these groups, 16 percent were of Hispanic ethnicity.[11] Of the 1,979,088 individuals under probation supervision by state agencies on the same date, 56 percent were white, 30 percent were African American, and 14 percent were "other," with slightly more than 10 percent of Hispanic ethnicity.[12]

Obviously, the number of minority (particularly African American) offenders under supervision is out of line with the numbers in the general U.S. population. It is also interesting to note the distinction between the percentages within racial groups from probation to prison. Whereas white offenders make up 56 percent of probationers, they represent only 43 percent of prisoners.

What are debated are the causes of the disproportionality. In his 1987 book, *The Myth of a Racist Criminal Justice System,* William Wilbanks proposed that the "perception of the criminal justice system as racist is a myth."[13] Wilbanks acknowledges that there are incidents of individual racism, but most studies he reviewed do not show sufficient evidence of racism, and he concludes, "prejudice and racism are not systematic."[14]

Minorities are disproportionately involved in crime, especially violent crime, both as the perpetrators and as the victims. Minorities in poverty-stricken, urban neighborhoods are most likely to be victims of violent crime. In a 1988 report, the Bureau of Justice Statistics noted that based on Uniform Crime Report homicide data, 1 out of every 179 white males will be murdered, whereas 1 out of every 30 African American males will be murdered.[15]

Crime is linked closely to poverty, drug use, and lack of opportunity for legitimate approaches to economic success. With crime more prevalent in African American and Hispanic neighborhoods, it would be expected that these groups would have higher arrest rates. Law enforcement efforts are always more intense in urban areas with high crime rates and high drug use. In a study of how the police respond to the war on drugs, it was noted that arrests for drug use and possession usually occur in the city rather than the suburbs and "have had a disproportionate effect on African Americans."[16] As an example, 42 percent of the young African American men in Washington, DC are in prison or jail or are under probation or parole supervision; and 70 percent are expected to be arrested by the time they reach the age of 35.[17]

Therefore, it appears that the disproportionate number of minorities under correctional supervision has less to do with racism within the criminal justice system than with social factors influencing crime, race, and social class. Even so, the high numbers of minorities in correctional systems still create a phenomenon that causes management problems for correctional administrators. Correctional administrators must strive for effective affirmative action programs to have a workforce that mirrors, to some extent, the client base. This not only enhances the potential for positive communications between staff and offenders but also reduces the perception by offenders that the system is racist and that they have a "right" to misbehave. Administrators must deal with the friction, tension, and separation among groups that result from the heterogeneity among offenders. In addition, staff must acknowledge and deal with the culture and subcultures that offenders bring with them, or that they develop while they are under correctional supervision.

Impact on Correctional Administrators

This issue of sentencing that results in more offenders being sent to prison for longer periods of time has an impact far beyond cost and resources directed to law enforcement, courts, corrections, and other elements of the criminal justice system. Although it can be argued that sentencing policy is outside the scope of responsibility for correctional administrators, it still must be dealt with and responded to by those managing correctional agencies and environments. First, administrators must acknowledge problems that result from current sentencing practices, such as an overrepresentation of minorities under correctional supervision, management of a prison population that will serve extremely long periods of time and have little motivation for good behavior, and provision of reasonably priced health care for older offenders with extensive health care needs. Second, administrators must consider policies and practices that can either be put in place to reduce the negative effects

An Overcrowded Prison Dormitory. A continued push for incarceration will result in a continuation of overcrowded prisons. (Courtesy of the Federal Bureau of Prisons)

of sentencing practices, or can begin a reconsideration of these practices if they prove to be costly and ineffective in reducing crime.

What can administrators do if they decided to become involved in the reconsideration of current sentencing policies? Some suggestions for changing the crime control policy is evident in the proposal to use "social support," by Cullen, Wright, and Chamlin.[18] These authors conceive **social support** as the process of transmitting various forms of capital—human, cultural, social, and material—to individuals or social units. The thesis is that involvement in crime is inversely related to the provision of social support. The authors suggest four ways that social support may contribute to the crime control agenda and that could be implemented by correctional administrators.

The first of these proposals is to provide early intervention programs to support at-risk children, parents, and their families. Juvenile correctional administrators deal almost totally with at-risk children. Adult correctional agencies deal with parents who have at-risk children because of the parents' involvement in the criminal justice system. Most correctional programs focus only on the offender and almost ignore the spouse and children. However, it would be relatively easy to link family issues to these programs, or begin programs in parenting skills specifically aimed at intervening with children to reduce their likelihood of delinquency and criminal involvement.

The second proposal is to invest in at-risk children through programs such as Big Brothers/Sisters and other nonprofit community programs that target emotional and material resources toward children. Correctional officials can reach out to private and church-based volunteer intervention programs to form partnerships and expand the services and support they can potentially provide.

The third proposal is to reaffirm rehabilitation. Cullen and colleagues suggest that, "One value of rehabilitation is that it is the only correctional philosophy that argues that the state should make an effort to support offenders both as an end in itself and as a means to the end of making society safer."[19] As noted in Chapter 5, there is now evidence of the effectiveness of rehabilitative programs in reducing recidivism, and public opinion polls indicate that citizens support rehabilitation as a concept and correctional goal.[20] There is no group better able to advocate the need for rehabilitation than correctional administrators directly involved in the delivery of these programs. In fact, if correctional administrators do not take the initiative and "reaffirm rehabilitation," then it is unlikely anyone else will do so.

Finally, the authors propose social and cultural reform, whereby people are asked to be more socially supportive, at the sacrifice of self-interest, or to replace the American dream of economic self-aggrandizement with one of looking out for the good of others. This is perhaps the most challenging of the authors' proposals and the most difficult for correctional administrators to substantively do anything about. However, it is important for those who work in social service agencies, whether family services or law enforcement, to recognize and model the importance of concern for others as an anchor of our cultural and social mores.

To summarize this section regarding sentencing as an issue that will confront correctional administrators over the next several years, it is important to understand the components that drive our current sentencing approaches and philosophies. These approaches result in longer sentences, overrepresentation of minorities under correctional supervision, and an "aging" of the supervised population. These issues can and must be dealt with by administrators. By reaching beyond the traditional scope of responsibility for corrections and considering proposals, such as those for social support, correctional administrators can implement programs that are more proactive than reactive. They can advocate and, therefore, influence policy makers regarding the importance of these proposals, and they can suggest the importance of alternatives to longer prison sentences as effective crime control agendas.

■ AGING OFFENDERS

Picture an 86-year-old man clutching a walker as he shuffles down a prison hallway. Not exactly the usual image of a dangerous killer locked up for the good of society. Chances are, it's not what the judge envisioned either when he sentenced John Bedarka, a Pennsylvania coal miner, to life without parole for shooting his wife's lover to death 30 years ago. But, Bedarka is still in prison . . . in frail health, severely depressed, and a threat to no one.[21] It is said that prison populations are a mirror of the general society. No more can this be so true in the age makeup of U.S. prisons. Those citizens 65 and older represent the fastest growing age group in the United States, reaching 34 million in the year 2000. In 1992, Americans over age 50 comprised only 26 percent of the population, but it is estimated that this age group will comprise 33 percent by the year 2010.[22] The demographics of the U.S. prison population reflects the same increase. In 1990, only 4.9 percent of the inmates in state and federal prisons were age 50 or older, and by 1998, this number had risen dramatically to 7.2 percent.[23] This change creates many issues in the management of offenders and the resources needed to respond to their needs. Obviously, older offenders have greater health care needs. Can older offenders be classified at a lower security level because they are less aggressive and frailer? Does it take a different type of staff, or staff with different training, to supervise older offenders? Are there adequate community facilities for older offenders who are released, and can no longer work and earn a living for themselves?

The most obvious and critical issues regarding older offenders are their declining medical condition and the cost to provide it. As was recently reported, "Because elderly people require more medical care, it costs nearly three times as much to incarcerate them, or about $65,000 a year per inmate."[24] Most prisons do not have a medical department set up to respond to the frequent and sometimes serious medical conditions presented by older offenders. As described in Chapter 10, most prison medical resources are only "clinics," similar to typical general practitioner physicians' offices, to treat routine illnesses. They neither have the staffing nor the equipment to respond to more serious medical problems, including depression, sexually transmitted diseases, tuberculosis and other infectious diseases, heart problems, and reduced circulation. These and many other illnesses result from the aging process and years of at-risk lifestyle choices such as tobacco use, extensive drug and alcohol use, and high-risk sexual behavior.

Prisons were envisioned for, and designed around, holding young and physically active inmates. Everything from prison architecture to recreation facilities were established without consideration for older inmates. Modern, campus-style, prison architecture emphasizes extensive space to spread out inmates over as much area as possible. However, older inmates with wheel chairs or with difficulty walking any distance have problems going the several hundred yards from one building to another, especially in northern states where the weather can be severe. Basketball, jogging,

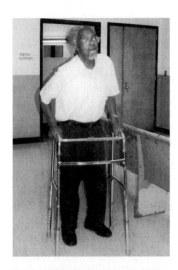

Elderly Inmate in an Ohio Prison. Older inmates now make up a larger proportion of the prison population than ever before. Age and deteriorating physical health of inmates cause many new issues for correctional administrators. (Courtesy of the Ohio Department of Rehabilitation and Correction)

or weight lifting often dominates recreation programs. There are few less-rigorous programs focused on maintaining flexibility for older inmates with less muscle strength or physical mobility. Work assignments suitable for older inmates can pose problems for correctional administrators. Although most prisons require inmates to work, traditional prison jobs, such as landscaping, or sanitation or food service work, offer few special accommodations for older inmates.

There is also the question of housing accommodations and assignments. To save space, prisons use bunk beds. Lower bunk assignments are the result of an inmate's good behavior and seniority. Older inmates cannot climb into upper bunks and, therefore, must be assigned lower bunks, even if their behavior and seniority do not warrant it. This reduces the number of lower bunks available for traditional assignments as an incentive for good behavior. For most prisons, there are two inmates assigned to each cell. Older inmates often do not want to cell with younger inmates (and vice versa), who have different habits and interests in radio or television stations. Younger inmates often have little tolerance for the nuances of older inmates, such as the need to go to the bathroom several times per night. These issues can build into serious tensions between younger and older inmates.

As noted in Chapter 6, the aging inmate population results in a need to reexamine security classifications. The higher the level of prison security, the higher the cost for prison operations. Do older inmates need the level of prison security classification their past crimes and history of violence warrant on risk assessment instruments, or can they be administratively reduced in security level because of their age? What do prison administrators have to do to protect older inmates from being victimized by younger and stronger predators? Is there special training that has to be provided to staff regarding the aging process and the effects of the prison environment on the elderly? Unfortunately, these questions have no easy or clear answers for the correctional administrator, who has to continually analyze these issues, and search for reasoned and pragmatic solutions.

JUVENILE OFFENDERS TRIED AND SENTENCED AS ADULTS

One of the outcomes of the get tough on criminals movement has been a push to treat serious juvenile offenders as adults as they are processed through the criminal justice system. Not only are public attitudes about adult criminals tougher, but there is also a great fear and concern that juvenile offenders are becoming more violent and dangerous. An increasing percentage of violent crime is now committed by youth. During the 1980s, murder arrests for juvenile offenders increased by 93 percent, and arrests for aggravated assault increased by 72 percent.[25] Demographics suggest that there will be a significant increase in the population of youths ages 10 to 18 during the early part of the twenty-first century. As a result, there is an even greater concern that juveniles will commit an increasing number of violent crimes. As juvenile crime receives increasing attention in the media, the public perception is that the juvenile justice system is not capable of coping with the gang-oriented, violent, juvenile offender.

The **juvenile justice system** was created more than 100 years ago specifically to separate juveniles from adult offenders. The court, under the concept of *parens patriae*, took over supervision of children when their parents failed to provide proper care and guidance. The juvenile court and correctional systems took responsibility for educating and nurturing delinquents, and they emphasized reform and rehabilitation. Rather than sending them to prison, as in the adult system, juvenile offenders were confined in *training schools.* Even though the concept of *parens patriae* is no longer applicable in juvenile courts, the concept for nurturing and reform continued until the 1980s, when the demand for punishment won out over rehabilitation for violent youthful offenders. As a result, many states enacted legislation to prosecute serious juvenile offenders as adults, and if they are found guilty and sentenced to a correctional institution, they are placed in an adult prison. By the end of the twentieth century, nearly all states had passed laws to permit the **waiver of juveniles to adult courts.** In some states, juveniles as young as age 13 can be tried as adults, and often prosecutors, rather than judges, have the authority to waive the case and have it transferred to an adult court.

Criminal processing of juveniles as adults creates many issues. Even though it results from a desire to punish juveniles, there still remains an interest in keeping youthful offenders separate from older, sophisticated adult criminals. In reporting on legislation that authorizes juveniles to be processed as adults, a 1995 National Institute of Corrections survey noted many requirements to maintain this separation. The report noted that

▌ Eighteen states have expanded the definitions of crimes or lowered the ages at which juveniles may be tried in adult court. Another six states have proposed, but not yet passed, such legislation.

▌ Two states (Colorado and Wisconsin) have authorized "youthful offender systems" to deal with serious offenders under age 18; another state (New Mexico) formally defined the categories "youthful offender" and "serious youthful offender," both specific to offenders under age 18.

▌ Three states have established a separate division of the justice system to prosecute or coordinate the state's response to juvenile crime.

▌ Five states have authorized new housing for offenders under age 18 or defined the circumstances under which they must be separated from adult offender.[26]

Herein lies the crux of the problem of processing juvenile offenders as adults. If serious or violent juvenile offenders are to be "bound over" to the adult system, but there is a requirement to either keep them separate from older offenders, or provide programs and activities designed to meet their needs as youth, there is really a third system created. This new system must be operated with almost separate resources and programs. Few adult correctional agencies have educational, vocational training and life-skills programs that meet the needs of young offenders. Similarly, most states do not have a large enough numbers of juveniles in their adult systems to make the development and presentations of such programs cost effective. When a state requires total separation of juveniles from adults, states generally designate one housing unit in an adult prison for juveniles. However, the logistics of inmate movement, meal service, medical care, and the provision of other ancillary services and programs makes total separation an almost impossible task.

The question of whether serious juvenile offenders should be tried and sentenced in adult courts is certainly one for debate. The American Correctional Association (ACA) standards note that the juvenile justice system has significantly different processes, procedures, and objectives from adult corrections, and these require specialized services and programs. James A. Gondles, executive director of ACA, has suggested that, "We will never, in my view, solve our problems on the back end with punishments. . . . Treating kids as adults solves very little; it's another quick-fix solution to a complex problem that took years to reach and will take years to resolve."[27]

Yet, it is generally recognized that many juveniles who are age 16 or 17 are not "children" in their physical maturity, willingness to commit violent acts, and danger to the public. Juvenile justice systems that try to protect and nurture them do not meet their needs and do not protect society from their potential violent acts. Unfortunately, although binding these youthful offenders over to the adult court system is not an ideal response, adult correctional administrators must now face philosophical, political, and operational issues as they try to put facilities and programs in place to handle these juvenile offenders.

■ WOMEN OFFENDERS

It is almost trite to suggest that women offenders create special issues for correctional administrators. Women offenders have been increasing both as prisoners and under community supervision more rapidly than male offenders, and by 1998, there was an estimated 950,000 women under the control of adult correctional agencies. Of this number, "Women represent about 21 percent of those on probation, 11 percent of those in local jails, just under 6 percent of those in prisons, and 12 percent of those on parole."[28] Not only does the increasing number of women under correctional supervision create significant issues but also women offenders have many more, and dramatically different, issues and needs than male offenders. And, correctional agencies are still struggling to identify and respond to these concerns.

The first issue for prison administrators is how to provide the same quantity and quality of correctional programs for female prisoners as is provided for male prisoners. In a lawsuit filed by federal prisoners entitled *Butler v. Reno,* female inmate plaintiffs argued gender discrimination by the Federal Bureau of Prisons in the denial of access to facilities, programs, and services available to similarly situated male inmates. The U.S. District Court for the District of Columbia agreed with the plaintiffs, and, in a 1995 stipulated order of settlement, the parties agreed that the Federal Bureau of Prisons would provide comparable programs, services, and facilities to both female and male inmates who are eligible for placement in minimum security prisons. These programs and services included maintaining similar staff–inmate ratios; providing work, educational, parent–child, and recreation program opportunities; providing comparable health care to male prisons; and ensuring a satisfactory number of minimum security space for females eligible for such placement. Although correctional agencies would not plan to intentionally discriminate against female offenders, the fact that there were few women in comparison to their male counterparts has resulted in the availability of fewer programs and services.

While growing in number, female prisoners still make up a relatively small portion of the nation's prison population. In most states, there are several male prisons but only one or two female prisons. This, in itself, causes problems, because females are placed further from their homes than men, making visiting for families more difficult. With fewer prisons, it is difficult to offer the same variety of programs, especially those that are expensive to establish and maintain, such as vocational training. In addition, with fewer prisons, there is not the same separation of inmates by security designation; therefore, female inmates usually have mixed security levels of inmates in their prisons.

These issues have been ignored for many years, but with the *Butler v. Reno* decision, and the increased public interest and visibility regarding female offender issues, correctional administrators have to find unique ways to try to create the same quality of correctional environment for women that they provide for men. Unfortunately, the solution to the problem of equal treatment almost resolves itself with the growth in the number and percentage of female inmates. Of the total population of state and federal prisons, the percentage of female inmates increased from 5.5 percent in 1994 to 6.7 percent in 1999.[29] The growth has caused the construction of new female prisons or the conversion of male prisons to hold female offenders. With a greater number of prisons, it will be easier to house women closer to their homes and to offer a greater variety of programs.

Female offenders have many problems that are not found with male offenders. Nearly six of ten women in state prisons have experienced physical or sexual abuses prior to their incarceration.[30] The majority of women (estimated to be 80 percent) who become incarcerated are mothers.[31] Within female prisons, there are issues of medical care and vocational training which differs from those traditionally present for male inmates. In addition, the development of a "culture" in a women's prison is considerably different from that in a male prison.[32] Female inmates expect a different style of communications with each other and with staff than male inmates. Correctional administrators must understand and be sensitive to the different needs of female offenders, and realize that the "one size fits all" prison operation is highly impractical for female inmates.

From the time a woman enters prison, they are likely to have a different situation than a man. Approximately one-fourth of the women who enter prison are either pregnant or had given birth within the past twelve months.[33] With the large number of female inmates who are mothers, there are feelings of guilt and isolation, as inmates feel they have abandoned their children, and must have their family members care for their children during their incarceration. Because there are usually fewer female than male prisons, the distance from home for women offenders is usually greater than for males, causing more difficulty in visiting by family and the children. And when the women receive visits from their children, the visiting conditions are not conducive to fostering a normal relationship between young children and their mothers. Most prison visiting areas provide seating similar to that in an airport waiting area, with no space for children to act like children, by running, playing, laughing and yelling.

To improve the opportunity for women to foster parental relationships with their children, many prisons have established **parenting programs** to aid mothers in continuing their normal roles as parents. Some programs include training classes for female inmates on how to improve their own parenting skills, and find ways to be effective and important parental figures, even from prison. Some parenting programs include special visiting situations where children may be able to spend several hours (in some cases overnight) with their mothers, go outside the normal visiting area, and use prison recreation and dining areas. Finally, some parenting programs create a role of mother as teacher emphasizing reading to children (even by audiotape) and being involved in their schoolwork.

One of the first such programs was initiated at the Federal Correctional Institution in Pleasanton, California. The MATCH (Mothers and Their Children) program focused on strengthening the mother–child bond by improving conditions for visiting, training in parenting skills and involvement in early child education, and improved prenatal care and referrals for social services for the children.[34] Another unique program is **Girl Scouts Behind Bars,** whereby incarcerated mothers can stay connected, assume parental responsibility, and be involved in a traditional community function of planning and attending Girl Scout meetings. Girl Scout chapters have been established in female prisons, and meetings (female inmates and their daughters) are held in the visiting room. These chapters are often linked to those in the community, so that the children can have the normal outside activities of the Girl Scouts, yet the incarcerated mothers can be involved in some meetings and activities. These programs are believed to be successful, because mothers and daughters often continue their involvement in Girl Scouts after the mothers' release from prison.[35]

There are many other differences in the needs and programs provided for female offenders. A national study of correctional programs for women offenders has identified characteristics about correctional programs that are successful.[36] Female offenders have been found to present less risk to institutional and community security than male offenders, and, therefore, risk classification instruments should be adjusted for the lower-risk levels.[37] The types of physical security presented in Chapter 8 for male inmates is not necessary for females, and therefore, a women's prison can be constructed for a lower cost than a similar security level prison for men.

Although a few of the larger states and the Federal Bureau of Prisons are already making adjustments for female offender needs, most states and local jails have yet confronted these problems. As the number of incarcerated women continues to grow, every jurisdiction will have to review and possibly modify how they assign and house females, the types of programs they provide, and the quality of medical care that is available. Although these modifications can be very expensive, by understanding risk and classification characteristics of females, and by modeling many successful programs that have been implemented in other agencies, these changes can be accomplished in a nondisruptive manner that benefits female offenders.

▰▰ MENTALLY ILL OFFENDERS

Over the past 30 years, the number of criminal offenders suffering from mental illness has been rising. Unfortunately, the solution to one problem has created another. In the 1950s, new **antipsychotic drugs** were developed, and by prescribing them to people suffering from mental illness, many patients were able to remain in the community rather than being placed in mental hospitals. These drugs, as a treatment for mental illness, seemed like a humane alternative to the wasted existence in a mental ward of a state hospital, where patients had little to do and often received little treatment. As a result of the ability of mental health patients to remain in the community, states closed their hospitals, and the number of mentally ill patients went from a high of 559,000 in 1955 to 69,000 in 1995.[38]

However, when these patients in the community stop taking their medication, problems result. There are several reasons those suffering from mental illness decide to stop taking their prescriptions. Many of these medicines have uncomfortable side effects, and if patients think they are doing better, they decide to stop taking the medicine. Sometimes, individuals lose their insurance coverage and cannot afford to buy the medicine. Without taking the medication, the symptoms of the mental illness return. Without the number of mental hospital beds and with the initiation of laws making it difficult to commit the mentally disturbed, many of these people end up without treatment, their behavior deteriorates, and they commit crimes. In place of the mental health system, they become clients of the criminal justice system.

A report issued by the U.S. Department of Justice, Bureau of Justice Statistics, estimated that there were 283,800 mentally ill offenders held in state and federal prisons and local jails at midyear 1998, and an additional 547,800 mentally ill individuals on probation.[39] These massive numbers put a tremendous burden on correctional administrators, who must develop programs to control, supervise, and treat these individuals in already overcrowded and underfunded situations.

In prison, these individuals create a dual problem for administrators. They have committed a criminal act, are often violent, and may be serving a long period of incarceration. Therefore, they require a high-security institutional placement and are housed with other offenders who have committed equally serious offenses who are serving equally long sentences. However, they are suffering from mental illness and must be diagnosed and treated while they are being held for their offenses. This combination of potentially violent, mentally ill prisoners, in high-security and probably overcrowded institutions, is a dangerous situation, which requires an inordinate amount of staff time and resources to manage.

Under probation and other community supervision, there are similar problems. Probation departments are organized to supervise the traditional criminal offenders, who need standard supervision to ensure they follow the conditions of their probation. However, the mentally ill require much more. They need to have a treatment program developed, receive counseling on maintenance of their medication, and require much more time and patience in supervising than the typical criminal offender. Most probation officers are not trained for these tasks and are not familiar with the mental health resources available for these offenders. Again, the overlap of criminality and mental illness creates a difficult dilemma for the correctional practitioner.

The key to dealing with these issues begins with partnerships between the state and local correctional agencies, and the state and local mental health service agencies. In most states, the correctional agency takes the responsibility for housing and providing treatment to mentally ill prisoners, whereas the state mental health departments provides support, staff training, and sometimes resources. Local mental health agencies can be used to provide counseling and support to probationers. The best results occur when this linkage between the correctional and mental health agencies is strong and both work toward common goals of treatment through counseling and medication to establish stability in behavior. If offenders remain stable, they can be managed through normal correctional procedures.

PRACTICAL PERSPECTIVES

Creating a State of the Art Mental Health Program for Offenders

Ohio has been recognized as a model of cooperation between the corrections and mental health state agencies. In the institutional setting, prisoners with serious mental illnesses are stabilized and distributed throughout the prisons rather than being housed in one separate location. In this manner, they have the same services and programs that are available to other inmates. However, Ohio was not always a model for such care, and until the past decade, there were many problems in the delivery of care to the mentally ill offender. In the early 1980s, two significant incidents brought attention to the problem. One was the murder of a staff member by an inmate with a history of mental health problems. The other was an attempted escape and hostage-taking by another inmate. During the trial for the second inmate, the defense attorney argued that he suffered from mental problems that were not responded to by the state department of corrections. Unfortunately, the jury believed the defense, and the inmate received only a minor sentence for his dangerous criminal acts.

Over the next several years, the Ohio Department of Rehabilitation and Corrections (DRC) and the Ohio Department of Mental Health (DMH) began to work closely together to identify resource and treatment needs, clarify roles, and implement effective programs. As a result, a team of individuals from both the correctional and mental health agencies developed a conceptual model of "holistic health care" that provides for

- Integrated medical, psychiatric, psychological, and chemical dependency service delivery.
- Continuity of care within DRC (the correctional agency) and upon release.
- An array of services, and
- Delivery of services by self-directed multi-disciplinary work teams.[40]

Particularly important is the **continuum of care** in the Ohio program. Correctional agencies need a variety of mental health programs in the prisons. The most intensive level of care is an "in-patient" prison hospital, operated very similarly to a mental health institution, where inmates with acute needs who often represent a risk to themselves or others, can receive aggressive treatment. A step below this level are short-term crisis units, which attempt to stabilize severe symptoms of mental illness, working toward either a return to a standard prison or (if the inmate requires more intensive treatment) a transfer to the prison mental health hospital. A third level is a residential unit within a standard prison, in which a cluster of inmates with mental illness live in a therapeutic milieu to receive treatment and counseling, yet still interact with other inmates for medical care, food service, or program participation. Finally, each standard prison provides outpatient services of counseling and supportive care so the mentally ill inmate can function in the general prison population.

In the community, the Ohio correctional and mental health agencies are further collaborating to provide services and programs for offenders with mental illness who are leaving prison. Prior to release, social workers work with the inmates to link them to mental health agencies in the community. Contacts with counties identify services available, and when they are not available, the counties apply for state funding to establish programs to increase the mental health treatment opportunities available for criminal offenders. The goal is to continue care from prison into the community and reduce the likelihood of recidivism.

Like Ohio, many states have developed excellent programs for inmates with mental health problems. However, there never seems to be enough available resources to handle the complications caused by large numbers of mentally ill individuals. With mandatory minimum sentences, three strikes laws, and longer sentences for violent and repeat offenders, the percentage of mentally ill offenders under correctional supervision is expected to continue to rise. The challenge for correctional administrators is to maintain a viable program to treat and control a very difficult group of offenders. In reality, managing mentally ill offenders is a roller coaster of successes and failures. Even after long periods of maintenance through counseling and medication, relapse rates are high. The treatment of mentally ill offenders requires resources, trained staff, appropriate facilities, and a great deal of patience.

EVALUATING EFFECTIVENESS

As noted in earlier chapters, in the future, there will be an increased level of scrutiny of correctional programs and operations. As a part of this scrutiny, there will be pressure to reduce the cost of corrections. With the growth in the number of prisons and the increase in the number of offenders under some type of correctional supervision, an ever-increasing percentage of tax dollars will have to be used to fund correctional operations. Elected officials and the public will demand accountability by correctional administrators of the large dollars they are spending. Although ideological arguments about the best way to punish, rehabilitate, and deter criminals will continue, the most important issue will become, "what are the most cost effective approaches?" Correctional administrators will need to be prepared to oversee studies that evaluate program and operational effectiveness, and to determine what delivers the most "bang for the buck."

Recidivism as a Measure of Outcome

Throughout the history of corrections, the expectation has always been that correctional activities should reduce **recidivism.** Although it is often argued that it is unrealistic to expect a correctional sanction or program to have a significant impact on the future criminality of offenders, it continues to be the measuring stick for effectiveness. It is common for legislators to ask a correctional administrator, "What impact does that program have on reducing crime?" The complex answer of how a program may make offenders more employable or may improve their self-image does not go far in the legislator's mind, unless those intermediate goals are associated with a reduction in recidivism.

There are many limits in the use of recidivism as an outcome measure. First, there are questions of how to define recidivism. Should it be defined as an offender committing any new crime, commission of a felony during the period of community supervision, or return to prison? The length of the follow-up is also an issue. Can a correctional sanction or program be expected to have an impact on an offender for three or even five years after the termination of the sanction or program? Is six months a more reasonable follow-up period? And finally, how does a research design control for the many external and internal factors that can affect recidivism rates?

Evaluations of correctional programs regularly use rates of arrest as the primary determination of whether a program or sanction is successful. The definition used has a lot to do with the level of perceived success of a program. With the possibility of wide variations in the definition, it becomes almost impossible to compare effectiveness of programs using recidivism rates. In fact, some researchers whimsically suggest that, "the best way to ensure a low recidivism rate is to define it very narrowly (e.g., incarceration in a state penal institution) and to use a very short follow-up period.[41]

Over the past decade, there has been a resurgence of interest in the effectiveness of correctional programs, in part because of improved sophistication of correctional outcome measures and more thoughtful evaluative designs. First, many rehabilitative programs that attempt to reduce recidivism now include a measure of "quality of the program" as a variable linked to success. One example to assess the quality of a correctional program is the Correctional Program Assessment Inventory, developed by Gendreau and Andrews.[42] The CPAI examines six elements within a program to assign a quality score: implementation and leadership; offender assessment and classification; program characteristics; characteristics and practices of staff; quality control; and other items, such as ethical considerations and level of support. By analyzing the quality of a program, all programs that target a certain area (such as drug abuse or sex offender treatment) are not considered the same in their comparison of outcome.

A second enhancement of correctional research is the use of **meta-analysis,** which is a way to quantify research results. Meta-analysis allows correctional researchers to examine many different outcome studies of programs, identify their individual indicators of success, and link those success indicators in a way that provides answers to more general policy issues. Gendreau, Goggin, and Smith help clarify what meta-analysis is and how it can be used:

What is meta-analysis? Consider how one would assess an individual's academic performance in undergraduate courses. Grades, of course, would be recorded as well as numerous other facts about the individual (i.e., age, gender, race, aptitude, study habits, types of courses, how they were taught, methods of grading, etc.). One can speculate about the individual's performance. If the grades were poor, was it due to poor study habits, "tough" courses, and so on? In order to obtain a more accurate assessment of the magnitude of the results (i.e., average grade) and how they may vary by age, study habits, and so forth across all undergraduates, then the data could be assessed on a sample of 100 students. Essentially, this is what meta-analysis does, but in this case, the individual represents one "research study."[43]

Importance for Correctional Administrators

For correctional administrators, these evaluative developments, along with the challenge of taxpayer accountability, make it even more important that research be conducted on the outcome of correctional sanctions and programs. For the past 20 years, administrators have complained about micromanagement by elected officials who often act on punitive ideology rather than on facts and informed discussion. However, it is incumbent on the correctional administrator to communicate research findings to these policy makers and to ensure they have available facts for informed decision making.

Administrators should devote resources to research studies which determine effectiveness. Most correctional agencies (even those with tens of thousands employees) have fewer than 10 full-time staff devoted to research and evaluation. And those researchers spend most of their time on creating reports of numbers of clients served or dollars spent, rather than how well things are working. Few agencies provide grants to universities to evaluate program outcomes, even when millions of dollars are targeted to implement a program. Correctional administrators should make every effort to ensure that thorough evaluation is a part of every new sanction or program. It is also important for correctional administrators to understand and know the effectiveness of sanctions and programs in other jurisdictions than their own. It is impossible for correctional administrators to effectively argue for programs, if they are not aware of studies that indicate success or failure.

THE USE OF TECHNOLOGY

Technology is the buzzword of the new millennium, even for corrections. Everywhere one looks, there are suggestions for the use of technology to make a job easier or change how things are done. With the information revolution, with personal computers and the Internet changing the way people shop, communicate, and work, technology impacts almost everything we do. Automobiles are equipped with high-tech devices to tell people where they are and how to get to where they want to go. There are "smart homes" that can be programmed to do certain tasks and make life easier for owners. Workplaces change almost daily with new equipment and operating systems.

However, corrections has been relatively slow to accept technological advances, even though there are an amazing variety of innovations that may have application for corrections. Several new technologies have been incorporated into correctional operations. Computers play a much greater role in predicting risk and maintaining information about offenders. Security systems are much more technologically sophisticated than they were even 10 years ago. Telemedicine is being used more extensively to reduce the need to take inmates outside a prison to be seen by a medical specialist. Video cameras are commonly used in prisons to more thoroughly monitor inmate movement and activities. Electronic monitoring of probationers has become an accepted practice in community supervision. However, these developments only touch the surface of what is available and could be used in a correctional situation.

Many technologies with potential correctional applications have been developed for military uses. As noted by Larry Cothran, executive officer of the California Department of Corrections Technology Transfer Committee, "the Cold War ended, and all of a sudden, you had a lot of companies trying to convert their military hardware to corrections and law enforcement."[44] It is entirely possible to completely redesign how correctional supervision is accomplished, almost like the science fiction movies in which inmates have something embedded in their heads that explodes if they leave the perimeter of the prison without it being deactivated.

These new technologies can change how perimeter fencing around a prison operates. Already, most California prisons have electronic fences that are lethal if someone comes in contact with them, changing the need for correctional officer surveillance from towers. There are systems in use that can detect even the smallest trace of illegal drugs on visitors entering a prison. There are heartbeat monitors that can detect an inmate hiding in a vehicle attempting to secretly leave the prison. Robots

Correctional Officer at a Security Console. Technology in prisons and for use in community supervision has significantly changed over the past 20 years. Issues of when and how to use technology, without undermining the importance of staff and offender interaction, must be addressed by correctional administrators. (Courtesy of the King County Department of Corrections)

with such monitors can also be used to count inmates and make sure they are in their cells when they should be. There is the potential for replacing electronic monitoring bracelets with sensors placed under the offender's skin that, using global positioning systems (GPS), can constantly monitor the movements of offenders, and potentially trigger an alarm or even shock them if they enter an area in which they are prohibited.

The most difficult issue for correctional administrators is how to use technology. Just because technology is available does not mean it will improve and advance the goals of corrections. First, many of the technologies are very expensive. Although marketed to promote financial savings through staff reduction or the elimination of expensive inmate escape hunts, some of the savings may never be realized. Correctional administrators may hear about an interesting technology and believe that its purchase and use may indeed save money; however, many of these applications have seldom been used, and they have never been fully evaluated in a correctional setting.

A second, even more difficult, issue is the philosophy surrounding the use of technology. It is possible to take away all privacy from offenders, constantly monitoring their activities and behavior. Some would argue that the elimination of their ability to commit further crimes is worth their loss of privacy. Others argue that offenders should be allowed some privacy and the opportunity to make decisions as to their behavior. The question arises as to whether a correctional system should control offenders' behavior through constant supervision and monitoring, or whether it should work to change attitudes and behavior through rehabilitative programs. There is also a question as to whether certain technologies are inhumane? The lethal electronic fences in California, which give off a lethal shock if someone tries to climb them, are an example. There are also many "stun guns" and shocking devices that are marketed to subdue violent offenders by confusing their central nervous systems.

Perhaps the most complex issue for correctional administrators to consider about technology is how much it should replace the people that now carry out correctional functions. Technology can supplement rather than replace staff, but technology is usually not cost effective unless it reduces the number of staff necessary to carry out a function. Corrections has always been a people business. It is people watching people, people communicating with people, and people trying to change people. Although technology can replace staff, it may also "depersonalize" the correctional environment. Many correctional agencies advocate and pursue a culture of positive interaction and communications among staff and offenders; they believe that such communications helps avoid tension and creates an atmosphere conducive to offender rehabilitation. Although the thoughtful use of technology does not have to significantly alter this type of correctional environment, administrators must consider how to appropriately mix technology and professional staff to reach the most favorable outcome.

The development of available technology for corrections is continuing at a rapid pace. As the private sector identifies corrections as a growing market for technology, there will be increased efforts to get correctional administrators to purchase and adopt these technologies. The challenge of a growing offender population, combined with pressures to reduce costs, will force consideration of how to mix the old and new ways to operate correctional agencies.

PRISONER REENTRY

As has been well established, there has been a tremendous growth in the prison population in the United States. In mid-2000, there were 1,254,577 adults in federal and state prisons and 596,485 in local jails.[45] Almost all of the attention is on the number of offenders *in* prison. Receiving little attention is the fact that there are approximately 600,000 prison inmates released each year from prison to the community.[46] In New York City alone, the New York State Department of Correctional Services releases approximately 25,000 people a year to the city, and the New York City jails release almost 100,000.[47] In California, there were 124,697 prisoners leaving prisons after completing their sentences, almost 10 times the number of releases only 20 years earlier.[48]

When there were only a few hundred thousand prisoners, and a few hundred thousand releasees per year, the number did not seem significant, and the issues surrounding the release of offenders were not overly challenging for communities. However, with the high number of offenders now returning to their communities, many without parole supervision, and some with no supervision, there has been a call for academics and correctional administrators to identify the impact of this phenomena on the offenders, their families, and their communities.[49] Many states have abolished parole and implemented determinate sentencing, whereby prisoners are automatically released after completing their full sentence minus any good time earned. One of the functions of a parole board is to examine prisoners "preparation" for release, including whether she or he has a place to live, a potential job, and family support. With determinate sentences, these factors are not relevant to release. When offenders have "done their time," they are released no matter what level support is available to them or how prepared they are for the community.

A study by the Vera Institute of Justice in New York City identified many issues that confront inmates released from prison.[50] The study included 88 randomly selected inmates released from state prisons in July 1999. Of the 88 people selected, 49 (56 percent) completed the study by allowing intermittent interviews to determine their progress and successful transition from prison to the community. Several issues were identified, including finding housing, ties with family and friends, finding a job, alcohol and drug abuse, continued involvement in crime, and the impact of parole supervision. It is interesting to note that, even at the point of release, the process had an ominous beginning. The study found that 50 out of the 66 who were interviewed on release reentered the community alone, with no one to meet them as they exited prison or got off the bus in New York City.[51]

Most offenders end up living with families or friends until they find jobs, accumulate some money, and then try to find their own residences. However, finding a job is often the most serious concern among ex-inmates, who have few job skills and little work history. Their age at release, their lack of employment at time of arrest, and the history of substance abuse problems make it difficult for them to find a good job. Many released inmates quickly return to substance abuse. Release is a stressful time, making it even more difficult to avoid a relapse to drug or alcohol abuse. All of these issues make it difficult for ex-inmates to avoid a return to crime, and, therefore, it is critical that prisons have programs to prepare inmates for what they will face on release and community services that are available to them upon their return.

Sociological issues regarding the community's response to the return of so many ex-inmates are beyond the scope of responsibility for the correctional administrator. What is the impact on social cohesion and community stability when several criminals are returned to a neighborhood? Anderson has identified how the attitudes and behaviors of ex-inmates are transmitted to those in the community on release and concluded that "family caretakers and role models disappear or decline in influence, and as unemployment and poverty become more persistent, the community, particularly its children, become vulnerable to a variety of social ills, including crime, drugs, family disorganization, generalized demoralization and unemployment."[52] In reviewing the effects of admitting and removing offenders from Tallahassee, Florida, in one year (1996) on the crime rate the following year (1997), Rose, Clear, and Scully found an increase in crime, and they questioned the deterrent and rehabilitative effect of prison. The authors suggest that releasing a large number of parolees to a community in one year destabilizes the community's ability to exert informal control over its members, because there is little opportunity for integration, there is increased isolation and anonymity, and ultimately the crime rate increases.[53]

Correctional administrators will have to deal with the results of further studies of the impact of prisoner release on communities and create in-prison programs, which, it is hoped, can address some of these issues. Findings of the community impact also will offer guidance for parole supervision policies and strategies. There is little yet known about the full impact of larger prison populations, and therefore larger release numbers on the communities. Yet, it is expected that this topic will receive increased attention, and demand specific responses for those who supervise correctional operations.

■ SUMMARY

The issues that face correctional administrators today and tomorrow reflect the continuing complication of their day-to-day tasks. Years ago, life for correctional administrators seemed rather simple: Maintain security and keep inmates from escaping. Most inmates served (by today's standards) relatively short periods of time. The small percentage of long-time inmates accepted their sentences and established a comfortable prison routine for both themselves and the prison staff. These "old cons" were admired by younger inmates and respected by staff. They followed the now-forgotten inmate code of "do your own time" and "don't rat on fellow inmates." In past years, inmates and staff understood their roles and didn't try to rock the boat or change the way things were done. Community supervision of probationers and parolees was fairly clear-cut, and most offenders completed their supervision successfully with few problems unless they committed a new felony.

Today, however, change is rapid, the offender population diverse, and it seems almost every offender requires some type of special handling. Few days go by without some type of crisis for the correctional administrator, either with budgets, staff problems, or offender conflicts. Perhaps the most important trait for successful correctional administrators is to be flexible and deal easily with change. Correctional administrators must be able to react quickly yet also anticipate problems and develop proactive solutions. Unfortunately, these challenges and issues are only going to increase and become more complicated. In the next chapter, the budgetary challenges and the need for new models of correctional management are considered. Are there different approaches that can be taken to operate prisons and supervise offenders in the community? Are there different ways for the public and private sector to partner in the delivery of correctional services? Can we "reinvent" corrections and find a better model for the future? The issues discussed in this chapter make it obvious that correctional administrators must consider and carefully evaluate different approaches for accomplishing their mission. Because limited budget resources further complicate these developing problems, in the next chapter, new approaches for funding of correctional agencies is addressed.

ENDNOTES

1. Camille Graham Camp and George M. Camp, *The Corrections Yearbook, 1999: Adult Corrections* (Middletown, CT: The Criminal Justice Institute, 1999), p. 3.
2. From the Gallup Organization, Inc. *The Gallup Poll (Online)*, available http://www.gallup.com/pol/indicators/indcrime.asp, 2 March 2001.
3. Camille Graham Camp and George M. Camp, *The Corrections Yearbook, 1998* (Middletown, CT: The Criminal Justice Institute, 1998), p. 57.
4. Michael Tonry, "Why Are U.S. Incarceration Rates So High?" *Crime and Delinquency* 45 no. 14 (October 1999): 445.
5. Bureau of Justice Statistics, *Drugs, Crime and the Justice System* (Washington, DC: National Institute of Justice, 1993), p. 2.
6. National Institute of Justice, *Drug Use Forecasting: Drugs and Crime, 1990, Annual Report* (Washington, DC: U.S. Department of Justice, 1991).
7. Bureau of Justice Statistics, *Drugs and Crime Facts, 1993* (Washington, DC: U.S. Department of Justice, August 1994), pp. 5–6.
8. Office of National Drug Control Policy, *The National Drug Control Strategy, 1997: FY 1998 Budget Summary* (Washington, DC, ONDCP, 1997).
9. Christina Jacqueline Johns, *Power, Ideology, and the War on Drugs: Nothing Succeeds Like Failure* (New York: Praeger, 1992), p. 174.
10. Charles Feldman, Headline News, "New L.A. Police Scandal: Sting Results in Officer's Arrest on Heroin Charges," http://cnn.com, 1 October 1999.
11. Camp and Camp, 1998, p. 12.
12. Ibid, p. 164.
13. William Wilbanks, *The Myth of a Racist Criminal Justice System,* (Monterey, CA: Brooks/Cole, 1987), p. 5.
14. Ibid., p. 6.
15. Bureau of Justice Statistics, *Report to the Nation on Crime and Justice*, 2nd ed. (Washington, DC: U.S. Department of Justice, 1988).
16. J. M. Klofas, "Drugs and Justice: The Impact of Drugs on Criminal Justice in a Metropolitan Community," *Crime and Delinquency* 39 no. 2 (1993): 204.
17. Forty-Two Percent of Young Black Men in Capital's Justice System," *New York Times* (18 April 1992): 114–124.
18. Francis T. Cullen, John Paul Wright, and Mitchell B. Chamlin, "Social Support and Social Reform: A Progressive Crime Control Agenda," *Crime and Delinquency* 45, no. 2 (1999): 188–207.

19. Ibid., p. 201.

20. Jody L. Sundt, Francis T. Cullen, Brandon K. Applegate, and Michael G. Turner, "The Tenacity of the Rehabilitative Ideal Revisited: Have Attitudes Toward Offender Treatment Changed?" *Criminal Justice and Behavior* 25 (1998): 426–442.

21. Tammerlin Drummond, "Cellblock Seniors: They Have Grown Old and Frail in Prison. Must They Still Be Locked Up?" *Time* 153, no.24 (21 June 1999): 60.

22. Kenneth Moritsugu, "Inmate Chronological Age Versus Physical Age, in *Long-Term Confinement and the Aging Inmate Population* (Washington, DC: Federal Bureau of Prisons, 1990).

23. Camp and Camp, 1998, p. 25.

24. Drummond, p. 60.

25. John J. Wilson and James C. Howell, *Comprehensive Strategy for Serious, Violent, and Chronic Juvenile Offenders: Program Summary* (Washington, DC: U.S. Department of Justice, Office of Juvenile Justice and Delinquency Prevention, 1993), p. 2.

26. LIS, Inc., *Offenders Under Age 18 in State Adult Correctional Systems: A National Picture* (Washington, DC: U.S. Department of Justice, National Institute of Corrections, 1995), p. 2.

27. James A. Gondles, Jr., "Kids Are Kids, Not Adults," Editorial, *Corrections Today* (June, 1997): 3.

28. Lawrence A. Greenfeld and Tracy L. Snell, "Women Offenders" (Washington, DC: Bureau of Justice Statistics, 1999), p. 6.

29. Camp and Camp, 1999, p. 14.

30. Greenfeld and Snell, p. 1.

31. Barbara Bloom, "Imprisoned Mothers," in *Children of Incarcerated Parents,* edited by K. Gabel and D. Johnson (New York: Lexington Books, 1995), p. 21. Also see R. Kiser, "Female Inmates and Their Families," *Federal Probation* 55 no. 3 (1991): 56–63

32. For more information regarding the culture of a female prison, see Mark S. Fleisher, Richard H. Rison, and David W. Helman, "Federal Inmates: A Growing Constituency in the Federal Bureau of Prisons," *Corrections Management Quarterly* 1 no. 4 (1997): 28–35.

33. George Church, "The View from Behind Bars," *Time* 22 (September 1990): 20–22.

34. J. Boudouris, *Parents in Prison: Addressing the Needs of Families* (Lanham, MD: American Correctional Association, 1996).

35. M. Moses, "The Girl Scouts Beyond Bars Program: Keeping Incarcerated Mothers and Their Daughters Together," in *Maternal Ties: A Selection of Programs for Female Offenders,* edited by C. Blinn (Lanham, MD: American Correctional Association, 1997), pp. 35–49.

36. Barbara A. Koons, John D. Burrow, Merry Morash, and Tim Bynum, "Expert and Offender Perceptions of Program Elements Linked to Successful Outcomes for Incarcerated Women," *Crime and Delinquency* 43 no. 4, (October 1997): 512–532.

37. Kathryn Ann Farr, "Classification for Female Inmates: Moving Forward," *Crime and Delinquency* 46 no. 1 (January 2000): 3–17.

38. "Prisons Replace Hospitals for the Nation's Mentally Ill," *New York Times* (5 March 1998), A-26.

39. Paula M. Ditton, "Mental Health and Treatment of Inmates and Probationers" (Washington, DC: U.S. Department of Justice, Bureau of Justice Statistics, 1999).

40. No author, "Mental Health Care in Ohio Corrections," unpublished monograph (Columbus, OH: Ohio Department of Rehabilitation and Corrections, 1997), p. 4.

41. Edward J. Latessa and Alexander Holsinger, "The Importance of Evaluating Correctional Programs: Assessing Outcome and Quality," *Corrections Management Quarterly* 2 no. 4 (1998): 23.

42. P. Gendreau and D. Andrews, *The Correctional Program Assessment Inventory,* 5th ed. (Saint John: University of New Brunswick, 1994).

43. Paul Gendreau, Claire Goggin, and Paula Smith, "Generating Rational Correctional Policies: An Introduction to Advances in Cumulating Knowledge," *Correctional Management Quarterly* 4 no. 2 (2000): 56–57.

44. Gabrielle deGroot, "Hot New Technologies: As the Military Downsizes, Private Technology Firms Begin Catering to the Corrections Industry," *Corrections Today* (July 1997): 60.

45. No author, "BJS Says Correctional Numbers Rose 44.6 Percent Since 1990," *Corrections Journal* 4 no. 11 (2000): 3.

46. See Camp and Camp, 1998. As of January 1, 1998, there were 1,249,595 inmates in state, federal, and District of Columbia prisons (p. 1). During 1997, there were 600,015 inmates released from these same adult correctional facilities (p. 59).

47. Marta Nelson, Perry Deess, Charlotte Allen, "The First Month Out: Post-Incarceration Experiences in New York City" (monograph, New York: The Vera Institute, September, 1999), p. i.

48. Joan R. Petersilia, "The Collateral Consequences of Prisoner Reentry in California: Effects on Children, Public Health, and Community" (monograph, April 2000), p. 1.

49. Joan Petersilia, "Parole and Prisoner Reentry in the United States," in *Prisons,* edited by Michael Tonry and Joan Petersilia (Chicago: University of Chicago Press, 1999), pp. 479–529.

50. See Nelson, Deess, and Allen.

51. Ibid., p. 5.

52. Elijah Anderson, *Streetwise: Race, Class, and Change in an Urban Community* (Chicago: University of Chicago Press, 1990), p. 4.

53. Dina R. Rose, Todd Clear and Kristen Scully, "Coercive Mobility and Crime: Incarceration and Social Disorganization," unpublished paper presented at the American Society of Criminology, Toronto, November, 1999.

▰ KEY TERMS

war on drugs	Girl Scouts Behind Bars
overrepresentation of minorities	antipsychotic drugs
social support	continuum of care

juvenile justice system

waiver of juveniles to adult courts

parenting programs

recidivism

meta-analysis

◼ YOU'RE THE CORRECTIONAL ADMINISTRATOR

1. You are the chief of correctional programs for a state correctional agency. A lawyer representing 200 inmates, all over age 50, in the state prisons comes to see you. The lawyer shows you a lawsuit that he is about to file alleging improper treatment and inhumane conditions. The suit alleges that as a result of the campus layout of the prisons, elderly inmates must walk several hundred yards to work, programs, and the dining room. It alleges a lack of medical care for health problems of the elderly. It includes an absence of work or recreation geared to their needs as well as many other allegations. He says instead of filing the suit, his clients will wait 60 days to see if you develop any plans to improve their situation. Unfortunately, you have been hearing some of the same issues from the wardens and know that the agency has not addressed these problems. What do you do? How do you determine whether there are unmet needs? How do you modify operations to meet needs that should be addressed?

2. You are the chief of mental health services for a state department of corrections. The director is under pressure from the governor and mental health advocates, who say that the department has ignored the needs of mentally ill inmates. You know their points have some merit, because the department does not have many specialized mental health programs. This issue has been heightened by two mentally ill inmates committing suicide by hanging themselves in the prisons over the past 60 days. In addition, a mentally ill inmate was raped in another prison. And an inmate suffering from mental illness murdered a staff member last week. How do you design an effective mental health program for inmates, and what resources can you seek or consult to establish and implement the program?

◼ WEB LINK EXERCISES

New Directions in Corrections: www.renewalinc.com

Go to the New Directions Web site for Renewal, Inc. Find out about Renewal and what services they offer to assist offenders in reentering the community as law-abiding and productive citizens. Describe the services you think are most helpful to offenders, and explain why.

15

Confronting the Increasing Costs of Corrections

INTRODUCTION

One of the most significant challenges for correctional administrators and other officials responsible for public budgets is the ever-increasing cost of correctional operations. With the increasing number of offenders under correctional supervision and with many factors driving up the per capita costs of operations, the amount of public funds that must be directed toward corrections threatens the availability of funds for other public purposes, and even the fiscal solvency of some local governments. The increased funding requirements for correctional agencies brings attention and pressures to elected officials to encourage correctional administrators to find ways to reduce budget requirements, and brings into question many policies and practices that the public believes create unnecessary expenditures.

As a result, correctional administrators try to find solutions to the budget dilemma. They examine ways to reduce their overall costs by "doing more with less" or by becoming more efficient in their operations. They look for ways to reduce demand for correctional services by finding alternatives to incarceration or by shortening supervision times. They look for ways to create revenue and to offset some of the increasing spending demands. And they look at nontraditional approaches to providing services, such as contracting with the private sector to reduce costs.

This chapter examines all of the aspects of increasing costs for corrections. First, the causes of increased correctional demands and budgets are examined. Second, the expenditures that are currently being committed to correctional agencies and the past trends in dollars for corrections are reviewed. Third, the methods by which agencies develop and monitor correctional budgets are investigated. Fourth, the alternatives available to correctional administrators to meet budget challenges are considered. Finally, the use of the private sector to provide correctional services and the potential for increased cost efficiency through this approach are examined.

INCREASES IN CORRECTIONAL BUDGETS

Correctional budgets have increased tremendously over the past decade. With crime rates decreasing over the same time period, correctional agencies supervise more offenders and, therefore, must have larger budgets. More offenders requires more prison beds, more employees for both community and institutional corrections, and the development of more intermediate sanctions. Although rational thinking would lead one to believe that the number of offenders under correctional supervision will decline soon, and therefore correctional budgets will be reduced, this has not yet occurred, and even though a few states are experiencing a decline in their prison populations, it is unlikely that any significant reduction in correctional budget needs will occur soon.

In the 1988 presidential election, George Bush successfully used the public's fear of crime as a campaign tool against Michael Dukakis. No one will soon forget the images of Willie Horton, presented as a dangerous offender who was **furloughed** from a Massachusetts prison by then-Governor Dukakis and committed a heinous violent crime. After elected president, Bush had to keep his campaign promises to be tough on crime and keep dangerous offenders in prison. In the 1990 federal budget process, the Bush administration added $2 billion of unrequested funds to the budget of the Federal Bureau of Prisons for prison construction. Not only were these prisons built, but the federal budget had to commit many more billions of funds over the next several decades to maintain and operate the prisons.

As other candidates for public office saw the effectiveness of **tough on crime policies,** with the promises of keeping dangerous offenders in prison, longer sentencing laws and funding for prison construction were passed by state legislatures throughout the United States. A decade later, many states wanted to turn back the clock and consider less costly sentencing approaches. Increasing costs of correctional budgets usually requires taking money out of other public budgets, such as education, social service programs, and those for improving deteriorating infrastructures. As Freeman suggests, "Tax revenues are not unlimited and, as correctional budgets have grown at the expense of other state agencies, elected officials have increasingly demanded that corrections assume a proactive role in reducing the burden on the taxpayer.[1] An examination of fiscal reports by the National Conference of State Legislatures noted that state spending on higher education experienced the greatest reduction during the 1990s, the period when state correctional spending had its fastest growth.[2]

In fiscal year 1991, state and federal adult correctional agencies budgets totaled $18.10 billion. By fiscal year 1998, these budgets increased 67 percent to $30.30 and represented 4.9 percent of the total budget of the jurisdiction.[3] This includes both operating and capital costs. The operating budget is that required for staff salaries, and to feed, clothe, and provide medical and other services to inmates. The capital budget is to build new prisons and expand the capacity to house more inmates. Figure 15–1 illustrates the tremendous increase in direct expenditures (not including intergovernmental expenditures such as federal grants) for all criminal justice

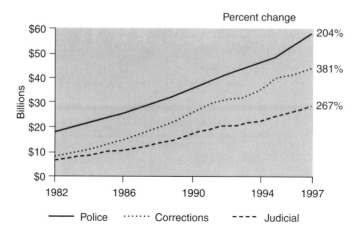

FIGURE 15-1 Direct expenditure by criminal justice function, 1982–1997.
Source: Justice Expenditure and Employment Extracts, Bureau of Justice Statistics,
www.ojp.usdoj.gov/bjs (1 February 2001).

functions. Correctional expenditure increases from 1982 through 1997 far exceeded the increase in police and judicial spending.

One informative fact about the increase in the overall spending for these adult correctional agencies is what has driven the increase. As one would expect, inflation and increases in employee salaries and benefits caused some of the budget increase. However, as reported in the *Corrections Yearbook, 1998,* the cost per inmate per day has only increased from $48.07 in 1990 to $55.51 in 1997, just more than a 15 percent increase.[4] During this period, the inmate population for these agencies increased 67 percent (from 750,000 to 1,250,000).[5] The increase in demand for services (housing more inmates) accounted for almost the entire increase in costs. Table 15–1 illustrates the total, operating, capital expenditures, and operating expenditures per inmate for state prisons during fiscal year 1996.

Just as budgets for prison operations have increased, the budgets for probation and parole functions have also increased. From fiscal year 1992 to fiscal year 1998, state correctional agencies reported funding for probation and parole agencies increased by 44 percent to more than $3.3 billion.[6] On January 1, 1998, these state agencies supervised 2.6 million offenders on probation or parole, at an average cost per day of community supervision of $3.54. These average costs include the following: (1) regular probation and parole supervision, (2) intensive supervision with more contacts by the officer with the offender than regular probation, (3) special supervision with programs such as a boot camp and substance abuse treatment, and (4) electronic monitoring of offenders using such devices as ankle bracelets or some other electronic technology to ascertain offenders' whereabouts.[7]

Correctional agency spending is expected to continue to increase for the next several years. With more than 83,000 new prison beds under construction in 1998[8] and another $3 billion budgeted for new construction in 1999,[9] there will be little reduction in the need to add dollars for prison operations in the new millennium. The issues quickly become how to find additional public funds for correctional

■ TABLE 15-1

State Prisons: Total, Operating, Capital Expenditures, and Operating Expenditures per Inmate, Fiscal Year 1996

Region and Jurisdiction	Expenditures (thousands of dollars)					Operating Expenditures (dollars per inmate)		Estimated Average Daily Number of Inmates, 1995–96
	Total	Operating	Percent of Total	Capital	Percent of Total	Per year	Per day	
Total	$22,033,214	$20,737,888	94%	$1,295,326	6%	$20,142	$55.18	1,029,595
Northeast	$5,083,959	$4,690,704	92%	$393,256	8%	$28,996	$79.44	161,773
Connecticut	497,838	475,367	94	22,471	6	31,912	87.43	14,896
Maine	51,713	48,206	93	3,507	7	33,711	92.36	1,430
Massachusetts	309,674	304,483	98	5,191	2	26,002	71.24	11,710
New Hampshire	42,970	42,429	99	541	1	20,839	57.09	2,036
New Jersey	839,308	827,115	98	12,193	2	30,773	84.31	26,878
New York	2,220,586	1,948,752	88	271,835	12	28,426	77.88	68,556
Pennsylvania	978,769	902,244	92	76,525	8	28,063	76.88	32,151
Rhode Island	109,596	108,683	99	913	1	35,739	97.92	3,041
Vermont	33,505	33,426	100	79	. . .	31,094	85.19	1,075
Midwest	$4,502,037	$4,254,686	94%	$247,351	6%	$21,919	$60.05	194,107
Illinois	740,423	732,824	99	7,599	1	19,351	53.02	37,870
Indiana	338,195	325,700	96	12,495	4	20,188	55.31	16,133
Iowa	146,069	143,774	98	2,295	2	24,286	66.54	5,920
Kansas	170,848	158,454	93	12,394	7	22,242	60.94	7,124
Michigan	1,167,610	1,161,142	99	6,468	1	28,067	76.89	41,371
Minnesota	185,983	184,359	99	1,624	1	37,825	103.63	4,874
Missouri	262,787	249,414	94	13,373	6	12,832	35.16	19,437
Nebraska	69,867	67,904	97	1,963	3	22,271	61.02	3,049
North Dakota	10,749	10,584	99	165	2	17,154	47.00	617
Ohio	1,014,917	873,584	86	141,333	14	19,613	53.74	44,540
South Dakota	34,152	33,582	98	570	2	17,787	48.73	1,888
Wisconsin	360,439	313,366	87	47,073	13	27,771	76.08	11,284
South	$7,442,584	$6,990,526	94%	$452,058	6%	$15,338	$42.02	455,756
Alabama	168,989	165,760	98	3,229	2	7,987	21.88	20,753
Arkansas	133,729	124,513	93	9,216	7	13,341	36.55	9,333
Delaware	87,961	87,253	99	707	1	17,987	49.28	4,851
District of Columbia	213,716	212,148	99	1,568	1	21,296	58.34	9,962
Florida	1,224,933	1,100,655	90	124,278	10	17,327	47.47	63,521
Georgia	560,358	547,490	98	12,868	2	15,933	43.65	34,363
Kentucky	208,706	198,775	95	9,931	5	16,320	44.71	12,180
Louisiana	316,245	313,463	99	2,783	1	12,304	33.71	25,476
Maryland	520,263	480,880	92	39,382	8	22,247	60.95	21,616
Mississippi	148,852	143,914	97	4,938	3	11,156	30.56	12,900
North Carolina	756,829	733,775	97	23,054	3	25,303	69.32	28,999
Oklahoma	198,290	193,567	98	4,723	2	10,601	29.04	18,260
South Carolina	315,539	277,868	88	37,671	12	13,977	38.29	19,880
Tennessee	350,575	349,177	100	1,398	. . .	22,904	62.75	15,245
Texas	1,713,935	1,565,214	91	148,721	9	12,215	33.47	128,140
Virginia	476,715	452,358	95	24,357	5	16,306	44.67	27,742
West Virginia	46,949	43,716	93	3,233	7	17,245	47.25	2,535
West	$5,004,632	$4,801,972	96%	$202,661	4%	$22,032	$60.36	217,959
Alaska	116,664	112,350	96	4,314	4	32,415	88.81	3,466
Arizona	418,094	409,167	98	8,927	2	19,091	52.30	21,433
California	3,031,047	2,918,845	96	112,202	4	21,385	58.59	136,492
Colorado	249,833	234,503	94	15,330	6	21,020	57.59	11,156
Hawaii	87,417	83,921	96	3,496	4	23,318	63.88	3,599
Idaho	56,957	55,017	97	1,940	3	16,277	44.60	3,380
Montana	42,448	41,875	99	573	1	20,782	56.94	2,015
Nevada	121,960	119,026	98	2,934	2	15,370	42.11	7,744
New Mexico	125,602	123,892	99	1,710	1	29,491	80.80	4,201
Oregon	254,330	253,421	100	909	. . .	31,837	87.22	7,960
Utah	113,394	111,808	99	1,585	1	32,361	88.66	3,455
Washington	357,862	311,122	87	46,740	13	26,662	73.05	11,669
Wyoming	29,025	27,024	93	2,001	7	19,456	53.30	1,389

Note: Expenditures exclude adult community corrections, juvenile corrections, and probation and parole services. Inmate counts used to calculate operating expenditures per inmate were based on prisoners under the jurisdiction of State correctional authorities from June 30, 1995, to June 30, 1996. Source: James J. Stephan, *State Prison Expenditures, 1996* (Washington, DC: Bureau of Justice Statistics, 1999), p. 2.

agency budget increases, and what options are available to add new prison beds and commit state taxpayer dollars for their operation. This situation creates a critical public policy challenge for correctional administrators, elected officials, and taxpayers who must foot the bill.

BUDGETARY AND PUBLIC POLICY CHALLENGES

Increased oversight by elected officials and a critical appraisal of how correctional agencies operate and spend their funds by the many interest groups that are affected by how much money is devoted to corrections or how much money is diverted from other public agencies can be expected from the dramatic increase in correctional agency budgets. Correctional agencies have operated and budgeted in very much the same manner throughout the entire history of corrections in the United States. Even with a number of different systems of public budgeting (line item budgeting, performance budgeting, planning–programming budgeting, and zero-based budgeting),[10] correctional budget development has basically been expense based and incremental.

With **expense-based budgets,** corrections agencies calculate how much it costs them for salaries, programs, and services and develop a budget based on these expenses. According to Phillips and McConnell, "A budget is a financial plan that serves as an estimate of future operations and, to some extent, as a means of control over those operations. It is a quantitative expression of the agency's or the prison's operating intentions. A budget translates intentions into numbers."[11] Although this is an accurate definition, it is also one that (without intending to do so) communicates many negatives of the correctional budget process.

Correctional agencies estimate the cost of their operations for the next or future fiscal years and ask the legislative body for that amount of money. If the state correctional agency has 10 prisons to operate, 10,000 inmates to feed and clothe, and employs 3,000 staff, administrators calculate the cost of these items, which becomes the budget request. They intend to continue doing business next year as they did in the past, and the budget provides for dollars required to conduct this business.

Correctional budgets are also **incremental,** in that the agency begins budget calculations by looking at what costs needed for operations last year and how much inflation or new prison beds will drive up the cost for the next year. The budget process seldom is designed to take any major policy issues into consideration. And when correctional budgets were relatively small, before they began to get so big that they required funds that elected officials would have liked to put into education, mental health, child care programs or even tax cuts, elected officials paid little attention to them.

Today, finding the money to fund correctional agencies has become a serious budget dilemma and, after some difficult choices are made, often results in a determination to find alternative approaches to future correctional operations. There are many options and policies that have recently been discussed and considered. Some seem to have promise, are politically attractive and supported, and may result in lowering correctional costs. Others may seem effective but have little political support. Or they may be politically attractive but have little effect on reducing the cost of correctional operations in a jurisdiction. Some of the alternative policies include the following:

▐ Reducing the offender or inmate population by reducing the length of sentences or the mandatory prison terms for certain offenses.
▐ Reducing the cost of daily operations of prisons or community correctional programs.
▐ Development of community sentencing alternatives to imprisonment.
▐ Reducing the cost of prison construction.
▐ Creating revenues in the correctional operations.
▐ Privatizing some services or operations.

REDUCING OFFENDER AND INMATE POPULATIONS

Many approaches to reducing the cost of corrections focus on community sanctions as alternatives to institutional sanctions. The first approach to reducing costs should consider whether society actually needs the high number of criminal offenders under supervision at any time. The most important goal of corrections is to protect society. Criminal sentences punish, deter, and incapacitate—by which fewer crimes are committed. The rapid increase in inmates and other offenders under correctional supervision has an important crime control aspect. Noting that the incarceration rate in the United States has grown more than four times since the early 1970s, Blumstein and Beck point out,

> There is no question that the nation has received some benefit from that growth in incarceration. At least for some crimes for which incarceration has a strong incapacitative effect, there is undoubtedly some crime reduction associated with increased incarceration . . . those benefits, however, must be weighed against the costs.[12]

The issue of cost is not a yes–no question of whether offenders should be sanctioned by imprisonment or community supervision, but for how long and in what combination of prison and community sanctions. As a result of the tough on crime mentality of many policy makers, sentences for imprisonment have lengthened, more offenders receive mandatory prison terms rather than probation, three strikes laws send repeat criminals to prison for life, opportunities for inmates to earn good time are reduced, there is longer postincarceration supervision, and both probation and parole are more likely to use additional approaches to supervision (electronic monitoring or intensive supervision), which all drive up costs. It is doubtful that lengthening prison sentences and "stacking" community supervision, when compared to the increase in cost, result in a proportionate reduction of crime and, therefore, increased safety to society. The accompanying Practical Perspectives case illustrates some of the dilemmas facing those trying to find options for reducing costs and the impact of even minor sentence modifications.

PRACTICAL PERSPECTIVES

Small Modifications Can Have Large Budget Implications

In one state experiencing a rapid increase in the number of offenders in prison, the state received a grant from the National Institute of Corrections to fund a prison overcrowding program. This program brought together legislators, judges, prosecutors, citizen groups, and correctional administrators to discuss the causes of the increase in prison population, to look for opportunities to reduce overcrowding, and to consider the need for more prison space while reducing the overall cost of the state correctional system. Many recommendations were suggested by the committee, one of which was a proposal to allow inmates to earn more good time for completion of drug abuse, educational, and vocational programs.

The state director of corrections began talking to legislators to explain the proposals and to urge their passage. One of the arguments was that if all inmates earned enough extra good time to reduce their sentences by only 90 days, it would save the state $500 million over 30 years. Legislators were shocked by these figures, but the director explained how they were calculated. The state held approximately 20,000 inmates, and reducing the sentence served by each for three months would, over time, reduce the population by 500 inmates. To build a 500 bed prison cost approximately $50 million, and it is estimated that construction costs represent only 10 percent of the overall operating costs of a prison over 30 years, or a total of $500 million. This represents how minor adjustments in time served can save massive amounts of dollars for state governments.

Unfortunately, it is politically difficult to do anything that reduces prison sentences, because many elected officials argue that extending sentences is necessary to make offenders accountable for their crimes. But as the example suggests, a lot of money can be saved by reducing sentences by 90 days, and the reduction would have very little impact on public safety. In writing about California's passage of three strikes legislation, Greenwood and colleagues suggest that legislators who found voting for the legislation politically attractive later reversed themselves and found that voting against funding the act's implementation was just as politically attractive.[13] It was presumed that voters would not like the resulting underfunding of education, environmental programs, and other social services that results from expanding prison costs for the three strikes bill. However, there has yet to be the first "voter revolution" about the lost opportunities by funding prisons to hold inmates serving longer sentences, and unfortunately, there is not likely to be any in the future. Caplow and Simon summarize the past and future projections of prison populations as follows:

While the rate of growth has slowed some in the 1990s, there is no reason to expect a reversal of directions any time soon. Indeed, while many states stiffened their criminal penalties during the 1980s, actual time served did not rise dramatically because of various offsetting administrative measures and court orders capping population. In the 1990s, these hidden brakes on prison population have been largely dismantled. . . . Growth in time served is likely to sustain growth in overall prison population even if prison admission rates should decline.[14]

REDUCING THE COST OF CORRECTIONAL OPERATIONS

As expenditures increase for correctional agencies and difficult choices must be made to not fund other preferred government operations, elected officials and the public express opinions on reducing the cost of current correctional operations. In a tough on crime climate with tough on criminals attitudes and rhetoric, it is not surprising that many people believe the costs of incarceration should be reduced by eliminating any programs or services that are not essential or may detract from the punitive aspect of the sentence. Additionally, correctional administrators know that they must do more with less and that their budgets will not continue to increase in direct proportion to the inmate population.

In this climate, one (or sometimes both) of two things occur. The legislative body may pass specific legislation that requires the elimination of programs, or it may refuse to provide funds for correctional activities it does not support. In several states the legislature has eliminated educational programs, recreational activities, or even staff performing security functions. Even when this does not occur, correctional administrators are often pressured to bring down the cost of confinement and must determine ways to reduce the budgets for prisons.

The California legislature has been very active in attempting to reduce funding for prisons. Without reducing the security of the prisons, the legislature directed that certain policies to modify security approaches and bring down costs should be enforced. In one action, California decided to stop using guard towers on perimeters and to replace them with lethal, electric fences. It was estimated that many prisons could reduce staffing in as many as 10 towers, saving almost 50 staff positions. It was estimated that this change in approach could save the state $40 million per year.[15]

In another action, California determined the need for many correctional officers could be reduced if gun ports were built inside of the prison in areas, such as the dining room and cell houses. The policy was modified to allow staff to shoot inmates to break up serious fights, rather than putting staff at risk by breaking up fights using less severe tactics. Unfortunately, this policy resulted in regular shooting incidents within California prisons, with correctional officers killing 36 inmates and wounding 207 others from 1989 until 1998.[16] From 1994 until 1998, only six inmates were fatally shot by staff in all other states, and all involved inmates trying to escape.[17]

One of the easiest targets for legislators has been to reduce inmate recreation or educational programs. Several states have banned weight lifting in prisons, believing it was a security risk because inmates strengthening themselves may make it difficult for staff to physically control the inmates. The issue, however, was really the negative image of inmates lifting weights in prison when they were supposed to be punished. In the late 1990s, the U.S. Congress did not ban weight lifting in federal prisons but added an amendment to the budget bills that no funds could be spent on inmate weight lifting or many other recreational activities.

Historically, many state prison agencies used **Pell grants** to fund inmate college programs. Pell grants began in the 1970s as a way for "disadvantaged populations" to receive funds for college courses. Inmates met the requirements for these grants, and most prisons had active college programs to motivate and improve inmate morale. In 1994, Congress specifically eliminated inmates from receiving Pell grants, and many active and proven college programs in prisons were eliminated.[18] Some jurisdictions kept college-level programs on a limited basis. However, in 2000, the Federal Bureau of Prisons proposed modifying their own rules to make inmates responsible for all college degree tuition costs.[19]

Another outcome of the pressure to reduce the costs of imprisonment has been the use of the private sector to own and operate prisons and house state or county inmates. The "privatization" of corrections is discussed further later. The threat of privatization has forced many public correctional agencies to reassess how they operate and to try to bring down costs to equate with those proposed by private companies. In 1996, the U.S. Congress required the Federal Bureau of Prisons (BOP) to contract for the private operation of one prison and assess the effectiveness of the contract. The BOP developed a request for proposal and contracted with the Wackenhut Corporation to operate the low-security Federal Correctional Institution at Taft, California.

To prepare for the evaluation of effectiveness, the BOP began to fund three of its similarly designed, low-security prisons at the same "inmate per day" rate that they were paying Wackenhut. This lead administrators at those three facilities to reduce staffing levels, to try to increase the inmate population (leading to more overcrowding), and to reduce recreational amenities and food costs to meet the operational costs of the private sector. On a broader scale, the BOP then initiated a plan for all prisons to begin to be budgeted on a "per capita" basis, rather than a line item budget basis.[20] By doing this, prison administrators began to reconsider how they operated and how to reduce their costs of confinement.

DEVELOPMENT OF COMMUNITY ALTERNATIVES TO PRISON

Many jurisdictions now have to confront the expense of sentencing policies that mandate certain offenders go to prison and lengthen sentences for others. Although some question whether public safety is improved by the large scale use of incarceration,[21] it would not be politically popular to try to reverse these decisions by shortening sentences and advocating probation for less severe offenders. Therefore, an in-between approach has been to find seemingly tough sanctions that allow offenders to be diverted from prison and remain in the community. These intermediate sanctions include intensive probation supervision, boot camp, and house arrest using electronic monitoring.

There are several reasons these intermediate sanctions have been widely adopted. First, although these penalties are not perceived as "punitive" by the public, they are supported for nonviolent offenders. Second, they are a less expensive sanction than imprisonment. And finally, they are believed to be more effective for "rehabilitating" offenders and allowing them to successfully remain in the community without returning to crime. Although it is arguable whether these three assumptions are true, they are widely enough accepted that elected officials and other criminal justice policy makers support their use.

The first interest of the public is to be protected, and they will not support any sanction that they do not believe punishes offenders and protects society. Surveys of public attitudes have found that the public will support the use of community sanctions if they believe they are effective. Sims, reporting on the findings from the 1995 and 1996 National Opinion Survey on Crime and Justice (NOSCJ), found that "while over half of the American public agrees that community corrections programs are too lenient, a much stronger majority appears to support certain programs that keep offenders in the community."[22]

If the public believes that community sanctions effectively protect them, they will support their use over imprisonment. An Ohio survey found support for

TABLE 15–2

Public Attitudes Toward Community Corrections

	Very Effective	Somewhat Effective	Not Very Effective	Not Effective at All
Regular probation supervision	16%	51%	22%	11%
Electronic monitoring of offenders	27	46	16	11
House arrest (home confinement)	13	42	23	21
Requiring offenders to pay fines instead of other penalties	12	36	31	21
Weekend jail sentences	11	36	27	25
Short-term boot camps	33	45	14	8
Requiring probationers to work so they can earn money to repay their victims	44	40	10	6
Requiring probationers to perform community services	29	48	16	7
Probation where offenders are monitored much more closely than offenders receiving the average level of supervision	20	53	18	9

Source: Barbara A. Sims, "Questions of Corrections: Public Attitudes Toward Prison and Community-Based Programs," *Corrections Management Quarterly* 1 no. 1 (1997): 54.

community corrections, but it was based on the public's recognition that prison space is scarce and expensive. The survey found that the public was in favor of using community correctional programs instead of paying for new prison construction.[23] Although they are not overwhelmingly supportive of sentences that use community placement for offenders, elected officials can use these findings to justify support for alternatives that are perceived to protect the public and rehabilitate offenders.

The NOSCJ survey asked questions about the public's perception of the effectiveness of certain community correctional programs. As indicated in Table 15–2, when the public was asked whether various types of community programs were effective at protecting citizens against crime, 73 percent indicated that intensive probation supervision was either "very effective" or "somewhat effective." Although only 55 percent similarly supported house arrest, 73 percent supported electronic monitoring of offenders. And boot camp was the most strongly supported; 78 percent of respondents believed them to be "very effective" or "somewhat effective."

Intensive supervision probationers (ISPs) involve intermediate sanctions that are believed to have promise in reducing costs. With intensive supervision, probationers who present a high risk of failure are placed in caseloads of smaller size than standard caseloads. The probationer is required to have considerably more contact with a probation officer and may have to report to the officer two or three times per week. In addition, officers do regular home and employment checks, urine analysis, and curfew checks. The focus is on closely monitoring the probationers' behavior, preventing them from criminal conduct, while maintaining them in the community rather than in prison. Although many studies consistently find a savings to the state or jurisdiction, they often find no reduction in recidivism with the use of ISPs. The following findings are summarized from a review of many ISP studies:

▌ ISPs have failed to alleviate prison crowding.
▌ Most ISP studies have found no significant differences between recidivism rates of ISP offenders and offenders with comparison groups.
▌ There appears to be a relationship between greater participation in treatment and employment programs and lower recidivism rates.
▌ ISPs appear to be more effective than regular supervision or prison in meeting offenders needs.
▌ ISPs that reflect certain principles of effective intervention are associated with lower rates of recidivism.
▌ ISPs do not provide an intermediate punishment.
▌ Although ISPs are less expensive than prison, they are more expensive than originally thought.[24]

Boot camps or **shock incarceration** is a way to divert young, first-time offenders from prison to a shortened stay in a military-style program emphasizing hard work, military drill, strict discipline, and physical training. As of January 1, 1999, 6,389 offenders were in boot camps operated by 32 correctional agencies.[25] Agencies reported the daily cost for 1998 at $58.06 and program length averaging five months.[26] This is higher than the 1998 reported daily cost in prisons of $56.26,[27] although the average prison stay for inmates released during 1998 was 29.1 months.[28] The alleged cost savings is not in the per day cost but in the overall cost of incarceration for the shorter boot camp period.

House arrest using electronic monitoring is another popular and inexpensive intermediate sanction used as an alternative to prison. With **house arrest,** offenders receive a "sentence" of detention in their own homes, and their compliance is often monitored electronically. With **electronic monitoring,** the offender wears a bracelet on the wrist or ankle, which confirms his or her presence in the residence through telephone lines.

A 1989 review of studies of electronic monitoring found that the average term of monitoring was 79 days; the longer the period of monitoring the greater the success; and that there was no significant difference is successful terminations among probationers, parolees, and those in other community corrections programs.[29] In other words, house arrest using electronic monitoring was as successful as prison and other more intensively supervised sanctions. In terms of cost savings, a National Council on Crime and Delinquency evaluation of Florida's Community Control Program (FCCP) found that not only did the FCCP participants have a lower new offense rate than similar offenders sentenced to prison and released without supervision but also for every 100 cases diverted from prison there was a savings of $250,000.[30]

Although intermediate sanctions may not always reduce further criminality among participants, most studies have shown these sanctions to be a cost effective (and equally safe) alternative to the use of prisons. As more studies identify key elements to success and as budgets for correctional operations continue to grow and demand cost cutting measures, it is likely that intermediate sanctions will play an even greater role in criminal sentencing. However, prisons continue to be built, and, correctional administrators continue to look for more economical methods of prison construction.

REDUCING THE COST OF PRISON CONSTRUCTION

Correctional administrators are continually pressured to find ways to reduce the cost of building prisons. There is no doubt that it is expensive to construct facilities that safely and securely house criminals; have sufficient space for operational needs such as food and medical services; and have program opportunities such as education, vocational training, and recreation. All of these activities require considerable space, and prison construction is not inexpensive.

As an example of prison architecture (illustrated in Chapter 12), the Federal Correctional Institution (FCI) in Greenville, Illinois, was opened in 1994. The facility is reported to include 357,000 square feet of space at the main medium security facility, 74,000 square feet at the minimum security camp, and 42,000 square feet of shared facility space such as the warehouse and central utility plant. The prison was constructed with 512 medium security cells and 128 minimum security inmate cubicles.[31] The cost of construction was approximately $62 million. With the Federal Bureau of Prisons calculating the **design capacity** of this prison at 768 medium security and 256 minimum security inmates, the combined total cost per inmate bed was more than $60,000. It must be understood, however, that the cost per bed includes the overall cost for constructing the prison as well as all of the space other than that used for cell or cubicle construction.

As correctional construction costs continued to rise as a percentage of state and local budgets, the public and elected officials began to question the cost and encouraged consideration of less expensive construction techniques or less space. As a result of this pressure, construction costs for prisons have increased little during the 1990s. These costs rose during the first few years of the 1990s and then declined in 1996 and 1997. In both maximum and medium security prisons, the 1997 cost was actually less than in 1990.[32]

There was also a considerable difference in construction costs among states. In 1997, prison beds under construction ranged for maximum security from $11,179 (Mississippi) to $128,000 (Washington), medium security from $11,000 (Florida) to $100,940 (Washington), and minimum security from $4,951 (Alabama) to $58,333 (Illinois).[33] Although several factors influence construction costs (climate, space requirements, construction type, and philosophy), the lower costs of construction in some states is obviously brought to the attention of correctional administrators in the more expensive states. Elected officials trying to save costs on correctional construction urge administrators to investigate the less expensive approaches to construction in some jurisdictions.

The biggest savings for prison construction is associated with space and type of security. The housing units make up far less than 50 percent of the total square footage at FCI, Greenville. If a jurisdiction decided they could do without space for education, prison industries, religious programming, drug abuse, and recreation, there would be considerable funds saved on construction. Additionally, if a jurisdiction determined that inmates with security designations above minimum (medium or even maximum) could safely be held in open dormitory space (cubicles) instead of cells, there would also be considerable construction savings. Apart from these questionable philosophical and policy considerations, jurisdictions look for other methods and opportunities to reduce construction costs, and several approaches have been successful, including the use of inmate labor for portions of the construction, design/build construction techniques, and the use of prototype prison design and construction.

All states use inmate labor to renovate space or even do small construction projects within existing prisons. This is a cost-effective way to renovate prisons, as well as excellent experience and training for the inmates. One reason it saves considerable dollars is because it is not necessary to bring outside construction crews and equipment into the prison, and develop what turns out to be expensive approaches to providing security for the construction project. If inmates do the work and correctional staff supervise their efforts, there is less need to provide security and to keep inmates away from the construction area.

However, a few states have tried to use inmate labor to reduce construction costs of new prisons. In the early 1990s, the Federal Bureau of Prisons contracted with private construction companies to build housing units and key operational areas such as food service and medical areas. The private contractors also built the outer shell of the program and activities buildings. The shells included the foundations, roofs, and unfinished walls. Inmates were then moved into the prison and completed the interiors of these buildings, including installing electrical wiring, heating and ventilation systems, and drywall ceilings and walls.

In the 1980s, when the state of California was confronted with a major construction program of bed space for almost 100,000 prisoners, it turned to inmate labor to reduce costs. "Poured-in-place" cement slabs were used for walls and ceilings. These slabs were long panels of concrete with vertical and horizontal iron bars linked inside the concrete to make them more secure and difficult to break. Inmates at existing institutions built forms for these slabs and poured the concrete. When they were ready, the panels were transported to the construction sites and assembled into the new prisons. During the same period, in Ohio inmates were used in existing prisons to construct materials for use in the new prisons. Inmates built steel grills to be placed over the glass windows as well as steel doors and frames for installation in the prisons.

Design/build is a rather new approach for government and prison construction. **Design/build** basically tries to consolidate responsibility for design and construction of a facility to "meet very tight construction schedules, guarantee budgets in the early phases of construction and simplify construction administration.[34] Design/build is an alternative to "design–bid–build," in which an architect designs the prison, bids are accepted for many portions of the prison from construction firms, and the winning bidders build the portion of the prison for which they received the bid. Each step is completed in sequence, and the average time of design and construction is 30 to 36 months. With design/build, "the entire scope of work—architectural and engineering design, construction, project management, cost management and quality control—[is] shared as a single-source responsibility by the designer and the builder under one individual contract.[35]

The belief is that design/build will reduce the construction schedule, because construction actually can begin on early phases (such as site preparation and underground utilities) even before the entire architectural and engineering designs are completed. It also has the advantage of providing a known fixed cost, because the entire project is bid to one contractor for a set price, rather than having 20 to 30 bids for small pieces of the construction pie. Although there are risks with this approach, both construction time and costs are usually reduced. In describing the use of a design/build for the U.S. Penitentiary in Coleman, Florida, Mary S. Galey, construction project administrator for the Bureau of Prisons, writes,

> The result was a design that more than meets the minimum needs of the BOP and still allows the contractor to construct the institution in an economical and efficient manner. Approximately 50 percent of the contract time has passed, the design is complete and the contractor is working with a schedule that has a construction completion date two months prior to the contract completion date.[36]

Finally, governments have been using **prototype prison construction** as a cost savings approach. The fact that many jurisdictions are building more than one prison of similar size and security level allows for a single design to be used for more than one prison.[37] Correctional agencies can use the prototype designs in a variety of ways. They can select one architect to develop a prison design for several different sites. This reduces the cost and time for architectural planning. The Federal Correctional Institutions at Greenville and Pekin, Illinois, are identical designs, with the only variations being a few color changes and slight adaptations for varying

Precast Cells in a New Prison Construction. One way administrators try to keep the cost of construction low is to use precast cells, which are brought to the construction site as a unit and stacked on one another. (Courtesy of the Pennsylvania Department of Corrections)

gradations between the two sites. Another prototypical approach is to use the same architectural design for certain portions of a prison, such as housing units, food service, or a program building.

What ever approaches are used to reduce construction costs, there is ample opportunity to save money. The sheer volume of construction over the next several years will be significant. The *1999 Corrections Yearbook* reports that on January 1, 1999, there were 41,368 total beds to be added to state and federal prisons at a cost of more than $1.9 billion.[38] Correctional agencies can select a variety of security and operations philosophies that have a meaningful impact on construction costs. And there are several approaches to construction that can reduce costs, including the use of inmate labor, design/build, and prototypical prison designs. And with a large amount of correctional budgets going toward prison construction, these cost reduction efforts can have significant monetary impact.

CREATING REVENUES IN CORRECTIONS

Seldom does one think of creating revenues when it comes to operating a correctional agency. However, many jurisdictions have become quite innovative in finding opportunities for creating revenue, and there are possibly many others that, although perhaps somewhat controversial, may be sources of income. In a chapter entitled "Enterprising Government: Earning Rather than Spending," the authors of *Reinventing Government* write,

> Our (government's) budget systems drive people to spend money, not to make it. And our employees oblige. We have 15 million trained spenders in American government, but few people who are trained to make money. . . . But can you imagine

the creativity they would turn loose if they thought as much about how to *make* money as they do about how to *spend* it?[39]

Since Osborne and Gaebler wrote about the need and ways to reinvent government, it has become quite popular to try to create revenue. The government often has unused products and services that could be sold to the private sector or even other government agencies. There is often the opportunity for government agencies to charge individuals fees for services, for example, to play on a recreational softball team, to use a public camp ground, or to tour a public building. With a bit of creativity, there are many ways that correctional agencies could create revenue. Agencies are charging offenders for supervision or for services, and are using offenders to produce products that can be sold for income or at least to reduce the cost of correctional operations.

The idea of charging offenders for services is not new, particularly for community corrections. Financial sanctions as a condition of probation have historically included fines and restitution to victims. More recently, probation agencies have begun to charge offenders for services (e.g., drug counseling, halfway house stays, work release programs) and for their supervision (e.g., electronic monitoring, intensive supervision, urine analysis). In 1980, only 10 states reported charging supervision or user fees, but this number has increased steadily to 25 states in 1986, and 41 by 1996.[40] For years, offenders in halfway houses had to contribute a portion of their income (often about 15 percent) to the cost of their room, board, and supervision. Although there are opponents of collecting fees from offenders, others argue that because offenders are allowed to remain in the community and stay in the workforce, they should contribute to the public cost for their supervision.

More recently, many jurisdictions approved a **cost of incarceration fee** for prisoners housed in local jails or state and federal prisons. The requirement for inmates to pay their own cost for being in prison has been well received by the public, yet it is fairly impractical and difficult to implement. There are very few inmates with the financial resources to pay what may end up being $50 per day to stay in prison or jail. Legislation authorizing payments usually releases indigent offenders from payment. And even when indigents have assets, prison administrators may calculate the cost to maintain inmates' families before determining whether the inmates have available resources to pay the state or county government. There are very few jurisdictions that have been successful at collecting the full cost of confinement from many inmates.

One fee that is widely used, and that was referenced in Chapter 9, is a fee for medical care. As reported in the *Corrections Yearbook,* as of January 1, 1999, 32 agencies charged prison inmates a minimal fee or copayment of two or three dollars for medical care.[41] These fees have two major benefits. The first is that collecting them raises money to help cover the rising cost of medical care for inmates. However, the more important benefit is the reduction in demand for medical services. Nevada, one of the first states to charge inmates a copayment, reviewed inmate use of medical resources from 1989 to 1991 and determined that the usage rate decreased by 76 percent in the maximum security prison and by 50 percent throughout the state.[42] The cost of medical care for inmates is extremely expensive, and there is ample opportunity for reduction. Table 15–3 illustrates state prison expenditures for medical care and other inmate services during fiscal year 1996. The total expenditures for medical care of the states reporting was more than $2 billion.

One way of creating revenue that is unlikely to ever again be used involves "leasing out" inmate labor to the private sector. However, every state has a prison industry program, in which inmates produce products that are sold to generate revenue and, in many cases, make a profit to help cover the cost of prison operation. In 1998, state and federally operated correctional industry sales were more than $1.5 billion and profits were more than $65 million.[43] There is much opposition from the private sector for allowing prison industries much freedom to produce goods for sale on the open market, and, therefore, most industries are only able to sell to other governmental agencies. However, with the increasing need for funds to expand correctional supervision and prison operations, states are extending the authorization for the sale of prison-made products.

Creation of revenues by correctional agencies is still very small, particularly in terms of the millions of offenders under the supervision of correctional agencies on any given day. However, there is an enormous opportunity to use this workforce to contribute to their own supervision or room and board. With the strong economy and low unemployment rate of the late 1990s and early 2000s, there will be an increasing willingness for the public to support the use of inmates for production of goods or delivery of services that can create revenue and reduce correctional costs. As one group of elected officials wishing to continue the prison boom look for ways to create revenue and reduce expenditures, another group will oppose allowing inmate labor to compete in the marketplace. It will be interesting to see which of these two groups will be successful in maintaining or expanding their position.

PRIVATIZING CORRECTIONS

Perhaps the most controversial approach to reducing the cost of corrections has been the **privatization** of correctional operations and programs, particularly the operation of prisons for profit by private companies. Although public correctional agencies contracting with the private sector for delivery of services is certainly not new, the ownership and operation of prisons by the private sector has a relatively short history. Generally, it is argued that the flexibility and market-driven nature of the private sector can lead to more cost-effective operation of prisons and other correctional programs. However, some question the moral and ethical foundations of profiting from taking away someone's freedom, and the turning over of what has traditionally been a governmental function. In the following sections, many issues of privatizing the nation's correctional operations are identified and discussed.

The History of the Private Sector in Corrections

The private sector has been involved in the administration of various correctional aspects for several centuries. When countries transported offenders to penal colonies, the offenders were often required to serve as indentured servants to

TABLE 15–3

State Prison Expenditures for Medical Care, Food Service, Inmate Programs, Utilities, and Transportation, Fiscal Year 1996

Region and Jurisdiction	Expenditures (thousands of dollars)				
	Medical Care	Food Service	Inmate Programs	Utilities	Transportation
National estimate	2,456,300	$1,112,900	$1,231,100	682,028	$197,000
Total, reporting states	$2,279,228	$1,107,672	$1,040,806	$682,028	$171,602
Northeast	$453,243	$203,305	$311,520	$154,748	$30,878
Connecticut	44,939	22,967	. . .	16,789	4,130
Maine	3,379	1,437	. . .	2,395	109
Massachusetts	39,850	9,406	. . .	8,476	1,914
New Hampshire	8,325	2,358	. . .	2,274	217
New Jersey	61,819	24,956	. . .	26,543	2,980
New York	163,454	70,050	. . .	64,025	19,061
Pennsylvania	119,522	65,686	. . .	30,675	. . .
Rhode Island	9,297	4,903	. . .	2,774	2,329
Vermont	3,658	1,543	. . .	796	137
Midwest	$394,325	$251,933	$156,765	$130,959	$32,119
Illinois	48,272	41,928	. . .	26,254	5,615
Indiana	. . .	16,687	. . .	9,198	1,730
Iowa	8,832	10,972	. . .	4,938	717
Kansas	16,647	9,750	. . .	4,787	1,441
Michigan	189,812	65,281	. . .	28,828	17,873
Minnesota	. . .	. . .	. . .	5,660	585
Missouri	24,867	14,887	. . .	11,535	1,562
Nebraska	3,577	3,083	. . .	1,841	278
North Dakota	622	660	. . .	485	85
Ohio	78,973	69,717	. . .	26,340	. . .
South Dakota	4,284	3,219	. . .	905	146
Wisconsin	18,439	15,750	. . .	10,187	2,086
South	$849,313	$366,799	$218,523	$259,944	$69,153
Alabama	21,535	6,389	. . .	8,091	1,644
Arkansas	17,972	7,215	. . .	5,858	637
Delaware	8,256	6,595	. . .	3,948	2,901
District of Columbia	21,804	14,776	. . .	9,496	4,763
Florida	194,594	81,813	. . .	37,213	24,976
Georgia	83,033	38,961	. . .	24,843	3,714
Kentucky	16,049	7,155	. . .	6,131	5,534
Louisiana	. . .	10,394	. . .	7,862	. . .
Maryland	37,380	17,594	. . .	19,188	3,064
Mississippi	15,153	8,468	. . .	5,163	1,143
North Carolina	76,634	28,151	. . .	22,971	3,250
Oklahoma	15,027	7,835	. . .	6,446	1,629
South Carolina	20,336	9,174	. . .	15,391	2,142
Tennessee	29,346	23,261	. . .	16,126	2,583
Texas	276,826	65,820	. . .	54,169	8,413
Virginia	. . .	29,998	. . .	14,644	2,334
West Virginia	5,367	3,201	. . .	2,406	425

Continued

TABLE 15-3 Continued

State Prison Expenditures for Medical Care, Food Service, Inmate Programs, Utilities, and Transportation, Fiscal Year 1996

Region and Jurisdiction	Expenditures (thousands of dollars)				
	Medical Care	Food Service	Inmate Programs	Utilities	Transportation
West	$582,348	$285,634	$353,997	$136,377	$39,453
Alaska	14,066	5,122	. . .	3,857	1,816
Arizona	39,703	23,797	. . .	12,033	. . .
California	378,031	177,614	. . .	78,686	25,565
Colorado	22,176	14,203	. . .	6,537	2,441
Hawaii	8,125	7,273	. . .	3,302	162
Idaho	7,128	3,512	. . .	1,455	369
Montana	4,030	2,100	. . .	805	362
Nevada	24,621	6,766	. . .	5,305	. . .
New Mexico	10,264	6,622	. . .	4,014	589
Oregon	14,463	10,438	. . .	6,245	2,157
Utah	10,868	4,163	. . .	2,936	1,136
Washington	43,140	22,661	. . .	10,445	4,856
Wyoming	5,734	1,362	. . .	757	. . .

Note: Figures include salaries or wages of correctional staff involved in the described activity. Detail may not add to total due to rounding. National estimates are based on ratio adjustments of total to covered inmate population. . . . Not able to separate from general operating expenditures.

Source: James J. Stephan, *State Prison Expenditures*, 1996 (Washington, DC: Bureau of Justice Statistics, 1999), p. 6.

individuals and businesses who had contractual agreements with the governments. Early prisons allowed businesses to contract for the use of prisoners as a labor source, with the funds offsetting the cost of prison operations. These contracts were ripe for abuse and led to federal legislation limiting the products of prison labor being sold on the open market.

However, as the contracting for services *from* inmates ended, contracting by public agencies for services *for* inmates began. With the development of an era of halfway houses during the late 1960s, the private sector formed alliances with public correctional agencies. By the 1980s, almost every state had contracts with privately operated halfway houses to provide residential services, supervision, and transitional programs for inmates leaving prison and returning to the community.[44] Today, the use of privately operated halfway houses is not seen as controversial, and it has expanded to house offenders serving probation sentences, short jail terms for DWI, and special needs offenders requiring drug abuse or mental health programming.

Many states have very small juvenile offender populations, and it was often cost effective to contract with small privately operated facilities rather than for the state to open juvenile facilities. Massachusetts actually closed all of its juvenile institutions in the early 1970s and contracted for delinquents to be housed in private community facilities. In 1984, it was reported that 65 percent of all juvenile facilities were private, housing approximately 32,000 offenders.[45] Juvenile offenders housed in privately operated correctional facilities has seldom been seen as controversial, partly because the nature of the juvenile justice system is not so much punishment as reformation.

The more controversial private sector involvement in corrections started with the contracting to house adult prisoners in private prisons. According to most reports, the first contract of this sort was initiated in 1984 and was a small, 250-bed facility operated by Corrections Corporation of America under contract with Hamilton County, Tennessee. Although it was considered an aberration with little chance for future expansion by most correctional administrators, this facility was soon followed by additional contracts for housing illegal aliens (contracted with the U.S. Immigration and Naturalization Service) and youth offenders (with the Federal Bureau of Prisons).

To ensure a clear understanding of what a private prison is, the following definition is provided: A **private prison** is any secure correctional facility, operated by other than a governmental agency and usually in a "for-profit" manner, which contracts with a governmental entity to provide security, housing, and programs for adult offenders. In a private prison, staff are not public employees; they are employees of the company that owns and operates the prison. The prison can be administered free from governmental policies for purchasing and personnel practices, although it will still be held to the same constitutional standard for treatment of inmates as a public prison.

The privatization of correctional facilities was spurred by the increasing number of inmates and the rapid need to build new prisons, the budgetary challenges required to fund these new prisons, and the Reagan era support of using the private sector to help downsize the scope of government:

> At that time, the prevailing political and economic philosophy encouraged government officials to turn to the private sector to administer public services, such as sanitation, health care, security, fire protection, and education. As a result of the introduction of free-market principles into the administration of public services, . . . the privatization of corrections appeared to be a new and novel approach to some old problems (i.e., overcrowding and mounting costs).[46]

The crunch to find financial resources for the expansion of prisons, the Reagan and Bush administrations' emphasis on less government, and the Clinton–Gore emphasis on improving government efficiency have all contributed to the interest in expanding the private sector delivery of traditional government services. By 1990, Logan reported that private prisons held more than 9,000 adult inmates.[47] By January 1, 1999, there were 57 privately operated facilities housing more than 27,000 adult prisoners at an average cost per day of $42.26.[48] Although this figure is considerably lower than the average cost of $56.46 per day for public prisons at the same date,[49] it is not a comparable figure. Private prisons have usually been contracted to house low-security prisoners, because approximately 95 percent of the inmates in private prisons on January 1, 1999, were either minimum or medium.[50] In contrast, approximately 68 percent of public prison inmates are medium security or lower, whereas 25 percent are close, high, or maximum security, and 6 percent are unclassified.[51]

How Private Prisons Function

When a jurisdiction decides to attempt to contract the placement of prisoners in a private prison, a formal legal and contractual process must begin. The first step is to determine the need for housing of inmates, both in terms of the number of inmates and security level required. Second, the correctional agency develops a **request for**

proposal (RFP), which outlines in detail the requirements, expectations, and standards to be met by the bidding companies. In the RFP, the agency will usually clarify the geographic area for which they will consider contracting for bed space. It is usually not necessary for the private prison to be located in the same jurisdiction as the correctional agency. It is not unusual for states to contract for bed space in a state some distance away.[52]

For a private company to own and operate a prison and contract for prisoners with a governmental agency, there must be **enabling statutes** by the state in which the private prison is located. A few states do not allow private prisons to operate within the state or limit the operation to contract with and house only prisoners from that state. Also, the state must pass legislation allowing the state to delegate by contract its correctional authority. In order to clarify responsibilities and avoid legal challenges,

> This statute must specifically address rules, regulations, licensing, policies, and procedures pertinent to the operation of private correctional facilities, as well as designate staff, facilities, budgets, and responsible agencies for the oversight of those rules, regulations, licensing, policies, and procedures. Enabling statues must grant judges authority to sentence defendants to private institutions; without such legislation, any sentence to a private prison would be subject to a jurisdictional challenge.[53]

The agency makes public the RFP, and any private company that meets the minimum requirements of experience and capabilities may submit a bid. Bids are usually evaluated on both cost and quality of service delivery, often rated by the companies past record and description of how they would operate the prison. The governmental jurisdiction then awards the contract, transports prisoners to the facility, and monitors compliance with contract provisions. These provisions are usually both general in nature, such as requiring the company to comply with American Correctional Association standards, and very specific, such as directing the availability of sick call for inmates or the number of calories per day in meals served.

There are several variations of operations by private companies as they comply with RFPs. First, the RFP may require a private company to own (already or build) a prison to house the inmates. Many times, a private company will build a large prison and then respond to RFPs from many jurisdictions to fill it. Very few problems result from having inmates from a variety of jurisdictions in the same facility. Second, a jurisdiction may already have a prison and may seek a private operator to manage the facility. Some jurisdictions prefer this approach, fearing that if contractual problems result with the private company, they can find another manager. However, if the company owns the prison, they must find available space elsewhere if the contract ends.

Finally, there are some governmental agencies that operate as private firms and respond to RFPs from other jurisdictions. Sechrest and Shichor refer to these as **public proprietary facilities** operated by "small jurisdictions without a strong economic base, thus making the (facilities) a potential source of income and employment."[54] These municipalities or counties pass bonds and build prisons specifically for contracting with other governmental jurisdictions. They often contract with one of the large private prison companies to manage them. However, the fact that they are owned by a governmental agency makes the contracts less bureaucratic to develop, and a response to an RFP can usually be avoided and a "direct award" to the public proprietary facility is legally allowable.

Issues in Prison Privatization

As noted earlier, privatizing the operation of prisons has been very controversial, and there are many arguments both for and against private involvement in corrections. Every discussion of private prisons includes pros and cons, benefits and costs, and advantages and disadvantages. These discussions usually include two general areas of issues: philosophical and pragmatic. The philosophical issues center around the distinction of roles between the private sector profit-making enterprises and government, ethics and corruption, and the larger public interest. The pragmatic arguments include cost effectiveness, quality of service, security and public protection, and liability.

Charles Logan, who has studied the operation of private prisons since they were initiated, identified 10 issues that are key to any deliberations regarding the use of private prisons. These issues are as follows:

1. **The propriety of proprietary prisons**—can the punishment of offenders be delegated to nonpublic agencies?
2. **Cost and efficiency**—are private prisons operated less expensively than public prisons?
3. **Quality**—does the profit motive diminish the drive for delivery of quality services and programs to inmates?
4. **Quantity**—does the involvement of the private sector to make a profit encourage the expansion of imprisonment beyond what is in the public interest?
5. **Flexibility**—does the fact that the private sector does not have to follow bureaucratic government policies for purchasing and personnel management increase efficiency?
6. **Security**—does the fact that an emphasis on profits and cost cutting undermine security for inmates, staff, and the community?
7. **Liability**—what impact does a government contracting with a private firm for housing inmates have on the liability of the government for violation of inmates' constitutional rights?
8. **Accountability and monitoring**—how will the private contractor be monitored to fulfill requirements and be held responsible if they do not?
9. **Corruption**—without the restraints inherent in government to reduce the likelihood of corruption, will there be an increase in private prisons?
10. **Dependence**—will the public sector become dependent on the private sector contract, and if so, how does this affect decision making?[55]

The first issue to address is the basic philosophical issue of whether private companies should be allowed to make a profit out of incarcerating criminal offenders. Many individuals and groups (such as the American Civil Liberties Union [ACLU]) argue that taking away an individual's freedom is the responsibility of the government and should not be abdicated to the lowest bidder. At this point, the U.S. Supreme Court has not clearly established whether government can transfer correctional functions to the private sector.[56] Logan notes, however, that the authority of government is derived from the consent of the governed and, therefore, may be delegated further with similar consent.[57] Although this question continues to be raised in every discussion of private prisons, it has generally been decided by the dozens of state and local governmental agencies that make use of the private sector to incarcerate inmates.

The second issue is the key one of cost efficiency. The major reason for involving the private sector in correctional operations is so that operations will cost less than if they are run by the government. There have been very few sound methodological studies to actually compare the cost and outcome of privately operated prisons. The earliest review of the Hamilton County, Tennessee, private prison suggested that it saved from 4 to 15 percent annually over the county operated penal farm costs.[58] In another study that examined costs comparing public and private prisons in Kentucky and Massachusetts, the researchers concluded that the private prisons appeared to be better managed than the public prisons.[59]

A study of costs over the fiscal year 1991–1992 comparing public and private facilities housing parole violators in the state of California resulted in a lower cost per day for private facilities. However, the authors state that,

> While the findings of this study are preliminary, when all factors are considered, they do not appear to be more supportive of the use of either the public or private proprietary facilities.... Considering comparative security levels, overhead, and hidden costs of [state] and [nonstate] facilities, the only conclusion at this time is that the relative costs of [these] operations are probably about the same.[60]

Recently, there have been questions by the California Controller's Officer regarding expenditures for private contracts. The contracting process was found to be flawed, and six private facilities ended up in court with the Department of Corrections to dispute cost and payments.[61]

Few studies that have examined the postrelease outcome between public and private prison inmates. In one Florida study comparing recidivism of releasees from private and public prisons, results favored the private prisons. Releasees from two private facilities were matched with releasees from public prisons. Recidivism from the private prisons was lower than that from the public prisons, and of those who reoffended, the crimes were less serious for the private prison releasees.[62]

Most of these studies have been plagued with poor research designs, a lack of complete data, or are very preliminary. In an attempt to capture the best available information comparing the cost effectiveness of public and private prison operations, the Government Accounting Office (GAO) conducted a comprehensive review of all completed studies. The GAO identified five studies that had been completed since 1991 on privately operated prisons in Texas, New Mexico, California, Tennessee, and Louisiana. The reviewers did not believe that three of these studies were sufficiently designed to use their results. The outcome from the remaining two studies indicated minimal or no differences between the public and private prison operations.[63]

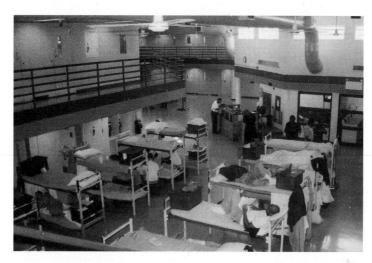

Can Privatization Reduce Overcrowded Prisons? Some private prison providers argue that contracting with the private sector can increase capacity, reduce overcrowding, and bring down the cost of incarceration. (Courtesy of the Ohio Department of Rehabilitation and Correction)

At this point, there can be no firm conclusions about the cost efficiency of private prisons compared to public prisons. More studies need to be conducted, with particular attention on outcome and a realistic comparison of costs. One study that has promise is being conducted by the Federal Bureau of Prisons to compare their first privately operated prison in Taft, California, with similar security-level federal prisons. Once it is completed, this study will add significantly to the literature and shed more light on the effectiveness of private prisons.

Some of the remaining issues are discussed in logical groupings as they relate to oversight and contractual considerations important to correctional managers. The first group includes the issues of "quality," "security," and "accountability and monitoring." The concern is whether a motive for profit making will reduce the emphasis on quality programs and service delivery, as well as overall security of a private prison. Although there are no firm conclusions that link profit to these issues, it has always been a concern of correctional administrators, and there is a developing perception that the concern may have some merit.

In the late 1990s, the District of Columbia contracted with Corrections Corporation of America (CCA) to house some of their prisoners at the Northeast Ohio Correctional Center, CCA's private prison in Youngstown, Ohio. In the first few years of operation, the prison inmates experienced several assaults, murders, and escapes, leading to an investigation of the prison's management practices by the U.S. Department of Justice. Although not specifically blaming the emphasis on making a profit for the mismanagement of the facility, the report alluded to the potential for profit to influence sound correctional practice and decisions.[64]

Since that report and the extensive media coverage of the CCA problems in Youngstown, many jurisdictions are reconsidering their support of privately operated prisons. Whereas jurisdictions must pass legislation to authorize placing inmates in private prisons, and in some states authorize even the locating and operating of any private prison, some states have passed bills limiting this authorization. In Ohio, the state legislature passed a bill requiring private prisons to meet all requirements for operations that state and local prisons must meet. In North Carolina and Pennsylvania, the states only allow private prisons to house inmates under contract from that state, rather than inmates from other jurisdictions. When private prisons experience few problems, there are few questions about the impact of profits. However, it is only natural that when problems of quality or security exist, the perception will be that the private operators sacrifice quality or security to enhance profits.

The most important element for correctional administrators considering contracting with the private sector is to be very specific in the RFP regarding the minimum levels of these programs and to build in procedures to monitor and hold the private sector accountable for meeting these levels. It is difficult to argue with the point of view of private prison managers, noting that they provide whatever services and quality the contractor builds into the RFP. They do not want to choose the standards expected but simply provide those specified and place a price and reasonable profit margin on meeting the jurisdiction's contract requirements.

One point that is seldom argued regarding the benefit of private prison operations is the flexibility that these facilities have over their public sector counterparts. Governmental agencies are usually overencumbered with bureaucracy and redundancy regarding purchasing and personnel management. To hire a correctional officer in a federal prison can take as long as one year from the time the officer candidate completes the job application, and up to six months for the prison that determines it needs to hire a new officer. Purchasing within governmental agencies is also archaic in approach and lacks the flexibility to make quick purchases when cost savings are available. One private sector warden noted, "One thing I love is the flexibility. If a truck with extra chicken not needed by the local supermarket pulls into my parking lot, and offers me a good deal, I can buy it on the spot. I could never do that as a public-sector warden."[65] In a general review of quantitative and qualitative data between a private prison in New Mexico compared with its previous operation by the state, private management was favored on many scales, including operational and administrative flexibility.[66]

However, one of the reasons that a great deal of government bureaucracy exists for personnel and purchasing is to reduce the likelihood of bribes, favoritism, and corruption that can occur in these areas. The lengthy requirements for fairness and inclusiveness by government agencies were put in place for a good reason, even if there is a collateral consequence of bureaucracy and lack of expediency. Therefore, private prisons, without these bureaucratic safeguards, are more at risk for corruption than the public sector. However, to date, this has not been a serious issue of the larger and more professional private prison operators. Even though there have been some isolated cases of prisoner abuse, blamed on a failure to do satisfactory background checks before hiring employees by private operators, the companies in which these occurred have gone out of business. Those remaining are reasonably diligent in checking candidates for employment for backgrounds that may indicate the potential for abuse or other corruption.

Again, correctional administrators who are worried about these issues can build safeguards into the RFP. Private companies will do whatever is required in terms of personnel hiring or purchase practices. It is unwise for the public agency seeking a private contract for prison operations to make these requirements too bureaucratic, because they will lose much of the financial benefit of flexibility. However, requiring certain background checks of personnel and minimum competition among bidders for contracts (for food, supplies, or materials) with the private prisons is reasonable and allows flexibility while reducing the potential for corruption. As one private operator notes in summarizing the value of private prisons:

> Private sector participation in the correctional profession elevates industry performance as a whole in several key respects: taxpayer cost savings, quality assurance, and operational effectiveness.[67]

The issue of liability when a governmental agency contracts with a private provider is complex and not yet clearly established through case law. It is generally accepted that the state or local government does not escape liability by simply contracting with a private provider for housing criminal offenders. The government maintains responsibility for the constitutional rights of all citizens, including prisoners. Private prisons under contract with government agencies act "under the color of the law," or with the power of the government. In general, pertinent case law indicates that governmental liability under the Federal Civil Rights Act (42 USC Section 1983) would most likely not be reduced by contracting with the private sector.[68]

In *Lugar v. Edmonson Oil Co.*, the U.S. Supreme Court determined that a party alleging a violation of their Constitutional rights must first show that the violating party was acting under the color of law.[69] When this has been established, both private contracts and the governmental agency can be held liable. (See *Medina v. O'Neill*[70]) In *Medina*, the Immigration and Naturalization Service detained stowaways on a vessel, placed some in a local jail, and placed others in the custody of a private company. When the illegal aliens attempted to escape, a private guard accidentally killed one of them. The Court found both the government and the private company liable for damages in the death.

Another concern is the dependence that may develop from the government contracting with a private firm for imprisoning offenders. The concern is if a contractor, for some reason, refuses to fulfill the contract requirements and decides to go bankrupt. The state may not have built space to house the inmates of concern in this case, expecting the company to fulfill its contractual obligations. However, if the firm is bankrupt, there is little the government can do to make it right, yet they still have to find a place to hold the inmates. Although this represents a "worst case scenario," it does raise questions of dependency. Therefore, states sometimes write contingencies into contracts or develop contingencies if the worst case occurs. Today, this is really an unlikely issue. No private firm has simply forfeited a contract and failed to perform. Also, there are so many private facilities that some space can usually be found that can be used in an emergency situation.

Perhaps the most difficult issue to address is the one of "quantity." Essentially, the question is whether the involvement of the private sector, as a profit-making entity in control of the imprisonment of offenders may somehow push for more, rather than less, incarceration. Sentencing policies and the increasing number of prisoners are always areas of public debate and dispute, and it is reasonable to examine the interest of private prison operators regarding these issues. In a recent article, David Shichor identified the issues and discussed problems of the free-market model in providing human services and the symbolic references of private prisons and corporate ethics.[71]

Earlier, Lilly and Knepper investigated the developing private correctional enterprise and illustrated similar commercial pressures for expansion to those that exist in the "military-industrial complex."[72] There is no doubt that successful private correctional companies have spent millions of dollars lobbying and educating elected officials in their role and performance. Although it is doubtful that private correctional companies would intentionally push for changes in sentencing that would end up sending more offenders to prison simply for the potential business, the private companies certainly could benefit from such laws. However, this issue is more of a perception than reality. There is no evidence that the involvement of private corrections influences overall sentencing policy.

The Future of Private Corrections

There are many factors that lead one to expect that the involvement of the private sector in correctional operations will continue to grow. First, the number of offenders under correctional supervision is expected to continue to rise. Second, tight budget constraints will force public officials to increasingly look for alternatives to the traditional approaches to managing offenders. Third, the continued lack of public confidence in the government's ability to perform essential services in a cost-efficient manner has lead many citizens to support "giving the private sector a chance."

Unfortunately, there is no credible evidence of the improved cost effectiveness of private correctional companies, nor is there a clear answer to many of the issues addressed in this chapter. There is, however, an acceptance of the role of the private sector in corrections today. The shadowy concerns about prisoner abuse, profit over quality, and unfulfilled commitments have not been realized to a significant level. In commenting on the lack of definitive findings about the effectiveness and other differences between public and private prisons, Gowdy notes,

> Nonetheless, the public's unsatisfactory view of today's penal system in terms of its costs and high recidivism rates are two factors that are likely to encourage further expansion of the private sector's role.[73]

■ SUMMARY

Why have correctional budgets increased so rapidly, and is there anything that can be done to slow down this increase? What are the pressures on correctional administrators as government budgets tighten, and what alternatives to increased spending are available to them? What is the role of correctional administrators in developing alternatives to incarceration, and what risks do they face by encouraging such alternatives? What non-traditional approaches can correctional administrators consider, and how much flexibility do they have in experimenting with or implementing these approaches? And, if they attempt to contract with the private sector to provide historically public correctional services, what are the issues that must be addressed in the contract award and monitoring?

All these questions have been addressed in this chapter, and they have prompted an examination and consideration of the complex administrative and political challenges that confront today and tomorrow's correctional administrator. Even with the strong economy of the 1990s and early 2000s, and with the resulting healthy budgets of many governmental jurisdictions, the growth of corrections and correctional budgets have outstripped the levels of available funds. Therefore, correctional administrators must respond to pressure to reduce costs or slow growth.

This pressure is unlikely to reduce in the number of offenders that any jurisdiction sends to prison. There is little political support for shortening sentences or even giving inmates more good time to reduce their sentences. Even if administrators are successful in implementing alternatives to imprisonment, it is likely only to slow the growth nationally, although a few states are seeing a decline in the inmate population since the turn of the twenty-first century. Although efforts to generate revenue is met with political and public opinion support, revenue enhancements are minute compared to budget increases and resource needs.

The most likely options for correctional administrators in responding to the challenges of tight budgets is to reduce their own daily costs of operation, to reduce costs of prison construction, and to privatize those services and needs for additional beds that are likely to be cost effective. The answer that seems simplest for elected officials and the public is to eliminate all prison "amenities," and the spending that goes with programs and activities that do not reduce recidivism or that detract from the punitive aspects of the sentence. However, cutting daily operational costs during a time of increasing growth and overcrowding creates a difficult dilemma for administrators. Inmate services have already been cut, and the extent to which such efforts can go without dramatically impacting both inmate and staff morale are questionable. Many of these amenities greatly improve the ability of administrators to manage prisoners, especially when inmates are serving extremely long sentences.

Reducing construction costs does offer a potential budget savings; correctional administrators can consider some of the techniques identified in this chapter as proven cost-reduction techniques. However, construction costs represent only a small percentage of the commitment of funds when a new prison is built when compared with the outlook of growth for a correctional agency.

Finally, correctional administrators are turning more and more often to the private sector to provide various services for offenders, for example, in the construction and operation of prisons. With thoughtful contracting, enhanced competition before the acceptance of a bid for the service, specific requirements for quality of service delivery, and clear and constant evaluation and monitoring of performance, the private sector can take some of the burden off correctional administrators in planning how to meet growth needs and maintain budget accountability. As popular as the use of private companies to operate prisons may seem, there still is no clear evidence of their cost effectiveness, however.

The future for correctional administrators in meeting budgetary challenges is cloudy and far from resolved. Although there are many alternatives that are being, and need to continue to be, explored, there is no panacea for resolving this issue. Although this creates stresses for, and taxes the abilities of, today's correctional administrators, future correctional administrators who want challenges are almost guaranteed them as well. Just as there is no end in sight to the growth in numbers and missions in the near future of corrections, there is no end in sight to the need to find more nontraditional approaches to providing needed services without "breaking the government budget bank."

ENDNOTES

1. Robert M. Freeman, *Correctional Organization and Management: Public Policy Challenges, Behavior, and Structure* (Boston, MA: Butterworth Heinemann, 1999), p. 108.
2. Sam C. Proband, "Corrections Leads State Budget Increases in FY 1997," *Overcrowded Times* 8 no. 4 (1997): 4.
3. Camile Graham Camp and George M. Camp, *The Corrections Yearbook, 1998* (Middletown, CT: Criminal Justice Institute, 1998), p. 87.
4. Ibid., p. 91.
5. Ibid., p. 5.
6. Ibid., pp. 182, 183.
7. Ibid., pp. 182–186.
8. Ibid., p. 77.
9. Ibid., p. 88.
10. For a description of these budget processes and corrections, see James G. Houston, *Correctional Management: Functions, Skills, and Systems,* 2nd ed. (Chicago, IL: Nelson-Hall Publishers, 1999), pp. 125–130.
11. Richard L. Phillips and Charles R. McConnell, *The Effective Corrections Manager: Maximizing Staff Performance in Demanding Times* (Gaithersburg, MD: Aspen Publishers, 1996), pp. 315–316.
12. Alfred Blumstein and Allen J. Beck, "Population Growth in U.S. Prisons, 1980–1996," in *Prisons,* edited by Michael Tonry and Joan Petersilia (Chicago, IL: University of Chicago Press, 1999), p. 18.
13. Peter Greenwood et. al., "Estimated Benefits and Costs of California's New Mandatory Sentencing Law," in *Three Strikes and You're Out,* edited by David Shichor and Dale K. Sechrest (Thousand Oaks, CA: Sage, 1996).
14. Theodore Caplow and Jonathan Simon, "Understanding Prison Policy and Population Trends," in *Prisons,* op. cit, p. 74.
15. Brian Hoffman, Gary Straughn, Jack Richardson, and Allen Randall, "California Electrified Fences: A New Concept in Prison Security," *Corrections Today* 58 no. 4 (1996): 67.
16. *Los Angeles Times,* "California Uses Deadly Force" (19 October 1998): 1.
17. Ibid.
18. John Linton, "Inmate Education Makes Sense," *Corrections Today* 60 no. 3 (1998): 18.

19. Steve Peacock, "BOP Proposes Inmates Pay All Tuition Costs for College," *Corrections Journal* 4 no. 10 (2000): 7.

20. With line item budgeting, agencies receive a certain amount for a variety of their operational areas, such as staff salaries, inmate food, and outside medical care. For a discussion of line item budgeting in corrections, see Houston, pp. 126–127.

21. See Joseph W. Rogers, "The Greatest Correctional Myth: Winning the War on Crime Through Incarceration," in *Public Policy, Crime, and Criminal Justice,* 2nd ed., edited by Barry W. Hancock and Paul M. Sharp (Upper Saddle River, NJ: Prentice Hall, 2000), pp. 308–321.

22. Barbara A. Sims, "Questions of Corrections: Public Attitudes Toward Prison and Community-Based Programs," *Corrections Management Quarterly* 1 no. 1 (1997): 55.

23. S. E. Skovan, J. E. Scott, and F. T. Cullen, "Prison Crowding: Public Attitudes Toward Strategies of Population Control," *Journal of Research in Crime and Delinquency* 25 no. 2 (1988): 150–169.

24. B. Fulton, E. J. Latessa, A. Stichman, and L. F. Travis, "The State of ISP: Research and Policy Implications," *Federal Probation* 61 no. 4 (April, 1997): 72.

25. Camile Graham Camp and George M. Camp, *The Corrections Yearbook, 1999: Adult Corrections* (Middletown, CT: Criminal Justice Institute, 1999), p. 121.

26. Ibid., pp. 122–123.

27. Ibid., p. 89.

28. Ibid., pp. 56–57.

29. Voncille Gowdy, *Intermediate Sanctions* (Washington, DC: U.S. Department of Justice, 1993).

30. D. Wagner and C. Baird, *Evaluation of the Florida Community Control Program* (Washington, DC: U.S. Department of Justice, 1993).

31. Federal Bureau of Prisons, *Greenville Federal Correctional Institution,* unpublished document, (Washington, DC: U.S. Department of Justice).

32. Camp and Camp, p. 79.

33. Camp and Camp, pp. 78–79.

34. Mark Reilly and Jim Grothoff, "Packaging the Process," *Corrections Today* 59 no. 2 (1997): 75.

35. James R. Conley, "Design/Build: The Future of Contracting," *Corrections Today* 62 no. 2 (2000): 118.

36. Mary S. Galey, "Design/Build: The BOP's View," *Corrections Today* 62 no. 2 (2000): 119.

37. For a description of the use of prototype prison or jail construction, see Thomas Beilen and Peter Krasnow, "Jail Prototype Leads to Faster Construction, Lower Costs," *Corrections Today* 58 no. 2 (1996): 128–131.

38. Camp and Camp, 1999, p. 76.

39. David Osborne and Ted Gaebler, *Reinventing Government: How the Entrepreneurial Spirit Is Transforming the Public Sector* (Reading, MA: Addison-Wesley, 1992), pp. 195–196.

40. C. S. Baird, D. A. Holien, and J. A. Bakke, *Fees for Probation Services* (Washington, DC: National Institute of Justice, 1986).

41. Camp and Camp, 1999, p. 89.

42. M. Nolan, "Medical Co-payment System: Nevada Department of Prisons" (paper presented at the seventeenth annual conference of the American Correctional Health Services Association, Salt Lake City, April 1992).

43. Camp and Camp, 1999, p. 107.

44. See Harry Allen, Evelyn Parks, Eric Carlson, and Richard Seiter, *Program Models, Halfway Houses* (Washington, DC: U.S. Department of Justice, 1978).

45. Edmund F. McGarrell and Timothy Flanagan, *Sourcebook of Criminal Justice Statistics, 1984* (Washington, DC: United States Department of Justice, 1985).

46. Michael Welch, *Corrections: A Critical Approach* (New York: McGraw-Hill Book Companies, 1996), p. 442.

47. Charles Logan, *Private Prisons: Cons and Pros* (New York: Oxford University Press, 1990).

48. Camp and Camp, 1999, pp. 92–93.

49. Ibid., p. 89.

50. Ibid., p. 93.

51. Ibid., p. 21.

52. Hawaii, for example, contracts for the housing of approximately 800 inmates with the Correctional Corporation of America in a prison located in Minnesota. Although this is inconvenient for administrators and inmate families, inmates do not have a right to be imprisoned close to their home state.

53. Ronald Becker, "The Privatization of Prisons," in *Prisons: Today and Tomorrow,* edited by Joycelyn M. Pollock (Gaithersburg, MD: Aspen Publishers, Inc., 1997), p. 395.

54. Dale K. Sechrest and David Shichor, "Comparing Public and Private Correctional Facilities in California: An Exploratory Study," in *Privatization and the Provision of Correctional Services: Context and Consequences,* edited by G. Larry Mays and Tara Gray (Cincinnati, OH: Anderson Publishing, Co., 1996), p. 135.

55. Logan.

56. Ira P. Robbins, "Privatization of Corrections: Defining the Issues," in *The Dilemmas of Corrections: Contemporary Readings,* edited by Kenneth C. Haas and Geoffrey P. Alpert 3rd ed. (Prospect Heights, IL: Waveland Press, 1995), pp. 592–594.

57. Logan, pp. 52–54.

58. Charles H. Logan, *Looking at Hidden Costs: Public and Private Corrections* (Washington, DC: National Institute of Justice Reports, 1989).

59. J. Hackett et. al., *Issues in Contracting for the Private Operation of Prisons and Jails* (Washington, DC: Department of Justice, 1987).

60. Sechrest and Shichor, pp. 148–149.

61. David Shichor and Dale K. Sechrest, "Quick Fixes in Corrections: Reconsidering Private and Public For-Profit Facilities," *Prison Journal* 75 no. 4 (December 1995): 457–478.

62. Lonn Lanza-Kaduce, Karen F. Parker, and Charles W. Thomas, "A Comparative Recidivism Analysis of Releasees from Private and Public Prisons," *Crime and Delinquency* 45 no. 1 (1999): 28–47.

63. U.S. Government Accounting Office, *Private and Public Prisons: Studies Comparing Operational Costs and/or Quality of Service* (Washington, DC: GAO, 1996).

64. John L. Clark, *Report to the Attorney General: Inspection and Review of the Northeast Ohio Correctional Center* (Washington, DC: Office of the Trustee for the District of Columbia, 1998).

65. Personal interview with John Brush, then a warden for the Correctional Corporation of America and previously a warden with the Federal Bureau of Prisons, August, 1996.

66. Charles H. Logan, "Public versus Private Prison Management: A Case Comparison," *Criminal Justice Review* 21 no. 1 (Spring 1996): 62–85.

67. Darrell K. Massengale, "Reinventing an Industry: Free Enterprise in Corrections," *Corrections Management Quarterly* 2 no. 2 (1998): 60.

68. Ira P. Robbins, "Privatization of Corrections: Defining the Issues," *Judicature* 69 no. 6 (April–May 1986): 325–331.

69. *Lugar v. Edmonson Oil Co.,* 457 US 922 (1982).

70. *Medina v. O'Neill,* 589, F. Supp. 1028 (1984).

71. David Shichor, "Private Prisons in Perspective: Some Conceptual Issues," *Howard Journal of Criminal Justice* 37 no. 1 (February 1998): 82–100.

72. Robert J. Lilly and Paul Knepper, "The Corrections-Commercial Complex," *Crime and Delinquency* 39 no. 2 (April 1993): 150–166.

73. Voncile B. Gowdy, "Should We Privatize Our Prisons? The Pros and Cons," *Corrections Management Quarterly* 1 no. 2 (1997): 61.

▓▓ KEY TERMS

furloughed

tough on crime policies

expense-based budgets

incremental budgets

Pell grants

intensive supervision probationers (ISP)

boot camp

shock incarceration

house arrest

electronic monitoring

design capacity

design/build

prototype prison construction

cost of incarceration fee

privatization

private prison

request for proposal (RFP)

enabling statutes

public propriety facilities

▓▓ YOU'RE THE CORRECTIONAL ADMINISTRATOR

1. You are the director of a state department of corrections, responsible for operating the state prisons, parole and probation supervision, and a variety of community sanctions that are alternatives to incarceration. Your prison inmate count has increased 25 percent over the past four years, the prisons are very overcrowded, and you are building new institutions to help with the overcrowding. However, your agency budget increases have not kept up with demand, and you have a higher inmate to staff ratio, meaning you have fewer staff available to manage the prisons. Legislative budget committees are asking you to reduce the costs of operation, because they do not want to have a tax increase to fund the increasing corrections budget. How do you develop a proactive plan to reduce the increased budget needs yet still operate all of the

state correctional functions in a safe and effective manner. Describe the plan
you would put in place over the next three years.

2. You are the contract administrator for a county correctional agency. The jail is
filled well beyond capacity, and the increases are expected to continue, at least
for the next three years. Instead of building a new jail, the county
commissioners have decided to contract with a private corrections company to
house the overflow of prisoners. There are already two companies that
operate jails and have space within a 100 mile radius of the county. They ask
you to prepare a request for proposal (RFP). How do you go about developing
the RFP? What do you put into the RFP to make sure you are getting the best
price and that you are getting the services needed to meet your responsibility
to house inmates in a manner that meets the constitutional requirements for
incarceration?

WEB LINK EXERCISES

Corrections Corporation of America or Wackenhut Corrections:
www.correctionscorp.com or www.wackenhut.com

Go to the Web site for either of these two private sector companies that operate
private prisons. Describe the purpose or mission for the company, and list the
benefits they suggest are available by the private sector involvement in public
corrections. Which two or three of these benefits do you believe are the most
realistic? Explain why.

CHAPTER

16

The Future and Correctional Administration

INTRODUCTION

In this textbook, there has been an examination of correctional administration from both broad and narrow perspectives, and through administrative, substantive, and philosophical issues. From the broad perspective, the history, philosophical developments, and attitudes and perceptions surrounding corrections and its administration have been reviewed. Conversely, policies and practices required to carry out critical correctional functions such as creating a safe and secure prison environment, managing dangerous and violent offenders, and providing adequate medical care to prisoners have also been described. Administrative activities such as strategic planning, the management of human resources, and budget development and administration have been considered. Substantive correctional issues such as classification of offenders, provision of treatment programs, and the operation of supermax prisons were addressed. And, the philosophical challenges within correctional administration, such as the importance of balancing punishment and rehabilitation, the political and public policy perspectives of corrections, and the need for new styles of correctional leadership were assessed.

One thing should be clear to readers of this textbook, corrections is not a static discipline. It is often suggested that the only thing correctional administrators can count on is that things will change. Consider the changes that have occurred regarding correctional issues over the past decade. The population of inmates in prisons and jails in the United States has more than doubled, and the budget and staff resources directed toward correctional agencies has increased proportionately. The makeup of the offender population is getting older, minorities and women are increasingly represented, and there is a larger proportion of offenders who are members of prison or street gangs. There is an increasing specialization within

469

correctional administration, including supermax prisons to house the most violent inmates, special units and prisons for sex offenders or inmates with mental or medical health problems, and risk and need assessments for offenders in the community to place them in specialized or intensive caseloads.

The frightening concern is that the pace of change that must be confronted and managed by correctional administrators is not likely to slow down. In fact, change will probably come even more rapidly, and change is likely to be dramatic during the early years of the twenty-first century. Some of the forces that have driven correctional change will continue to impact correctional agencies, and other forces are changing in their intensity and direction. There are many new correctional concepts that are being considered and will have to be evaluated. Those that prove valuable will be incorporated into the landscape or agenda of correctional administration. Experimental criminology, restorative justice, new penology, a rebirth of the rehabilitative ideology, a downturn in the number of inmates, and continued change in the offender makeup all will need to be examined and addressed over the next few years. There is no question about it, corrections and the challenges for correctional administrators, will continue to change.

WHERE ARE WE TODAY?

Unfortunately, many uninformed people have a fairly negative perception of corrections as lacking professionalism, effectiveness, and responsiveness to the public's interests and offenders' needs. Although these perceptions are far from the truth, during the 1990s, there was a general lack of support for what corrections accomplished. Corrections appeared to have little focus and seemed to help no one; there was dissatisfaction from offenders and offender groups, victims and victim's rights groups, the public and their elected officials, and even correctional administrators themselves. This situation prompted the state of Vermont to survey public opinion. Vermont correctional administrators were surprised and disappointed by what they found out.

> The upshot was that the criminal justice system was thoroughly disgusted with our inability to hold anyone to their minimum sentence release date. The media castigated us nightly as "the revolving door," using "corrections math," and the victims community declared us to be the enemy. Our staff morale was shot. Quite clearly, the problem wasn't us. It was everybody else. It was their fault. They just didn't understand us.[1]

As a result of this realization, Vermont began to redefine the problem it faced and began to educate the public about how corrections really functioned, including approaches that could better meet the needs of victims, the public, and offenders. Their efforts are described in the discussion of restorative justice.

In reality, corrections not only made considerable progress during the last three or four decades of the twentieth century but they also made adjustments to better reflect the public's desire for a change in policies and approaches. Reforms and improved operations came in many areas of correctional administration. Several new prisons were constructed to keep up with the increased number of inmates. These new prisons were economic boons to their communities and were often more cost efficient to operate than older prisons. Within the prisons, there were improvements in operational areas such as medical care and food service. Corrections leaped forward in professionalism, aided by the American Correctional Association (ACA) accreditation process. Risk assessment instruments improved decision making concerning inmate prison classification, release on parole, and supervision in the community. Correctional staff became better trained, better educated, and better represented by minorities and women.

During the 1990s, correctional agencies doubled their capacities and doubled the number of prisons they operated. Between 1990 and 1998, 410 new prisons were opened by state and federal correctional agencies.[2] From 1991 to 1999, more than 750,000 new prison beds were under construction by these correctional agencies.[3] The new prisons provided correctional agencies opportunities to improve the environment for staff and inmates; to implement new programs and create new management styles and cultures; and to improve cost efficiency by increasing the number of inmates housed, incorporating technology, and improving visibility and ease of monitoring inmates.

As noted previously, one of the most important areas for the reform and improvement of correctional organizations and their administrations has been accreditation by the American Correctional Association (ACA). By January 1, 1999, 517 state and federal prisons in 25 agencies[4] (36 percent of the total of 1,419 prisons[5] in all state and federal agencies open on that date), had been accredited by ACA. ACA standards required for accreditation include all areas of security, treatment, operations, human resource management, and the general administration of prisons. Therefore, ACA accreditation demonstrates that these prisons are meeting the accepted professional standards in all of these areas. Even though 64 percent of prisons are not accredited, this does not mean these prisons are not professionally operated or do not meet constitutional standards. In fact, with the active involvement of federal courts in reviewing complaints by inmates, correctional agencies have been proactive in meeting professional standards rather than fighting expensive lawsuits they may lose, resulting in the agency having to change operations anyway. Although it was not unusual to find correctional agencies operating prisons that were obviously unprofessional and inhumane in the 1950s and even 1960s, it is highly unusual to find such prisons today.

Although risk assessments, discussed in Chapter 6, to aid in classifying inmates and predicting risk to the community are used in almost every correctional agency today, there are concerns that their use may have gone too far in replacing experienced and professional judgments. These risk instruments are used to evaluate prisoners' security levels, to aid in parole release decisions, and to assign supervision levels to community offenders. There is little dispute that these instruments have improved decision making within correctional agencies. The instruments have also made correctional decisions understandable to offenders and to the general public. They have improved the ability to assign inmates to appropriate settings with physical security that reduces escapes and violence. And they have allowed community corrections administrators to align scarce resources with the offenders with the greatest risks and needs.

As noted in Chapter 11 corrections is a "people" business, and staff are the most valuable resource available to correctional agencies. Prior to the 1970s, there was little focus on the importance of recruiting staff committed to a career in corrections, or staff with experience, demeanor, and education that could contribute to the long-term quality of the agencies. Today, human resource management tasks are extremely valuable to correctional agencies. In many correctional agencies, the quality of training and focus on staff development rivals most Fortune 500 companies. As the saying goes, "necessity is the mother of invention." Correctional agencies, confronted with growth and an increasing complexity of operations, had to invest in the human resource divisions. Otherwise, they would not have a high-quality staff, able to work in a difficult environment, and able to lead these agencies into the new millennium.

The importance of workforce diversity has also been addressed. Community correctional agencies have historically had better representation of minority and female staff than their prison counterparts. As of January 1, 1999, state and federally operated probation and parole agencies had 53 percent female staff, 21.1 percent African American staff, and 6.3 percent Hispanic staff.[6] While not at levels of community agencies, the percent of minority prison staff has been increasing. The percentage of female prison staff increased from 27 percent in 1991 to more than 32 percent in 1999, whereas the percentage of nonwhite staff increased from 23.3 percent to 29.6 percent over the same period.[7]

Although correctional reforms over the past few decades are impressive, they are likely to be insignificant compared with the change and restructuring that will be required by correctional agencies over the next few decades. The many challenges and issues expected to confront correctional administrators were described in Chapter 14. These issues regarding sentencing, aging offenders, juvenile offenders, women offenders, mentally ill offenders, effectiveness and accountability, technology, and prisoner reentry will challenge even the most talented and experienced correctional administrators. Throughout the remainder of this chapter, we examine expectations for the future and developing concepts that will influence corrections and transform the work of correctional administrators.

■■■■ WHERE ARE WE GOING IN THE FUTURE?

There are different opinions as to where corrections is headed in the future. On one hand, there are those who suggest the future of corrections is bleak, because the many problems that have confronted correctional administrators over the past decade are expected to intensify. On the other hand, are those who believe the worst is past and that many problematic trends, such as the increase in the number of inmates and community offenders, are likely to decline. Both sides of this argument are examined and some of the current circumstances that may set the tone for the future are considered.

Why do some consider the future of corrections dismal? Crouch suggests that even with a decline in crime rates, there is unlikely to be a decline in rates of incarceration.[8] He suggests two factors that make a decline in the number of offenders in prison uncertain. With the construction of so many prisons and expansion of prison capacity, Crouch believes it will be difficult for officials to not use these facilities to full capacity. Second, he believes that the prevailing conservative political ideology will continue, with more legislation to lengthen prison sentences or legislation requiring mandatory prison sentences for more crimes. Welch agrees with the dismal prediction, noting that even with massive prison construction levels, overcrowding and inadequate services and programs persist. He suggests

> Even worse, the immediate future for corrections looks bleak since prevailing political, economic, and technological forces contribute to the vastly expanding correctional enterprise.[9]

Welch continues his dreary prediction of the future of corrections by suggesting that the overuse of incarceration will continue because of what Feeley and Simon refer to as the **new penology.**[10] In a 1992 article, these authors proposed how corrections had changed from using clinical judgments, focusing on offender rehabilitation and emphasizing reducing recidivism, to the identification of high-risk offender groups and the development of controls to prevent the further commission of crimes by these groups. These authors suggest the following approach for such controls:

> Among them are low frills, no-service custodial centers; various forms of electronic monitoring systems that impose a form of custody without walls; and new statistical techniques for assessing risk and predicting dangerousness. These new forms of control are not anchored in aspirations to rehabilitate, reintegrate, retrain, provide employment, or the like. They are justified in more blunt terms: variable detention depending upon risk assessment.[11]

Although this may sound too futuristic and like a violation of individuals rights, it is really not a distant step from current operations and approaches taken to administer correctional sanctions. The new penology advocates the use of prediction tables and actuarial instruments to identify individuals with a high risk for committing crimes, and the elimination or restriction of their freedom in order to control their behavior, and therefore, prevent them from committing new crimes. This practice is little different from some practices currently used. Individuals charged with crimes are often considered for bond based on actuarial predictions of their dangerousness. In Chapter 6, selective incapacitation was described as a practice in using risk assessment, and preventing the release on bond of offenders who present a likelihood of reoffending. In fact, in studies of selective incapacitation, there have even been calculations of the number and types of crimes that could be avoided, and the potential dollars saved, by not releasing offenders with the greatest risk of reoffending.

The more positive predictions for the future of corrections are primarily based on the fact that the rapid increase in incarceration appears to have slowed. Although the number of prisoners in adult and federal prisons has risen steadily over the past 15 years, there is some evidence that the rate of growth may have peaked. Table 16–1 illustrates the percentage of growth in the state and federal prison population from 1990 through 1999. If the annual increases for the first nine years were averaged in three-year blocks, the growth for 1990 to 1992 was 7.4 percent for 1993 to 1995 was 7.6 percent, and for 1996 to 1998 was 4.9 percent. The growth for 1999 was only 3.4 percent.

████████ **TABLE 16-1**

Change in the State and Federal Prison Populations, 1990–1999.			
	Annual Increase in the Number of Prisoners		
Years	Custody	Jurisdiction	Percentage Change
1990	60,000	61,555	8.6%
1991	49,153	51,640	6.7
1992	58,031	56,941	6.9
1993	58,815	64,992	7.4
1994	80,766	84,258	8.7
1995	88,395	71,172	6.7
1996	49,222	57,494	5.1
1997	48,800	58,785	5.0
1998	47,905	58,420	4.7
1999	36,957	43,796	3.4
Average annual increase.			
1990–99	60,168	65,867	6.5%

Note: In years in which states changed their reporting methods, counts based on comparable methods were used to calculate the annual increase and percentage change. The average annual increases were calculated on the revised counts in 1999.
Source: Allen J. Beck, *Prisoners in 1999*, (Washington, DC: US Department of Justice, Bureau of Justice Statistics, 2000), p. 3.

    This apparent decline in the annual growth in the number of people in prison is not yet enough of a trend on which to base major policy decisions or to reverse any plans to add prison capacity. However, a few states have found they do not need all of the prison beds they have been constructing. North Carolina recently constructed three new prisons but delayed their opening until the prison population increased and they needed the beds, and Texas (for a time) had more than 6,000 new beds sitting empty because of the limited prison population growth.[12] Combine these developments with the fact that a few states (Alaska, California, Connecticut, Delaware, Hawaii, Maryland, North Carolina, and Pennsylvania) had negligible growth during the last two years of the 1990s,[13] whereas Ohio has actually had a decline of almost 3,000 in the number of prison inmates,[14] and this decline of prisoner growth warrants more review.

    There are several factors that may be influencing the slowing increase in incarceration, including decreasing crime rates, an increase in community alternative sentences, a good economic climate, positive demographic trends, a softening of punitive sentencing ideologies, and the fact that many criminals are already in prison. Crime rates are highly correlated to demographics, and they are higher when there is a high proportion of the U.S. population between the high-crime ages of 15 and 30. Much of the increase in the crime rates during the 1970s and early 1980s was the result of the baby boomers entering their late teens in the late 1960s, and continuing to commit crimes during their high-risk crime age. As the philosophy for sanctioning criminals evolved from one of extensive use of community sanctions to a greater use of imprisonment during the 1980s, these baby boomers, with second and third convictions, ended up being sentenced to prison for long periods of time. During the 1990s, the baby boomers "aged out" of the high-risk age for committing crimes. However, the first decade of the new millennium could witness a return to rising crime rates, because a wave of "echo boomers," children of the baby boomers, will move into this high-crime age.

As state correctional agencies became almost overwhelmed with prisoners during the late 1980s and early 1990s, they began to work aggressively with local county courts and correctional agencies to create alternatives to prison. These alternatives provided options for judges to effectively sanction offenders yet keep them in the community. With the massive increases in the number of offenders sent to prison, it would be expected that the probation population would decline. However, just the opposite occurred. From a 1990 population of 2,670,234 offenders on probation, there were 3,077,861 probationers on January 1, 1996,[15] and the 2000 population on probation was projected to increase to 3,661,032.[16] States such as Ohio have invested heavily in community corrections, providing grants to local governments to create intensive probation programs, build community facilities to house probationers who would otherwise have been sent to prison, and increase the use of house arrest and electronic monitoring.

Following this trend, many of the **Community Corrections Acts** passed in the 1970s are regaining interest.[17] These acts created incentives for counties to develop local alternatives for handling offenders in the community, rather than sending them to state prisons. During the 1970s, it was believed that offenders and their families would be better off if they remained in the community. Today, the acts are again becoming popular. However, the popularity is because of the high cost to society for the extensive use of imprisonment. By 2000, California correctional agency budgets were projected to require 18 percent of the entire state budget.[18] Fabelo suggests that the public safety returns for incarceration are becoming marginal, and the public and elected officials support for building more prisons is declining.[19] He notes that technology, such as geographic location systems, is becoming available and can be effectively used for less costly supervision of offenders in the community.

It is hoped that these alternatives to imprisonment will effectively reduce the number of nonserious offenders sent to prisons. However, correctional administrators are concerned that if there is a successful diversion of minor offenders from prison sentences to sentences served in the community, the makeup of prisons will dramatically change. As noted by Wilkinson

> If, indeed, community sanctions are imposed on non-violent offenders, prisons will increasingly become repositories for the more violent, predatory and remorseless criminals. A greater concentration of violent offenders may create more tension among inmates and between inmates and staff. Added incidents of violence can be anticipated, resulting in more injuries or worse, and a requirement for more disciplinary cells. . . . By developing "supermax" prisons, we can isolate problem offenders in one facility.[20]

Although the punitive atmosphere dominated criminal sentencing for the past two decades, there is some realization that tough on crime criminal sentencing may have gone too far. There is an increasing number of judges (federal, state, and county) who have expressed their frustration with mandatory, minimum prison sentences for first-time drug offenders and life imprisonment for even minor felonies under three strike provisions. Judges, required to use sentencing guidelines and follow specific laws mandating prison sentences, often bemoan the lack of options available to them and the overzealous prison sentences that they must give to some relatively minor offenders.

The classic case illustrating the "overreach" of mandatory prison terms was the 1995 sentencing of Jerry Williams under the California Three-Strikes Law. Williams had two prior felony convictions involving violence, when he stole a piece of pizza from four children. His theft of pizza did not involve the use of a weapon. The judge, under the mandatory California law, had to sentence Williams to 25 years in prison. The cost to the state for his incarceration for stealing a piece of pizza is estimated to be $500,000. Another unintended problem resulting from the California Three-Strikes Law is that offenders with two prior convictions are refusing to plea bargain. They know that because of their prior two convictions, any new felony results in their receiving either a 25-year or life sentence. As a result of their unwillingness to plead guilty and their demands for trials, the court systems are becoming engulfed in trials for relatively simple cases. The Jerry Williams sentence for stealing a piece of pizza and the overall impact on cost and court delays resulting from the California Three-Strikes Law have generated considerable discussion regarding the problems resulting from mandatory prison terms and from taking away almost all judicial discretion to consider mitigating circumstances in sentencing offenders.

One possible reason for the reduction in the number of new prisoners is that most of the habitual offenders who commit a large portion of crimes are already in prison. Proponents of imprisonment point to declining crime rates as the successes of these tough sentencing policies. They argue that although prisons are expensive, they are worth the cost, and increasing the use of imprisonment reduces crime and saves money. Opponents note that changing demographics, better economic times, and declining drug use and drug crimes have more to do with crime rates than imprisonment policies.[21] The extensive use of imprisonment as a sanction for criminal offenders has certainly prevented the commission of several crimes. The important policy questions, however, are whether the cost of incarcerating offenders caught in the "prison net" for such long periods of time is worth the expense and at what point does society reach a "diminishing return" on the investment in more prisons.[22]

There are many developments that will impact the future of corrections. Some of these developments may result in reducing reliance on imprisonment as the primary criminal sanction. Others may change the activities or priorities of correctional administrators. At this point, no one can be certain of the true impact of these developments, and they will continue to be discussed, debated, tested, and evaluated. Throughout the remainder of this chapter, the developing concepts that are likely to influence the future for correctional administrators are examined.

EXPERIMENTAL CRIMINOLOGY AND A RETURN TO SOCIALIZATION

One of the reasons that society relies so much on imprisonment as a crime control policy is to avoid the risk of offenders remaining in the community and possibly continuing to victimize others. Placing offenders in the community does not simply create a risk for potential victims, it also creates a political risk for policy makers and a career risk for correctional administrators. It is difficult for those who create or implement crime policies to increase the use of community corrections, knowing that they also increase the risk of crime in the community. This is particularly difficult, because there are few controlled experiments testing the outcome of various sanctions and few definitive results that can be used to aid and protect policy makers who wish to increase the use of community sanctions. The use of **random field testing (RFT)** has seldom been used to evaluate the effectiveness of different criminal sanctions. With a random field test, offenders randomly receive sentences of either community placement or imprisonment, their results are identified, and the sanctions are compared to determine effectiveness in preventing future crimes. As one can imagine, there are many legal and ethical questions about randomly assigning offenders a sentence. However, Sherman has recently argued that such RFTs should be more seriously considered. Sherman notes how many advances in medicine relied on random experiments, and that without such experimentation, there is unlikely to be a move away from reliance on imprisonment:

> After two decades, the small number of RFTs evaluating crime prevention and alternatives to incarceration . . . have failed to persuade the relevant audiences of funding agencies, criminologists, agency officials, and program innovators of the wisdom of employing RFT designs in testing new programs.[23]

Sherman's suggested use of RFTs to better identify successful sanctions for criminals is called **experimental criminology.** His suggestion is interesting for two reasons. First, there are potentially significant benefits that can result from the use of controlled experiments (including random assignment) to evaluate criminal sentencing practices. Although it would be difficult to test, a rational hypothesis is that because of the preventative value of prisons in crime control, and especially during times of intense public and media interest regarding crime, few criminal justice policy makers will risk diverting large numbers of offenders from prison without conclusive evidence that these actions do not significantly jeopardize public safety. If there was random field testing of various criminal sanctions, and there was conclusive evidence that the less expensive and less intrusive community supervision of offenders could protect society as effectively as prison (at least for relatively minor or moderately criminal offenders), it would be much easier for policy makers to decide to expand the use of community options to imprisonment.

Another interesting point regarding Sherman's suggested use of RFT for criminal justice is his discussion of **socialization.** Sherman notes that of the three basic mechanisms for obtaining compliance with laws (socialization, deterrence, and incapacitation), "the one with the greatest evidence and theoretical promise is socialization."[24] Socialization of offenders involves the immersion of offenders in programs to train or teach them how to successfully function in society by finding and holding a job, by taking responsibility for their families and children, and by avoiding the use of drugs and other illegal substances. Sherman suggests these strategies should also include procedural changes during arrest and prosecution to show greater respect to offenders, the use of moral appeals to offenders' recognition of the harm caused by their actions, court-ordered counseling regarding moral appeals during probation, and the use of restitution to require offenders to repay their victims for the losses associated with the crime.[25]

Sherman proposes that because most first-time offenders are not sent to prison and because most repeat offenders generally end up in prison, a focus on socialization at the point of arrest and prosecution for first offenders holds promise. Therefore, there is tremendous potential to implement programs of socialization for first-time offenders, those most at risk to end up in prison at a later time. However, with today's focus on punishment, deterrence, and accountability, even first-time offenders are likely to receive a sanction that does not include programs designed to socialize them for success in the community. Socialization strategies can be implemented within the criminal justice system, and many socialization programs are within the authority of correctional administrators to implement. The next section discusses a relatively new concept in sentencing criminal offenders: restorative justice. Restorative justice includes many of the elements that Sherman advocates should be implemented using socialization strategies.

RESTORATIVE JUSTICE

Restorative justice is a concept that has been gaining acceptance, and many states and counties are creating restorative justice alternative models for sentencing offenders. The **restorative justice** approach is based on the fact that traditional sentencing and punishing of offenders does little for society and the victims of crimes, because it focuses only on offenders in a punitive and reactive manner. As noted, victims have been left out of the criminal justice process, although victim rights efforts have recently been urging the implementation of programs to assist victims and ensure their voices are heard throughout the process. Restorative justice also has been spurred on by the high cost of imprisonment, particularly when used for nonviolent offenders. It seems unreasonable for society to spend large amounts of money to punish and incarcerate offenders who represent little risk to their communities, while the offenders do nothing to "make right" the harms they have caused.

Restorative justice models of sentencing are designed to shift the focus away from being reactive and punishment oriented, from being costly to taxpayers, and from a lack of involvement by the victims. Such models are targeted to hold offenders accountable for the harm they have done and to have them take responsibility to repair damage. Freeman defines restorative justice, "as a process that focuses on the injury resulting from the crime and works to repair that injury by shifting the role of the offender from passive recipient of punishment to active participant in reparation."[26]

This move to repair the harm done by criminal acts is the first of two key elements of a restorative justice system. The second element is the active involvement of the victim in determining the proper sanction for the crime. Minnesota was one of the first states to implement restorative justice sentencing approaches. A deputy commissioner for the Minnesota Department of Corrections writes,

> Restorative justice is a philosophical framework that seeks to set up processes that promote the repair of harm. It balances the needs of three primary stakeholders: the victim, the offender, and the community. This is contrasted with a justice system that seeks as its primary aim to catch, convict, and punish offenders. As restorative justice initiatives are articulated and applied in communities, most often the philosophy is embraced as common sense, good neighborly principles. Restorative values include responsibility, accountability, and participation by all who have a stake in the outcome, repairing the harm, making things right, and supporting the victim.[27]

The restorative justice emphasis on offender accountability and reparation can take place at any point in the traditional criminal justice and correctional systems. However, they may have the most value during sentencing. In a pure restorative justice model, the offender and victim both participate in the decision regarding adjudication of the offense. The focus while determining the sentence is on how to repair the damage and what the offender can do to make up for the crime committed. The victim provides input on what is appropriate. Victims may want an apology, may seek restitution, or may want a punitive sentence of imprisonment. The offender must accept responsibility, by recognizing the damage that has been caused and agreeing to a reparative approach to correct the harm.

There may be hesitancy by some to accept the inclusion of both the victim and offender in the process; some believe that offenders may not be sincere or that victims may be intimidated. Although the two participants do not necessarily have to "come together" to discuss reparation, it is generally believed that this face-to-face discussion goes a long way in furthering the feeling of involvement by the victim, and forcing the offender to "put a face to the crime committed." The public supports restorative justice; public opinion surveys generally conclude that, "the process of mediating conflict between crime victims and offenders provides many benefits to the parties involved, the community, and the justice system."[28]

When the Vermont Department of Corrections identified the lack of confidence and support they had from the general public, one of the primary approaches they initiated was the implementation of a restorative justice sentencing model. The department administrators designed "two kinds of sentencing tracks, each to address a different sentencing purpose."[29] As illustrated in Figure 16–1, those offenders who commit serious crimes are placed in the risk management track, which is directed toward identifying the risk posed and providing a range of security, treatment, supervision, and surveillance to manage that risk and protect the public. The focus of a prison sentence for these offenders is "incapacitation."

Offenders who commit nonviolent offenses are usually placed in the reparative track, which provides programs and sanctions created by boards of community members, with an emphasis on repairing the damage of the crime while holding the offender accountable for the offense. The probation sanctions include acts such as an apology, paying restitution to the victim, and performing community service by the offender. An intermediate sanction includes more intensive community supervision, under the supervision of the parole board. If offenders fail to perform the reparative acts or meet the conditions of this community supervision, they are

	Probation	Intermediate Sanction	Prison
Risk Management	Supervision Counseling Referral	Day treatment center Intensive substance abuse Life management Supervision Community restitution	Incapacitation and treatment (violent, sex, education, MH)
Reparative	Reparative board Apology Restitution Community service	Reparative board, supervised Community service Work crew	Community Service Work Camp

FIGURE 16–1   Vermont Department of Corrections sentencing tracks.
Source: John G. Perry and John F. Gorczyk, "Restructuring Corrections: Using Market
Research in Vermont," *Corrections Management Quarterly,* 1 no. 3 (1997): 33.

expeditiously sent to prison through the parole revocation process, requiring a lesser standard of proof and allowing lesser representation for offenders than a probation violation. In the reparative track, a sentence of imprisonment is usually in a minimum security facility, and even the imprisonment maintains a focus on reparation through community work.

As noted earlier, restorative justice models can be emphasized throughout the correctional process. Correctional agencies have implemented ways in which victims can be informed and involved in decisions about offenders, even offenders who are sentenced to prison. For most states and the Federal Bureau of Prisons, any victim who requests such will be notified of the impending release of an offender. Some states provide the opportunity for victims to make their views known before a parole hearing, or even to attend the hearing and make a personal statement. In addition to continued involvement of victims in the correctional process, many jurisdictions find other ways for offenders to focus on reparation during their sentences.

The Federal Bureau of Prisons (BOP) has been very successful in collecting fines and restitution from inmates and from offenders under community supervision. The BOP includes the responsibility for paying judgments in their management decisions regarding inmates. Inmates know that if they do not create a payment schedule (even for small amounts such as $25 per month) and make regular payments, their lack of responsibility will be considered when they request preferred housing assignments or work in correctional industries. Ohio has extensively involved prison inmates in community service work jobs. The program began in 1991 and during the first eight years Ohio inmates performed 4.2 million hours of community service work.[30] In addition to performing this work, a study of Ohio inmates performing community service indicated a "positive statistical significance with regard to participation in community service and recidivism. In essence, prisoners with *any* experience in community service were reimprisoned less often than those who had *none.*"[31]

Restorative justice concepts are quickly spreading throughout the United States. Not only have they been proven effective in the Ohio study but they also have the support of the general public. In Vermont, restorative justice approaches were created to respond to the lack of satisfaction by citizens in the activities of the corrections department, and as a way to involve citizens and victims without spending large sums of money to build and operate new prisons. Restorative justice sentencing models are more proactive than traditional sentencing, they focus on the community rather than only the offender, and they emphasize repairing the damage from the crime more than punishing the offender.[32] Because of these positive aspects, it is expected that restorative justice programs will continue to grow in the future.

A RENEWAL IN THE REHABILITATIVE IDEOLOGY

In addition to a move toward the principles of restorative justice, there is also a renewed interest in rehabilitation. Throughout the past two decades, a punitive attitude about crime, sentencing, and offenders seems prevalent. The public perception was that offenders were treated too softly, and by toughening sentences and making sanctions more punitive, the deterrent effect of criminal sanctions could be increased. In a 1996 review of public attitudes regarding crime control approaches over the past 20 years, it was discovered that citizens favored three approaches: (1) harsher sentences for offenders, (2) increased use of the death penalty, and (3) increased gun control. Retribution was ranked as the most important purpose of sentencing adult criminals by 53 percent of respondents, although rehabilitation was ranked as most important by 21 percent of respondents.[33]

Although there is no more recent data to indicate these attitudes have softened or that the public now ranks rehabilitation as more important than retribution, there is evidence of movement in this direction. And there is increasing evidence of the potential for positive results from treatment programs. In Chapter 5, the variety of programs that are offered to offenders and studies that identified statistically significant positive findings from the delivery of correctional treatment were discussed. In addition, Chapter 14 described issues evaluating the effectiveness of correctional programs and services, and the new evaluative strategies for increasing the sophistication of study designs and measurements of outcomes.

Overall, there have been two major developments in this regard. First, there are many studies, or meta-analyses of studies, that have shown successful outcomes from correctional treatment programs.[34] Second, there are ways to determine the quality of the programs and to link program quality to outcome. The results indicate that improved program quality and careful matching of offenders' personal characteristics to the type of program or service contributes to a positive treatment outcome.[35] These findings encourage confidence in treatment by providers and correctional administrators, and result in an increased momentum to continue current programs and begin new ones.

There is also a public acceptance of treatment programs for offenders. A 1997 survey of citizen attitudes in Ohio indicated strong support for correctional treatment programs and strong support for rehabilitation as the primary purpose for a sentence of imprisonment.[36] With findings of success in reducing recidivism and with a softening of punitive attitudes toward rehabilitation, it is likely that correctional administrators may be more successful in arguing for additional resources to implement treatment programs for offenders. If this occurs, a renewed interest in rehabilitation will benefit offenders, correctional administrators, and the general public.

SUMMARY

This concludes our discussion of the future of correctional administration, and concludes this textbook and our overall examination of the challenges facing correctional administrators. Throughout this textbook, there is an emphasis on looking forward. It is important to understand the past, and how correctional theories evolve and are integrated into correctional practices. Correctional administrators must understand *why* they do things as well as *how* they are done. By learning from the past and integrating knowledge and experience with predictions of future challenges, correctional administrators will be prepared to proactively set agendas in the future, rather than have agendas set by outside forces.

This chapter reviewed many topics. First, you examined the status of correctional administration today. There have been tremendous changes and improvements in correctional administration over the past three to four decades. Those who have worked in corrections during some of this period are well aware of the changes and should be commended for the increase in sophistication and professionalism that has occurred. In almost every discipline and in all types of public and private agencies there have been a multitude of technological developments, changes in management and leadership styles, and improvements in staff quality and sophistication. However, few disciplines or categories of public or private agencies have advanced as much as corrections. There have been improvements in facilities (new prisons), services (medical, housing, and food service), professionalism, risk analysis and decision making, human resource management (staff training, quality, and diversity), and the ability to plan and prepare for future challenges.

You examined the two conflicting perceptions of the future of correctional administration. The dire outlook is based on the challenge of meeting a continued growth in the number of incarcerated inmates. Some argue that this is a positive trend, that imprisonment is the most effective method for protecting the public from criminals. However, others recognize that continuing to increase the dollars directed to prison operations takes money away from other public needs, and an overreliance on incarceration undermines the initiative to consider and carefully evaluate less costly, but perhaps just as effective, community sanctions. The more optimistic look at the future finds a developing trend toward reducing the reliance on incarceration. Although the pendulum may not have swung away from imprisonment toward community correctional approaches, some believe the rapid increase in the number of inmates is slowing and may soon "top out."

Concluding this chapter and the look into the future was a discussion of issues that are increasingly being considered and implemented. Perhaps experimental criminology, using random field testing, may never be fully accepted. However, it represents an interesting option, and, even its discussion, will probably result in more research and the use of quasi-experimental tests of various levels of criminal sanctions. What is most important is that policy makers analyze and understand the overall impact of their decisions, and weigh factors such as public safety, cost, and the long-term impact of building new prisons before they commit to changes in criminal sentencing and correctional operations.

The collateral discussion of socialization also presents an interesting alternative for responding to criminals and crime. Socialization includes a proactive vision of how to handle offenders. It also is a good "lead" into a discussion of restorative justice. With restorative justice focusing on reparation for the crime rather than simply punishment for the offender, the community and victims are more fully involved and justice is more likely served. Restorative justice is promising for several reasons. It has the support of the general public, who have long had a sense that neither the victim nor the community benefited from the traditional approaches to handling offenders. Restorative justice is economical; it can bring money into the system, rather than continuously increasing expenditures. It holds offenders accountable for their crimes, forcing them to face the damages they have caused, and to accept responsibility for that damage. Finally, restorative justice *simply makes good sense.* There are few involved in the criminal justice system (offenders, prosecutors, victims, correctional administrators) who do not respond positively to restorative justice techniques, whether they are carried out at the time of sentencing or at some later time in the correctional process.

Another promising development is the perceived renewed interest in rehabilitation. Unfortunately, correctional administrators, to some extent, rejected rehabilitation as a correctional goal during the past 20 years. Perhaps this was because of the inability to force offenders to change, the lack of research indicating a link between rehabilitation and reduced recidivism, or a desire to avoid appearing soft on criminals. For whatever reasons, current correctional administrators seem more willing to support and argue for funding for rehabilitation programs. This development is very important. A successful correctional environment is one that *balances* the importance of punishment and rehabilitation in correctional practices. With the trend toward punishment as a correctional goal throughout the 1990s, there was a danger of losing rehabilitation as an accepted part of correctional practice.

This concludes the study of correctional administration. The goal of this textbook has been to give future correctional administrators an overall understanding of how theory and practice are integrated. The first part of the text provided descriptions of the key components of correctional administration, including leadership, management, vision, and strategic planning. In Part 2, theories and practices regarding the management of offenders were presented. Correctional goals of punishment, deterrence, incapacitation, and rehabilitation must be intertwined in both community and institutional correctional settings in order to meet the overall mission of protecting the public. The delivery of correctional programs and services, their operation, and how they contribute to the correctional mission was examined. There was a description of how classification and risk assessment are used to guide decision making and to place offenders in an environment that meets their individual needs and the needs of the community.

In Part 3 of the text, the management of the prison setting was explored. Correctional administrators can easily become overwhelmed by the complex challenges of managing a prison. This section included a description of how prisons and staff are organized to accomplish work within a prison. There were extensive discussions of the way in which prison administrators create a safe and secure environment, and manage violent inmates. Basic services that must be provided to inmates, including housing, medical care, and food service, were discussed.

The management of correctional staff, the most important resource for a correctional agency, was examined in the first chapter in Part 4. Key activities and issues regarding human resource management and staff development were described. With a large percentage of correctional budgets going to staff salaries, it would be imprudent to not invest in this resource by emphasizing professionalism, diversity, training, and personal development. Also included was a chapter depicting the value of effective supervision, the impact that supervision has on employee performance, and the challenge in becoming an effective supervisor. Extremely important for correctional administration is the trend toward empowering, rather than merely supervising, staff. Empowerment does not come naturally, nor does it come without a thoughtful plan for implementation. However, agencies that have successfully empowered their staff know that the effort is worthwhile. The final chapter in Part 4 on managing staff explained their role in corrections and described potential career opportunities. Additionally, there was a discussion of the importance of leadership and the types of actions that leaders can take to support and motivate their staff.

In addition to this chapter reviewing the future of correctional administration, Part 5 included a critique of the many issues that will confront correctional administrators over the coming decades. Also, the challenge of the increasing cost of corrections and the alternative approaches for reducing costs were examined. As the volume of tax dollars devoted to corrections increases, the opportunity of using these funds in other public arenas is increasingly recognized. This recognition results in pressure on correctional administrators to find new and less expensive approaches to fulfill their missions without jeopardizing the safety of the public.

Overall, correctional administration is a profession facing significant challenges, conflicting goals, and increasing visibility in the public and political arena. This text was written because of my career enjoyment of working in corrections for more than 25 years. There is fulfillment that results from meeting difficult challenges, yet there is disappointment that results from failure, whether that failure is real or perceived by others. However, there is never a dull day in the life of a correctional administrator. Hopefully, reading this book and studying correctional administration will help prepare you to accept the challenges that will confront correctional administrators for the next several years.

ENDNOTES

1. John G. Perry and John F. Gorczyk, "Restructuring Corrections: Using Market Research in Vermont," *Corrections Management Quarterly*, 1 no. 3 (1997): 27.

2. Camille Graham Camp and George M. Camp, *The Corrections Yearbook, 1999: Adult Corrections* (Middletown, CT: Criminal Justice Institute, 1999), p. 74.

3. Ibid., p. 77.

4. Ibid., p. 82.

5. Ibid., p. 67.

6. Ibid., pp. 199–200.

7. Ibid., p. 133.

8. Ben M. Crouch, "Looking Back to See the Future of Corrections," *The Prison Journal*, 76 no. 4 (December 1996): 471.

9. Michael Welch, *Corrections: A Critical Approach* (New York: McGraw-Hill, 1996), p. 448.

10. For a complete description of the "new penology," see Malcolm M. Feeley and Jonathan Simon, "The New Penology: Notes on the Emerging Strategy of Corrections and Its Implications," *Criminology*, 30 no. 4 (1992): 449–474.

11. Ibid., p. 457.

12. Penelope Lemov, "The End of the Prison Boom," *Governing* (Washington, DC: Congressional Quarterly, Inc., August 1997), pp. 32–33.

13. Camp and Camp, p. 2.

14. Personal conversations with Ohio Department of Rehabilitation and Corrections officials, (26 February 2001).

15. Bureau of Justice Statistics, "Nation's Probation and Parole Population Reached Almost 3.9 Million Last Year" (Washington, DC: U.S. Department of Justice, 1997), p. 5.

16. Thomas Bonczar and L. Glaze, *Probation and Parole in the United States, 1998* (Washington, DC: U.S. Department of Justice, 1999), p. 1.

17. For a description of Community Corrections Acts and how they may be refined for future use, see Kay M. Harris, "Key Differences Among Community Corrections Acts in the United States: An Overview, *Prison Journal,* 76 no. 2 (June 1996): 192–238.

18. Phillip G. Zimbardo, *Transforming California's Prisons into Expensive Old Age Homes for Felons: Enormous Hidden Costs and Consequences for California's Taxpayers* (San Francisco, CA: Center on Juvenile and Criminal Justice, 1994), pp. 7–8.

19. Tony Fabelo, "Whatever Is Next after the Prison-Building Boom Will Be Next in Texas," *Prison Journal,* 76 no. 4 (December 1996): 475–483.

20. Reginald A. Wilkinson, "The Future of Adult Corrections" (unpublished testimony provided to the National Council on Crime and Delinquency's Conference entitled, Reducing Crime in America: The Agenda for the Twenty-first Century, 5 December 1997).

21. For a good review of crime control policies, see James Houston and William W. Parsons, *Criminal Justice and the Policy Process* (Chicago, IL: Nelson-Hall, 1997).

22. For a discussion of the value of imprisonment on crime control, see Charles Oliver, "Costs of Crime and Punishment: More Prisons Save Money, But Only up to a Point," *Investors Business Daily,* (20 May 1996).

23. Lawrence W. Sherman, "Reducing Incarceration Rates: The Promise of Experimental Criminology," *Crime and Delinquency* 46 no. 3 (July 2000): 300.

24. Ibid., p. 305.

25. Ibid., pp. 306–309.

26. Robert M. Freeman, *Correctional Organization and Management: Public Policy Challenges, Behavior, and Structure* (Boston, MA: Butterworth Heinemann, 1999), p. 397.

27. Mark Carey, "Overcoming Fear, Misunderstanding, and NIMBY Through Restorative Covenants, *Corrections Management Quarterly* 4 no. 3 (2000): 12.

28. Myron Steele and Thomas J. Quinn, "Restorative Justice: Including Victims in Community Corrections," in *The Dilemmas of Corrections: Contemporary Readings*, edited by Kenneth C. Haas and Geoffrey P. Alpert (Prospect Heights, IL: Waveland Press, 1995), p. 530.

29. Perry and Gorczyk, p. 32.

30. Reginald A. Wilkinson, "The Impact of Community Service Work on Ohio State Prisoners: A Restorative Justice Perspective and Overview," *Corrections Management Quarterly* 4 no. 3 (2000): 30.

31. Ibid.

32. For an overview and many articles regarding the topic of restorative justice, see the Summer 2000 issue of *Corrections Management Quarterly* 4 no. 3.

33. Timothy J. Flanagan and Dennis R. Longmire, editors, *Americans View Crime and Justice: A National Public Opinion Survey*, (Thousand Oaks, CA: Sage Publications, 1996).

34. For examples of studies that indicate a positive treatment effect, see Francis T. Cullen and Brandon K. Applegate, editors, *Offender Rehabilitation: Effective Treatment Intervention*, (Aldershot, UK: Ashgate, 1997). Also see Gerald G. Gaes, "Correctional Treatment," *The Handbook of Crime and Punishment*, edited by Michael Tonry (New York: Oxford University Press, 1998), pp. 712–738; particularly Vernon L. Quinsey, "Treatment of Sex Offenders," pp. 403–425. Also see Douglas S. Lipton, "Prison-Based Therapeutic Communities: Their Success with Drug-Abusing Offenders," *National Institute of Justice Journal* (February 1996), pp. 12–20.

35. For discussions of qualitative assessments of treatment programs and matching of offenders to program services, see Sharon Levrant, Francis T. Cullen, Betsy Fulton, and John Wozniak, "Reconsidering Restorative Justice: The Corruption of Benevolence Revisited?" *Crime and Delinquency* 45 (1999): 3–27. Also see Edward J. Latessa and Alexander Holsinger, "The Importance of Evaluating Correctional Programs: Assessing Outcome and Quality," *Corrections Management Quarterly* 2 no. 4 (1998): 22–29; Paul Gendreau and Donald Andrews, *The Correctional Program Assessment Inventory*, 5th ed. (Saint John: University of New Brunswick, 1994); Paul Gendreau, Claire Goggin, and Paula Smith, "Generating Rational Correctional Policies: An Introduction to Advances in Cumulating Knowledge," *Correctional Management Quarterly* 4 no. 2 (2000): 52–60.

36. Brandon K. Applegate, Francis T. Cullen, and Bonnie S. Fisher, "Public Support for Correctional Treatment," *Prison Journal* 77 no. 3 (1997): 237–258.

KEY TERMS

new penology
Community Corrections Acts
random field testing (RFT)

experimental criminology
socialization
restorative justice

YOU'RE THE CORRECTIONAL ADMINISTRATOR

1. You are the chief of planning for a state correctional agency that includes both community and institutional corrections. You have been asked by the director of the agency to create an issue paper that speculates into the future and generates a new paradigm for the management of the agency. You are to identify one assumption (for instance, there will be a shift to restorative justice or the agency's primary mission will be the rehabilitation of offenders) that will impact the way the agency is managed in 20 years. Discuss this topic in a small group, and then identify the one major assumption that will drive the agency in the future. Then, describe how the agency should reorganize or change staffing or management to meet this new mission.

2. You are the court administrator for a medium-size county. The judges are very interested in creating a restorative justice model of sentencing. They really do not know much about it nor do they have any idea how to implement it. They ask you to create an organizational model for implementing restorative justice. Who do you involve in a discussion of how a restorative justice model should be implemented, and what role would the individuals or groups play in the discussion? Describe how you would set up a restorative justice model to present to the judges. Include the steps and processes that would be included and the individuals that would be involved. Specifically discuss the role of victims and your recommendations as to whether the victim would ever sit down personally with the offender to discuss ways to repair damages caused by a crime.

WEB LINK EXERCISES

American Correctional Association (ACA): www.corrections.com/aca/

Go to the Web site for the ACA. Find the section on accreditation. Identify what the ACA describes as the benefits of accreditation. Which two of the benefits suggested do you think would be the most beneficial to correctional administrators, and why?

Index